Infinite Horizons
The Life and Times of Horace Holley

But he who makes the mighty effort, . . . he who has the supreme courage and strength to gain the summit, for him the invisible becomes visible; for him the infinite divine horizons are unfolded, and that which was hidden behind the mountains is revealed.

Horace Holley

INFINITE HORIZONS
THE LIFE AND TIMES OF HORACE HOLLEY

Kathryn Jewett Hogenson

GEORGE RONALD
OXFORD

George Ronald, Publisher
Oxford
www.grbooks.com

© Kathryn Jewett Hogenson 2022
All Rights Reserved

A catalogue record for this book is available from the British Library

ISBN 978-0-85398-651-5

Cover design Steiner Graphics

CONTENTS

Acknowledgements		vii
Prologue		xi
1	The Book	1
2	Words, Words, Words, and an Encounter	9
3	Paris	37
4	Turmoil	62
5	The Poet Returns	77
6	The Early Years of the Bahá'í Faith in New York	99
7	The Covenant	125
8	New York City Paves the Way	160
9	The Birth Pangs of the New Ordering of the World	190
10	Building the World Anew Is a Messy Business	221
11	Understanding the Quest for World Peace. The Continuing Education of Horace Holley	252
12	Spiritual Conquest in the Midst of War	282
13	Institution of the Learned	322
14	The Promised Land	352
Bibliography		385
Notes and References		397
Index		469
About the Author		489

This work is dedicated with immeasurable gratitude to
The National Spiritual Assembly of the Bahá'ís of the United States

and to
the memory of Claire Vreeland
and to her descendants who continue her legacy of service to
the Cause of God

ACKNOWLEDGEMENTS

When I decided to write a biography of Horace Holley in 2010, the greatest champion of the project was my editor at George Ronald, May Hofman. She had a strong personal interest in Horace Holley because her mother, Marion Holley Hofman, was not only his friend, but a distant relation. Throughout the decade that followed, May was consistently my prod, my cheerleader and my helper as well as my talented editor. I am forever in her debt.

Horace Holley led me to a remarkable woman, Claire Vreeland, who had attempted to publish his biography years before I became interested in him as a subject. She was from Horace's hometown, Torrington, Connecticut, and a journalist for a local newspaper. When she learned about the Bahá'í Faith from her son, Paul Vreeland, and his wife, she whole-heartedly embraced it. To her delight, she discovered that a native son of Torrington was an important Bahá'í and set out to learn more about him. How fortunate for posterity that she did, for she set out on her search for information when many who had known Horace were still able to provide their accounts. She connected with his niece, Polly Doremus, and nephew, Irving Holley, Jr., both children of Horace's closest sibling, Irving. They shared Claire's enthusiasm for the book and provided her with documents, recollections and photographs from the Holley family, which undoubtedly would have been lost without Claire's careful stewardship. Irving Holley, Jr., was a professor of history at Duke University and later donated other Holley family papers to the Connecticut Historical Society in Hartford. Both Polly and Irving have since passed away.

After learning about Claire's research and writing, my husband, Gary Hogenson, and I arranged to visit with her. She was an absolute delight despite her advanced age. Spunky, engaging, brilliant – a happy ball of sunshine – we enjoyed every minute we spent with her. It began a friendship that lasted until shortly before her passing in 2015. She provided some of her research and I would telephone her from time to time to discuss Horace and ask questions. Following her death her son, Paul, sent the remaining items from her Horace research to me. She never gave up the prospect of publishing the biography. Her tenacity and inquisitiveness as well as her love for the subject shone through her letters as she gathered Horace's story. This telling of Horace's life would be poorer and less engaging without the contribution of her research.

What I also found in Claire was a believer deeply dedicated to the Bahá'í Faith and always willing to serve it. Her descendants are much the same and have worked tirelessly to promote the Cause in multiple countries using many means, including their talents for writing. For this reason, I feel that it only befitting to dedicate this work to them.

Paul Vreeland performed another invaluable service for me: reading the manuscript and offering editorial comments and corrections. His mastery of the English written word far surpasses mine, so I am grateful for the many hours he spent carefully scrutinizing my scribblings.

This is the day to work in groups. No project the size of this book could have been accomplished without the input and assistance of many people. While I was the primary parent, many others played significant roles in bringing about the birth of this book. My husband, Gary Hogenson, and our daughter, Elizabeth Hogenson, assisted with research as well as editing the manuscript. In addition, Penelope Walker, Maureen Haghighi, and Kenneth Bowers read part or all of the manuscript.

All historians are greatly in the debt of archivists. I wish to especially mention those serving at the US Bahá'í National Archives: Edward Sevcik, Roger Dahl, and Lewis Walker who expended many hours on my behalf. Furthermore, I was ably assisted by staff at the Connecticut Historical Society, the Williams College Archives, the Stanford University Archives, the archives of the National Spiritual Assembly of the Republic of Ireland, the Torrington Historical Society, and by the archivist of the New York City Bahá'í archives, Anita Graves. Lawrenceville Academy has made its archives accessible online. I am grateful to the National Spiritual Assembly of the United States and the Spiritual Assembly of New York, New York for granting permission for me to look at their institutional records. Duane Troxel assisted with providing photographs from the collection held by the United States National

Spiritual Assembly. Jaque Bookwalter, Edward and Ellen Price, and Albert and Joan Lincoln kindly provided hospitality when I had to spend time away from home to carry out research.

Duane Troxel, Joel Nizin, Robert Weinberg, Hussein Ahdieh, Earl Redman, Brent Poirier and Jan Teofil Jasion provided material from their own research. My sister, Nell Chenault, a librarian at Virginia Commonwealth University, helped to locate material. My brother, Edward Jewett, and cousin, David Purdy, provided information and insights into the administration of Episcopal parishes in the United States. My friends and family, especially my children, including my daughter, Mary Hogenson, were supportive in countless ways throughout the years as I worked on this project. Poets Bret Breneman and John Hatcher assisted me to better understand Horace's poetry and literary world during his period as a professional writer.

Throughout this project, many people have shared stories with me about Horace. Most were fleeting memories from childhood or youth, but all of these recollections put together helped bring him to life within my mind. I wish to especially acknowledge Hooper Dunbar, Manucher Javid, Loretta Voeltz, Bernard and Donald Streets, and Joanne Thomas Tahzib who took the time to speak with me about their memories.

Finally, I wish to acknowledge the other staff at George Ronald, especially Erica Leith, for their roles in bringing this book into being. It was in very capable hands.

PROLOGUE

This book was written with an eye to the future. Today's reader will, I hope, find it interesting, informative, and inspiring; but future generations will be able to appreciate its relevance more fully. Horace Holley increasingly spent his energies and talents on building a better world, one he knew he would never live long enough to see. Someone had to lay the basic foundation for a world at peace, and he was willing to dedicate his life to doing so. Yet this is not simply the story of someone who was exceptionally farsighted, it is the tale of a man who lived inside his head, and through putting his thinking into words and action, set in motion revolutionary changes. The life and times of Horace Hotchkiss Holley were full of exciting events, as well as quiet, but significant moments of reflection. He stood in the centre of many transitions: in the arts, in war and peace, but most of all, in the development of a new religion – the Bahá'í Faith. His footprints are to be found in the narratives of others because he was too modest to name-drop or trumpet his own accomplishments. He seemed to be everywhere.

In 1913, at the age of twenty-six, Horace published a slim volume, *Bahaism: The Modern Social Religion*. At the time he was working as a poet and art gallery proprietor in Paris. His little book was one of the first attempts by an American Bahá'í to create an introductory work about the Bahá'í Faith for the public. The Faith, born in Iran in 1844, claimed that its Prophet-Founder, Bahá'u'lláh, was the Promised One, the Return of Christ, the Voice of God for this Age, and Horace had accepted this claim with his whole heart. Bahá'u'lláh's Son, 'Abdu'l-Bahá, who was then the Head of the Faith, praised Horace's book as yet another milestone in the process of bringing His Father's religion to the attention of the peoples of the West. Within His response, 'Abdu'l-Bahá made a remarkable prediction about the future of the budding author.

Thank thou God that thou art confirmed and assisted; thy aim is to render service to the Kingdom of Abhá, and thy object is the promotion of the teachings of Bahá'u'lláh. Although the glory and greatness of this service is not known for the present, but in future ages it shall assume most great importance and attract the attention of the most great scholars.[1]

Until now, this prediction – that Horace's services to the Bahá'í Faith would be carefully studied – has remained largely unfulfilled, though not from lack of interest. Partial attempts have been made to examine his life; however, those who have tried to write more than a summary have found him to be a formidable subject, not easily captured because of the many facets of his life as well as the breadth of his published works and speeches. This challenge is compounded by the fact that Horace's life encompasses the sweeping story of the development of the North American Bahá'í community between 1914 and 1959. He is a constant presence, like a bright thread running through a tapestry, that connects the events of the Bahá'í Faith during its formative period. It is also impossible to ignore what was happening in the world during Horace's lifetime, because he became more involved in the greater world than the average person.

Four overarching themes run through Horace's life. The one with widest general appeal is his development as a creative writer during a fertile time when the arts in the West were passing through a major turning point. Surprisingly, just as he was becoming well-known in creative circles, he chose to abandon that path, never to return. Nonetheless, his brief time as a poet, essayist and art gallery manager was integral to the development of his unusual ability to read the times, to perceive and understand what was happening around him in the wider world and to think at depths seldom plumbed by the average person. His association with other artistic and literary luminaries and his concerted efforts to hone his skills as a wordsmith, created a writer of unusual depth. But rather than employ his pen to create literature, he changed direction and put it to work in the service of advancing the betterment of humanity.

A second theme is Horace's inner struggle to develop his spiritual capacities and improve his own character. As a bright, amiable son of New England, from his youth he was well liked and seemed to have an

PROLOGUE

easy road ahead of him, perhaps in an academic setting. From a young age, he was known for his quick wit, which, when combined with his extensive knowledge of language, added humour to any occasion. Nevertheless, beneath his quiet but funny exterior, dwelt a soul determined to unravel the existential mysteries of life. From the moment Horace first learned about Bahá'u'lláh and accepted Him as his Guiding Light, a spark ignited within him that became a roaring fire through focused exertion. His inner spiritual quest was strewn with formidable obstacles and pain; but he always persevered, never faltered, never wavered. Though imperceptible at first, his concentration on understanding and applying spiritual teachings within himself took hold of his being until the transformation was so complete that by late middle age, those who met him noticed that he was no longer the old Horace. There was a marked difference in his very countenance. The word often used to describe him was 'luminous'. Little wonder, then, that in 1951, Shoghi Effendi appointed him to the first contingent of those named as Hands of the Cause of God.[2]

The third major theme of Horace's life demonstrates his desire to make the world a better place, through promoting the ideals and teachings of the Bahá'í Faith both within the community of believers and to the public at large, especially among leaders of thought. Securing world peace was perhaps his greatest interest and desire. He spent many years exploring how the establishment of international institutions could bring that about, ultimately concluding that a world government based upon spiritual principles wedded to the elimination of elements of national sovereignty was the only solution. His views on this developed over decades and were largely inspired by Bahá'u'lláh, who taught that the time has come for the peoples of the earth to unite. The unity the Bahá'í Faith sought was not the sort of unity to be feared, such as tyrants have tried to impose. No, the teachings Horace embraced promised that, with the elimination of war, the other scourges men have visited upon each other such as prejudice, injustice, oppression, and enslavement would be eradicated as well. This vision of a world at peace, of a reign of justice, was not meant as a pious hope; it was a promise that Bahá'u'lláh stated with authority could be attained with effort and changes in attitude and heart. The key prerequisite to reaching the Golden Age was the widespread acceptance of the simple truth that mankind is one; that is, that no person or group is superior to any other and no one should have rights denied to others. It became Horace's mission in life to act upon and spread this vital principle. In the process, he confronted head-on the evils of racial prejudice and misogyny, of economic oppression, and unbridled nationalism connected to militarism.

There was one injunction of Bahá'u'lláh which became Horace's dominant goal in life: the establishment of an institution, an international governing council, that would be able to direct the affairs of mankind based upon spiritual principles. It would be capable of promoting and maintaining the longed-for day when love, justice, and unity would reign throughout the planet. This new entity would be elected by representatives of all countries and territories of the world. From the time when Horace first met 'Abdu'l-Bahá in 1911, laying the groundwork for the establishment of that embryo of a future world government – the Universal House of Justice – became his overarching objective. He lived long enough to take part in the final preparations for the establishment of that international institution decreed by Bahá'u'lláh. Alas, he died less than three years before his efforts bore fruit when the Universal House of Justice was first elected in 1963. This is the fourth theme of his life: his efforts to begin the construction of the Bahá'í Administrative Order which he believed in the fullness of time would become the system adopted by the peoples of the world to govern the planet. As the old structures administering the nations were being torn down through two World Wars, he was among the handful of devoted Bahá'ís quietly, and unnoticed, busily building up the new. He was among the main individuals laying down the foundation stones. God had not left humanity alone during its time of dire need. There was a heaven-sent blueprint, and he was a champion builder starting the erection of the edifice that would govern mankind in the future, that would save it. He worked tirelessly on building the Kingdom of God on earth.

The story that follows cannot do justice to the unique life of one who was part of a turning point in history and left his indelible imprint on it. As the fortunes of the Bahá'í Faith rise, as the numbers of its adherents and supporters increase such that it becomes one of the most consequential of the world's religions, and as its capacity to remake society grows, Horace Holley's accomplishments will be judged with greater clarity. Only then will humanity acknowledge the debt it owes to this quiet spiritual giant.

I

THE BOOK

I pray Thee, Lord, for some great work to do,
Full worth the years I wait beneath the sky
                                    Horace Holley[1]

Important events, world-shaking events are seldom announced with the beating of drums, blasts of trumpets or exploding fireworks. More likely, they are quiet, trivial, everyday happenings that go unnoticed even by the participants until their true worth is revealed days, years, or centuries later.

One such incident took place over the North Atlantic in May 1909 as the *SS Merion*, an American Line passenger ship, made a routine crossing from Liverpool, England to her home port of Philadelphia, Pennsylvania. No one recorded where it happened. Did it occur in the upper-class dining room? In a lounge with tufted seating? While strolling on a deck? Why bother noting for posterity such a minor detail of an insignificant transaction? Over time, however, the event would prove not only life-changing but world-altering. It was the loan of a book.

The owner of the book was an American beauty, Bertha Herbert – an extraordinarily accomplished woman of the world. The recipient was a twenty-two-year-old college student from Connecticut, eight years her junior, Horace Holley. Horace was not looking for such a book. In fact, he was not originally scheduled to be on that ship, but the Wheel of Fate, the unseen forces of the universe, had decreed otherwise.

In the retelling of the loan, one detail is usually missing; Horace was not travelling alone. He and his favourite brother, Irving Holley, three years older than Horace, were returning home to Torrington, Connecticut, following a two-month vacation in their ancestral homeland, the British Isles. Horace had never travelled beyond the borders of the United States, or even far from the region of New England. The brothers enjoyed their adventure immensely. They explored the Isle of Britannia from London to the West Country, from Scotland and Wales to Oxford and Windsor, taking in as much as time and funds allowed: bookshops, museums, cathedrals, sessions of Parliament, the theatre, hiking and restaurants.[2] The money for their excursion was supposed to be spent on school tuition; nevertheless, as frivolous as the trip may have seemed to frugal relatives, it was critically needed therapy, for the brothers were both mourning the recent loss of the mother whom they adored. They were adrift, rudderless.

When the Holleys first booked their passages, they also scheduled their return voyage to the United States; however, an unexpected message from Williams College reached Horace in London, causing the brothers to change their plans and return home earlier. The cable informed him that, despite his semester-long absence from school, he had been named editor-in-chief of Williams' literary journal for the following academic year. This was a high honour, especially for such a prestigious school with its reputation for excellence. Horace was eager to dive into that work, so they modified their plans and booked tickets on the *SS Merion*, sailing from the port of Liverpool on 19 May.[3]

Aboard ship, how could Horace and Irving fail to notice Bertha? Her name appeared just above 'Holley' on the upper-class passenger list. She stood out in any crowded room. Tall, slender, with dark hair, a fair complexion, and deep brown shining eyes, her neighbours in her hometown, Bayfield, Wisconsin, considered her a striking beauty.[4] Not only lovely to gaze upon, Bertha was also a trained portrait artist, the head of the interior design department for the Wanamaker's Department Store,[5] and a connoisseur of fashion and colour. This beauty was anything but dull. With exotic, far-ranging interests,[6] she was an efflorescent butterfly.

Horace was tall like his relatives, with blue eyes, brown hair, a fair complexion, and angular features. He was so thin that his high school classmates called him 'Pole'. No one, other than perhaps his mother, ever considered him handsome. He made up for his lack of a beguiling appearance with humour, for he was often the 'life of the party'.[7] His quick mind enhanced his strong wit. Horace was an above average student, excelling in the subjects that interested him the most: history, literature, and social sciences.[8] By far his greatest natural gift was a talent for words, both written and spoken. Poetry easily flowed from his pen. If an occasion required a poem, he was the one asked to write it, even though a reviewer for the Williams College newspaper said that, while Horace's poems were excellent, there was a sameness of tone because of his 'leaning toward the philosophical and religious'.[9] His abilities as a writer as well as his conscientiousness and organized mind had earned him the journal editorship. Friendly, but quiet, Horace had no difficulty getting along with classmates and teachers.

* * * * *

The book loaned to him was about the life of the leader of a new religion, not a usual theme to offer a young bachelor. Both of the Holley brothers were innately religious; thus, one unanswered element of the historic loan is the question: which traveller first brought up the topic of religion that led to it? An incident which happened two years earlier might provide a plausible answer. Bertha attended a reception in Paris hosted by another native of Wisconsin.[10] Among the guests were a well-to-do English matron, Sara, Lady Blomfield,[11] and her daughter, Mary, minor members of the British aristocracy. Mother and daughter were sitting together on a couch when Bertha, without the preliminary introduction required by proper etiquette, approached them and sat down between the two. The brash American neglected to engage in customary small talk, but at once jumped into what may well have been a practised spiel.

'If I look happy, it is because I *am* happy. I have found the desire of my heart! I should like to tell you why I am so happy. May I?'

The captive audience could hardly say 'no' to so surprising an opening. Lady Blomfield remembered that at that moment Bertha's face 'glowed'.

'It is true! True!'

Did the startled women begin to feel slightly uncomfortable as this awkward social situation unfolded? Imagine their amazement at what Bertha said next.

'We have been taught to believe that a great Messenger would again be sent to the world. He would set forth to gather together all the peoples of good will in every race, nation, and religion on earth. Now is the appointed time! He has come! He has come!'

If only the facial expressions of Bertha's two listeners had been captured at that moment! As sincere practising Christians, they surely believed in the Second Coming of the Christ, but it may never have occurred to them that the Second Coming would touch their own lives.

Lady Blomfield later said of that instant, 'These amazing words struck a chord to which my inner consciousness instantly responded.' Deep within her being, she knew Bertha spoke the truth. 'Great awe and intense exaltation' took hold of her 'with an overwhelming force'.[12] This brief encounter with Bertha set the Blomfields' lives on a different path. It would have been appropriate if, at that moment, fireworks had exploded over London to mark the encounter, because, with little fanfare, Lady Blomfield would alter the future of Great Britain through her tireless work there to establish the Bahá'í community upon a firm foundation.[13]

It seems from the only account of the occasion that Bertha failed to mention the name of the newest Messenger of God, Bahá'u'lláh. She did, however, tell her two listeners about His Son, 'Abbás Effendi, better known by the title He chose for Himself, 'Abdu'l-Bahá – Servant of Bahá – who was at that moment a prisoner of conscience of the Ottoman Empire held in the prison-city 'Akká in Palestine. She quoted His own words to them, 'For the Cause of God, I am a prisoner.'

With such a forthright introduction, the Blomfields wanted to learn more. Bertha did not offer them any literature, only the address of a British artist who had just returned to Paris from a visit to 'Abdu'l-Bahá. Her mission completed, Bertha rose to leave. While heading to the door, she turned around and returned to the Blomfields still seated on the sofa. Bertha had forgotten to exchange addresses in order to arrange an appointment. That accomplished, Bertha walked out of their lives. Lady Blomfield never mentions seeing Bertha again, despite the incalculable debt owed to her for the message she imparted to them.[14]

Did Bertha use a variation of this approach to introduce Horace and Irving to the Bahá'í Faith? It was Horace, not his more conventionally religious brother, who accepted the loan of the book.

* * * * *

As a first effort to write a biography of 'Abdu'l-Bahá in English, the book was lengthy. Flipping through it, Horace would have noted that it contained a foreword by the distinguished Cambridge University Orientalist, Edward Granville Browne, at the time the only Western scholar to have investigated the Bahá'í Faith. The author, Myron Phelps, was a New York lawyer who had made an extended visit to the ancient city of 'Akká in Palestine to meet 'Abdu'l-Bahá. The thick volume sympathetically focused upon the obscure religious sage from Iran, attracting Western readers as another exotic tale straight out of the Arabian Nights folktales. In the Muslim world, however, the book was deemed dangerous contraband by religious and government authorities, for 'Abdu'l-Bahá was a prisoner of conscience. To illustrate, a few years earlier government officials in Beirut, Lebanon, (then part of the Ottoman Empire) had confiscated the copy of Phelps's book owned by William Jennings Bryan, an important American politician, Democratic Party Presidential Nominee, and future Secretary of State, while he was travelling through the Levant. Bryan had visited 'Abdu'l-Bahá at His home shortly before his copy was seized. He asked the U.S. Consulate officials to intervene with Ottoman authorities to get it back, protesting all the while against Turkish censorship of religious literature.[15]

The book had a cumbersome twenty-nine-word title: *Life and Teachings of Abbas Effendi: A Study of the Religion of the Babis, or Beha'is Founded by the Persian Bab and by His Successors, Beha Ullah and Abbas Effendi*;[16] despite this, it sold well enough to have a second edition. Even though it focused upon 'Abdu'l-Bahá rather than upon His Father, Bahá'u'lláh, the Faith's founder, it provided English readers with an adequate, but not entirely accurate, summary of the Bahá'í Faith.

As Horace moved from Browne's intriguing introduction with its first-hand account of meeting with early believers, including Bahá'u'lláh Himself, and on to the main body of the book, he encountered an arresting prediction at the opening of Phelps's introduction: that the Bahá'í Faith would be important to the world in the near future.

> To the student of the development of human thought, there is probably not in the world to-day another place so interesting as the small city of Akka in northern Palestine; for there may be investigated, still in its youth and under the fostering care of one of its founders, a religious Faith which gives promise of becoming, at no very distant time, one of the recognized great religions of the world.[17]

Phelps's introduction provided a brief history of the Faith and the story of how he came to visit the backwater town of 'Akká. The logic of the Bahá'í teachings impressed him; they even seemed to him to agree with modern science. He was likewise astonished to find that a religion born in backward Persia espoused social teachings such as the elimination of prejudices of all kinds, which were progressive and even ahead of the times. More so than other religions, Bahá'í was notably liberal in its attitudes towards other faiths, recognizing others as also being divine in origin. The Bahá'í Faith professed to be a renewal of those earlier messages.[18]

Phelps begins the first chapter with a question; one which would capture the attention of any Christian reader: what would it really be like if Christ came again? From there, Phelps provides a first-hand account of the Christ-like daily affairs of 'Abdu'l-Bahá, Father to the poor, the sick, the troubled – a sage, a holy man living in great simplicity in an ancient town that seemed to have changed little since the days when the Nazarene walked the nearby hills and valleys.

As an adventurous youth, Horace would have found much of the book to be exciting because most of it is comprised of a first-person narrative of the history of the Faith as seen through the eyes of one who lived it, the sister of 'Abdu'l-Bahá, Bahíyyih Khánum. It was every bit as much a page turner as the best of novels. Phelps did not hear her tale himself because Islamic custom forbade men who were not part of the household from being in the presence of a woman from a good family. Fortunately, his female travelling companion wrote down her story. What Bahíyyih Khánum told her guest was inspiring, mystical, heroic, and heart-breaking. The barbaric persecution of the small but growing band of Bahá'ís was, to a twentieth-century American, an echo of the dark past of humankind, so Horace the Connecticut Yankee must have found it difficult to believe that such official persecution of the innocent had not yet been eradicated from the world.

Phelps had arranged in Egypt to have a small sampling of Bahá'í scripture translated into English, mostly extracts from the book *Hidden Words*, which he included in the last section of the book. Even though the renderings into English were clumsy, these snippets of scripture provided a glimpse of the vast ocean of Bahá'u'lláh's writings.

All in all, Phelps and Browne concluded that the Bahá'í Faith was progressive and noteworthy, but both men, however, categorized it as merely a purer version of Christianity that had not yet suffered from corruption as had earlier religions. Neither of them had gained an accurate, comprehensive understanding of the authoritative teachings of the Faith.

Like all readers, Horace read the book through his own unique lens. He had been immersed from birth in the Congregational Church, one of the last tangible American remnants of the Puritans who settled his corner of the New World as religious refugees.

Both sides of Horace's family were active members of the Congregationalist Church going back for generations. His paternal grandfather contributed a major share of the cost of the construction of the church where, as a child, Horace attended Sunday School classes[19] and sang in the choir. This Protestant immersion did not end when Horace continued his education away from home. Williams College, even though founded as a secular school, maintained a close association with the Congregationalists, whose church was directly across the street from the main campus. The required curriculum included religious studies, and attendance at worship services was compulsory.[20] Horace's high school, Lawrenceville Academy, had been established by Presbyterians, a denomination which linked arms with the Congregationalists during the nineteenth century. It too required attendance at chapel services, which often meant listening quietly to lengthy sermons. Horace had been thoroughly indoctrinated into Puritan Protestant Christianity.

Phelps's description of the persecution of the Bahá'ís may have evoked within Horace the oft-told stories of how his own ancestors fled England during the early 1630s for the wilderness of America to escape religious persecution.[21] The ferocious persecution of early Bahá'ís bore many similarities to the horrific maltreatment of dissenting sects within Christian Europe.[22] One cardinal trait of New Englanders is a long memory – it was the descendants of the Puritans who wrote the country's first history books and established its first universities. The Phelps book alerted Horace that the old evil, religious intolerance was on the rise once again, but this time in the Islamic world.

* * * * *

What effect did the book have upon Horace? Decades later he had this to say:

The wisdom, the universality of spirit and the profound love expressed in 'Abdu'l-Bahá, persecuted leader of a new religion, captivated me. He stood apart from the epic heroes and thinkers of history and brought a new dimension to my inexperienced, naïve liberal culture.[23]

'The pattern of life since then', he reflected during the last years his life, 'has been a series of efforts to find out what the Bahá'í World Faith is, what it means, and how it functions.'[24] While many others would also search to understand what it 'is' and 'what it means', few would pay as much attention as Horace to 'how it functions', the critical component of the teachings of the Faith necessary to remaking the world into a new system for organizing life on the planet, 'the one Haven of abiding felicity and Peace'.[25] Working towards that exalted goal would become his great life's work – laying the foundation for a future world government based upon spiritual principles capable of advancing and maintaining world peace.

Horace's investigation of the Bahá'í Faith was more than an academic exercise. Through his encounter with it, he began an arduous inner search and examination. His spiritual path would run through countless twists and turns, including along dark, deep valleys carved out for him by tests. After many travails and much introspection, he arrived at the realization that the Faith could not be reduced to a mere formula or 'well-turned phrase'. Instead, 'Gradually my ventures proved to me that I myself was to be encompassed, re-oriented, remoulded in all the realms of being'.[26]

Had Horace been able to gaze into the future as he first flipped through the hefty book in his hand there on board the *Merion*, he would have been astonished to learn that he would actually meet the primary subject of the book, 'Abdu'l-Bahá, not once but many times. 'Abdu'l-Bahá would become his Guiding Light, and, under His tutelage, Horace would dedicate his life to the service of the Bahá'í Cause and the betterment of humanity.

2

WORDS, WORDS, WORDS, AND AN ENCOUNTER

A staff, a knapsack and a book
Gathered at dawn, I start upon the road,
The world before, my pain within.
                    Horace Holley[1]

When the Holley brothers disembarked from the *SS Merion* at Philadelphia, they exchanged addresses with Bertha. Their new friend was returning to New York City while they headed home to Connecticut.

To make up his lost semester, Horace enrolled in summer classes at Columbia University. From its campus in New York's Upper West Side, he used his free time to explore sights and landmarks in Manhattan and the neighbouring boroughs by taking trollies, ferries, and subways. He relished lazy moments 'sprawling awhile under a tree along the Hudson River' where he could watch the steady parade of boat traffic. The Metropolitan Museum of Art was a favourite destination. And then there was time spent with Bertha, whom he gladly accompanied to her favourite restaurants, where she knew the food was good and cheap.[2] The daughter of a ship's captain from the Great Lakes, Bertha had found big cities to her liking and could introduce Horace to her view of New York. Like her, despite growing up in a small town, he embraced the city.

There is no record of Horace attending Bahá'í gatherings that summer, probably because several of the families which regularly hosted meetings were away on extended travel.[3] He may, however, have made the acquaintance of a few of the hundred or so Bahá'ís in New York. Other than what he could find in the Columbia library, he would have made little progress in learning more about the Faith during that stay in Manhattan.

* * * * *

To understand Horace's future, it is important to first know more about his past. It begins not with the Hudson River, but with the Naugatuck, whose shallow, swiftly flowing stream raced downhill through his hometown. The power of that river is what first attracted industrialists at the dawn of the Machine Age to the village of Wolcottville – for the river could supply energy to mills and water to foundries. His grandfather, Francis Newman Holley, was among those who transformed the village into a town by constructing a woollen mill along the river. As the town grew, its name was changed to Torrington.[4]

Horace was born on 7 April 1887 within sound of the rushing Naugatuck in a fine home on Prospect Street built by his grandfather on the hillside just above the main business district. Francis Holley was a natural born entrepreneur. Besides the mill, he helped establish a railway spur to Torrington as well as a bank, which he served as president. Through his leadership in the business community and in civic associations, he became a leading citizen of the town; he was also elected to public office and served as a pillar of his church.[5] Even though Francis Holley had passed away before Horace was born, that grandfather's shadow still towered over Horace's family. It was the wealth that remained from his grandfather's estate that had made it possible for Horace and Irving to visit Great Britain and attend college.[6]

Every family of achievers has members who struggle to get along in the world, which was the unfortunate lot of Horace's father, Edward Hotchkiss Holley. Horace never got to know his father well, his memories would have been only those of a young child. The family characteristics that made it possible for some Holleys to prosper by-passed his father's generation only to reappear in Horace's eldest brother, Francis Newman (Frank) Holley II. Edward first tried his hand as a merchant but failed. Then he took up dairy farming and the operation of a large creamery near Philadelphia, but again was unsuccessful. Finally, Edward returned with his growing family to Torrington, where he became part owner of a knife and cutlery factory.[7] It was during that period that Horace was born. Though his father – a lover of church architecture, a poetry patron, and a well-educated dreamer,[8] had a reputation for amiability and a good character, he was a poor provider. Horace stated years later that, 'My father was – as far as I can judge today – a nervous intellectual type who found it easier to live in the abstract than in the concrete world.'[9] Edward's career making blades was short-lived because the most unfortunate of Holley family hereditary traits manifested in him – mental illness. Horace remembered that when he was about four or five years old, a great deal of sorrow came over his family.[10] His father was sent away to an asylum in Hartford, where he died when Horace was twelve.[11] It would not be the last time mental illness would devastate Horace's life.

Fortunately, Horace's father married a strong, resourceful, practical woman, Ellen Martha Wheeler, known as Nellie. Born in nearby Salisbury, her roots in the Litchfield region of Connecticut were just as deep as those of her husband's family. The Wheelers were middle-class solid citizens who ensured Nellie received a high school education, sufficient for her to work briefly as a schoolteacher prior to her marriage. When her husband became mentally unstable and no longer capable of earning a living, she took matters into her own hands and started making lady's hats, becoming the town's most sought after milliner.[12] But hats alone were not enough to provide for a family with five children, so the eldest son, Frank, left school at age fourteen to work in a brass factory owned by a relative[13] and assisted his mother with raising his four younger siblings: Lawrence, Lillian, Irving, and Horace. The baby of the family,[14] Horace came to consider his brother Frank a substitute father.[15]

Even though his mother and older brother faced immense challenges, including the 1893 economic depression which gripped the country, Horace stated, 'What a wonderful youth we had together . . . ! It comes over me in a great flood sometimes, a stab that is sharpened by joy and gratitude as well as pain. All the working and playing together, the adventures, the friends – the boyhood of it all!'[16] Nellie created a loving home environment – 'The miracle mother wrought' as Horace later recalled.[17] True, the family had no choice but to sell the elegant Holley residence and move to a smaller home, but there were loving aunts, uncles and cousins nearby who also cared about the Holley children enough to assist them financially even after they became adults. As a boy, Horace explored the streets and alleys of Torrington and hiked along the banks of the river. He did not have far to go by bicycle to reach rolling farmland, rocky hills, and shady woodlands. He enjoyed singing in his church choir and tried to learn to play the guitar. Not a born athlete, he preferred watching team sports to taking part in them, even though he had enough of an interest as a spectator to give a play-by-play account of a football game. Card games, especially Bridge, which he played to the end of his life, were a favourite diversion. He also learned to dance, a skill that attracted girls.

Horace was keenly interested in current affairs from the time he was young, avidly reading whatever periodicals and newspapers were available to him. Nevertheless, his travel experiences were limited to rural New England. He came from the same stock of English settlers as did most of the people he knew during his formative years – people who had a reputation for hard work, an emphasis on the importance of education, a no-nonsense moral sensibility, and sparse use of spoken words. They were a tough lot able to endure the coldest of winters and the rockiest of grounds.[18] Horace never forgot where he came from, for he was proud to wear the mantle of a Connecticut Yankee.[19] When teased about his regional identity, he remarked, 'I think a person who isn't one thing or another is nothing . . . It's the local <u>smell</u> that makes poetry beautiful.'[20]

However, the world that enveloped Horace during his youth was changing swifter than the flow of the Naugatuck, for he was born just as the United States opened its doors wider, spurring a thirty-year period of mass immigration that would transform the ethnic make-up of Torrington, making it much more diverse. Other revolutions were taking place, for Horace also was born into the Machine Age, so as a child he had one foot in an older way of living and the other in the future. Automobiles were replacing the horse and buggies; oil lamps were being put away into attics as electric lights illumined parlours; and, along the unpaved streets, electric wires were strung between poles, providing perches for flocks of birds. Furthermore, the time of his birth marked the end of the American frontier for there was no more wildernesses left to conquer in the United States. The physical world seemed to be rapidly shrinking as people the earth over grasped the revolutionary concept that it might be possible to manage the completely explored planet. Horace took all of this in. Yet, despite his inquisitive mind, his copious reading, it would take an illness for Horace to be given the opportunity to explore first-hand the wider world and the wonders of his age.

During Horace's next-to-last year of high school, he became ill, forcing an extended absence from school.[21] This calamity strengthened his bond with his mother, for he loved sitting with her and talking during the evenings.²² On the other hand, it created a serious dilemma: how best to continue his education? His family knew he was bright; however, after missing an extended period from school, an alternative needed to be found to enable him to continue without stifling his interest in learning by forcing him to repeat earlier lessons. Fortuitously, his sister was engaged to marry a graduate of Lawrenceville Academy.²³ That boarding school was unusual because it had adopted progressive educational methods copied from innovative schools in Europe. It had devised a 'house system' whereby students lived in buildings smaller than conventional dormitories in groups of about thirty, making it possible to create a homelike, close-knit environment. Its overall success and sterling academic reputation attracted students from many of the most prominent, accomplished, and wealthiest families in the country. Somehow, funds were found to send Horace to Lawrenceville, and he left Torrington for the first time.

Though not as significant as the loan of the book six years later, Horace's change of schools proved to be one of the greatest blessings of his life. He blossomed. Faculty and classmates recognized his abilities and the fatherless youth established close relationships with several adults willing to take an interest in him and guide him.²⁴

The academy could have been 'in China', as Horace told his mother,²⁵ so different was it from the world of his childhood. Life on campus was lively, stimulating, and intellectually robust – exactly what Horace needed. He had no difficulty fitting in. He said little, but when he spoke up, it was often to make a funny comment.²⁶

After graduating from Lawrenceville in 1906, Horace enrolled at Williams College, a small, elite school for men nestled in a valley within the Berkshire hills of western Massachusetts. The choice was probably as much his family's as it was his because many of his most accomplished ancestors had attended the school, including the one with whom he shared his name, the Reverend Horace Holley. His great-great-uncle had been widely known during the early nineteenth century as a great intellect, a freethinker, and a progressive reformer, whose unorthodox theological ideas got him into trouble with conservative forces while serving as a clergyman and President of the University of Transylvania, Kentucky.²⁷ Horace was aware of the achievements of his namesake and that he was walking in his footsteps at Williams.²⁸ Like his illustrious ancestor, he was attracted to the study of religion and the life of the mind. The Holley family had also produced other achievers – mainly Williams graduates, including successful businessmen, war heroes, pathfinders, and politicians. Horace knew his family's history, and it was a source of pride and identity for him.

Williams College, like Lawrenceville Academy, patterned its programme after European educational models, in Williams' case the Universities of Oxford and Cambridge. Each student worked one-on-one with a tutor besides attending regular lectures. Horace's experience at Williams mirrored his at Lawrenceville. As before, he offered his services to school publications as both writer and staff member willing to take on the other tasks of publishing such as dealing with printers and advertisers. He joined a social fraternity, sang in the choir, and took part in the interdenominational Protestant religious services of the Young Men's Christian Association chapter in addition to its recreational activities.[29]

Horace continued to thrive at Williams until almost the end of the spring semester of his second year when, without warning, his life was turned upside down. On 18 June 1908, college officials received a telegram from his brother, Frank, informing them of the sudden death earlier that day of their mother, the rock of Horace's world. The telegram asked the school officials to convey this terrible news to him.[30]

Nellie Holley was devoted to her children, so when Horace's sister, Lillie, needed her mother's help with the birth of her first child, she and her husband asked Nellie to join them at a naval station on a tiny island off the eastern coast of Puerto Rico.[31] While in the Caribbean, Nellie contracted malaria.[32] By the time she returned home, she was very weak, so the family sent her to a sanitorium.

Somewhat improved, she moved to the small lake cottage in the mountains owned by her son, Irving.[33] The Holleys hoped the clean air and carefree nature of that family retreat would restore her good health. Instead, even as her strength returned, she died unexpectedly from a massive stroke at age 55.[34]

Less than two months before her passing, Nellie had written her youngest child what would be her last birthday greeting to him. She noted that his birthday in 1908 was special, because he was turning twenty-one, the age he legally became an adult. This milestone prompted her to tell him how proud she was of him, and to extol his upright character and honesty. She said that he made the world a happier place because of his cheerful disposition, unlike those who saw the world through 'blue glasses'. She added that he had been a comfort to her and offered her blessings. Besides these tender, motherly expressions of affection, Nellie made an unusual prediction – that her son 'will have fame, if not fortune'.[35]

Horace never wrote about his mother's death and the effect it had on him. Anyone who searches among his writings for accounts of those dearest to him and of those who produced the most profound impacts on his life will never find a poem, an essay, a play, or a letter that explores those deepest of feelings. In the most private place of his being, Horace walled away certain people from his pen. His mother resided there where only a select few would join her.

There was nothing to do but to go on with life without the loving, encouraging presence of Nellie Holley. Grief-stricken, Horace returned to school for the first semester of his third year, but somehow it was not the same. As Irving described their mood when the two brothers celebrated Christmas at the end of the semester, 'we felt our respective schools held no further advantage to us . . .'[36] The brothers put aside their studies and sailed to England.

* * * * *

After nine months away from Williams College, Horace was ready to return to campus at the end of the summer of 1909 with his head full of all that he had experienced in Great Britain and New York. The trauma of his mother's death was slowly retreating into the background and having just completed the most eventful period of his life, the Horace who returned to Williams was more worldly, more sophisticated than the Horace who had left the previous Christmas. He had only two more semesters remaining to complete his Bachelor of Arts degree. He plunged into the work of editor-in-chief of the literary magazine and resumed his previous college activities. However, as the October frosts turned the trees on campus from deep green to scarlet, orange, and gold, he received another piece of unexpected news that brought his world to a complete standstill, for it was more momentous than the loss of his mother. He was going to be a father. Bertha informed him she was pregnant.

The only moral choice was to marry, quickly and quietly. His decision made, Horace withdrew from Williams. The simple wedding ceremony was carried out with little celebration on 29 October at the prominent Grace Episcopal Church in Manhattan officiated by an Episcopal minister who was a family friend. Frank and Bertha's older sister served as the required two witnesses.[37] Those who knew Horace were probably astonished by the turn of events, and they were probably even more surprised by the couple's plans. The newspaper announcement of their marriage stated that they were leaving immediately for France where Horace intended to complete his studies at the famous university, the Sorbonne – a wish sincerely made that would never be fulfilled. Once again, they were sailing across the Atlantic, but this time as husband and wife headed to the port of Antwerp.[38]

* * * * *

The newlyweds began touring continental Europe, a journey that Horace would only have dreamed of a few months earlier. They proceeded directly to one of Bertha's favourite places, Paris, staying from early November until early January. It delighted Horace to be introduced to a wide stratum of Parisian society, many of whom he could call upon to assist him as an aspiring writer. Most likely, these were prior acquaintances and friends of Bertha's from her previous sojourns in the City of Light.[39] Among those, it is likely he met at least a few members of the Paris Bahá'í community.

Though Horace's first visit to Paris lasted only two months, the Bahá'í community there would play a significant role in his life, not only while he was in Europe, but in later years when he would live again in the United States. In 1909, a significant number of the pillars of the Paris Bahá'í community were Americans drawn to that international capital of the arts to study and work in the creative professions. When the Faith was first brought to Paris in 1898 by a group of Americans on their way to the Holy Land, they introduced it to a New Yorker living there, May Bolles. She became the mother of the Paris community, setting it upon a firm foundation before departing for Canada after her marriage to William Sutherland Maxwell.[40] The Maxwell family continued to influence the believers in Paris and would later become important to Horace. May and the other early Parisian Bahá'ís had connections to the Ecole de Beaux Arts and to the artistic community.

Over time, the community added Bahá'í students from Iran studying in schools in the region surrounding the city, as well as French citizens and expatriates from countries other than the United States. The make-up of the Paris Bahá'í community increasingly reflected the cosmopolitan mix of the general population in the region of the French capital.[41] This community enjoyed a special blessing because, from its inception, Paris was the usual stopover for those travelling between the Holy Land and the United States and England.

The most important members of the community – friends of Bertha's – included the first French Bahá'í: the lawyer, translator and scholar Hippolyte Dreyfus; and his future wife: the American heiress, sculptor, and scholar Laura Clifford Barney. She was the daughter of renowned portrait artist Alice Pike Barney, who had executed a pastel portrait of Bertha shortly before she met Horace.[42] The year after Myron Phelps, the author of the book loaned to Horace on board ship, had visited 'Abdu'l-Bahá, Laura Barney visited 'Akká for an extended period, during which she became fluent in Persian. She undertook one particular service during her time in the Holy Land, for which posterity will be forever grateful. While joining 'Abdu'l-Bahá for His midday meals – His 'tired moments' – she systematically asked Him important questions about a variety of subjects, especially those of interest to Christians. His secretary carefully recorded the answers. With the help of Hippolyte Dreyfus, she edited and produced from the notes of these 'table talks' the classic book, *Some Answered Questions*, which was first published in London in 1908. She and Hippolyte had also travelled together throughout Iran to visit sites associated with historic events of the Faith.[43] Horace wanted to hear everything they could tell him about the Faith.

The Holleys left Paris soon after the Christmas holidays, just in time to miss the Great Paris Flood of 1910 – the worst flooding of the Seine River in centuries. On their way south to Italy, they stopped for ten days in Lausanne, Switzerland, the most foreign place Horace had yet visited outside the United States. Its museums and cafés, the myriad languages and unfamiliar customs of fashionable Europe added to his other new cultural experiences of the previous twelve months. It was almost too much for the young Yankee to absorb. Like all those who travel far from their homelands, Horace started paying attention to the differences between the people of New England and those of other ethnic groups. The youth from Connecticut wrote to his brother that, 'My ideas have all been taken out of their little boxes, taken apart, tested, put together again. Only now I begin to realize the thoroughness of the test. I see better where I stand, what is "mine own", and what is foreign in me.'[44] Horace was taking the first inner steps towards becoming a citizen of the world.

During early February, the couple searched for a place to live in another Mecca for the arts – Florence, Italy. Horace was enchanted by the city! What a spot for a budding poet and an artist! Every street corner whispered the artistic genius of the Renaissance. The art and architecture adorning the city, along with the natural beauty of Tuscany, continued to inspire and attract artists. He wrote back to his Connecticut relations about the joys of a Tuscan spring.

> Spring is fully arrived, bag and baggage. Hot sun, garden planted with potatoes, spinach and onions, due April 10, and the borders of flowers in luxurious color. Finest town in the world. Worth a year of life to get the view from ones own roof.[45]

Horace had little first-hand experience of Roman Catholicism until coming to France and Italy other than to observe from afar the comings and goings of the two Catholic churches in Torrington, whose congregations were composed primarily of recent immigrants.[46] Over the centuries, the Catholic Church developed many rituals often grounded in cultural traits which seemed alien to Horace with his American Protestant roots. His Puritan ancestors considered Catholic ceremonies, especially many elements of the Mass, to be idolatrous. That spring of 1910, while awaiting the birth of their baby, Holy Week arrived – the week in between the Christian Holy Days of Palm Sunday and Easter. Streets filled with processions and church ceremonies showcased a pomp and pageantry missing from austere Congregationalist churches. The Puritans forbade the wearing of clerical robes, of religious statues, of elaborately decorated churches. Instead, simplicity was their watchword – quite the opposite from the colourful Catholics, especially in Italy, where each locality had its own unique traditions for celebrating Holy Week. In Florence, an elaborate ceremony known as the *Scoppio del Carro* commemorates an event from the First Crusade. White, garland-laden oxen pull a magnificently decorated cart carrying an ornate

Horace Holley (left) and Irving Holley (seated right) with Horace's college friend, Sid Wilson, a Rhodes Scholar studying at Oxford University, enjoy boating on the Cherwell at Oxford, 1909

Horace Holley touring Stratford-on Avon, England in 1909

'The Decorator', 1909, pastel on canvas portrait by Alice Pike Barney of Bertha Herbert Holley. The artist was the mother of the Holleys' friend, Laura Clifford Dreyfus-Barney

Horace Holley's father, Edward Hotchkiss Holley, as a young man

Horace Holley's mother, Ellen 'Nellie' Wheeler Holley

Horace Holley's birthplace, originally the home of his grandfather, Frances Newman Holley, Torrington, Connecticut. Horace lived in this house the first years of his life

Overview of Torrington, Connecticut

1889 drawing of Torrington, Connecticut showing the path of the river through the town

The Holley family children, December 1890. Horace Holley (seated on velvet chair) as a three-year-old with his siblings, seated left to right: Frank, Irving, Liliane (Lily); standing: Lawrence

Horace Holley as a baby

Horace Holley with his bicycle

Horace Holley as a school-aged boy

Francis 'Frank' Newman Holley, eldest of the Holley children who served as a father figure to Horace after their father became ill and died

Horace Holley when a student at Williams College

*Horace Holley, second from left, with friends at Williams College.
Note the fraternity symbol draped on the piano*

tower through the city accompanied by drummers, banners, and revellers in historic costumes as well as the usual officials and others who always seem to be part of any parade. On Easter Sunday, the tower explodes with fireworks in the Piazza del Duomo. The fireworks are timed to coincide with moments in the Easter Mass held in the cathedral. Horace found this Florentine observance of the most sacred period of the Christian calendar both fascinating and amusing.[47]

* * * * *

Horace's religious background is an indispensable element of his story, for the milieu which moulded him would also shape his response to the Bahá'í Faith and the contributions he would later make to its organic evolution. His family history is that of Puritan forbears from England who settled the region of New England – that small area of the nation that played an oversized role in the development of the American psyche.

The creation story of his country that Horace would have learned as a boy went like this. The Puritan Fathers re-enacted the Biblical Exodus of the Hebrews when they fled from persecution in the Egypt of England to the Promised Land in the wilderness of America. There, they built a new society, a City on a Hill,[48] that became a beacon of hope, a New Jerusalem. Essential to the story is the understanding that Americans were a chosen people with a God-given destiny to remake the world in the image of Protestant Christianity.[49] In fact, the icon for the narrative, Plymouth Rock, a large boulder on the Massachusetts shoreline, owes its place in American lore in part to Horace's great-great-uncle Reverend Horace Holley.[50]

How and why did the Puritan movement begin and what did they believe? It was an outgrowth of the greater movement termed the Protestant Reformation. The top tier of the Catholic Church hierarchy centred at Rome grew wealthy and corrupt over time as many of the teachings of Jesus of Nazareth, the carpenter Messiah, were gradually forgotten, ignored, or altered. The worst blow to the spiritual mission of the Church was its acquisition of political power. Inevitably, when the Church exercised temporal control of large swathes of Europe, Popes were chosen from among the ranks of military men and politicians rather than from the clergy. One of the earliest of the Christian scholars to question doctrines of the Church when Catholicism was the state religion of Western Europe was the Englishman John Wycliffe in the fourteenth century. He boldly defied Church authorities by translating portions of the New Testament into English, a great crime against a Church which restricted the language of the Bible to Latin, a language inaccessible to the average person. All but educated Catholic elites had to rely upon clergy to explain their religion. Wycliffe's boldest heresy was to challenge the existence of the Papacy. He argued that Christian doctrine and practice should be based solely upon the scriptures, which were silent about ecclesiastical hierarchy. Wycliffe's teachings attracted followers and influenced the thinking of Christians throughout Europe. Many who agreed with him were hunted and persecuted. Wycliffe, however, escaped certain execution by dying of natural causes. In one last attempt to discredit him, authorities exhumed his body and burned it.

True ideas cannot die by fire. Flames shoot them heavenward and scatter them further afield. The torch lit by Wycliffe was but one of a growing number that illumined the path for other reformers such as Jan Hus in Bohemia, Martin Luther in Germany, and John Calvin in Geneva. Wycliffe laid the foundation for William Tyndale's English translation of the Bible a century later. Tyndale's exemplary efforts to bring the word of God to the masses were rewarded by his being pursued across Europe and burned at the stake by order of King Henry VIII of England. Those who improved upon Tyndale's translation suffered similar fates. Over the course of the sixteenth century the Reformation took greater hold in England, going through periods of official favour and official sanction. Contraband vernacular translations of the Bible were balm to the souls of many Christians as the recently invented printing press produced untold copies, thousands of which were smuggled into longing hands in England. These early translations served as the foundation stones of the official English translation of the Bible, known as the King James Version, the one which Horace studied as a youth. Little wonder that this fight to gain access to the Bible in the languages of the people resulted in an emphasis on reading scripture and questioning of any doctrine not found in it. Reliance upon the holy texts became a core principle for the Puritans. It followed that everyone should be taught to read, hence Puritans put great effort into fostering literacy.[51] Once they reached America's shores, they wasted little time in establishing significant educational institutions, beginning with Harvard College in 1636.⁵²

Protestants in England became increasingly frustrated over the course of the sixteenth century when the official church in their country, the newly established Church of England, failed to adopt many reforms from the Reformation even though Henry VIII had severed the English Church from the Papacy. The English Protestants therefore sought not to reject the Anglican Church, but to 'purify' it. For these 'Puritans', true Christians had to experience a mystical relationship with the Almighty after which they should live righteous lives with their faith permeating, outwardly and inwardly, every aspect of their being. The responsibility of individual believers to act morally created what came to be known as the Protestant 'work ethic' – the idea that each person had a religious duty to practise discipline and thrift and to work hard. Puritans who established colonies in New England also believed that the moral teachings of the Bible should also form the basis of community life and the civil laws.⁵³ This conception of a Biblically based life for both individuals and the community was the ideological sea in which Horace swam. One of the leading scholars of American religious history summarized this Puritan legacy:

> ... the future of the United States was settled and to a large degree shaped by those who brought with them a very special form of radical Protestantism which combined a strenuous moral precisionism, a deep commitment to evangelical experientialism, and a determination to make the state responsible for the support of these moral and religious ideas. The United States became, therefore, the land *par excellence* of revivalism, moral 'legalism' and a 'gospel' of work that was undergirded by the so-called Puritan Ethic.⁵⁴

Little wonder, then, coming from such a background, that the idea of a new world order established upon spiritual principles was not new to Horace; his ancestors had already attempted it, with limited success.

* * * * *

The Holleys' honeymoon lasted at least until Hertha Holley was born in June 1910, coinciding with the period when Horace's classmates were celebrating their graduation from Williams. His earlier ambitions were swept away by the beauty of the new creation – his little daughter.

> Dream after dream, and hope retires to hope,
> The multitudes for whom I once aspired
> United in the child I now adore?[55]

Even though the Holleys liked Florence, living there stretched their meagre budget, so they decamped south to the more reasonably priced and equally picturesque medieval town of Siena where they took up residence in a cottage on the grounds of a decrepit castle set upon a hill from which they could gaze across the scenic rolling countryside. It was time to establish a nest within which they could engage in their chosen vocations and raise their baby.

No poet ever had a more romantic setting within which to perfect his craft than Horace did in Italy. He would sit at a table in the garden of their small house, his little daughter playing at his feet, and write while his beautiful wife painted his portrait and illustrated and illumined his compositions. Taking breaks from his writing, he took long walks alone through the Tuscan countryside to bask in the landscape's beauty. He became enthralled by the local farmers with their slower, simpler ways of life, little changed from those of their ancestors. He revelled in the whole of his experiences that were Italy.

> *In Italy*
> A beggar slept among the weeds
> And Hertha said to me:
> 'God loves the tare, if anywhere,
> In Italy.'[56]

How to get started as a professional writer? The best way for writers of poetry to be noticed was to submit their works to magazines before publishing a collection of them as a book, so Horace sent poems and essays to journals in the United States and England. In 1911 a handful of his works were published, first in the magazine *The Century Illustrated Monthly Magazine*.[57] Unfortunately, he discovered that the payments he received for his compositions were too small to support a family. He wrote to his brother about his realization that, as a married man with a child, he could not follow the Bohemian existence he might otherwise enjoy; to glory in poverty while pursuing his art. Undertaking the life of a writer would be more challenging than he had originally thought. He was transitioning from a carefree youth to a responsible adult and was introspective enough to notice the change.

> An important change, one of the most important in a man's life, has come over me . . . The element that distinguishes the man from the boy, and even the intelligent man from the unintelligent or helpless man, is the possession of a firm, definite plan for the conduct of his life. It is the element which distinguishes the house built upon a rock from that one built in the sand. For more than a year I have been a boy in a man's position, and for lack of a satisfactory plan have felt myself living precariously in a house the first storm could blow away. Now, by a combination of chance, need and desire, I have within a few days strode out from hesitation and doubt to certainty, to enthusiasm.[58]

Horace seized upon a strategy to improve his writing. To begin, he would write only poetry. Next, he would compose works in prose, and finally he would pen a play.[59] He stated that he intended to write a novel after completing those first three phases, but if he began one, no trace of it survives.

Even though Horace had received a progressive education, his studies still drew heavily from the writings of ancient Greeks and Romans and the canon of English writers from earlier centuries. During his halcyon Italian years, Horace's poetry continued to be influenced by the writing fashions of the nineteenth century – formulaic writing that won him accolades as a student. He had difficulty extricating his poetry from older styles employing rhyme, metre, and rhythm. Writing is as much craft as art, so he had to make a conscious effort to practise and experiment in order to liberate his writing voice. He also kept abreast of what other writers were publishing.

Within the year, Horace had completed enough poems to produce a book, *The Inner Garden*. His wife both illustrated and illuminated it with pen and ink drawings in the fashionable art nouveau style. It was a modest beginning.

Horace was setting out to establish a career as a full-time poet just when that branch of English literature was taking a sharp turn. Poetry as an art form had become stale, out of touch with the times, particularly with the changes wrought by the industrial age that had set in motion earth-shaking social upheavals undermining the very foundations of society. There were still peasants working the farms of their ancestors, such as Horace's neighbours in Siena, but increasingly those people of the land as well as the village craftsmen were sending their adolescent children to the cities to work in factories. Verses extolling springtime in the meadow and love under the moonlight seemed sentimental, unserious. A new cadre of poets from Horace's generation were coming into their own as part of a greater movement to bring the arts into the modern age. Toward the end of the late nineteenth century, writers and artists tried to portray life realistically, while the poets of Horace's time sought to go a step further by portraying realism through an exploration of the effects of modernity on the unconscious – to explore the thinking behind outer physical reality.[60] As Horace took up writing as a profession, a group of expatriate Americans socializing in a pub in London challenged each other to write poetry that seemed more in tune with the times. Ezra Pound emerged as the leader of this group of literary revolutionaries. Pound would have his own encounter with 'Abdu'l-Bahá and become an obstacle to Horace's success in the literary world, even as Horace adopted some of the ideas espoused by this fledgling school of poets.

In the United States during this same period, two members of groups suffering relentless discrimination would launch significant alternative outlets for poets by establishing publications which promoted a diversity of voices. The first was Harriet Munroe, who was slighted as a poet by the powers running the Columbian Exhibition in 1893 solely because she was a woman. This formidable, independent woman of Chicago refused to be silenced as a writer by prejudice against her sex. In 1912, she established *Poetry Magazine*, which quickly became the most influential of all poetry journals, making her, as its editor, the 'grande dame' of American poetry. She understood how to sell poetry by combining works that appealed to wider audiences with more challenging, innovative, and controversial pieces.[61] She liked Horace's writing and included a good number of his poems in editions of her magazine. The other poet who opened doors for other writers was William Stanley Braithwaite of Boston,[62] a brilliant African-American with a sixth-grade education who believed the world's literary heritage belonged to all peoples. In 1913, Braithwaite began publishing annual anthologies of poetry in order to reform and revive an art which he felt was being strangled by the poor judgement of editors. Braithwaite's keen eye for talent became widely respected among publishers of all races and his anthologies became bestsellers. His capacity broke through colour barriers. Braithwaite included Horace's poems in his anthologies and Horace admired the man whose utopian vision was of a community of writers devoted to beauty which welcomed everyone. Writing to Braithwaite in 1915, Horace praised and encouraged him, saying:

> Through the busy streets of our cities you have made pass a new procession, the singers; to the farthest field and the loneliest hill you have brought the sight of a nation's vision. For the first time can all the poets of one race[63] become acquainted with one another, thus learning to regard poetry as an ever-larger, ever more varied ministry. . . the seeds of creation strike into friendly soil . . . you have established a relationship with the very sources of life in our race.[64]

Besides these two publishing outlets, a number of publications that became known collectively as the 'little magazines' sprang up in London, Chicago and New York. These modest magazines concentrated on *avant-garde* art and literature. None had long lives because they never attracted enough subscribers to survive financially. Their influence on the canon of English literature was considerable, for many of the most acclaimed writers of the time were first published within them. Many of Horace's poems were published in these journals over the next five years, and he would also advertise in several and sell them in his Paris gallery.

Ezra Pound's group in England adopted the name 'Imagists', and Pound himself sought to exert his influence over editors of literary journals, in an attempt to be the one to decide whose poetry was worthy and whose was not. Horace inexplicably found himself linked with the Imagists, though he never considered his works to be part of that poetry school. This movement, which came to include H.D. (Hilda Doolittle), Richard Aldington and Amy Lowell, believed verse should emulate the simple directness of Japanese Haiku and contemporary French poetry.

They scoffed at standard rules of rhyme and rhythm, utilizing precise words that conveyed meaning without considering whether the words rhymed. Ironically, even though the Imagists sought to break free from the chains of earlier forms of poetry, they imposed their own rules.[65]

Anyone publishing a book for sale to the public must expect a variety of reactions. All Horace's books of poetry were reviewed in newspapers and journals, so he had to become inured to public criticism. This included a scolding in the prestigious, internationally read London *Times Literary Review* because the reviewer did not like his use of the free verse genre of poetry.[66] When Horace published his second book, *Creation: Post-Impressionist Poems*, it was critiqued by the deviser and keeper of the list of Imagist rules, Richard Aldington in *The Egoist* magazine. Aldington's essay, 'Modern Poetry and the Imagist', appeared as the topmost item on the front page where it could not be missed. He begins by lamenting that the reading public readily purchased novels but would no longer pay for poetry. Aldington then jumps to a review of Horace's latest book, beginning with an overall assessment of Horace's work: namely that 'the poems aren't much good'. He says that Horace's 'poems are mostly cosmic' and written in free verse, guessing that Horace must have been overly influenced by the American poet Walt Whitman, and that his language was sometimes 'pompous and inflated'. After providing a couplet as an example, Aldington pushes the knife in further by saying, 'Now I firmly believe that this sort of writing accounts for the terrible indifference of many educated people towards poetry.' But then, after further dissecting Horace's writing, Aldington half-apologizes: 'I do not wish to slate Mr. Holley more than he deserves' and goes on to quote a couplet from his poem 'Hertha' which Mr. Aldington admired.[67] While it was flattering to be prominently featured in such an influential journal, Horace felt stung for having been used as a negative example. He responded in the best possible way – with humour. His letter to the journal concluded with a poem he wrote to make light of the Imagists and their rules, and it was published in the following issue. The poem has been reprinted multiple times in works exploring the Imagism movement.

> *The Mice*
> In the world's cupboard
> The scamper of little feet,
> A new sound.

O busy, sharp-teethed mice
Nibbling your anxious bellies full,
Fear not:
The Cat was belled long since
By mice of a bolder generation!

Nay rather beware the tightness of your own tummies,
Little mice,
Since already you have eaten the Greek Anthology
And now your glistening white teeth
Gnaw the fat tomes of Chinese Wisdom.

What would you do with the Lute of Jade,
O little mice?
This is indeed a dainty luncheon,
O little mice,
    O Imagists![68]

Fortunately, other reviewers did not share Aldington's negative opinion of Horace's poetry.[69] A different review of the same compilation of poems said:

> Horace Holley recently published a book with Kennerly (hail the publishers!) 'Creation.' These post-impressionist poems are permeated with that glad, healthy satisfaction with life as it is and a faith in the future that characterized the older New Englanders, Emerson and Thoreau. Holley strengthens the American crew with his added powerful oar.[70]

Horace never wanted to be categorized. He did, however, become more and more a practitioner of *vers libre* – free verse – without metre or rhyme. He also experimented with blank verse. Another reviewer in a 1915 anthology lamented that American writers had been slower to adopt free verse than their European counterparts. This poetry form had been championed a generation earlier by Whitman, who had dared American writers to be more innovative, but those following in his wake had imitated him rather than breaking new ground. That second reviewer therefore found Horace's poetry to be a welcome change:

> ... The sensuous and emotional elements of his unrhymed stanzas are blended with a fine intellectualism that here and there dilates suddenly to spread before us a vision of – 'Carcassonne'. A casual study of his verse will teach the student of *vers libre* that the secret of this form lies in not only the rhythmic foot as opposed to the metrical foot, but in a sixth sense of the value of the words. You may turn to Yeats and you will see what is meant; and if you read Isaiah and the Psalms of David, and Whitman's 'Lilacs', you will be fully persuaded that true *vers libre* is for the poet who is born with the sense of the magic of words.
>
> In Mr. Holley's 'Les Morts', in 'They', 'The Blue Girl' and 'Souls' one finds somewhat of this magic.[71]

Harriet Munroe herself reviewed Horace's republished compilation which combined his earlier *Creation* volume with poems written after the first printing. (*Divination and Creation* was the new title.) She described Horace as 'the young poet and dreamer', adding that, 'Rarely have I read a first book of poems so keen with spiritual passion. The poet feels more than he can say, perhaps, but the beauty he divines and dreams is joy and pain to him, emotion that makes life almost an impossible ecstasy.' But her review went on to instruct him that, while he showed great promise, there was room for improvement.

> If the poet's art fails him often, if we have turgid lines that seem to crush the finer ones, we may reasonably hope for more measured control in his next book . . . The later work shows finer taste and a more stript and clarified style.[72]

Even though Ezra Pound never cared much for Horace's poetry, he liked Horace personally, describing him as 'amiable'.[73]

Though Horace thought of himself primarily as a poet, it can be argued that his essays were his best works. He began by writing about women's suffrage; a controversial topic in 1910, in an essay published in *The Freewoman*. As the husband of a suffragette, how could he fail to express his solidarity with this vital issue?! The practice of writing poetry affected his ability to turn a phrase, to condense his thinking when writing prose. Most of his essays written while he was in his twenties focused upon the arts, not only writing but painting and sculpture as well. He also began a book on the subject that he never finished.[74]

* * * * *

During the summer of 1910, while the Holleys were adjusting to the joys and responsibilities of parenthood, the recently installed reform government in Istanbul confirmed to the Turkish officials in Palestine that 'Abdu'l-Bahá, at age sixty-six, was a free man. He had been a prisoner of conscience since childhood. For the first time in forty-two years, He could legally depart from the Ottoman Province of Syria. He wasted no time. After an extended period of rest in Egypt to regain His health, He set out for His longed-for destination – the West – where He intended to strengthen the small but growing bands of converts in Europe and the United States and further spread His Father's teachings. His precarious health, however, intervened, further delaying his departure. The years of deprivations, of malnourishment, of mistreatment and harsh living conditions had made the normal infirmities of age more extreme. After months of additional rest, He was finally on His way across the Mediterranean Sea headed for Marseilles, France.

When 'Abdu'l-Bahá's disembarked from his steamship in August 1911, almost a year after leaving Haifa, he was met by a jubilant Hippolyte Dreyfus-Barney. Hippolyte and his new wife, Laura Dreyfus-Barney (the couple had combined their last names) were given the honour of hosting 'Abdu'l-Bahá at Thonon-les-Bains, his first European destination. That small resort town on the French shores of Lake Geneva (Lake Leman) may have seemed a surprising choice since no Bahá'ís lived there, but it was renowned for its curative mineral waters and thermal baths, which were used to treat a variety of ailments, including one that severely afflicted 'Abdu'l-Bahá, rheumatism. Besides which, it was late summer when those who could afford to do so left the cities of Europe for the scenery and wholesome air of the countryside. Bahá'ís, as well as wealthy, prominent people from Iran, were escaping the heat of summer in the pleasant environs around the banks of the lake.

The telegram that arrived at the Holley's Siena cottage one day in late August must have seemed to Bertha and Horace to be a thunderclap on a clear blue-sky day. In Italy, they had been removed from Bahá'í fellowship, from any reminder of 'Abdu'l-Bahá and the teachings of the Faith.

Unexpectedly, the telegram they received from their friend, Hippolyte, was an invitation to meet 'Abdu'l-Bahá, not in the Holy Land, but in Thonon across the lake from Lausanne. It was only a long day's train ride away. The family did not hesitate. They packed their bags, bundled their baby daughter, and caught a train headed north through the Alps to the popular resort town. Horace was going to meet the Man first introduced to him two years earlier on the pages of the Phelps book in the middle of the Atlantic Ocean.

The journey itself was a preparation, a mental cleansing for Horace as the majestic scenery of the snow-laden Alpine peaks swept away the cares of daily life in Siena from his thoughts. After winding through the rugged terrain of the mountains, the train raced downhill toward the sparkling blue lake tucked between France and Switzerland. It was Tuesday, 29 August. They climbed down from the train, taking firm hold of Hertha, and, carrying their luggage, made their way toward the imposing, white, five-storey Hotel du Parc. The lawns of the park adjoining the hotel spread around it like a giant green skirt. There were people scattered about at little tables enjoying the late August weather, the lovely scene completed by music drifting across the gardens from a nearby bandstand.

As the family approached the hotel, they spied a group of people sitting together on the lawn focused upon one man seated in the middle. A handful of the men were attired in unfamiliar oriental dress. Just at that moment, Hippolyte arose from among them and made eye contact with Bertha Holley. Then the rest of the group stood up as one to greet the Holleys striding across the grass towards them.

And there HE was. Horace had never seen a photograph of 'Abdu'l-Bahá, in fact, had never formed a mental image of Him, but he could pick Him out from the crowd instantly.

> I saw among them a stately old man, robed in a cream-coloured gown, his white hair and beard shining in the sun. He displayed a beauty of stature, an inevitable harmony of attitude and dress I had never seen nor thought of in men. Without having visualized the Master, I knew that this was He.[75]

It was more than visual recognition; it was a spiritual recognition. Horace had never experienced anything like it.

> My whole body underwent a shock. My heart leaped, my knees weakened, a thrill of acute, receptive feeling flowed from head to foot. I seemed to have turned into some most sensitive sense-organ, as if eyes and ears were not enough for this sublime impression. In every part of me I stood aware of 'Abdu'l-Bahá's presence.[76]

Horace found himself overcome with emotion, a response he had probably not expected. Something new was being born within him.

> From sheer happiness I wanted to cry – it seemed the most suitable form of self-expression at my command. While my own personality was flowing away, a new being, not my own assumed its place. A glory, as it were from the summits of human nature poured into me, and I was conscious of a most intense impulse to admire.[77]

Without even having heard 'Abdu'l-Bahá speak, Horace immediately understood at the greatest depths of his being that he was in the presence of One who was much, much more than a mere sage.

> In 'Abdu'l-Baha, I felt the awful[78] [awe-inspiring] presence of Baha'u'llah, and, as my thoughts returned to activity, I realized that I had thus drawn as near as man now may to pure spirit and pure being.[79]

The fleeting moments that passed as Horace strode across the lawn to meet 'Abdu'l-Bahá for the first time would, for the rest of his life, serve as the scales upon which he would weigh all aspects of life. With those brief steps, he had been transformed forever.

> This wonderful experience came to me beyond my own volition. I had entered the Master's presence and become the servant of a higher will for its own purpose. Even my memory of that temporary change of being bears strange authority over me. I *know* what men can become; and that single overcharged moment, shining out from the dark mountain-mass of all past time, reflects like a mirror I can turn upon all circumstances to consider their worth by an intelligence purer than my own.[80]

Other believers were there as well, including Americans whom Horace probably had never met before.[81] More arrived as the visit continued. 'Abdu'l-Bahá also brought His own entourage, including Siyyid Asadu'lláh-i-Qumí, whose loving and kind gestures of friendship towards the Holleys left a deep impression on them.

The Western believers were given ample opportunities to ask questions, but Horace found he had no desire to do so; in fact, his questions were answered without him needing to ask. Instead, he only wanted to soak up the radiance of 'Abdu'l-Bahá's very being.

> I yielded to a feeling of reverence which contained more than the solution of intellectual or moral problems. To look upon so wonderful a human being, to respond utterly to the charm of his presence – this brought me continual happiness. I had no fear that its effects would pass away and leave me unchanged. I was content to remain in the background.[82]

Throughout the next two days, Horace the poet noted every detail: 'Abdu'l-Bahá's gestures, His 'stately rhythmic speech', the respectful way that the other hotel guests – primarily well-to-do Westerners – treated One who 'appeared like some just king that very moment descended from his throne to mingle with a devoted people'.[83] He observed that 'Abdu'l-Bahá was even more impressive as He walked than when seated. 'Abdu'l-Bahá answered serious questions but He also 'laughed heartily' for within him was no trace of asceticism or 'useless misery'.

> The divine element in Him does not feed at the expense of the human element, but by its own abundance, as if He had attained His spiritual development by fulfilling His social relations with the utmost ardour.[84]

Inevitably, it wasn't long before Horace the Christian-Bahá'í compared 'Abdu'l-Bahá to Jesus Christ.

The following morning as Horace strolled through the town of Thonon, he realized the events of the previous twenty-four hours had 'invested the commonplace with new significance'. All things had been made new for him: '. . . I was conscious of a new sympathy for individuals and a new series of ties by which all men are joined in one common destiny.'⁸⁵

The last day of their visit, as 'Abdu'l-Bahá prepared to depart for first Geneva and then London, Bertha and Horace, along with the other Western believers, were each presented with ring stones bearing a Bahá'í symbol, referred to as the Greatest Name. Horace returned his to 'Abdu'l-Bahá with the request that it be given instead to his little daughter along with a blessing. 'Abdu'l-Bahá readily agreed to that request. Horace understood the ring stone did not possess magical powers, only that it was a remembrance of his family's visit with 'Abdu'l-Bahá.⁸⁶

Years later, Horace confided to those near to him that he cried every day in Thonon. He knew that during that fleeting visit, 'Abdu'l-Bahá recreated him.⁸⁷

* * * * *

In the weeks and months following that brief visit to Lake Leman, Horace had many new ideas to mull over and interpret within the solitude of his Siena garden. In November, he produced a small pamphlet of his ode, 'The Return of Religion', which he dedicated to 'Abdu'l-Bahá. The fragrances of his little garden invoked within him a vision of the coming of God's Messengers which he likened to the sweet aromas of the flowers available only to those with keen senses capable of picking up their scent. His work explored the theme of the progressive unfoldment of divine revelation through God's chosen Messengers and Prophets across the centuries: 'The prophets in one fellowship return . . .' Through the medium of poetry, Horace tried to articulate how his inner being had been profoundly altered by his brief time with 'Abdu'l-Bahá.

> Deeper than sense and farther than our blood
> These odors penetrate,
> Which pierce within our soul's most secret mood
> And change our fate;
> Incorporate
> Henceforth with all we feel and think and do,
> Thereby with what we are.
> Once more we feel an aspiration rise
> From depths of our own nature to renew
> Its marriage-vows with God . . .

Almost as soon as Horace returned to Siena, he penned a written account of his visit to Thonon. He concluded his narrative with a parting sentence which is usually overlooked by those studying his memorialization of that historic occasion. Horace was already conceptualizing the future, pondering the time when 'Abdu'l-Bahá would pass from this world, leaving behind believers such as himself. He wrote:

> . . . we men and women, heirs of Bahá'u'lláh's manifestation, labour to erect the House of Justice amid the increasing charity and enthusiasm of the world.[88]

The Holleys would have other opportunities to be with 'Abdu'l-Bahá in Paris in 1913, but unlike Horace's detailed account of the meeting in Thonon, the only incident Horace ever recorded from the many gatherings with 'Abdu'l-Bahá he attended was a minor one which took place at an apartment within sight of the Eiffel Tower.[89]

> . . . When I entered the room the Master was standing at the window looking out. Tea was being served. When the Master turned around He seemed tired. He asked if there were questions. Someone requested Him to explain 'eternity'.
> The Master said: We live on the earth, and the earth revolves on its axis once in twenty-four hours, and that is a <u>day</u>. The earth revolves around the sun every 365 days, and that is a <u>year</u>. On the sun there is neither <u>day</u> nor <u>year</u>.[90]

That account of 'Abdu'l-Bahá speaking of eternity would be the last time Horace would relate any of his own first-hand experiences in His presence. For his own encounters with 'Abdu'l-Bahá would be safely tucked away deep into that space where he kept the most important people in his life, the place where his mother already dwelt within him.

* * * * *

Horace's first encounter with 'Abdu'l-Bahá had opened for him a new vision, that of a world at peace, a just world where all of the peoples across the globe had come together to create a world government which would usher in and maintain the golden age of humanity. He had seen with his own eyes how the Faith could bring together the East and the West into perfect harmony. He wanted that to be universal.

> The test which the Orient passes upon the servant of a Prophet is spiritual wisdom; we [Westerners] concern ourselves more with questions of power and effectiveness. From their alliance – from wisdom made effectual, and power grown wise – we must derive the future cosmopolitan virtue. Only, now while the East and West are exchanging their ideals, is this consummation possible.[91]

Constructing this new reality would become his unspoken goal to the end of his life. He would become a champion builder of that new world civilisation. His vision was greater than that of the Puritan 'City on a Hill', for he wanted to hasten the arrival of the long-awaited Kingdom of God on Earth.

. . . For two days, on terms of rare intimacy, I met an older man whose nature personified and exemplified the creative type, the self-conscious, self-directed poetic nature of my earliest and profoundest ideal.

The effect his mere presence had upon me was immense. Our first meeting shocked my entire being. It was a moral cataclysm not less astonishing in result than the toppling of old mountains in a sudden whirlpool of the sea. But the thunder and jar of the change seemed outside, though close and imminent, and not within me. Within, I gained a startling clarity of perception. My thought seemed to go out and mingle with his. I saw myself, and life, as he must regard himself and life habitually: as I never before had witnessed them, and as I never could have seen them by my own effort. This man's nature somehow projected its unity upon me like a vision. And in the supreme arrogance of real humility I seized upon it as a vision of my true self. He had given me a perspective outside either fragment of the divided nature I had previously been compelled to accept as self. I looked down as from a tower, and there, not too far away, the two winding paths met, the overgrown, baffling jungle gave way to open ground. But the vision cruelly hurt and tormented me. It cut away, and bound together; it shattered, and restored. I could not escape it.

Horace Holley[1]

3

PARIS

O wind, be favorable to my small bark;
For my sake, ocean, lay your tempest-foam.
For me the last sun flickers; nearing home,
Kind stars, direct my harbor through the dark.
Only within our lonely soul
God thrust a secret and a goal.

Horace Holley[2]

When the Holleys returned home from Thonon at the beginning of autumn, 1911, the idyllic nest they had created in Siena seemed to Horace to be out of sync – off kilter. He had enjoyed the year-long retreat, a period of 'an equal degree of endeavour and relapse, labour and repose',[3] but it was time for a change. Looking around his family's cozy little cottage, he noted the 'puritanically bare writing table by the window, a deep lounging chair by the fire; pen and manuscript conspicuous to hand, but pipe and novel ready also'.[4] They no longer suited him as they were. The inner shifts wrought by his brief time with 'Abdu'l-Bahá had transformed him into a more serious person, a more determined person, no longer content to leisurely pursue his addiction to writing poetry. He lost no time in reordering the room, starting with his pipe. Grabbing it, he flung it through a window, 'drawing in, almost reverently, a deep breath of cool October air'.[5]

Returning to an unfinished manuscript he had begun before the life-altering trip, Horace continued to bring himself to account. Could the New Horace subdue completely the Old Horace?

> . . . True, that battle had many skirmishes. Doubts rose hideous from the original slime of life, and ridicule confronted me in the dark; but against all the stupor and opposition I held one impregnable defence, a conscious joy.[6]

There was something else coming to life within him – a growing realisation of the oneness of all things. This awakening perception brought forth unexplored insights about the meaning of morality and what morality had to do with him as a writer.

> Just here I first grew aware of a Morality for art. Morality as a system of conduct, obedience to some outer standard or authority, had never interested me. I had resolved to make myself creative as an artist, if that were possible, and felt that this determination had nothing to do with ten or any other number of commandments. Morality in general has no bearing on creation, which is personal and dynamic, but only on goodness, which is static and conventional, and as soon as I discovered this I ceased to give the matter any concern. The word had even become distasteful; yet to my surprise I had suddenly turned Moral.[7]

For the first time, he saw an alternative pathway stretched out before him, one that was more satisfying, illuminating, capable of making him not only a better writer, but a better person.

> I had learned that the union of thought, action and will can produce a richer, more fertile, and more spontaneous personality. I learned that self can create self, directed onward through the days in accordance with a definite and useful plan; that one's own being will respond to conscious artistry and yield a result showing forth the artist's desire not differently than a poet's words or a sculptor's marble. I learned about the creative process itself; how it is a function of spiritual growth or decay, accurately tracing to those fitted to observe, the soul's onward course toward self-control or self-abandonment. No great work of art but represents some signal victory or defeat suffered by that mysterious being.[8]

All of his life, Horace had worked on developing his skill with words, constructing images on paper like a master craftsman. His reward was praise from his instructors and the publication of the fruit of his labours by editors. Remote Siena had few distractions other than its beauty. However, the longer Horace remained there, the more he suspected that Tuscany was not providing him with the life experiences that would reveal significant insights to convey through his words. Nothing he published captured the hearts of his readers. No one memorized his verses or set them to music. They had failed to become part of the collective consciousness. Years later, when he was settled into another kind of life in New York City, Horace contemplated the trajectory of modern poetry, and, though not said directly, reconsidered his own period as a reclusive writer in Italy. He theorized that the public was no longer interested in modern poetry, and that its rejection could be traced to poets abandoning contact with ordinary people and the work-a-day world. Looking back, he observed that even two generations before him, writers like Shelley, Keats, Byron and the Brownings had escaped the ugliness of modern industrialism by fleeing to Italy. Those Romantic poets sought sanctuaries where beauty still existed, just as Horace had done almost a century later. Other writers, who were unable to run away, found another kind of refuge in places constructed within their own minds. 'Poetry has consequently come to mean one thing, daily life another.'[9] To Horace, this constituted an abandonment of the poets' duty. 'They betrayed life into the hands of brutal, redeeming waste; they betrayed poetry itself into the hands of a vain, sterile ideal.'[10] His insight was that to be a true poet meant to be of the world, not apart from it.

> . . . the creative imagination, like a woman's body, is sterile until fertilized by contact with living forces. The poet is but one loop in the electric current, and though he is the particular loop which represents the filament able to send forth illumination, nevertheless the source of its energy lies in the circuit as a whole. Thus it is for the very stuff and essence of poetry that the poet has been compelled to re-unite with the world.[11]

* * * * *

In the interval since the Holleys' visit with 'Abdu'l-Bahá, autumn had come and gone, and the winter festival of Christmas had arrived. The Holleys had made friends in their cloistered world on the outskirts of Siena, and this year they hosted a Yuletide party for the Christian Holy Day celebrating the birth of Jesus. Everyone in the immediate environs of Castello delle Quattro Torri was invited, including the owner of the castle and his servants. Local peasants – mainly farmers, an Italian captain and his wife, babes in arms, and an elderly gardener – all were the honoured guests of the Holleys in their best American egalitarian manner. Within the limits of their purse, Bertha and Horace put much effort into festively decorating their cramped home for the approximately thirty guests. There were small Christmas trees decorated with shiny ornaments and dangling toys and a 'Congregational Sunday School' quantity of candles. At the appointed hour of 8:30 in the evening, guests started to arrive. In groups of twos and threes, they set down their lanterns and candles outside the door of the cottage and joined the revelry. Hertha adorned the party with the captivating charm of a one-year-old as she was lifted up and carried round and round a lighted Christmas tree. Each guest received a token gift from the Holleys: the children got fruit and candies, the owner of the castle received a sketch of the fortress landmark executed by Bertha, while the other adults received scarfs, tobacco, a shawl, or the like. Horace remarked that he did not remember when he had enjoyed himself so 'thoroughly and refreshingly'. It was a holiday unlike any he had ever experienced in Connecticut. He admitted in a letter to a relative that he had come to the realization that he had a new appreciation for and understanding of people from another culture who, at first, had seemed strange to him.

After their guests departed, the Holleys sat near the fire sipping coffee while eating a brandy-soaked[12] cake baked by Bertha, which Horace set alight. It was time to exchange Christmas presents as a family. Horace received a miniature portrait of their daughter from his wife, which she had painted in secret to surprise him, an embroidered silk waistcoat, and a book he had wanted for some time. She also had a jeweller set a stone with a Bahá'í symbol into a ring for him. The stone, a gift from 'Abdu'l-Bahá, was especially dear. In describing his new ring, he referred to 'Abdu'l-Bahá as 'the Persian saint whom I reverence like a father'.[13] The Holleys were still Christian-Bahá'ís.

Horace's Puritan ancestors disapproved of the celebration of Christmas because the New Testament gave neither the date of Jesus's birth nor called for an annual observance of the event. Over the centuries, American views about Christian doctrine changed, and so too did the celebration of Christmas, which increasingly took on trappings resurrected from ancient pagan traditions. Curiously, it was Horace's great-great-uncle, Orville Holley (brother to Reverend Horace Holley) who sped up the conversion of the American celebration of Christmas from a religious observance into a secular winter festival by publishing for the first time the poem which began, 'T'was The Night Before Christmas . . .'[14] That popular poem cemented the details of the Santa Claus story into the folklore of the world.

The Holley celebration of a Christian Holy Day would not have raised an eyebrow among the small bands of Bahá'ís in Europe and the United States because they too continued to observe the traditions and holidays of their religious and cultural backgrounds. A formal enrolment process for the converts in the West did not yet exist. Bahá'ís, such as the Holleys, understood that in accepting Bahá'u'lláh they did not have to discard their belief in and love for Jesus. They believed Bahá'u'lláh was truly the long-awaited Return of Christ. Therefore, most of the Christians attracted to the Bahá'í Faith at that time retained their formal memberships in churches, like the Holleys, whose knowledge of the Bahá'í Faith continued to be rudimentary despite their time with 'Abdu'l-Bahá. Back home in Siena, the Holleys existed in a Catholic world, with no other believers with whom to commune and further their understanding of the Bahá'í Faith.

Enchantment fades with the passing of time. So it was with the Holleys' infatuation with Italy. Or perhaps the couple reached the inevitable conclusion that Horace's inheritance and tiny royalties would never be enough to support them; practical concerns took priority over romantic preferences. Bertha's ambitions required a city where she could solicit clients if she were to succeed as a portrait artist. But there was more; she had become increasingly interested in fashion design, using what she had learned about lines and colour from composing images of people.[15] Both of the Holleys needed the stimulation and fellowship of other creative souls. In May 1912[16] they packed up their growing accumulation of possessions and returned to Paris, a move which would provide them with an opportunity to be part of an active Bahá'í community. Horace's Bahá'í education was about to accelerate.

* * * * *

'Abdu'l-Bahá left Thonon, France and its nearby neighbour, Geneva, not for Paris, but for London, where he spent the month of September. During that first of two visits to the capital of the British Empire, He gave a public speech for the first time in His life.[17] This well-received talk was followed by numerous others in churches, universities, lecture halls and parlours. He also met with people from all levels of society and attracted extensive coverage in the news media. On 3 October 1911, He left London for Paris. As in England, 'Abdu'l-Bahá addressed a variety of religious and secular organizations, met a wide assortment of people, and gave interviews to the press. In addition, many people from Iran, the country of His birth, sought Him out, especially Persian students receiving a Western education in the environs of Paris. The French capital was a favourite place for members of the Persian royal family and other wealthy Persians, who were among those who made a point of meeting with Him. In December, He returned to Egypt because His health could not tolerate the cold, damp winters of Western Europe.

During His time in Paris in 1911, 'Abdu'l-Bahá spoke on an extensive variety of topics, from prayer and life after death to current events. The Dreyfus-Barneys served as translators; Hippolyte rendered the talks into French while Laura explained them in English. Because every word He uttered was precious, they were carefully recorded and transcribed. A number of those notes were later published, especially in the first Bahá'í magazine, *Star of the West*, based in the United States, which included articles about Bahá'í activities throughout the world. A broader, more authentic picture of the Faith was coming into clearer view.

* * * * *

Horace's career as a writer coincided with the end of what is remembered in Europe as the *Belle Époque* and what American historians call either the Progressive Age or the Gilded Age. During the period straddling the nineteenth and twentieth centuries, industrialists became the new royalty, accumulating levels of wealth far surpassing that of kings – hence the name 'Gilded Age'. This development exacerbated extreme disparities in wealth and poverty, which in turn created and worsened social ills. Countering the problems spawned by industrialization was the emergence of progressive social movements directed towards overcoming the challenges faced by rising numbers of urban poor and displaced people. Europe was also contending with this new prosperous industrial class, the nouveau riche, and the concomitant social changes.

Ironically, amid such social upheavals, the continent was experiencing a blessed condition that was rare for Europe – peace. For the first time in centuries, a generation of Europeans had come of age without suffering through a major war. A traveller could go from country to country within Europe without a visa. Not only commerce, but the arts and sciences flourished in this stable environment. While most European countries still had hereditary royalty, elements of governance were increasingly democratic, and there were a growing number of elected legislatures with real, rather than simply advisory, power. Deep problems remained, but on the surface, the period was later remembered as a wonderful time to be alive. Western European civilization flowered, and it seemed that the *Belle Époque* – the Beautiful Period – would go on indefinitely.[18]

In 1912, London, as capital of the far-flung British Empire, was the administrative and commercial centre of the world, but Paris was its cultural heart. For more than half a century, the city on the Seine served as a matrix for artists, writers, composers, actors, and dancers. By the time the Holleys arrived, artistic freedom in Paris had become so liberal that even works deemed scandalous for flouting morality could be seen in prominent theatres and in respectable art galleries. Its artists and creative thinkers were the advance guard of originality, far ahead of their counterparts in other countries, including New York and London.[19] No wonder Paris was where Bertha most wanted to be.[20] Horace referred to it as 'the most cosmopolitan city in the world'.[21]

Horace and Bertha spent days scouring the neighbourhoods of Paris, searching for a flat which accommodated not only their desire to be around other creative people but also fit their purse. They secured a temporary apartment at 16 Rue Boissonade in an area preferred by artists, writers and expatriate Americans residing in the Left Bank's Latin Quarter.[22] At that time, the street was a cul-de-sac opening onto Boulevard Raspail and ending at a garden which separated it from Boulevard Montparnasse.[23] Perhaps their American Bahá'í friends, the Impressionist painter F. Edwin Scott and his wife, helped the Holleys locate the residence since the Scotts lived across the street at no. 17. The Scotts, who were among the pillars of the Paris Bahá'í community, hosted many gatherings in Edwin's atelier.[24] An excited Horace wrote to his family in Connecticut that it was the couple's first unfurnished residence as a family, which they hurriedly outfitted with furniture purchased as bargains from an American leaving the city. Bertha, a former interior designer, decorated it, leading Horace to remark that his wife could 'make a "home-palatial" out of a heap of colored cloth'.[25] As their fortunes improved, so did their accommodations. They moved months later to another apartment within the Latin Quarter,[26] and Bertha leased a studio.[27]

Bertha established a clothing business, creating dressing gowns and capes for American women of means living in Paris. It was an exciting time to be in fashion design because women's clothing was advancing rapidly to reflect the transformation of their social status as the suffrage movement won victories for women's rights. Tight fitting, floor-length gowns reinforced with constricting undergarments were being replaced by dresses that were shorter in length, practical, and more comfortable. Bertha was not only interested in creating innovative clothing for women; colour was her passion, influenced by artists of the Fauvist Movement – painters such as Matisse,[28] who used vivid colour in unnaturalistic and expressionistic ways. She extended this love for vibrant fabrics to a line of decorative items for the home, especially pillows.

Making a go of designing alluring clothing required the cultivation of a paying clientele among socially prominent women who would not only purchase Bertha's creations, but who would subtly advertise her designs by wearing them in public.[29] She staged events to exhibit her work and took advantage of opportunities to appear at social occasions where the Holleys could befriend potential clients. Within less than two years, the number of orders for her garments and pillows required a growing number of seamstresses. Unlike the Holley factories in Connecticut, there were no economies of scale because each article of clothing was customized for the specific client. For start-up capital, Horace had to again dip into his diminishing inheritance. He served as manager for his wife's business, and, reminiscent of his mother's millinery business, their home served as Bertha's workshop until she could afford a studio.

The Holleys established a second business to provide employment for Horace, the Ashnur Galerie of Art. The gallery, located at 211 Boulevard Raspail, was a short walking distance from their first home and close to the busy commercial intersection with Boulevard Montparnasse. It was also within sight of the Café du Dôme, the hub for American writers and artists. That café, like several others nearby, provided a space for ideas to spread, and connections to be made over steaming cups of coffee and cold sandwiches – just the place to meet artists who could be persuaded to sell their works through Horace's gallery. The modest storefront the Holleys rented at the street level of an apartment building was suitable for displaying a small collection of paintings, sculpture, embroidery, pottery, jewellery, and other works by contemporary, Post-Impressionist artists and craftsmen – the more modern, the better. To announce the gallery's opening, Horace composed and published an essay on the importance of art and distributed it as an advertisement. It concluded with, 'The freedom of self-expression achieved by any people is the index to its spiritual sanity.'[30] The Ashnur became known informally as the 'American Art Gallery'. It served as the Paris sales outlet for the English and French journals of the art and literature world and Horace allowed artists and writers to post announcements. Despite the gallery's favourable location within the hub of creativity, wealthy, fashionable people were unlikely to walk past, because the neighbourhood at the time was run-down.[31]

Managing his gallery in 1912 satisfied the entrepreneurial streak Horace had inherited from his family and placed him in contact with the community of artists and other imaginative thinkers drawn to the French capital during the years preceding the Great War. His knowledge of art and artists rapidly expanded as he became acquainted with luminaries such as Pablo Picasso[32] and as he gained a deeper understanding of the movements emerging in painting and sculpture. Tending his shop provided him with spans of free time between browsers and paying customers – time enough to jot down a poem or an idea, to read a book or to peruse a journal. A new set of questions began to swirl through his mind. What is the essence of art? What is a painter or sculptor attempting to achieve through the stroke of his brush or a hammer against chisel? Why is art important? He wrote an essay about the purchase of a painting that explored whether the woman who bought the work of art was truly worthy of owning it.[33] To his mind, a work of art was far more than an adornment; it was a living embodiment of the artist who created it. The artwork becomes a gift from the artist to another human being. Through deliberate observation of and reflection upon the creation, something of the artist is transferred to the unconscious being of the observer, but only if the observer is willing to take in the meaning of the work. Therefore, he concluded, the mere exchange of money should not determine the ownership of art. Horace believed that 'art is the medium for transferring the fulness and meaning of life from one to another personality'.[34] He asked whether 'we moderns can learn soon enough to make wealth incidental to life, or whether . . . a misdirected civilization will topple of its own weight . . .'[35] Had other forces of history not intervened first, this idealistic attitude toward the sale of artistic creations would have probably doomed the financial viability of Horace's gallery – and Horace's thinking would have astonished his grandfather Holley.

One visitor to the Ashnur Galerie wrote an account of the day he first met Horace. The American writer John Gould Fletcher, a young, well-educated wanderer, was exploring the sights of Europe while trying to determine the direction of his life. Aimlessly strolling down the sidewalk, he noticed Horace's shop with its paintings displayed in the front window, and, out of curiosity, walked inside, where he 'had the good fortune to meet an American who, like myself was then an exile living in Paris'.

> I was walking along the Boulevard Raspail when the sight of a shop window, where two or three pictures, painted in a manner akin to that of Cezanne and Matisse, were displayed, brought me to a halt. When I discovered that this was an art gallery, I went in. A tall, gaunt-looking young man, of about the same age as myself, with blue eyes and dark hair, arose from a desk at the back and addressed me in French.[36] I replied somewhat haltingly, whereupon he instantly laughed, apologized, and went on in English as American as my own. It turned out that he . . . had been brought to Paris by his American wife, a clever dress designer who served her large clientele of wealthy Americans there. Having nothing in particular to do, he had opened this small gallery, whose entire stock in trade, so far as I could see, consisted of the works of two exiled Scotsmen and one expatriated American. Horace Holley – this was my new friend's name – had also, like myself, cherished ambitions of becoming a poet, and had published a small volume, *Post-Impressionist Poems*, during that year in London. The gallery he was now running was well stocked with the works of his three painters – J.S. Peploe, whose art for a time enjoyed a considerable vogue in London, Anne

Estelle Rice, an American expatriate, one of whose pictures shown in the Independents a few months before my visit had achieved a scandalous success, requiring protection by the police from the threatened assaults of spectators, and finally, John Duncan Fergusson, who, as I recall, still lives and exhibits occasionally in London.

Holley knew all these painters personally, and offered me a letter of introduction to the one I considered the best – Fergusson – which instantly raised him high in my regard. I formed the habit, during my stay, of calling on him often and hearing him tell anecdotes of his own life in Paris, as well as incidents from the lives of these famous painters.[37]

During the short period when the Ashnur Galerie was a going business, the most significant artists promoted there were two of the four[38] Scottish colourists, Samuel John Peploe and John Duncan Fergusson. Fergusson especially was considered one of the leading British artists of the period. Another exhibitor, American, Anne Estelle Rice, a member of the Fauvist Movement, is remembered for her use of colour. Other artists who exhibited at the Ashnur included Jerome S. Blum and Charles Winzer, also Americans.

The primary artists associated with the Ashnur Gallery were also regular contributors to the British arts magazine *Rhythm*, one of the little magazines run by friends of Ezra Pound. In addition to Pound, the magazine included a number of up-and-coming writers such as Katherine Mansfield.[39] Horace advertised the gallery and published in that magazine. *Rhythm* was a good example of the many intersections between the graphic and literary arts at that time.

It is quite likely that a number of the Holleys' connections within the art and literary community originated with their friends, the Barney family. Laura Dreyfus-Barney had an sister, Natalie Barney, a poet, who hosted a legendary literary salon on Fridays in her Paris home. The list of those known to have attended is a who's who of the most noteworthy writers and artists of Western Europe and the United States. Unlike her religious and upright younger sister, Laura, Natalie was notorious for her open flouting of moral conventions of the time. Even though Natalie met 'Abdu'l-Bahá during His time in Paris and knew many of the Bahá'ís, probably including the Holleys, there is no evidence that she ever became seriously interested in the Faith. However, she was an unavoidable, dominating presence among the Dreyfus-Barneys' friends in the art world.[40]

* * * * *

In early Spring 1912, 'Abdu'l-Bahá again boarded a ship embarking from Egypt heading northwest; however, this time He stopped in Europe only long enough to change ships because His destination was New York City. After years of fervent entreaties from His American flock, He was on His way to visit them. For ten months He toured North America from coast to coast. At the end of that unforgettable visit, He was visibly exhausted but pleased with His American sojourn when He boarded the SS *Celtic* to sail for England. His historic tour of North America had been an unqualified triumph which would yield unlimited fruits with the passing of time. For the American believers, it had been an exhilarating, whirlwind Bahá'í education.[41]

His second visit to the British Isles was also successful despite His weariness. The strenuous schedule was enough to bring on exhaustion for anyone His age, but to this was added the onset of a cold, damp British winter which further affected His precarious health. Nevertheless, rather than escape to the warm, dry air of Egypt, He continued His work of furthering His Father's Faith, undaunted by His physical ailments.

Accompanied by British believers grief-stricken at His imminent departure, He entered Victoria Station on the morning of 21 January and there bid them farewell for the last time. The train took him to the Port of Newhaven, where He boarded a steamer sailing for the French port of Dieppe. From there He took another train, this time destined for the Saint Lazare Station in the heart of Paris. The night was cold and rainy, but inclement weather was not enough to discourage fifty people from anxiously awaiting His arrival. Thus began 'Abdu'l-Bahá's second visit to Paris, one that would extend until summer and provide the Holleys with ample opportunities to be with Him again. Of all the places He visited in the West, He spent the most time in Paris – longer even than the months He spent in New York.

There are undoubtedly many reasons 'Abdu'l-Bahá lingered in Paris. Ironically, He frequently told His entourage that the people there were less interested in Him and His message than the Americans and British.

Unlike His previous stops during His Western journey, He received only a smattering of invitations from leaders and clergy during His second visit to France. However, He had other reasons to be there. For one, His daughter, Rúhá, needed a throat operation, so He summoned her to join Him and attended to her care for several months. Perhaps His greatest attraction to Paris was to take advantage of its role as a hub for high-profile visitors from the Ottoman, Egyptian and Persian empires. At that time, the French had a heavy footprint in the Orient. It was possible for Him to privately meet with a significant number of key people from Iran, Turkey and Egypt in Paris, something that was impossible for Him to do in Haifa owing to the complexities of politics. Furthermore, though He could not travel to His homeland where the majority of Bahá'ís were to be found, He could meet with Iranian believers in Paris, including a number of young Bahá'í students.

His daily schedule developed a rhythm which allowed Parisian Bahá'ís, such as Horace, the ability to know when He was likely to be available. 'Abdu'l-Bahá would meet with visitors in the morning at His apartment, and around noon He would give a brief talk to whoever was there. Afternoons usually included a walk or drive through one of Paris's large public parks, calling upon people He wanted to see and receiving more visitors. If not too fatigued, He accepted invitations for the evening or spent it tending to correspondence. The Paris Bahá'í community held two regular weekly meetings, one on Mondays during the early evening hours at the home of the Holleys' neighbours, the Scotts, and the other, a Friday evening gathering at the Dreyfus-Barney home. (Frequently, the Sandersons hosted Bahá'í meetings, but during 'Abdu'l-Bahá's 1913 visit, this family took care of His daughter and her companions during the period of her medical treatment.) Occasionally, 'Abdu'l-Bahá attended these regularly scheduled meetings but had to curtail His participation after becoming ill. Several times when He could not attend Bahá'í community gatherings, He deputized someone to go on His behalf and to speak on a particular topic.

* * * * *

Horace's education in the Faith expanded during his time with 'Abdu'l-Bahá in Paris, and it had a French flavour. In His remarks, 'Abdu'l-Bahá often compared France with the United States and Great Britain, especially when speaking candidly to His travel companions and the closest Western friends, such as the Holleys. He knew that each country required a different emphasis of message. In the United States, His foremost topic was the oneness of mankind, placing special attention upon the need to bring the black and white races together. Due to the legacy of slavery, racial prejudice remained America's greatest and most intractable spiritual blemish. The theme He ofttimes repeated in England was the need to eliminate war and establish universal peace. In France, He confronted an entirely different spiritual disease: agnosticism and atheism. He did not intend by those labels only those who openly avowed their rejection or questioning of religion; instead, He included those who turn away from the life of the spirit in less overt ways by failing to make spirituality part of their daily lives, even if they continue to observe religious traditions. Indifference is just as harmful as denial.

Throughout history, there have been people who, for a variety of reasons, cannot accept the existence of a Supreme Being. As a well-educated American living in Europe, Horace had certainly encountered such people and been exposed to their thinking. For at least one hundred and fifty years before 'Abdu'l-Bahá's visit to Paris, many influential educated elites of Europe had rejected belief in God, and their published works helped to give atheism a patina of respectability. Many factors contributed to this denunciation of religion. Formal education included the study of Greek and Roman classics in their original languages, written by ancient pagans. This classic literature, pre-dating the widespread establishment of Christianity, was often more familiar to the educated than the text of the Bible. Secondly, the Enlightenment, an intellectual movement that emphasized the use of reason and the scientific method, led historians to a dispassionate study of religious history. The resulting works dispelled myths about the purity of the early centuries of Christianity. Hagiographies of the lives and works of saints were dismissed as little better than fairy tales. Even the story of the life of Jesus came under sceptical scrutiny. Adding to this revolution in religious thought were rapid advances in scientific knowledge which called into question many teachings of the Bible about the creation of the earth and its geologic history. Scholars took apart and examined the Biblical story of the creation of the universe with critical eyes, much as they would any secular text. Perhaps the greatest damage to the religious beliefs of the intelligentsia came not from scientists and theologians, but from the writings

Horace Holley playing with Hertha Holley as a baby during the time in Italy

Hotel du Parc at Thonon-les-Bains, France where Horace Holley first met 'Abdu'l-Bahá in 1911

Hertha Holley as a toddler with Bertha Holley. 'Abdu'l-Bahá delighted in Hertha as a young child

Horace holding his daughter, Hertha, 1912, the year the family moved to Paris

Informal picture of Hertha Holley looking at a book in May 1913, Paris

'Abdu'l-Bahá (foreground) in Paris in 1913 with his entourage and other Persians, posing under the Eiffel Tower. His English translator, Ahmad Sohrab, is third from the right

Hippolyte and Laura Dreyfus-Barney, pillars of the Paris Bahá'í community and friends of the Holley family

Horace Holley in front of the Ashnur Galerie in Paris, which he managed. The business, informally referred to as the 'American Gallery', specialized in Post-Impressionist art

The cottage the Holleys rented during the summer of 1914 as World War I was beginning. The Holley family are standing in front and the second woman is most likely the English nanny

of philosophers who argued that the existence of a Supreme Being was irrational. And if such a Being did exist, He was not interested in controlling the evolution of the world of matter, which came about through natural selection, not through a grand design – a point they asserted had been proven by Charles Darwin. They rejected even the proof of causality; that is, the argument that the universe could not create itself.

The long history of abuses inflicted upon humanity in the name of religion by ecclesiastical authorities further strengthened the arguments of the atheists. During the period of the Reformation and Counter-reformation, horrific wars sparked by disagreements on Christian doctrine were fought throughout Europe, especially in France. Staggering numbers of people died, and cities were laid waste in the name of Jesus. Relentless persecution of French Protestants intensified during the long reign of King Louis XIV, causing many to flee to the safety of North America. Later, during the period of the French Revolution, Christianity briefly became illegal in France under the rule of radical anarchists who seized control of the government and executed the monarch. Church property was confiscated, desecrated and looted, thousands of clergymen were executed, and nunneries and monasteries were forcibly closed. To further humiliate the shrinking numbers of avowed Christians, officials carried out pagan rituals in the public squares of Paris. The crowning blow came when French troops under the command of Napoleon Bonaparte marched on the Vatican, looted its treasures, captured Pope Pius VI, and took him back to France as a prisoner where he died while in captivity. Even though this repudiation of Christianity was partially reversed a few years later, many of France's elites never returned wholeheartedly to Christianity. In the century that followed, measures taken by the French government severed the church's remaining official ties to the state, further eroding Catholicism's privileged position in France. Except for peasants in the countryside and the remnants of the old ruling families, a sizeable percentage of Frenchmen considered religion to be a dangerous force, best subjugated or ignored.[42] This history explains in part how great was the spiritual battle 'Abdu'l-Bahá was fighting during His many months in Paris.

'Abdu'l-Bahá had interacted with the people of Paris during His 1911 visit, which gave Him opportunities to take the pulse of the French society in which the Holleys were immersed. The following year, He made this remark while He was in New York City:

> Paris is most beautiful in outward appearance. The evidences of material civilization there are very great, but the spiritual civilization is far behind. I found the people of that city submerged and drowning in a sea of materialism. Their conversations and discussions were limited to natural and physical phenomena, without mention of God. I was greatly astonished. Most of the scholars, professors and learned men proved to be materialists. I said to them, 'I am surprised and astonished that men of such perceptive caliber and evident knowledge should still be captives of nature, not recognizing the self-evident Reality.'[43]

Again and again during His second visit to Paris, 'Abdu'l-Bahá made virtually identical remarks to His travelling companions and close associates about the spiritual state of Paris. He had to fortify the French believers by giving them the tools required to remain steadfast in a dark sea of materialism, lest they too drown in it.

Horace's writings are evidence that if he had ever flirted with agnosticism or atheism, his interest had been short-lived. During his years as a student, he was exposed to many works espousing negative views towards belief in the existence of a Supreme Being who fashioned the universe with a grand design. How could he not be subjected to these ideas when the canons of literature and the writings of historians and social scientists of the early twentieth century were replete with works questioning or rejecting the existence of God, much less a divine plan? It is telling that Horace named his first-born 'Hertha' after the Mother Earth Goddess of Algernon Charles Swinburne's mystical poem by that name.[44] In the words of one commentator, Swinburne, an avowed atheist, wrote his favourite and most famous poem 'Hertha' as 'a meditation upon a godless universe', one 'without a personal god' even though it is written in the style of a religious invocation.[45] Later, Horace would open his introductory work on the Bahá'í Faith with a discussion of western agnosticism and atheism, beginning with the writings of Matthew Arnold. Horace's opinion was that this 'intellectual despair' had run its course and that a revival of religious faith was underway.

* * * * *

On Sunday morning, 26 January, the Holleys put on the good clothes they would have worn to a church, taking care to dress warmly for the damp cold of a Paris winter day. They had just returned from a visit to Switzerland. Two-and-a-half-year-old Hertha held tight to her parents as they made their way to 30 rue Saint-Didier. The triangular-shaped building where two streets joined was a beautiful relic from the past, with its small balconies ornamented with wrought-iron railings. As they entered the hotel lobby, they were greeted by the warmth of a fire across from the front door. Already people were there waiting to see 'Abdu'l-Bahá in His rented rooms, including other Americans. The Holleys had not seen 'Abdu'l-Bahá since their time with Him in Thonon seventeen months earlier. The weather outside was grey, but inside the small hotel all was sunshine.

During their visit that morning, 'Abdu'l-Bahá treated Hertha as if He were her adoring grandfather, with hugs, kisses and candy treats. Horace mentioned to Him that he was writing a book about the Bahá'í Faith from the perspective of economics. Others asked 'Abdu'l-Bahá about spreading the teachings of the Faith. At midday, He paused from speaking with individual visitors to deliver a talk to the assembled guests in His sitting area. That day He spoke about the Manifestations of God; that is, those Messengers of the Almighty sent to mankind to explain God's Will. These included Adam, Abraham, Moses, Jesus, and Muhammad in addition to the two recent Manifestations, the Báb and Bahá'u'lláh.

For almost five months in 1913, Horace was present with 'Abdu'l-Bahá at many gatherings. The records of those who attended each meeting are incomplete, but the Holleys are recorded by name a handful of times. It can be assumed that one or both Holleys attended the meetings at the home of the Scotts since they lived not far from them. There are indications that 'Abdu'l-Bahá visited Horace's nearby art gallery.[46] The Holleys heard Him discuss a wide variety of topics. For example, when they visited 'Abdu'l-Bahá a second time, He talked about how the sacred scriptures counteract superstition and prejudice.[47]

The Holleys brought along Hertha when they visited 'Abdu'l-Bahá on 20 February. While He was in the midst of speaking, Hertha suddenly dashed to Him. 'Abdu'l-Bahá lifted her up in the air and embraced her. Turning back to His audience, He recalled how much the little girl reminded him of his own young son, Ḥusayn, who had died at about age five. He recalled His treasured memories of that little boy climbing into His bed to be close to his Father.⁴⁸ Returning to His midday topic, 'Abdu'l-Bahá once again spoke of the materialism that had overtaken Europe and snuffed out its spirituality. He likened France to a beautiful tree which produced no fruit. He called upon those present to strive day and night to breathe a new spirit – the Love of God – into Europe, setting it alight to become a spiritual conflagration.⁴⁹ Whenever He gave a talk, as on that morning, He became animated. He would walk a bit, pause, and close His eyes, then move before a window and gesture with the sweep of a hand to illustrate a point. Sometimes He would move His turban to the edge of His eyebrow and peer through his lashes. Then He would smile and raise His hands to the sky, palms facing upwards. His voice would change, becoming that of one in authority issuing a command. Then His voice would alter again, becoming a soothing, "pleading gentleness' as though it was music from heaven.⁵⁰ His listeners were mesmerized.

When Horace made another visit to 'Abdu'l-Bahá on 19 May, he met other visitors who had just arrived from the United States. They were eager to report to 'Abdu'l-Bahá about the Bahá'í National Convention, which had just concluded. Their account made Him happy. Laura Dreyfus-Barney soon entered the little suite of rooms, bearing a magnificent bouquet of roses to further brighten the small space, already decked out with flowers from other admirers. Then it was Horace's turn to ask a question. Judging from the answer, it was a deep, important question based upon Horace's study of Charles Darwin's theory of evolution through natural selection, a pervasive ideology among many educated people and one often used to challenge belief in God. 'Abdu'l-Bahá's response as recorded that day was:

> In the spiritual mirror, the virtues of the world of humanity are visible. Just as the intellectual law unravels the mysteries of phenomena, similarly, the spiritual law acquires the ideal principles of humanity. Just as in the world of nature the 'survival of the fittest', likewise in the spiritual world there are the perfections of the divine realm. Just as order and peace are continued in a community through the strong hand of law, in the same manner the world of humanity exists through the acquirement of divine and spiritual virtues. The struggle for existence insures the growth and development of the species, likewise the spiritual law secures the unfoldment and progress of the spirit.⁵¹

In response to another question, perhaps also put to Him by Horace, 'Abdu'l-Bahá spoke about the material world as a great prison for the souls of men. Only through adherence to Divine Law can a man free himself from all the negative aspects and traits which derive from life in the material world. Ironically, abiding within the constraints imposed by Divine Law results in true freedom because it fosters life born of the spirit. That brief explanation about the importance of Divine Law would have more meaning for Horace twenty years later. Next, someone asked a question about spiritual happiness. His response was that there are three paths to happiness: tests and ordeals, perseverance along the spiritual path, and faith, the last being the speediest road to true happiness. He also addressed questions about the various stages of life and about the trials of the martyrs.[52]

* * * * *

In April, 'Abdu'l-Bahá left Paris for a month to travel to Germany to meet with that nascent Bahá'í community which had implored Him to come. He next accepted an invitation to visit Hungary from members of a family that were not Bahá'ís. From there, He travelled to Austria. At the close of the month, He returned for a third and final visit to Paris, arriving on 1 May 1913. Bertha was among those waiting to welcome Him as His train pulled into the Gare de l'Est (East Train Station) at 9:15 that evening.

The toddler, Hertha, had not seen 'Abdu'l-Bahá for more than a month when, on 4 May, the Holleys paid Him another visit. He had to coax her with candies until she again warmed to Him. This became a game where she would take a piece of candy from His hand, cross the room, and hand it to Laura Dreyfus-Barney. A little later, the child would retrieve the candies piece-by-piece from Laura and return them to 'Abdu'l-Bahá. When it was mentioned that Horace's book on the Faith would soon be published, 'Abdu'l-Bahá pointed to Hertha and said that the child was another book by Horace – a living book, a book from God. Bertha then brought up the subject of health and healing. 'Abdu'l-Bahá explained in detail that most ailments of the body require material means for healing, but some illnesses are brought on by spiritual sickness and these especially respond to prayer. It was thought naïve to believe that healing could come only through prayer. This topic led to a discussion comparing the material world with the spiritual world. The body of man is subject to decomposition, no matter how well he takes care of his health. He urged His listeners to turn to God and be assured that their prayers would be answered.[53]

During 'Abdu'l-Bahá's remaining six weeks in France, Horace was nearing the completion of his first book of prose, an exploration of the Bahá'í Faith as the answer to the social ills of society viewed through the lens of economics. He read excerpts at gatherings of the Paris Bahá'í community and answered 'Abdu'l-Bahá's questions about the progress of the manuscript at a meeting of the friends on 19 May. 'Abdu'l-Bahá responded that during the time of Christ, there were no books written about His Teachings, yet in this day, already a number of books had been written about the Faith, which showed the greatness of the Cause.[54]

As 'Abdu'l-Bahá's visit to the West drew to a close, the Holleys were granted an interview with Him on 25 May, this time at the ornate Baltimore Hotel. Throughout 'Abdu'l-Bahá's time in Paris, a number of individuals who would play a significant role in Horace's life later came to see Him and probably met Horace. For example, that morning, the Holleys met – probably for the first time – Fanny Knobloch, an American who had visited her ancestral homeland, Germany, in order to see her sister who was living there to spread the Faith. She had journeyed to Paris to spend more time with 'Abdu'l-Bahá. Fanny and her relatives in Washington DC would be among Horace's significant friends in a few years.

Most likely, the 25 May interview was the last opportunity Horace had to speak individually with 'Abdu'l-Bahá. The topic that 'Abdu'l-Bahá wished to discuss with him, the Bahá'í House of Worship, then under construction near Chicago, probably surprised Horace. The Holleys had no plans to return to live in the United States, but 'Abdu'l-Bahá knew that His guidance on that topic would become vital to Horace in the future.

At last, after more than two years of travel in the West, 'Abdu'l-Bahá began His journey eastward towards home, departing Paris on the morning of 12 June. It seems likely that at least one of the Holleys was among the fifty people who waited for him at the Gare de Lyon train station to bid him a last tearful goodbye. He took the time to speak briefly to each one. Then He was gone.

In writing his book, Horace tried to summarize 'Abdu'l-Bahá, calling Him 'Ambassador to Humanity', the title given 'Abdu'l-Bahá by one of those who heard Him speak in Washington DC, which seemed the most appropriate of many titles. Horace, nonetheless, shied away from endeavouring to capture the majesty and mystery of 'Abdu'l-Bahá; even the greatest of poets would fail at the attempt. Instead, Horace focused on the relevance of the message of 'Abdu'l-Bahá to the requirements of the hour.

> . . . But how different the mission, how different the method, how different the man! If any generation could distinguish out, while still living, the nature most richly and most potently endowed with its best forces, ours has that privilege. In 'Abdu'l-Bahá we have a mirror focusing all that is most significant, suppressing all that is irrelevant, of our time.[55]

Later in 1913, following 'Abdu'l-Bahá's final departure from Europe, Horace published *The Modern Social Religion*, to assist those seeking spiritual truth. It was more a reflection of the thinking of the twenty-six-year-old Horace than a faithful exposition of the teachings of the Faith. Published in London by Sidgwick & Jackson, Ltd., it was a timely book needed and welcomed by English-speaking believers.

Horace begins his book by acknowledging the previous century's trends toward agnosticism and atheism, but states that he perceives a return to spirituality during the early years of the twentieth century.[56] Horace believed that a great battle was raging in the West as to which would be the best means of solving the ills of society: the teachings of Christianity or the adoption of economic Socialism. He posits that the Bahá'í Faith fulfils both the needs of the spirit as well as those of society. While the book's broad themes are primarily faithful to the teachings of the Faith, the chapter recounting the lives of the Báb, Bahá'u'lláh and 'Abdu'l-Bahá, is the most accurate, although the narrative has errors. His mistakes and misconceptions are understandable because very little authoritative material was available in English, and those few translations of Bahá'í scripture he could study failed to capture either the exact words or the spirit of the teachings as they were given in Arabic or Persian.

Most of Horace's narrative concentrated on carefully articulating why a new universal religion was necessary. He couched his explanations in the modern language of evolution, natural science, psychology, and social science. The Bahá'í Faith was presented as the logical next step in both the material and spiritual evolution of mankind as a species (he preferred to use the word 'race').[57] Though clearly concerned with social justice and social reform, especially the rights of women and universal education, Horace was also interested in the mystical, and so he attempted to prove that the Bahá'í Faith was the answer to the ills of the world because it offered both material and spiritual solutions.

> Bahaism desires a new social order in which the development of spiritualized men and women shall be the primary purpose; not supermen, whose nature is essentially hostile to the many, but that order of free beings representing our own ideals achieved in daily life and common things. To such an order we already potentially belong, and the highest human fellowship the earth will ever contain will not be other than our own kind, released and inspired by participation in a co-operative society.[58]

Like most Western Bahá'ís at the time, Horace viewed the Bahá'í Faith as a movement, not as an independent world religion. He had not yet fully grasped that Bahá'u'lláh spoke with the authority of God and that the Bahá'í Faith was not influenced by earlier movements or ideas. Horace wrote that the Faith was 'a reaction . . . against an immediate condition'[59] and likened it in some of its essentials to the Protestant Reformation. A cursory reading of the book reveals that he continued to be a 'Christian-Bahá'í 'and wrote the work for a Christian audience.

The appendix of the book not only provides insights as to which publications Horace read but also gives a comprehensive overview of the Bahá'í literature available in the West in 1913. Inexplicably absent from his list of publications was the book that had introduced Horace to the Bahá'í Faith, Myron Phelps's *The Life and Teachings of Abbas Effendi*.[60] Undoubtedly, he had discovered the book's deficiencies as his own knowledge of the Cause expanded.

Despite its inadequacies, 'Abdu'l-Bahá extolled Horace's book in a Tablet to him in which He stated that as He had heard others praise the book highly, He hoped that it would be translated into Persian so that He Himself could read it. He showers Horace with praise and encouragement before making what must have been a startling prediction, a prophetic statement which probably left Horace perplexed.

Thank thou God that thou art confirmed and assisted; thy aim is to render service to the Kingdom of ABHA, and thy object is the promotion of the Teachings of BAHA'O'LLAH. Although the glory and greatness of this service is not known for the present, but in future ages it shall assume most great importance and will attract the attention of the most great scholars. Therefore, strive more and more as much as thou canst in this service, so that it may become the cause of thy everlasting glory and in the Kingdom of ABHA thou mayest shine like unto a star.[61]

Horace's greatest reward was writing the book itself, for the effort had required him to focus his considerable intellectual powers upon the exploration of what it meant to be a Bahá'í. A reviewer in *The Christian Commonwealth* (London) called it 'A work which may influence to no small degree the trend of religious reform . . . Mr. Holley's book is worthy of its great theme.'[62] Despite other positive reviews, sales were modest and within a few years, negligible.

* * * * *

The following spring, Horace and an American college student, Jack McClure, spending a year in Paris,[63] publicly sparred within the pages of one of the little literary magazines, *The Egoist*, about questions of religious truth.

McClure, who aspired to be a writer, fired the opening salvo with an essay recounting ongoing debates with Horace about religion. He did not name Horace, referring to him only as his friend 'the Bahaist'. His argument was actually that of pantheism. McClure claimed that what some people called God was in fact nature – the material world's forces that have always existed and will continue to exist. Thus, human beings are at one with all life on the planet, neither higher nor lower than any other aspect of the physical universe.

Horace responded by first identifying himself as McClure's unnamed 'Bahaist' friend and claiming 'the privilege of a reply'. While he admitted that the creatures of the world do change physically over time, he explained that each evolves according to its kind. He set forth the proposition that it is not the gift of reason which separates *homo sapiens* from other creatures, for animals employ reason, instead it is the ability of human beings to be cognizant of spiritual reality. He then launches into a discussion of spiritual reality and the dual nature of human beings: both material and spiritual. Coming back to the question of evolution, he states, 'Man *is* a Time-product. Evolution *is* attempting to discard men for a superior type. But men themselves contain the organism for infinite further development. It is poor thinking to imagine that superman must be organically different from man.'[64]

Characteristically, after carefully deconstructing his friend's theories, Horace ends his essay with a tribute to McClure. 'But I do not mean to be critical. It is such a relief to find a man in McClure's temperament in the Egoist, that I am tempted to destroy this letter and content myself with a glad *Hurrah! The Egoist has found an ego at last!*'[65]

Horace's willingness to forthrightly discuss his beliefs in major literary journals was consistent with his poetry, which often spoke of God and spiritual themes, subjects quite out of fashion – writing that would never win him admirers among those seeking to define modern poetry, especially Ezra Pound and his colleagues. This was ironic because Pound had met with 'Abdu'l-Bahá in England in 1911. He said this about that meeting: 'I went to conduct an inquisition & came away feeling that questions would have been an impertinence.' 'Abdu'l-Bahá was 'more important than Cezanne, & not the least like you'd expect of an oriental religious now' and 'he is a dear old man'. Though Pound was not won over by the encounter, he did come away with respect for 'Abdu'l-Bahá even as he continued to dismiss the Faith off-hand. Speaking of the Bahá'ís, he told a friend, 'The whole point is that they have *done* instead of talking, and a persian [sic] movement for religious unity that claims the feminine soul equal to the male, & puts Christ above Buddha, to the horror of the Theosophists, is worth while [sic]. Even if a lot of silly people do get mixed up in it.'[66]

The contrast between Pound's and Horace's responses to meeting 'Abdu'l-Bahá is a reminder that not everyone sees with the same eyes. Pound was drawn to the occult, but not to religion. Driven by other ambitions, Pound would place obstacles on the ladder to literary success for poets such as Horace whose writings explored the spiritual aspects of life.

* * * * *

As the Holleys and their Parisian friends basked in the afterglow of 'Abdu'l-Bahá's departure, storm clouds were rapidly building on the eastern horizon. 'Abdu'l-Bahá had warned the peoples of the West repeatedly that if immediate measures were not taken to end the antagonisms between rival nations – especially between Great Britain and Germany – a great conflagration was inevitable, and it would not be long in coming. He advised his listeners that a thought of war should be replaced by a stronger thought of peace. But His warnings went unheeded. His prediction of a approaching great calamity was about to come true. The Holleys would soon be refugees.

4

TURMOIL

Homeward
There is no other bosom for a grown man
To sob his whole heart-bursting grief upon
Than the sweet motherhood of his own native race;
No voice to call him back from loneliness
Than his own language, uttered from the first
   comfortings of love
By the hushed lips of poets and faithful women
Speaking into the great darkness
That he, in his dark time, may turn homeward
   again and find
The world's heart warmly near.

Horace Holley

While 'Abdu'l-Bahá was still in France in 1913, He received news of a speech delivered by the American Secretary of State, William Jennings Bryan. He was keenly interested in Bryan because the popular politician had visited Him in 'Akká and owned a copy of the Phelps book, *Life and Teachings of Abbas Effendi*. 'Abdu'l-Bahá reciprocated his visit while crossing the United States in 1912, by making a brief detour to the Bryan home in Nebraska. Bryan was away that day, but his wife Mary, his partner in all that he did, warmly welcomed the unexpected visitor from the Holy Land and undoubtedly gave her husband a full report of 'Abdu'l-Bahá's visit.

Devoutly religious Bryan was a pacifist and in 1913 was scurrying around the world, especially Europe, using his best skills as a lawyer to persuade governments to sign bilateral arbitration treaties with the United States. These treaties required a twelve-month cooling-off period during which all disputes would be submitted to an investigative tribunal. During the period just before the onset of World War I, Bryan's efforts would garner 30 treaties, including with most of the major nations of Europe. Alas, the idealist could not secure agreements with bellicose Germany and the Austro-Hungarian Empire.[1]

On 23 May, the *New York Herald* newspaper ran an article about a speech Secretary Bryan had delivered to a military group on 14 May. That article reached 'Abdu'l-Bahá in Paris. He was pleased with His friend Bryan, whose talk spoke of battleships of the future composed of the material of friendship, captained by the Prince of Peace, navigated by the compass of the heart, and firing shells of good will propelled by the gunpowder of love.[2] When this article was read aloud to 'Abdu'l-Bahá and assembled visitors, He discussed Bryan's talk. According to His translator, 'Abdu'l-Bahá responded to the *New York Herald* article by commenting:

> The Spirit of this age demands the establishment of universal Peace. No power on earth can withstand before it. God has destined that Peace must reign in this age and it will come to pass. Let the advocates of Peace work with greater zeal and courage for the Lord of Hosts is their supporter. In this radiant century and merciful age, the ears are opened, the hearts are awakened, the eyes are seeing and the consciounces [sic] are stirred. The age of strangeness has passed, the century of friendship has arrived. The dark hours have disappeared and the luminary of unity hath dawned. Now is the time to be illumined with the rays of the sun of the solidarity of the human race. This is not the hour to take life. This is the hour to impart life; this is the hour of self-sacrifice for the commonweal of humanity.[3]

Throughout His time in the West, 'Abdu'l-Bahá expounded upon the theme of peace because He knew humanity was careening toward an unfathomable calamity. A 1912 newspaper interview quoted Him as saying, 'All Europe is an armed camp. These warlike preparations will necessarily culminate in a great war. The very armaments themselves are productive of war. This great arsenal must go ablaze. There is nothing of the nature of prophecy about such a view . . . it is based on reasoning solely.'[4]

Horace's facility with French meant he was not confined during his years in Paris within the bubble of English speakers; this would be an advantage as 1914 unfolded. That year, he began to write a regular column for the French arts journal, *Les Soirées de Paris*, focused upon what was happening in the arts in England and the United States. This significant journal had been founded by a group of notable writers and artists led by Guillaume Apollinaire, the famous poet and art critic (and friend of the Barneys.) Its offices were located a short walk from his gallery at 278 Boulevard Raspail, so Horace stopped there frequently. This put him in contact with many luminaries of the French art and literary world who kept him abreast of current events from a French viewpoint. He particularly loved to loiter at their offices on Wednesday afternoons when submissions for the upcoming issue arrived.[5] Horace had a bit of fun with this French journal. For at least one issue, he created a mischievous French penname, O. W. Gambedoo, which allowed him to write a tongue-in-cheek assessment of English-speaking poets. The mystery author states he is friends with John Gould Fletcher and praises his writing.[6] Unfortunately, Horace's venture into anonymous writing only lasted one issue, because events were about to overtake his brief venture writing for the French magazine.

In 1914, those paying attention to the public discourse in speeches and the media would have easily noted the growing animosity between Great Britain and France and their nemesis, Germany, and concluded that the European powers were racing dangerously towards a precipice. The arts community of Paris, however, was not paying attention. The artists and writers on both sides of the Atlantic mostly ignored the warning signs of the approaching conflagration, preferring to believe, as many among the intelligentsia did, that the countries of Europe had become too interconnected to raise up arms against each other. It would be uncivilized.[7] And were there not well-organized peace movements pressuring the governments of Europe as well as the United States to avoid armed conflict? Horace had always been a student of politics eager to keep abreast of the developments of the day, including the opinions to be found in political journals and newspapers. He had heard 'Abdu'l-Bahá Himself warn of the imminent dangers facing the people of Europe and was conversant with the Bahá'í programme that would eliminate them. Horace wrote about the coming conflict in *The Modern Social Religion*, at least eighteen months prior to the outbreak of hostilities, for he had taken to heart the warnings he heard from the lips of 'Abdu'l-Bahá. Horace identified England and Germany as the most likely belligerents and posited that only a world federation could prevent the coming clash of arms: 'Could England and Germany be dissolved into a synthesis larger than either and including both, this fateful war-cloud would instantly become a very harmless mass of smoke and vapour.'[8]

Despite Horace's anticipation that war was coming, he and his family associated within the rarefied atmosphere of the elite – that of their wealthy clients, and even more so the intellectuals and artists within whose circles they revolved. This was also true of the Parisian Bahá'í community, composed as it was primarily of well-to-do expatriates and friends such as Hippolyte Dreyfus, who, though a native of France, was ethnically Jewish and thus unrepresentative of most of his countrymen. In a neighbourhood such as the Latin Quarter, which was a world apart from the other areas of Paris, chats with their local grocers and other vendors would probably not have given the Holleys an accurate sense of the undercurrents flowing through the general population. Many ordinary citizens were growing more conservative and nationalistic as they longed for the old ways of life discarded during the industrial age, at the same time as their 'betters' were pushing reform and trying to throw off stifling traditions of all sorts. As the younger generation of Europeans looked backward, their deep feelings of ethnic and national pride increased. Many wished to return to a romanticized mythical time of national greatness and comforting customs that their parents had gladly jettisoned for the benefits of modernity. In fact, most people of the West were unaffected by or uninterested in the writers, artists, and the *avant-garde* trends that obsessed the Holleys and which would be appreciated and adopted by the general population only years later.[9] Little wonder that within their orbit of acquaintances, it was easy for the Holleys to turn away from the warning signs that should have accelerated changes to their personal lives and businesses.

* * * * *

It was April in Paris in 1914, and Horace was in high spirits. The Holleys were well settled into their home, their businesses were beginning to flourish, and their social circles were expanding. A growing number of Horace's writings were appearing in print. Life was fine and suggested a bright future. That month Horace wrote to Irving describing his domestic bliss, stating that he admired his newly married brother's household virtues because he completely lacked them himself. Horace's idea of a good place to live was a shelter within which to eat and sleep with 'the least possible trouble', a small studio apartment would do nicely. Bertha held opposing preferences. With great care, she had transformed their Parisian nest into a lovely home with hand-painted wall hangings and curtains, furniture she had enamelled and adorned with a multitude of colourful, embroidered cushions. The couple enjoyed entertaining, and even hosted a costume party; but mainly they offered guests tea on Sundays or coffee 'of an evening'. One must wonder how Irving imagined his brother's social life when Horace described his friends:

> Our friends are all nationalities and types, but each one representing some definite force. We go to few houses, but each is the centre of an interesting group. Saturday afternoons, for example, Bertha loves to go to Princess Eristoff's,[10] where we always meet unusual people. We met the Princes Bourbon (Spanish royal family) there, and numbers of artists, musicians, and revolutionists.[11]

Bertha had created a niche in the fashion world designing jackets, opera coats, and dressing gowns made of embroidered silks. She had already held a successful exhibition of her designs at the Hotel Astoria in Paris the previous February and had received an offer to host another at a major summer resort in August. Her goal was to open a shop on Rue de la Paix, with Horace as its business manager.[12] Horace was floating a book, *The Dynamics of Art*, around publishing houses and outlining a play written in verse. The toddler Hertha had become known as the 'modern art baby' who, naturally, was 'bewitchingly' dressed by her mother. The Holleys had already leased a cottage in the country for the month of August, where the lively four-year-old could explore nature with her father. They would travel back and forth to Paris as business required, and because they had rented their Paris apartment to others for late summer, they would use Bertha's studio as their Parisian base.

*****

The Holleys' plans were about to collide with other plans. As the family looked forward to their summer activities, German generals were busy honing a strategy known as the Schlieffen Plan, to facilitate the invasion of France, to reclaim borderlands they considered rightfully German, and to avenge affronts to Teutonic honour. The German military assumed that the tiny, neutral country of Belgium would not offer resistance, and that a sweep into France would be swift and decisive. The French military were occupied with finalizing their own defensive plans. They correctly assumed the Germans would attack by marching through Belgium, so they planned to counterattack Germany's left flank through the Ardennes and invade Germany's soft underbelly.[13] The military of both countries had been waiting a long time for an opportunity to put their plans into action. Their years of preparation were at an end.

On 28 June, while making a state visit to the city of Sarajevo in the Balkans, the heir to the Austrian-Hungarian throne, Archduke Ferdinand, and his wife were gunned down by a Serbian nationalist. News of the assassination was of little interest to Parisian society. When the wealthy American writer Edith Wharton, who was hosting a garden party in Paris, received word of the assassination, her guests shrugged and continued their chatter about 'the last play, the newest exhibition, the Louvre's most recent acquisitions'.[14] Nonetheless, the Austrians could not ignore the crime and threatened revenge upon the Slavs of Serbia by issuing an ultimatum on 23 July and declaring war on the 28th. Serbia's Slavic brothers, the Russians, felt compelled to come to Serbia's aid. The entry of Russia into this skirmish gave Germany the excuse it needed to execute its Schlieffen Plan, first by declaring war on Russia on 1 August, then by invading Luxembourg the next day. Its armies invaded Belgium on 3 August; the same day Germany declared war on France.

The German goal was to overrun France while its ally, Austria, attacked Russia. German armies rolled through neutral Belgium; but rather than making a swift, easy passage, they encountered resistance from the Belgian army and from irregular civilian fighters. German troops responded by carrying out atrocities against innocent men, women, and children – acts of barbarity that Europeans incorrectly believed were no longer possible on a continent that only weeks before had epitomized enlightened refinement and the apex of human civilization. Not only did the Germans kill thousands of unarmed civilians, they wantonly destroyed the cities and towns, including cultural treasures. Except for England, which subsequently declared war on Germany, most of the world looked on in horror yet failed to rush to the aid of little Belgium.

Even though armies were on the move, the Holleys were obligated to continue with their holiday plans. They departed Paris, making the short journey by train to their summer cottage in the hamlet of Poigny, which would serve as much as a refuge as it would a holiday location for the little family. Every morning during the weeks prior to their departure, Horace left home before breakfast to purchase newspapers to keep abreast of the war. Expecting the worst, the Holleys made arrangements for their business affairs should trouble come. Their luggage included a full box of provisions, since they were uncertain how long they would be away from Paris.[15]

As soon as they arrived in Poigny, Horace headed to the Post Office where he hastily penned a letter to his eldest brother, Frank, in which he related where they were, which bank held their funds, and their plans should the politicians fail to avert all-out warfare. It was 1 August, the day Germany declared war on Russia and the day after the popular socialist leader and anti-war advocate, Jean Jaurés, was assassinated in a Paris market. Horace heard it was to be the last day civilians would be allowed to travel by train according to the normal schedule. He was already devising means of sending mail back to Paris should the postal system shut down. His letter described organized chaos as school buildings and other empty spaces were requisitioned to billet troops. He even anticipated that their Paris apartment would soon be taken for that purpose. But he assured his American relatives in Connecticut, that they need not worry because he and Bertha were prepared for disorder. 'We have food and money for a long time . . . Whatever happens we can get through with whole skins at least.'[16]

Their trip to the country by train had given the Holleys a glimpse of what was actually happening, not just what was being reported in the newspapers.

> . . . An Army Captain told me last night that the chances were 20 to 1 that a civil revolution would break out in Paris immediately War was declared. The Station was held by a company fully armed, as we entered it this morning. All along the line we met troop trains and trains of various munitions, going to the front . . . Driving

out from Rambouillet to Poigny, we passed many farmers trudging to the railroad, change of shoes and stockings on their back, some accompanied by weeping women, who had been recalled to their regiment by telegraph. Very few expected or hoped any longer that war can be avoided.[17]

By the time Horace wrote to Irving again two weeks later, Great Britain had fully entered the conflict, and the fires of battle were spreading across other regions of the continent. Unknown to the French public, the border areas of France were already ablaze. With the world collapsing around him, Horace's letter to Irving was focused on congratulating his brother and his wife on the birth of their first child and on giving advice for managing the sleeping patterns of a newborn. 'Gee, I never thought I'd be handing out advice of this kind, like a wise old grandmother!' He ended by reminding his brother of their carefree days together at 8 Prospect Street when they were a complete family together and how far they had come from those happy times in a small New England city.[18] A letter from Irving crossed his in the mail, reaching Horace the next day. It must have expressed the anxiety of the relatives as it contained a sincere offer of hospitality to Horace and his family should they need to return to the United States. Horace was grateful but certain that leaving France was 'not a necessity but a luxury'. However, he assured his brother that they would not be foolish and would leave for the United States if 'circumstances turn against France to a wholly unexpected degree. . .' While he understood his brothers' concerns about the war, he assured Irving that being resident in Europe 'soon changes one's ideas unfortunately'. He concluded by stating, 'Let us hope it will be the last war of all!'[19]

Away from the fighting in their three-roomed thatched cottage with its garden, the Holleys enjoyed the fresh air and the leisurely pace of rural French life throughout most of the month of August – even assisting local farmers with bringing in their harvest. The war was all but forgotten as French newspapers continued to provide encouraging reports, reassuring the public that the homeland's borders were impregnable – reports deliberately failing to give the true state of the war, to reduce fear. Horace turned his thoughts from the turmoil of current events to the peace of writing a novel, expecting to enjoy an enforced lengthy holiday all the while expecting to return to Paris within another month, the war happily won.[20] But as the end of August approached, so did the German armies, which, having laid waste to Belgium, were rapidly advancing on Paris.

Bertha returned to Paris on 25 August to see off friends sailing for America. The next day she dispatched a frantic telegram to her husband asking him to return to Paris at once. Leaving Hertha with her British nanny, Horace spent five hours at the Rambouillet train station, trying to secure a seat on any train headed toward Paris. For the first time, he saw with his own eyes the gravity of the situation, and he was shocked. Trains filled with retreating French and British troops, many of whom were wounded, passed by the station, as did trains packed with Belgian refugees. He learned from British soldiers that the allied armies were in retreat and that the fighting was not far away from Poigny, that their numbers had been decimated in fierce fighting and that no reinforcements came to their rescue, yet they remained determined to fight on. Worse, both an elderly Belgian refugee and a French Corporal recounted to him the atrocities they had witnessed first-hand. Whispered the refugee, '*I have no wish to live. I have seen what no human being can look upon and continue to believe in the value of life. . .*' The Frenchman related to him the torching of an ambulance full of wounded.[21] Once aboard, Horace witnessed from the train's window men digging entrenchments not twenty kilometres from his summer cottage.

Safely reunited with his wife, Bertha informed him she had been advised to bring their daughter to Paris or to take her further south. Horace hurried back to the train station to return to the cottage to retrieve Hertha; but, after three hours of waiting, found that the first seat available was at 4:30 the next morning. He and Bertha used the time to hastily pack and to withdraw money from the bank – they had the good fortune of dealing with the only bank in Paris that was not imposing a $50 limit on withdrawals.

On Monday 31 August, Horace, with Hertha and her nanny in tow, returned to Paris. He had observed a woman weeping uncontrollably at one train station because she could not buy a ticket after many hours of waiting. This sparked the concern that he and his family might become stranded in Paris – a possibility he was ready to face himself, but which he was determined should not be the fate of his young daughter, even should he have to pay a taxi to take them away from the fighting. During his return to Poigny, Bertha spent the day in Paris trying to get train tickets for their escape south. She waited in line all morning and, when it was finally her turn at the ticket booth, she was informed she would have to come back the next morning.

As soon as the family were reunited at the apartment at 9:30 that evening, Bertha and Horace instructed the nanny to put Hertha to bed and to continue the packing while they went back out into the city to find a way to escape. It was 10:30 p.m. They encountered a friend who told them about a Russian who could arrange passage to Spain. They hailed a taxi and rushed there, only to find the Russian sleeping. Rousing him, they learned they were too late, the southern route was no longer open. The Russian also informed them that parts of Paris had been bombed earlier that day and that there was little prospect of getting out of the city. The Holleys hurried back to their waiting cab and had it take them to train stations around the city hoping to secure passage. At 12:30 a.m. they arrived at the St Lazare station, scene of 'Abdu'l-Bahá's arrival eighteen months earlier. Horace determinedly strode through the baggage room and then forced his way into the English ticket office, which was packed full of Americans and British citizens who had already spent a day and night there waiting for tickets. Horace decided the family should head north to England rather than try to go south, no matter the cost. Miraculously, he was able to purchase tickets for the port of Le Havre on a 3:30 a.m. train. Despite the tickets, there was no assurance that they would have seats, nor that they would obtain passage on the boats crossing the Channel.

The Holleys dashed back home, woke and dressed Hertha, grabbed their hastily packed luggage, and together with their nanny, dashed back to the St Lazare Station. On their way, the taxi's tyre blew out and the spare one did not work, but the driver drove anyway on the wheel's wooden rim. As they made the journey through the sleeping City of Lights, Horace was astonished at the blackness and emptiness of Paris.

> We arrived there at 2:55 A.M. through a city of which every strategic point – bridges, public buildings, etc – was in complete darkness. Absolute quiet and calm. I shall never forget that trip across the Place de la Concorde and the Seine. It can be described only by comparing it with one of those half-familiar, half-strange places seen in dreams. In all Paris I had not seen a dozen taxis that night.[22]

By the time they arrived at the station, the gates to the platform were already open and the surging crowd had filled every space on the train. Somehow, they found a place to sit – a miracle of sorts. Having obtained transport to the coast, they faced their next worry: finding passage across the English Channel. Their fellow passengers informed them that Le Havre was already jammed with refugees seeking passage to England. As the train lumbered north, they passed French cavalry, artillery and supply wagons headed toward Paris. Were they in retreat? Were they reinforcements for the defence of the city? At each stop along the way to the coast more people fleeing the fighting crammed into the already overcrowded cars. Horace wrote his family from the train, 'I have been 30 hours without sleep and on short rations, but I was never so thoroughly alert in my life.'[23]

As the train headed northward towards its destination, Horace pondered the meaning of the war – a topic he would return to many times over the decades that followed. 'It comes over me with the intensity of a religious faith that this war in its true relation to human affairs is not a conflict between jealous races, it is not a treaty fight – it is a war against war.' He then discusses the importance of disarming Germany. 'Only so will the roots of war and "armed peace" be torn from the ground.'[24]

When the train pulled into the station at Le Havre, Horace rushed to the ticket office for ships sailing for England. Adding to the family's worries, in the confusion of their departure, their trunks were lost. Bertha and the nanny took four-year-old Hertha to find food while Horace waited in line for hours to secure passage out of France by boat. Finally, it was his turn at the ticket window. Everything seemed in order until the agent insisted upon knowing their British nanny's address in England. There would be no sale without it, and Horace had no idea what it was. The women were half a mile away at a café. He had an idea. He asked the agent to excuse him for a moment. He rushed to a nearby train and pretended to talk to a woman through a window where the agent could see him. He returned to the agent with a London address he made up in his head. Satisfied, the agent sold him the precious tickets. Remarking later about the incident, Horace said, 'I don't believe it was a very immoral lie!'[25]

Le Havre was overrun with troops – French, British, and Belgian. How Horace admired them, especially the short-of-stature Belgians who were ill-dressed and equipped! Those battered warriors had 'such an air of conscious responsibility and determination! You felt that they knew the world's eyes were upon them and they will prove themselves even. The crowds went wild over them.'[26]

Late that evening, the family boarded the ship. Unable to secure a cabin, they huddled on deck in the company of many other passengers. It was cold. Children were crying. Horace noted small black objects floating in the water as the moon shone upon it which he recognized with a start to be British mines.[27] A wave of emotion swept over him as he pondered the great military forces at work and the protection provided by the British navy – a protection making their passage across the English Channel possible. They arrived at the port of Southampton at 5:30 in the morning. The sunrise was beautiful. The ship made its way cautiously toward the harbour, carefully steering away from mines, barely discernible in the early light. As they approached the docks, they watched four British naval cruisers – 'great ships with heavy guns' – embark in a single line. Other warships rode at anchor.[28]

The first thing Horace did when the family arrived in London was to head to the telegraph office, where he cabled Frank to inform his nervous American relations of their safe arrival. He learned from a clerk at that office that thousands of anxious messages were arriving daily from Americans worried about their loved ones in Europe.[29] He found lodging for himself in the attic of the 'Poetry Bookshop'[30] in London while Bertha and Hertha went to stay for a time with friends in the English countryside and the nanny returned to her mother.

While in London during the next month, Horace had another experience that brought out a further tragic element of armed conflict between nations. The Holleys visited with an unnamed friend who was a Member of Parliament and a published authority on diplomatic history. Their friend's wife was proud to be German. The poor family had close relatives fighting in both the German and French armies.[31] While the family was having tea with the Holleys, their son, fresh from training in the British Army, arrived in uniform with his rifle, and started to talk about his desire to kill Germans, unaware that his mother was present. His quietly weeping mother, who believed the cause of her homeland was a just one, was horrified.[32]

This first-hand experience with war fired Horace's spirit. He was delighted to be in a place with reliable news of the fighting. He tried to assess the tenor of the times among the British, even attending the

'Nation's Call to Duty' rally hosted by the Lord Mayor of London. Rallies such as this were held throughout the British Empire to stimulate patriotic support of the war effort. The most prominent of the speakers at that London rally was Prime Minister H. H. Asquith. The other speakers included a who's who of leading English politicians. Horace recorded this historic period for his American friends and relations back in Connecticut.

> ... I went about London, feeling the temper of the people and reveling in the vast choice of newspapers. Somehow, too, I felt a sudden reaction from my tension at Paris, especially as the German line of advance seems to have changed its direction. At first I could not realize the apparent indifference of the English at this war. I wanted to stop men on the street and ask them if in heaven's name they did not know their country was at war. But very quickly I appreciated the fact that this indifference was only on the surface. If nothing else could prove it the great Guild Hall meeting yesterday was more than proof enough that the English not only realize that they are at war but will fight to a finish. The Hall itself reminded me of my own college chapel at Williams, but a chapel richly hung with old battle flags and decorated with statues of men famous before we were a separate nation. How I felt the power radiating out from the oratory of men not only influential but cultivated, not only magnanimous but stirred to the heart's last depth! I need not go into detail about the meeting because of course the papers will have it. But I can't help mentioning something I heard cried out amid the shouts of enthusiasm greeting Churchill. 'Your mother was an American[33] – hurrah!'[34]

The Holleys' stay in England was brief. At first, upon learning that the German march on Paris had been stopped, they hoped to return to their home from where Horace intended to bicycle through the battlefields,[35] but as the weeks went by, that option seemed less prudent. By 3 November, they were aboard the ocean liner *Minnetonka* as it steamed into the port of New York – after a blessedly safe crossing amidst the early days of war.[36] This ship's luck would run out less than three years later when, as a troopship, she would be torpedoed and sunk by a German U-boat. Perhaps it was during this very crossing, with the

Holleys on board, that its captain thought his ship was being tracked closely by a German cruiser, and so decided to make a risky full-steam run for New York through the fog of Nantucket with the *Minnetonka*'s lights out and its fog-horn silent. The engines worked so hard that the ship's decks shook.37 The Holleys and their fellow passengers breathed a collective sigh of relief at the sight of the New York City skyline and the Statue of Liberty, with the war and the perils of the Atlantic at their backs. But for the Holleys, one immediate fear would be replaced by another, less tangible one – their uncertain future.

Horace never forgot his first-hand experience with the horrors of war. Though his brush with the war was brief, its effect upon him was lasting and profound. The cause of world peace became a passion and, as a Bahá'í, he understood that international institutions had to be established in order to achieve it. He would often look back at what was at first called the Great War and later referred to as World War I and contemplate what it meant. War became a theme of his poetry. By the time the fighting stopped, the unrelenting, futile, wasteful, mass carnage of trench-warfare had devoured millions of Europe's youths. In 1916, as America debated whether to enter the conflict, he began a poem entitled 'War' with these words:

> What heart can hold the heartbreak of this war?
> Its sorrow, more excessive than the sea,
> Breaks every dike of feeling.38

The idea of returning to live in America – even visiting the United States – was not something the Holleys had entertained or even desired. Several years earlier, Horace had written to his brothers that he wished to visit the United States to see his family, but his finances prevented it. Besides which, Bertha loved France and her life there. Only a war could remove Bertha from Paris. And then there was their daughter. Four-and-a-half-year-old Hertha had never set foot in America, had never met her aunts, uncles, and cousins. How would she adjust to life in a land foreign to her?

The naïve, untried youth who had sailed from that same port city for France five years earlier no longer existed. In the autumn of 1909, he had been a recently orphaned Christian-Bahá'í university student wrestling with life's great themes. On the day he set sail he had been married only a few days to an older woman he had known for less than six months. He returned to New York City a seasoned husband, a father, a published writer of growing renown, an art merchant, and an experienced traveller with a network of friends among the arts community on both sides of the Atlantic. His earlier interest in the new religion, the Bahá'í Faith, had been nurtured and strengthened through his times with 'Abdu'l-Bahá in France, and his spiritual understanding and commitment to the Faith were deeper, wider, more developed. He had already published his first introductory book about the Faith. He was all of twenty-seven years of age.

Horace was hardly off the ship when he began reflecting upon his five-year sojourn in Europe, marking it as a pivotal period of his life, concluding that his arrival in France in late 1909 signified the end of his adolescence. Though his youth had prepared him for a rigorous life of the mind, it was the period of early adulthood that was for him a period of true self-discovery – a time when he was no longer under the tutelage of teachers, professors, and mentors, unless one considered the authors whose works he ravenously devoured to be his teachers. Seldom had a young man at just that stage of life had such a rich milieu in which to deeply ponder life's hidden meanings than did Horace during his European years. Back in New York, he realized through introspection that those years had been a period of adjusting his inner desires to the realities of life. He wrote, 'The first five years after adolescence are spent in accommodating one's instinctive, innate preference to the casual requirements of environment. That accommodation almost invariably consists in establishing a new psychic centre at the expense of the natural one.'[39] So what was that new psychic centre within the young writer?

5

THE POET RETURNS

Now as from a long arduous journey
Have I returned
Homeward within myself
And loose from aching shoulder the pressing straps,
And lay my burden down, my wisdom,
Content with home.

       Horace Holley[1]

The only thing that Horace had to do to recognize how much New York City had changed during his five-year absence was to look around. Towering over the skyline was the new sixty-storey Woolworth Building, the tallest building in the world – soon to be eclipsed by other skyscrapers under construction. These leviathans owed their existence to recent developments in elevator technology and the invention of the steel frame. In 1914, no other city in the world had such a soaring skyline – a portrait of the future. From the moment Horace and his family left the docks and stepped onto New York's thoroughfares, he must have wondered what had happened to the horse-drawn carriages and wagons because they had mostly been replaced by machines: trams, buses, trucks, and automobiles.[2] Engineering had advanced, and prices had fallen thanks to the efficiencies of Henry Ford's automotive assembly lines – an industrial innovation that was transforming manufacturing and making all kinds of technologies affordable. Instead of strolling the park-like boulevards that crisscrossed Paris, the Holleys were dwarfed by a grid work of masonry canyons that stretched straight into the horizon. This upstart on the Hudson was not yet the world centre of the arts, but it had snatched the crown of King of Commerce from London. New York was the New World flexing its muscles.

 New York City is an unwieldy metropolis. Its five boroughs, spread across islands and peninsulas, are separated by the deep channels of the Hudson, East and Harlem Rivers where they converge and empty into the Atlantic Ocean. This favourable geography gave the city one of the largest natural deep-water ports in the world. Despite consisting of five districts, the common image of New York is the island of Manhattan, with its skyscrapers planted firmly in the city's unusual bedrock. That island would be Horace's home for the next quarter century.[3]

* * * * *

In the beginning, Horace was not reconciled to moving back to the United States, a sentiment expressed gloomily in his poem 'New York (By an "artist refugee")'. The poem employed images of Greek warriors returning home at the end of the Trojan War drawn from Homer's classic tale, the *Iliad*. He had faced an uncertain future when he embarked from New York for France in 1909 and now, five years later, he returned with greater confidence that he and Bertha could meet this unexpected new challenge. Any certainty that he and his family could resume the lives they left behind in Europe, was, alas, mistaken. For as difficult as the past three months had been, an unforeseen storm, more turbulent than what he had recently experienced, was about to appear on the horizon.

Untethered from his art gallery and Paris routine, Horace used his time to put pen to paper. He started writing while lodging at the Poetry Bookshop in London and continued during late autumn in New York. Judging by the volume of articles published during the first half of 1915, his output during the last months of 1914 and winter of 1915 was prodigious. He composed new poetry and wrote essays on a variety of topics, especially about the arts.[4] One essay discussed American writers like himself returning from Europe because of the War.[5] Another mused about art and life. A third rebuked the purveyors of taste in America for failing to appreciate its native sons' contributions to the decorative arts.[6] And there were others. Horace the writer was running full steam.

* * * * *

In December 1914, the Holleys rented a studio apartment in midtown Manhattan at 19 East 48th Street, a suitable location from which to relaunch Bertha's career as a women's fashion designer.[7] It was located close enough to Central Park for Hertha to enjoy outings and an easy walk from the new (1911) monumental Main Branch of the New York Public Library in Bryant Park – a magnet for Horace. Their small home gave Bertha proximity to department stores and clothing boutiques, as well as to the Garment District. The couple immediately set to work to re-establish the clothing business they had left behind in Paris.

The following April, Bertha asked her husband for funds to invest in a scheme that promised a good rate of return within a short period. She had learned about this money-making opportunity through a friend who could facilitate the investment. Horace agreed and turned over to his wife's friend a sizeable portion of their savings.

Saturday, 8 May began uneventfully for the Holley family. That spring afternoon, Bertha informed her husband that she and Hertha were going to visit friends in Bronxville, a neighbourhood known for its arts colony. Horace thought nothing of it. Evening came, and the two had not returned home. Finally, at 10:00 that night Bertha and their daughter came through the door. Bertha was visibly agitated. She had a confession to make. In what must have been the most awkward conversation of their marriage, she admitted she had left that day, not to see friends, but to leave Horace by running away to Montreal with the man to whom they had entrusted their money. The man never showed up as promised at Grand Central Station. Bertha had to be candid about what happened because their funds were gone, along with the man with whom she had developed an attachment.[8]

This direct lightning strike pierced Horace to the core of his being. There had been no hints in any of his intimate letters to his brothers that cracks had appeared in the marriage's foundation. He, for one, always seemed content – even genuinely happy – with his family life. The two were independent people who gave each other wide latitude to participate in activities apart from each other. He was proud of his wife's achievements and always spoke of her with affection. If Horace had been unaware of the depths of his wife's dissatisfaction with the marriage, that reality now squarely confronted him. The couple discussed their feelings into the night. While it was true that Bertha had betrayed him, he could not ignore his wife's unhappiness with the marriage. They agreed to reconcile. He would forgive her, she would remain in their marriage, and together they would make a fresh start.[9]

But, involving as it did another man, how could they really put this incident behind them? How could trust be rebuilt? Where is the balm that can alleviate the pain of such deep wounds? Horace knew but one source of consolation and guidance: 'Abdu'l-Bahá. He poured out his heart to his Master and, despite the War, dispatched the letter to the Holy Land. Because of the unpredictability of mail coming from Palestine, it was many months before he received a reply. The message would fortify him through all the troubles he would face in life. 'Abdu'l-Bahá's response, dated 20 March 1916, did not promise Horace a future better than the one he faced. Instead, it instructed him on how to confront tests. 'Abdu'l-Bahá likened life to navigating a ship sailing through wild storms and tranquil seas. This was the way God trained souls. Horace should be appreciative that he was being strengthened and enriched by these trials, for 'Abdu'l-Bahá warned that consistently calm waters meant the sailor was nearing his journey's end. Just as he should be thankful for whatever befell him, he should find joy from participating in a united Bahá'í community, and not from ephemeral pursuits that gave temporary pleasure. And he should remain with his wife, with feelings of gratitude in his heart for his family.

> To Mr. Horace Holley
> Upon him be greeting and praise!
> O thou fruit-bearing tree in the Paradise of Glory!
> Thy detailed letter was perused. All that thou hast written was a cry raised from the depth of a sincere heart. As thou hast written, it was for some time that like the nightingale during the autumnal season thou wert unable to sing and warble to the beauty of the rose, but praise be to God that thou art again inspired with the thrills of new songs and the stimuli of new melodies. It is natural that a passenger on board the steamer and sa[i]ling on the great ocean may now witness the tumultuous waves of a wild storm and in the freedom and joyousness of his heart ride on the white crest of the iridescent and pearly foam – watching a world of surging waters battling against the sky – and anon behold the sea, tranquil its surface like a mirror, reflecting therein the blue dome of heaven. These experiences are the natural requirements of one's journey. They have always been conducive to the enrichment of human nature. But on the other hand if the tranquility become permanent and the traveler totally deprived of the wonderful sight of the waves – the sea not

being stirred by the blowing of the winds – this state is undesireable and reprehensible – for it is indicative of the fact that one's journey has come to an end. Praise be to God that thou art again a waving sea – the waves rising higher, ascending to loftier heights, thy head is full of new tumults and thy tongue raising a new acclamation. It is hoped that this time through the wafting of the breezes of the Paradise of Abha thy cheerfulness, thy enthusiasm, thy spiritual commotion and thy ideal intoxication may become greater and more intense than the first.

What thou hast written is true: Today my joy and happiness consists in the firmness and steadfastness of the believers of God, the attraction of the hearts with the Fragrances of God, the detachment of the people from the inordinate desires of passion and self and their complete dependence on and communication with the Kingdom of God.

There is no doubt that we do not find real joy and happiness through the songs of the singers, the music of the musicians and the flowers of the rose-garden, nay rather our delight and exhileration [sic] consists in the anthems of unity and the chorus of harmony raised from the assemblages of the friends of God, singing in the heavenly rose-garden, their voices reaching to the ears of the people of the world and creating a divine attitude of beatitude and ecstasy. Therefore I hope that like unto lyre and harp thou mayst raise the lays of joy and the melody of thanksgiving in this rose-garden of the Kingdom, and associate and consort with thy beloved wife and be ever happy and full of beatitude. Kiss on my behalf the two cheeks of thy dear child. I hope that she may be educated and receive divine instruction in the school of God.

Upon thee be greeting and praise!

(sig.) Abdul Baha Abbas

(Trans. By M. Ahmad Sohrab, Haifa, Syria, March 20th 1916)[10]

Horace wrote to a friend that, while he had 'not hoped for the privilege of a tablet' when he wrote to 'Abdu'l-Bahá, he 'must read and study this tablet many times'.[11] Armed with 'Abdu'l-Bahá's guidance, the couple attempted to move forward together. Horace continued to serve as Bertha's business manager. He wrote an article, 'The Art of the Dress', to advertise her innovative clothing ideas.[12] She patented a dress design,[13] and he patented a self-tying necktie.[14] Months after the marital crisis, Bertha was pregnant again. On 16 July 1916, the Holley's welcomed another daughter, Marcia (also called Betty), who was a more robust baby than her sister had been. At about the time of Marcia's birth the Holleys bought a house in the Long Island suburbs to provide a better environment for their children.[15] Outwardly, it appeared the family was again sailing through tranquil seas.

* * * * *

The American literary community was already familiar with Horace before his return from Europe. Like him, many American writers had spent time in Paris and London before the War and were acquainted with authors on both sides of the Atlantic. It did not take long after settling into New York before Horace was associating with many creative minds who were transforming the arts. A handful of these members of the *avant-garde* established an artists' colony on the outskirts of the small farming community of Ridgefield, New Jersey, across the Hudson River and behind the Palisades – the dramatic, stone cliffs along the west side of the river. Situated on a large property with rolling meadows and orchards, it was directly across the Hudson from Ulysses S. Grant's tomb in Manhattan's Morningside Heights neighbourhood and hence it was christened 'Grantwood'. Rustic, white-washed, clapboard shacks, and one proper large stone house dotted the property.

The first to take up residence at Grantwood were the writer and publisher Alfred Kreymborg, and the artists Man Ray and Samuel Halpert. Horace was a friend of Kreymborg's, the primary host of social gatherings for writers held in lower Manhattan and at Grantwood. On Sundays from June into the autumn of 1915, Kreymborg and his wife welcomed refugees from the torrid heat of concrete Manhattan to their two-room shack near a cliff. Horace was a regular. Kreymborg described his friend as 'thin and ascetic as a vegetarian'.[16] Horace brought along a fellow poet whom he introduced to the group, Skipwith Cannéll, who had just returned from London and Paris. Much to the amusement of their audience seated on the grass, Cannéll and his wife, a professional dancer, would impersonate the American poets they had left behind in Europe – poets familiar to the picnickers through their works, but whom many had not yet met. Drawing the most enthusiastic response was Mrs Cannéll's mimicking of the poet Ezra Pound, the menacing presence hovering over all English-speaking poets seeking to be published.[17]

To reach this bucolic spot in the boondocks, Horace would take a ferry across the Hudson to the New Jersey side, and then ride a trolley to the top of the Palisades. After a brief walk through open countryside, he would arrive at a patch of woods, where he would follow a path for about ten minutes, emerging back into the open on the side of a hill offering a panoramic view of the valley below.[18] The scenery alone must have had a restorative effect on the Torrington poet who loved nature.

One of the most notable regular participants – and the only one to arrive by car – was the local physician and poet, William Carlos Williams, his old, two-seater Ford automobile trailing dust to announce his arrival. Williams' enormous size (matching his reputation as a poet) dwarfed everyone.[19] As the summer turned to fall, other picknickers included the poet and author of works for children Mary Carolyn Davies; the poet Marianne Moore; the writer Orrick Johns; and the painter of the controversial canvas *The Nude Descending a Stairway*, Marcel Duchamp – who usually turned up accompanied by the art collector, critic and poet Walter Arensberg.[20] Normally present were Man Ray, the innovative photographer still residing in the orchard, and another noted photographer and sometime Ridgefield resident, Alfred Stieglitz.[21] Rounding out the gatherings were a host of other writers, artists, and intellectuals.

Guests brought sandwiches to share, and some brought folded papers, which they slipped inconspicuously into Kreymborg's hands or pockets. These crumpled sheets were their works in progress. That July, Kreymborg published the inaugural issue of his new literary journal, *Others: A Magazine of the New Verse*, which included several of Horace's poems. Kreymborg's goal was to encourage his fellow poets to experiment by providing them with a platform to showcase ground-breaking works. The première issue immediately created a sensation in the literary world and attracted budding writers, some of whom would become famous after being introduced by that journal.[22] Contributors to *Others*, including Horace, formed the core group of those drawn to Grantwood and, in colder weather, to the Kreymborg home in Greenwich Village. Kreymborg realized that his guests – geniuses all – were too shy to read their own works during these casual social gatherings. He understood how each, including Horace, was uncertain how their most recent compositions would be received. Between games of softball and tennis, it was left to Kreymborg, his thick glasses perched toward the end of his nose, to read the drafts aloud to the friends lounging about on the ground. The readings would spark remarkable, light-hearted discussions on writing and art. When among their peers, these creative thinkers, accustomed to working in isolation, gained the assurance that there were others in the world who understood them. Kreymborg recorded his memory of the sessions:

> They enjoyed talking shop most of all, but their discussions spread an evasive levity over the serious current of their actual thought. Like most every other cultural activity of the new soil, the intercourse of these people was a novel experience. They had to approach it warily and grow up to the art of conversation with a painstaking, self-conscious *tempo* similar to their development as artists. It was not a lack of self-confidence which dictated so shy a contact, but a joyous bewilderment in the discovery that other men and women were working in a field they themselves felt they had chosen in solitude. Without any affected modesty, each seemed positive that the other fellow was a better poet than himself, and this attitude engendered a regard which expressed itself in silence or a quiet, ungainly phrase.[23]

Summing up the get-togethers at Grantwood, William Carlos Williams wrote that, 'It doesn't sound exciting, but it was. Our parties were cheap – a few drinks, a sandwich or so – coffee but the yeast of new work in the realm of the poem was tremendously stirring.'[24] Horace never gained a better education in the craft of writing than during those fleeting Sundays he spent in the orchards of New Jersey.

Perhaps inspired to greater effort through association with his new acquaintances, Horace continued to compose a variety of works at a gallop. It would be fair to say that 1916 was the apex of his brief career as a poet. His lengthy poem 'Cross Patch', about the life of a spirited young horsewoman worn down by societal conventions constraining women, was published that year in *Poetry: A Magazine of Verse*.[25] The *Publishers Weekly* described the poem as a short story told in verse.[26] 'Cross Patch' dealt with a theme Horace explored more directly in prose in a small book – actually a lengthy essay – entitled *The Social Principle*, published later that year.²⁷ He opined that human beings cease to be their authentic selves after adolescence because society requires conformity to certain norms. Artists are among the few people who can escape this repressive homogenization. The heroine in 'Cross Patch' remains true to herself but pays a heart-wrenching price for her individuality. The poem received honourable mention in the magazine's annual awards, a considerable honour because it was one of the country's most prestigious poetry award programmes.²⁸

In *The Social Principle* Horace explored the transition from a focus on the sanctity of the individual to that of the interdependence of all men. He asserted that the time had come for human beings to learn to become part of a collective, no longer developing simply as individuals. 'For it is true, and invariably true, that in proportion as an individual lacks awareness of others he loses awareness even of himself.'²⁹

Furthermore, Horace expounded upon another of his favourite themes: the ordering of society and the roles various types of individuals play. He had an unfortunate lifelong habit of categorizing people into 'types'. In *The Social Principle*, he devised the following orders of men: the man of action, the executive, the artist, the philosopher, the mystic and the prophet or Messiah. He proposed that the relationship which should govern the interplay between all these components of humanity should be based upon and manifest Christ's admonition to love one another. Had the people of the world obeyed Jesus, each category of man would have realized his potential and played his role in creating a better social reality. As true Christians, they would have discovered the truth that 'as right relations are developed, the love concept not only appears more possible, but its true range grows apparent'.³⁰ The world had become an exceedingly dark place despite its material progress because of mankind's failure to implement the spiritual law of 'love'.

> And yet, after all, the world of electric light, of X-ray and aeroplane, is also the world of poverty and war. Only superficially does this era differ from the past; the same motives, if not the same manner, actuate life, and the progress we achieve with our right hand we destroy, or at least sully, with our left.³¹

Despite turning away from Christ's teachings, humanity was not doomed. Horace closes his essay with an amazing proposition – arguing that, for the first time in history, it was possible for humankind to eradicate the twin scourges that had plagued it from time immemorial: poverty and war.

> Two problems confront modern society, poverty and war. To state that these are not new problems but very old ones, as many insist, brings the reply that while poverty and war have always been present in society as conditions, these conditions were never before confronted but evaded.[32]

He hypothesized that Christ's teachings had tempered the course of Christendom over the centuries. For example, the glorification of war had lessened to such a degree that by the twentieth century most people would willingly go to war only in cases of defence. If racial hatred were to be eradicated and economic advantage could no longer be gained through armed conflict, even defensive war would no longer be necessary.

> Thus universal peace has already established itself as revelation, as mystical experience, as abstract principle and more and more as artistic motive . . . It stands for us a problem not of the moral and intellectual being, but a condition inherent in the social order itself.

The doctrines put forward by religion, mystics and philosophers shaped public opinion, and were reinforced through the work of artists. What remained was to find a practical means of 'rendering peace not only possible but inevitable'.[33] This required organization – 'systems tending of themselves to make order and efficiency'.[34] Without stating it explicitly, he was pointing the way towards the goal he set out at the end of his published account of his first encounter with 'Abdu'l-Bahá, namely, the establishment of a spiritual world government – the Universal House of Justice.

The Social Principle also included a shorter essay on Christianity, 'The Beginning of an Era', which had appeared a few months earlier in the respected intellectual symposium, *The Forum* magazine.[35] Many of its readers may have found the primary idea explored in that second essay to be startling and audacious – even disturbing. Horace argued that Christianity as a religious force propelling humanity forward was spent. The time had come for a new religion to supersede Christianity, though he did not mention the Bahá'í Faith by name. He set forth why a new religion had become necessary, asserting that the Great War had revealed that the concept of the 'sanctity of the individual' had been replaced by the concept of 'interdependence of men'.[36]

> The Great War, like the fall of the Roman Empire, is only the visible manifestation of a change going on throughout every aspect of human life. It is the physical projection of a universal spiritual drama. It is not Germans and English who are fighting, according to the reality of that drama; it is the Old World and the New, the Christian Era and an Era still so young that it has not yet been named.[37]

An advertisement for *The Social Principle* described it as 'a restatement of the Christian teaching of love thy neighbor', and that it 'demonstrates man's right to be his best self, and not something else which society unphilosophically wants him to be'.[38] There were no signs that his little book influenced many readers. Horace lamented to a Bahá'í editor that *The Social Principle* only sold about six or seven hundred copies. 'All our efforts . . . are more or less tentative, don't you think, until the time comes when the spirit of real inquiry has been awakened in the world. If my book helps in any way to point to the real Book, I shall be most happy.'[39]

That same year, 1916, Horace also published a collection of one-act plays entitled *Read-Aloud Plays*. He confided to his brother Irving that they were autobiographical,[40] but he need not have confessed that because anyone familiar with Horace's life would readily recognize they were primarily derived from his own experiences. Set in New England, Italy, Paris and New York, the plays explored themes that ran through his published essays: the meaning of art, the lot of an artist, what it is to be a writer, intimate relationships, inner development, and getting along in society. His principal characters' speeches allowed Horace the playwright to philosophize through their voices. These short works, two of which originated as short stories, were intended to be performed in intimate settings, such as a parlour or library, by a few people reading aloud. He tried these works out with different groups ranging from two to six people and found the plays to be satisfying even without a stage.

He became convinced that 'the homage all literature pays the drama if we identify the drama with the stage' was unnecessary and hoped other playwrights would follow his lead.[41] The works show Horace to be a better essayist than a playwright; but as windows into Horace's thoughts, they are invaluable. Oddly, the topic left untouched was God and religion, a frequent element of his poetry.

After this fertile period of writing, Horace remarked that

> When I look at this list of books I wonder how . . . I ever found time and strength to turn out so many in this time. But I also feel as if I had only just begun to work, and as if most of what I have written to now were only an apprenticeship. My underlying principles are at last getting clear, and I feel that they can be applied in every conceivable way . . .[42]

* * * * *

Back during the summer of 1914, when war was on the verge of breaking out in Europe, the President of the United States, Woodrow Wilson, was distracted from conducting the business of the nation by the final illness and death of his wife. Overcome with grief, he sank into depression. It is doubtful, however, whether there was anything he, or any other American leader, could have done to stop the fast-moving cataclysm during the decisive month of July.[43] Once he regained his footing, Wilson took steps to keep his country out of the conflict, despite the desire of the majority of the population – including Horace – to side with England and France against Germany. In his bid for re-election in 1916, Wilson ran on his pledge of American neutrality. Among Horace's motives for writing *The Social Principle*, which discussed the War, was his desire to add his voice to those advocating an end to the hostilities. Horace avidly followed Wilson's speeches and had probably met the President more than once when Wilson served as President of Princeton University, located close to Lawrenceville Academy. Horace was present when Wilson spoke at Williams College.[44] A few months before the United States entered the War, Horace continued to believe that Wilson would maintain neutrality, saying, 'President Wilson has entered upon the chief Bahai work, events are aiming at a tremendous climax. We must exert ourselves to avoid peace being established and accepted as a mere ethical or sociological ideal, without a spiritual basis and purpose.'[45]

Among the loudest voices demanding that America stay out of the war was the publisher and writer Max Eastman. Like Horace, Eastman had studied at Williams College (a few years ahead of Horace) and was part of the Grantwood group.[46] Eastman had Wilson's ear, as did a handful of peace activists.[47] The Holleys ran advertisements for Bertha's business in Eastman's periodicals, and given their overlapping circles, it is likely that Horace and Eastman were acquaintances.

In 1917, Wilson decided he could no longer keep the United States out of the War after a German telegram to Mexico was intercepted and published in the press. The note urged Mexico to enter the War on Germany's side in order to reclaim territory the United States had taken from it almost a century earlier. Wilson had been moving toward war because of the unrestricted sinking of ships from neutral countries by German submarines, and the telegram was the tipping point. Wilson had heeded the advice of peace activists for three years; now he and his Cabinet turned on those former political allies, demanding their unqualified support for the war effort. Laws and regulations were put into place to stifle opposition. Americans of German descent were threatened by mobs and men of draft age were harassed if not in uniform. Horace had reason to be wary because, in New York, vigilantes pulled men his age off public transportation and forcibly took them to army enlistment stations. A curtain of fear fell over the country as people became guarded in their speech and careful with their actions.

One of the most public victims of government persecution was Max Eastman, whose influential, left-leaning, Greenwich Village-based publication, *The Masses*,[48] strongly opposed the War after the country entered the conflict. Eastman was singled out for prosecution by the US Postmaster General because his magazine had a wide readership. The government forced him to cease its publication and, to make an example of him, brought criminal charges against him under the Sedition Act. Following two sensational trials which made him the notorious emblem of the dissenters, he was acquitted, but the government pressure on him was ruining him.[49] Amid this turmoil, Eastman established another publication, *Liberator*. No doubt to show his repulsion at Eastman's treatment, Horace took a brave stand by allowing the *Liberator* to publish his statement endorsing advertising in that controversial journal, a step that connected him to Eastman. Horace affirmed that the advertisements he had placed in Eastman's publication had brought business to Bertha, saying, 'My intention in this advertising at first was merely to connect Mrs. Holley's new idea of dress with the movement of justifiable, evolutionary radicalism which THE LIBERATOR represents.'[50] Though he did not agree with much of Eastman's political leanings,[51] Horace was willing to publicly stand up to injustice, even if by doing so he risked becoming a target as well.

Unlike Eastman, Horace's thinking about the promotion of peace had evolved since the beginning of the War and he no longer felt it appropriate for Bahá'ís to be active in the organized movements working to pressure governments to end the hostilities immediately. He had concluded that associating the Faith with particular peace groups, other than to praise their ideals, was not useful.

> On the train I thought over various things, and it occurred to me that inasmuch as the Master has refrained from instructing us specifically about the war, confining His teaching to the principles of love and peace and the Message, since the war undoubtedly must run its course so as to bring the desired effect among the nations – therefore I believe that perhaps we are wasting our energy in asking the assistance of any person to attend our meetings and bring their own message, no matter how fine and true from the world's point of view.[52]

New Yorkers were constantly reminded of the War even though it was being fought across the ocean, because many of the troops sailing for Europe paraded down the city's avenues on their way to the docks, and countless wounded returned home through New York. By the time the country was fully mobilized, the conclusion of the War was in sight. On 11 November 1918, the guns of the exhausted belligerents fell silent. One horror was over, but another had already taken its place in the last months before the armistice – a world-wide influenza epidemic. It had arrived in New York without warning in September 1918. Even though this contagious disease caused widespread closures of businesses, large gatherings, and public events for only a few months, waves of people contracted it and staggering numbers died, especially young adults. Death often came within hours of its onset. As Horace walked the streets, most of the people he passed on the sidewalks had their mouths covered by home-made, white cloth masks. This unseen terror would not abate until the spring of 1919.[53]

Horace harboured passionate feelings about the conflict, especially deep anger towards Germany. As returning troops marched down Broadway as heroes, the uncomfortable question arose whether or not England had actually been saved by America's late entrance into the War. Had American involvement really been necessary? There were those who argued that giving the United States any credit for the outcome of the War was misplaced nationalism. In response to a letter published in the *New York Times* condemning this form of 'Americanism', Horace wrote a letter to the editor stating:

> Accepting the obvious definition: that 'Americanism' stands for the good rather than the ill of America, and for American success rather than American failure, the average American is quite convinced today that 'Americanism' must work not only for domestic stability; but stability among our international relationships. No sane man has the slightest intention of permitting prejudice to lead into another world war, nor ignorance to drift into one.[54]

* * * * *

Throughout much of the Great War, the Bahá'ís across the world were rudderless. 'Abdu'l-Bahá was once again in danger as the Holy Land was subjected to martial law under the command of the ruthless, cold-hearted Turkish General, Jamál Páshá. Except for rare intervals, 'Abdu'l-Bahá could neither send nor receive correspondence reliably, much less could He permit visitors. Enemies of the Faith seized the opportunity to be rid of 'Abdu'l-Bahá and filled Jamál Páshá's head with lies about Him and His objectives. Despite a favourable meeting between 'Abdu'l-Bahá and the Turkish commander, the machinations of the Faith's enemies continued, undermining the positive effects of their brief encounter. Jamál Páshá openly announced his intention to crucify 'Abdu'l-Bahá.[55] All who loved and admired 'Abdu'l-Bahá worried constantly. Occasionally, a message from the Holy Land would get out, followed by another period of uneasy silence.

The War had spread far beyond the bounds of Europe, especially when the Ottoman Empire entered it on the side of Germany and Austria. Battles were fought in North Africa and the Middle East. Haifa and 'Akká became so dangerous that for some months 'Abdu'l-Bahá removed His family and the other believers to a nearby Druze village in the hill country. Before the War ended, He and the other Bahá'ís in the Holy Land would be liberated from the clutches of the Turks by the British Army under the command of General Edmund Allenby.

'Abdu'l-Bahá, ever calm in the midst of any crisis, used this enforced period of inactivity to write messages to the American and Canadian communities. Collectively, they were a monumental directive for the spiritual conquest of the planet, known as the *Tablets of the Divine Plan*. Through them, He charged the small band of believers in North America to take up the banner of the Faith and carry it to the four corners of the earth. The first group of messages, composed in 1916, focused upon spreading the Faith within the United States and Canada. These were copied onto postcards to avoid difficulties with government censors, making it possible for them to successfully reach United States and Canada. They were quickly disseminated and printed in the *Star of the West*. This first batch addressed different regions of the United States with messages tailored to the needs and circumstances of each. Horace was appointed to the New York committee to begin to put into action the Tablet addressed to the Northeastern states.[56]

Additional messages were written in 1917, while it was impossible to dispatch them from the Holy Land. This second group contained Tablets naming 120 specific countries and territories to be opened to the Faith, an undertaking which had to be deferred for almost two decades.

Assisting 'Abdu'l-Bahá throughout the War was his American-educated secretary, Ahmad Sohrab. This bright, ambitious young man had also served as a translator during some of 'Abdu'l-Bahá's western journeys, including His 1913 visit to Paris during which he came to know the Holley family. Sohrab was eager to return to the United States, so as soon as Palestine was liberated and it became safe to depart, he requested permission to return to New York to deliver the last batch of precious Tablets. The copies he carried were not on postcards, but beautifully rendered onto individual parchments by a trained calligrapher. The precious documents were rolled as scrolls and placed in a metal tube for safe travel.[57]

Sohrab, the voice of 'Abdu'l-Bahá for many American believers, received a hero's welcome in New York. With the collection of the Tablets of the Divine Plan complete, it seemed befitting to hold a large celebration to fête this essential charter. The Eleventh Annual Convention of the Baháʼís of the United States and Canada was scheduled to be held in New York in April 1919, during the Festival of Riḍván. It would be the first national gathering since the end of the War and the liberation of ʻAbdu'l-Bahá – a joyous occasion which would be well attended, as well as an opportunity to celebrate, honour and promulgate the Tablets.

The imposing Hotel McAlpin on Herald Square, the largest hotel in the world when it was completed in 1912, was chosen as the site for the historic Convention. Horace served on the publicity committee and Bertha on the special committee tasked with dramatically revealing the parchment Tablets in their beautiful frames. When it was time for the highly anticipated unveiling of the Tablets, the hall was full to overflowing. With soft music wafting through the room, three young girls, accompanied by beautiful young women, ceremoniously drew open the curtains on cue to show the parchments. It was a never-to-be-forgotten moment. Featured prominently throughout the programme was Sohrab, who, as courier and translator, was called upon to regale the audience with stories about how the Tablets were written during the darkest days of the War. Other speakers included several locally prominent clergymen and the popular Lebanese writer, Kahlil Gibran, an admirer of ʻAbdu'l-Bahá who had sketched His portrait when He visited New York.[58]

Opening the world to the Faith while simultaneously continuing the work on the construction of the House of Worship outside Chicago – the equivalent of raising a cathedral – surely fired the imaginations of those present. The active believers in North America numbered only in the hundreds and most, like the Holleys, were of modest means. Before them stood a soaring mountain range they had been told to climb, and the practical considerations were overwhelming. The vision of growth was breath-taking and glorious. How to begin? These stalwart believers were well familiar with assistance and confirmations from the spiritual realm, and they would need to invoke aid from angels to accomplish their newly assigned tasks.

Horace's greatest impression of that historic National Convention was of the crowd who attended, representing a broad array of the people of America.

> The Bahá'í Convention lingers in my memory as the supreme Crowd, the unity which is music, and healing and power.
>
> It means little to mention who were there. I would not willingly resolve that perfect concert into its little, single notes. At moments it seemed as though everyone of mankind was a part of that Crowd. All the types were there, if not all the individuals. As in the Ark, no kind and sort had been left behind.[59]

The Bahá'ís knew well that their meeting to plan the spiritual conquest of the planet was being held at the same time as the Paris Peace Conference. In the Hall of Mirrors at the Palace of Versailles, governments and representatives of many peoples and nations were haggling over the reordering of the globe in the War's aftermath. President Wilson was leading the way with his Fourteen Points – proposals wildly acclaimed by the European public, who hoped that implementing those American ideals would bring about lasting peace and a modicum of justice for ethnic minorities.[60] Wilson's list included a call for the establishment of a League of Nations and for the self-determination of ethnic groups. In a letter to a Bahá'í in Iran, 'Abdu'l-Bahá praised Wilson's proposals, but noted that twelve of the Fourteen Points had been put forward by Bahá'u'lláh decades earlier and widely circulated. That this same divine guidance was now being advocated by no less an international figure as President Wilson was a sign that God was at work in the world. 'Consider how the law of God is being spread by ideal forces.'[61]

* * * * *

The Holleys' new baby daughter, the few acclamations Horace received as a writer, the growing success of Bertha's business, the home in the suburbs – all should have pointed to better days for the family. But the Holleys' reconciliation was short-lived. 'Don't ever read a novel,' Horace confided to his brother, Irving, 'and think it is more subtly tragic than life. If I could speak out and tell you all the intermingled truth and falsehood, desire and necessity, joy and sorrow that bind me to every day, you would have a three volume story of continual amazement.'[62] Horace and Bertha separated in 1918 and divorced acrimoniously in 1919. Bertha took their young daughters and left Horace with their considerable debts, which would take more than a decade of concerted effort to repay.⁶³ A poem written earlier perhaps foreshadowed the end of the marriage.

> *Confession*
> The first hour with her, even the first,
> I felt
> A leaf in some lone forest crisp and fall.
> A wiser man were warned.
> I stayed;
> And straightway, like a strange eclipse,
> All things lost luster in her presence,
> Lost luster, darkening – days, events, and I.
> And still I was not warned.
> Yet, in my new remorse
> (What else but I the knife that tortured her?)
> I asked – why had I changed?
> What hardened, what edged my heart,
> What drove it home?
> No will of mine.
> Then, as the darkness thickened and grew mad,
> Walling us two in one close coffin
> (A cenotaph, I said!),
> The brooding whisper I meant became a scream
> And suddenly from that terror lightning broke
> Our sunless worlds apart; and she was gone.
> And she was gone.
> Now, as I turn from the world's reproach
> Seared like the fields against the new seeds' sowing,
> One thing I say of that mad winter –
> One thing, the last:
> 'Poor child . . . *She was* the tragedy . . . before it came.'⁶⁴

Separated from his family, Horace had to face that he needed a steady income. For most of the marriage, Bertha had been the primary breadwinner, even though he had served as her business manager. His inheritance had provided their start-up capital and operating funds, and it had been supplemented toward the end of the marriage by bank loans taken out in his name. He continued to earn occasional royalties and fees from his writing, but hardly enough to support two households. He also knew he had to reconsider his choice of career as a writer. Not only had it failed to catapult him to literary success, but it had put little more than meagre bread and water on his table.

In Horace's play *The Genius*, a teenaged boy searches for a reclusive New England writer whom he esteems. The man had experienced considerable success at the beginning of his career, but then had faltered, as did his marriage. The writer explains to his sixteen-year-old admirer from New York City why he escaped to a cabin in the country.

> Brilliance – I'll tell you what that was, at least for me, I wrote several things that people called 'brilliant' . . . From about sixteen on I had been acutely miserable – physically miserable. I never knew when I wouldn't actually cave in. I felt like a bankrupt living on borrowed money. Of course, it's plain enough now – the revolt of starved nerves. I cared only for my mind, grew only in that, and the rest of me withered up like a stalk in dry soil . . . But nobody pointed out the truth of it all to me, and I scorned to give my body a thought. People predicted a brilliant future – for me, crying inside! Then I married . . . A decorative girl, you know. She wanted to be the wife of a great man . . . We didn't get along. There was an honest streak in me somewhere which hated deception. I couldn't play the part of 'brilliant' young poet with any success. She was at me all the while to write more of the same thing. And I didn't want to. The difference between the 'great' man I was supposed to be and the sick child I really was, began to torture. I knew I oughtn't to go on any further if I wanted to do anything real . . .[65]

When Horace separated from Bertha, he first moved to a hotel and then to a little apartment in the rectory of the chapel of St Mark's in the Bowery Episcopal Church on East 10th Street.[66] His protagonist in *The Genius* speaks of how the daily routine of life became a saving grace after his marriage failed, which was no doubt true for Horace. Getting on with the elemental routines of life hides anger, hurt, and regret.

> Hunger. That was my salvation. Simple, elemental, unescapable appetite. You see I had no servant, no one at all. So I had to get up and work to prepare my food . . . It was very strange. Compared

with this life, my life before had been like living in a locked box. Some one to do everything for me except think, and consequently I thought too much.[67]

Despite Horace's new routine, the failure of his marriage and the separation from his children were devastating. He expressed his inner suffering to the one person who had always understood him and loved him unconditionally, his brother, Irving.

> There is a strange influence in pain, purifying and revealing, which makes it vital beyond the reach of all 'philosophies of success'. It changes us in ourselves, and in such a way that we become more conscious of something that 'wants to be known'. I guess all we can do is to let it sink in as deeply as possible, without trying to steer the boat too determinedly in one direction; though probably wiser people gain control and learn how to develop it from stage to stage.[68]

To earn money, Horace started writing articles for an industrial trade journal, *Iron Age*, learning the advertising business at the same time by selling ad space. His entrance into the field of advertising coincided with the first glimmerings of the formative age of that industry. The first commercial radio broadcasting companies were about to expand the modes of advertising. His on-the-job apprenticeship in developing effective publicity would be a boon to the fledgling Bahá'í community in its efforts to become more widely known and to attract new adherents. However, working for an employer made him long for the lengthy period of his past self-employment when he had arranged his time as he pleased. As he lamented to one Bahá'í friend, 'It seems terrible to me to have to spend the best hours of my day at work upon apparently unimportant things of business when I might be attempting to write about the Bahai teachings, but there must be some wisdom in it.'[69]

* * * * *

Despite the unhappy ending of his marriage and the changes the divorce thrust upon him, Horace never soured on the institution of marriage itself. Indeed, he was optimistic. The character of the writer in his *The Genius* expressed his thinking.

... Of course, there is such a thing as the wrong woman. She makes a man a fraction. The better she is in herself, the less she leaves him to live by. One twentieth is less than one half. But the right woman! She multiplies a man . . .[70]

Horace's ship had sailed through a hurricane, and he was a better seaman for it. As his craft moved into calmer waters, it was time to survey his future anew, and alone.

Flight
As sky to the hawk's wing be,
O Life, for me!
Space yielding space and height
   compelling height,
To poise and free
The ardor of my flight!

Give me the sky
Of the hawk's wing, Life!
– And does a voice reply:
'To the hawk's wing – to the
   hawk's wing,
Sky?[71]

6

THE EARLY YEARS OF THE BAHÁ'Í FAITH IN NEW YORK

All the world in miniature is represented in New York.
If New York can be united all the world can be united.
Horace Holley[1]

Throughout the quarter of a century Horace lived in Manhattan, New York City was the North American hub for the Bahá'í Faith, taking over that position from Chicago.[2] Because of its unique advantages, New York initiated and developed many facets of local Bahá'í community life that would be adopted by its sister communities across the entire planet. Horace was one of the principal drivers of the establishment and refinement of these essential foundations of Bahá'í communities, which would have implications for a future world civilization.

Even though the number of active members[3] in New York varied between fifty and one hundred during that formative period, this was significantly more than any other community in the United States and Canada – even in Europe.[4] New York was the most important seaport on the Atlantic Coast, so many Bahá'ís travelling to and from the World Centre in the Holy Land passed through its docks, usually taking time to connect with their fellow believers while in the city. New Yorkers thus often heard news sooner than others. Unlike the large Bahá'í communities in Iran which suffered relentless persecution, this infant urban community was blessed with religious freedom, for that right was enshrined by law into the Bill of Rights of the US Constitution. It could therefore establish and expand its institutions without fear of outside interference. It was also blessed with a significant number of individuals of capacity, means, devotion, and steadfastness. Its large membership meant that its gatherings had higher attendance than could be accommodated in any but the most spacious of homes, so, as a community, it had to develop capacities not yet required by its sister localities. Early on it had to manage renting and maintaining facilities, devising means of efficiently and inexpensively communicating with at least a hundred households spread throughout the sprawling city, and soliciting and managing substantial funds. New York tried various approaches to managing its community long before other cities and towns had to consider the issues arising from large numbers. With these advantages, New York City contained within it the perfect combination of elements to experiment with and create grassroots Bahá'í institutions and means of operating.[5]

Horace started attending Bahá'í meetings within two weeks of his arrival in New York.[6] He must have noticed immediately that his new home community differed from Paris. This was due to the differences in history and makeup of the two cities. The most notable distinction was that the New York Bahá'ís had both a governing body and a regular gathering for devotions, business, and fellowship called a Nineteen Day Feast; Paris had neither.[7] The state of the New York community in November 1914 – the starting point for Horace – was the culmination of fifteen years of experimentation as well as episodes when the group's unity had been tested. To appreciate Horace's contributions to the development of Bahá'í community life, it is necessary to explore the history of the New York Bahá'í community.

In October 1915, less than a year after the Holleys moved to Manhattan, the founder of the New York Bahá'í community, Arthur Pillsbury Dodge, died. It is likely that neither Horace nor Bertha knew him well, though they undoubtedly heard stories about him from old-timers, especially during the weeks following his funeral. They were certainly acquainted with his family, especially his widow. Dodge's death was a major turning point for the New York Bahá'ís, and marked the end of its pioneer days. The community was fortunate to owe its establishment to a man with Dodge's praiseworthy qualities and strength of character. He was a 'Renaissance man' with multiple talents and creative interests who dabbled in a variety of professions. His efforts and spiritual devotion garnered for him the posthumous, honorary title, 'Disciple of 'Abdu'l-Bahá'.[8] Dodge first learned of the Faith in 1897 while living in Chicago. His teacher was none other than the Lebanese Bahá'í who first taught the Faith systematically within the Western hemisphere, Ibrahim George Kheiralla. When Dodge moved to Manhattan shortly after taking Kheiralla's class, he told his friends and neighbours about the new Faith and opened his home to inquirers. Before long there were enough interested people to form a class, so in 1898, he invited Kheiralla to visit New York to serve as its teacher. That same year, the growing band of Bahá'ís elected officers, though not a governing committee. In 1900, the Dodges strengthened their commitment to the Cause by making a pilgrimage to 'Akká where 'Abdu'l-Bahá Himself tutored and guided them. When they returned, they used their fuller and more accurate understanding of Bahá'u'lláh's teachings to set New York's community on firmer footing.[9]

By late 1900, the Faith's roots in the New York area had grown deep and wide, enough so that the expanding coterie of believers recognized a need for organization, not simply officers. However, no authoritative template or guidance was available for them to follow. With limited Bahá'í writings yet translated into English, their overall knowledge of the Faith in general, much less its teachings about administration, was superficial. The Kenosha, Wisconsin Bahá'í community had been the first to have an elected governing council;[10] nonetheless, the New Yorkers looked to Chicago as a model even though its Board of Counsel had been elected for the first time only nine months earlier, in March. Chicago, likewise, having no example to follow, devised its governing committee based upon its knowledge of how a typical American civic organization set up an executive board.[11] This method of concocting a system of governance by borrowing from the surrounding world is reminiscent of the approach the early Christians used to establish their administration. In the absence of any express teachings from Jesus Himself, the church fathers imitated the civil institutions of the Roman world. The first Bahá'í teachers 'Abdu'l-Bahá sent to the United States provided cursory guidance about administering the community, but it turned out that some of their directives were misleading or incorrect. Their most unfortunate mistake was proclaiming that women were ineligible to serve on Bahá'í governing bodies.[12] These Persian teachers were not helpful with administration because they knew little about it themselves since it had yet to be fully established in Iran. Little wonder then, that for decades, Bahá'í institutions in the United States turned to the widely used handbook for parliamentary procedures, *Robert's Rules of Order*.[13] When Horace joined the Board of Counsel, he found it functioning much like any civic body, for it had barely changed over the previous sixteen years. Indeed, it was struggling as best it could to manage the community. When any issue arose for which there was no definitive guidance, it made up its own answer.

Administration was no small matter for Bahá'ís. Bahá'u'lláh called upon His followers to establish a new world order that would foster peace, justice, and unity and make it possible to establish a golden age for all of humanity. These lofty goals were unattainable without a visible order functioning according to spiritual principles. Bahá'u'lláh in his Book of Laws ordained that each community be governed by an elected Local House of Justice.[14] These would be overseen by an elected international supreme body, the Universal House of Justice. Beyond His injunctions to bring those institutions into existence, Bahá'u'lláh did not provide details. He did, however, elevate the practice of consulting upon all matters in an open, fair manner – a collective search for truth – to the level of an essential spiritual truth, giving it a status far above that of a mere good practice. Consultation was a divine law.

During His own lifetime, Bahá'u'lláh laid the groundwork for the future administration of His Cause by appointing four exceptional believers in Iran to serve in a new role with the title 'Hand of the Cause of God'. They were directed to serve as guides, leaders, examples, teachers to the other believers in Bahá'u'lláh's Iranian homeland, the cradle of the Faith and its largest Bahá'í community. As these four Hands gained experience and evinced increasing capacity, He instructed them to organize consultations with other believers to reach decisions related to the spreading and administration of the Faith. In 1899, seven years after Bahá'u'lláh's passing, 'Abdu'l-Bahá asked the Hands of the Cause to appoint a group of trustworthy, capable believers in the region of Tehran to serve as a preliminary governing council. He specified that all four Hands were to be included among the membership. That council is now considered to have been the first Spiritual Assembly to come into existence.[15] The small groups of believers on the other side of the world were unaware of this first step in the establishment of an administrative order.

In New York in 1900, the time for action had arrived. On 1 December, Orosco C. Woolson, Jr.[16] and Charles E. Sprague[17] sent a printed notice to the Bahá'ís throughout the greater New York area, including the New Jersey suburbs, inviting them to attend a meeting on Friday, 7 December at Carnegie Hall. An unfurnished studio had been rented on the 8th floor of the famous concert hall large enough to accommodate a crowd. The stated purpose of the gathering was to elect a Board of Counsel.[18] For years after, the New York community held its annual meetings and elections on 7 December, until informed that such meetings should be held according to the Bahá'í calendar in late April, during the period of the Riḍván Festival.

By-laws had already been prepared before the meeting by Hooper Harris, a lawyer and prominent member of the community – a future friend and colleague of Horace. Hooper read them aloud to the friends gathered at Carnegie Hall. Despite this attempt to set rules for the election, the voting process was not conducted smoothly. Those receiving the highest number of votes during that historic election were: O. C. Woolson, Jr., W. Hooper Harris, Andrew Hutchinson, William H. Hoar – another Disciple of 'Abdu'l-Bahá and one of the first believers in America to learn of the Faith, Edwin A. Putnam, M. W. Neal, Howard MacNutt, and Mírzá Raffe. Anton Haddad from Lebanon, the first Bahá'í to set foot in the West[19] (though not the first teacher) was designated to serve as an honorary member and advisor. When Harris asked those present to affirm their belief that 'Abdu'l-Bahá was the Centre of the Covenant, Mr Neal realized he could not do so and asked to be excused from serving. He was replaced by Frank Osborne. In compliance with erroneous instructions of the teachers from the Middle East, only men were elected, though the women present voted. Hooper Harris's wife, Gertrude Harris, therefore proposed the creation of a Women's Auxiliary. One of those present remembers that the meeting was far from harmonious,[20] in part because there were no Bahá'í election principles to guide the participants or the proceedings. Most of the people involved in this historic event were still active members of the New York community in 1914 and several served with Horace on the Board of Counsel and later the Local Spiritual Assembly. It was a chaotic yet worthy beginning.

The Board of Counsel, as the New Yorkers named it, initially, had two primary functions: manage the finances of the community and promote the printing and distribution of Bahá'í literature.[21] Establishing a treasury was a critical first order of business. However, before it could solicit funds, it had to gain the trust of those it served so that they would willingly make contributions.[22] Those present at the 1900 election well understood the need to establish a treasury because they were all asked to help pay for the rental of the meeting room. Fourteen years later when the Holleys arrived, the agenda of the Board was still focused principally upon money, organizing meetings, and literature.

In 1909, the same year Horace first learned of the Faith, a notable member of the New York Board of Counsel made a pilgrimage to the Holy Land. Mountfort Mills, who would become one of Horace's dearest friends, was a brilliant, insightful lawyer who had been born in Boston. Mills was thirteen years older than Horace and would serve with him on several Bahá'í institutions over many decades. Mills would also make significant contributions to the Faith. While he was visiting the Holy Land, he took advantage of the opportunity to ask 'Abdu'l-Bahá a series of essential questions about administration. Ever the lawyer, he wanted details. 'Abdu'l-Bahá's most significant answer to Mills was in response to questions about the authority of the councils then governing a handful of American Bahá'í communities. Could these bodies demand and expect obedience to their decisions? Could these elected bodies decide questions of doctrine? Were they the same as the institutions called for by Bahá'u'lláh? 'Abdu'l-Bahá responded that the governing institutions in the West, such as the Board of Counsel, should not be considered as local Houses of Justice; they were only temporary. The time was not yet ripe for the divinely ordained institutions decreed by Bahá'u'lláh to come into existence. They could only be established when the Bahá'í community had many more members. In the meantime, the principal duty of the Boards was to foster the spread of the Faith. The Boards could, however, attend to practical matters such as helping those in need, publishing Bahá'í materials, and promoting the construction of the House of Worship; but, lacking the spiritual station of Local Spiritual Assemblies, they could neither command obedience nor decide about what constituted the authoritative teachings of the Cause. 'Abdu'l-Bahá advised that the Boards should neither incorporate nor have constitutions, though in the future it would be necessary for the Local and National Houses of Justice to do so. Mountfort recorded 'Abdu'l-Bahá's statement that, 'The first duty is to direct the attention of hearts to God.'[23]

'Abdu'l-Bahá clarified one controversial point for Mountfort Mills – one that was important to both Bertha and Horace as public advocates for women's right to vote. He corrected the earlier guidance from the Persian visitors by directing not only that women could, but that they should serve on the governing committees at both the national and local levels.[24] Once Mountfort returned to the United States, he spread this guidance about women serving on local executive committees. The New York Board of Counsel was not satisfied with Mill's oral report that women were eligible to serve on elected institutions. To verify it, the Board asked the Temple Unity Executive Committee to send an inquiry to 'Abdu'l-Bahá on its behalf so the answer would be in writing.[25] With hindsight, women's right to vote and serve on institutions seems obvious, however, women did not win the right to vote in civil elections until the passage of the 19th Amendment to the United States Constitution in 1920. And then, after years of efforts in state after state to gain ratification, the deciding vote was cast by one Tennessee legislator who changed his mind at the last minute – it was that close. The Bahá'í Faith taught the abolition of all forms of prejudice, but in 1909 the adherents in the West reflected the currents of thought swirling around them. At the time when women began to serve on Bahá'í institutions, many religious congregations and civic organizations kept them apart from men in what were usually called 'ladies' auxiliaries'. Horace was elected to the Board of Counsel in 1917 and may have served the previous year as well. By the time he became a member, the president of the Board was a woman, Mrs A. I. Breed, and four of the nine members were female.[26]

Following His 1912 visits to New York, 'Abdu'l-Bahá commented upon the city and its Board of Counsel, which He referred to as the House of Spirituality, emphasizing how important that community was to Him.

> Thou hast written that the House of Spirituality in New York is splendidly confirmed and consequently the number of the friends is increasing. This news imparted great joy. My hope is that New York may become the Center of this Great Cause; the Glad tidings of the Kingdom of God would encompass (it); the Banner of the Oneness of the world of humanity would be raised, and the Divine Teachings would pitch their Pavilion in that city. In my trip to America I spent a long time at New York. I went to Washington and returned to New York. I went to Chicago and came back to New York. I visited California and went back to New York. From this it becomes evident that I feel the utmost attachment to New York.[27]

* * * * *

Horace had immediately begun to take an active part in the Bahá'í community as soon as he returned to the United States. When elected to the Board a year or so later, he was quickly given responsibilities. By that point, the Board had broadened its agenda beyond the management of gatherings and finances. Horace was put on the committee appointed to carry out the Tablets of the Divine Plan for the northeastern region. He also served as chairman of its publicity committee,[28] and on the finance committee.[29] Horace was interested in establishing weekly meetings for inquirers and offered to be responsible for those.[30] There were already weekly devotional gatherings and community meetings besides monthly meetings to foster the construction of the House of Worship.[31] Most of these meetings were held in homes. Horace took on responsibility for finding large rooms to rent for gatherings when a big attendance could be expected. He was also among the few New Yorkers frequently asked to address large gatherings.[32]

In 1917, Horace asked the Board to take an action which showed his avid interest in current affairs and foreshadowed his later efforts to bring the Faith into the public square and to the attention of prominent people. President Wilson had made a noteworthy speech before the United States Senate about the War and the country's response. The address called for a 'League for Peace' that would 'create a peace that is worth guaranteeing and preserving, a peace that will win the approval of mankind . . .'[33] Wilson's address put into words one of the greatest longings of Horace's heart, so he asked the Board to write the President a letter of thanks on behalf of the New York Bahá'í community.[34]

* * * * *

The Holleys had no experience with Nineteen Day Feasts until they returned to New York. The concept of regularly held community meetings scheduled according to the Bahá'í calendar was first introduced in the West by the New York community. Horace would be instrumental in further developing this bedrock gathering of all Bahá'í communities worldwide because of his keen interest in improving consultation and communication within the large New York community.

New Yorkers first learned about the Nineteen Day Feasts, in 1905, when three of its community members, Howard MacNutt, his wife, accompanied by Julia M. Grundy, visited the Holy Land. These three were still pillars of the community at the time the Holleys arrived. During their pilgrimage, 'Abdu'l-Bahá made a point of requesting that the Americans attend a gathering of believers scheduled for the following evening. It was a never-to-be-forgotten Feast during which the simple, but delicious, Persian rice dish pilau was served on large, flat platters. 'Abdu'l-Bahá went from person to person seated at the tables, putting overflowing spoonful after spoonful on their plates Himself. He joked with them about being in prison along with Him – for He was then back under house arrest[35] – calling them the prisoners of love. He pointed out that He was teaching the lesson of servitude and sacrifice. After the meal, talks were given, including one by Howard MacNutt, and the other Westerners revelled in the melodic chanting of the Holy Word even though they did not understand it. Though the Western and Eastern believers could not speak the same languages, they all understood the language of love as they sat together at the long wooden tables. The Americans did not realize it at the time, but the type of gathering they took part in had been ordained by the Báb and subsequently ratified by Bahá'u'lláh, to be held every nineteen days to create and strengthen the bonds of affection between the believers. The next day 'Abdu'l-Bahá spoke to the Americans about the Feast and charged them to take the concept of the Nineteen Day Feast back to America.[36] He is reported as saying:

> I shall never forget the beautiful meeting last night. You must meet together in this way in America. Be true, loyal servants of God. Arise to serve His Cause. These are divine meetings, and the Bounties which surround the Kingdom of Heaven will descend upon you. The same Spirit of Love and Life which fills the Supreme Concourse will fill your meetings. This is a time of trouble and testing to all the believers.[37]

Obedient to 'Abdu'l-Bahá's instructions, Howard MacNutt brought the matter of meetings every nineteen days to the Board of Counsel on 5 May 1905.[38] With the Board's approval, the MacNutts held the first Nineteen Day Feast in the West on 23 May 1905 at their spacious Brooklyn home. During that historic occasion, which was attended by nineteen people,[39] the returning pilgrims read aloud the words they had heard 'Abdu'l-Bahá speak at the Feast in 'Akká. These meetings became the centrepiece of Bahá'í life, first in Brooklyn and then throughout the New York area. Recounting the second one held at the home of the Fleming family, Andrew Fleming remembered that 'we all read tablets from copies sent to different believers and Mr. Mac Nutt gave a short talk. After that we held them at different houses until they became so large that only at [sic] Mr. Mac Nutt's house could accommodate them, and that continued until we were merged with the New York Assembly.'[40]

One of those impressed by those early historic Nineteen Day Feasts was an indomitable believer from the New York community, Isabella Brittingham, another Disciple of 'Abdu'l-Bahá, whom Horace would come to know along with her husband, James Brittingham. Isabella was the one person primarily responsible for spreading the idea of the Nineteen Day Feast throughout North America during her years of travelling as a Bahá'í teacher.[41] These regularly scheduled devotional gatherings were quickly adopted, becoming the focal point of Bahá'í community life. Another element was added to these gatherings in 1916 when Horace, together with Howard Colby Ives, proposed to the New York Board of Counsel that the committee responsible for the Feasts also take on the responsibility of soliciting recommendations from the community members attending the gatherings. These would then be conveyed to the Board, creating another path for communication. The Board agreed. This was the first known instance of adding a business element to the Feasts.[42]

* * * * *

An administrative structure to govern the United States at the national level had begun to take shape weeks before Horace first encountered the Faith. No national committee came into existence until March 1909, even though several larger Bahá'í communities, such as Chicago, Kenosha, Wisconsin, and New York City had elected governing councils almost a decade earlier. Ironically, the establishment of an indirectly elected national body sprang from a specific need with no thought of creating an overarching governing body for the entire country.

It all began with a building. Less than ten years after four people in the city of Chicago formed the first Bahá'í group in the Western hemisphere, 'Abdu'l-Bahá asked the American believers to build a House of Worship.

He had in mind not a modest building for meetings, such as the many humble and not so humble Christian churches which dotted the United States. No, the structure He envisioned would be a large, nine-sided dome with nine identical doors and surrounded by nine gardens. This magnificent edifice would be a 'Dawning Place of the Mention of God',[43] a sacred space set aside exclusively for prayer, meditation, and the study of scripture. The only music within its walls would come from the human voice; and there would be no sermons or rituals. It was a request to build the Bahá'í equivalent of a cathedral. Such an unusual, monumental building was already under construction in 'Ishqábád in modern-day Turkmenistan; and 'Abdu'l-Bahá assured the believers in America that they were capable of meeting the daunting task He set before them.

On the first day of the new year of the Bahá'í calendar, 21 March 1909, at the same time as Horace and his brother were concluding their British adventure, thirty-nine representatives of Bahá'í communities across the United States gathered in the third-floor billiard room of the spacious home of Corinne True in Chicago, and selected a group to oversee this enormous project.[44] The new institution they brought into being was awkwardly named the Bahá'í Temple Unity. Among the nine original Executive Board members they selected were Horace's friends Mountfort Mills and Roy Wilhelm.[45] Present, but not selected for the Board, was a young lawyer from Boston, who would also play an important role in Horace's future service, Alfred Lunt. Within a few years, Lunt would become secretary of the Executive Board. The Board's membership was chosen to ensure that the main Bahá'í communities across the country were all represented. Temple Unity's sole purpose would be to foster and coordinate the erection of the House of Worship on a site that had already been chosen on the outskirts of Chicago.[46] By default, this first nationally elected committee filled the role of a national Bahá'í council. It would be elected annually at a National Convention until 1925, when it was at last replaced by a true governing body for North America, the National Spiritual Assembly.[47] For years, the annual Conventions would make decisions and, in between the gatherings, the Executive Board would implement them, with no authority to go beyond the will of the Convention. Bahá'í communities in big cities, including New York, took turns hosting these annual Conventions. Horace began attending them occasionally as an elected delegate within a few years of settling in New York. The story of how

Temple Unity was replaced in 1922 by the National Spiritual Assembly and the pivotal role Horace would play in the development of that new institution would become the most significant aspect of his life.

* * * * *

In 1914, the unofficial headquarters of the American Bahá'í community was the business office of Roy Wilhelm in lower Manhattan near Wall Street – heart of the country's commerce and home to New York's stock exchange. Roy was a coffee broker who bought and sold coffee beans in the global market. His office was well equipped to manage routine international correspondence, so naturally, Bahá'í cables and letters were sent and received from the Holy Land using that business address. Tall and thin like Horace, this middle-aged bachelor lived across the Hudson River in New Jersey with his Bahá'í parents. Roy was practical with common sense; and, like Horace, possessed a keen wit; for example, he signed correspondence to friends with the name A. Fragrant Bean. Always pleasant company and folksy in his banter, he was liked by everyone. Roy had been privileged to spend many days with 'Abdu'l-Bahá, both in the Holy Land and the United States and had been honoured to provide Him with the use of his West Englewood home and its extensive grounds for a large picnic, an event which 'Abdu'l-Bahá ordained to be held annually as a remembrance of His time in the New World.[48]

The memory of a particular visit to Roy Wilhelm's office during the early days of the Great War remained indelibly etched in Horace's mind many years later. That day, Roy had just received a letter from Haifa and was visibly excited by its contents as he handed it to Horace. Perusing it, Horace was struck by 'Abdu'l-Bahá's uncanny ability to pierce through the smoke of the War and see into the future.[49]

> All the people of the world are, as thou dost observe, in the sleep of negligence. They have forgotten God altogether. They are all busy in war and strife. They are undergoing misery and destruction. They are, like unto the loathsome worms, trying to lodge in the depth of the ground, while a single flood of rain sweeps all their nests and lodging away. Nevertheless, they do not come to their senses. Where is the majesty of the Emperor of Russia? Where is the might of the German Emperor? Where is the greatness of the Emperor of

Austria? In a short time all these palaces were turned into ruins and all these pretentious edifices underwent destruction. They left no fruit and no trace, save eternal ruin.⁵⁰

When the Great War was halted in November 1918, the German dynasty, the Russian dynasty, and the Austro-Hungarian branch of the Hapsburg dynasty were gone forever. Swept away along with them was a way of life thousands of years old, during which hereditary autocrats and aristocrats dominated the peoples of the world. Other dynasties, including the Ottoman Sultanate and the ancient line ruling China, also came to an exhausted end, vanishing without so much as a whimper. As Horace reflected, '. . . the Master saw the end in the beginning, and into the Tablet He brought into the hearts of the believers that the basis of our modern civilization had already been destroyed.'⁵¹

The War generated a short-lived revival of religious faith. Church attendance soared during the War as those with loved ones on the battlefield supplicated for divine deliverance. After the soldiers returned home, however, they and their families became less interested in matters of the spirit.⁵² Those who had experienced combat had seen hell. Taking stock of the wreckage, the lives lost, the misery of those left behind, mankind was appalled at the War's cost in blood and treasure. Much of France and Belgium, especially, were smouldering ruins. Countless numbers of the youth of Europe were dead or maimed. How could a vaunted civilization such as had sprung from Europe, with its foundation based in Christianity, become so barbarous, so uncivilized? It was a time for soul-searching; but that quest for answers was not carried out in the churches, for Christian institutions had done nothing to prevent the war. It became easier to turn away than to think deeply about the catastrophe because the immensity of it was beyond contemplation. Instead, people looked for fun, to escape, to tear off the restraints of propriety and forget the disaster. Ironically, this mood hit the United States at the very moment that alcoholic beverages became legally prohibited. This meant that a titillating element of danger was mixed with forbidden cocktails, as many partied to forget the collapse of the pre-War world. The bars of New York were replaced by hidden, illegal bars called 'Speak-Easys' and the alcohol continued to flow.

Worst of all, the War had not only failed to heal the racial divide in the United States, it exacerbated it just as the mass migration of blacks from the cotton fields of the South to the industrial cities of the north accelerated. The grandchildren of former slaves were still denied equality half a century after emancipation. Previous advancements in racial justice were swept away during President Wilson's administration as Wilson rolled back gains that Blacks such as Louis Gregory, an active Bahá'í who was a lawyer, had made in holding responsible government and military positions. Black citizens had assumed when the country went to war and their sons acquitted themselves well on the battlefield – as did the New York-based all-black unit, the Harlem Hellfighters – it would be impossible to deny their true worth as human beings any longer. Finally, they would attain their full rights as citizens, which they had long been promised but had always been denied. This expectation, unfortunately, proved little more than wishful thinking. In 1919, race riots broke out in many cities across the country. One of the worst of these occurred in Chicago when a Black youth accidentally swam along a portion of the Lake Michigan beaches reserved for Whites. A mob killed the innocent young man which further sparked Whites attacking Black neighbourhoods and setting them on fire. More than 500 died and at least a thousand Black citizens became homeless. Dr Zia Bagdadi, a Bahá'í living in Chicago, rushed into the flames to assist Black Bahá'ís and other victims.[53]

The Bahá'í community had a moral obligation to respond to the racial violence of 1919. Throughout His journey across America, 'Abdu'l-Bahá had frequently addressed the spiritual sickness of racial prejudice afflicting the country, warning that if that dire disease was not cured, blood would run in the streets. Now it had. In 1921, while Mrs Agnes Parsons of Washington DC was on pilgrimage, 'Abdu'l-Bahá instructed the well-connected, wealthy, white socialite, to organize a Race Amity Conference in the nation's capital. This successful event would be the first of many Race Amity Conferences held in various locations over the next decade to address the heart-breaking, unjust plight of the Black community. This issue was important to Horace, so he eagerly took part in the meetings. These gatherings also highlighted the important work of the New York Bahá'í community in the predominantly Black Harlem neighbourhood, where the Bahá'í philosopher, writer and first African-American Rhodes Scholar, Alain LeRoy Locke, was a guiding light in what became known as the Harlem Renaissance. New York's Bahá'í community was unusual for most religious congregations in the city because it was racially integrated. As we shall see, working for racial amity and justice would be a never-ending project for the Bahá'ís, including Horace, for decades into the future.

As the conflict between Blacks and Whites intensified, other rifts within society opened wider. For example, fundamental disagreements about political and economic philosophies led to terrorist attacks by groups with extreme agendas. The most infamous of these was the 1920 bombing of Wall Street, which occurred not far from Roy Wilhelm's office, which ignited a period called the 'Red Scare'.[54] The abuses of unbridled capitalism, resulting in extremes of wealth and poverty, had made the economic concept of socialism and its more radical version, communism, attractive. There were also groups ascribing to the more nihilistic philosophy, anarchism. Those espousing those philosophies came to be treated as enemies of the country in the wake of the terrorist incidents.[55] For example, Max Eastman, mentioned earlier, whom Horace had tried to help during the War, had long been closely associated with outspoken socialists, as were other members of New York's creative community who were part of Horace's circle of friends in the arts. It became dangerous to espouse those philosophies.

Thus, the two years following the end of the Great War were chaotic, a condition exacerbated by lack of leadership from the White House. President Wilson had focused his attention on the Paris Peace Conference and his drive to bring the United States into the newly established League of Nations rather than the day-to-day governance of the country. Within months of his return from Paris, he became severely incapacitated by a massive stroke. Concealing his true condition, his wife and close aids secretly managed the country on his behalf. By the time Wilson's term of office ended, the effects of his inability to carry out his office were apparent. In 1920, with the promise of returning the country to 'normalcy', Warren Harding was elected to replace Wilson, during the first presidential election in which all adult women finally had the right to vote. Harding began his brief tenure in office by confronting the sharp economic downturn which had started at the end of Wilson's term – a recession so severe that Horace feared losing his job with his advertising firm employer.[56] Fortunately, Harding righted the ship of state, and the hard times of 1920 did not last long. The economy improved and general prosperity was in sight.

* * * * *

In 1919, with the war over and civilian travel resuming, 'Abdu'l-Bahá granted permission for pilgrims to again visit the Holy Land. Eager American believers lost no time in making the journey halfway across the globe. His relationship to the Western believers had evolved during the War and the American communities were once again receiving guidance conveyed through returning pilgrims. Horace described this renewed connection to 'Abdu'l-Bahá and the modification of the tone of His guidance.

> Here in New York we are tremendously interested in the return of two friends from visiting Abdul Baha in Haifa, Palestine. The big point now seems to be that he no longer will answer mere personal questions, or decide things for us, but wants people to be grounded in the principles of true unity and take responsibility for making these understood. As for America, the feeling is that every effort must be made to bring about better relations between whites and blacks, or disasters will result.[57]

* * * * *

Amid these turbulent times, there was one person who brought calm and stability to Horace's world. A special young woman among those attending Bahá'í gatherings in New York caught Horace's eye in 1919 following the end of his marriage. Doris Pascal was the opposite of Bertha. Short in stature, a brunette with pleasing looks, though not a great beauty, she had a practical turn of mind. Doris was more patron of the arts than artist; however, she enjoyed writing poetry and came from a family devoted to an assortment of the arts. Perhaps it was this shared interest combined with their mutual, unwavering devotion to the Faith that attracted them to each other. Doris was energetic, amiable – a cheerful person with a sense of fun who appreciated Horace's dry wit.

Doris first met Horace and his family in Paris in 1913 at the first Bahá'í gathering she ever attended. 'Abdu'l-Bahá was the speaker. Those few hours in the presence of 'Abdu'l-Bahá transformed her life, pointing her down a new path that would lead her to Horace again. Thinking back to that pivotal day, she remembered, 'I was spiritually asleep at the time, but while I was listening to the Master's talk I felt as if Jesus were speaking and I thought that the Master was saying what Jesus would have said.' When 'Abdu'l-Bahá finished His remarks, the others got up and followed Him out of the room, but Doris remained seated, lost in thought. Before she knew it, 'Abdu'l-Bahá returned, walked straight to her, and startled her with a kiss on the forehead.[58]

The War drove Doris from Europe back to the United States, where she found a job as an office worker in New York. It is likely her acquaintance with Horace was renewed at Bahá'í gatherings.

It happened that a friend who was an architect invited her to tour his own newly constructed home he had designed. He arranged her visit to his stylishly appointed residence at a time when he could not be present to host her. To her delight, as she wandered through the house, she spied a device she had never used before – a telephone. A daring impulse got the better of her – she tried it out. The only person she knew who had a telephone number was Horace, so she picked up the receiver of the miraculous contraption and called him. He dropped what he was doing and rushed over to join her at the house. Some months later, on 25 September 1919, they married in Greenwich, Connecticut.[59] To look at them, they appeared to be an odd couple. She seemed half his height and was on the round side. He was tall and excessively skinny. She was outgoing and a lively companion. He was quiet and reserved. Doris, like Horace, was steady and trustworthy. She became devoted to her husband. Unlike his relationship with Bertha, Horace took on the role of head of the household, and Doris became his assistant. Theirs was a genuinely affectionate marriage that would endure until Horace's passing, over forty years later. He wrote to his brother Irving informing him of his marriage stating, 'Doris is absolutely the girl and I am quite happy.'[60]

Doris had an unusual pedigree. Her father, Goodridge Sinderby Bowen, was born in Barbados, an island colony in the British West Indies that would gain its independence in 1966. The Bowens had deep roots in the Caribbean going back to the early days of European settlement. They were renowned among the old English families for their musical talents, a trait her father inherited.[61] The problem her ambitious and talented father faced as a pianist was that in London those born in the colonies were treated as second-class. So, Bowen assumed the stage name Julian Pascal when he worked as a professional musician. He also created a London-based past. Under the name of Bowen, Goodridge married Annette Sterner from England in New York in 1892. Though there are hints that Doris, like her father, was born in Barbados, her family narrative insisted she was born in London in 1894.[62] While still a small child, her family moved from London to New York, which became her true hometown. She was the eldest child, with two younger brothers, Ernest and Gordon, and a sister, Elsa. Her parents' marriage ended in divorce. Her father would remarry, but her mother never did.[63] Records show that when Doris married Horace, she used the last name Bowen.

Doris's father taught at the Guildhall School of Music in London and continued teaching after the family moved to New York. By the time her father relocated to Los Angeles in 1912, he was among the country's foremost pianists, having toured in several countries as well as throughout the United States.[64]

Doris's mother[65] never achieved the fame of her father but garnered some public recognition from her efforts in the promotion and preservation of handicrafts, especially the weaving of tapestries and other textiles.[66] Her youngest brother, Gordon, shared their mother's love of antiques and furnishings, working for years as an unsuccessful antique dealer. He also had a brief career as an actor, landing a few minor roles in the New York theatre. His difficulties in life, usually the result of excessive drinking, landed him on the Holleys' doorstep. The eldest of her two brothers, Ernest, was a successful novelist, playwright and screenwriter who became head of the Screenwriter's Guild in Hollywood while under contract to big film studios.[67] As a successful professional writer, Ernest was Horace's kindred spirit, so the brothers-in-law became friends despite living on opposite coasts.

Soon after the 1919 wedding, Doris became pregnant. Their son, Horace Holley Junior, was born prematurely on 30 May 1920, and struggled for life for ten hours. He died the next day. A few friends accompanied Horace to St Mark's-in-the-Bowery Episcopal Church, to lay to rest his infant son in the church vaults.[68] Horace had to sell a few pieces of furniture in order to pay for the baby's burial.[69] He and Doris never had any other children.

The Holleys turned to a church to bury their son because they were unfamiliar with the requirements of Bahá'í burial and, in a crowded city like New York with few cemeteries, St Mark's could provide a place to bury their child. Other early Bahá'ís, too, turned to churches to carry out necessary life tasks such as weddings and funerals because the Bahá'í Faith in the United States could not yet perform marriages recognized by civil law and they lacked a religious ritual for burials. Bahá'ís in the West continued to refer to the Faith as a movement, not a religion, even using the term 'movement' on the stationery of their governing counsels. Many Western believers retained membership in churches and saw no contradiction in doing so. A number of the Bahá'ís in New York, including Doris and Horace, were on the membership rolls of St Mark's in lower Manhattan, then led by Reverend Doctor William Norman Guthrie.[70] A few Bahá'ís, such as Juliet Thompson, were members of the neighbouring Episcopal Church of the Ascension on the edge of Greenwich Village. It was at that church that 'Abdu'l-Bahá gave His first public address in North America in 1912 at the invitation of Reverend Doctor Percy Stickney Grant. Both clergymen, who were close colleagues, were attracted to the Faith. Dr Guthrie invited the New York Bahá'í community to use his congregation's facilities for meetings. Before accepting this generous offer, the New Yorkers asked permission from 'Abdu'l-Bahá, who cabled His consent, 'Accept invitation, Church Episcopal. Hold Sunday afternoon meetings.'[71] Dr Guthrie became an informal advisor to the New York believers, including to the Board of Counsel itself,[72] apparently with the blessing of 'Abdu'l-Bahá who had advised Edward Kinney that 'whatever Dr Guthrie deems advisable, concur with him and put in practice . . .'[73] Horace, along with Mountfort Mills, would rise through the ranks of the lay positions at the church and one of their close Bahá'í friends, Edward 'Saffa' Kinney,[74] served as organist.[75]

St Mark's was an unusual church. Located in the East Village neighbourhood on the oldest site of continuous religious practice in Manhattan, it is the city's second oldest church. Furthermore, it is situated on the spot where the leader of the seventeenth century Dutch Colony, New Amsterdam, Peter Stuyvesant, had his farm[76] and where that famous Dutch leader is buried within the vaults of the church. Over the centuries, the area surrounding St Mark's became less fashionable as its congregation moved to newer neighbourhoods in the north of the island. By the early twentieth century, the church had to offer something enticing to retain its well-to-do congregation, and Guthrie was the magnet.[77] He had a doctorate in literature as well as a liberal education in theology. He adored the arts. His sermons were as much college lectures in the humanities as they were summons to the life of the spirit. The church, under Guthrie's leadership, gained a reputation as 'the poets' church', one which it still retains. In a *New York Times* article, Guthrie stated that 'The way to get people to go to church is by making an appeal to them through art. The solution of the church problem in this country must be approached from the aesthetic side.'[78] His worship services were unconventional and not altogether Christian because he was wont to add elements drawn from other religions, such as Buddhism and Native American religious practices. One never knew what to expect at St Mark's.

Dr Guthrie's passion for paintings got the Bahá'í community into a bit of trouble. They held a weekly meeting in the church's chapel on Sunday afternoons, in compliance with 'Abdu'l-Bahá's instructions. To make that space more befitting for uses other than Christian worship services, Guthrie commissioned an out-of-work artist to decorate a large theatre curtain, which could be used with the church's portable stage. Guthrie asked the artist to paint a copy of Sandro Botticelli's classic painting, *Spring (Primavera)*. While Guthrie was travelling in Europe, the painter completed his copy of the nude cherubs and semi-nude nymphs enlarged to an eight-foot scale and installed it in the chapel. Soon after, the Bahá'ís held a large, well-publicized gathering in that space, the first event at the chapel after the painting was in place. As fate would have it, a newspaper reporter arrived unannounced to learn more about the Bahá'í Faith. The resulting article focused not upon the topic of the meeting but upon the curtain's scandalously dressed women in transparent gossamer. The reporter termed the figures as 'the Ten Gods of the Bahais' and used the image to mock the Faith. Mortified by the embarrassment the painting had caused his Bahá'í friends, Guthrie was impressed at how they handled this turn of events. None of the Bahá'ís said anything about the painting to Guthrie or any other church official, but within less than a week, they had acquired a large cloth to cover the image for their next meeting. Guthrie apologized and praised the Bahá'ís for 'the Christian charity and the marvelous prompt self help of these extraordianary[sic] virtuous people! Had one ever heard of such neighbors, such friendly tenants, humble accepters of underserved ridicule!' The Bahá'í community went a step further and offered the church a curtain to cover the nave with its altar whenever the main sanctuary was used for purposes other than Christian worship so that the church could avoid the appearance of irreverence. It was gratefully accepted.[79]

*****

In 1919, Horace began the decades-long struggle to provide for two households. Albeit more lucrative, the world of advertising was far removed from that of poets and literary writers – in fact, many looked upon it with suspicion, comparing advertisers to hucksters selling cure-alls. His affable nature, well-trained mind, and conscientiousness made him a trusted, valued employee.[80] He rolled up his sleeves and went to work, taking on multiple jobs to support his family. He left the industrial trade magazine *Iron Age* after about two years to take a better job as a copy editor for the Philip Kobbe Advertising Agency, and then moved on to the Redfield Advertising Agency in 1921, where he was Chief of the Copy Department.[81] All three positions came with growing levels of responsibility that required occasional travel.[82]

Few periods of history have witnessed changes in daily life as rapid as those that occurred during the years immediately following the end of the Great War, much of it because of the miracle of harnessing electricity. The electrification of urban areas now made it possible for the average household to purchase consumer appliances. First a family would install electric lights. Next, they would purchase an electric toaster and an iron. Before long, life without an electric stove or refrigerator seemed unbearable. Inventors might have been the heroes of the age, but it was the advertising agencies which brought their vision of the future to the ordinary citizen. Labour-saving devices affected everyday life by freeing millions from the drudgery of countless tasks. Travel became faster and safer. Communication became easier and quicker. Clothing became more practical and comfortable. The night was conquered for the first time in human history. Leisure became possible for the masses. It was the job of Horace and his colleagues in the advertising industry to make the public aware of how new-fangled contraptions could improve their lives. Advertisers stood at the leading edge of technology, looking toward the future.[83]

*****

The vision of the Bahá'í Faith, of its mission, of the possibilities of what the Bahá'í community could achieve, was becoming clearer to Horace as he passed through his mid-thirties. He had endured a heart-breaking personal calamity and had watched as the world was torn apart by conflict. No longer overtaken by the introspection inherent to writing poetry, he refocused his thoughts, less on himself and more on the wider world. He became more conscious of the signs around him pointing to the oneness of humanity – the foundational teaching of Bahá'u'lláh. That primal concept started to take hold of him. He expressed these burgeoning insights in a watershed letter to Irving, the most religious of his brothers who had become an active Episcopalian in their hometown in Connecticut. Until about 1916, Horace seldom mentioned the Faith in his correspondence. He begins his letter by discussing the situation in the United States after the war, especially the sharp economic downturn, and then explores the interconnectedness of mankind.

> It looks to me as though the general readjustment were going farther and deeper than most people think, or at least admit. If we measure the extent of the possibility of change by the standard of the collective consciousness – that is, if we estimate how much more change must be accomplished before the average person gets the idea that life is co-operative in purpose and method rather than competitive – the extent of readjustment is staggering. Personally, I think that this is the true standard, and that an entirely new direction must be given all our activities before the world will reach equilibrium. The thing surrounds the individual on all sides, and makes each of us feel pretty helpless at times, but it's reasonable to think that a nucleus of right-thinking and right-acting people will eventually be formed to lay the foundations for the new cycle. In the last analysis, civilization rests not on machinery nor money, but on thoughts and the desires that mold them. That's why it seems to so many of us down here that the whole present scheme of things is dangling by a pretty weak thread, and must, whether more or less calmly or more or less violently, come to earth – rest on a firmer basis of mutual understanding. Of course, we have to go on doing our best at the job we have, but a man is foolish to bank his life entirely upon material factors today. If there was ever a time for taking every opportunity to arrive at some inner truth, it's right now. Everywhere the people

without a satisfying and calming vision are at each other's throats. And that's how the eternal division comes, separating people, not by classes or creeds, but by qualities.

What a group of us down here is trying to do is to build up the faith in a civilization resting upon eternal, impersonal standards – and grasp it as firmly that whatever happens around us, we'll see and feel nothing except the defeat of selfish influence and the approach of reality. Perhaps you wont [sic] 'get' this at all, yet somehow I think you will, and that you have already worked out your own philosophy to meet the demands of this dissolving age.[84]

Horace's desire to share the Bahá'í Faith with his closest brother reflected his growing urge to write a second book about the Faith. He wanted to introduce the new religion so persuasively that its readers would be inclined to accept its truths.[85] Seven years had passed since he had published his first Bahá'í book, *The Modern Social Religion*. In January 1921, *Bahai: The Spirit of the Age* was published in New York by Brentano's and in London by Kegan, Paul, Trench, Trubner & Co., Ltd. It is unquestionably a more mature exposition of the Faith than his first introductory book.[86] Its enhanced readability not only demonstrated that his skills as a wordsmith had improved, but that scribbling advertising copy for the masses rather than writing poetry for the erudite had heightened his capacity to reach a general audience. The book's opening essay, 'The Cosmic Trinity', draws as much from science as it does from theology. He particularly uses the attributes of electricity – that mysterious intangible force bringing to life the gadgets rapidly transforming everyday life – to discuss abstract spiritual truths. The first section of the book could be categorized as a lengthy sermon rather than an essay, as it examines of the nature of man through spiritual concepts. Deceptively simple scientific images such as the orbit of earth around the sun and the basic science of rainbows give the reader unusual insights into weighty subjects such as the Will of God and God's Covenant with mankind.[87] What most distinguishes the second book from the first is the inclusion of entire Tablets and talks from Bahá'u'lláh and 'Abdu'l-Bahá. Many more authoritative Bahá'í writings had been translated into English since 1913, so Horace filled his second book with those, rather than his own musings. However, with the texts available a century later, the later book still contains misconceptions about aspects of Bahá'í teachings, especially regarding the stations of the Báb, Bahá'u'lláh and 'Abdu'l-Bahá.[88] This was not Horace's fault, however, for his errors were common ones that had not yet been corrected through the Bahá'í guidance available in 1920.

Overall, it would be fair to describe *Bahai: The Spirit of the Age* as a missionary tract in the same sense as the four Gospels of the New Testament are recognized now as the equivalent of modern pamphlets to attract and keep converts. After setting forth basic proofs in his first section, the latter sections are addressed to specific religious groups to speak to their particular teachings from a Bahá'í perspective. The inclusion among these of metaphysical and mystical American sects, including Christian Scientists, New Thought adherents and Theosophists, should not be taken to mean that Horace was personally attracted to the metaphysical, for a review of his life shows that it was not at all his focus. It is possible that he may have attended a few meetings of the Theosophical Society,[89] but more likely his inclusion of chapters targeted at particular groups provides a window into the type of people who came to Bahá'í public meetings in New York – primarily the liberal minded, the mystical, with a fair sprinkling of eccentrics. Theosophy, in particular, was a common waystation for many of the early Western believers on their path to finding the Bahá'í Faith.[90]

At the end of *Bahai: The Spirit of the Age*, Horace makes a point of including two messages of 'Abdu'l-Bahá, setting them apart from the other themes because he thought they deserved special attention. The second of these is a lengthy letter in the form of a prayer written to the Persian Bahá'í community during World War I. In it, 'Abdu'l-Bahá discusses the War and the calamities confronting humanity, explaining that these can be remedied only by mankind turning to God. The Great War and its meaning never were far from Horace's thoughts.

The leading item in the concluding section of the book is an account of a talk 'Abdu'l-Bahá delivered at a Society of Friends meeting in England on 12 January 1913, in which He expounded upon the practice of meditation. Horace's singling out this particular address of the multitude of those given by 'Abdu'l-Bahá in the West may provide a clue about his own devotional life. Finding moments of solitude to reflect deeply while in a meditative state must not have been easy within the crowded spaces and hectic pace of New York City life. It is clear to the reader, however, that the insights contained within *Bahai: The Spirit of the Age* are the fruit of intense study and reflection upon the spiritual nature of man and the universe.

The publication of this popular book marks the beginning of a brief but fertile period during which Horace explored spiritual themes in essays published in the *Star of the West* and other Bahá'í periodicals. A handful of these gems resonate a century later as much as they did when first published and they have continued to be studied and republished by later generations. A few years later, these articles impressed Shoghi Effendi so much that he commented upon their 'beauty and force', and encouraged Horace to write more.[91]

As 1921 rolled on, Horace's life regained a rhythm and a purpose. He had adjusted to his new circumstances – a new wife, new arrangements to see his daughters, new responsibilities in the Bahá'í community, a new profession – all the while doing his best to serve his Maker and keep everyone happy. He had sailed through rough seas, and the worst storms seemed to be behind him.

But then a telegram arrived at Roy Wilhelm's office in the late fall of 1921. It was dispatched from the Holy Land by the beloved sister and right hand of 'Abdu'l-Bahá, Bahíyyih Khánum. She announced to the world-wide Bahá'í community that the One who was their Guiding Light, the Centre of their world, had died suddenly on 28 November after a brief illness. Bahá'ís from Tehran to London, from San Francisco to Sydney, from Cairo to Tokyo, were first stunned and then, as the news sunk into their hearts, stricken with a grief beyond consolation. The world, it seemed, had stopped turning.

A day or so after Horace learned of 'Abdu'l-Bahá's passing, he penned this reflection:

> *Abdul Baha voiced and made eloquent the spiritual aspiration that lies dumb in the hearts of men. He embodied in vigorous, triumphant maturity that ideal which in others is but a sleep and a forgetting. Men of every race, creed, class and color in the world are devoted to Abdul Baha, because Abdul Baha has been a pure mirror reflecting only the noblest and highest qualities of each. He has taught mankind more than mere cessation from warfare and strife – the influence of the humility of Abdul Baha has been to create a positive vision of righteousness which shall never die. The physical death of Abdul Baha is like the physical death of the seed; and from this seed there will arise a stately tree whose fruits of knowledge and of love shall, God willing, provide a feast for every hungry heart. Abdul Baha lived forty years in the Holy Land – and in that forty years he made Holy the entire world.*
>
> Horace Holley
30 November 1921[1]

7

THE COVENANT

The United States is a nation born through rebellion. Obedience to any institution has never come easily to its citizenry. Many Americans, such as Horace, were descendants of those who had braved the perils of oceans and hostile environments in order to liberate themselves and their progeny from the strict control of others. The United States population spread across a vast continent until, by the late nineteenth century, there was no more frontier to conquer for freethinkers seeking complete independence through remote living. With such a heritage, inevitably, broad swathes of American citizens believed deep down that they had a right to complain about anything so long as they did not resort to violence. It should be no surprise, given this widely held attitude that there was a God-given right to unbridled freedom, that those who converted to the Bahá'í Faith were freethinkers who valued their independence and nonconformity. Maybe it is no wonder, then, that a significant number of American believers struggled to grasp the meaning of the Covenant of Bahá'u'lláh.

This Covenant, an essential element of Bahá'u'lláh's teachings, required that those who accept Bahá'u'lláh as God's Messenger for this day also recognize His appointed successor, 'Abdu'l-Bahá, and the one 'Abdu'l-Bahá chose to succeed Him, Shoghi Effendi. Adherents were also to accept the authority of the Universal House of Justice once it came into existence, as well as the authority, guidance, and decisions of national and local Bahá'í elected institutions. The reward for obedience was the continuation of divine guidance long after Bahá'u'lláh had departed this earthly plane. His Covenant would forever protect His Faith from schism, a malady which had crippled and inhibited the efficacy of earlier religions. Contained within the Covenant of Bahá'u'lláh was the promise that these appointed successors, especially the Universal House of Justice, would be inspired and guided by God. Obedience would not only strengthen unity but also allow the spiritual blessings stemming from divine guidance to take effect in the world.

One event that took place in New York in 1912 had taken on the status of a legend. Horace was familiar with the story because it had become the mother tale for the New York Bahá'í community. Juliet Thompson, a pillar of that community, who was probably an old acquaintance of Bertha Holley since both were portrait artists, was one of the central characters. Though born in New York,[2] Juliet spent most of her formative years in Washington DC, where she met the Barneys who introduced her to the Faith. Like the Holleys, she was invited to visit 'Abdu'l-Bahá at Thonon-les-Bains in 1911. Unfortunately, the Holleys and Juliet missed meeting there by a few hours because she had just left when they arrived. Like the Holleys' Paris neighbour, the painter Edwin Scott, her atelier was large enough to accommodate sizeable Bahá'í gatherings. For decades, she generously opened her old brick townhouse in Greenwich Village for weekly meetings and was thrilled when given the opportunity to host 'Abdu'l-Bahá multiple times in her studio.[3]

When Shoghi Effendi surveyed the history of 'Abdu'l-Bahá's historic visit to the West, he singled out the events of the legendary day in New York as among the most significant of 'Abdu'l-Bahá's actions, for on 19 June 1912 He announced His station as Centre of the Covenant to His Western flock. The first episode of that historic day began in the early afternoon. 'Abdu'l-Bahá had finally granted Juliet's persistent entreaties to paint His portrait. He came to her third-floor studio to pose for her. Seated in a corner of the room, He settled Himself as best He could into the chair which she had designated for Him while she worked quickly on her prepared canvas. His time was precious, and He had warned her He could not spare much of it for the picture.

Joining the artist and her subject that day was one of Juliet's most cherished friends, Lua Moore Getsinger, whose devotion to 'Abdu'l-Bahá was boundless. During her first pilgrimage to the Holy Land in 1898, she and her husband were privileged to be the first Western believers to meet 'Abdu'l-Bahá in person. She had since visited Him a handful of times, including one visit that lasted almost a year, during which she learned to speak Persian. Both women were in paradise that afternoon.

When 'Abdu'l-Bahá mentioned that He wanted to sleep, Juliet nodded her assent, assuring Him she could continue her work as He dozed. Once He fell asleep, however, she found she could no longer make her brushes move across the canvas. She could only stare at Him, enraptured by every detail of His napping visage. His form was as still as if carved of marble. Power and divine grace radiated from that reposing figure. Suddenly, He awoke. The instant His eyes opened, the room changed and appeared to pitch like a ship sailing through a storm. His very countenance seemed to be ablaze. Startled, Juliet and Lua both shook uncontrollably and sobbed in awe and fear. 'Abdu'l-Bahá turned to Lua and addressed her in Persian. Her tears rolling down her cheeks, she responded in the same language that she understood. But that was not sufficient acknowledgement. 'Abdu'l-Bahá had to be certain that Lua truly comprehended, so He summoned His interpreter from downstairs.[4] Juliet, transfixed as she watched this unfolding mystical event, later recorded that, 'Never shall I forget that moment, the flashing eyes of 'Abdu'l-Bahá, the reverberations of His voice, the Power that still rocked the room. God of lightning and thunder! I thought.'[5]

But what came next was even more earth-shaking.

> I appoint you, Lua, Herald of the Covenant. And I AM THE COVENANT, appointed by Bahá'u'lláh. And no one can refute His Word. This is the Testament of Bahá'u'lláh. You will find it in the Holy Book of Aqdas. Go forth and proclaim, 'This is THE COVENANT OF GOD in your midst.'[6]

As swiftly as the momentous incident began, it passed. 'Abdu'l-Bahá resumed being altogether human – even more human than before. But the day was not yet over.[7]

Later that afternoon, appearing before a group of believers gathered at His own accommodations, 'Abdu'l-Bahá spoke about His station as the Centre of the Covenant. He directed that Bahá'u'lláh's Tablet of the Branch, newly translated into English, be read aloud to the friends for the first time. This weighty Tablet of Bahá'u'lláh set forth in unmistakable language 'Abdu'l-Bahá's unique station.[8]

Months later, 'Abdu'l-Bahá sent a Tablet of His own to the New York Bahá'í community which contained these words:

> Deliver my greeting and praise and my abundant longings to my beloved ones in that city (New York) which hath become the City of the Covenant and the town of the Love of God.[9]

In Shoghi Effendi's majestic history of the first century of the Bahá'í Faith, *God Passes By*, he spoke of 'the dynamic affirmation by Him of the implications of the Covenant instituted by Bahá'u'lláh, following the reading of the newly translated Tablet of the Branch, in a general assembly of His followers in New York, designated henceforth as the "City of the Covenant"', explaining that the events of that notable day in New York were among the most significant of 'Abdu'l-Bahá's deeds during His historic visit to the West.[10]

What did 'Abdu'l-Bahá mean by the title 'City of the Covenant'? During Horace's time in New York, the city would earn its name, as he, through his membership on the National and Local Spiritual Assemblies, would be called upon to deal with one crisis after another. When he discussed this title of his adopted home, Horace said, 'In the world of true religion, a title or epithet has the authority of a command,' and, 'Thus Abdul Baha gave New York a spiritual significance when he called it the City of the Covenant.' He commented, 'Perhaps the believers in New York have been slow to appreciate the truly unequalled privilege of living in Abdul Baha's City.'[11]

* * * * *

As fate would have it, on the historic night of 27 November 1921, three of Horace's friends from the City of the Covenant were in Haifa when 'Abdu'l-Bahá ascended to the other worlds of God. Dr Florian Krug, a prominent surgeon born and raised in Germany, and his American wife, Grace, had been privileged to host 'Abdu'l-Bahá in their Manhattan home during His 1912 visit. Dr Krug, known for his forceful personality, originally opposed his wife's involvement with the new religion, but when he met 'Abdu'l-Bahá, his heart awakened until he finally became a stalwart believer who devoted his life to the Cause. The Krugs had come to the Holy Land with the intention of settling there to serve 'Abdu'l-Bahá. The other New Yorker was a youth residing temporarily in Haifa to carry out a special assignment on behalf of Roy Wilhelm. Twenty-five-year-old electrician Curtis Kelsey was sent to Palestine along with the equipment necessary to illuminate the buildings at the World Centre with electric lights, including the two Holy Shrines. After months of work, this capable young man had already completed most of that task, during which he had become a full member of the staff serving at the World Centre of the Faith. In those first hours following 'Abdu'l-Bahá's sudden death in the midwatch of the night, these three friends of Horace found themselves at the centre of a world-shaking event.

With the clarity of hindsight, the Bahá'ís realized that 'Abdu'l-Bahá made comments to a handful of individuals over the course of the last months of His life to prepare them because He knew that His earthly ministry was drawing to a close. However, most of those to whom He directed remarks were blinded or unwilling to read His statements aright and so were unprepared for His impending death. Even during His last days, when He exhibited symptoms of illness, the seriousness of His condition remained unrecognized. It was assumed it would pass. Thus, His two daughters who were attending Him during the wee hours of 27 and 28 November were surprised when He took His flight to God's other worlds. Dr Krug was hastily summoned from bed. He confirmed 'Abdu'l-Bahá's ascension and closed His eyes. As the household awoke to the calamitous news, inconsolable wailing could be heard from every side. His sister, Bahíyyih Khánum, summoned Curtis and told him to take 'Abdu'l-Bahá's automobile and drive to the other side of the Bay to inform the Bahá'ís in 'Akká.

'Abdu'l-Bahá's funeral on 29 November united the contending factions of British-controlled Palestine in shared grief, perhaps for the first time in the region's sad history. People of all religions, ethnicities and social classes loved 'Abdu'l-Bahá as if He were their own Father. The cities of Haifa and 'Akká came to a standstill as the long procession following the coffin wound its way up the mountain to the Shrine of the Báb. The street in front of 'Abdu'l-Bahá's home was crammed full with people. Among the religious leaders who gave speeches extolling Him were Christians, Jews, Muslims, and Druze. The British authorities sent high-ranking representatives and sincere condolences. Reports of His death sped across the world's telegraph wires and were spread further afield by newspapers, especially in those places in the West which He had graced with a visit. One did not need to be an adherent of the Faith to recognize that an irreplaceable voice for peace and unity was now silent.[12]

As the terrible realization of this immeasurable loss overcame the initial emotional numbness, the question uppermost in the minds of all Bahá'ís was a simple one: what next? Believers across the globe knew that Bahá'u'lláh had ordained the establishment of an international, indirectly elected, governing body, the Universal House of Justice; that institution, however, did not yet exist. The smattering of Bahá'í governing committees in less than a dozen countries had little authority, especially at any national level. Should the founding of the House of Justice be the next step? If so, who had the authority to initiate it?

At the time of 'Abdu'l-Bahá's passing, none of His sons were still living, all having died as babies or young children. His angelic younger brother, Mírzá Mihdí, had died decades before. Many of His male relatives, especially His half-brothers and cousins, had shown by their actions to be His most unrelenting, vicious enemies because of deep-seated jealousies and worldly ambitions. Their machinations, misdeeds and treachery had left Him with no alternative but to remove each and every one of them from the body of the Faith. 'Abdu'l-Bahá left behind adult daughters and young grandchildren. His eldest grandson was a graduate student studying at Oxford University. This remarkable twenty-four-year-old, Shoghi Effendi, collapsed when he learned of his Grandfather's death the moment he glimpsed a telegram with the news lying open on a receptionist's desk in the London office of a Bahá'í. As the eldest male descendant, Shoghi Effendi was suddenly head of his family. After a brief rest to restore his spirits, he hurried home to Haifa, where a greater shock awaited him.

When Shoghi Effendi arrived on 29 December, his beloved great-aunt, Bahíyyih Khánum, greeted him with the news that His Grandfather had left a sealed envelope with his name on it. Upon opening it, he found a Will which named him as his Grandfather's successor – Head of the Bahá'í Faith. Moreover, Shoghi Effendi was appointed to fill a new position with the hereditary title Guardian, and when the Universal House of Justice was established, he was to serve as its chairman. Prior to reading the Will, Shoghi Effendi had never received any indication that His Grandfather had any future position in mind for him. He had served his Grandfather as a secretary and aide, and his only ambition was to continue that service, especially as a much-needed English translator.

Fortunately, there was one person Shoghi Effendi could rely upon – one who could advise and encourage him, Bahíyyih Khánum, the Greatest Holy Leaf and daughter of Bahá'u'lláh. She was closer to him than his mother. She had seen it all – the full panoply of the unfoldment of the Bahá'í Faith from its earliest days when she was a child in Tehran, through the horrors of the persecution which followed the Báb's martyrdom, the confiscation of all of her family's wealth and their homelessness, her Father's unbearable imprisonments and exiles, the rise and spread of her Father's Faith, betrayals by members of her own family, and her Brother's triumphant expansion of the Cause into the West, even as He dealt with the faithlessness of His close kin. As a believer, she was unrivalled in her devotion, her steadfastness, her inner spiritual development, and her keen insights into the verities of the Faith. Though tiny of stature, she was the great woman of the Bahá'í Dispensation, the equal of Mary Magdalene of Christianity and Fatimah of Islam. Having announced 'Abdu'l-Bahá's passing to the world, the task fell to her to send a second historic telegram to the Bahá'ís of America announcing 'In Will Shoghi Effendi appointed Guardian of Cause and Head of House of Justice'.[13]

Horace's friend Roy Wilhelm wrote his first impressions of the young Guardian after spending time with him in Haifa a few months after 'Abdu'l-Bahá's death:

> Shoghi Effendi is a most interesting character study. He is, I presume about twenty-three, small of stature, a singular sweetness of countenance and character, possessing extraordinary brilliance of mind and perception, it seems to me for one of his years. His quickness too is remarkable. He makes it constantly evident that he wishes authority to rest in the body of the Bahá'ís at large. It seems to me that we should as far as possible shield him from the multitudinous perplexities which continually were presented and pressed upon 'Abdu'l-Bahá from all quarters of the globe – else his sympathetic mind will be so overburdened that his health may not be equal to the strain, and in any event his time and attention diverted from the most important matters – of bringing into operation the terms of the Will and Testament.[14]

Within less than a month after his return home, Shoghi Effendi opened his first letter to the Western believers with these immortal words, 'At this early hour when the morning light is just breaking upon the Holy Land, whilst the gloom of the dear Master's[15] bereavement is still hanging thick upon the hearts, I feel as if my soul turns in yearning love and full of hope to that great company of His loved ones across the seas, who now share with us all the agonies of His separation.'[16] What heart is so chilled that it would not instantly warm to such sentiments? Horace now had a new pole star who would guide him unerringly and unfailingly for over three decades. He would develop an extraordinary working relationship with the Guardian despite the separation of thousands of miles. His love and admiration for and devotion to Shoghi Effendi would become so profound that it would be beyond mere words to express, even for a talented wordsmith. The Guardian would join that special place in his heart with those most dear to him.

* * * * *

One of the first tasks facing the new Guardian was the promulgation of the Will and Testament of 'Abdu'l-Bahá. It was a lengthy document in three parts, each section written at different times between 1901 and 1908 while He was a prisoner under house arrest in imminent danger of being executed. The paper and ink of at least one section was damaged when it was hidden for a time in a water cistern. The most delicate and vital task would be to prove the authenticity of the Will to the generality of believers to such a degree that no one could doubt its authority.

On the morning of 3 January 1922, nine men – most of them members of 'Abdu'l-Bahá's family, gathered at the home of one of His daughters located next to 'Abdu'l-Bahá's house. They inspected the Will, its seals, signatures and especially its handwriting, and collectively judged it authentic. It was then read aloud and one of those present was instructed to make an accurate copy. Four days later, it was read in Persian to a group of believers from Iran, India, Egypt, England, Italy, Germany, America, and Japan. The third and most significant reading of the Will occurred as part of carrying out the local custom of hosting a feast on the fortieth day after a death. The luncheon, held in the spacious home of 'Abdu'l-Bahá, included among the guests many dignitaries, government officials, and local religious leaders. At the conclusion of the banquet held in the commodious central hall, the Will was once again read aloud. It was the first public announcement that Shoghi Effendi had been appointed as successor. Because of his profound sense of humility and propriety, the grieving Guardian did not attend any of these three gatherings.[17]

The Will had to be translated into English with painstaking accuracy. Emogene Hoagg, a Californian with secretarial skills, aided by Ethel Rosenberg, a British believer with a working knowledge of Persian, lost no time in assisting Shoghi Effendi with this critical task. The Will was the charter outlining the administration of the Faith, so it was essential that the generality of believers receive copies of it as quickly as possible to prevent disunity and schisms from developing during the period of transition. Bahá'ís worldwide would need to immediately study the Will and Testament closely; consequently, Shoghi Effendi settled upon translating what he considered the most significant excerpts first in order that those sections could be distributed quickly. For this abridged version, he included only one of the multiple sections of the Will establishing his own role as Head of the Faith – the least weighty of those sections.[18] By late February, one copy of the extracts from the Will had been mailed to each country with an organized Bahá'í community.[19] Roy Wilhelm, who arrived in Haifa just as the interim document was completed, mailed the copy for North America to his office assistant and fellow believer, Nellie Lloyd. It arrived in New York on 25 February and was turned over to the Temple Unity Executive Board the following day.[20]

The Temple Unity Executive Board, along with the New York Board of Counsel, immediately set to work to determine how to best disseminate the abridged version of the Will and Testament to the friends. Horace, as secretary of the New York Board, served as its intermediary to the Temple Unity Executive Board. The Board had received a cable from Haifa on 23 February instructing it to advise Bahá'í communities across the country that, temporarily, the Will and Testament of 'Abdu'l-Bahá should be kept privately within each Bahá'í community[21] because of fears that enemies within and without would attack the Faith during this perilous period. The Board, therefore, directed that the precious charter be read aloud to each community and each believer should be given free access to study it. However, it was not to be copied, nor should excerpts be lifted from it. New York's Board acted swiftly by calling a meeting to introduce the extracts to the believers on 6 March.[22] The New York Board strongly recommended that it should be printed and distributed as soon as possible 'as garbled versions may be issued by enemies at any moment'.[23]

These precautions proved to be justified. A supporter of 'Abdu'l-Bahá's half-brother and arch-enemy, Muḥammad-'Alí, visited the offices of the

New York Herald and *New York World* newspapers and told reporters lies about the state of the Faith and the succession.[24] Muḥammad-'Alí's claims to be the rightful head of the Faith appeared in those papers at about the time the excerpts of the Will arrived in New York. Alfred Lunt, secretary of the Temple Unity Executive Board, contacted those newspapers to give them the facts and minimize the damage.[25] Horace also reached out to those newspapers but suggested that 'the most effective reply to these false articles is by supplying the press with articles of positive and constructive value'.[26]

At the same time that Horace was working with Lunt to arrange both the printing and careful distribution of 'Abdu'l-Bahá's Will and Testament in America, important consultations were taking place in the Holy Land. Shoghi Effendi had summoned a select group of trustworthy, level-headed believers to Haifa. Among them were three members of the Temple Unity Executive Committee: Roy Wilhelm, Charles Mason Remey[27] and Mountfort Mills. Corinne True, another member of the Committee, was also present, but True and her daughter had come as pilgrims and only participated in the less formal consultations during meals. The Guardian chose Lady Blomfield, Wellesley Tudor-Pole and Ethel Rosenberg to represent England; the Dreyfus-Barneys to represent France; and Consul Schwarz and his wife, Alice, to represent Germany. He invited two believers from Iran, but the Persian representatives arrived late and missed the consultations with the Westerners. The distinguished Arab believer Siyyid Muṣṭafá Rúmí, was also summoned by Shoghi Effendi, but he too arrived late from Burma and missed the consultations.[28] Another friend of Horace who was already present in Haifa was Ruth Randall from Boston.

Shoghi Effendi was much younger than these veteran leaders and had spent most of the preceding years away from Haifa studying at universities, so he was still untried and little known to them. He had multiple reasons for calling the group together. First, he wished to acquaint these key individuals with the contents of the Will and to allow them to examine the original document so they could attest to its authenticity when back among the other members of their home communities. Several of the Westerners had a working knowledge of Persian and all had received original writings from 'Abdu'l-Bahá, so they were familiar with His handwriting and writing style.

The Guardian had another purpose: to consult with these devoted, stalwart, and capable pillars of the Faith about what to do next. The big question he wished to address was: should he immediately commence the establishment of the Universal House of Justice? Even the British government's authorities in Palestine were pressuring him to set up the House of Justice so that an institution, rather than individuals, would hold title to Bahá'í properties. Those called to Haifa expected that preliminary plans for the formation of the supreme international governing body would be the focus of discussion in addition to matters related to carrying out the Will.[29] Shoghi Effendi restricted the key sessions to Mountfort Mills, Roy Wilhelm, the Dreyfus-Barneys, Lady Blomfield, Major Tudor-Pole, and the Schwarzes. Even though first-hand notes from those closed-door discussions have never been found, what can be gleaned from accounts of those who were present in Haifa at the time is that, at first, they all agreed that establishment of the international governing body seemed the logical and best course of action. But through further consultation, it became evident that the foundation for that supreme institution had not yet been laid. No true national or local Spiritual Assemblies existed to either elect it or support it. The way forward came into focus and the consultants reached a consensus. As a first step, Shoghi Effendi charged them to bring about the election of national and local Spiritual Assemblies in their home countries at gatherings scheduled to take place that spring.[30]

While meeting with this esteemed group, Shoghi Effendi completed the full English translation of the Will and Testament. Having finished that urgent task, on 5 March, he addressed a lengthy letter to the believers in North America. It spoke of the period of transition through which the Faith was passing and the power of the love that 'Abdu'l-Bahá was 'extending to us from on high'. With His death, it was more imperative than ever that the friends become united. Appealing to their undying love for 'Abdu'l-Bahá, he reminded them that 'The eyes of the world, now that the sublime Personality of the Master has been removed from this visible plane are turned with eager anticipation to us who are named after His name, and on whom rest primarily the responsibility to keep burning the torch that He has lit in this world.'[31]

Next, the Guardian turned to the principal emphasis of his letter: the establishment of local and national Spiritual Assemblies. The time had arrived to strengthen those bodies already in existence and bring others into being. He stated unequivocally that these embryonic institutions would develop into the local and national Houses of Justice called for by Bahá'u'lláh in the Kitáb-i-Aqdas and by 'Abdu'l-Bahá in His Will and Testament. Because the American believers did not have access to the scriptural authority for these institutions in English, he included a selection of newly translated passages from Bahá'u'lláh and 'Abdu'l-Bahá, particularly those setting forth the spiritual principles governing the functioning of Bahá'í institutions, including consultation. He ended with advice for determining when a matter should be referred to a local Spiritual Assembly, and when it fell under the jurisdiction of a national Spiritual Assembly, as well as when it might be appropriate to appoint a committee. Shoghi Effendi deemed this broad guidance to be sufficient to begin establishing the Bahá'í Administrative Order – the divinely ordained system which in the fullness of time would unite and govern the world. He would convey more precise details and guidance over the course of the next five years, much of it deriving from the crucible of experience.

*****

Throughout religious history, schisms often erupted during transfers of authority when individuals and factions vied for control. Shortly after Bahá'u'lláh died in 1892, 'Abdu'l-Bahá's half-brothers, half-sisters, and cousins arose to oppose Him. Their plan was to establish a caliphate which they would control as its members in flagrant disregard of Bahá'u'lláh's incontestable written instructions that 'Abdu'l-Bahá was to be His successor. Of necessity, the Will and Testament of 'Abdu'l-Bahá contained a lengthy exposition of the perfidy of His eldest half-brother, Muḥammad-'Alí, in order to explain why he had forfeited any right to succeed Him. Muḥammad-'Alí's unrelenting, despicable actions over the entire course of 'Abdu'l-Bahá's ministry not only violated the Covenant of their Father but tarnished the good name of the Faith. At the time of 'Abdu'l-Bahá's passing, that half-brother remained unrepentant and undeterred. Taking advantage of the opportunity presented by 'Abdu'l-Bahá's unexpected death, Muḥammad-'Alí lost no time in putting forward his claim to what he considered to be his birthright under Islamic law as eldest male descendant of Bahá'u'lláh, contrary to 'Abdu'l-Bahá's Will. Over the next decade, others would also question the right of Shoghi Effendi to succeed to the position of Head of the

Faith. Indeed, in His last letter to the American believers, 'Abdu'l-Bahá warned His Western flock against those who would violate the Covenant and instructed them to stay clear of them.[32]

During this crucial period, the Americans were not left without wise counsel and accompaniment. In 1920, 'Abdu'l-Bahá had sent a learned Bahá'í historian from Iran, Mírzá Asad'u'lláh Fáḍil Mázindarání, known to the Western believers as Jináb-i-Fáḍil (often spelled Jenabe Fazel),[33] to the United States to assist the struggling community with its outreach to the public. He arrived just in time to attend the 1920 National Convention when the architectural design for the House of Worship was chosen by a vote of the delegates. He remained in the United States for more than a year, travelling around the country to help deepen the Americans' understanding of their Faith as well as to give talks to the public. On his way home to Iran in 1921, he stopped in the Holy Land just prior to 'Abdu'l-Bahá's passing and a few months later was called back to consult with Shoghi Effendi.[34] In February 1923, Shoghi Effendi sent him back to the United States as his emissary with instructions. Horace reported that Jináb-i-Fáḍil met with the Bahá'ís from throughout the metropolitan New York region at St Mark's Hall on 23 February: 'He said that he had come to assist the American friends to cooperate with Shoghi Effendi in carrying out the plan drawn up by Abdul Baha in his last Tablets and Testament.'[35] His charge was to visit Bahá'í communities across the country to aid them with establishing Spiritual Assemblies in accordance with the Will and Testament. He told those present that 'the House of Justice will be built on the foundations of the present Spiritual Assemblies, and as the Houses of Justice are to be strong, therefore the foundations must be deeply laid and made firm.'[36]

* * * * *

Shoghi Effendi had another worry. During the Great War when all communication with 'Abdu'l-Bahá was cut off, a divergent faction tore apart regions of the American Bahá'í community. It began in Chicago when a small clique created their own community within the city, removing themselves from under the authority of the House of Spirituality. The members of this group, collectively referred to as the 'Reading Room', preferred to focus upon the mystical aspects of the Faith. They also opposed its organization, though ironically, they formed their own governing committee and tried to have its representatives take the place of the Chicago House of Spirituality at the next National Convention. Regrettably, tact, love, and wisdom were not used to work with the members of the Reading Room. A committee of inquiry[37] was appointed by the House of Spirituality, which expeditiously arrived at the heavy-handed verdict that the members of the Reading Room were violating the Covenant of Bahá'u'lláh – an extreme condemnation requiring excommunication.

The manner in which the committee had approached the wayward Chicagoans appalled many onlookers, who concluded that its report was tainted by the haste in which it was produced and ratified. Only 'Abdu'l-Bahá had the authority to decide that someone was a Covenant-breaker – a fact apparently unknown to the Americans at the time. The investigation was perceived as an unwarranted witch-hunt. The actual issue of the errant group became lost in the dispute over how the committee went about its work. The controversy, pitting community against sister community, reached a climax at the 1918 National Convention. Though the West Coast Bahá'ís were not affected significantly by this matter, whole communities within the Midwest and East Coast became estranged and mistrustful of each other.

The following year, with the War over and guidance at last streaming from the Holy Land, the 1919 Convention focused upon reconciliation. Nonetheless, feelings continued to be raw, and distrust lingered. Shoghi Effendi later alluded to this situation in his 5 March 1922 letter, when he called on the friends to stop judging each other and to put aside the past in order to move the Faith forward in unity.[38] Horace's opinion about the matter is unknown, other than that he was concerned about the danger inherent in any attempt to create separate groups within a Bahá'í community.[39] Ironically, there were individuals on both sides who would be named either Hands of the Cause of God or Disciples of 'Abdu'l-Bahá and who would come to work arm-in-arm in the years ahead. That they could put aside this sad episode is a testament to the guidance of 'Abdu'l-Bahá and the Guardian and their own developing spiritual maturity.

* * * * *

After years of concerted effort at honing his abilities as a wordsmith, by 1919 Horace had shifted from writing secular poems and essays to articles exploring religious themes for Bahá'í publications. That year, while he was still in the midst of personal problems, Eugene and Wandeyne Deuth, a married couple who were also members of the New York Bahá'í community, established a new Bahá'í magazine, *Reality*.[40] How could Horace fail to be drawn to it! He submitted an article for its first issue and agreed to serve as a consulting editor. The New York flavour of the magazine differentiated it from the international Bahá'í journal, *Star of the West*. What really excited Horace was that the Deuths had purchased a printing press to establish a publishing business. Horace was thrilled at the prospect of putting that press to good use, for he had employed all of his connections in the publishing world to resolve a persistent, urgent need of the Bahá'í Faith in the West – printing Bahá'í materials economically. The Deuths generously offered their business office as a New York Bahá'í Library where Bahá'í meetings could be held after working hours. It was a prime midtown Manhattan location at 416 Madison Avenue, not far from his office. *Reality* seemed heaven-sent. Innocently begun with the best of motives, within a few short years it would bring about the first big test the City of the Covenant would confront. Through *Reality*, Horace would take on a new role – one he would carry out again and again for the rest of his life – defender of the Faith.

Eugene Jeno Deuth was a minor aristocrat[41] from Hungary, who had established a prosperous import-export business based in New York. His wife, Wandeyne (Margaret) Deuth, was an active Bahá'í born and raised in Kentucky. This middle-aged couple worked as a team to create their publication and publishing business. Even though the imposing Eugene was the spokesman for the family, Wandeyne was the more strong-willed of the two and apparently the one behind most of the decisions.[42]

When *Reality* began monthly publication in 1919, it was gratefully welcomed by New York Bahá'ís as an alternative to *Star of the West*, which had fallen into a slump in the interim before new management would improve it.[43] Unlike *Star of the West*, *Reality* was aimed at a general audience, and published items from both Bahá'í and non-Bahá'í authors. It did, however, always include a section devoted to Bahá'í activities in the metropolitan New York area, especially those open to the public. Horace became a regular contributor, submitting articles and poems with religious themes. The magazine was given the unofficial blessing of the Bahá'í New York Board of Counsel, which reviewed in advance the section reporting on its local community. 'Abdu'l-Bahá Himself encouraged the Bahá'ís to support it.⁴⁴ When its September 1921 edition ran a request for readers to purchase stock in the journal, the appeal included a reminder of 'Abdu'l-Bahá's praise of *Reality* – and that He had made a sizeable contribution to it of seventy pounds.⁴⁵ In its third issue, Horace waxed ecstatic over the new periodical and the opening of its offices as a Bahá'í centre in a good location in midtown Manhattan, adding, 'May all the believers recognize in Reality one of the universal contacts which the Cause requires with the general public. Reality has no other object than to invite inquiries and awaken interest.'⁴⁶

To allay concerns that *Reality* was competing with the official publication, *Star of the West*, in March 1922 Horace, as secretary of the New York Board of Counsel and member of the editorial board, penned an editorial praising the magazine while clarifying that it was not an official organ of the Bahá'í community.

By 1921, the circulation of the journal had grown and the publishing work had expanded, so the Deuths hired a business manager, Herold S. Robinson.⁴⁷ Robinson was not a Bahá'í, though he was sympathetic with most of its ideals. His primary concern was making the journal profitable, which meant increasing the number of subscribers – especially among the Bahá'í community – and the number of paying advertisers. In early 1922, the Deuths sold their publishing business to Robinson, while retaining their positions as the magazine's editors. They then travelled to Europe for an extended period, leaving *Reality* in Robinson's care. By the time they returned, the situation at the magazine had changed. Foremost was the appointment of a new editor-in-chief, Mary Hanford Ford, who had previously served as the arts editor.⁴⁸ Ford was a well-known and often controversial Bahá'í who had authored many books and articles on a variety of topics. She was especially drawn to the mystical and to efforts to reform society. This forceful woman was also a sought-after lecturer outside of the Bahá'í community, because her wide-ranging interests included passionate support for social movements, such as the women's suffrage crusade. Despite all she brought to the role of editor, Ford lasted only a few months. By the end of the summer, another force dominated *Reality* magazine.

A peculiar man of genius from Washington DC, Dr Harrison Gray Dyar, took over the magazine, steering it over the rocky shoals of the next stage of its life. This new co-owner and editor had a passion for building brick-lined tunnels under his homes. He was dedicated to studying insects, especially mosquitos. Despite the scientific community's respect for Dyar's many achievements while employed by the Smithsonian Institute as a leading researcher in the study of insects, his personal behaviour got him into trouble. His infamy increased when a vehicle travelling on a public street in the vicinity of DuPont Circle fell into one of his tunnels. The authorities were appalled to discover his warren of tunnels running beneath the nation's capital. All published accounts about him agree that Harrison Gray Dyar was eccentric – brilliant and multi-talented, but exceedingly eccentric. The son and heir of a wealthy family, Dyar had earned a degree in chemistry from the Massachusetts Institute of Technology and a doctorate in entomology from Columbia University.[49]

Dyar's second wife, Wellesca Pollock Allen, given the name Aseyeh by 'Abdu'l-Bahá, became a committed Bahá'í in 1901 during the earliest years of the Faith in the West, and had made a pilgrimage to the Holy Land in 1907.[50] When 'Abdu'l-Bahá visited Washington DC in 1912, He called on the Dyars. Even though Harrison Dyar could never give his whole-hearted allegiance to any group – wishing to remain a freethinker and free agent – he found the social teachings of 'Abdu'l-Bahá to be in line with his own ideas. He gave lectures on Bahá'í topics for the Washington DC Bahá'í community. Involvement with *Reality* provided an opportunity to liberally promote his own conceptions to a wider audience. He and Robinson were kindred spirits in their ideals and motives. And Dyar was willing to fund the journal.

When he began his work as editor of *Reality*, Dyar's greatest obstacle quickly became the Bahá'í Administrative Order which had been established only months earlier. 'Abdu'l-Bahá's Will and Testament was being circulated and studied, the National Spiritual Assembly of the United States and Canada had been elected for the first time, and in larger cities such as Washington DC and New York, Local Spiritual Assemblies were being established. The Will of 'Abdu'l-Bahá demanded obedience to these nascent institutions as well as total fealty and obedience to Shoghi Effendi. To Dyar's thinking, organization was a harmful perversion of the Bahá'í Movement. He hated the word 'obedience'. In his mind, Bahá'í was not a religion, but a bundle of good ideas that if widely spread and implemented would transform the world into a better place.

Organization, especially one demanding unequivocal compliance, was, to his mind, a hindrance that impeded the spread of the ideals which he believed Bahá'í stood for. Dyar saw no reason why any governing board should define the Bahá'í Faith, for it was his unwavering conviction that each individual attracted to the teachings of 'Abdu'l-Bahá had the right to define the Bahá'í Movement for himself.

Horace continued as a consulting editor even after Dyar became an owner of *Reality*, though most of his fellow Bahá'ís who had shared that role were replaced by others who were not Bahá'ís. But after seeing the August 1922 edition, Horace decided he had to withdraw his support.[51] That month the masthead displayed the words 'THE BAHAI MAGAZINE' over the top of the name *Reality*.[52] The New York Spiritual Assembly, which Horace served as secretary, asked the owners to remove any statement connecting the magazine to the Faith. Robinson and Dyar complied with this request in the September issue, adding on the title page the words 'The Management and Editors of REALITY magazine are solely responsible for its contents'.[53] This prompted Horace to write a letter on behalf of the New York Assembly thanking them for their cooperation. It was a kind, encouraging letter that the Assembly probably assumed would be seen only by the magazine owners and staff.[54] But this was not how Robinson and Dyar believed conversations should be conducted. The Assembly's letter was published, including its letterhead, followed by an open letter to the Assembly signed by Robinson attacking the very existence of the New York Spiritual Assembly and championing the Bahá'í principle of 'independent investigation of truth'. The magazine was not an official Bahá'í organ because, since the Faith was incapable of being organized, there could never be an official magazine. He said:

> REALITY stands only upon the Bahai Principles as expounded by Abdul Baha. It is willing to co-operate with any individual or group of individuals who will help us to promote these great Bahai Principles; outside of that, it is not interested in organization, officers, or officials. The Bahai Principles are the thing we are fighting for, and are greater than any individual organization.[55]

Further intensifying this attack upon the Assembly, Dyar wrote an article for the same issue, 'The Twelve Basic Bahá'í Principles', outlining his own vision of the Bahá'í Faith.[56]

That first response to a Bahá'í institution in the October issue marked the start of Dyar digging another kind of tunnel, one that would head steadily downward and ultimately undermine the journal's stability even as he sought to destroy the underpinnings of the Bahá'í institutions. The letter signed by Robinson quoted a widely circulated statement attributed to 'Abdu'l-Bahá that the Bahá'í Faith could not be organized. In response, a Canadian believer wrote a letter to the editor clarifying that the alleged statement from 'Abdu'l-Bahá was a mistranslation. What He had really said was that the Faith could not be confined within an organization. Asked to explain this further, 'Abdu'l-Bahá had remarked that of course the Faith had to be organized just as every household requires organization, but His important point was that the organization of the Faith would not operate rigidly.[57] Dyar replied that that was a distinction without a difference and dug the tunnel deeper by claiming it could only have a spiritual organization, not a tangible one with structure.[58]

With the Bahá'í Faith still in its earliest days, with most of its sacred scripture still unpublished, it was necessary that a means of authenticating any assertion of what it stood for be in place. 'Abdu'l-Bahá had therefore established the principle that all Bahá'í publications had to be reviewed in advance to ensure that the purity of the Bahá'í teachings would not be diluted or adulterated. In his very first letter containing significant guidance about Bahá'í administration, dated 5 March 1922, Shoghi Effendi reiterated this requirement for all Bahá'í publications and placed the responsibility for establishing review processes upon the Bahá'í Assemblies about to be elected that year.[59] This constraint was an anathema to Dyar and Robinson, who wanted to publish anything they wished and label it Bahá'í.

The magazine was well known to Bahá'ís from coast to coast, and so growing alarm about its change in tone and attack on the New York Assembly became the business of the National Spiritual Assembly, then also based in New York. In response to the exchange in the December 1922 issue, the National Assembly informed the Bahá'ís nationwide that *Reality* was not an official Bahá'í publication and that its content was not subject to review by the Bahá'í institutions. It then began a quiet effort to win over Dyar and Robinson by assigning people such as Mountfort Mills and the scholar Jináb-i-Fáḍil to meet with them privately. This approach of presenting information and using gentle persuasion backfired because Dyar wrote his own version of those conversations and published them.

Dyar began seeking more dirt about the Faith to shovel as he deepened his tunnel that was rapidly causing a collapse of any remaining goodwill between the magazine and the Bahá'í community. Over the course of the next two years, he would pull apart the Will and Testament of 'Abdu'l-Bahá,[60] question the divine authority of Bahá'u'lláh, and allow an article questioning the authorship of some of Bahá'u'lláh's most important writings to be run in the magazine.[61] He explored in print episodes of Covenant-breaking, especially that of Muhammad-'Alí. Not surprisingly, advocates for that enemy of Shoghi Effendi contacted the magazine, assuming it to be an ally. Dyar wrote an article analysing who had the better claim to succeed 'Abdu'l-Bahá, Muhammad-'Alí or Shoghi Effendi, deciding that Shoghi Effendi was the more liberal of the two and so the better choice. Nonetheless, he allowed Muhammad-'Alí's associates to have their say, including Ibrahim Kheiralla, the teacher who had first introduced the Faith in the United States in 1892 before turning against 'Abdu'l-Bahá in an attempt to seize control of the American community. This public recounting of the problems the Faith had endured because of a few misguided, ambitious individuals was deeply troubling.[62] Shoghi Effendi sent a verbal message to the National Assembly through a returning pilgrim that he thought Dyar to be more dangerous than most critics of the Faith because he was highly intelligent and had a public platform with which to convey his ideas.[63] Dyar admitted that his access to authentic Bahá'í writings was limited, because most were not yet available in English. Thus, his analysis was based upon snippets of Bahá'í scripture and unauthenticated talks of 'Abdu'l-Bahá as well as his own imagination.

In July 1924, four members of the National Assembly, including Horace, joined Herold Robinson for lunch at a restaurant. Robinson made an offer that if the Bahá'í Faith would buy a substantial interest in the magazine, its editorial policy would align more closely with the Faith. A few weeks later, Dyar and his wife met with the National Assembly. It was clear to the Assembly members that his attitude had not changed but had instead hardened. He insisted that anyone should be allowed to call himself a Bahá'í. To him, the Bahá'í Cause was divided into two groups: those following the Administrative Order which he termed the 'Bahá'í Religion', and those who followed only the social principles of the Faith, which he labelled the 'Bahá'í Movement'. Why not co-exist peacefully?⁶⁴

Based upon guidance from Shoghi Effendi, the National Assembly and the New York Assembly decided that the best course of action was to ignore both Dyar and the magazine. As Shoghi Effendi advised:

> Concerning the magazine 'Reality,' I feel we must make it unmistak[e]ably plain to those in charge of it that the Bahá'ís would gladly and gratefully respond to the invitation to cooperate with those that are responsible for it immediately they are fully satisfied that nothing is or will be published by them, whether in the magazine or elsewhere, that would, however indirectly, prejudice or reflect upon their conception of what the Bahá'í Movement is or stands for. Should this be refused, and unfriendly and harmful matters be published against them, the attitude of all of us should be a definite refusal to help and absolute non-interference, as well as the absence of any form of retaliation which will instead of achieving our end defeat our purpose. We should leave him in the hands of God.⁶⁵

Horace's fellow New Yorkers turned to him during a community meeting to help them understand why they should no longer support a journal that seemed to promote Bahá'í ideals. He responded that even though by 1925 the magazine had appeared more conciliatory, there was never a full acceptance of 'Abdu'l-Bahá's teachings, for it was 'not real cooperation, it is merely the parasite feeding on the strength of the larger organism'. He told his friends that the Bahá'ís had a proven means to protect the Faith from those who would harm or use the Cause in untoward ways: to remain aloof from them.⁶⁶

> The one quality the Bahá'í should emphasize is the quality of surrender. It is for the Bahá'í to be perfectly serene and if this surrender goes into the depth of our nature and is founded upon absolute awareness as well as faith, I know this Cause will grow. The Cause is established upon a basis of consultation and unity and I think all the friends now can begin turning their back on anything that might have happened in the past and carry this beautiful spirit and this wonderful message to those they meet from day to day.⁶⁷

After losing Bahá'ís as its core group of subscribers, *Reality* moved further and further into metaphysical and occult topics and advertisements. The magazine ceased publication shortly after Dyar's death in 1929.[68] Until then, the Bahá'í community, especially in New York, had to endure and minimize the damage it caused to its image and teachings. This brief tempest was a foretaste of a much greater challenge to the Covenant that emerged as the controversy surrounding *Reality* faded. In fact, the instigator of the next test, Ahmad Sohrab, became a consulting editor of *Reality* during the months of 1922 when its articles attacked the institutions of the Faith. His willingness to countenance these attacks was a glimpse into his inner opinions, which were about to be made manifest.

* * * * *

The test brought about by Ahmad Sohrab would, at its outset, be much more subtle and consequently more difficult to navigate; because at its centre was the one individual that many New York Bahá'ís not only trusted and admired but loved.[69] How could they fail to be beguiled by the former secretary and English translator of 'Abdu'l-Bahá? Small of stature, he possessed an oversized personality with an ambition to match. Charming, intelligent, cunning, and a gifted storyteller, he was delightful company, especially when recounting tales from his eight years in the presence of 'Abdu'l-Bahá. Ahmad always offered up good ideas,[70] was not shy about taking initiative, and was a natural leader who easily attracted a following. Despite these praiseworthy attributes, he was driven by intense ambition. This was apparent as early as 1911, when friends were commenting on what they perceived as his arrogance.[71]

When 'Abdu'l-Bahá sent the great Bahá'í scholar and sage, Mírzá Abu'l-Faḍl-i-Gulpáygání, to inspire and train the Western believers during the earliest days of the American Bahá'í community in 1901, He also sent Ali-Kuli Khan, a youth who spoke English, to assist the great man. The work of serving the daily needs of the scholar while at the same time carrying out the translation of correspondence between Western believers and the Holy Land proved too much for Khan, so he wrote to 'Abdu'l-Bahá to request that He also send Ahmad Sohrab, an eager young teenager, to the United States to help tend to the household needs of Faḍl.⁷² 'Abdu'l-Bahá sent Sohrab with the instruction that he was to return to Egypt with Faḍl.⁷³ But in his first major act of defiance, young Ahmad remained in the United States where he found work with the Persian Legation in Washington DC. He continued to improve his knowledge of English and became a translator.⁷⁴ Almost a decade later, during 'Abdu'l-Bahá's ten-month journey through North America, he served intermittently as one of His translators and aides before being sent back to Egypt in 1912 by 'Abdu'l-Bahá. When 'Abdu'l-Bahá returned to Paris in 1913, He no longer had a translator, so Sohrab was summoned to join Him for the remainder of His travels in Europe. He returned with 'Abdu'l-Bahá first to Egypt then to Haifa, where he continued to serve as English translator and secretary until the end of the Great War. Immediately after the hostilities ceased, Sohrab begged for permission to return to United States, and 'Abdu'l-Bahá acceded. Arriving in Manhattan with the second batch of the Tablets of the Divine Plan in his luggage, Sohrab became an instant Bahá'í celebrity, the hero who had braved the War with 'Abdu'l-Bahá.

For many of those who met 'Abdu'l-Bahá during His Western journeys, Sohrab was His voice. As the primary translator of most correspondence in English following 'Abdu'l-Bahá's return to the Holy Land, he was aware of the contents of confidential letters sent to 'Abdu'l-Bahá. Of course, Ahmad would have known what was in Horace's letter describing his marital problems as well as 'Abdu'l-Bahá's response to him. Sohrab also frequently contributed articles to the *Star of the West* in which he normally began with his own spiritual message and then related the current situation in the Holy Land. What the friends loved best about him was his desire to chronicle everything 'Abdu'l-Bahá did and spoke. He would write lengthy letters to American Bahá'ís giving detailed accounts of a day in the life of the One he was serving. Among the thornier issues before the National Spiritual Assembly was whether his 'diaries' could be published with the blessings of the Bahá'í institutions, a decision Shoghi Effendi left to the judgement of the National Assembly with the admonition that none of the words of 'Abdu'l-Bahá as recounted by Ahmad should be considered exact, authoritative quotations.⁷⁵ As time passed, Sohrab unashamedly took credit for the words of Bahá'u'lláh and 'Abdu'l-Bahá⁷⁶ as well as plagiarized well-known authors who were not connected with the Faith.⁷⁷

At the time the first Assemblies were elected in 1922, Sohrab was living in Los Angeles trying to earn a living as an actor and lecturer.[78] He was elected the first secretary of that Assembly. Unfortunately, another of 'Abdu'l-Bahá's former translators, Dr Amin Fareed, was also living there and Sohrab appeared to be friendly towards him even though Fareed had been expelled from the Faith by 'Abdu'l-Bahá for multiple transgressions and the Bahá'ís were admonished to avoid him. Ahmad denied associating with this enemy of the Cause, responding that his interactions with Fareed were due more to the rules of courtesy than a desire to ally with him.[79]

By 1923 Sohrab was back in New York, connected with *Reality* magazine, and becoming a formidable force. About two years later, he became acquainted with a wealthy new believer, Julie Chanler, who in short order became attached to this exotic smooth-talker with his close connections to 'Abdu'l-Bahá.

Julia Lynch Olin Chanler,[80] who had been taught from infancy how to steer through the upper crust of society, married well twice. Her father was a distinguished attorney who served for a time as President of Wesleyan University and her first husband was a wealthy New York financier. She jumped further up the social ladder with her second marriage to Lewis Stuyvesant Chanler,[81] former Lieutenant Governor of New York and another prominent lawyer. Lewis was a descendant of the first multi-millionaire of the United States, John Jacob Astor, and also of Peter Stuyvesant, the famous final Governor of the New Amsterdam Dutch Colony before it was taken over by the British. Lewis was New York City royalty.

In 1925, Chanler reconnected with an old friend and another lady of means, Loulie Mathews. Mathews had become an ardent Bahá'í during the intervening years, and was holding weekly introductory meetings about the Faith at her home. After some months of becoming reacquainted, Mathews enticed Chanler to attend one of her gatherings. The speaker for that particular meeting was the charismatic and always interesting Mary Hanford Ford, mentioned previously. Julie was drawn to the ideals of the Faith and decided at the urging of Mathews to enrol. The new convert next travelled to the Holy Land to meet the women of the Holy Family, as well as Shoghi Effendi.[82] Buoyed by her experiences as a pilgrim, her enthusiasm for the Faith and desire to promote its ideals knew no bounds.

At about the time Julie Chanler visited the Holy Land, she became friends with Ahmad. She and her husband became his patrons, providing Sohrab with funds to rent locations for his lectures and to publicize them. His talks were popular, attracting not only Bahá'ís but the general public. Often the venues, including hotel meeting rooms, were filled. Sohrab was enchanting, entertaining, and full of ideas to save the world. The principles of the Faith he espoused attracted many of those who heard him, and some wished to know more about the Bahá'í Faith, for Ahmad never failed to mention Bahá'u'lláh as the source of his convictions. The Bahá'ís who attended were delighted with his success and felt that Sohrab's presentations should receive the unqualified support of the Bahá'í institutions, especially because they generated more interest among the populace than the other public Bahá'í gatherings in the city.

The New York Assembly faced a quandary. Sohrab's gatherings were drawing crowds and generating a growing number of serious inquiries about the Faith, even converts; but he had deliberately avoided bringing them under the supervision of the Bahá'í institutions, even while portraying them as though they were official Bahá'í activities. More distressing were comments reported back to the Assembly that Sohrab refused to recognize the authority of the New York Assembly. To his mind, how could this Assembly, composed of people who knew less than he did, advise or direct him – he who had spent eight years serving 'Abdu'l-Bahá day and night as a personal secretary? Equally distressing, Sohrab made assertions about the Faith during his presentations that did not seem to accord with the Assembly's understanding of the teachings of the Faith. There was also the issue of Ahmad quoting 'Abdu'l-Bahá. Indeed, he had spent many hours in the company of the Master, but his assertions as to what was said could not be authenticated. Both 'Abdu'l-Bahá Himself and the Guardian had warned against accepting unauthenticated oral statements.

Sohrab requested permission to use the rented rooms the New York Bahá'í community used as a Bahá'í Centre to give his lectures. The hesitant Assembly granted his request, but with conditions. When it became evident that he was not complying with the terms laid down by the Assembly and continuing to make distressing statements during his meetings, the Assembly withdrew its permission to use the rooms.

The storm which had been building for years intensified as Ahmad became more vocal in his rejection of Bahá'í administration. He told his supporters he had been treated harshly by the Assembly, especially by its officers – that no love or kindness sprang from the Assembly, only harsh judgement. He convinced them that the Assembly's reactions to him were wholly unwarranted. Horace was among those Sohrab criticized and blamed.

The idea of any split within the Bahá'í community innately repelled Horace. His reactions to both the Reading Room incident, which nearly split Chicago, and the attempt by Dyar to create two different Bahá'í movements, brought forth an inner determination to do whatever he could to prevent such mischief from ever taking effect. He was well aware of 'Abdu'l-Bahá's last letter to the American community, which arrived after His death. It contained a clear warning to all of His Bahá'í children to avoid those who would break apart the Faith, saying:

> O ye beloved ones! Guard the Cause of God! Let no sweetness of tongue beguile you – nay, rather consider the motive of every soul, and ponder the thought he cherisheth. Be ye straightway mindful and on your guard.[83]

Horace had first met Ahmad in Paris and held nothing against him personally, but as National Assembly Secretary, he was privy to Shoghi Effendi's admonitions that Sohrab should be closely watched.

Julie Chanler agreed with her friends among the New Yorker Bahá'ís that the tension between the New York Assembly and Sohrab was nothing more than a personality conflict between Horace and Ahmad – two strong-willed individuals – so she hatched a plan to solve this clash of titans. Ever the hostess, she resolved to bring the two together over a friendly dinner so that they could patch up their differences and then all would be well.[84] She had already planned a Christmas Eve banquet and invited many Bahá'ís, including Horace. But to make certain that this holiday party achieved the desired effect of reconciling Horace and Ahmad, she invited the two men to join her for lunch earlier that day at the popular Sherry's Restaurant in the Hotel New Netherland. She later recalled that luncheon:

> We had a table by the big Christmas tree and talked far into the afternoon. Mr. Holley was reserved but conciliatory; Sohrab was frankly critical of the Bahá'í Administration and its congealed

methods. I was between the two, hoping that a basis for future cooperation between them might be established right on the spot. It was evident that the difference was basic, the one being absorbed in administrative procedure, the other believing that tight organization in spiritual matters was completely inappropriate. Both had come to this meeting with misgivings.[85]

Julie had glimmerings of hope that her scheme was succeeding as the afternoon wore on:

> As hour succeeded hour in the dimly lighted dining room, festooned with Christmas decorations that always impart a sense of happy anticipation, I felt that these two men who, without question, were the leading personalities in the Bahai movement, were falling into a pattern of agreement. Each realized the accomplishments of the other; both were concentrated on the Cause; the atmosphere of Christmas hung heavy about us. When we arose from the table I had the impression that this Christmas Eve was a starting point for great developments in the near future.[86]

Horace and Julie walked a few blocks together after they left the restaurant. She asked him if, at the dinner later that evening, he might say a few words about the luncheon and make positive comments about Ahmad, indicating that he was now fully back in the fold. She understood Horace's response to be that he would do as she requested.

The Christmas Eve dinner was a merry celebration. After the sumptuous meal, the stuffed guests repaired to the drawing room where little gifts awaited them, spread beneath the Chanlers' Christmas tree. Presents were exchanged and everyone was in a jovial holiday mood. Judging the atmosphere to be just what she needed, Julie turned to Horace and asked him to speak. It was for her, the moment she had been anxiously anticipating, 'My heart was beating high for I believed that he was about to make a statement of major importance.' But she was about to be disappointed. Horace arose and stood silently before the tree for what seemed to his hostess to be an eternity. After the long silence, he said: 'I wish you all a Merry Christmas.' He then sat down. Julie's heart sank. Her attempt to change Horace's opinion of Ahmad had failed.[87]

By 1929, the New York Assembly was increasingly uncertain what to do next. It had tried quiet diplomacy, kindness, and giving Sohrab the use of the Bahá'í Centre, but the situation continued to deteriorate. It knew that many who were following him, especially the Chanlers, were doing so with the best of motives. There was a growing chorus, which included long-time pillars of the New York community, that the Assembly should simply bend to Ahmad and support his work to spread the Faith, for surely he was far better versed in the teachings of the Faith than those serving on the Local Assembly. Moreover, he was successful. Already, because of Sohrab, the Assembly had learned a difficult lesson: that it bore the responsibility for everything that happened within its community, especially at its Bahá'í Centre. This included approving in advance any publicity for Bahá'í gatherings – another condition Sohrab refused to accept.[88] It reached the conclusion that it was time to seek assistance from the National Assembly.[89] Once the New York Assembly appealed for help to its senior institution, it assumed it should take no further action until given direction.[90]

The National Assembly had been quietly monitoring the situation for some time. At the end of 1929, it received the following cable from Shoghi Effendi, which came to Horace as secretary of the National Assembly:

FEEL STRONGLY AHMAD SOHRAB SHOULD UPHOLD UNCONDITIONALLY AUTHORITY LOCAL AND NATIONAL ASSEMBLY HAVE IN NO LETTER OF MINE DEPARTED FROM THIS BASIC PRINCIPLE WHICH ALONE SAFEGUARDS UNITY OF CAUSE SHOGHI.[91]

In order to be certain of Sohrab's attitude toward the institutions, the National Assembly asked Amelia Collins, who knew him from California, to meet with him. She reported he was not loyal to the Bahá'í institutions and was unequivocal in his desire to work apart from them.[92]

The general approach taken by the National Assembly was to be slow to react to Sohrab and to be exceedingly kind to those in his orbit, especially his patroness, Julie Chanler, who had begged Shoghi Effendi to be patient with Ahmad's meetings so that he could prove their worth. The Guardian had responded to her that he would allow his activities to continue for a time, but he emphasized that she and Ahmad had to accept without reservation the authority of Bahá'í institutions.[93] This forbearance only emboldened Sohrab, who started mailing his own writings to Bahá'í communities throughout the West, including communities in Australia and New Zealand. Alarms rang from many quarters as those receiving his missives were horrified that he was challenging the authority of the Administrative Order.[94] The Guardian instructed the National Assembly to manage the situation and it then directed the New York Assembly to be more careful and kinder in its interactions with Ahmad and his supporters.

The challenges Sohrab and others[95] posed to the validity and authority of Bahá'í Administration during this period provided the Guardian with an opportunity to further educate the National Assembly in the verities of the teachings of the Faith. His unpublished letter to the Assembly of 27 February 1929 was his first attempt in English to explore in greater depth the Covenant and its relationship to Bahá'í institutions. The important points in that letter would be repeated in the years ahead – reusing even much of the letter's language. Commenting upon those who try to undermine the unity of the Faith, he advised that it was in reality 'a blessing in disguise' and that 'every storm of mischief' instead had the result of assisting the Faith to 'proclaim to all the world the exalted character of its precepts, the completeness of its unity, the uniqueness of its position, and the pervasiveness of its influence'.[96]

> We should feel truly thankful for such futile attempts to undermine our beloved Faith – attempts that protrude their ugly face from time to time, seem for a while able to create a breach in the ranks of the faithful, recede finally into the obscurity of oblivion, and are thought of no more. Such incidents we should regard as the interpositions of Providence, designed to fortify our faith, to clarify our vision, and to deepen our understanding of the essentials of His Divine Revelations.[97]

Shoghi Effendi stressed that those questioning the Administrative Order showed a lack of understanding of the totality of the Faith.

> It should be remembered by every follower of the Cause that the system of Bahá'í administration is not an innovation imposed arbitrarily upon the Bahá'ís of the world since the Master's passing, but

derives its authority from the Will and Testament of 'Abdu'l-Bahá, is specifically prescribed in unnumbered Tablets, and rests in some of its essential features upon the explicit provisions of the Kitáb-i-Aqdas. It thus unifies and correlates the principles separately laid down by Bahá'u'lláh and 'Abdu'l-Bahá, and is indissolubly bound with the essential verities of the Faith. To dissociate the administrative principles of the Cause from the purely spiritual and humanitarian teachings would be tantamount to a mutilation of the body of the Cause, a separation that can only result in the disintegration of its component parts, and the extinction of the Faith itself.[98]

While the National and Local Assemblies considered what they should do to bring Sohrab and his champions back into the light, he and the Chanlers seized upon a new tack. Because their gatherings were gaining in attendance, in 1929 they decided to form their own organization, which they named the New History Society. In 1911 while still a youth, Sohrab had been the moving force behind the formation of the Persian-American Educational Society, based in Washington DC. That association held several conferences before fading away. Through it, however, he gained experience in founding and running an organization.

The newly established New History Society added to the problems before the Assemblies. Sohrab's well-attended meetings had moved from the Bahá'í Centre and the Chanlers' home to large hotel meeting rooms. In January 1930, they were able to book prominent speakers to address the Society's meetings. For example, one held in the ballroom of the Ritz-Carlton Hotel featured the farewell address of Rabindranath Tagore, the famous Indian poet and philosopher, as he was about to depart the country. The *New York Times* reported that over two thousand people crowded into the hotel, and hundreds were turned away for lack of space. Helen Keller, the blind and deaf sage, was present and also spoke. The press portrayed the event as a Bahá'í gathering. The Society's programme the following week featured Albert Einstein, the world-famous physicist and author of the Theory of Relativity.[99] When Shoghi Effendi learned of these successes, he replied through his secretary that: 'The reason why the New History Society could win over some of the friends was because a superficial view of their activities showed signs of great success in the field of teaching. If the Assembly had used the services of all the friends in intensive constructive work, they would have not deserted us and found interest in other camps.'[100]

With the New History Society gaining momentum, action became more urgent. The National Assembly discussed the matter in its annual report published in the April 1930 *Bahai News Letter*. It recounted its consultation with both Shoghi Effendi and the New York Assembly quoting the clear admonition of the Guardian that 'every individual endeavoring to teach the principles of the Cause should adhere to the form and spirit of Bahá'í administration as the sole basis of unity of the Cause'. However, Shoghi Effendi had also 'pointed out the need of loving wisdom in dealing with individuals who are sincere in their efforts to render service even though mistaken and misguided in some of their views and methods'.[101] The National Assembly reported that it continued to pursue understanding and cooperation with the New History Society and had taken concrete steps to ensure that members of the public who were attracted to the Faith through the Society's activities would be warmly welcomed into the Faith and appropriately guided. The friends were urged 'to hold an attitude of good-will and serene patience pending the complete solution of the problem'.[102] But as the spring became summer, this conciliatory statement was no longer sufficient.

In June, after considering another letter from Shoghi Effendi about Sohrab and his organization, the National Assembly concluded that developments necessitated a definite statement about the New History Society and its relationship to the Cause.[103] To lay the groundwork for the statement, the August edition of the *Bahai News Letter* began with an editorial, drafted mainly by Horace, exploring the role and authority of local Spiritual Assemblies, including lessons from experiences of the previous ten years. This was followed by the National Assembly's official statement regarding the New History Society and Sohrab. The statement began with a brief history of the institutions' efforts to work cooperatively with Ahmad. It assured the friends that its new policy was not made in haste but only after concerted attempts 'to bring about full and frank consultation with the leaders of the New History Society'. It said that it had become 'the responsibility of the National Assembly to inform the friends that the activities conducted by Ahmad Sohrab through the New History Society are to be considered as entirely independent of the Cause, as outside the jurisdiction of the Local and National Assembly, and hence in no wise entitled to the cooperation of the Bahá'ís'.¹⁰⁴ In conclusion, the National Assembly urged loyalty to Bahá'í institutions while demonstrating unfailing kindness and goodwill in all interactions with individuals.¹⁰⁵ The Guardian sent a cable signalling his approval of this action.¹⁰⁶ But when the National Assembly's policy statement was read aloud at the following New York City Nineteen Day Feast, it ignited an explosion of passionate anger.

A group of Sohrab's most assertive Bahá'í supporters requested to meet in person with the National Spiritual Assembly at its August meeting. They levelled charge after charge against the New York Assembly and made harsh allegations against two of its officers, including Horace.¹⁰⁷ The National Assembly then invited the New York Assembly to meet with it at Green Acre in October and furnished New York with the notes of the August meeting. This upset the New York Assembly, especially because its members felt that those complaining should have first brought their issues to the Local Assembly. Horace urged calm and, as a member of the New York Assembly, recommended sending a lengthy letter to the National Assembly, laying out the history of the matter and refuting in detail all the accusations the group of malcontents had brought against it.¹⁰⁸ This emotional and delicate matter became a bounty and blessing. For the first time, it provided the practical opportunity for the new institutions to examine the relationship between the National Assembly and a local Assembly, including where the jurisdiction of the national and local bodies stopped and how appeals from a local Assembly to the National Assembly should be handled.¹⁰⁹ Both institutions gained insights from the New History Society test that would improve their handling of future difficult matters. In the end, the National Assembly determined that, while some mistakes had been made by the Local Assembly, especially in the tone it assumed in its relationship with community members, the New York Assembly had done nothing wrong.

The Guardian and the two Assemblies had stepped lightly in their dealings with Sohrab because of fear of hurting well-intentioned believers who were under his spell. The patience shown was due primarily to that concern, especially regarding Julie Chanler. Sohrab, however, knew what he was doing and so Shoghi Effendi was consistent in his insistence that he must state unequivocally his loyalty to the institutions of the Faith. When a believer sympathetic to Ahmad wrote to Shoghi Effendi that the New York Assembly appeared to be gradually becoming more favourable towards him and the New History Society, in a letter written on his behalf the Guardian replied: 'This is to solve the problem in the wrong way. It is not the Assembly that has to be won to the cause of some rebellious person, but that person brought back under the authority of the Assembly.'[110] Learning to accept the decision of an Assembly, even when it appeared to be wrong, was a hard lesson, but it was the only approach that would ensure that unity would not be broken.

Ahmad Sohrab's activities had not only injured the Cause in New York, but in other countries which received reports of his activities. The Guardian wrote in his own handwriting a note to Roy Wilhelm that he grieved 'to hear of the confused situation in New York'. And that he felt Ahmad 'will now exert his utmost to cause a split and bring about a schism in New York'.[111] The Guardian gave instructions directly to the New York Assembly a few months later in 1931, saying: 'Never compromise with Ahmad, stand firmly, but also ignore his very presence in New York. Neither take measures against them nor help them.' Instead, the Assembly should focus its entire attention upon 'teaching and other constructive work, and you will see how unity will be achieved, those of the friends, who have erred will be drawn back into active participation with the Assembly and the whole problem will die out'.[112]

The Guardian instructed the National Assembly to take primary responsibility for dealing with Sohrab because, should it fall instead to Shoghi Effendi, he feared many new believers would misunderstand his action. The Guardian had, however, long since determined that Sohrab was not faithful to the Will and Testament of 'Abdu'l-Bahá. He advised that the best course of action was for the National Assembly to show forth complete indifference to him and his activities. Shoghi Effendi also deplored the waste of energies spent by the friends in supporting Sohrab and his ephemeral activities rather than whole-heartedly pursuing constructive teaching work, which would yield truly lasting results.[113] The New York Assembly's responsibility was to uphold the decision of the National Assembly that 'the moment the New York friends are convinced that Ahmad is not going to turn and obey the Will and Testament, they must ignore those involved completely. There must be no delay about this as soon as this conviction is reached.'[114] By the time the National Assembly issued this directive in April 1931, Sohrab had lost interest in using the Bahá'í Centre – one point of contention – and most of his supporters within the New York Bahá'í community were gradually moving away from him and the New History Society.[115]

Unfortunately, the New York Bahá'í community would have to continue to endure Sohrab's activities, and the New History Society, much longer than it had to watch the misguided success of *Reality* magazine. The New History Society thrived for years with the Chanlers' financial support, as well as their connections to prominent people. It rented bigger halls for larger meetings, attracted widespread press coverage of its activities, and created a public reading room and information centre in a storefront at a conspicuous Manhattan location. The New History Society naturally confused the public that saw two disparate groups, each claiming to be the Bahá'í Faith in New York.[116]

Because of the earlier difficulties with Dyar, Horace had suggested to Shoghi Effendi that the name 'Bahá'í' be trademarked. With the Guardian's enthusiastic approval, this was carried out. This became helpful years later when problems with Sohrab arose again. Armed with what it thought was legal protection for the good name of the Faith, in 1941 the National Spiritual Assembly brought a lawsuit against the New History Society for infringement of the trademarked name 'Bahá'í'.[117] A New York Court held that it could not decide religious questions, thus the New History Society could continue to use the name. In response, the National Assembly released an additional statement about the New History Society in order to further distance the Faith from it. This action proved especially useful a few years later when the New History Society claimed that the Bahá'í writings provided religious grounds for its members to be exempt from military conscription. This stance was contrary to the policy that the National Assembly conveyed to the government during World War II. By the early 1950s, Sohrab had joined forces with other Covenant-breakers, especially the family of 'Abdu'l-Bahá in the Holy Land who had opposed the One he had served, all the while claiming to be a devoted Bahá'í.[118] Summing up the decades of battles with Sohrab, the Guardian stated in a letter in 1941 that Sohrab was 'no doubt the most subtle, resourceful and indefatigable enemy the Faith has had in America'. Even though the New York Assembly and National Assembly became less concerned with Sohrab over the next two decades, Horace would have to confront his machinations again in the 1950s in his role as Hand of the Cause when Ahmad created new troubles for the Faith, including in the Holy Land.[119] The damage Sohrab caused over the course of many decades was incalculable.

Sohrab died in New York on 20 April 1958, the eve of the day on which local Spiritual Assemblies are elected annually throughout the world.[120] With his death at age 68, the New History Society faded, leaving hardly a trace.[121] His former wife and only child had become estranged from him long before – both even stopped using his family name.[122]

The New York Bahá'í community, with Horace often the one serving at its helm, had navigated through two major storms throughout the first decade that it had a Spiritual Assembly. As the troubles with Sohrab subsided, the Guardian acknowledged its voyage through turbulent waters. In a letter to the New York Assembly, his secretary wrote, 'The steadfastness with which the New York friends withstood all the recent attempts to undermine the unity of the Cause is truly remarkable and will be undoubtedly a source of incalculable blessings for all believers.' The letter concluded with this poignant handwritten postscript:

> Your letter, carrying the welcome news of the steadfastness and continued activities of the New York believers greatly rejoiced my heart. Despite severe tests, and in the face of powerful and insidious opposition, the 'City of the Covenant' has proved itself worthy of the position bestowed upon it by 'Abdu'l-Bahá. The foundations of the spiritual citadel which His hands laid down remain firm and impregnable. The History Society, its promoters and originators, like many others that have preceded them, will sink into utter oblivion, while the Order which the hand of Bahá'u'lláh has reared will continue to develop and prosper. How sad the lot of those who have allowed the glitter of a transitory and superficial success to obscure their vision of the future glories of the Cause! Many will no doubt realize their mistake and rejoin the fold. Yours is the priceless blessing of having failed to deviate from the straight and narrow Path. May He continue to guide your steps and sustain your high endeavors.
> Your true brother,
> Shoghi[123]

8

NEW YORK CITY PAVES THE WAY

The myriad crises which arose during the first years following the death of 'Abdu'l-Bahá probably would have been less severe if the believers in the West had possessed two things. First, most of the Bahá'ís in the Occident did not have more than a cursory knowledge of the essential verities of the Faith. This deficit was largely due to lack of translations of the Sacred Writings into English. Secondly, this situation could have been ameliorated if the communities in the West had been strong enough to provide spiritual support to those struggling with the rapid changes within the Faith during that pivotal period. This second deficiency was in large measure due to lack of administration based upon Bahá'í principles. In late 1921, there was an urgent need to educate the friends and strengthen their communities so that they would become robust spiritual havens capable of assisting the friends to remain steadfast. It fell to New York City, as the largest and most organized of the Western Bahá'í communities, to find solutions to both problems. Of course, this meant Horace became intimately involved in both educational and administrative developments, for it was New York that paved the way for all other Bahá'í communities.

* * * * *

After the design of the Temple was chosen in 1920, Horace concluded that the next focus should be upon the printed word, that is: 'publishing the Divine Word, publishing books and pamphlets about the Cause, publishing the bulletin or newspaper of the Cause, and publishing the Bahai Magazine, or universal public expression of the Cause'. For, 'Publishing opens the highways along which the blessed feet of the Teachers can swiftly go, and Teaching creates the means by which the Temple can be gloriously completed.'[1] Since he arrived in New York

City, Horace had been keenly interested in spreading the teachings of Bahá'u'lláh through books, journals, and pamphlets. His service in this field was about to consume much more of his energy.

In the early 1920s, Horace's pen produced a significant number of Bahá'í essays, which were published primarily in the journal *Star of the West*.[2] On his own initiative, he also compiled English translations of writings from Bahá'u'lláh and 'Abdu'l-Bahá into a single volume entitled *Bahá'í Scriptures: Selections from the Utterances of Bahá'u'lláh and 'Abdu'l-Bahá*.[3] This personal project, completed before the first Assemblies were elected in 1922,[4] was an arduous task underwritten by a loan from his brother, Irving.[5] As the first book in English that could be studied in much the same way as the Bible or other Holy Scriptures, it was monumental. Horace posits in its introduction that readers of the book might be familiar with 'Abdu'l-Bahá from His travels a decade earlier, but they were less likely to have encountered the true source of His teachings, Bahá'u'lláh; thus, the book was organized so that the words of the Father would be read before studying those of His Son.[6] Horace hoped the book would be studied carefully, paying attention to 'what seems [sic] little details but really are very important: for example, the very first utterance of Abdul Baha . . . is his supplication to realize the condition of servitude.'[7] Horace also apologized in the introduction for the inadequacies of the translations in that those available to him 'must be considered as a king in rags, since the Arabic and Persian originals are declared by all who have had access to them to be of the most exalted beauty and the most moving force.'[8] The anthology was gratefully received because it fulfilled a need.[9] One reader – a new believer – called it her 'meat and drink'.[10] Shoghi Effendi approved of *Bahá'í Scriptures*, saying that he felt certain it would arouse interest in the Cause, and he hoped others would produce similar publications.[11] Over the next two decades, as more and more authoritative translations became available, the deficiencies of *Bahá'í Scriptures* became apparent. Horace considered different options, such as revising his initial volume or substituting a new compilation for it.[12] Twenty years later, in 1943, Horace used the original concept of *Bahá'í Scriptures* to create an expanded, authoritative compilation entitled *Bahá'í World Faith: Selected Writings of Bahá'u'lláh and 'Abdu'l-Bahá*.[13] Like its predecessor, this second collection of sacred texts served for many years as a primary source of Bahá'í scripture in English –'a World Bible revealed for men of all races and lands'.[14]

The exercise of producing a compilation of Sacred Texts inspired Horace to write an essay, 'The Writings of Bahá'u'lláh', for the *Star of the West*.[15] It represents the culmination of decades of writing and thinking about the process and power of putting words on paper. In it, he discusses the customary approach to studying literature – focusing upon the work itself rather than upon the creator of the work. That approach, he felt, was flawed, for his understanding – gleaned from his own creative methods – was that the creator knows well that his work, no matter how good, never fully makes manifest the inspirations from which the creation had its birth. Likening writers to musical instruments, he postulates that 'Authors differ vastly as to what notes sound through their work and what notes remain silent.'[16] Only the creator is aware of those unearthly silent notes he could not bring forth through his tangible handiwork, and this knowledge frustrates him. Creators, therefore, will always be dissatisfied with their creations.

> . . . any person who has ever actually felt the creative impulse within his own consciousness realizes that the work produced, even at is best, renders only a fraction of the significance that impulse contained. During creation, the author feels an infinite resource opened within him, a resource which the work created never satisfactorily records.[17]

After discussing how William Shakespeare – considered the greatest of all writers in the English language – was limited by his own human experience, Horace then expounds on the difference in essence between the fruit of the pen of Bahá'u'lláh and that of gifted writers.[18] Bahá'u'lláh's Writings can never be read as one would read other works because only His Writings include the silent notes that originate from the infinite – a trait no normal human being can ever express.

> By minds limited to customary closed circle of experience, these writings can be read over and over without understanding. The supreme benefit of reading them, indeed, is to learn merely how they are to be read . . . No comparison between Bahá'u'lláh and other writers is possible.[19]

Drawing upon his own Christian background, Horace then compares the Writings of Bahá'u'lláh to the utterances of Christ.

The words of Jesus are the manifestation of the Christ – the power of men to respond infinitely to the infinite power of God. But Bahá'u'lláh's message does not *repeat* the message of Christ – it *completes* that message.[20]

Summarizing his thoughts, Horace provides a glorious exposition of the power and sublime character of Bahá'u'lláh's Sacred Texts, which have no equal in the world's literature or works on philosophy.

... in the writings of Bahá'u'lláh there is an influence not dwelling elsewhere in literature or philosophy. That influence permeates and proceeds from a literary and philosophic form, but the power of the influence well-nigh shatters the cup of speech. Here is Truth, in distinction to facts; Reality in distinction to logic; immovable Power in distinction to emotion. Our categories and our systems fail to contain this writing, as engineers would fail to dam the sea. Our critical faculties even prevent us from approaching its outpouring effect, for its very purpose is to create new faculties as standards in the mind. It is a Mystery; but not secretive; a Revelation, but not argumentative; Love, but not enticement. In numberless passages the flame burns visibly forth and the wine intoxicates. It is a spiritual geography for the searching mind, a home for the heart outworn . . .[21]

* * * * *

The New York Board of Counsel began to use the name Spiritual Assembly[22] before it was entitled to assume that appellation because it was not yet more than an organizing committee. When, in 1922, New York's governing body was elected, it finally had the right to assume the title and spiritual role of Local Spiritual Assembly. The newborn, divinely ordained Assembly was a bud that would blossom into a Local House of Justice in the fullness of time. From the moment of its birth, it became the body to which the believers within the boundaries of New York City were obliged to turn with a posture of obedience. No longer a board of directors, it was a wholly new entity, different in its essence, although its membership and election process changed very little from the old Board of Counsel. Horace was elected to that nascent Assembly and chosen its first secretary.[23]

Although the archived minutes of the New York Board of Counsel are incomplete, comparing them to the minutes of the Local Assembly after 1922 reveals that a genuine transformation had taken place. The butterfly had emerged from its cocoon. The Board had conducted its business as a typical American civic organization such as the Rotary Club, a Women's Club, or the Chamber of Commerce. Occasionally it provided guidance to members of its community, but it lacked the compelling authority needed to elicit the loving obedience of those it served. It focused primarily on managing funds and making certain that arrangements were in place for meetings. From the outset, the Spiritual Assembly, on the other hand, understood that it was an institution ordained by God which must function at a higher level, ever conscious of the spiritual principles of the Faith, especially the teachings regarding consultation. Unity became its watchword. For decades, both the Board of Counsel and the Assembly employed the procedural rules set forth in *Robert's Rules of Order*, a widely used guidebook for conducting meetings. Hence, the minutes of both are replete with formal motions and seconding of motions. But a student of the early minutes of the New York Assembly will be struck by the difference in tone and focus after the change of 1922.[24]

* * * * *

Scant attention had been paid to developing Bahá'í community life before the election of the first Local Assemblies. In the 1920s, the Nineteen Day Feast was the centre of community life – the one meeting open only to adherents that was like a coming together of a family. When it first established these gatherings almost two decades earlier, the New Yorkers knew they were intended to be held every nineteen days; however, the New York community found the nineteen day interval to be impractical. Notifying its large community of the changing dates, times, and locations was a costly, time-consuming chore. Settling on a fixed date and place was a less complicated solution; thus, the New York Feast was regularly scheduled on the nineteenth of each Gregorian month at the Bahá'í Centre. The friends took turns arranging the programme and providing refreshments. Only in 1925 did the community begin to hold the Feasts every nineteen days in conformity with the Bahá'í calendar and in obedience to the guidance of Shoghi Effendi.

In the beginning, the New York Nineteen Day Feast was a devotional and social gathering that always included food – usually a dinner. It became apparent over time that the Feasts afforded opportunities to channel community recommendations through the Feast Committee to the Board of Counsel. Over the years, these monthly meetings increasingly strengthened the bonds between community members and the Board, as they also became a conduit for disseminating news about Bahá'í activities in other localities, as well as information about issues of interest. Naturally, ideas were shared on how to best advance the work of the Faith.[25]

As the New York Spiritual Assembly's work grew, it became obvious that it needed a means to communicate with the friends in the metropolitan area and, in turn, a way for those they served to raise their concerns and pass on their ideas. With its many members spread over a wide geographic area, this free exchange between the Assembly and its community could not be facilitated easily, even at the Feasts. To send a letter to everyone by mail was expensive and time-consuming. Consultation between 30 to 100 people at gatherings was difficult, insufficient, and unwieldy. Because it found that there was not adequate time to conduct the business of the community at the monthly Feasts, the Assembly decided to hold a special meeting on the first Tuesday of each month that would be devoted exclusively to community business. By establishing a separate business meeting, the Feasts could remain focused upon worship and fellowship.[26] These additional 'community meetings' were initially popular, but attendance dropped within a few months.[27] The Assembly then agreed to increase the frequency of Feasts by holding them every nineteen days and to add a business segment between the devotions and food. This proved to be the best solution.[28] The Feasts now not only provided a regular forum for community consultation, but the spiritual atmosphere created by prayers, readings of scripture, and music elevated the tone of the business session.

* * * * *

The New York community was responsible for a momentous innovation that would lay a solid foundation for all Local Assemblies: a governing charter for legal incorporation. The New York Board of Counsel first explored incorporating in 1917 but was advised by 'Abdu'l-Bahá that it was not yet time to do so.[29] Considering the changes in Bahá'í administration after 1922, in 1925 the New York Assembly asked the National Spiritual Assembly about the possibility of incorporating.[30] The National Assembly responded that it indeed wanted Local Assemblies to incorporate, but that it also wanted that process to be uniform throughout both Canada and the United States. Furthermore, the National Assembly felt it should be the first institution to incorporate, but its efforts were hampered by legal impediments.[31] By 1930, the New York Assembly had received permission to proceed.[32] Horace, Mountfort Mills (an attorney), and other New York Assembly members began the work of drafting the document that would become By-Laws for a Local Spiritual Assembly, a type of constitution or charter. Naturally, Horace and Mountfort, who were both serving on the National Assembly, used the newly drafted Declaration of Trust of the National Assembly as their guide. The By-Laws were adopted and signed by the New York Assembly on 12 November 1931[33] and unanimously ratified by the New York community at a Nineteen Day Feast on 3 January 1932.[34] It was then reviewed by the National Assembly and accepted with modifications. Once finalized, the document was published in *The Bahá'í World* for people the world over to study as an inspiring example.[35]

The Guardian was exceedingly pleased with New York's By-Laws, as he stated in a letter to the New York Assembly:

> . . . I have read and re-read most carefully the final draft of the By-Laws drawn up by that highly-talented, much-loved servant of Bahá'u'lláh, Mountfort Mills, and feel I have nothing substantial to add to this first and very creditable attempt at codifying the principles of general Bahá'í administration. I heartily and unhesitatingly commend it to the earnest perusal of, and its loyal adoption by, every National Bahá'í Spiritual Assembly, whether constituted in the East or in the West.[36]

The Guardian then astonished the New York City Assembly by charging it with the task of dispatching copies of its By-Laws to Bahá'í Assemblies across the world.

> I would ask you particularly to send copies of the text of this

document of fundamental importance accompanied by copies of the Declaration of Trust and the text of the Indenture of Trust, to every existing National Spiritual Assembly, with my insistent request to study the provisions, comprehend its implications, and endeavor to incorporate it, to the extent that their own circumstances permit, within the framework of their own national activities . . .[37]

Lest they doubt the significance of their accomplishment, the Guardian painted for them a picture of how their By-Laws would help to bring about the eventual establishment of the Universal House of Justice.

You can hardly realize how substantially it will contribute to pave the way for the elaboration of the beginnings of the constitution of the worldwide Bahá'í Community that will form the permanent basis upon which the blest and sanctified edifice of the first International House of Justice will securely rest and flourish.[38]

Shoghi Effendi then provided New York with general guidance about the role of a Local Spiritual Assembly – guidance which would be shared with millions of Local Assemblies around the world for centuries to come as the Faith spreads to all corners of the globe. It set out their duties as 'the trusted ones of the merciful'.

I would specifically remind you that in the text of the said By-Laws which to the outside world represents the expression of the aspirations, the motives and objects that animate the collective responsibilities as willing ministers, faithful stewards and loyal trustees to those who have chosen them. Let it be made clear to every inquiring reader that among the most outstanding and sacred duties incumbent upon those who have been called upon to initiate, direct and coordinate the affairs of the Cause, are those that require them to win by every means in their power the confidence and affection of those whom it is their privilege to serve. Theirs is the duty to investigate and acquaint themselves with the considered views, the prevailing sentiments, the personal convictions of those whose welfare it is their solemn obligation to promote. Theirs is the duty to purge once for all their deliberations and the general conduct of their affairs from that air of self-contained aloofness, from the suspicion of secrecy, the stifling atmosphere of dictatorial assertiveness, in short, from every word and deed that might savor of partiality, self-centeredness and prejudice. Theirs is the duty, while retaining the sacred and exclusive right of final decision in their hands, to invite discussion, provide information, ventilate grievances, welcome advice from even the most humble and insignificant members of the Bahá'í family, expose their motives, set forth their plans, justify their actions, revise if necessary their verdict, foster the sense of interdependence and co-partnership, of understanding and mutual confidence between them on one hand and all local Assemblies and individual believers on the other.[39]

Thus, the New York By-Laws became the model constitution for all Local Spiritual Assemblies everywhere and for all time, which also meant that it could never modify them without the permission of the Guardian and National Spiritual Assembly.[40] Ironically, the Chicago Assembly registered its By-Laws with its government first, winning the distinction of being the first incorporated Local Assembly. However, Chicago used the By-Laws drafted by New York.[41] New York was not far behind, submitting its document to its state government on 31 March 1932.[42] Shoghi Effendi requested that a photograph be made of the New York Spiritual Assembly to memorialize its role in creating the essential charter and he informed Horace that a copy of the New York certificate of incorporation as well as its By-Laws had been framed and were placed on display at the Mansion at Bahjí – a distinct honour.[43] Horace served as chairman of the New York Assembly throughout this noteworthy undertaking.[44]

Its constitution placed the New York community on firm footing, but there was still much to learn, especially about Bahá'í consultation – the basis of all collective decision-making. According to Assembly minutes, Horace often advocated for increasing the amount of consultation between the Assembly and the community it served, suggesting that the members should get to know the sentiments of the believers by putting forth greater efforts to interact with them. He also reminded his colleagues of the confidential nature of their meetings and that decisions should not be made when others who were not members of the Assembly were present.[45] These admonitions would become standard operating principles for all Assemblies, but in small communities where the active believers were all members of the Assembly, those points were not yet as relevant.

* * * * *

As the largest community in North America, New York City assisted the National Spiritual Assembly to clarify how national committees should interact with Local Assemblies. In 1930, New York challenged the right of the National Teaching Committee to hold regional conferences organized by a group from the region appointed by the Committee. This seemed to the New York Assembly to clash with its own responsibilities by creating a 'duality of Bahá'í interest and of Bahá'í authority in each local community'. It asserted that its complaint was based upon principle because 'every departure from the organic laws of the Cause tends towards the weakness and disintegration of a Bahá'í community'. It reminded the National Teaching Committee that 'Believers residing in small communities cannot appreciate the many problems arising in communities such as New York.'[46] Horace added his own voice to this matter in a separate letter to Alfred Lunt in which he expressed concerns that if a national committee was allowed, without first gaining permission from the National Assembly, to subdivide the country into regions and appoint subcommittees for each, inadvertently it 'could build up a political machine'. Referring to the problems then enveloping New York City because of the renegade New History Society, he said, 'If, for instance, the New History outfit were to organize through independent Bahá'í groups throughout the country for its work, it might become a serious menace.'[47] Because of New York's objections, the National Assembly instructed its Committee to be more respectful of the rights of Local Assemblies, soliciting their assistance and input before solidifying their plans. The National Assembly did not wish to stifle initiative but wished to 'gradually and surely lead toward a closer contact of the organized assemblies with the various national departments of the work'. This would be more in accord with the spiritual principles, 'so that all the organs and parts are in the closest relationship and cooperation, but this cannot be expected to be brought about overnight'. The National Assembly's letter ended with a postscript stating that 'The assertion of authority unwisely done, disturbs the balance and crucifies initiative. It is the challenging problem of Bahai administration unless we follow the wonderful balance set by Shoghi Effendi.'[48]

Even as New York sparked a conversation about the limitations of national committees, so it also generated guidance from Shoghi Effendi about the limitations of Local Assemblies. When the Assembly sent him its local newsletter, he thanked the Assembly through his secretary, stating that he wished to continue to receive it. But a note of caution was included because New York City's resourcefulness might be perceived to be eclipsing those of the national administration.

> While fully conscious of the importance of such Bahá'í local organs in bringing more unity and cooperation among individual believers and groups, Shoghi Effendi feels that great care should be taken lest local activities of this nature tend to develop to an extent that would jeopardize the national activities of the Faith. Just as the local Bahá'í fund must under all circumstances be subordinated to the national fund, so also every local circular letter should be considered as subsidiary to the national report of Bahá'í activities in every country. Such a coordination between local and national efforts is indispensable, not only because of its economic advantages, but essentially due to the fact that upon the application of the principle underlying this process must inevitably depend the effective working of the entire administrative machinery of the Faith. There is order, coordination and system in the Cause, and not a jungle of conflicting interests and of continually clashing wills.[49]

* * * * *

The earliest Bahá'í gatherings in the New York metropolitan area could only be held in the homes that could accommodate sizeable gatherings. It was perhaps the only community in the United States with enough active members to regularly need a space larger than the average home parlour. As numbers grew, the community rented rooms as needed and used the facilities of St Mark's-in-the-Bowery Episcopal Church. The publishing offices of *Reality* magazine also served as another meeting venue for several years. Finally, in 1924, the community leased rooms on a monthly basis. In their eagerness to decorate this first Bahá'í centre, believers donated pictures of 'Abdu'l-Bahá to fill the walls. This bounty quickly overwhelmed the space. Of course, no one wanted their own offering removed. The matter finally was brought to the Local Spiritual Assembly, which decided that only one picture would be hung at a time and that the picture should be alternated every nineteen days.[50] Having a facility also required the community to maintain and manage it. Fortunately, among the New Yorkers were a few volunteers willing to assume responsibility for booking and supervising meetings. There was also the ongoing issue of scheduling responsible believers to be present several hours each day so that the centre could be open for those wishing to learn about the Faith.[51]

The problem of meeting space was solved, but not the greater one – the geographic expanse of the community. Over the years, New York's centres were located in central Manhattan, forcing those who lived in the outer boroughs to go to great effort to attend meetings. Even when travelling by train and the subway system, it was an arduous journey. The incorporated city is spread over 302.64 square miles (783.83 square kilometres), and the island of Manhattan alone was 22.83 square miles (59.13 square kilometres). These measurements did not include the surrounding suburbs, where many believers who participated in New York activities lived.

The size of its membership created other challenges for New York when it came time for elections. There were more than one hundred active believers scattered throughout the city's boroughs,[52] and at least twice that number were on the membership list. How could the average believer know whom to vote for when it was impossible to know everyone? One early solution was taking nominations during the election meeting. It was quite normal for at least a handful of the nominees to ask to be removed from the list because they did not think they would be able to serve. They learned from experience that allowing believers to have their names removed from the list of those who were eligible to serve was contrary to the unfolding instructions of Shoghi Effendi. In order to preserve the right of each Bahá'í to vote for whomever his or her heart and head dictated, there should be no nominations or electioneering. The solution New York devised, which would later be adopted by other communities as they grew, was to have a copy of the membership list available to the electorate during the voting.[53]

In 1934, the Guardian acknowledged in his handwritten note at the close of a letter to the New York Spiritual Assembly, its contributions to the development of local Bahá'í communities, saying, 'You have by your acts, your spirit and example consolidated the foundations of the administrative order of our glorious Faith.'[54]

* * * * *

For the two decades after World War I, not only was the New York Bahá'í community the largest in the West, but it was the most demographically diverse. This was the period of the Great Migration when thousands of descendants of African slaves moved from the rural southern region of the country to its industrial northern and midwestern cities. Adding to this mix were millions of immigrants from the poorer regions of Europe. The masses crowding its tenements in lower Manhattan, were considered racially white, even the darker skinned ethnic groups from the Mediterranean region. Prejudice against immigrants was a problem – especially against Catholics and Jews – but it was far less virulent than prejudice against Blacks born in the United States. Slavery was America's original sin, which had deformed the character of the nation. 'Abdu'l-Bahá confronted the disease of racial prejudice repeatedly during His journey across North America, and Shoghi Effendi continued admonishing the Bahá'ís in the United States to do everything in their power to eradicate what he termed America's 'Most Vital and Challenging Issue'. From its formative period, New York City's Bahá'í community included Black members, especially from the Harlem neighbourhood and the borough of Brooklyn. With cultural differences mixed in with subtle and not-so-subtle prejudices, ensuring true unity within the New York Bahá'í community required constant sensitivity, concerted effort, and vigilance.

According to renowned historian Paul Johnson, by the 1920s Harlem had become a city within a city and the unofficial capital of Black America. Between 1910 and 1920, New York City's Black population increased from 91,709 to 152,467 and over the next ten years jumped to 327,706. Most were migrants from the Southern states. At the turn of the twentieth century, Harlem was still a predominantly White, middle-class neighbourhood. With the influx of migrants from the South, by the end of the 1920s Harlem was no longer a prosperous community; it was predominantly Black and much of it had become a slum because of unbridled overcrowding. The rapid arrival of Black neighbours caused the White residents to flee –118,792 of them in the 1920s alone. Blacks became 12 per cent of the population of Manhattan Island. These farmers and tradesmen from the Southern states were joined by other black immigrants from the Caribbean, who were not welcomed by their new Southern neighbours.[55] These demographic changes inevitably affected the predominantly White New York City Bahá'í community.

A movement which came to be known as the 'Harlem Renaissance' – the Golden Age of Black American culture – had its birth in New York City during the first decades of the twentieth century as the Black population swelled. Its philosophical leader was the philosopher, writer and first Black Rhodes scholar, Alain LeRoy Locke. Dr Locke, a Bahá'í, had made a pilgrimage to the Holy Land to meet 'Abdu'l-Bahá and enjoyed a close relationship with Shoghi Effendi. Despite the challenges spawned by the Great Migration, it was a time when music, dance, art, fashion, literature, theatre, and politics flowered within the Black community. White New Yorkers loved to take the subway to Harlem for a night out at its dinner clubs where they enjoyed hot jazz and fried chicken, and in the process gained a love for elements of Black culture. The influence of this cultural renaissance on the wider society continues to be incalculable, especially its impact on the performing arts. It also provided intellectual foundations for the waves of civil rights movements spread across the rest of the century. Locke, Louis Gregory, and other Bahá'ís played a part in this significant movement.

Horace was fervently interested in racial justice and equality. His hometown's most famous native son was John Brown, the abolitionist who was considered to be a sainted martyr in the Northern states and the devil incarnate in the South where he tried to spark a violent slave rebellion. Brown, though born in Torrington, Connecticut, did not grow up there. He returned, however, as an adult to do business and had dealings with Horace's grandfather, Francis Holley. According to family lore, Brown visited the Holley family home. Horace's heart was sympathetic towards the plight of Black people, but until moving to New York, his surroundings afforded limited opportunities to become acquainted with them as friends. The one Black he came to know well was fellow National Assembly member, Louis Gregory, the son of slaves. His lack of first-hand knowledge did not prevent Horace from developing an intense interest in efforts to eliminate the persecution of

Black citizens by law and social mores. While living in New York City, Horace experienced first-hand the wages of racism – both overt and subtle – even within the Bahá'í community.

'Abdu'l-Bahá gave His most noteworthy talks about racial unity during His visits to Washington DC, which, despite being the nation's capital, was Southern by culture and racially segregated. The evening of 11 May 1912, hours after returning to New York City from Washington, He spoke to New York believers about the oppression of Blacks in America, reiterating what He had said in Washington.[56]

> God maketh no distinction between the white and the black. If the hearts are pure both are acceptable unto Him. God is no respecter of persons on account of either color or race. All colors are acceptable to Him, be they white, black, or yellow. Inasmuch as all were created in the image of God, we must bring ourselves to realize that all embody divine possibilities.[57]

When 'Abdu'l-Bahá directed Agnes Parsons of Washington DC to organize a Race Amity Conference in her racially divided city, she asked Horace to participate. He sent sincere apologies that his employment made it impossible to travel on the dates of the Conference, but as an advertising professional, he willingly reviewed the programme for her together with his friend Mountfort Mills. He gave his approval, saying,

> We did go over it, most carefully, realizing through how many rocks and whirlpools of prejudice and misunderstanding you had to steer, and we really marveled at the success with which you kept to the Bahá'í principles without making it appear a 'Bahai' occasion.[58]

Even though Horace missed the historic first Race Amity Conference, in 1924 the New York City Bahá'í community held its own. It featured an impressive ensemble of speakers including Jane Addams, the famous social worker from Chicago; James Weldon Johnson, national secretary of the NAACP,[59] the country's foremost civil rights organization; and the distinguished anthropologist, Dr Franz Boas from Columbia University, who scientifically debunked the idea of a 'superior race' and advocated for interracial marriage. Horace, Mountfort Mills, and Roy Wilhelm assisted with arrangements and spoke at the conference.

Other organizations, including the National Urban League and League of Women Voters, took part. The primary topic was relations between Blacks and Whites; however, the conference also touched upon issues affecting other races as well.[60]

The New York Baháʼí community held other Inter-Racial Amity Conferences, including one in 1927 at the Nazarene Congregational Church in Brooklyn with its predominantly Black congregation. The talks were interspersed by negro spirituals performed by the church choir. Horace, the first speaker, addressed the topic, 'The Origins of Prejudice'.

Holding this important Baháʼí event in a Black, Christian Church was emblematic of the New York Baháʼí community's initial interaction with the Black segment of the city's population. From its early days, it associated with Black churches, especially the Nazarene Church and its founder, Reverend Henry H. Proctor.[61] New York's first Local Spiritual Assembly included among its nine members not only Horace, but also a Black member, Reverend Richard Manuel Bolden, founder of the First Emanuel Church in Harlem, and a published author on religious topics.[62] Bolden started a group called the Rainbow Circle, which carried out social events to promote loving interaction between the races. He also held Baháʼí gatherings at his church on Sunday afternoons.[63]

While Horace was serving on the Local Assembly, it appointed a Harlem Teaching Committee and, a few years later, added a Race Amity Committee. The Assembly frequently asked Louis Gregory to come to New York to assist with the work in Harlem,[64] recognizing that plans for the teaching work in that neighbourhood had to consider that 'peculiar circumstances prevail there'.[65] To its credit, the Assembly also treated Harlem as an integral part of its greater teaching plan for the city. It strove to find an appropriate meeting location for the neighbourhood and worked to ensure that White members participated in the Harlem teaching efforts, not just Black believers.[66] It devoted most of one of its meetings to consulting with a Black believer, Sadie Oglesby from Boston, to hear her report about race relations in America soon after she returned from the Holy Land where she had discussed the matter extensively with Shoghi Effendi. Horace attended her presentation.[67] One problem the Assembly encountered in working with the Black community was that the Baháʼís naturally associated with all kinds of people, including immigrants from the Caribbean and Africa, but these groups of Blacks were not welcomed by Blacks from the United States – an issue within Harlem that spilled over into the Bahá'í community.[68] It also had to deal with reports of incidents at Bahá'í gatherings which were perceived by community members to be racist.[69]

In 1930, the New York Assembly reported to Shoghi Effendi that the Race Amity work had helped it overcome the negative effects it suffered because of the New History Society, commenting, 'The fact that our community is the largest and most varied Bahá'í group in America surely creates special opportunities for service among believers of all races, classes and types.'[70]

Though organized primarily by the National Race Amity Committee, one of the crowning Bahá'í race amity events held in New York City was a banquet to honour the work of the NAACP and the Urban League. About 150 people attended the gathering held on 27 February 1932, including the famous civil rights leader, W. E. B. DuBois, who afterwards sent a note of thanks stating that he considered the event to be a true accomplishment. Horace was among the speakers at that evening's programme, which was presided over by Louis Gregory and Loulie Mathews. The National Amity Committee judged that event to be an achievement second only to the first Race Amity Conference in Washington in 1921.[71]

New York City was not only racially diverse; it was also ethnically, economically, culturally and socially diverse. People from every continent passed through it, and many stayed. During the first half of the twentieth century, it was the primary port through which most immigrants entered the United States and were processed at the government facility on Ellis Island. Many of those millions of arrivals could not afford to continue travel into the interior of the country and settled in decrepit tenement housing on the lower East Side of Manhattan. They created enclaves of various nationalities street by street, with each city block becoming little different from the homeland of its residents. English, if spoken at all, was a second language. Yiddish, Italian, Russian, Irish, and dozens of other tongues could be heard throughout most of Manhattan. In addition to various ethnic groups, the Bahá'í community included those from all levels of society. There were members with comfortable wealth and members employed as manual labourers as well as a few in dire need who turned to the Assembly for material assistance.

Learning to put the principle of the oneness of mankind into action within a community as varied as New York City was a challenge causing many people to feel uncomfortable. Horace addressed this in a talk to the New York community in 1931. He first pointed out that all groups are based upon the principle of exclusion. You must be a relative to be part of a family, you must be an engineer to be part of that professional society, you must be a resident to be part of a neighbourhood organization. This was where the Bahá'í Faith was different. 'No one can be excluded from a Bahai community who enters with the faith in the teachings of Baha'u'llah.'[72] This was a root cause of the problem of creating unity within the Bahá'í community.

> Therefore in such an inclusive movement the individual entering for the first time has the experience of meeting just the types of persons who are perhaps strangest or most difficult for him. At one of the earlier talks the question was raised from the floor as to why a certain sentiment of friendliness and cordial love which some of the friends were conscious of in the Bahai community of different cities years ago seemed to be absent in the city of New York. It seems quite obvious. In the first place the Bahai community does not exist to sanction any particular personality. It does not exist in order to lend exclusive encouragement to any particular view.[73]

The problem lay not with the diversity of the community but with the spiritual development of each individual.

> In order to receive the experience of this newer and freer association with other people we must give up all of our human ego of our previous limited social experience. And so as a community grows to a point of maturity and responsibility it is inevitable that those entering it will for a time feel the burden of forever accommodating themselves to a universal point of view. It is much easier for any human being to belong to a group which sanctions certain forms of prejudice – where certain social and economical problems are never raised; where the association of the members are for limited times and in special places and when you put on your overcoat and hat you leave the responsibilities of that movement behind.
>
> All that is very much easier than the experience of a new quality of

human association in which each one of us must encounter oppositions which are in reality not oppositions but the sensitiveness of our own undeveloped souls. We call it opposition; we might call it enmity; but in reality it is our own sensitiveness to the impact of truth.[74]

He went on to say that without the difficulties of learning to get along with diverse types of people, there is no inner growth. But simply becoming a part of a diverse group was far from enough to create unity. The group had to be held together by a spiritual bond, with the controlling principle being the oneness of mankind.

In the Bahai cause the individuals come in not as social entities; they do not come in as political or economical or credal personalities; they come in as quickened souls. That is why in the power of Baha'u'llah there is a bond between the minds and heart of people which when we become adult in the cause and spiritually conscious enables us to associate usefully with other believers . . .[75]

This was not merely a matter of the psychology of group dynamics, for Horace raised the vision of his listeners to the mystical nature of spiritual association.

There is a profound mystery in the association of people in a Bahai community for the reason that the selective power at work is a universal power. It has picked us up because we can rid ourselves of the prejudices that are the dead hand of the past. This power permeating a body of a few hundred people will in that body evolve a collective intelligence, a collective will, a collective vision which can in time produce a manifestation of human power superior to anything in the organized world today . . .

History gives us age after age the example of a little group of truly devoted followers who stand firm and steadfast while around them all things decay. And they are upheld by this power of spiritual faith and when the situation clears and the old order is sufficiently renounced, the basis of the new age is found in the conscious faith of a very small proportion of the inhabitants of the land.[76]

* * * * *

The Holley family a year or so before the marital separation (1916 or 1917). Horace is holding Marcia and Hertha is seated on Bertha's lap

Hertha Holley (left) and Marcia Holley (right), the daughters of Horace Holley

Doris Pascal (Bowen) at about the time of her marriage to Horace Holley in 1918

Horace and Doris Holley at about the time of their marriage in 1918

Doris Holley

Left to right: Frank, Irving and Horace Holley enjoying time together in May 1922 in Torrington. Their fourth brother, Lawrence, lived in the Western United States; consequently, he became increasingly detached from his family in the East

As one who enjoyed nature, Horace Holley was delighted whenever his small apartments in Manhattan afforded him access to the building roof, as in this 1922 photograph of him

Perhaps the first photograph ever taken of the National Spiritual Assembly of the United States and Canada. It was taken on 1 July 1923 at the New Jersey home of Roy Wilhelm, who probably took the photograph. In the foreground: Agnes Parsons. Left to right: Alfred Lunt, Louis Gregory, Henry Randall, Horace Holley, Corinne True, Charles Mason Remey and Jenabe Fazel (Mírzá Asadu'lláh Fáḍil Mázandarání). Fazel was sent by Shoghi Effendi to serve as a consultant to the National Assembly, among his other tasks, but he did not serve on it

Participants at the 1925 National Convention held at Green Acre, Eliot, Maine. According to Shoghi Effendi, the election held during that gathering marked the true beginning of the National Spiritual Assembly for the United States and Canada

Green Acre Inn, Eliot, Maine, undated. The Holleys lived at Green Acre for one year and spent summer months there for many decades

Horace and Doris Holley with Siegfried 'Fred' Schopflocher, probably taken at Green Acre

1926 meeting of the National Spiritual Assembly at the Wilhelm Evergreen Cabin in New Jersey. Others who were not members were also present in the photograph. Seated left to right: Hamedeh Khan, Florence Morton, Amelia Collins, Keith Ransom-Kehler. Standing left to right: Roy Wilhelm, Allen McDaniel, Horace Holley, Ali-Kuli Khan, Laurie Wilhelm, Siegfried Schopflocher

Meeting of the National Spiritual Assembly at the Wilhelm property in New Jersey, 29 June 1930. Bertha Herklotz, who was the Spiritual Assembly's first paid administrative staff member, posed with the Assembly. Front row, left to right: Allen McDaniel, Siegfried Schopflocher, Amelia Collins, Florence Morton, Bertha Herklotz, Louis Gregory; back row, left to right: Alfred Lunt, Horace Holley, Roy Wilhelm

Since 1913, the New York Bahá'í community had enjoyed an informal association with the Saint Mark's-in-the-Bowery Episcopal Church and its minister, Dr William Norman Guthrie. This relationship with the affluent, predominantly White congregation continued for years even after the Assembly rented rooms in another area to serve as a Bahá'í centre. A handful of the pillars of the Bahá'í community were also formally enrolled members of St Mark's and involved in its administration. Mountfort Mills served as Senior Warden, the highest Episcopal lay position, which serves as the intermediary between the clergy and the congregation. Horace served as Junior Warden, another important lay position with responsibility for managing church facilities. They held these positions at the same time they were serving as officers of the National Spiritual Assembly. Edward 'Saffa' Kinney, a professional church organist and composer, served as St Mark's choirmaster. The prominent roles played by Bahá'ís had not gone unnoticed. Guthrie defended their leadership positions, for these three were his friends and allies in his ongoing fight with the New York Bishop who was trying to rein in Guthrie's *avant-garde* and non-Christian worship services.

Reverend Doctor Guthrie was an unusual combination of religious leader and scholar of the humanities. He held advanced degrees in both and published many books and articles. He came from a family of freethinkers and reformers; his maternal grandmother was the remarkable writer and social reformer Fanny Wright.[77] When he was young, he studied at the most liberal of American Episcopal seminaries in the United States at that time, The University of the South, usually referred to as Sewanee.[78] He took a job in the seminary's outreach operation during which he supervised a young seminarian from Ireland, George Townshend. Townshend would later become a Bahá'í and be named a Hand of the Cause by Shoghi Effendi. Townshend and Guthrie maintained a lifelong friendship through correspondence, which included discussions about their mutual interest in the Bahá'í Faith.[79]

Guthrie taught literature at Sewanee, the University of Cincinnati in Ohio, and then at the University of Chicago. He also served as rector of a church in California. In 1911, he was offered the job of rector of prestigious St Mark's.

Guthrie was by nature attracted to other freethinkers. One haven for individuals such as Guthrie was the spiritual retreat centre, Green Acre, which was part of the Chautauqua circuit of summer programmes for the liberal-minded seekers after spiritual truth. At the time Guthrie took part in the programmes at that retreat near Portsmouth, New Hampshire, it was attracting 'Emersonians, Whitmanites, and various seekers of spirituality through poetry, art and music' as well as those involved in the New Thought movement.[80] During the early days of Green Acre before its founder, Sarah Farmer, learned of the Bahá'í Faith, Guthrie and his wife would pack up their young children and take them to the summer sessions held at that unspoiled spot near the Atlantic Ocean. There the Guthries would join other students with unusual religious inclinations, absorbing stimulating talks while enjoying the fresh air and the natural beauty of the Piscataqua River. Like many who came to Green Acre, the Guthrie family camped along its slopes in tents. Their association with Green Acre, however, was short-lived. During the second summer they vacationed there a tragic incident upset the Guthries. A student from Harvard University, unaware of the dangers of the river, made the mistake of swimming in the rapid tide flowing past the retreat's grounds and drowned before Green Acre's rowboats could be unchained to rescue him. It seemed to the Guthries that the managers at Green Acre were more concerned about the possible theft of the boats than the need for them to be readily available to rescue people from the river. Believing the accident was grossly mishandled by Farmer and the other Green Acre managers, the Guthries severed their association with the retreat.[81]

Guthrie became interested in 'Abdu'l-Bahá during His time in New York in 1912. It is unknown if Guthrie attended any of 'Abdu'l-Bahá's talks or met Him. He scheduled a private audience with 'Abdu'l-Bahá at the Kinney's large home on Riverside Drive. When he arrived that afternoon, he was informed that 'Abdu'l-Bahá had left for a walk to meditate along the top of the cliff overlooking the Hudson River. The Bahá'ís considered 'Abdu'l-Bahá's decision to forgo the appointment as providential, and so refused to fetch Him.[82]

When the Holleys moved to New York, they followed the example of other Bahá'ís and joined St Mark's where Horace and Norman Guthrie developed a close friendship. The two had many common interests, ideals, and goals. As one of Guthrie's college friends described Norman, 'Your interest, constitutional or temperamental, is in the exceptional, the bizarre, the outré, the exotic; wherefore you are appealed to in literature specially by men and women who point out stars in the intellectual firmament that common eyes are disqualified to see . . .'[83] Norman's sermons provided Horace with intellectual stimulation, for they were more often college lectures on literature than religious expositions. The liberality of St Mark's put no doctrinal constraints on the Bahá'í worshippers.

St Mark's usual Christian church services were held on Sunday mornings and the Bahá'í services were held later that day in the mid-afternoon. It made for a satisfying day full of spiritual upliftment. Guthrie loved planning Bahá'í services, which followed the form of Protestant church services, but he inserted Bahá'í writings and prayers where Biblical text would normally be used. He especially enjoyed holding a Bahá'í service the afternoon of Easter Sunday.[84] He would send requests and suggestions to the Bahá'í Board of Counsel and later the Spiritual Assembly. The Bahá'í community welcomed his participation in their meetings and occasionally asked him to address events, including the special occasion when the Tablets of the Divine Plan were unveiled in 1919. Horace was happy to be of service to St Mark's through his friend.

Guthrie suspected, but never fully appreciated, that the Bahá'í Faith teaches that to be a true Christian in this day means to embrace Bahá'u'lláh. This did not require a rejection of Christ, instead, it required a deeper understanding of Him as one of an endless stream of Divine Messengers. The more people converted to the Faith, the fewer would remain with Christianity. He described his own view of the New York Bahá'í community in his memoirs.

> To me they were Spiritual Kindred, earnest, sympathetic friends of God. If the religious support they needed must reach to them from Jesus indirectly by the way of 'The Bab' a modern Persian martyre [sic], successor of Abdul Baha who dwelt at the foot of Mount Carmel, how should that disconcert me? Strange always are the ways of the spirit, which no reverent man will venture to judge or delimit.[85]

Guthrie's association with Bahá'ís finally led to trouble with his supervising Bishop[86] and was commented upon unsympathetically by New York newspapers.[87]

Horace was not simply a member of St Mark's lay council, the vestry, he was Junior Warden, making him the manager of the church's real estate holdings and facilities.[88] It was an enormous responsibility for which he received remuneration, though it is unclear whether Horace received the use of a church-owned apartment at a reduced rent or if he was paid, or both.[89] At any other church in New York, serving as Junior Warden would have required little work, but not at St Mark's. Its primary church building had been constructed during the late eighteenth century when most of Manhattan Island was still farmland or woodlands, making it possible for the church to acquire land surrounding its chapel. This legacy increased when Guthrie convinced the vestry to purchase derelict apartment buildings adjoining the church property which he intended to rent cheaply to creative people such as artists and writers. The church owned multiple apartment buildings as well as a second imposing church building a few blocks from the original St Mark's; thus, as its Junior Warden, Horace was managing a small real estate empire. At various times, the Holleys occupied church apartments, including a spacious, attractive one next to the church he especially liked that had a little garden in the rear of the building.[90] While Junior Warden, he had an opportunity to renew his acquaintance with the famous architect Frank Lloyd Wright, whom he had met years before in Florence, Italy. Horace served as the church's liaison when St Mark's commissioned Wright to design a high-rise apartment building.[91] Horace was also a member of the committee that oversaw the church finances and he led a campaign to raise funds for the church endowment.[92] The knowledge and experience Horace gained managing real estate, finances, and fund raising would serve him well as secretary of the National Spiritual Assembly.

How much did Horace's service within the administration of an Episcopal church affect his ideas about Bahá'í administration? A brief history of the Episcopal Church (the American branch of the Church of England) is necessary in order to appreciate how it differed from that of his Puritan religious heritage, especially considering that the Episcopal Church was historically the nemesis of his Puritan ancestors.

The Church of England – the Anglican Church – came into being not because of the Protestant Reformation but solely because King Henry VIII wanted a divorce from his first wife. Ironically, while young, Henry had openly opposed the Reformation by penning a tract against it, for which he was awarded the title 'Defender of the Faith' by the Pope. But he had a problem. The teachings of Jesus set forth clearly in the Gospels forbade remarriage while a prior spouse yet lived, and he needed to remarry to produce a male heir. The church had long gotten around this inconvenient divine law by allowing the Pope to grant annulments – a decree that the marriage was defective, and so the union was null and void. When Henry requested that the Pope annul his marriage of many years to his Spanish-princess wife, geopolitics took precedence, so the Pope refused. Henry was not a man accustomed to being denied what he desired; so, in a fit of anger, he broke the English church away from the authority of the Pope. The Church of England was born. The monarch took the place of the Pope as its head. It has since become known as the Anglican Church. After Henry's death, other British sovereigns allowed some Protestant theology to seep into the Church of England,[93] making it a hybrid – neither completely Catholic in its doctrines nor completely Protestant, though it kept many of the outward trappings of Catholicism. Bertha and Horace were married in an Episcopal Church, foreshadowing the significant role that the American branch of the Anglican Communion would play in Horace's life for almost two decades.[94]

Unlike most Protestant denominations whose congregations are governed at the local level, the Episcopal Church has a hierarchy like its mother Roman Catholic Church, centred on the authority of bishops. The Anglican Communion's highest-ranking clergyman internationally is not a Pope, but the Archbishop of Canterbury. Episcopalian Church services were to follow the instructions and forms laid out in the *Book of Common Prayer*, a manual tacitly approved by the British monarch. It retained most of the formal, ritualistic worship services of Catholicism, unlike other Protestant denominations that sprang directly from the Reformation.

Though Horace was formally enrolled in St Mark's, he did not participate in its communion services or partake of the sacraments, for he was always forthright about his belief in Bahá'u'lláh as the Manifestation of God for this day.[95] Despite Horace's half-way acceptance of church membership, Guthrie once described him as 'a highly ethical person' and 'a poet, a critic, a meta-physician, a wit', adding that he 'enjoyed his company'.[96]

Horace's friendship with Guthrie started to unravel just as the Great Depression began to strangle the economic life of the country, creating a general milieu of stress that affected the church. Their disagreements originated in a controversial mental health clinic – The Body and Soul Clinic – founded in part by Guthrie, which used the church facilities to provide free care. The liberal-minded congregation was committed to being of service to the economically depressed neighbourhood surrounding its main sanctuary building, but many members became increasingly uncomfortable and disconcerted when mentally ill patients roamed the grounds and congregated within the church. Patients were often found sleeping in the sanctuary and otherwise treating the sacred space before the altar irreverently. The church's membership declined sharply because of the clinic. After years of tolerating this situation, a rebellion erupted among St Mark's members who demanded that the clinic find another location. Horace pointed out that a fully equipped hospital stood empty less than a block away.[97]

Once the foundations of the church began to shake, the gentle rumblings escalated to a severe earthquake when the 1931 audit of the church's finances was submitted to the vestry. It showed that Guthrie, known to be a spendthrift, was rapidly running through church funds at a time when donations were declining in parallel with the economic downslide of the general economy. Worse, there were funds that passed through Guthrie's hands that were unaccounted for. The vestry, with Horace at its helm, was justifiably alarmed and decided that Guthrie should be nudged into retirement before the most iconic, historic Episcopal Church in New York lost its shrinking congregation altogether and had to go into bankruptcy.[98]

Practical considerations of church management were important when determining what to do about the clinic and finances, but to Horace the primary consideration was a spiritual principle. As he put it, 'What is a church; how should a church be used in order to fulfill its religious mission?'[99] He answered his own question stating that a church was not the place to manage all social needs; government was the entity responsible for that. Instead, the role of the church was 'the cultivation of spiritually conscious human beings'.[100] He added: 'A church must be a wellspring of the water of spiritual knowledge. When this highest of missions is fulfilled, the humanitarian functions of an ordered society will be properly discharged.'[101]

Guthrie wrote to Horace of his dismay that, despite their friendship, Horace had been among the advocates for removing the clinic from the church. He scolded Horace and told him he needed to convert back to the Gospel and use his intellect less and his heart more.[102] Horace responded with a carefully reasoned letter setting out the problems with the clinic and reminding Guthrie that even he was afraid of some of the unsavoury elements drawn to it. In fact, Horace related that he and another vestry officer had received credible death threats from fanatical proponents of the clinic.[103] He also defended himself against Guthrie's charge that he believed in neither the church nor the priest, saying:

> I infer that you are charging me with being unduly under the influence of my family background in the Congregational Church. As far as I myself can judge, the most lasting influence I retain from that source is the conviction that Christianity makes every human being morally responsible for his own life and conduct under one divine standard . . . In other words, from my view, a priest does not escape or transcend the obligations laid upon every other man . . .[104]

Horace noted the bad publicity the church received because of its controversies and asserted that he had tried to ameliorate it but laid the blame for it on Guthrie.[105]

Guthrie refused to leave his post as rector without a fight. He blamed Horace for the troubles because Horace had become one of the primary spokesmen for the vestry. Journalists have always loved a controversy and the local papers made the happenings at St Mark's big news. Horace was mentioned by name in several newspaper articles.[106] When the battle reached its climax, Guthrie used the one element of the Episcopal Church which he had railed against his entire career – the precise church rules. He recruited allies to become church members solely to vote on his side. When the matter of his continued role as head of St Mark's was put to a vote of the congregation in 1933, the vestry lost, and its members were replaced by Guthrie's supporters, an action which ultimately was settled in a court of law.[107] One immediate consequence for Horace was that he and Doris had to move to an apartment that was not owned by the church.[108] Thus, they severed their remaining ties with St Mark's.

* * * * *

A seemingly minor event several years earlier had taken place half a world away in Egypt, which would lead to the emancipation of the

Baháʼí Faith from Islam and would affect all Baháʼí ties to other religions. Not only the Holleys, but all Baháʼís who still retained memberships or associations with churches, were about to be asked to sever those connections and be loyal exclusively to the Baháʼí Faith. It began with a decision in a small village to harass the Faith. In 1925 in Egypt, local Muslim authorities decided to pressure the Baháʼís living among them by insisting that Baháʼí marriages to Muslims were invalid. This case was appealed to the highest Islamic Court in that country, one of the most influential religious authorities in the entire Islamic world. The high court upheld the local decision against the Baháʼís by affirming that the marriages were void. But the case did not stop there because, significantly, it specifically upheld the lower court judgement that the Baháʼís were not Muslim heretics because they were not Muslims at all. Islamic authorities had officially, albeit inadvertently, recognized the Baháʼí Faith as an independent world religion.[109] Shoghi Effendi lost no time in making the most of this otherwise unfavourable verdict, emphasizing that 'This decision . . . may be regarded as an initial step taken by our very opponents in the path of the eventual universal acceptance of the Baháʼí Faith, as one of the independent recognized religious systems of the world.'[110]

As more and more Islamic governments and religious authorities followed the lead of the Egyptian court and refused to recognize the Baháʼí Faith as a branch of Islam, a long-awaited development came into view: the recognition of the Faith as an independent religion. Shoghi Effendi became concerned that as long as Baháʼís continued their membership in other religious groups, this positive progress would be impeded. His Grandfather, ʻAbduʼl-Bahá, to the end of His life continued to adhere to many Muslim practices, such as attending the noonday services on Fridays and keeping the Muslim Fast during Ramadan. The Guardian had not followed his Grandfather's example, because he was convinced that the time had come to begin removing the remaining connections to the religious environment from which the Baháʼí Faith had emerged.

Looking back upon this period, Rúḥíyyih Khánum, the wife of Shoghi Effendi, commented:

> . . . that he, Shoghi Effendi, the beloved, eldest grandson, was His [ʻAbduʼl-Bahá's] successor and First Guardian of the Cause of God. Saddled with this great weight, crushed by this great blow,

he turned his eyes to the Bahá'í world. He beheld a widely diversified, loosely organized community, scattered in various parts of the globe, and with members in about twenty countries. These people, loyal, devoted and sincere though they were, were still, to a great extent living in their parent religion's house, so to speak; there were Christian Bahá'ís, Jewish Bahá'ís, Muhammadan Bahá'ís and so on. They believed in the Bahá'í Faith but were intimately connected with their former churches. Like fruit on a tree, they were a new crop but still stuck to the old branch. This was true East and West alike. That was the point to which the Faith had evolved at the time of the Master's ascension.[111]

On 15 June 1935, Shoghi Effendi called upon all believers to follow his lead and separate from 'outworn creeds'.[112] He made it clear that this new requirement should not be understood as disparaging the religions established by earlier Divine Messengers. He said:

> ... our Cause unreservedly recognizes the Divine origin of all the religions that preceded it and upholds the spiritual truths which lie at their very core and are common to them all, its institutions, whether administrative, religious or humanitarian, must, if their distinctive character is to be maintained and recognized, be increasingly divorced from outworn creeds.[113]

This new requirement that the believers detach themselves from their earlier religions raised concerns and questions among the North Americas Bahá'ís, so the National Assembly drafted a preliminary statement to respond to inquiries and submitted it to Shoghi Effendi for approval before promulgating it. The statement was most likely composed primarily by Horace as the secretary and scribe of the National Assembly. As he set out to explain to his fellow believers why they should willingly relinquish their church and synagogue memberships, the task must have caused him to reflect on his own involvement in the Congregational and Episcopal Churches as a Bahá'í. He had attempted during his affiliation with St Mark's to pour new wine into old wineskins, and the skins had burst.

The National Assembly's statement, 'Concerning Membership in Non-Bahá'í Religious Organizations', which was published in the

March 1936 edition of *Bahá'í News*, sought to elevate the understanding of the North American believers, to help them appreciate that relinquishing church memberships was not an arbitrary mandate but part of the larger goal of making the world anew. It quoted letters from the Guardian which explained that the Administrative Order was not merely the means of managing the Faith, but the embryonic structure of a future Bahá'í World Commonwealth. The National Assembly said:

> ... a Bahá'í is not merely a member of a revealed Religion, he is also a citizen in a World Order even though that Order today is still in its infancy and still obscured by the shadows thrown by the institutions, habits and attitudes derived from the past. But since the aim and end has been made known, our devotion and loyalty must surely express itself, not in clinging to views and thoughts emanating from the past, but in pressing forward in response to the needs of the new creation.[114]

The New York Bahá'í community eased out of its close association with St Mark's-in-the-Bowery Church, a process made easier because it had its own meeting rooms. Its functioning Assembly was incorporated and capable of providing not only guidance but loving pastoral care. In a few years it would be granted the right to conduct weddings that would be recognized by the State of New York, no longer relying on officiation by a clergyman or government official to make them legal. It had become familiar with Bahá'í burial laws and could carry them out without assistance. For more than a decade, its members had studied the volumes of guidance and new authoritative translations of Sacred Texts flowing forth like a torrent from the Holy Land. Connections with churches such as St Mark's and those with Black congregations in Brooklyn and Harlem had played a positive role during the community's infancy. Now, it stood firmly on its own, having developed a vibrant community life. It was on the path to becoming a vital component of the spiritual life of the city it served.

In the religion of Bahá'u'lláh we have a divine-human Revealer, as in other religions of prophetic type, whose authentic utterances constitute a body of spiritual law; but unlike previous dispensations, the Bahá'í teachings create a social structure capable of bringing the spiritual laws into practical effect. There is thus no inherent division and antagonism between mysticism and organization as hitherto has always prevented the fruitage of the will of God in man. Replacing individual 'conscience' (that last refuge of egoism and first impetus to insanity) by the collective consciousness of the Spiritual Assembly, the Bahá'í Faith supplements personal belief by the habit of loyal co-operation and the instinct of consultation. Social beings are produced, instead of limited egos, but by the attainment, not the repudiation, of true inner experience. Spiritual experience today, thanks to Bahá'u'lláh, is no mere subjective affirmation of 'higher self' or self-created concept of God, but consists in knowledge of and obedience to the body of Bahá'í teachings. The mystical and the practical are become one, to the confusion of those who prefer either attitude alone, without the balance. Since states of development differ, and understandings are diverse, the institution of the Spiritual Assembly reconciles every set of opposites and makes possible a degree of sanity and effective co-operation such as never existed before.

Horace Holley[1]

9

THE BIRTH PANGS OF THE NEW ORDERING OF THE WORLD

Shoghi Effendi was overburdened and in a hurry during the early months of 1922. Not only was he continuing to grieve the recent loss of 'Abdu'l-Bahá, as were his fellow believers everywhere, but he was also now carrying the load of responsibilities that came with being the Head of the Faith. This weight soon became heavier due to the actions of enemies of the Faith. The key to the Shrine of Bahá'u'lláh, the most sacred of all Bahá'í Holy places, was forcibly confiscated by rebellious relatives who had been expelled from the Faith. Another important Holy Place, the House of Bahá'u'lláh in Baghdad, was seized by Shi'ih clergy. At the same time, the Western Bahá'í communities confronted Shoghi Effendi with a different assortment of critical problems which could not be deferred to a less tumultuous time. A preponderance of Western believers had based their allegiance to the Faith primarily upon the personage of 'Abdu'l-Bahá. Now that He was gone, this allegiance needed to be transferred as soon as possible to elected Bahá'í institutions lest Bahá'ís in the fragile Western communities began to drift away from the Faith or turn to opportunistic individuals seeking leadership. Shoghi Effendi's dilemma was that the essential institutions which had been prescribed by Bahá'u'lláh had not yet been established.

Ready or not, the time had come when Spiritual Assemblies had to be brought into being with all due haste. That February and March, Shoghi Effendi invited particular Western believers from among those he had summoned to Haifa to accompany him on private walks through the olive groves and hillsides of Mount Carmel. As they surveyed the verdant beauty of early spring while gazing upon the Galilean hills across the Bay, he tutored them in his soothing, gentle voice, providing insights into the spiritual principles underpinning the administrative bodies that were about to be created and giving specific instructions in answer to their questions. Mealtimes when all the Westerners – those summoned and those in Haifa for other reasons – were together provided an informal opportunity for the Guardian to expound further on the requirements of the coming months.

Hardly three months had passed since the death of 'Abdu'l-Bahá, when Shoghi Effendi penned a long letter to his co-workers in North America which began with a rousing call to action, stating:

> At this grave and momentous period through which the Cause of God in conformity with the Divine Wisdom is passing, it is the sacred duty of every one of us to endeavour to realize the full significance of this Hour of Transition, and then to make a supreme resolve to arise steadfastly for the fulfilment of our sacred obligations.[2]

Immediately after completing this his first directive to the West focused upon Bahá'í administration, he used the hours sitting around the table with his guests to explain the letter's weighty contents. This seminal letter included new translations from Bahá'u'lláh's writings to confirm to the Western believers that Bahá'u'lláh Himself had ordained the establishment of Assemblies and provided governing principles for His Administrative Order. Though the letter lacked details such as how to carry out an election or organize administrative tasks, the basic principles essential to make a start were all there, including the spiritual law of consultation – the underpinning of all decision-making in the Faith. The goal of the Faith of Bahá'u'lláh was to transform the world into a new civilization – a New World Order – which could only come about through a revolution in the way in which life on the planet was organized. The institutions about to come into being for the first time were the precious seeds.

A new and significant concept for the Western believers was the foundational principle that the Faith's institutions were as much a part of the essential spiritual teachings as any other aspect of the religion; consequently, all believers were enjoined to support and obey them unreservedly. For Americans in particular, whose previous Christian denominations were born in the fires of the Reformation, strict obedience to religious authority made them uneasy. Inevitably, this would result in severe tests.

Shoghi Effendi charged Roy Wilhelm and Mountfort Mills, Ethel

Rosenberg, and the Schwarzes to ensure that National Assemblies were appropriately elected in the United States and Canada (as one Assembly), Great Britain and Germany, respectively, at their upcoming National Conventions. He provided scant instructions as to how these elections should be conducted. Those details could wait and would evolve with experience. It was important to simply make a start. A few weeks later, Shoghi Effendi sent cables to remind the American community that the two most pressing needs of the hour were completing the House of Worship and teaching. This would be the last guidance that community would receive prior to its National Convention which began on 24 April 1922.

Exhausted in body and spirit, Shoghi Effendi slipped away from the Holy Land during early April and retreated to a remote Alpine region of Switzerland where he hoped to recover his health and steady his emotions in the clear mountain air after enduring the unbearable stress and ardours of the previous months. As he scaled the steep mountain slopes day after day, he rigorously examined his own inner being to prepare himself spiritually and mentally for the burdens he bore. There was no choice but to strive mightily to conquer any aspect of his own character that he found wanting, which would make him unable or unworthy to carry out the immense responsibilities so unexpectedly thrust upon him.

Before the Guardian departed from Haifa, he announced on 7 April that he had placed the reins of the Faith into the capable hands of the foremost woman of the Bahá'í Dispensation, his Great-Aunt, Bahíyyih Khánum. This momentous creation of a regency came at the very moment the first National and Local Spiritual Assemblies were coming into existence and taking their first tentative steps to organize their work. These embryonic institutions found they could rely upon Bahíyyih Khánum's wise guidance during the crucial months following the first elections. On 16 December 1922, Shoghi Effendi wrote to his North American flock: 'Now that my long hours of rest and meditation are happily at an end, I turn my face with renewed hope and vigor to that continent the soil of which is pregnant with those seeds that our beloved Master has so tenderly and so profusely scattered in the past.'[3] He was pleased with the news that awaited him from America when he returned to his work.[4]

* * * * *

Between 1908 and 1922, the business of the American Bahá'í community was conducted at the national level by the Executive Board of the Bahá'í Temple Unity, which was elected annually by delegates representing the larger Bahá'í localities.[5] The National Convention served as a sort of legislature, which, like many state legislatures in the United States, met briefly once a year. The Executive Board would then spend the following twelve months carrying out the resolutions of the previous Convention. Speaking of the Convention's relationship to the Executive Board, Horace said that, 'As the Convention can be called the soul of the Cause in North America, so the Unity Board can be likened to its mind.'[6] Because the primary purpose of the Executive Board was to promote and arrange for the construction of the House of Worship, it had no choice but to incorporate so that it could sign contracts, open bank accounts, and own land. Lawyers serving as members of the Executive Board[7] assisted with drafting the articles of incorporation which Temple Unity adopted as a formal constitution and submitted for ratification to the State of Illinois. After the incorporation, Conventions were conducted in strict conformity with the provisions of the constitution, and the Board could not legally stray far from the decisions voted upon by the delegates. The Board found these constraints difficult when unforeseen matters required action during the intervals between Conventions. Temple Unity, as organized, quickly became unwieldy.

In 1920, Horace crafted a proposal for a committee structure that would make the Temple Unity Board a more effective national governing body. The inspiration for his scheme arose from serving on the Board's 'Idea Committee'. He drafted a lengthy document that laid out detailed suggestions, complete with organizational charts, and plans for the establishment of nine committees, each devoted to a particular task such as teaching, publishing, the House of Worship, publicity, and finance. Each of the nine members of the Executive Board would be assigned to a committee. These recommendations were widely circulated among the most active Bahá'ís. At the next Convention in 1921, Horace, as a delegate and member of its Committee on Permanent Committees, addressed the gathering to explain the recommended organizational structure. The Faith was growing and developing, and its administration should reflect those realities. He persuasively argued that there was also a need for local governing councils to adopt a similar approach. His suggestions were adopted, but never implemented because they were about to become immaterial.

At that same Convention, the Organization Committee recommended revising the charter and by-laws to reflect the growing authority and responsibility 'Abdu'l-Bahá had placed on the Executive Board; thus, a committee was appointed to draft amendments and present them at the 1922 Convention for consideration.[8] No one in the spring of 1922 could foresee that a year later, the proposed changes would be totally obsolete – irrelevant – just like Horace's grand organizational charts. The days of Bahá'í Temple Unity were numbered.

* * * * *

It is rare when those taking part in an event appreciate, while it is happening, the moment's historical significance and its implications for the future. Those privileged to attend the 1922 National Convention well knew that that gathering would be long remembered because its purpose was not simply to foster the construction of the Mother Temple of the West but to bring into being the first National Spiritual Assembly for the United States and Canada. Horace was not elected a delegate that year, so he did not attend, but he grasped the importance of that assemblage as it was underway. He probably never imagined, however, that it would set in motion forces that would change the trajectory of his own life.

Like the Temple Unity conventions before it, there were two days of business meetings. Consultation was concluded at the end of the afternoon sessions, and the evenings were more like Christian revival meetings opened to the public. Rousing musical performances interspersed with spirited speeches would stir the emotions of the audience and remind the delegates why they were proud to be Bahá'ís. Cheerfulness was not the emotion most in evidence in 1922, however. The entire community, especially those who were the backbone of the Faith, continued to mourn the passing of 'Abdu'l-Bahá. It had only been six months since that devastating loss. Therefore, the sessions of the Convention that normally brought joy were given over to remembering and extolling the One whom they loved dearly, now departed from their midst. It was also time to consider well the role of the new institution, the Guardianship, and to learn more about the one now filling that role, Shoghi Effendi. Most of the Americans who had been in the Holy

Land either at the time of the passing of 'Abdu'l-Bahá or in the months that followed attended the Convention. They stood before their enraptured listeners and took turns recounting what they witnessed and what they heard from those who were in the Holy Land that fateful night of 28 November. These accounts filled the pages of the Convention report later published in *Star of the West*, which related nothing about the historic election other than to give its results.

The transcript of the 1922 business sessions shows that the gravity of the proceedings aroused in the delegates enhanced spiritual maturity and an unwavering determination to carry out their weighty tasks in conformity with spiritual principles. No doubt, recalling fresh memories of 'Abdu'l-Bahá created a tone of reverence which blanketed the entire Convention and its Congress.[9] The first business session befittingly opened with a recitation of the Tablet of Visitation for 'Abdu'l-Bahá often recited at His resting place. Then, before considering any other item on the agenda, Shoghi Effendi's 5 March letter regarding Bahá'í administration was read aloud in its entirety and discussed. Those who had just returned from Haifa gave accounts of what Shoghi Effendi had said to them and how he had explained certain passages of that letter. Generally, the friends had been warned to be cautious about accepting oral reports of statements by the Head of the Faith, but this time, those who had met with Shoghi Effendi were able to verify what was reported. During the ensuing consultation, the Convention voted to prepare a document pledging loyalty to the Guardian and affirming the community's willingness to abide by the charters of the Bahá'í Faith, including 'Abdu'l-Bahá's Will and Testament.[10] Before mailing the statement, it was decided to widely circulate it so that it could be signed by believers from throughout North America.[11] Those privileged to be with Shoghi Effendi in the Holy Land all declared without reservation that he was an extraordinary individual who, despite his youth, projected a seamless continuance of the spirit of his Grandfather.[12]

The one point highlighted emphatically by those returning from Haifa was the supreme authority of the National Assembly with regard to all matters under its jurisdiction. It could only be overridden by Shoghi Effendi. No longer would the Convention be a body for legislating. That responsibility would fall solely upon the newly established institution. This led to questions about the role of the Convention in the future, but there were no authoritative answers.[13]

Confusion overtook the Convention when the time arrived to vote for the National Spiritual Assembly rather than the Executive Board of the Temple Unity. A lawyer from the old Executive Board reminded the Convention that voting procedures were still regulated by the Illinois articles of incorporation. Did that legal document control the proceedings? If so, how much of it was no longer relevant and needed to be amended?[14] A motion was adopted to legally amend the incorporation to reflect the change to the National Assembly with its broader powers and the elimination of the Executive Board. This led to another issue regarding the new National Assembly; during the three months when four of the members of the Executive Board were in the Holy Land, the Board could not reach a quorum to make decisions, resulting in delays and problems. To prevent this from recurring, it was proposed that the National Assembly have more than nine members. Shoghi Effendi's informal remarks seemed to allow for that possibility. Yet under the articles of incorporation, the Executive Board had to be made up of exactly nine members. Did that old legal requirement also control the number of National Assembly members? The United States and Canada covered a vast landmass that was difficult to traverse, making it almost impossible for members from across the continent to come together. Could this problem be solved through the election of alternate members or by allowing members to designate proxies? Those returning from Haifa provided uncertain guidance on these points as they struggled to accurately recall Shoghi Effendi's response to that question. The delegates even discussed whether to leave this issue to the discretion of the National Assembly after it was formed.[15]

Distance affected more than the question of attaining a quorum. It inhibited the ability of the delegates to choose the best candidates when marking their ballots. Already, those living on the West Coast complained of being excluded because most gatherings were held in Chicago or – worse still – at locations along the Northeast Coast. All adult believers in the two countries were eligible for election. How could the delegates from the Los Angeles community become familiar with believers in Montreal, Washington DC, Philadelphia, or Miami? A proposal was made that, for this first election, a straw vote be taken so the 63 delegates could have names of worthy individuals brought to their attention before proceeding to a final vote. The previous year, nominations had been taken from the floor, and nominees stated whether they would be able to serve if elected.[16] A straw vote seemed an improvement because names could be put forward anonymously. In the absence of authoritative guidance, the Convention adopted that approach. The articles of incorporation required that the members of the Executive Board each receive a majority, not just a plurality of votes. When the tellers reported the results of the straw vote, eight of the top nine vote-getters had received more than a majority of the votes, and the ninth was one vote shy. There were calls to accept the first vote as final, but after much discussion, it was determined that that would violate the spirit of the straw vote, and so another vote was taken. The results were the same, except the second time, all nine received a majority.[17] Horace, even though absent from the Convention, received votes in the initial straw vote, but not in the second vote.[18]

Other than two members, the first National Assembly's membership was unchanged from that of the Executive Board of Temple Unity from the previous year. The individual receiving the highest number of votes was the wealthy Chicago housewife[19] and 'Mother of the Temple', Corinne True. Also elected was the well-to-do homemaker[20] and the primary pillar of the Cause in California, Ella Goodall Cooper, who had been part of the first Western pilgrimage in 1899. Alfred 'Fred' Lunt, a Harvard-educated lawyer, and William Randall, an elderly, wealthy business owner, were from Boston. Another combination of lawyer and businessman, Mountfort Mills and Roy Wilhelm from the New York metropolitan area, were elected. Architect Charles Mason Remey and a lawyer who was the son of slaves, Louis Gregory, were elected from Washington DC. Rounding out the membership was the Persian medical doctor, Zia Bagdadi, whose distinguished Bahá'í family served the World Centre from their post in nearby Beirut, Lebanon. In the coming years, each of these individuals would play a significant role in Horace's life. Ella Goodall and Louis Gregory were the only members who had not served on the Executive Board the year before.[21] Mountfort Mills was elected chairman and Fred Lunt, secretary – offices they had held under the old Board. The National Assembly's first official letterhead was an example of the uncertainty about its new status just as the new entity continued to be wedded to the legal structure of the former Board. In large letters it stated at the top of the page: 'Mashreq'ul Azkar'. Below that in smaller type is 'Bahai Temple Unity'. Off to the side in even smaller type were the words 'National Spiritual Assembly', with the members listed by name below it.

The question before the National Spiritual Assembly was what to do first. Ella Cooper summed it up in a letter to Mountfort Mills, stating, 'what momentous work we are engaged in these great yet difficult days!'[22]

* * * * *

Horace, a whole-hearted advocate for organization, nonetheless repeated in his 1920 proposal for Temple Unity the widely held misunderstanding among American believers that 'the Bahai Movement is not an organization, but on the contrary the spirit of organization . . .'[23] He based this on the mistranslation of an authoritative statement by 'Abdu'l-Bahá which was circulating among Western believers. The gist of the mistranslation was that the Bahá'í Faith could not be organized. This was later corrected because the English translation did not capture 'Abdu'l-Bahá's full meaning in the slightest – He had said the Cause could not be confined within an organization. But the damage had been done as that statement became the mantra of free spirits who eschewed any type of authority or structure. That mistranslation was in part responsible for significant numbers of Bahá'ís in North America questioning the wisdom of the establishment of National and Local Spiritual Assemblies. By January 1923, it was apparent to the National Assembly that it must take steps to allay those misgivings, so it appointed a task force to draft a document to provide the scriptural basis for Bahá'í administration. The result became the lead article in the March issue of the *Star of the West* entitled, 'Bahai Organization: The Basis in the Revealed Word'.[24] It began by explaining the reason for the article: 'In this day when many liberal minded people rebel against the restraint to which they sincerely think organization subjects them – it is well to present some of the vital needs for organization which the Bahai Teachings make evident.'[25]

It took time for the believers in the West to study and digest the Will and Testament of 'Abdu'l-Bahá supplemented by excerpts from other Sacred Texts translated by the Guardian. Moreover, building the administrative bodies required details. Who was eligible to vote? Was a majority or plurality needed for election? Were meetings confidential? Who had the right to use official stationery? What were the roles of officers? What was the relationship between the National Assembly and

Local Assemblies? The foundation was firm, but inevitably, experience generated questions. Between 1922 and 1927, Shoghi Effendi wrote a number of general letters on administration in addition to answering specific questions. He was authorized in the Will and Testament to interpret the Sacred Texts, but not to legislate. He chose not to answer some inquiries, deferring them to the Universal House of Justice. If a question required creating a policy not covered in the Writings, sometimes he would provide an interim solution, with the understanding that the House of Justice could later change it. By the end of those productive five years, the Guardian had set in place the most vital aspects of administration.

Once the Assemblies began to function and to make decisions on a variety of issues, another question arose in the minds of many believers. The Faith came from God but was administered by mortals. Believers asked, 'must we obey *those* people because we know the members of Assemblies are flawed human beings like ourselves?' Even among the members of the Assemblies, those in the minority did not always support decisions wholeheartedly, inhibiting their success. Personal conflicts between individual members were unavoidable, testing the limits of the Bahá'í spirit of goodwill. Serving on Spiritual Assemblies would often become a burden, not a joy.

The National Spiritual Assembly had a difficult first year. It failed to create harmony among its members, nor did it produce concrete plans of action for the believers to follow. Horace expressed his personal concerns to the secretary of the National Assembly, Fred Lunt.

> . . . since the ascension of Abdul Baha, the National Spiritual Assembly has been unable to bring a unifying and inspiring spirit to the scattered Assemblies and friends, or set up definite programs of action that would bring out the reserve of spiritual longing that lies in the hearts of all. Doubtless I should not even feel this regret, but it comes from the confidence that in this age organizing capacity is pretty closely related to spiritual faithfulness, since the very expression of this Cause is the spirit of organization applied to all the conditions of life. Therefore, I await the call of that trumpet which will sound with unmistakeable [sic] power when we have a unity that comes from oneness, and not from a majority rule which is invariably burdened with the resistance of the minority. Majority

rule has blinded us to the real meaning of political democracy, and I trust it will soon pass away from all deliberations among Bahais.[26]

Shoghi Effendi set out in a letter dated 12 March 1923 a lengthy list of the tasks and responsibilities of Assemblies, emphasizing that expanding the membership by fostering teaching was their most essential duty.[27] For the United States and Canada there was also the ongoing responsibility of completing the construction of the House of Worship on the shore of Lake Michigan. Progress had slowed due to lack of funds – a problem to be tackled by the National Assembly. The new national institution was given responsibility for the review of Bahá'í publications and for ensuring that the monthly newsletter and other important Bahá'í publications were drafted, edited, printed, and distributed. Publications were always a concern because only a handful of believers, including Horace, had training and experience in writing, publishing and publicity. The crisis stemming from the loss of the House of Bahá'u'lláh in Baghdad gave the National Assembly its first international agenda item when the Guardian assigned it tasks to assist with the effort to regain that future centre of pilgrimage. It was also charged with protecting the American community from Orientals associated with the enemies of the Faith. One member of the National Assembly remarked that 'the Bahai work, always strenuous, seems to be increasing to such an extent that each day is filled to overflowing with unexpected and pressing demands'.[28]

* * * * *

Though Horace probably did not sense it at the time, the 1923 National Convention was a major turning point in his life, for he was elected to the National Spiritual Assembly for the first time. Aged 36, he was its youngest member. Horace would serve on that institution continuously until the end of 1959 – making his membership on that body his life's greatest work. Ironically, Horace did not attend that National Convention and so missed the first meeting.

That 1923 Convention reflected the changes and challenges of the previous year as the infant institutions at the national and local levels tried to understand and carry out their mandates. In order to assist with that second national election, Shoghi Effendi once again dispatched the wise and learned Jináb-i-Fáḍil Mazindarání to the United States from Iran. He arrived in time to attend the Convention in Chicago and accompany its deliberations as the Guardian's representative. One National Assembly member noted that Fáḍil's 'never-failing sweetness and gentle suggestions always appeared to assist us at the psychological moment'.[29] Having learned from the previous Convention's uncertainties, one priority in 1923 was to modify the incorporation of the Bahá'í Temple Unity to align it more closely with the unfolding requirements of the Bahá'í administration – a legal project which could only be finished years later.

*****

Horace was presented with two opportunities to serve during the early months of 1924. The first came about through the government-sponsored British Empire Exhibition. Representatives of all religions were invited to make a presentation at the conference of the 'Living Religions within the British Empire'. Shoghi Effendi and the newly established National Assembly of the British Isles considered this opportunity 'to arouse and stimulate interest among the enlightened public' to be too important to miss.[30] He requested that the National Assembly of the United States and Canada prepare the paper to be read at that gathering, though someone else would be asked to read it.[31] Horace was chosen by the National Assembly to be the primary draughtsman. His well-crafted general summary of the Faith was read to the conference by Mountfort Mills and widely circulated.[32]

The second noteworthy service arose from the National Assembly's decision to ask Horace to serve as acting secretary while Fred Lunt was temporarily relieved from that office so that he could tend to a family crisis.[33] That brief taste of the work of the secretariat proved to be such a challenge that Horace wrote to Fred that 'any secretary of the N. S. A. not able to give full time to this work should be ranked among the martyrs of the Cause!'[34] Grateful to have the volume of his work acknowledged, Fred replied, 'I was glad that a practical demonstration of this has come home to you as I know you are always frank and fair in your judgment.'[35] His colleagues must have approved of how Horace carried out the work, for when it came time to elect officers following the 1924 election, he was elected for the first time to the office of secretary. Except for a brief period when his own personal concerns required relinquishing it, he would serve in that position for more than thirty-three years. Lunt, who had served as secretary of the Temple Unity Executive Board for years, would forever hold the distinction of being the first secretary of the National Spiritual Assembly.

It became apparent to those assembled for the 1924 Convention that the National Assembly was not meeting as frequently as it should. The most formidable obstacle to regular meetings was the geographic spread of the members. Residing across the continent, from coast to coast and into its heartland, travel became too onerous and expensive for the members. Commercial civilian air travel was costly, unreliable, and not yet widely available. The previous year, the National Assembly had only met five times, and only one of those meetings had all nine members present. The Assembly resorted to allowing alternates to serve as consultants in the absence of the elected members.[36] Solutions were put forward during Convention consultation such as increasing the number of members to make it easier to get a quorum, paying the travelling expenses of the members, and taking geographic location into consideration when voting. A returning pilgrim put an end to some of these ideas by reporting Shoghi Effendi's expressed desire that the membership should be representative of the entire two countries (the United States and Canada) and that the ability of a member to pay for his or her own travel expenses should not be a factor.

Shoghi Effendi had also told the recent pilgrim that it was important that the election of the National Assembly should be undertaken only through the power of the Holy Spirit and with prayer.[37] These last comments subtly reflected the underlying problem confronting the delegates – continuing disunity within the community. Ever since 1922, the national elections had been marred by electioneering as factions sought to gain the upper hand. The Guardian was fully aware of this state of affairs, depressing him to the point of becoming so physically ill that he had to leave Haifa to regain his health. The Convention listened to the reading of a letter from Bahíyyih Khánum in her role as regent for her great-nephew, Shoghi Effendi, in which she passionately implored the friends in America to become united, lest they doom their beloved Faith.[38]

In 1925, the National Convention was held on the picturesque grounds of the Green Acre Bahá'í School in Eliot, Maine, rather than in Illinois. This lovely venue was chosen that year primarily to celebrate, after years of litigation, the victory of gaining full ownership of that historic facility on the banks of the mile-wide Piscataqua River across from Portsmouth, New Hampshire. 'Abdu'l-Bahá had stayed for a week in its four-storey Inn in 1912, and a growing number of smaller buildings, including cottages, were springing up along its gently rolling lawns that sloped down to the swiftly flowing river. It was the one spot in all of North America where, once any believer set foot upon its ground, there was a feeling of being home – of being on turf that represented the Bahá'í promises for that future, that was blessed with the presence and prayers of 'Abdu'l-Bahá.

The 1925 election was especially noteworthy because it marked the first time the Guardian fully approved of the manner in which the election was conducted; that is, there were no nominations, results were determined by plurality rather than a majority, and, for the first time, delegates could vote by absentee ballot when they were unable to attend the Convention – expanding the possible individuals who could serve. Attachments – primarily legal and financial – to the old Temple Unity were slowly being dissolved. At last, the Guardian stated that the National Spiritual Assembly was a body worthy of the name. Even though the National Assembly was first elected in 1922, it continues to count its years from 1925 when Shoghi Effendi acknowledged that it was truly a National Assembly.

* * * * *

During his first year as secretary, Horace carried out his responsibilities from his small apartment in New York during his off-hours while continuing to work for the Redfield Advertising Agency. Over the course of the previous three years, the work of the National Assembly had steadily increased, so New York believer Bertha L. Herklotz had been hired to assist with the clerical work of the National Assembly. She became the first true staff member other than the caretakers of the Temple property and Green Acre. Bertha, the unmarried daughter of German immigrants and a professional stenographer,[39] also served with Horace on the New York Assembly. It was not long before even her assistance was not enough to enable Horace and Doris to keep up with the Faith's steadily expanding administrative work.

In 1925 the National Assembly asked Horace to give up his employment at the Redfield Agency and serve full time as secretary.[40] The salary he was offered included payment for Doris' services as well. They were asked to move to Green Acre, where they would be given the use of a small cottage and the Faith would furnish the coal to heat it.[41] For a man responsible for supporting two households and still climbing out of debt, this was a consequential request. Living in Maine would also make it more difficult to see his daughters. But there was another aspect to the move – an emotional one – because Horace had an inner attachment to Manhattan, especially to the neighbourhoods on the lower part of the island. It was the place where he felt he belonged, and now he was being asked by the Faith he loved more than life itself, to leave.

When Horace first returned to the United States from Europe, he wrote an unpublished one-act play entitled, 'I Want to Live in Greenwich Village'. The story revolves around a conversation between a young woman from a small town in Connecticut and her conventional parents. Like normal parents, they expected their daughter to marry, settle down in her hometown and become much like everyone else in their orbit of friends and family. This is not at all what she wanted; her heart's desire was to move to the Greenwich Village neighbourhood of New York City. Her parents were shocked, for 'The Village' had a notorious reputation as a place overrun by those with loose morals and who were not only radical thinkers, but unhinged. Their daughter was unmoved by her parent's misgivings. On the verge of tears, she explained that she was not like most people. She was not content to define herself solely by how she made her living. She wanted to find inner joy, inner happiness – to fill an emptiness deep inside of her which could not be explained in mere words. She had never found kindred spirits in her little town, but she was certain that they were out there in the world, and she was determined to find them and live among them. Greenwich Village seemed to her the logical place to look.

> <u>Inwardness</u> is change, because it's growth. Then I knew I couldn't find what I wanted in this town . . . I thought and thought what to do. Where were the others – those I wanted as friends –who knew what the emptiness was for, what's in it you can work on, and get strength from, and become, the same as in the outward, people become their jobs . . . Then it came over me that the inward people

need each other, just as the outward people do – that they must have their place, their city, their work, their lives . . .[42]

During the two and a half decades Horace lived in New York – like a homing pigeon – he repeatedly found his way to Greenwich Village, even for a time living in an apartment facing Washington Square, the park around which the life of The Village revolved. He loved being among creative people, the hangouts such as Polly's Restaurant reminiscent of his days near the Café Dome in Paris, the little bookstores filled with *avant-garde* literature, and the odd assortment of people passing by the grand George Washington Arch that symbolized the neighbourhood.[43] Washington Square Park even had a statue of another illustrious Holley[44] who was a distant relation, which was a source of pride to him. He was where he belonged. Over time, however, his desires and needs had matured. Service had become more important than self-fulfilment. When the National Assembly asked him to leave Greenwich Village, Horace dutifully closed the door to his former life and put his trust in God. He and Doris packed their belongings and moved to rural Maine. He had already given up his career as a writer to serve the Faith, now he was letting go of yet another inner desire.

Horace reflected upon his personal sacrifices for the Cause in a letter he wrote to console Mason Remey, who was still smarting from the decision to use an architectural design for the House of Worship other than one from among those he submitted.

> . . . As a writer, or perhaps I should say as one who likes to write, I know something of the terrifically complex inner experiences which a creative mind goes through when the esthetic sense comes into conflict with some unusual spiritual situation. I am certain that other types of people cannot appreciate this particular and most exquisite form of agony. The strange thing is that those of us who have been most certain of the special manner in which we were qualified to serve the Cause have been the ones who had to learn the difficult lesson that some other method of service might be more acceptable to 'Abdu'l-Bahá. Why these things should be, we none of us can fully understand, but the outcome is a more deeply seated obedience, when the victory has been won, than would be possible in any other way or under any other conditions.[45]

Shoghi Effendi expressed his own appreciation for the sacrifices both Holleys made in moving to Maine in a handwritten postscript at the bottom of a letter to the National Assembly: 'I wish to add expressions of my deep gratitude to you and Mrs. Holley for your painstaking, valuable and devoted efforts during the past year that has witnessed so many significant and vital events in the history of the Cause. Your services will ever be remembered by me with feelings of pride & gratitude.'[46] In another letter, he went farther in expressing his true assessment of Horace's capacity and his determination that it should be put to good use to advance the Faith. In 1926, lamenting his own need for capable assistants, the Guardian wrote a personal note to Horace at the bottom of another official letter stating, 'I have often felt the extreme desirability of having a collaborator like you working by my side here in Haifa. The loss of . . . is keenly felt by me and my hope is that the conditions here and abroad will enable me to establish the work in Haifa upon a more systematic basis. I am waiting for a favourable time.'[47] That favourable time would not come until after the Guardian's passing, for Horace was always deemed too valuable to the work of one of the most important Bahá'í communities to take him away from it.[48] He would however have an opportunity – though brief – to serve in the Holy Land.

Horace had already developed a love for Green Acre by the time he and Doris moved there in the fall of 1925. In the months prior to the move, he had travelled to Buffalo, Detroit, and Chicago, and was preparing for other trips on behalf of the National Assembly. This hectic pace made his little cottage on the hill above the water a haven. As soon as he was settled, he wrote to his brother Irving about his new life in the woods telling him that 'you couldn't ask for a more comfortable home. The view in front sweeps down across Green Acre to the river, in back through fields to pine woods against the horizon a half mile away.'[49] Doris had someone to assist her with the housekeeping so that she could help him with his work for the National Assembly, because 'there's enough for us both, and then some'.[50]

The Holleys enjoyed living in Maine, but by May 1926, the National Assembly concluded that Green Acre was too isolated to serve as its headquarters,[51] and so, at the end of that summer, the Holleys left the forest by the sea and returned to the bustle of Manhattan. Initially, the National Assembly rented office space at 129 East 10th Street, but in 1928, in order to economize, it asked Horace to allow that lease to lapse and to rent a post office for the National Assembly's address.⁵² Throughout much of the next decade, the Holley's small apartments – often consisting of only one room – would serve as the national office.⁵³ As he commented in 1927 to a friend, 'The work of national secretary is capable of infinite expansion,' and he was happy to carry it out.⁵⁴

* * * * *

Increasingly, the work of the Faith exhausted Horace and affected his health – which had never been robust. There was a Bahá'í osteopathic physician in Geneva, New York, Dr Albert Heist, who had a far-flung reputation as an exceptional healer.⁵⁵ Among the believers in the area near his clinic were Willard and Doris McKay, who owned a fruit farm outside of Geneva where they enjoyed hosting Bahá'í gatherings. The McKays, both younger than Horace and without children, had become Bahá'ís shortly after the passing of 'Abdu'l-Bahá. They quickly began to actively serve the Cause and became acquainted with the Holleys at National Conventions, Green Acre and Bahá'í gatherings in New York City. The McKays were not surprised when the Holleys arrived in Geneva that June 1928 because when Doris McKay was in New York a few months earlier, she had noticed that Horace did not look well. The McKays invited them to stay at their home for the several weeks Horace was receiving treatment. It took little persuasion to convince the Holleys that Horace could best restore his health in the quiet of the McKays' orchards and the simplicity of their rustic farmhouse. His hostess later recalled that the Holleys' visit coincided with cherry-picking time when truckloads of Italians would descend upon their groves. Despite his need for rest, Horace was determined to be of use. First, he cut the McKays' lawn. Then he undertook mending the wooden front porch steps even though he knew almost nothing about carpentry. A pattern for the boards was cut out by his hostess's seamstress mother, which he used to guide his saw after balancing the wood on a chair. In the process, he sliced through the arm of the chair. With his cackling chortle, he and his hosts howled with laughter at his ineptitude.⁵⁶

Doris McKay observed that while Horace was their guest, he was 'relaxed but not idle'.⁵⁷ No wonder Horace was rundown and ill, for his normal energy seemed 'fantastic' and the amount of work he produced 'superhuman'.⁵⁸ When she asked him about his exceptional power, he told her that he would sometimes receive what he termed an 'energy zone', which when it operated within him, gave him more than usual capacity to work.[59]

The McKays also observed first-hand the close ties binding the Holleys as a couple. Both loved the word of God. Doris enjoyed reading Bahá'í scripture out loud. Horace, exhausted from a day spent outside exploring the farm, would settle into a comfortable chair and silently reread *Bahá'í Scriptures*. Willard was, like Horace, well-educated and had been employed as a university instructor, so he relished engaging in long elevated conversations with Horace in the isolation of his farmstead. The fresh air and tranquillity of the country, mixed with the loving care of the McKays, rebuilt Horace's health, so that by the end of June the Holleys were able to return to Manhattan and their arduous work for the Cause.[60]

* * * * *

In the early months of 1929 when the state of the American economy showed no signs of faltering, Horace began to struggle to meet all of his financial responsibilities while engaged full time by the Faith.[61] He was supporting his daughters, who were now teenagers, as well their mother and Doris. When it came time to elect officers for the year, Horace asked to resign as secretary, citing personal reasons, so that he could obtain other employment. He assured the National Assembly that he would continue to serve the Faith as best he could as a member of the Assembly, but without pay. His fellow National Assembly members asked him to defer this for a few months.[62] As soon as Shoghi Effendi learned of Horace's request to resign, he immediately sent a cable addressed to Horace. Interestingly, the cable was not sent directly to Horace but to another member of the National Assembly to ensure the other members would see its contents. It read:

> MUCH PERTURBED YOUR WITHDRAWAL BOTH FOR FUNDAMENTAL PRINCIPLE INVOLVED AND LOSS OF YOUR UNIQUE SECRETARIAL GIFTS BEG RECONSIDERATION
> LOVE SHOGHI[63]

Horace and his wife consulted further about their situation. At the next meeting, he announced that he would agree to continue as secretary, but without pay, so that he could accept other employment. This offer was gratefully accepted.[64]

Just before the next annual election, sensing that Horace might again request to be released from his office, Shoghi Effendi again appealed to Horace to continue as secretary in a handwritten postscript. He told his 'dear-coworker' that he truly deplored his resignation and hoped that he would 'in the days to come arrange your work and affairs in such a manner as to be able to lend increasing assistance to the ever-extending activities of the Cause.'[65]

Reticent to disclose his personal problems, Horace was apparently not completely candid with the National Assembly about his circumstances. About a year earlier, Horace had received a playful letter from his eldest daughter, Hertha, in which she remarked that she wanted to muss his hair, going on to tease him about the amount of printer's ink consumed by his books. The letter disclosed to her father her plans to travel to Europe later that summer, writing that she would probably stay through the winter in order to study French.[66] Like her father, eighteen-year-old Hertha was intelligent with a sense of humour, and had wide-ranging interests, especially the arts. Horace, no doubt, was delighted that Hertha would finally be returning to the places where she had spent the first years of her life. But any hopes Horace may have entertained that his daughter would have an enjoyable time in Europe came to an end during the winter of 1928 when he began to receive distressing reports[67] – first intimations of a seven-year ordeal that would end tragically. While Hertha was in France, the old Holley family nemesis took hold of her – mental illness. Several doctors were consulted. Their unanimous conclusion was that she was not capable of safely returning to the United States. Even had those attending to her care given consent for her to travel, it would have been difficult to obtain permission from a ship's captain to bring on board a person actively suffering from mental illness.[68] Letters and cables would reach Horace reporting that his daughter's condition had improved, only to be followed soon after by others reporting relapses. Once she was settled in a sanitorium in Geneva, Switzerland, she stabilized, and her thinking slowly became closer to normal. By 1930, Hertha's illness had taxed Horace's emotions and finances to the breaking point as he struggled to raise funds to pay for Hertha's care in the midst of the first year of the Great Depression.[69] He could not afford to go to Europe to tend to his daughter, so he asked Mountfort Mills to arrange to visit her on his behalf because he resided part-time in Geneva.[70] Horace also contacted the noted Bahá'í psychologist and philosopher, Dr Auguste Forel, to request that he accept Hertha as a patient, and so she came under Forel's expert care.[71]

After the 1930 election, the National Assembly established a three-person Secretariat when Horace informed them that he could no longer serve as secretary. Even though Fred Lunt was elected to replace Horace as the titular secretary, Horace and another member assisted Fred with the work. Two believers from the New York area, Bertha Herklotz and Roushan Wilkinson, were engaged to help with the clerical work.[72] The Guardian informed the Assembly that he was satisfied with this arrangement because it meant that Horace's invaluable services would not be completely lost, although he was unsure if a committee would prove to be practical. By that time, the Guardian seemed to have learned more details about Horace's family problems because he addressed a personal note to Horace in his postscript, saying

> I am very glad to hear of the formation of a national Secretariat, and I trust that it will be productive of the best results. I am also glad to know that your connection with the Secretariat is maintained and I will pray that your personal domestic problems may soon be eliminated, that you may continue to render your extremely valuable services to our beloved Faith.
> Your true brother Shoghi[73]

At last, in 1932, Bertha and Marcia sailed to France to bring Hertha back to the United States,[74] where she could remain under the care of doctors. As the ship carrying his eldest daughter docked in New York, it must have seemed to Horace that the worst episode of this nightmare was over and that his talented child would soon get on with her life as a budding adult. Relieved, he was ready to resume service as secretary of the National Assembly if elected to that office again.

* * * * *

The National Assembly was still constrained by the incorporation of the Temple Unity. The By-Laws of that entity could only be changed at the annual Conventions with proper legal notice given in advance to the delegates. When the Convention voted in 1924 to amend the Temple Unity charter so that the National Assembly could exercise greater control over the national affairs, it still did not completely bring the old incorporation into alignment with the requirements of the Bahá'í Administrative Order. The old Executive Board of Temple Unity had to exist for a time, at least on paper, to meet the legal requirements of the laws of Illinois, even though the National Assembly appointed its members instead of having it elected by the Convention.[75] The title to the Temple property was held by that Executive Board. This legal entanglement impeded the National Assembly's ability to incorporate and take full control of funds and real estate. The lawyers on the National Assembly set out to resolve these issues by drafting a new constitution that could be submitted to the Guardian for approval. Horace, though not a lawyer, became intimately involved with this project. His lawyer colleague, Mountfort, commenting upon the ease with which Horace immersed himself in the complexity of incorporation, teasingly remarked, 'I get the impression in some way that you were just reaching for your hat one fine day to go out and have the Assembly incorporated.'[76]

The aptly named Alice Greenacre, a Chicago lawyer, was hired to carry out the incorporation. She presented the National Assembly with multiple options, including asking the United States Congress to pass a private bill incorporating the Faith nationwide.[77] States other than Illinois were explored, but what should be done for the Commonwealth of Canada? Finally, the National Assembly settled upon using a voluntary trust by creating a document called a Declaration of Trust which it would submit to the State of Illinois.[78] This type of legal document seemed especially fitting because in the Kitáb-i-Aqdas, Bahá'u'lláh said of the members of the Spiritual Assemblies that, it 'behoveth them to be the trusted ones of the Merciful among men and to regard themselves as the guardians appointed of God for all that dwell on earth'.[79]

The Guardian informed the National Assembly of specific points that should be included in the Declaration of Trust and its accompanying By-Laws, for example:

> It should be pointed out in the by-laws that in any locality where the number of recognized believers is exactly nine these automatically

constitute a Spiritual Assembly. It should also be pointed out in the by-laws that whatever is not specifically referred to therein is left entirely to the discretion of the National Assembly, who are free to delegate such discretionary powers as they see fit to the Local Assemblies within their jurisdiction.[80]

After reviewing a preliminary draft, Shoghi Effendi instructed the Assembly to consider additional issues before completing the legal document. He needed to purchase parcels of land in Palestine, especially in the areas bordering the twin Holy Shrines. Shoghi Effendi was in a rush to bring this about because Jews fleeing increasing persecution in Europe were rapidly building on the slopes of Mount Carmel, encroaching on land he wished to acquire to protect the Shrine of the Báb and to complete the World Centre. His plan was to safeguard these strategic plots by placing their ownership under the name of the National Assembly of the United States and Canada, thereby making it an international affair should any person or entity try to wrest them from the Faith.

> He is desirous that our National Assembly should appear upon the public records here as the owner of property on Mount Carmel in its own name, not in the name of private individuals as Trustees for it.[81]

The Declaration of Trust was modified to accommodate that additional requirement. Shortly thereafter those changes proved their usefulness when the North American National Assembly was given legal title to the Eastern Pilgrim House within the shadow of the Shrine of the Báb in Haifa.[82] At the same time, the Guardian recognized that the documents had to conform to the requirements of American and Canadian law, stating: 'But most important, he feels, is to choose what is best for the larger work of the Assembly in the United States and Canada.'[83]

When changes were made to the documents in order to conform to Illinois law, the Guardian questioned them because he feared the incorporation was not broad enough to encompass the full range of the powers and responsibilities of the National Assembly.[84] Over the course of the years, amendments would be made to the Declaration of Trust to bring its provisions into conformity with the expanding requirements of the National Assembly. The possibility of amendment deliberately included in the document was one of its virtues. But it was vital that all amendments to the Declaration of Trust be approved by the Guardian because it would serve as the template for all other National Assemblies throughout the world.

Almost a century later, the American Declaration of Trust and By-Laws have been translated into dozens of languages and used by Baháʼí communities all over the globe to incorporate or register the Faith with their governments. Rúḥíyyih Khánum, wife of Shoghi Effendi, called the incorporation of the North American community 'one of the great milestones in Baháʼí history . . .'[85]

In a foreword to the Declaration of Trust and its By-Laws which Horace wrote for *The Baháʼí World*, he likened the Declaration to the famous Mayflower Compact, the first foundational legal document in United States history, which was also written in the form of a trust. When English settlers reached the coast of Massachusetts in 1620 on the ship the *Mayflower*, before going ashore they consulted together and drafted a covenant to bind themselves under a new democratic government. Every element of the National Assembly's Constitution along with its By-Laws was based solely upon principles enunciated by the Guardian. Though cloaked in the language of law, these were truly spiritual documents.

> The Declaration, in fact, is nothing more or less than a legal parallel of those moral and spiritual laws of unity inherent in the fulness of the Baháʼí Revelation and making it the fulfilment of the ideal of Religion in the social as well as spiritual realm. Because in the Baháʼí Faith this perfect correspondence exists between spiritual and social laws, the Baháʼís believe that administrative success is identical with moral success; and that nothing less than the true Baháʼí spirit of devotion and sacrifice can inspire with effective power the world-wide body of unity, revealed by Baháʼu'lláh.[86]

In numerous letters as well as in his magnificent history of the Faith, *God Passes By*,[87] Shoghi Effendi spoke with glowing pride of the monumental achievements of the National Spiritual Assembly of the United States and Canada and of the Spiritual Assembly of New York City in putting Baháʼí administration on a firm footing, both legally and within the Baháʼí community, by drafting constitutions and obtaining governmental recognition of the Faith through incorporation. His first letter endorsing the final draft of the National Assembly's Declaration of Trust offers an excellent example of his delight at what they had accomplished.

> As already intimated, I have read and re-read most carefully the final draft of the By-Laws... and feel I have nothing substantial to add to this first and very creditable attempt at codifying the principles of general Bahá'í administration. I heartily and unhesitatingly commend it to the earnest perusal of, and its loyal adoption by, every National Bahá'í Spiritual Assembly, whether constituted in the East or in the West. I would ask you particularly to send copies of the text of this document of fundamental importance accompanied by copies of the Declaration of Trust and the text of the Indenture of Trust, to every existing National Spiritual Assembly, with my insistent request to study the provisions, comprehend its implications, and endeavor to incorporate it, to the extent that their own circumstances permit, within the framework of their own national activities. You can but faintly imagine how comforting a stimulant and how helpful a guide its publication and circulation will be to those patient and toiling workers in Eastern lands, and particularly Persia, who in the midst of uncertainties and almost insuperable obstacles are straining every nerve in order to establish the world order ushered in by Bahá'u'lláh. You can hardly realize how substantially it will contribute to pave the way for the elaboration of the beginnings of the constitution of the worldwide Bahá'í Community that will form the permanent basis upon which the blest and sanctified edifice of the first International House of Justice will securely rest and flourish.[88]

In the process of untangling and dissolving the legal arrangements of Temple Unity, one issue was particularly delicate and controversial, namely, control of the funds expressly earmarked for the House of Worship.[89] Ever since 1909, the primary goal for raising money was to build the Temple. That continued to be important; however, after 1922 money was also necessary for the general work of a growing religious community. The transfer of the Temple accounts to the National Assembly's treasurer was carried out with some reluctance on the part

THE BIRTH PANGS OF THE NEW ORDERING OF THE WORLD

of the old members of Temple Unity, especially because they perceived that the members of the new body, who in cases such as Horace, represented the coming of age of the next generation of believers, were not solely focused on the House of Worship and so 'not keenly alive to the importance of the Temple work . . .'[90]

* * * * *

A decade after it was established, the National Assembly continued to grapple with the vast distances under its jurisdiction. From the beginning, it had members residing on the West Coast while its centres of activity were based in either New York or Chicago. Small wonder if the West Coast members often felt left out, which caused friction within the Assembly. One example, Nellie French, an affluent member from Pasadena, California, travelled on the fastest trains available to attend a meeting in New York. Of the eleven days she was away from home, eight were spent travelling.[91] The delegates revisited this issue in 1933, but it was pointed out once more that the Guardian wanted the membership of the National Assembly to represent the diversity of the two countries. This laudable goal was achieved only at the price of fewer meetings, since the Assembly continued to struggle with attaining a quorum. Much of the time, it met with only the five members from the East Coast. Correspondence proved to be an inadequate substitute for participation in consultations, and those at a meeting often forgot to share important information with the absent members. For several years, the National Assembly allowed absent members to give a proxy to someone else. It also permitted the Convention to elect alternate members. Sometimes, if someone was present at a meeting, but not a member, the National Assembly would ask that person to take part in consultation so that more points of view could be examined, though those extra participants could not vote.

Another vexing issue for the National Assembly with communities in the north of Canada and on the tip of Florida was how to communicate with those it served. Not only did it have to devise means to convey its messages, but it also had to be able to elicit what was in the hearts of those it served. It had to learn how to convey its decisions in a manner which did not seem overly autocratic, especially during the first decade when many Bahá'ís were still uncertain about giving unreserved allegiance to the institutions. This skill of corresponding appropriately was even more sensitive when it came to communicating with the nascent Local Spiritual Assemblies which were just learning to crawl. Horace shared his thoughts about this conundrum with his colleague Fred Lunt.

> ... [there] is the delicate question of where constructive leadership ends and where dictation begins. The guiding principle is always Shoghi Effendi's words that power is vested in the local Assemblies, while authority is vested in the National Assemblies. Of course, we would not care to exercise any authority that would tend to weaken the power of the local Assemblies, as the N. S. A. derives from them and weakens through their weakness.[92]

Just as in New York City, where Horace frequently suggested new ways to foster better communication between the Local Spiritual Assembly and its community, he pondered how to foster a spirit of unity through consultation and disseminating information at the national level. He proposed a national Bahá'í bulletin to serve as the voice of the National Assembly.[93] Even though the *Star of the West* reached many American households, its focus was on a global readership. The National Assembly approved of his idea and made him editor of the *Bahá'í News Bulletin* which was launched in December 1924, continuing publication until 1990.

Horace had another idea to assist the fledgling Assemblies. Between 1922 and 1927 Shoghi Effendi sent letter after letter with invaluable guidance and insights about Bahá'í administration. If this correspondence could be compiled, edited, and published in the first issue of the News Bulletin, it could serve as 'a clear guide and "primer" for the instruction and reference of the local Spiritual Assemblies.'[94] Within the next few years, Horace expanded this essential compilation as other letters were received from the Guardian, and published it as *Bahá'í Administration*, a timeless work which included the most significant of the Guardian's letters to America during the 1920s and up until 1932. He wrote the introduction and was permitted to give titles and subheadings to the letters to make them easier to follow. In his 1927 introduction to the work, Horace states that it is primarily a reference book, but he hopes that it will interest non-Bahá'ís, for: 'The method of

Bahá'í administration, with its provision of local, national and international units, is the most perfect plan of worldwide spiritual unity ever evolved.'[95]

* * * * *

The Faith had first taken hold in Chicago, the heartland of the United States, and that metropolis continued to be critical to the Bahá'í community because it was the most central location for the Canadians as well as Americans, and the House of Worship for the continent was rising on its outskirts. After the completion of the basement in 1922, with its large central meeting room known as Foundation Hall, National Conventions as well as other gatherings open to the public began to be held there. Even though the dome was yet to be erected, being able to utilize the lower area of the structure was a great achievement and bounty. Horace had opportunities to explore the Temple site a number of times during the early days of the National Assembly, where he no doubt called to mind when during a private meeting with 'Abdu'l-Bahá in Paris in 1913, he had unexpectedly received guidance about the future Mother Temple of the West.

Most of the members of the Temple Committee appointed by the National Assembly resided in the Chicago area, and many of them had previously served on the Temple Unity Executive Board. The Committee had evolved from being the main executive body of the Faith in North America to one of many committees appointed and managed by the National Assembly, its authority now limited to matters related to the land, construction matters, and the maintenance of the building. Learning to function as a committee rather than as an independent body did not come easily for some of the long-time members of Temple Unity. The National Assembly found it had to exercise tact and patience regarding House of Worship issues.[96] Furthermore, as a result of changes in membership of the National Assembly, the officers now resided in New York, Boston and Washington DC, shifting the administration from the Midwest to the Northeast, especially to New York.

Some members of the Chicago community found it difficult to accept these changes. There were also vestiges of discontent left over from the Chicago-based Reading Room affair as well as disruptive personality conflicts swirling through and weakening that important

Bahá'í community. The sole member of the National Assembly living in the metropolitan Chicago area wrote candidly of undercurrents questioning the authority of the National Assembly circulating within the City of Chicago.[97] Horace responded by reminding his colleague that he, as a National Assembly member, was in a position to see first-hand how carefully the National Assembly was approaching its work. He explained his own understanding of the Covenant of Bahá'u'lláh and what it required of all believers. Obedience to and respect for the institutions was a spiritual test that separated the firm believers from those of weaker faith. Horace hoped his colleague would assist his fellow Chicagoans to recognize that they were being tested and help them become steadfast in the Covenant.

> Under these conditions one must choose to which attitude one is going to attribute the most weight and which view one is going to consider most seriously. Either we have got to become imbued with a faith that the N.S.A., irrespective or [sic] its personalities, occupies a position of responsibility for which there is no substitute in this country, and go ahead carefully but firmly and courageously, or else relinquish this responsibility and merely mark time in accordance with the expressed or unexpressed views of the other party. It is my deepest hope that the others will come to see that obedience to the Covenant today is first an understanding of, and next a sympathy for the organization and methods of service as established by Shoghi Effendi, but even if this should not happen I feel that we have no right to destroy the function of the National Spiritual Assembly for the sake of a negative attitude the end of which is inevitable failure.
>
> It may well be that the Bahá'í organization has come as a kind of Day of Judgment for certain souls who attribute to themselves a spiritual station so high that in their hearts they cannot admit any superior authority. You will remember the talk of 'Abdu'l-Bahá gave in this country in which he explained that obedience to him was obedience to Bahá'u'llh [sic]... just as in the case of an ambassador sent by a king to a foreign country. The N.S.A. is Shoghi Effendi's representative to this country and unwillingness to cooperate with that body is nothing less than disobedience to the Guardian. Since it is only Shoghi Effendi who can bring about the success of the Cause, should we not with all our power turn to his positive instructions

and his expressed hopes, and forget entirely the shadows thrown by the unhappy souls which seem to exist in the Cause?

What did Horace believe was the best approach for the National Assembly to deal with the naysayers? He believed that some of the difficulties would eventually erupt into a crisis, and that in the meantime, the Assembly should become a spiritual centre the friends would turn to.

> The situation will come to a crisis sooner or later, but some N.S.A. must become a center of positive effort irrespective of personalities, and why should we leave this to some future body? The great majority of the friends desire progress and understand the spiritual conditions required for it, and if a crisis does come I am sure that everything which we have done to improve the work will be confirmed . . .[98]

From its infancy, the greatest challenge confronting the National Assembly was establishing unity among its members. Its first years had been especially rocky as personalities clashed and old issues stung. Unbridled electioneering eroded trust. The advice given to the National Assembly by Shoghi Effendi as its birth-year was coming to an end in 1923 rang true and would forever be a guide.

> Many and grave may be the obstacles, whether from within or from without, which we shall have to encounter in the days to come, but we feel sure that if we but maintain consistently before our eyes a broad and noble vision of its significance and vital necessity in these days, and above all its universality and all-conquering power, we shall be enabled to surmount them, one and all, and by the Power of the Faith, carry the Ark of the Covenant to its Haven of Safety and Triumph.[99]

Shoghi Effendi called upon the members of the National Assembly to take up the urgent task of bringing about unity by first banishing 'every trace of the animosity and mistrust of the past' from their hearts so that they could form 'one united front, and combat, wisely and tactfully, every force that might darken the spirit of the Movement, cause division in its ranks, and narrow it by dogmatic and sectarian belief'.[100] He then stated unequivocally that 'It is primarily upon the elected members of the National Spiritual Assemblies through the Bahá'í world that this highly important duty devolves . . .'[101] This call to unity seemed at first glance to be a simple matter. But as human beings, Horace and his fellow members would find it difficult to achieve.

10

BUILDING THE WORLD ANEW IS A MESSY BUSINESS

From its inception, the National Spiritual Assembly recognized it had two primary projects to foster and manage: complete the construction of the House of Worship and increase the number and locations of avowed believers. In 1926, it devised a strategy called the Plan of Unified Action to achieve those goals, the first of an endless series of plans to further the development of the Faith. Even before that Plan was adopted, the twin goals were apparent if not formally stated. The Guardian wholeheartedly approved of the Plan of Unified Action and applauded this first initiative by a National Assembly to create goals.[1]

Of the two objectives, one was most urgent – the raising of funds to begin the first phase of the construction of the dome of the Temple. The building's foundation, including the basement area with its large meeting room, was already complete and in use by 1922, but the structure above ground remained an eyesore because it appeared to be an untidy black mound surrounded by a dirt lake.

The other aim, to increase the number of avowed believers, was a challenge at a time when society was turning away from churches. The National Assembly knew it must devise means of stimulating the believers to arise and tell others about Bahá'u'lláh, for the overarching goal of remaking the world through His teachings would never be attained without more adherents.

Teaching the Faith is a service to God enjoined upon all Bahá'ís; therefore, it should have been a source of unity because every believer could teach. However, there were different approaches to introducing the Faith. Unfortunately, some of the friends had their own ideas about what would attract inquirers, and they clung to their methodologies as though all other approaches were not only ineffective but contrary to the teachings. Some, such as renowned teachers Mary Hanford Ford and

Albert Vail, stressed the mystical – even supernatural – aspects of the Cause. Others, such as Louis Gregory and Horace, preferred to introduce Bahá'u'lláh through His social teachings regarding world peace, the elimination of prejudices, and the spiritual solution to economic problems. (That last topic was especially popular during the financially difficult years of the 1930s.) Horace, like other teachers, often combined both in his talks to Bahá'ís, but he preferred discussing the social teachings with non-Bahá'ís. What some believers failed to grasp was that these two approaches were complementary. Each teacher needed to consider the particular listener. Those who wished to introduce the social teachings of the Faith found that the ideas were often more readily received by the movers and shakers of society when they were not cloaked in religious terminology. For those drawn to the more esoteric, spiritual teachings, a more forthright approach to introducing religious teachings seemed the most effective. Not surprisingly, in larger communities such as New York, the believers gravitated to members who shared their preferences for either the mystical or social teachings. This unintended separation into groups created factions within a community whose *sine qua non* was supposed to be unity.[2] One way to address this problem was through training programmes for teachers that would engender in them a comprehensive approach. However, when teacher training first began in the 1920, the delicate issue arose as to whether Bahá'í teachers should be 'approved' or 'certified'.

From the early days of the Bahá'í Faith in the United States, gifted teachers of the Cause had arisen through the ranks of the believers. These were Bahá'ís who possessed not only extensive knowledge of the Faith, but the capacity to convey that knowledge in a manner that opened hearts. A handful of those believers travelled around the United States and Canada giving public talks and meeting with gatherings of Bahá'ís and with the public. Most legendary of these was the one given the title 'Mother Teacher of the West' by 'Abdu'l-Bahá: Lua Getsinger, the one mentioned previously that He had also named Herald of the Covenant that fateful day in New York in 1912. A trained actress and on fire with devotion, Lua touched many a soul during the first days of the Faith in the West as she travelled from place to place with the financial assistance of a wealthy family in California.[3] Others followed in her path: Isabella Brittingham, Howard Colby Ives and his wife Mabel Rice-Wray Ives, and Howard MacNutt from the New York City area;

Elizabeth Greenleaf from Massachusetts; Orcella Rexford from California; and May Maxwell and Lorol 'Kitty' Schopflocher from Canada.

By the time the National Spiritual Assembly began its work, the two primary travelling teachers in North America were Albert Vail, a graduate of Harvard Divinity School and ordained Unitarian minister from Illinois, and Louis Gregory, from South Carolina who as the son of slaves had graduated from Howard University Law School. Albert and Louis were employed by the National Spiritual Assembly so they could devote their time to the Faith. The National Teaching Committee supervised their work, directing where they should visit. Both were gifted writers who also produced many articles for Bahá'í publications. For example, Louis reported the National Conventions for the *Star of the West* and Albert contributed many articles to that periodical and was its editor for about a year. Communities would take advantage of a visit from any of the outstanding travelling speakers by renting a meeting room and inviting the public to the talks through newspaper advertisements and other publicity. Horace, as secretary of the National Assembly, was placed in the position of traffic-controller, receiving requests for teachers and forwarding them on, then receiving reports of visits to convey to the Assembly. He became the one person on the National Assembly with the big picture.

This system of travelling teachers had many benefits, especially in making it possible to introduce the Faith in regions of the country where there were no Bahá'ís. However, it also spawned passivity among many of the friends, who waited for an accomplished travelling teacher to come to their community before mentioning the Faith to others. Only when a travelling teacher was scheduled would they take action. The problem of deferring to travelling teachers needed a remedy if the institutions were to spur the entire community to arise to teach. The Tablets of the Divine Plan had charged the North American community with the primary responsibility for the spiritual conquest of the planet. A handful of teachers, no matter how capable, could never carry out such a crusade. With the Local Assemblies beginning to assume their basic responsibilities, it was time to wean the friends from the practice of full-time, paid teachers.

Compensating teachers for carrying out a spiritual duty had been controversial for many years.[4] One of the emphatic teachings of the Faith is that each believer should earn his living because work, according to Bahá'í scripture, had an elevated status. If the tasks of life were performed in the proper spirit, they became a form of worship. An oft-cited praiseworthy example of earning a living in conjunction with teaching was that of John and Clara Dunn, who moved from Seattle, Washington to Australia, in response to the Tablets of the Divine Plan. The Dunns were already advanced in age when they decided to introduce the Faith to the Antipodes. Hyde Dunn secured employment as a travelling sales agent for a food company, using his business travels to spread the Bahá'í message across much of Australia. Also, Martha Root, a journalist from Pittsburgh, Pennsylvania, circled the earth multiple times to spread the Cause by earning her expenses selling articles to publications. Another example was Orcella Rexford, who gave paid lectures on health and other topics as she criss-crossed the country, which funded her Bahá'í work.

Covering the expenses of travelling teachers required sizeable sums of money. The fastest way to travel between cities was by train. In order to economize, the National Assembly investigated special railway passes for clergy offered by railway companies, but this presented dilemmas. The first problem was determining who should be eligible for the limited number of passes. Should they be given only to travelling teachers, members of the National Assembly, or national committee members? Then there was the problem of the railways requiring that the passes should only be allocated to clerics with proof of ordination.[5] This created a quandary for a religion forbidden by its teachings to have clergy. This was already an issue because, to many people, Gregory and Vail appeared to be Bahá'í clergy. Clergy railway passes might serve to reinforce that misconception.

Shoghi Effendi turned his attention to training an army of teachers after he was satisfied that Local Assemblies were established and functioning at an acceptable level. It became the dominant theme in his general letters. With Green Acre now owned by the Cause and other locations being used as training facilities, such as the Geyserville property in California, the Guardian promoted intensive training at Bahá'í summer schools as a solution to increasing the number of capable teachers, saying: 'Green Acre is to be developed into a centre where teachers are created to go out into the field as able servants.'[6] The National Assembly agreed that there was a need to hold training sessions to improve the capacity of believers to spread the Cause and it considered not just summer schools but looked to other spaces as well. For example, teaching conferences were held in conjunction with the National Conventions, replacing the Congress for the general public. Regional teaching committees began to organize training sessions as well. These efforts intensified after the adoption of the Plan of Unified Action. Again, Horace was active in coordinating these efforts and often served as a lecturer, especially at Green Acre. He also prepared study outlines for the Sacred Texts that individuals could use at home.

* * * * *

Challenges from within rarely appear with full force at the outset. There is often a period of quiet waiting and watchfulness by those who are uncomfortable with change. Therefore, it was not wholly ironic that during its earliest years the greatest challenge to the authority of the National Spiritual Assembly came from the very person who had served as its first secretary, Alfred 'Fred' Lunt. Again, Horace was placed in the middle of a tragic drama.

The crash of the New York stock market in October 1929 is often used to mark the beginning of the Great Depression. However, the market rebounded within months and the economy, though jittery, did not seem out of control at the beginning of 1930. President Calvin Coolidge left office when the economy was still on a relatively solid foundation, except for the reckless trading – gambling – unleashed within the equities markets. The new President, Herbert Hoover, was a civil engineer and successful business executive, who had an innate ability to organize. Like President Woodrow Wilson a decade earlier, Hoover believed in social engineering, the concept that the government should rely upon the advice of experts to undertake deliberate societal change. Even though Hoover was a member of the opposing party, Wilson had turned to this brilliant man to manage the delivery of relief materials to the millions of people suffering in Europe in the years following the War. Hoover was applauded for the deft manner in which he accomplished his task. Surely a man of his capacities could rescue the economy. His administration set to work implementing measures – many of which were experimental – to reverse the economic downturn. These government programmes and policies had little effect. By 1932, what had appeared at first to be a normal correction of the business cycle had become a full-blown depression. Ironically, analysis by economic experts decades later would determine that it was government intervention itself that had prevented recovery – a reality seen by Shoghi Effendi at the time. The price of misjudgement was that multitudes lost their jobs, and many of those who retained their positions were forced to accept reductions in pay. Family farms and homes went into foreclosure. More than a million people, including hundreds of thousands of children, became homeless. Wandering the country, many set up squalid camps even in the parks of New York City. An angry populace staring hopelessly at their diminished wealth, overwhelmingly voted Hoover out of office with the anticipation that Franklin D. Roosevelt would be their saviour. But he repackaged the same remedies tried by Hoover and added other government programmes for good measure, swelling government intervention into many aspects of American daily life. Again, after limited improvement, the economy worsened.[7] In 1932 and throughout 1933, everyone in the country was in a bad mood – the Baháʼís included.

Among those struggling financially in the early 1930s was Fred Lunt, who was serving as secretary of the National Assembly during the time Horace was tending to his family problems. Lunt was born in 1878 in Beverly, Massachusetts into a middle-class family. His father was a businessman and later an assessor for a city.[8] Fred had established his own law practice in Boston after being rejected or expelled by large law firms that were leery of his public association with his strange religion. He had a large family to support, and as the Depression deepened, making a living through a small law practice became increasingly difficult. Even his corporate clients were short on funds.[9]

Horace and Fred should have been easy friends and natural allies. Both were sons of New England with deep ties to that region, both had been given elite educations, and both were intensely interested in current affairs, economics, and government. Both were passionately devoted to the Baháʼí Faith to such a degree that they were willing to make substantial personal sacrifices to serve it. Both served as secretary of the National Assembly. The longer they served together on that institution, however, the harder it was for them to get along personally.[10] This problem was not just between Fred and Horace; many other members found Fred difficult to work with, going back as far as his service on the Temple Unity Executive Board and the National Assembly prior to Horace's election.[11]

One clue as to why Lunt could not work well with his colleagues on the National Assembly becomes evident from his *New York Times* obituary, which omits his prominent service to the Bahá'í Faith. The headline read: 'Ex-head of National Republican League was 59'. Politics was another of Fred's passions. He had been head of the Republican Club at Harvard, and a delegate to the Republican National Convention while 'Abdu'l-Bahá was visiting the United States in 1912. He worked on presidential campaigns in 1908, 1916, and 1924, this last time while a member of the National Assembly.[12] Though he was not the only American Bahá'í engaged in political activity prior to 1932, when it was expressly forbidden, he was certainly the most visible.

In American partisan politics, if a decision is made that others believe to be wrong, the opposing party wastes no time in denouncing it publicly, making a fuss in newspapers and using the issue as a lever to win the next election and oust those who were responsible for it. The winner could then reverse course without regard to whether or not the original decision was correct. This approach is the opposite of how the Bahá'í Administrative Order functions, for it requires unqualified acceptance of and obedience to all decisions made by elected Assemblies, even if it appears to some that a decision is wrong. Moving forward together in unified obedience quickly makes mistakes obvious while averting schism and ill-feelings. Thus an obvious mistake can easily be corrected. Years of involvement with a political party permeated Fred's thinking, so he struggled to align himself with the attitudes required for Bahá'í service. The longer he served on the National Assembly, the more frequently he found himself at odds with the rest of the members. His colleagues felt he was not open-minded and that as the years went on, his ability to process information was diminishing. This latter problem may have been due in part to the considerable stress he was under and perhaps to the beginning stages of a heart disease that would bring about his untimely death. A growing number of conflicts alienated Fred from the other eight members of the Assembly, leading eventually to his open agitation against the institution itself outside of meetings.[13]

Fred Lunt had attended the founding meeting of Temple Unity in 1909 and served from its early years on its Executive Board, usually as an officer. He never forgot the 1920 annual Convention during which the delegates, rather than the Executive Board, carried out 'Abdu'l-Bahá's assignment to select the architectural design for the House of

Worship from among the many submitted proposals – the most significant decision ever made by a Baháʼí Convention – believing that that Convention should be a model for the future. The Executive Board when he served on it had always been subservient to the Convention. The powers of the Executive Board were suspended when the Convention was in session. To Americans such as Fred, having a legislative body meet briefly once a year was not odd; in fact, it mimicked the rhythm of most state legislatures, whose enactments were carried out during the rest of the year by the executive branches of state governments. Lunt was certain that the solution to the decisions of the National Assembly that he disliked was simple: overturn them by majority vote at the next Convention.

*****

One decision that Fred strongly opposed was releasing from service the two full-time paid travelling teachers in 1932. Albert Vail and Louis Gregory were well-loved, gifted teachers who confirmed countless converts. Both traversed the country, giving lectures and otherwise strengthening local Baháʼí communities. Gregory's work was especially important because he focused on spreading the Faith's teachings about race amity and bringing the Cause to the attention of the Black population. His journeys throughout the South when it was still in the grips of legally sanctioned racial segregation and oppression, often enforced through extrajudicial lynching of any Black citizen who tried to better his station in life, placed Louis in grave physical danger. With exemplary courage, Louis never hesitated to continue his travels because he and the National Assembly well understood how vital they were to bringing the healing message of Baháʼu'lláh to that backward region of the country. Horace appended a personal note to him on an official letter, expressing his own admiration for Louis' efforts, saying, 'The conditions of danger and sacrifice under which you are teaching, seem to me to approximate more closely the early days of the Revelation in Persia than can be found anywhere else in the West at this time. God bless you!'[14]

Unquestionably, the work of the paid teachers was important, but by 1931 Shoghi Effendi decided that the teaching work should be subordinated to the construction of the House of Worship. The promise of a magnificent House of Worship was a source of pride to Bahá'ís the world over. Thousands of postcards with a picture of the architectural drawing had been distributed far and wide. But after more than a decade that promise was far from fulfilled. Not only did the Faith still lack its 'Silent Teacher' but failing to finish the edifice was becoming an embarrassment. The good name of the Faith was dependent on completing at least the outside of the superstructure. Only a handful of believers in North America had the means to make large contributions, and as the Depression deepened those donors found it difficult to contribute as they had during the more prosperous 1920s. To resume construction, cuts had to be made to other expenses wherever possible, including the funds allocated to the teaching work. This meant, for example, suspending contributions from the National Fund to assist the travels of international teacher Martha Root, and financial support to the international Bahá'í office in Geneva, Switzerland, which represented the Cause to international organizations.[15]

In considering the matter of paid teachers and expenses, the National Assembly had other factors to ponder. It was aware of the unhealthy dependence upon the subsidized teachers. It became obvious that the Depression had hastened the inevitable time when the generality of believers would have to arise to carry out that crucial work as part of their daily Bahá'í service. Money was not required to tell one's neighbour or co-worker about the Cause of Bahá'u'lláh. The reason stated in the Assembly's minutes for its decision to release Vail and Gregory was that their services were needed only until the Temple structure was complete. Perhaps some members assumed that the 'Silent Teacher' would be sufficient to bring the Faith to the attention of the public.[16] It also stated in its minutes that 'It was the sense of the meeting that self-support in the Bahá'í Cause is not merely a factor conforming to the economic condition of the National Fund at the present time, but also to the spiritual principles of the Cause.'[17] Despite its dire financial constraints, the Assembly knew that, in the throes of the nation-wide economic crisis, neither Vail nor Gregory were likely to easily secure alternative employment, so it decided that both should receive ten months of severance pay – rare generosity during the Depression.[18]

Neither Vail nor Gregory quietly accepted the National Assembly's decision, and both were quick to engage supporters to come to their rescue. When voices were raised questioning the wisdom of the decision, the National Assembly laid the matter before Shoghi Effendi, asking if it should rescind its decision to eliminate the institution of paid national teachers, though it added that it was not inclined to reverse the decision. Vail insisted he had been instructed by 'Abdu'l-Bahá to leave his post as a Christian minister to serve the Faith, though there was no firm evidence to support that claim. The National Assembly wanted to do 'everything possible to retain Albert's loyalty and activity', stating to Shoghi Effendi that 'the situation is so delicate that we are afraid that anything we might write or say to Albert would be misunderstood'.[19]

Vail believed with some accuracy that the Guardian was behind the decision.[20] When he went on pilgrimage for the first time, he had watched 'Abdu'l-Bahá correct Shoghi Effendi, who was then still a minor. It immediately occurred to Vail that Shoghi Effendi was not perfect and all-knowing like his Grandfather. Thus, when the Guardian became Head of the Faith, Vail's allegiance to him was tentative. His attitude was the same towards the Local and National Spiritual Assemblies when they assumed the roles previously held by the Temple Unity Executive Board. He never fully understood the need for obedience to elected institutions made up of people who were less knowledgeable than he was. Years earlier, 'Abdu'l-Bahá had informed Albert that in the future, he would become blind. Vail therefore set about memorizing as much of the Bahá'í Writings as possible, believing that, at some point in his life, he would lose his eyesight. It did not occur to him that 'Abdu'l-Bahá was referring to a different blindness. Albert never lost his physical sight, but despite many loving attempts to keep him within the Bahá'í community, he turned away from the Faith and rejoined the Unitarian ministry.[21] Despite this estrangement, he continued to tell people about Bahá'u'lláh to the end of his life.[22]

Louis Gregory had a different theory about the decision. He passionately believed that Horace was to blame and had been plotting to bring it about for years. He set out this hypothesis in a frank letter to the National Assembly, composed with the blessing and encouragement of Fred Lunt. In it, he expressed his opinion that the decision was unjust and ill-timed because his efforts in the South were bearing fruit amid the increasing hardships of the times. Had he written only to the National Assembly or the Guardian about his feelings, the matter could have been dealt with delicately and wisely. But he also expressed them openly, especially around Boston and Green Acre. Rather than criticize the institution, he let it be known that he believed Horace alone was responsible for his release from service, spreading the false idea that Horace single-handedly controlled the Assembly. It was true that other members of the Assembly often relied on Horace because of his knowledge and experience, but the National Assembly was composed of strong-willed, assertive people who would not be led by one member. The National Assembly directed its chairman, Allen McDaniel, to speak with Louis on its behalf. This conversation occurred some months after the initial shock rocked Louis, and by then Allen found that his attitude was slowly changing. Louis began to recognize that the decision was made by a deliberative corporate body after consultation, and not by a single member. He also accepted that financial realities made the decision unavoidable.[23] A few months after meeting with McDaniel, Louis apologized to Horace for his sharp attacks on him in a letter to the National Assembly, writing, 'I regret any grief that may have come to you or others from any comments of mine. The fact that my own feelings may have been wounded does not justify one, in the light of the teachings, of being hurtful to others.'[24] Both men put this sad episode behind them and, over the years, drew closer as friends, especially when Louis re-joined the membership of the National Assembly.

* * * * *

A rebellion of those opposed to the authority of the National Assembly was percolating. It was centred mainly in the Boston area, home of Fred Lunt and many of the friends who agreed with his positions on a variety of subjects. Others were in the New York area. In the minds of some believers, Horace was associated with another group. Inevitably, the two would clash. And that is what happened at the 1933 National Convention.

Fred Lunt's sympathisers quietly approached delegates to ensure that he would be elected chairman of the Convention. Fred used that position to talk, filling much of the consultation time with his own comments. He allowed non-delegates to have the floor and a small number of individuals to monopolize the Convention sessions. The agenda set in advance by the National Assembly was ignored as the Convention bounced from one topic to another. The delegates, especially Fred's friends, still believed that they were part of a legislative body called upon to make decisions, rather than part of a consultative institution that was authorized only to give suggestions to the National Assembly. Resolution after resolution was proposed, ad hoc committees were hastily formed to investigate each proposal during the period of the Convention, and decisions were rendered by vote as though each matter at hand was settled once and for all. The other eight outgoing members of the previous National Assembly sat in Foundation Hall silently observing this. They were all dismayed. Elected secretary of the Convention, Horace seldom spoke unless his office required it, and then kept his remarks brief.[25] The Convention was out of control. Worse, away from the official sessions, gossip, rumours, and backbiting were rampant.[26]

The Convention had one universal effect – those who attended left stirred up. One friend wrote to Horace saying, 'Wasn't it an awful Convention! . . . "The flag of unity is not yet unfurled." How the Supreme Concourse must have wept over us in Baha'u'llah's Temple!'[27]

In the Convention's aftermath, Allen McDaniel wrote to Horace and recommended that the National Assembly send a report to Shoghi Effendi as soon as possible, saying 'It is clearly evident from the recent Convention that Fred Lunt and several others hold the view that the Convention is the time and place for a relatively few of the believers to air personal grievances and to function on the personal plane,' and he recommended that the Assembly ask the Guardian for guidance.[28]

The report Horace sent to Haifa explained it was the considered view of the majority of the members of the Assembly that the National Convention had never evolved along with the other components of the Administrative Order. He characterized what had happened as an effort by a small but aggressive group to gain control of the Convention.

> Immediately on opening, the Convention seemed to come under the influence of a relatively small group of delegates and non-delegates who had apparently made up their minds to accomplish certain specific results. The agenda was either put aside or made the vehicle for carrying out these plans for a period of two days. During that time the majority of delegates remained silent, and appeared uneasy and disturbed by the existence of many cross currents of personal emotion and will. The time of the election was changed, clearly to allow more opportunity for influencing the result. Delegates were

approached and urged to voice certain complaints, and the inability of Assembly members residing in the West to attend every meeting was expounded at length.[29]

The National Assembly held a special session in the midst of the Convention and decided not to intervene, even though the rights of the majority of delegates were being trampled upon by a few people. After more than a day of being dominated by a minority, other delegates started to voice their concerns about the flow of the proceedings, insisting that the Convention return to its essential business. When the results of the election were announced, there were no changes to the membership; Fred Lunt, the leader of the insurgents, received the least number of votes of the nine. It was apparent from the expression on the faces of his allies that the election results were a surprise to those who had tried to change the make-up of the Assembly. This entire episode seemed to Horace – speaking freely as an individual within the letter to the Guardian – to indicate a strong need for greater study of the fundamental principles of Bahá'í administration. He concluded the articles on that subject appearing in *Bahá'í News* had not been enough to educate the believers.[30]

The basic problem appeared to the National Assembly to be a lack of understanding about the differing roles played by the Assembly and the annual Conventions; roles which had changed after 1922.

> After attending ten consecutive Conventions, I can state without reservation that all Bahá'í matters in America have been brought into the circle of unity except the Convention, which remains psychologically almost where it was in the days of the Bahá'í Temple Unity.[31]

While the National Assembly awaited a response from Haifa, exasperated, it devised a strategy to prevent future Conventions from getting out of control. It decided to propose amending Article VIII, Section 7 of the By-Laws to eliminate the election of Convention officers by the delegates. Instead, the officers of the outgoing National Assembly would fill those positions. With its own chairman moderating the consultation, the Convention would carry out its mission of making suggestions, not decisions. No longer would it be possible to hijack a

Convention. Fred Lunt was vehemently opposed to the change and was probably the member who cast the sole dissenting vote.[32] The National Assembly expected to be criticized for this change but, as Horace commented to the Guardian,

> Our own view is that the Convention almost every year has been invaded by negative and political elements which, by reason of the previous Convention procedure, have exerted an influence entirely out of proportion to their real value to the Cause, and that the amendment is an essential protection to the entire body of delegates against the disturbance either consciously or unconsciously fomented by a very few.[33]

* * * * *

In His Will and Testament, 'Abdu'l-Bahá warned the believers 'to take the greatest care of Shoghi Effendi . . . that no dust of despondency and sorrow may stain his radiant nature . . .',[34] for his heart was like a barometer. The slightest report of disunity would affect not only the Guardian's mood, but his health, sometimes sending him to bed. One can imagine the dire effect the reports of the 1933 Convention had on him.

Troubles cannot wait. The National Assembly had much to do to restore the unity lost at the Convention; however, the ongoing problem of distance stood in its way, making it impossible to get a quorum. In July, because of the chairman's health problems, only four members were able to attend the scheduled meeting, not enough to conduct business. These four members consulted but had to leave their conclusions to be ratified at a future meeting. As Horace related to Shoghi Effendi, 'we felt it necessary to make every possible effort to contribute to the continuance of the work'.[35] Getting a quorum continued to hamper the Assembly throughout the tumultuous 1933 to 1934 term of service.[36]

An alarmed Shoghi Effendi rose to the occasion by providing clear answers to the North American community through the National Spiritual Assembly.

> . . . the supreme body in the United States and Canada, whose privilege and function is to lay down, amend and abrogate the

administrative principles of the Faith with the approval of the Guardian, is not the Convention, however representative it may be, but the N.S.A.[37]

Despite its overarching authority, the National Assembly was cautioned not to inhibit the delegates.

> . . . it is the sacred obligation and the primary function of the National Assembly not to restrict under any circumstances, the freedom of the assembled delegates, whose twofold function is to elect their national representatives and to submit to them any recommendations they may feel inclined to make.[38]

The letter, however, emphasized that the annual National Convention was not a legislature.

> The function of the Convention is purely advisory and though the advice it gives is not binding in its effect on those on whom rest the final decision in purely administrative matters, yet, the utmost caution and care should be exercised lest anything should hamper the delegates in the full and free exercise of their function.[39]

Shoghi Effendi recommended that the National Assembly's decision to amend the By-Laws so that its own officers would serve as the officers of the Convention be given further thought in light of his guidance, though he did not directly overrule it. The delegates had the right to elect their officers. Should the National Assembly instead appoint the officers, it would appear that the outgoing National Assembly members were 'seeking to direct the course of the discussion in a manner that would be conducive to their own personal interests'.[40]

A postscript in Shoghi Effendi's own hand at the end of the letter reiterated the 'undisputed authority of America's supreme Bahá'í administrative body', while he reaffirmed 'the untrammelled freedom of individual believers and delegates to exercise their functions'. He concluded by cautioning that 'utmost care and vigilance should be exercised lest any fresh misunderstandings arise regarding these fundamental issues'.[41]

On the day that the letter was written to the National Assembly, another was written on behalf of Shoghi Effendi to Alfred Lunt containing many of the same points. The second also addressed one point Lunt had raised in his letter to the Guardian, the role of prominent individuals. This was not a simple matter for him to understand in a Faith where all individuals serving on elected institutions were equal, not only regarding their fellow members, but equal to those they served. The same principle applied to those dedicated to teaching the Cause full-time. The institutions, as corporate entities, were the ones with a high station in the community of believers.

> Regarding the principle that the Cause must not be allowed to center around any Bahá'í personality, the Guardian wishes to make it clear that it was never intended that well qualified individual teachers should not receive from local Assemblies every encouragement and facilities to address the public. What the Guardian meant was that the personality and popularity of such a speaker should never be allowed to eclipse the authority, or detract from the influence of the body of the elected representatives in every local community. Such an individual should not only seek the approval, advice and assistance of the body that represents the Cause in his locality, but should strive to attribute any credit he may obtain to the collective wisdom and capacity of the Assembly under whose jurisdiction he performs his services. Assemblies and not individuals constitute the bed-rock on which the Administration is built. Everything else must be subordinated to, and be made to serve and advance the best interests of these elected custodians and promoters of the Laws of Bahá'u'lláh.[42]

Had Fred Lunt taken to heart the response he received from the Guardian and considered all issues settled, unity could have been restored quickly. But that is not what happened next.

Any criticism of Bahá'í administrative institutions was contrary to the very spirit of the Covenant of Bahá'u'lláh, because it undermined the authority of those institutions. The Bahá'í administrative structure included appropriate occasions such as the Nineteen Day Feast, when the friends could point out problems and offer suggestions, and there was also a right to appeal a decision of an Assembly. The Assemblies were warned against wielding dictatorial authority, just as the friends were enjoined to be supportive of all decisions of the Assemblies. Not that these local and national Assemblies were infallible; this injunction was necessary to prevent the greater harms arising from disunity.

Horace realized that there was another element to the principle of accepting rule by the majority: timeliness. In a talk to the New York City community in 1931, he related how he remembered 'Abdu'l-Bahá explaining the importance of submission to the will of the majority:

> . . . as Abdul Baha says, if a situation arises in which an individual is convinced by all the wisdom and all the intelligence and all the experience at his command that he is right and the group is wrong, nevertheless he has to yield up that individual sense of right for the sake of the collective wisdom. Now how can we reconcile this apparent fallacy? It seems to me that the truth has more than two or three dimensions. One way of understanding the mystery implied in the master's [sic] command is that a certain proposal, we will say, is made and is rejected by the law of consultation. That proposal may have been put forward by the wisest one of the group. It may be rejected because the others are incapable of understanding or appreciating it. Why then should the wise one yield his sense of right to the group? It is because, I feel, in matters of that kind truth is conditioned by another factor and that is time. A thing can be theoretically right and yet not valid until the conditions are ready for it, and there if in a given set of circumstances an individual may put forward a proposal which is rejected by a law of consultation, we may be sure the time for the proposal was not right. It was a tremendous thing which Shogi [sic] Effendi said to Mrs. Maxwell in Haifa some years ago. 'Let the friends remember that the spirit of Baha'u'llah confirms only the result of spiritual consultation.'[43]

The Guardian had explained in unequivocal language that the Convention was a separate Bahá'í institution with its own responsibilities and limitations. After studying his letter, the National Assembly rescinded its earlier decision to eliminate the election of Convention officers by the delegates. It also decided that the By-Laws did not accurately reflect their new and more complete understanding of the role of the Convention. It therefore reexamined that document with an eye to bringing it into conformity with Shoghi Effendi's August letter.

The issue underlying the division within the community was

fundamental. Those who wanted to bring back a strong National Convention with the right to override decisions of the National Assembly did so because they were afraid of vesting all national authority solely in a group of nine people, even though they were elected.[44] They wanted the Convention to have the ability to check that authority through more than a ballot box, just as the American Government with its three-pronged structure – legislature, executive, judiciary – was carefully designed to be a system of checks and balances. The history of the United States Republic is a story of the push and pull between those favouring a strong central government and those insisting that authority should rest primarily at the local level based upon the adage, 'the government which governs best governs least'. Those fearing that a powerful National Assembly would exert its authority with a heavy hand failed to appreciate that the Guardian and, later, the Universal House of Justice would provide the check on Local and National Assemblies. Having annual elections for the local and national bodies also meant that an Assembly that had lost the confidence of those it served would not keep the same membership for long.

Fred Lunt viewed the National Assembly's interest in revising the section of the By-Laws dealing with the Convention as another opportunity to cement his understanding of the Convention as co-equal to the Assembly. He wrote again to Shoghi Effendi. The response he received showed that there were limits to Shoghi Effendi's patience with Lunt's persistent criticism of the National Assembly and his unwillingness to wholeheartedly accept his guidance.

> In regard to your criticism of the Article VIII of the By-Laws of the National Spiritual Assembly, the Guardian wishes you to know that since this is a secondary matter arising out of the general principle he has already laid down in one of his latest communications addressed to you and to the National Spiritual Assembly concerning the power of the delegates and the relation of these to the National Assembly, he does not think it is necessary for him to enter into these details which by their very nature fall within the jurisdiction of the National Spiritual Assembly. It is to that body which you should submit any criticism, whether in regard to the provisions of the Constitution, or in connection with any other phase of the administrative work of the Cause. It is not for the Guardian to enter

into matters of detail. His overwhelming and pressing duties, and the very nature of his position as the supreme Guardian of the Faith, make it impossible for him to interfere in affairs of a local character, and of a relatively secondary importance. It is for you, as one of the distinguished members of the highest administrative body of the Cause in the States, to remind your fellow-members of what is their duty to consider and to act upon. The Guardian lays down the general principle, and it is for the National Assembly to direct all Local Assemblies and groups as to the best way they can apply it to their local conditions.[45]

Lunt, nonetheless, continued to be dissatisfied. In April, shortly before the 1934 Convention, he penned a letter on behalf of the Boston Spiritual Assembly which was critical of the National Assembly. It was sent to Bahá'í communities across the United States and Canada. Other members of the Boston Assembly later reported that Lunt wrote and sent the letter on his own without the Assembly's approval,[46] though several of the Boston members agreed with its contents. This public criticism of the National Assembly as an institution by one of its members raised the issue of how to work harmoniously with Fred to a higher level. The National Assembly determined it had no other option but to act. It once again sought the guidance of Shoghi Effendi before sending a letter to all Local Assemblies which, though not addressing Lunt's letter specifically, provided definitive guidance about administrative principles. Horace candidly stated in a letter to the Guardian that:

> There is no doubt that the Annual Convention still stirs up a great deal of self-consciousness among the friends. Year after year it serves as the stage for egoistic performance, directed in some cases toward the end of electing certain believers and in others toward the end of preventing certain believers from being re-elected. The National Spiritual Assembly itself must bear the chief responsibility, in that collectively it has failed to rise above the clamor and stand firmly united for the true principles underlying the various personal issues which are raised. This year the situation appears to have come to a climax, and I am convinced that the National Spiritual Assembly by an overwhelming majority will assert and insist upon correct procedure without the slightest regard for any personal considerations.

In the days of Baha'i Temple Unity the Conventions were largely dominated by human politics operated behind the screen of false piety. That is the element which still lingers among some of the old believers, and the justification advanced is that the Convention, in some mysterious way, is a separate and superior Baha'i body, as it was perhaps at the time the Master instructed the Convention, rather than Baha'i Temple Unity, to select the Temple design.[47]

In response to an individual who wrote to Shoghi Effendi about Lunt's Boston letter, the Guardian's secretary responded on his behalf that:

As to the problem which has arisen in connection with the News Letter published and circulated by the Boston Assembly, the Guardian has already written about it to your N. S. A., expressing the view that under no circumstances should any local Assembly be given the right to criticize and much less oppose, the policy duly adopted and approved by the N. S. A. It is his hope that henceforth the problem of the relationship between the N. S. A. and the local Assemblies in matters of this nature will, in the light of his instructions, be carefully understood by individuals and Assemblies alike.[48]

* * * * *

The 1934 National Convention was long remembered as a low point in the development of the Faith in the United States. Just before it convened, Horace was convinced that the steps taken by the National Assembly would prevent problems, as he candidly wrote to a friend, 'I do not believe this convention will be as hellish as the last one, because by now the National Assembly has learned that it must intervene when the delegates go off the track.'[49] His optimism misjudged the spirit of the moment.

In response to the Boston circular, the National Assembly decided to present two straightforward statements to the delegates immediately before the official opening of the Convention. The first was a comprehensive statement about the spiritual nature of the Convention, its parameters, and prerogatives. It clarified that those who were not delegates could not take part directly in the consultation, even though they could be present as observers. The second statement, which addressed the Boston letter, was so blunt that it elicited a vehement reaction when read aloud to the attendees.

The National Assembly was frustrated that the comments and actions of delegates were indicative that they were either ignorant of or ignoring the guidance of the Guardian. It had attempted to educate all the community about Bahá'í administration by printing Shoghi Effendi's letters in the February 1930 edition of *Bahá'í News*. In the wake of the 1933 Convention, it republished the same guidance with the addition of the Guardian's August 1933 clarifications about the nature and role of the Convention. For good measure, this was republished twice, in the November 1933, and again in the February 1934 editions of *Bahá'í News*. To ensure that those who had not yet studied that guidance had another opportunity to become familiar with it, the Assembly reemphasized the Guardian's guidance in its first statement to the 1934 Convention. The tone of the opening paragraphs did not hide the Assembly's exasperation with the delegates' prior failure to abide by the words of Shoghi Effendi.

The second statement prepared for the 1934 Convention reflected the National Assembly's institutional growing pains, especially its incomplete understanding of when candour was warranted and when it was not. To understand why the National Assembly issued the statement, it must be understood that, from the beginning, all Bahá'í institutions make their decisions in confidence. It is vital to protecting that confidentiality that all members are prohibited from sharing what transpired in the council chamber unless the Assembly gives them permission to do so. Having assurance of confidentiality makes it possible for members to speak frankly and for sensitive information to be shared. Inevitably, it seemed unfair to members that, whenever the institution was criticized, they were enjoined from explaining or defending its decisions. Fred had violated the trust of the Assembly by repeatedly reporting to others what transpired confidentially in the meetings. What was worse, he misrepresented the Assembly's decisions and motivations. The Assembly bore his behaviour with patient silence for years, but when the Boston letter containing misinformation as well as sharp criticism of the institution was widely disseminated, it decided it must defend itself. Years later, other institutions – not yet born in 1934 – could have assisted the Assembly rendering public defence unnecessary,[50] but the Assembly had few options at the time, other than to allow the situation to fester as it was.

The National Assembly's written response to Lunt's challenges to its authority got directly to the point.

> The general letter broadcast by the Boston Assembly in April brings to the surface and makes public a condition which challenges the integrity of the administrative structure of the Cause in America. That letter can only be understood when it is read against the proper background. To see in it merely a circular letter prepared and issued by a local Spiritual Assembly is to see but a small part of the questions actually involved. That letter, in reality, is an act of public rebellion against the National Spiritual Assembly by one of its members – the enlargement and reinforcement of the attitude of disaffection of a minority against the majority of his own Assembly. It is, moreover, a direct disobedience to one of the Guardian's specific instructions.[51]

The statement provided a general history of the problems and provided the Bahá'í principles that applied, including, 'The [National] Assembly recognizes no "minority" but only the unity established by decisive vote.'[52] It reported that, after the previous Convention, the National Assembly had been informed by multiple delegates that they had been approached improperly in order to influence their vote in the annual election. It listed other problems from the previous year, including that its business sessions had been dominated by a few assertive voices, leaving little space for contrary viewpoints. The most disturbing reports to reach the National Assembly after the Convention stated that vague rumours questioning the character of individual believers were quietly spread during the social periods outside of the formal proceedings.[53]

In response to the allegations of the Boston letter, the National Assembly reported what had occurred during the past year regarding the possibility of amending the By-Laws and recounted its exchange with Shoghi Effendi regarding that issue. The National Assembly asserted the Boston letter addressing this confidential correspondence was proof that a member of the National Assembly was involved in drafting it. Fred Lunt was never named throughout the statement, but it was obvious to whom it referred. The National Assembly expressed consternation that one of its members used a Local Assembly to 'spread the spirit of disaffection broadcast among the friends', especially when that member had been unequivocally instructed by the Guardian to direct his concerns only to the National Assembly.⁵⁴ The sentiments in the Boston letter seemed reminiscent of partisan politics and had created factions. A letter to the chairman of the National Assembly written on behalf of Shoghi Effendi, which warned against factions, was quoted:

> The Cause is not and should never be considered as a political organization led by party leaders. It is a divine institution whose responsible administrators should consider themselves as mere channels whereby God protects and guides His Faith. The administration should never be allowed to become a bone of contention between individuals and groups. It stands above human personalities and transcends the scope of their limited and inevitably selfish ideas. Its custodians should continually purge themselves of every trace of personal desire or interest and become wholly imbued with the spirit of love, of cooperation and of genuine self-sacrifice.⁵⁵

At the end of the letter to the chairman, Shoghi Effendi, in his own handwriting, expressed that the controversy in the United States had upset him and reminded the National Assembly that the entire Bahá'í world was watching what happened in America. The Assembly further quoted from that same note, that, 'The supreme authority, essential unity and harmonious functioning of the highest administrative institution in that land must at all costs be maintained. Nothing must be allowed to happen that would in the least impair its effectiveness, lower its prestige, or undermine its authority.'⁵⁶

The National Assembly ended its plainspoken statement by declaring that it had laid bare the situation, which had gone on for years, to place it squarely in the hands of the delegates. It called upon them to put aside loyalty to personalities and to focus instead upon what was best for the Cause.

To the surprise of those attending the Convention, the National Assembly had both statements read aloud before the Convention was formally called to order. Halfway through the reading of the second statement, Fred Lunt abruptly interrupted, claiming that the National Assembly had no right to read anything before the Convention was convened, claiming that the acting chairman had broken a promise to him not to do so. Neither assertion was true.

As expected, the National Assembly's second statement sparked an uproar. Fred Lunt was given the floor and then addressed the Convention for about an hour and twenty minutes without pause, during which he restated the points in the Boston letter – essentially that the National Assembly was attempting to deprive the delegates of their rights and was concealing this intention. One of Fred's friends then made a resolution that the statement of the National Assembly be erased from the Convention's official record as an act of magnanimity and kindness and, by vote, it was adopted. In response, the National Assembly met and drafted another statement to the delegates, which was even more frank than the previous statement, this time naming names. It explicitly reiterated that only the Guardian could reverse an action of the National Assembly, not a Local Assembly or the Convention. It upheld its decision to report its complaint against its member saying that what had transpired confirmed the wisdom of that decision, for Lunt 'has carried a spirit of partisanship and of contempt for the institution of the N.S.A. and scattered it like embers of suspicion into the hearts of the Baha'is'. It went on to say, 'He has done his utmost to influence the result of the annual election, posing as the champion of the rights of delegates while flagrantly overriding the Guardian's instructions concerning the spiritual character of Baha'i elections.'[57]

The National Assembly agreed with the resolution that magnanimity and kindness were important, but only 'up to a point'. Above all, the Assembly had to 'uphold the integrity of the institution itself. The sole issue before the National Assembly, and consequently the sole issue before the delegates, is whether the American Baha'is are concerned with personality or with the upbuilding of the permanent institutions of the Cause.'[58]

When the votes of the annual election were tallied, the National Spiritual Assembly's membership had not changed. Fred Lunt and his other eight colleagues would have to try harder to get along. Both sides felt vindicated.[59]

As a delegate elected to represent the Boston community, Lunt returned home and, reported what had transpired to his community. He took that opportunity to further criticize the National Assembly. The 1934 Convention had been just another skirmish in a conflict that was not yet over.

Shortly after the Convention, the National Assembly received the following supportive note from the Guardian in his own hand.

I wish to reaffirm in clear and categorical language, the principle already enunciated upholding the supreme authority of the National Assembly in all matters that affect the interests of the Faith in that land. There can be no conflict of authority, no duality under any form or circumstances in any sphere of Baha'i jurisdiction whether local, national or international. The National Assembly, however, although the sole interpreter of its Declaration of Trust and By-Laws, is directly and morally responsible if it allows any body or institution within its jurisdiction to abuse its privileges or to decline in the exercise of its rights and privileges. It is the trusted guardian and the mainspring of the manifold activities and interests of every national community in the Baha'i world. It constitutes the sole link that binds these communities to the International House of Justice, the supreme administrative body in the Dispensation of Baha'u'llah.[60]

Over the next month, credible reports reached the National Assembly from Boston that Lunt's attitude and behaviour were the same despite all that had occurred at the Convention. He continued to openly rail against the National Assembly at local meetings. Firm, decisive action appeared to be the only solution to an intractable problem. The National Assembly consulted and then took the drastic, unprecedented action of expelling Fred from its membership. It took no immediate steps to announce the expulsion to the community because it first wanted to obtain the approval and guidance of the Guardian, whom the Assembly cabled immediately. Though Lunt was not present during the consultation and vote, he arrived at the meeting later that day and was informed of the decision 'in a very quiet and dignified way'. Shocked, Lunt informed his allies at once.[61] He then wrote a letter of appeal to the National Assembly[62] and followed it with a letter to all of the delegates. The effect of Lunt's own letters was to announce his removal far and wide.

Horace wrote a letter on behalf of the National Assembly to Shoghi Effendi, explaining the most recent events and enclosing two reports about Fred from Boston, including one from the Boston Assembly's chairman, as well as Lunt's letter to the delegates. He reminded Shoghi Effendi that Lunt had 'never been in any spiritual sense a member of the N.S.A., but has pursued a course of his own which at almost every critical point has deviated from the course taken by the body as a whole. As long as the National Assembly asserted no internal discipline this independent course caused a great deal of confusion but never culminated in open rebellion until a standard of unity and loyalty was definitely established.'[63] The true reason for Fred's removal was that for at least a decade, many institution members had found it difficult to work with him. He did not seem to be thinking clearly, which Horace thought might indicate some 'abnormal mentality'. The letter concluded by saying, 'It is the conviction of the N.S.A. that the case is utterly hopeless. We do not regard his lack of truthfulness as lies or deceit in the usual meaning of the word but as a deviation from normal reality with which we are unable to deal as members of the N.A.'[64]

A cablegram from the Guardian dated 13 July 1934 was unequivocal. The National Assembly was required to reconsider removing Fred Lunt from its membership.

> . . . VIEW GRAVE CONCERN CONSEQUENCE DRASTIC ACTION FEEL ABSOLUTE NECESSITY RECONSIDER SITUATION ENABLE LUNT RETAIN MEMBERSHIP SHOGHI[65]

The cable was followed by a letter reemphasizing the importance of the National Assembly reconsidering its decision because,

> He feels that at the present juncture in the development of the Administration such an action on the part of the N.S.A. would not only create misunderstandings and misapprehensions as to its real nature and purpose, but would in addition greatly depress and cause much spiritual harm to one of its members who has already attained such a distinction both in the teaching & administrative fields of service.[66]

Shoghi Effendi pointed out that by being magnanimous towards Lunt, the National Assembly 'would considerably add to its power and influence by demonstrating the true spirit which animates its deliberations and decisions'.[67]

As secretary, Horace was privy to confidential information about challenges within the community. Unfortunately, as the spokesman for the institution, he was often the target of those who were upset with the decisions of the National Assembly. As Fred stirred up his supporters in both the New York area and Boston, Horace candidly expressed to a former National Assembly member his own exasperation with what seemed an endless problem, not just with Lunt, but with other malcontents within the community.

> Lord! The problems in the Cause! (I'm thinking now of Boston and Fred Lunt) Sometimes I wonder whether it wouldn't be better if the delegates elected only kindergarten teachers or physicians and psychologists to the N.S.A. We poor laymen, trying to uphold the fundamental principles, are continually surrounded by conditions and attitudes that resemble a nursery when they don't resemble an asylum!
> Well, we'll keep struggling.[68]

With the grave matter before it, the National Assembly moved its next meeting to Chicago so that members from the West Coast could attend. In the interim, the West Coast members debated among themselves how best to proceed. George Latimer from Portland and Leroy Ioas from San Francisco met together and discussed the issue at length, concluding that the Guardian's cable was not so much a command as it was a call to reconsider the Assembly's decision. In their joint letter to their colleagues, they stated that 'under the present situation, and without a change in his attitude, we could not conscientiously vote to continue his membership'.[69]

At its next meeting, the National Assembly reconsidered the Lunt matter as the Guardian requested, and then sent the following cable to Shoghi Effendi.

> ADMONITION RECONSIDER LUNT MEMBERSHIP CONSCIENTIOUSLY HEEDED. CONTINUED AGITATION AND UNCHANGED DISRUPTIVE SPIRIT COMPEL ASSEMBLY REAFFIRM ITS ACTION. STOP. ASSEMBLY MAKING NO PUBLIC STATEMENT PENDING YOUR FINAL DECISION.[70]

The Guardian responded that he did not approve of the Assembly's reaffirmation of the expulsion, and so to solve the situation, he himself would appeal to Alfred Lunt to stop criticizing the National Assembly.

As more reports of the disunity seizing the American Bahá'í community reached the Holy Land, the Guardian sent the most forthright statement yet, which the National Assembly printed in a prominent spot in *Bahá'í News*.

> Present controversy agitating American believers if unchecked will through its inevitable world-wide repercussions inflict irreparable injury (upon) Cause (of) Baha'u'llah. Nothing short (of the) following measures can avert threatening danger: retention (of) Lunt's membership, and inflexible resolve by whomsoever directly or remotely concerned (to) refrain from slightest criticism, expressed or implied, that must necessarily impair (the) undivided authority (of the) institution (of the) National Assembly. Even barest reference to issues involved should be instantly dropped (and) forgotten. Concentrate precious energies (upon) uninterrupted prosecution (of) divinely appointed enterprise. Appeal entire community (to) heed (my) passionate entreaty (and) grave warning.
> (Signed) Shoghi
> Haifa, Palestine,
> August 20, 1934[71]

The day after that cable was received, the National Assembly sent the Guardian a response:

> IMMEDIATE COMPLETE OBEDIENCE FROM ASSEMBLY[72]

Shoghi Effendi well appreciated that the National Assembly had been through an emotionally wrenching controversy. Disunity within the body of the institution not only retarded the ability of the Assembly to carry out its vital work, but deeply hurt the hearts of its members. For most of the members of the National Assembly, Lunt was an old friend. None of them had forgotten his many achievements and his long-time dedication to the Cause of God. The Guardian's response to the Assembly's cable, especially his signature, conveyed his feelings towards the National Assembly.

> PROFOUNDLY APPRECIATE ASSEMBLYS EXEMPLARY RESPONSE LOVE SHOGHI[73]

Alfred Lunt would remain on the National Assembly until 1937, at which time his health made it impossible for him to continue serving. He passed away in August of that year. In his cable responding to Lunt's death, Shoghi Effendi extolled the 'esteemed well-beloved Lunt', adding that 'Future generations will appraise his manifold outstanding contributions to rise and establishment Faith Bahá'u'lláh American Continent'.[74] He requested that the entire membership of the National Spiritual Assembly visit his grave in Boston to pay tribute to him on behalf of the Guardian because of the significant role he had played in the establishment and development of the National Assembly. The troubles were forgotten, and only his achievements would be remembered, for he had earned the distinction of being the first secretary the National Spiritual Assembly, the foundation of the future National House of Justice which would in an age to come become the primary national governing body serving millions. He was a champion builder of that foundation.

* * * * *

From the time of the first election of a National Spiritual Assembly in 1922, there had been episodes during which individuals or minority groups sought to influence the outcome of its membership through electioneering. Far into the future, stifling such practices imported from the greater society into the sacred space of Bahá'í elections would continue to vex Bahá'í institutions. Horace shared a conversation he had had with a former member of the National Assembly on that topic.

> He told me yesterday that it was discouraging to him to see political tactics apparently succeed our honest NSA work. This is a very deep spiritual problem for a Baha'i. We all meet it in one form or another. I am wrestling with it . . . Anyhow, I'm praying that we will touch together a new height of understanding. Somehow the institutions of a Divine Faith have been established, and must develop, in a human community that possesses so much weakness and is the victim of its own immaturity. The institutions are like boats that must pass through terrible rapids before they emerge into the sea. There are rocks outside, & sometimes the crew itself is grievously divided. And meanwhile the world releases all the turbulence of the day of judgment! All I can say is, it is a holy and surpassing privilege

to cherish and protect these institutions of the Most Great Peace, &
<u>to</u> <u>have</u> <u>their</u> <u>qualities</u> even when not a member . . . That is reality –
all else is froth of human imagination and desire.⁷⁵

Looking back as the year 1934 drew to a close, it seemed as though the National Assembly had been suffering from a grave, life-threatening fever. Finally, the fever broke in the heat of summer, and recuperation began. Perhaps the true underlying cause of the strongly held differences of opinion was a basic lack of understanding of the verities of the Faith.⁷⁶ Two years earlier, a small number of Western women who were all pillars of their communities arrived at the same time in the Holy Land as pilgrims. When they met together informally with Shoghi Effendi and conversed about the situations in their home communities, especially in the United States, the Guardian was flabbergasted to learn that the knowledge and understanding of basic beliefs of the Cause was shallow and often incorrect among many Western believers. This was not only true regarding the spiritual vision and nature of the Administrative Order, but also regarding the divinely ordained stations of the Central Figures of the Faith: Bahá'u'lláh, the Báb, and 'Abdu'l-Bahá.⁷⁷ The station of 'Abdu'l-Bahá was particularly confusing because to those from Christian backgrounds who met Him, His perfections and mystical powers seemed to be proof that He was the Return of Jesus.

Shoghi Effendi remedied this problem by penning his immortal work, *The Dispensation of Bahá'u'lláh*, promulgated in 1934. He devoted in-depth discussions to each of the Central Figures and one to Bahá'í administration, including newly translated excerpts from the Sacred Texts. When it was republished within a collection of his letters in 1938, the Guardian gave Horace permission to add titles and subtitles to the text. Shoghi Effendi's wife, Rúḥíyyih <u>Kh</u>ánum, later wrote that *The Dispensation of Bahá'u'lláh* 'burst upon the Bahá'ís like a blinding white light' and that she knew from her husband's own comments that 'he considered he had said all he had to say, in many ways, in the *Dispensation*'.⁷⁸

In the end, the sad chapter centering on Alfred Lunt played a decisive role in developing the capacities of Bahá'í institutions. New guidance regarding the role of the Convention, the appealing of decisions of the National Assembly, and the authority of the institutions, not only in relationship to individuals but to each other, were provided by the Guardian over the course of the two years it took to resolve the matter. This invaluable guidance became an essential resource to the Baháʼí community worldwide forever. The National Assembly itself learned that unity was always the most important consideration, even when an individual member seemed unbearable.

Horace continued to serve as secretary of the National Assembly for another quarter of a century. Never during those later years would the National Assembly confront an internal problem as severe as that posed by its first secretary. As the early believers whose understandings of the Faith were formed during the Temple Unity period passed from the scene, the next generation of Baháʼís raised up under the Administrative Order took their place with clearer appreciation of what the institutions were and how as individuals they should respond to them.

11

UNDERSTANDING THE QUEST FOR WORLD PEACE: THE CONTINUING EDUCATION OF HORACE HOLLEY

The search for a principle of unity capable of binding together the peoples of the world in some valid and creative relationship is undeniably the essential matter confronting the present generation.
Horace Holley[1]

One time at Green Acre, Horace spoke to a group of youth about insights. He advised his listeners to act as quickly as possible whenever they received a flash of insight or an idea, even if only to jot down the thought, because those quick bursts of mental light were gifts from God.[2] A significant example of the insights springing from the fountain of inspirations continuously flowing from Horace's busy mind was one he gingerly shared with Shoghi Effendi in 1924. He proposed an annual yearbook extolling and explaining the accomplishments of the worldwide Bahá'í community during the previous year. Such a work might not only educate and inspire the believers but could inform the public of the teachings and advancement of the Faith.[3] Shoghi Effendi lost no time in implementing this suggestion and placed much of the responsibility for carrying it out upon Horace's shoulders. The first volume of the *Bahá'í Year Book* appeared in 1925. Though published under the supervision of the National Spiritual Assembly of the United States and Canada, its true Editor-in-Chief was the Guardian.

In 1925 when Horace began to work full-time for the National Assembly from his cottage at Green Acre, he wrote with more than a little pride to his brother Irving about this new worldwide publication, for he found his writing projects for the Faith to be 'intensely interesting'. Already, he was looking long into the future by describing *The Bahá'í World* as an annual publication 'which will develop into something of international interest as time goes on, with a board of editors representing the Bahais of all countries'.[4] His remarks proved to be prophetic, for at the time of this writing, *The Bahá'í World* continues as a digital publication of the Bahá'í World Centre.

Perusing his first copy of the yearbook delighted Shoghi Effendi. He gave Horace full credit for its quality in a letter written on his behalf which read, 'The speedy completion, the perfect order and the appealing tone of the work, owes, he feels sure, its perfect polish greatly if not entirely to your able pen . . .' The letter conveyed that the book 'has served only to heighten and enhance his esteem and deep admiration for you and your deeply-appreciated service'.[5] That praise served as encouragement to keep Horace working, for the rest of the letter was comprised of detailed instructions for the next volume. This marked the beginning of a decades-long close association between the Guardian and Horace as the publication became dear to both hearts. Shoghi Effendi described *The Bahá'í World* as

> eminently readable and attractive in its features, reliable and authoritative in the material it contains, up-to-date, comprehensive and accurate in the mass of information it gives, concise and persuasive in its treatment of the fundamental aspects of the Cause, thoroughly representative in the illustrations and photographs it reveals – it stands unexcelled and unapproached by any publication of its kind in the varied literature of our beloved Cause.[6]

Routinely, the work on each edition began with Shoghi Effendi's secretary sending Horace the points to be included in the section of the summary of the achievements of the international Bahá'í community. This important element of each edition was always the second major section following the opening section on the aims and purposes of the Bahá'í Faith, which Horace also drafted.[7] The outline of the topics to include in the narrative contained only sparse details, anticipating that Horace would seek the information necessary to draft a coherent, comprehensive article.[8] To gather this information, Horace corresponded with Bahá'ís all over the world.[9] This extensive work on *The Bahá'í World*, therefore, provided him with an unusual glimpse into Shoghi Effendi's big picture of the overall state of the Cause – an invaluable vantage point which he could share with the National Assembly. The

Assembly was responsible for appointing an editorial board to assist with gathering and editing the material for each issue; however, the bulk of the work fell to Horace. He learned to delegate and to accompany those appointed to the board who lacked his expertise by gently instructing them how to carry out their tasks.[10]

With each passing year, the working relationship between Shoghi Effendi and Horace became more finely tuned, even though the two had never met. By the 1930s, the size of the publication had increased significantly, reflecting the growth of the community as well as the enhanced level of activity under the direction of the Guardian. *The Bahá'í World* also began to be published biennially rather than annually because of the labour and funds required to produce each edition. As Horace had envisioned when he proposed the yearbook, it found its way onto the shelves of libraries and into the hands of noteworthy people, especially in the West. After seven years of collaboration between Shoghi Effendi and Horace on producing *The Bahá'í World*, the Guardian's secretary wrote to Horace:

> It is surely a blessing for Shoghi Effendi to have people like you on whom he could rely for achieving things that time does not permit him to undertake in person. Were it not for your competence and his reliance upon your efficiency and judgment he would have to do the work of *The Bahá'í World* alone and thereby neglect many of his other duties. He is still more thankful to God when he sees you hunger for service and enjoy being over-burdened. May the Master send him many of such competent and self-sacrificing helpers.[11]

Shoghi Effendi himself echoed his secretary in his loving, handwritten postscript which said that he was 'deeply aware of the complexity and strenuous character of the work you have undertaken for *The Bahá'í World*'.[12]

* * * * *

The intended audience of *The Bahá'í World* was both Bahá'ís and those who, though not adherents, were sympathetic to its ideals. Horace, nevertheless, continued to nurse a nagging, unsatisfied desire to reach leaders of thought with the Message of Bahá'u'lláh so that its social teachings would be implemented centuries before the Faith became among the dominant world religions. This was undoubtedly the vision he and others had shared for *Reality* magazine when it was established in 1921. So far, Bahá'í periodicals were produced by and for members of the Bahá'í community and held little interest for the public. Horace was convinced that the only way to reach the upper strata of society with the Message of Bahá'u'lláh was through sharing the principles without reference to the religious source.

Either directly or as a member of Assemblies, Horace was keenly involved in most efforts to produce Bahá'í literature in English and so was always alert to opportunities to spread the Faith through the printed word. For instance, he found himself involved as a member of the New York Assembly when fellow New Yorker Howard MacNutt worked diligently to compile the talks of 'Abdu'l-Bahá given during His 1912 visit to the United States and Canada. The result was *The Promulgation of Universal Peace*, which was initially published in two volumes: the first appearing in 1922 and the second in 1925. This wonderful collection quickly became an important addition to the standard literature of the Faith – almost but not quite at the level of the Sacred Texts.[13] However, Horace thought it was not tuned finely enough to suit as an introductory text. Therefore, in 1927, while at Green Acre, he curated a second compilation, *Foundations of World Unity*, selecting from among 'Abdu'l-Bahá's myriad talks given in Europe and America as well as from His letters to individuals. He chose the content carefully to reflect the broad range of the spiritual and social teachings of the Cause without the repetition found in MacNutt's comprehensive compilation that by design included all authenticated talks. In his introduction to *Foundations*, Horace likened 'Abdu'l-Bahá to a Rosetta Stone 'inscribed with the human story in three languages – the language of the mind, the language of the heart, and the language of the spirit'.[14] Though first compiled in the 1920s and printed privately for use as a teaching resource,[15] *Foundations of World Unity* was not published as a book until 1945.

* * * * *

During His tour of the United States and Canada, 'Abdu'l-Bahá spoke numerous times about the prerequisites for world peace, setting forth the comprehensive Bahá'í peace plan. By request, He addressed several large peace societies in New York City and was invited to deliver a speech before the prestigious, invitation-only, annual Lake Mohonk Conference on International Arbitration held at a resort several hours' journey from Manhattan. His talks at Columbia University in New York and Leland Stanford University in California were bookends to His momentous journey across the continent in that these two similar lectures restated most of His other speeches on world peace.[16] His discourses on social and world trends made a lasting impression on Leroy Ioas, a young businessman living in San Francisco in the early 1920s, who would join Horace as a member of the National Spiritual Assembly in 1932 and remain his close friend to the last days of Horace's life.

Leroy was full of high ideals and abounding energy. Intelligent and resolute, he had never been afforded an opportunity for an advanced education. Nevertheless, with his penchant for hard work married to great innate capacity, he steadily rose through the ranks of executives in the railway industry.[17] Horace recognized Leroy's spiritual strengths and knowledge gained through applied self-study, telling his younger colleague that he was 'one of the few real students of the Teachings in their historical background and social setting'.[18]

Like Horace, Leroy possessed a keen interest in the wider world, especially issues related to current trends and events. His desire to ameliorate the evils and injustices around him led the young Californian to seek a means of bringing the teachings of the Faith to the attention of leaders of society. He was familiar with the 'World Unity' dinners hosted by the Portland, Oregon community, through the efforts of his friend George Latimer – another friend and future National Assembly member.[19] Leroy proposed that the San Francisco Spiritual Assembly sponsor a World Unity Conference that would address not only world peace, but racial and sexual equality. The scholarly, notable speakers who agreed to take part were almost all non-Bahá'ís. That conference, held in 1925 in one of the city's most prominent hotels, was a success, attracting large audiences and widespread positive publicity.

Ioas provided the National Spiritual Assembly with a comprehensive report of the conference with his suggestion that similar World Unity Conferences be held in other communities. The National Assembly enthusiastically adopted the idea and established a committee to assist other localities with holding them. Those appointed were Horace,

Florence Reed Morton, treasurer of the National Assembly, and writer and heiress Mary Rumsey Movius.[20] The workforce and all funds were to be supplied by the sponsoring local communities, but the national committee would aid in the promotion of each conference and offer other assistance, including speakers.

Horace was eager to take on responsibilities for the World Unity Conferences, for he had never forgotten his family's brush with the horrors of World War I in 1914. He wanted to do everything in his power to ensure that the Great War would be the last war. In October 1925, he had written to Albert Vail requesting 'Abdu'l-Bahá's Tablet addressed to the peace organization at The Hague, because Horace had heard that it prophesied that another war was coming and he was eager to bring it to the attention of the National Assembly, saying, 'We can all realize that in the present condition of the world the problem of making public such a prophecy places a great responsibility upon us . . .'[21] Some months later, after learning about the San Francisco conference, Horace wrote to Shoghi Effendi about his desire to reach out to organizations and movements that advocated many of the principles of the Faith. While the Guardian agreed that this was a worthy effort, he sounded a note of caution in the response written on his behalf.

> You mentioned in your letter your intention to come in contact with the representatives of movements who are akin to the Cause in the principles they advocate. Shoghi Effendi trusts that in all such communications and activities you would maintain the prestige and superiority of the Cause. We should never compromise our principles for some temporary benefits we are apt to reap. It is very important to bring the Cause to the attention of such leaders of thought and for this purpose we have to come in touch with them, but our aim should be to draw them to the Cause rather than follow their footsteps. Being fully confident of your judgment and wisdom, Shoghi Effendi hopes you will undertake such work, but at the same time safeguard the interest of the Cause.[22]

During 1926 and 1927, eighteen communities held World Unity Conferences, including Worcester, Massachusetts; New York, New York; Montreal, Canada; Cleveland and Dayton, Ohio; Hartford and New Haven, Connecticut; Chicago, Illinois; Portsmouth, New Hampshire;

and Buffalo, New York. They all followed the format of the San Francisco Conference with three consecutive nights of programmes featuring a diversity of speakers on topics based upon Bahá'í principles. Most of the speakers were not Bahá'ís and included clergy, prominent academics, authors, and politicians – including the first woman to serve in the Canadian Parliament.[23] Some conferences were held in church buildings, others on university campuses such as Brown University and Cornell University, and a few in hotels. Most attracted sizeable audiences and positive newspaper coverage.

Similar to San Francisco, the World Unity Conferences provided valuable experience that enlarged the capacities of the host communities. They created opportunities for fledgling Bahá'í groups to generate local publicity and bring the nascent Faith to the attention of civic leaders as a new and growing force for good. Horace took part in several conferences as a speaker and, no doubt, used his knowledge of advertising to assist them. Though the conferences were on the whole fruitful, just as in San Francisco, human and material resources were stretched to the limit. Shoghi Effendi urged the American community to follow up with those attendees who showed the greatest interest;[24] this guidance, however, was seldom implemented systematically because most of the host communities lacked the resources or knowhow to do so. The sessions stimulated thinking and generated good will, but these intangible achievements were fleeting.

As the series of conferences drew to an end and the attention of the Bahá'ís turned to other matters, the National Assembly's World Unity Committee concluded that the conferences should mark only the beginning of a continuous effort to bring the teachings of the Faith to leaders of thought. All three committee members were motivated by a sense of urgency springing from 'Abdu'l-Bahá's warning that another war greater than the last one was coming; and each was convinced that bringing the Bahá'í message to their fellow citizens, especially leaders and scholars, could prevent it.[25] During a long car ride, Horace and Florence Morton consulted at length and hatched a plan to continue the World Unity Conferences by establishing a World Unity Foundation. A formal organization could not only sponsor conferences and provide speakers to other events but might launch a grass-roots movement. A growing army of local chapters committed to waging peace could be tied together and supported through the Foundation's central office and its journal, *World Unity*. The concept seemed logical, simple, and sound. Florence and Mary Movius, two intelligent, capable businesswomen, were willing to fund the organization until the endeavour became self-supporting through a growing membership and magazine subscriptions. In 1927, the United States was prospering under the light touch of President Calvin Coolidge, and no dark clouds were visible on the North American horizon. The National Assembly approved this proposal but decided that it should be an individual initiative rather than an official activity of the Faith. It issued statements in *Bahá'í News* explaining the Foundation and encouraging the Bahá'í community to support its work.[26]

Full of high expectations, Horace shared the plans for the World Unity Foundation and its journal with Shoghi Effendi, stating his hopes that these would be influential 'for conveying the ideal and principles of world unity . . .'[27] Initially, Horace had advocated that changes be made to the *Bahá'í Magazine* so that it would appeal to the audience he hoped to reach with *World Unity*, but that recommendation had been rejected because the publication served other aims. However, he envisioned the new magazine to be a part of the old one and continued to anticipate that in the future the two would merge. Appealing to Shoghi Effendi for his blessing, guidance and prayers, he remarked, 'You, who see deeper into the realities of things than we, and estimate more accurately the power of all the forces working in the world, can give us much needed advice and counsel if you will, and assist us to assure the friends that the magazine will serve without harming any of the established activities of the Cause.'[28] Horace stated, with misplaced optimism, that 'The time required of me in this work does not detract from my work as secretary.'[29] That concluding sentence was what most interested Shoghi Effendi, because he was especially concerned that this new enterprise would take Horace away from his indispensable Bahá'í work.

Each of the three founding members[30] made important contributions to the new endeavour. Florence Morton, a trained landscape architect who had inherited and ran a large factory, provided most of the funding, and served as treasurer. Horace, with his professional background in writing, publishing, and advertising, assumed the management of the journal. Mary Movius, an elderly writer, real estate heiress, and another source of funds, became president of the board of directors. Though Horace had the vision and most of the required skills to serve as the overall head of the Foundation, he lacked the time because of his responsibilities as secretary of the National Assembly. He was also not well known or connected in the circles they wished to access. He therefore suggested that they hire Dr John Herman Randall to be the Foundation's public face as director and editor. Randall was an ordained Baptist minister and associate pastor of The Community Church, a prominent, non-denominational, liberal church in New York City.[31] A gifted, widely sought-after orator and author of many philosophical, religious, and psychological books, Randall was keenly interested in and sympathetic towards the Bahá'í Faith, even though he was not a professed believer.[32] He had been a presenter at several of the World Unity Conferences and shared their underlying ideals. These four then established the non-profit corporation, the World Unity Foundation, with Randall as director and editor of the journal.[33]

As a young man, John Randall had happened to be in the audience when the historic first public mention of Bahá'u'lláh in the West was made during a speech given at the Parliament of World Religions in Chicago in 1893. He attended many Bahá'í conferences over the years and was often asked to participate as a speaker. In 1912, 'Abdu'l-Bahá spoke at Randall's church,[34] and Randall was so taken by Him that in 1922 he compiled a small book of 'Abdu'l-Bahá's talks given in New York.[35] Randall was enthusiastic about being involved with the World Unity endeavour in part because he was at a turning point as a clergyman and seeking another outlet for his aspirations.[36] While visiting Europe the summer prior to beginning his work as director and editor of the World Unity Foundation and its journal, he commented to Horace that, from his reading of European newspapers, it seemed evident to him that the opinion leaders in Europe were moving in the direction of unity and cooperation but did not know how to bring those conditions into reality. The World Unity Foundation seemed to be just what the times needed.

> This is just where we come in to emphasize & make clear that the spirit making for unity must of necessity come first, it cannot be born in the consciousness of men before any 'plan' can succeed. I am more than ever convinced, Horace, that we are beginning at the right end of this world problem, which is only another way of saying that Baha'ullah [sic] was indeed God's prophet to this age.[37]

Horace was enthusiastic about working with Randall because he saw in him a kindred spirit and potential close friend, saying, 'I can't tell you how I look forward at the prospect of being your co-worker from now on.'[38] John confided he had been warned by others about becoming entangled in an organization controlled by the Faith, but Horace assured him of the Foundation's independence, explaining that it was the branch of the Bahá'í Faith devoted only to spreading the ideals of the Cause, and was otherwise unrelated to other aspects of the Faith such as building the Temple in Chicago. He suggested to John that 'Let's just learn how to spend ourselves most effectively for the spread of the new spiritual message.'[39]

Horace's proposed job description for Randall as head of the Foundation and chief editor of the journal was that he 'should represent the character and purpose of the magazine in the eyes of the general public'.[40] Furthermore, he should contribute one article to each edition and use his wide network of influential people to solicit articles and subscribers. As Horace told John, he himself would oversee the office staff of the journal, work with the printer, create a tentative table of contents for each issue, edit submissions, and correct printer's galleys; in other words, his 'part would be rather in the nature of a office executive responsible for the publishing details and co-editor with you in passing upon contributions'.[41] He assured his colleague that 'desk work suits me to the utmost. The World Unity movement can throw all the drudgery of that kind on me and I will be happy, while you will personify the movement . . .'[42]

The original plan was that John, working full time for the Foundation, would ensure that World Unity Conferences were held all over the country. Speeches from those gatherings would provide content for the journal, and conference participants would be encouraged to form self-supporting local chapters to carry forward the work of spreading the cause of peace. None of this went as planned, despite a few early successes. For example, the speakers rarely followed through with submitting written versions of their talks to the magazine. Local committees often dissolved within a year, and even when they continued, they expected to be subsidized financially by the national organization.[43] Inadequate resources meant that attention to the innumerable details required to attract and retain a growing membership was impossible.[44] In truth, none of the four directors had experience with building an organization with local chapters and a growing membership other than from their Bahá'í experiences, which in 1927 was minimal.

In October 1927, the first issue of *World Unity* was published, providing an expansive view of the world and current international affairs. Its stated theme was 'Interpreting the New Age, Creating the World Outlook'.[45] Early issues of the magazine covered not only significant peace topics such as the League of Nations and the ground-breaking Paris Pact of 1928 (the Kellogg-Briand Pact) – the first attempt to make war illegal, but also articles about countries and religions of the world unfamiliar to the average Westerner, the arts and sciences, and other topics which would engender a sense of world citizenship. Contributors by and large were not Bahá'ís, though the three Bahá'í directors tried to ensure that all articles reflected or were compatible with Bahá'í teachings. The editors ensured that 'Abdu'l-Bahá's talks and writings were sprinkled throughout the editions. A number of the individuals featured in the magazine were leading peace activists: Hamilton Holt, Edwin D. Mead and Lucia Ames Mead, and Theodore Marburg, several of whom had heard 'Abdu'l-Bahá speak. A few had served as presenters at World Unity Conferences, including Dr David Starr Jordan and Rabbi Rudolf I. Coffee. Though most of the content was written for the magazine, some was derived from speeches or other publications. Over seven years, the magazine published articles by notables such as Nobel Peace Prize recipient Norman Angell; eminent sociologist and advisor to President Wilson, Herbert Adolphus Miller; scholar of international law Philip Quincy Wright; a foremost scholar on auxiliary languages who had heard 'Abdu'l-Bahá speak in California, Albert Léon Guérard; the first president of the Republic of Korea, Syngman Rhee; the well-known writer and philosopher Bertrand Russell; expert on US foreign policy and official historian of the San Francisco Conference to establish the United Nations, Dexter Perkins; former Secretary of State and Chief Justice of the Supreme Court of the United States, Charles Evans Hughes; philosopher and influential social reformer John Dewey; socialist, pacifist and US presidential candidate Norman Thomas; the executive director of the League of Nations Association, Philip C. Nash; and a leader of the preeminent American civil rights organization, the NAACP (National Association for the Advancement of Colored People), Robert W. Bagnell. The famous architect Frank Lloyd Wright designed one version of the masthead and also submitted a book review at Horace's request.[46] One of the most praiseworthy attributes of the journal was its inclusion of well-reasoned articles by contributors who were not well known and who otherwise would not have been afforded a nationwide platform for their voices.[47]

There were, however, two aspects of the work of the Foundation that proved problematic. First, its stated objectives were lofty but vague. For example, the subheading for the magazine was 'a monthly magazine promoting the international mind'. This allowed for wide participation in the Foundation's work but did not clarify what exactly it stood for. In 1932, this omission was rectified, first by promoting the Bahá'í concept of a world federation and then by adopting the tenets set forth in 'Abdu'l-Bahá's 1919 Tablet to the Central Organization for Durable Peace in The Hague. The second challenge was that, from its inception, the founders feared that tying *World Unity* to the Bahá'í Faith would not only repel some readers who otherwise shared Bahá'í ideals, but cause their primary target audience, leaders of thought, to dismiss it. The Bahá'í background of the Foundation became so well concealed that over the years, those scholars who have written about it concluded that Randall was its sole founder and proponent.[48] This indirect approach also confused and dismayed many Bahá'ís.

Beginning in 1933, Horace strategically included articles touching upon the spiritual teachings of the Bahá'í Faith,[49] so that during its last years of publication, it became more openly a Bahá'í journal. Horace used his personal connections to solicit articles and subscribers. An especially noteworthy example of his efforts resulted from a small dinner party the Holleys hosted for Louis Gregory and Samuel A. Allen and his wife. The Allens were interested in learning more about the Faith. Samuel Allen was head of the New York Urban League, one of the most important civil rights organizations in the city. Over the course of the evening, Horace proposed that *World Unity* could publish articles that spoke the truth about the plight of the Black citizens of the country, and Allen readily agreed to furnish them. Horace hoped the articles would lead to public meetings about racial issues, and he offered to take part in them.[50] This small dinner party in a tiny New York apartment was noteworthy at the time, because rarely did a White family host Black friends.

Almost from its birth, the World Unity Foundation and its journal were opposed by a handful of believers, who were very vocal about their disapproval. This created misconceptions and bad feelings which haunted the World Unity Foundation to the end. Racial discrimination was usually among the topics addressed through its work, however, adding it to other topics diluted it. Louis Gregory, for example, was alarmed that resources he felt should be directed only toward race amity work were being diverted by the Foundation. Others were distressed by the Foundation's indirect approach to delivering the Bahá'í message, which they believed should be conveyed overtly. Simply putting forward Bahá'í social teachings without crediting Bahá'u'lláh was, to some, not only insufficient, but wrong.[51] Others objected to Horace receiving a small salary for his work on the magazine while employed full time as secretary of the National Assembly.[52] This background noise of discontent hampered the Foundation's ability to gain the full backing of the Bahá'í community even though its work was often reported and promoted in the *Bahá'í News*.

The debates sparked by the World Unity Conferences and the World Unity Foundation came to the attention of Shoghi Effendi. In a letter written on his behalf to the National Spiritual Assembly, Shoghi Effendi discussed at length the thorniest of the controversies: teaching methods. Referring to those World Unity Conferences carried out by Bahá'í communities, he stated that 'I desire to assure you of my heartfelt appreciation of such a splendid conception'. He then explored why a variety of approaches to spreading Bahá'u'lláh's teachings, both direct and indirect, was appropriate and desirable if executed with thoughtful care under the supervision of a National Spiritual Assembly.[53] Directly exploring the Conferences, the letter explained that there were two ways to spread the Cause.

> . . . it appears increasingly evident that as the Movement grows in strength and power the National Spiritual Assemblies should be encouraged, if circumstances permit and the means at their disposal justify, to resort to the twofold method of directly and indirectly winning the enlightened public to the unqualified acceptance of the Bahá'í Faith. The one method would assume an open, decisive and challenging tone. The other, without implying in any manner the slightest departure from strict loyalty to the Cause of God, would be progressive and cautious. Experience will reveal the fact that each of the methods in its own special way might suit a particular

temperament and class of people, and that each in the present state of a constantly fluctuating society, should be judiciously attempted and utilized.⁵⁴

The letter asked the friends to consider the example of 'Abdu'l-Bahá who adopted His manner of conveying Bahá'í truths to the listener: 'if we but call to mind the practice generally adopted by 'Abdu'l-Bahá, we cannot fail to perceive the wisdom, nay the necessity, of gradually and cautiously disclosing to the eyes of an unbelieving world the implications of a Truth which, by its own challenging nature, it is so difficult for it to comprehend and embrace'.⁵⁵

* * * * *

In early 1929, when the World Unity enterprise seemed to prosper, Shoghi Effendi sent a letter to the National Spiritual Assembly that would have a profound impact on Horace. It was the first of a series of letters he would write almost annually through 1936 to which Horace gave the collective title of 'World Order letters'. The Guardian permitted him to add titles and subtitles to these lengthy essays, and to write an introduction when they were published as a collection in 1937 as *The World Order of Bahá'u'lláh*.⁵⁶ These letters were promulgated one by one just as Horace was reading and thinking deeply about the world situation as part of his work on *World Unity*. He compared Shoghi Effendi's perspective on the present and future challenges facing humanity with that of the esteemed non-Bahá'í contributors to the magazine, and he had no doubt as to which was superior. These epistles from the Holy Land exhilarated Horace, who remarked, 'If Bahá'ís want inspiration they had better spend a lot of time with these great letters!'⁵⁷

Among the World Order letters was a special one published in 1934 which became entitled *The Dispensation of Bahá'u'lláh*. It was more of a booklet than a letter. Horace, who helped arrange its publication as a pamphlet, described it as giving 'the fundamental teachings about the station of Bahá'u'lláh, the Báb, the Master⁵⁸ and also the relations of the Guardian and the Universal House of Justice',⁵⁹ going on say that

It is a wonderful document, and removes a lot of misconceptions which have been floating around for years. I feel that it will initiate a new and stronger era of teaching, and probably was written for that very purpose.[60]

The letters, read in sequence, also show Shoghi Effendi's expanding confidence and capacity. Each successive letter is longer and more complex; the first letter is one quarter the length of the last. This evolution also reflects the increasing capacity of the readers. His extraordinary ability to view events from the perspective of trends lasting hundreds, even thousands, of years, and to apply spiritual principles to all that was happening in the world, was not simply profound, it was breath-taking. Horace commented upon this feat in his introduction, stating:

> Shoghi Effendi's exposition of the Teachings, his unique realization of the ultimate aim and purpose of Bahá'u'lláh's Revelation, are no static commentary upon a sacred text but the very essence of world statesmanship evoked in the hour of man's direst need. No longer do the Bahá'ís require 'Abdu'l-Bahá's written Testament to prove the existence of the Guardianship – the successive communications from Shoghi Effendi, and especially those devoted to the subject of World Order, in themselves contain the highest demonstration that Bahá'u'lláh's Spirit continues to bless His Cause and assure its victory in the reconciliation of the peoples of earth and their union in 'one Faith and one Order'.[61]

The late 1920s through the early years of the 1930s proved to be a period of intense education for Horace as his focus shifted from the arts to current affairs, especially political and economic issues. He was reading, thinking, and absorbing, writing, and then thinking again. The more his views aligned with those of Shoghi Effendi, the less he was influenced by perspectives and ideas from non-Bahá'í sources. One of his dearest friends, Florence Morton, remarked openly about the change she observed in his thinking, saying, 'Horace, you are gaining so remarkably in intellectual and spiritual power, that you are fairly towering above us all, and your brain is so fertile that there is nothing that cannot be attained by the Magazine.'[62]

The letter Shoghi Effendi dispatched on the first day of the Bahá'í New Year in 1932, which Horace titled, 'The Golden Age of the Cause of Bahá'u'lláh', contained an unexpected new injunction – one which shook Horace and his friends managing the Foundation and journal. Even though Bahá'ís had long been asked to avoid becoming entangled in politics, now it was forbidden.

> Let them refrain from associating themselves, whether by word or by deed, with the political pursuits of their respective nations, with the policies of their governments and the schemes and programs of parties and factions.[63]

This edict created many questions, including whether Bahá'ís could vote in civil elections, an unresolved issue which dominated the consultation at the following National Convention.[64] Horace accepted this new directive without reservation and, as the secretary of the National Assembly, he was responsible for explaining it to the community through articles in *Bahá'í News*. The articles in *World Unity* did not shy away from politics in their discussions on world issues, and being compelled to avoid it upset his fellow directors who wanted to effect change through political action. As long as *World Unity* was soliciting articles from politicians, it would be impossible to completely dissociate the journal from partisan advocacy. Mary Movius, President of the World Unity Board of Directors, wrote to Horace about her distress at being asked to refrain from speaking or writing about politics, informing him that she had heard other believers express similar sentiments. She implored Horace to explain Shoghi Effendi's injunction to her, for it 'seems that all the liberty the human race has been fighting for all these thousands of years is to [be] wiped out by one command'. She remembered words she had heard 'Abdu'l-Bahá say in Paris, to the effect that some of the best Bahá'ís in the world are ones who never heard the word Bahá'í.[65] Surely, the non-Bahá'í authors of *World Unity* were worthy of being given a public platform.

During this period, when the Bahá'ís were adjusting to the prohibition against political involvement, Horace learned a lesson about what that admonition meant. He wrote an editorial for *World Unity*, 'The Clue to World Strife', for its October 1933 issue[66] in which he explored Communism and Fascism. At the time, the Soviet Union and Italy were controlled by these political parties respectively. The authoritarian regimes theoretically based upon economic theories were upsetting the international order and were partly responsible for emerging armed conflicts. Horace and his fellow directors believed the essay was so important that it was sold as a separate broadside. He submitted it to Shoghi Effendi hoping that it would be included in the upcoming issue of *The Bahá'í World*. No doubt, he was surprised and chastened by the response written on the Guardian's behalf. While praising the clarity of the essay, it stated that to include such an article in a Bahá'í publication would surely undermine the security of Bahá'í communities in other countries, for example, the Bahá'í community of Italy then enduring hardships under the Fascist regime of Mussolini. 'To open a criticism of any political philosophy actually in vogue may create unforeseen difficulties by making the authorities think that the Bahá'ís are secretly engaged in political activities with which they pretend to have no connection of any sort.'[67] The rebuke did not stop there, for the article, which was on the whole a defence of democracy, demonstrated that Horace did not yet understand the Bahá'í teachings on government.

> The Cause stands neither for the democratic liberalism of the West which has proved, particularly since the war, to be a partial failure, nor for the absolutistic and authoritarian philosophy of the Idealists of the 19th C., of which Fascism is a direct descendant. The Bahá'í Faith is neither wholly democratic nor solely aristocratic nor monarchial. It combines all three elements and has a philosophy of its own which tries to combine various systems of political organizations. [this entire portion of the handwritten letter is underlined][68]

Though the original plan for the World Unity enterprise seemed attainable when it was hatched in 1926, the situation of the country and the world changed with unforeseen swiftness. Just as the Foundation and journal were gaining traction, an insurmountable obstacle appeared in their path: the Great Depression of the 1930s, which plunged much of the world into unremitting, deep economic chaos. When the government closed the banks in 1933, Florence Morton could no longer pay her factory employees, much less continue to fund the World Unity Foundation. Mary Movius's real estate fortune lost most of its value as property prices plunged. At first, economies were made by reducing Randall's expenses by confining his travel to the New York City area. Next, all office staff were either released from service or forced to take reductions in pay. Horace carried on as best he could, even when the funds to keep the magazine going became precariously low. He would not allow their efforts in the cause of peace to fail, convinced as he was that their goals remained vital, urgent, and heaven-sent. Resolved to carry on, he said to Florence that 'we are aware of the Providential forces guiding events and can therefore feel faith that every worthy service will be protected. You can count on my determination and energy to the very last ditch.'[69]

Determined though he was to continue the World Unity work, Horace slowly began to recognize that their goal of changing the course of world events was naïve, even if well intended. The World Order letters had expanded his vision, making the Foundation's efforts seem less important, less worthy, because anything it could hope to achieve paled in comparison with the goals and efficacy of the Faith. In the end, there was only one power that could rescue mankind from perdition – the revelation of Bahá'u'lláh.

> The belief which many friendly observers of the Faith have expressed, namely that the mission of this Cause is to introduce into society the leaven of a more liberal and universal outlook, a mission to be fulfilled when the 'Bahá'í principles' have won general acceptance – this attitude, which has conditioned a certain number of Bahá'ís, at least in the West, has lost its force with the rise of knowledge concerning the world order of Bahá'u'lláh emanating from the Testament of 'Abdu'l-Bahá. The Bahá'ís have been carried beyond that critical point of development, with its temptation to relax from the early zeal of teaching, overlook the vital importance of their own organic unity, and judge the progress of the Faith by criterions established in the non-Bahá'í realms of society. Their present realization, that the new wine cannot be held in old bottles, stands as a land-mark in the evolution of the Bahá'í community . . .
>
> To summarize this subject briefly, it is noted that the Bahá'í community has come to see more and more clearly its essential separation from a world which has lost control of its own destiny. The followers of Bahá'u'lláh have been given knowledge that another war is inevitable; they consequently are striving to build upon the foundations which can alone endure.[70]

Much to the relief of the other directors, Randall resigned from the Foundation at the end of 1932. It had become painfully obvious that his primary skills were public speaking and networking, and that he was incapable of managing and growing an organization.[71] The Foundation as an organization never materialized. Randall had merely gone from speaking engagement to speaking engagement with no attempt to consolidate the interest he stimulated. From the outset, by default, Horace had assumed most of Randall's executive responsibilities.[72] Hoping to save the journal, Horace officially became editor, a position he had been carrying out without the title virtually from the publication's birth.[73] It became necessary more than once for him to use his personal funds to keep the magazine afloat even though he was already overwhelmed with financial problems.[74]

Despite Horace's concerted efforts, the times were against the survival of World Unity Foundation and its publication. The United States Presidents during the 1920s – all progressive Republicans – had promoted America abroad as a do-good country, uninterested in taking the lands of others, yet willing to come to the aid of its neighbours. But when the economic depression hit, the international missionary zeal of Quaker pacifist President Herbert Hoover changed to policies that protected only the United States, especially by imposing tariffs to aid industries – which unintentionally punished America's trading partners. The damage to the rest of the world caused by these short-sighted policies was incalculable. When Franklin Delano Roosevelt was elected in a landslide in 1932, to the strains of the upbeat song, 'Happy Days are Here Again', he promised even greater isolation from the world. It was time for America to solve its own problems before helping other countries. The struggling League of Nations became all but irrelevant, and with it the dream of an international body that could avert conflicts between nations faded away. The world's rapid march towards the next worldwide war was already underway. Peace movements, though active, were unfocused and could not compete with rising militarism and nationalism.[75] Horace commented in an editorial, 'The road along which the world peace movement has travelled since the European War has come to a dead end.'[76]

Subscriptions to the few magazines promoting the ideals of universal brotherhood had become luxury items even the most sympathetic reader could ill afford. No matter the strivings of the World Unity Foundation proponents – even sacrificially, their constrained resources were never enough to sustain and expand their early successes. They continued the work under a cloud of impending failure with the expectation that some good would come from it. As Movius wrote to Holley, 'I like extremely the editorials you are writing for "World Unity," and only hope they will bear fruit. They will, undoubtedly, even if we never hear of it.'[77]

Prior to conceiving the Foundation and journal, Horace had approached the staff of the *Bahá'í Magazine* about adding content that would appeal to the non-Bahá'í public, to no avail. Hoping to salvage the readership and influence of *World Unity* magazine, Horace went further than his earlier suggestion by proposing a merger. *World Unity* with its many subscribers – primarily universities, libraries, and peace societies[78] – and its access to influential authors could contribute those resources to the *Bahá'í Magazine*, which would increase its readership and quality. Because each journal was based upon differing approaches and audiences, the editor of the *Bahá'í Magazine*, Dr Stanwood Cobb, a leader in the field of education, could not envision how the two could be compatibly combined. Undeterred, Horace wrote to Shoghi Effendi about his proposal, suggesting that a new magazine be created with a different name. The Guardian unreservedly approved of the plan and the National Assembly appointed a committee to work out the details. In the meantime, Horace continued the publication of *World Unity* as best he could.

Even though Shoghi Effendi never directed Horace and his colleagues to abandon the World Unity Foundation and its journal, his correspondence with Horace more than once hinted at his concern that it would curtail Horace's capacity to carry out the more vital work of the Cause. Finally, in a letter to Horace written on his behalf, the Guardian expressed his true feelings more frankly, saying that, despite changing the content of the magazine to make it more Bahá'í, 'as it stands, however, it surely involves a good deal of waste of energy, and it is for you to do your best to remedy that situation. Your new policy is, indeed, an important step in this direction. But it should be carried to its logical and inevitable end.'[79] As the Foundation was winding down, Horace finally understood what Shoghi Effendi had been trying to say to him from the beginning of the World Unity enterprise – that his concern was not about the misdirection of material resources, but of human resources.[80] In relating this epiphany to Florence Morton, he wrote that 'I trust I am not victim to any vanity when I say that the only fair interpretation I can arrive at is that Shoghi Effendi wants me to be working for a magazine directly serving the Cause,' and that 'what Shoghi Effendi wants most is to have those responsible for World Unity begin to concentrate their energies and resources on direct Bahá'í service'.[81] When the Guardian approved the merger of *World Unity* and *The Bahá'í Magazine*, Horace was filled with 'great joy and gratitude', saying, 'Shoghi Effendi is a wonderful Commander in Chief, and by following his vision we will all make the greatest possible contribution to the success of the Cause.'[82]

At last, in 1935, after an extended consultation under the auspices of the National Assembly, the two magazines ceased as separate publications and a new entity, *World Order*, was born.[83] It ran from 1935 to 1949, and was revived in 1966, publishing steadily until 2007. Expressing his vision for the new publication, Horace commented, 'What I most ardently long for is that, in the future, the Guardian can use World Unity to convey his great World Order letters not only to the believers but also to the general public! Let's pray for that speedy consummation.'[84]

After the merger, Horace took responsibility for three issues of *World Order* each year, and Stanwood Cobb edited the others. Horace's issues continued to feature articles from non-Bahá'í authors while Cobb's editions primarily used Bahá'í authors. Non-Bahá'í readers of *World Order* initially applauded the issues that were similar to *World Unity*,[85] but as the overall content became increasingly oriented towards the Faith, they dropped their subscriptions. In 1935, only a handful of believers were capable of writing for a publication,[86] and, alas, their level of writing generally did not rise to the quality previously found in *World Unity*. This was hardly surprising because Horace had drawn upon the world's writers without regard to their religion. Retaining *World Unity's* high standards was simply impossible, though it was the best effort the Faith could put forth. Like *World Unity*, *World Order's* informative articles covered a wide range of topics aimed at the educated public, but as an explicitly Bahá'í organ under the auspices of the National Spiritual Assembly, it never gained as broad a readership as *World Unity*.

Did the World Unity Foundation and its journal have any impact at all? The most prominent American clergyman of the time, head of the Riverside Church in New York City, Harry Emerson Fosdick, said of *World Unity* magazine that it represented 'one of the most serious endeavors . . . to use journalism to educate the people as to the nature of the world community in which we are living'.[87] Warren F. Kuehl, perhaps the foremost scholar of internationalists during the early twentieth century, mentioned the magazine as one of only a handful at the time discussing issues promoting peace through international order, noting that it seemed unique in its advocacy of a world federation.[88] Another scholar of diplomatic history, Anne L. Day, concluded that World Unity's primary contribution was creating a space for lesser-known people interested in international peace to put forth their ideas.[89]

> . . . the conferences and the magazine helped foster a world outlook without prejudice and a faith in humanity which survived the horrors of World War II. World Unity Magazine gave young scholars a medium to which they could hone their insights toward global humanitarian values, thus broadening consciousness to recognize the moral and spiritual equality, 'to realize that the interests of all men are mutual interests'.[90]

After the World Unity endeavour was well and truly finished, Florence Morton proposed to her old friend that Green Acre hold a special programme each year intended for non-Bahá'ís that addressed social issues. Horace responded by reminding her of the lessons learned from World Unity; namely, that to be successful, it would require human resources and funds, both for promoting attendance and engaging outside lecturers. He could not see – peering into the immediate future – how the Faith could afford such an annual programme. He then explored her proposal in greater detail. 'What it comes down to is', he concluded, 'that the bigger the idea, the more thoroughly must it be carried out.'[91]

As the World Unity Foundation was being dissolved in 1935, armies were marching across an expanding number of hot spots in Europe, Africa, and Asia. Before long, much of the globe would be plunged into the most horrible conflict mankind had ever experienced.

* * * * *

The following year, 1936, Horace inserted a thin strip of yellow paper into the envelope containing a business letter to his colleague, Leroy Ioas. It read simply:

Leroy: My daughter Hertha died Monday morning. She was twenty five years old and had been terribly ill for nearly seven years. The Master loved her very much as a baby in Paris. Horace[92]

Having reached middle age, Horace seldom wrote poetry, so his grief apparently was not expressed in verse. However, when his daughter was an infant and the world seemed full of the promise of good things to come, he penned a poem setting out his happy hopes for his baby daughter as she embarked upon life.

Hertha
She will grow
Beautiful.
Beauty will come to her
Given, like sun and rain;
Will go from her
Freely, like laughter.
She will be
Center, circumference to a great joy
Swiftly passing, repassing
Like water in and from a limpid well.
She is of the new generation, new;
Torch for the flame of passion,
Flame for the torch of love.

She will grow
Beautiful.
No, beauty itself will grow
Like her.[93]

Sadly, Hertha's early death springing from the effects of her seven-year struggle with mental illness did not end Horace's struggles with that old Holley family foe. His only surviving child, Marcia, started to exhibit psychiatric problems in her early twenties, latent tendencies probably brought to the surface by the trauma of her older sister's death. Like her sister, Marcia would improve, then relapse. During her better days, Marcia was bright, funny, and interested in the world, much like her father and sister.[94] She would spend most of her life in facilities for

1930 New York City Race Amity Conference held at the Urban League offices in Harlem. Both Horace and Doris Holley participated.

Spiritual Assembly of the Bahá'ís of New York in 1932. Standing from left to right: Edward Kinney, Horace Holley and Hooper Harris. Seated: Marie Little. Loulie Matthews, Orphelia Crum, Julia Threlkeld, Bertha Hurklotz, and Marie Moore

Alfred 'Fred' Lunt, first secretary of the National Spiritual Assembly of the United States and Canada

Mountfort Mills, member of the National Spiritual Assembly and close friend to Horace Holley. Mills was a lawyer based in New York City who greatly assisted Shoghi Effendi

St Mark's-in-the-Bowery Episcopal Church, where many Bahá'í meetings were held between about 1913 and 1935. 1936 photograph

William Norman Guthrie, brilliant and controversial rector of St Mark's-in-the-Bowery Episcopal Church in New York City, who had a longtime interest in the Bahá'í Faith

John Herman Randall, president of the World Unity Foundation, and clergyman

Florence Reed Morton, treasurer of the National Spiritual Assembly and co-founder, with Horace and two others, of the World Unity Foundation. She and Horace were close friends

Ahmad Sohrab, secretary and translator to 'Abdu'l-Bahá who rebelled against Shoghi Effendi and the Bahá'í Administrative Order. Together with Julia Chanler, he founded the New History Society to compete with the Bahá'í Faith in New York City

The National Spiritual Assembly consulting in the 1930s

Members of the National Spiritual Assembly at Green Acre, where the institution met at least once every summer. Left to right: Siegfried Schopflocher, Roy Wilhelm, Dorothy Baker, Amelia Collins, Allen McDaniel, Louis Gregory, Horace Holley. All but McDaniel would be named Hands of the Cause of God

The National Spiritual Assembly as the exterior ornamentation was being installed on the House of Worship, 1933. Seated left to right: Nellie French, Leroy Ioas; standing left to right: Carl Scheffler, George Latimer, Siegfried Schopflocher, Horace Holley, Allen McDaniel, Roy Wilhelm, Alfred Lunt

Marcia (Betty) Holley at the beach at Cannes, France when a teenager

Horace Holley enjoying the sunshine and magnificent river views at Green Acre

impaired adults unable to function without care, passing away in 2002 in Connecticut.[95] Horace tucked away his daughters into that portion of his heart that was too deep to ever bring them back to the surface to be examined and discussed.

Earlier in the same year that he would lose Hertha to mental illness, Horace wrote a comforting letter to another family who had a much-loved member struggling with similar challenges. He said:

> It is all particularly poignant to me because in my family, too, there has been more than one case of mental disturbance, and some of my relatives have suffered a great deal from worry about it, feeling always the possibility of assassination by the unseen foe. So you see how parallel the situations are. But I can assure you . . . that for people like you and me, the attitude of worry is negative and needless. We must go forward in activity and faith and not for one minute stand in the shadow of personal dread. The whole world is in the direst condition, and the Cause will have to triumph inwardly and outwardly over all that is sinister, confusing and dreadful. To be able to transmute the substance of defeat into the essence of victory is our special job. Mental confusion and despair is inevitably the concomitant of the existing state of mind in the world. It is overwhelming to everything on earth except conscious faith.
>
> Please accept my loving sympathy and also my positive assurance. A Baha'i can never be a hapless victim of any situation.
>
> Horace[96]

This period – especially the years 1932 to 1934 – was an especially troubling time for Horace and his family. Hertha was a constant worry and Doris had serious problems within her own family which required not only her attention,[97] but Horace's too. Hertha's care and burial drained the last of Horace's savings[98] amid financial hard times, which forced him to take on multiple jobs. He was coping simultaneously with problems generated by strong-willed men: Alfred Lunt, William Norman Guthrie, John Herman Randall, and especially Ahmad Sohrab. His dream of changing the world through the World Unity Foundation and its journal evaporated. Each of those stories had to be told separately, even though they were all going on at the same time. Yet Horace emerged from those terrible years stronger in faith, with much more profound insights, and consistently hopeful for better days ahead. There were times when he was frustrated and expressed his feelings candidly to those he was close to, but he never showed despair. He accepted that the forces of the universe under the direction of the Almighty were directing the fortunes of humanity, including his own affairs.

The image of Horace throughout his New York years is always the same: a pale, thin, lanky man with a small moustache hunched over a typewriter surrounded by stacks of letters, newspapers, magazines, and books scattered across his wooden desk and any other available surface. Pens, pencils, a bottle of ink and knife to sharpen the pencils are at the ready. Never far from where he sits, a lit cigarette dangles precariously on the edge of a full ashtray, emitting a thin line of smoke. The tap, tap, tap of typewriter keys jostles the table, interrupted by zings when he throws the carriage. Occasionally he pauses to take a sip from a lukewarm cup of black coffee Doris served him twenty minutes earlier, but lunch holds no interest for him. There is too much to do – so many letters to write, articles to draft or edit, cables to send and talks to compose. Once in a while, he stands up, stretches, and walks over to a window to gaze upon the out-of-doors – a place he seldom visits any more. He glances at his watch. Is it time to leave for a meeting? How long will it take to get there by bus, subway, on foot? He checks his pocket for the coins he will need for fares. Then he returns to his table and the endless paperwork. As he remarked to a friend, 'You don't know how I have to figure every hour of time in order to get all my work done!'[99]

Horace could not have carried out his work without Doris as his assistant. She typed many of his writings and generally served as his secretary. She was invaluable, not only because of her dedication to him and his work, but because she was also a gifted writer who could improve upon his drafts. Indeed, others sought her assistance with their writing.[100] The Holleys were a team.

* * * * *

In 1935, after asking the friends world-wide to sever their ties to their former religions, Shoghi Effendi wrote a second letter to the believers in the West with an additional requirement: the time had come for them to adhere to some of the laws of the Faith set down in Bahá'u'lláh's book of laws, the Kitáb-i-Aqdas.[101]

> The laws revealed by Bahá'u'lláh in the Aqdas are, whenever practicable and not in direct conflict with the Civil Law of the land, absolutely binding on every believer or Bahá'í institution whether in the East or in the West.¹⁰²

Specifically, Bahá'ís were enjoined to abstain from consuming alcoholic beverages, to adhere to most of the requirements of Bahá'í marriage and burial, and to refrain from the use of mind-altering substances such as heroin or marijuana. They were to remain chaste before marriage and faithful to their spouse after marriage. In January 1936, the Guardian enjoined the believers in the West to recite their daily obligatory prayer and to observe the Nineteen Day Fast.

> Certain laws, such as fasting, obligatory prayers, the consent of the parents before marriage, avoidance of alcoholic drinks, monogamy, should be regarded by all believers as universally and vitally applicable at the present time. Others have been formulated in anticipation of a state of society destined to emerge from the chaotic conditions that prevail today.¹⁰³

Over the course of seven years through his World Order letters, Shoghi Effendi had provided an in-depth tutorial on the verities of the Faith, its goals, and its vision of the world it was striving to bring into existence. Now he was calling upon the Bahá'ís to bring their behaviour into conformity with the high standards of such a pure, holy, and sanctified Cause that they might be worthy to assist with ushering in the New World Order. Horace had already cut his church ties and given up any connection he had to politics; now he would obediently avoid alcohol. But he still could enjoy his cigarettes and coffee.

Miraculously, despite the economic challenges facing the believers, donations continued to flow to the Temple project, and the superstructure was built. Nineteen years to the day from when 'Abdu'l-Bahá laid the cornerstone, a gathering was held within the unfinished shell on 1 May 1931 to dedicate the dome.¹⁰⁴ But the shell was far from complete, and the financial situation of the country was getting worse. At points during the Depression, the Temple would be one of the few monumental building projects ongoing in the United States. When in 1934 the last ornamental panel sheathing the dome was in place at last – a remarkable achievement that involved the development of new building techniques – Horace remarked,

> The Temple dome is at last finished, and its beauty is even more than expectation. Here at last is a demonstration of the Cause of which we can be fully proud. Now what we have got to do is to make the communities unified enough to demonstrate the Cause on the human plane – the final task of religion on earth!105

The second half of the 1930s arrived with a new set of worries that would affect all Americans. President Roosevelt and his cadre of experts had hastily created new government agencies, convinced that these would bring an end to the Depression. In an all-out struggle to restore prosperity, the central government exerted more control over not only the economy but daily life. For brief intervals, economic recovery seemed to be in sight. The financial losses sustained in 1929 were slowly being recouped. High levels of unemployment, however, remained an intractable problem because employers had learned to make do with fewer workers and were not ready to expand their businesses after high business taxes were imposed by the Roosevelt Administration. In 1937, the stock market crashed again, plummeting the economy into another steep nosedive. To make matters worse, that same year civil war was raging in Spain, Germany's military mobilization and bellicosity became an increasing menace, and Japan invaded China.106 Doris was especially anxious about the situation in Europe because her mother had returned to live in England. Her mother sent her a reassuring letter stating that 'the war situation is just the same as it was six months ago'. She reported that according to a friend with connections to the military and Home Civil Service, 'no one thinks it is dangerous'.107 Horace certainly disagreed with his mother-in-law's rosy assessment, because of 'Abdu'l-Bahá's prediction that another war, far worse than the Great War, was inevitable.108

When Horace turned 50 in 1937, his life was fully devoted to serving the Bahá'í Faith. Any vestiges of worldly ambition had been wrung from him, and his only remaining aim was to carry out his service in a manner pleasing to his guiding star, Shoghi Effendi. The affection and admiration he held for the Guardian was returned. In 1938, Shoghi Effendi sent Horace a cable stating:

ASSURE YOU OF EVERDEEPENING ADMIRATION YOUR UNRIVALLED SERVICES
LOVE ABIDING GRATITUDE SHOGHI[109]

* * * * *

The House of Worship had become a Chicago landmark and images of its beauty were already being used by the wider community. The National Assembly turned its attention to how the building would be used and how would it serve the surrounding area. In 1938, the National Assembly studied guidance from 'Abdu'l-Bahá about the buildings that should surround the Temple. The House of Worship embodied worship, while those structures in its vicinity should exemplify the companion attribute of service. Among the buildings which 'Abdu'l-Bahá said should stand in the shadow of the Temple was one dedicated to the administration of the Faith.[110] The National Assembly determined that the unique and dignified architect's studio already erected across the street from the House of Worship could suitably serve as its seat – a Bahá'í Ḥaẓíratu'l-Quds. This building on the shore of Lake Michigan was owned by the Faith and had been used not only as the architect's studio, but as his residence during the design phase. The Temple's custodian and his family were currently residing in it.

The delegates at the 1938 Convention voted to recommend that the National Assembly establish a national headquarters next to the House of Worship[111] and the National Assembly's 1939 decision to carry that out was whole-heartedly endorsed by Shoghi Effendi. In his own hand, the Guardian wrote that, with the approaching completion of the Temple, the National Assembly's resolution

> to establish within its hallowed precincts and in the heart of the North American continent the Administrative Seat of their beloved Faith cannot but denote henceforward a closer association, a more constant communion, and a higher degree of coordination between the two primary agencies providentially ordained for the enrichment of their spiritual life and for the conduct and regulation of their administrative affairs.[112]

Horace indicated he and Doris were willing to relocate from their beloved New York City. The Guardian reacted to this decision in a cable saying DELIGHTED WELCOME TRANSFERENCE TEMPLE AREA LOVING APPRECIATION,[113] and so it was decided that the secretary of the National Assembly should live close to the Temple in the rural village of Wilmette,[114] many miles from the urban centre of Chicago.

Shoghi Effendi was well aware of the personal sacrifice the Holleys were making. Though not born in New York City, Doris had grown up there and so for her it was her true hometown. He sent a cable through Roy Wilhelm which read,

> HORACE DORRIS [SIC] CARE WILHEMITE NEW YORK
> AWARE PROFOUNDLY APPRECIATE SACRIFICE PERSONAL CONVENIENCE INVOLVED TRANSFERENCE TEMPLE VICINITY DEEPEST LOVE SHOGHI[115]

It was time to close a chapter of their lives. Doris and Horace finished packing their last boxes and carried them downstairs and out of their four-storey apartment building to their automobile, parked as close as possible to the door. Back inside, they ascended the stairs one last time to survey their now empty tiny New York apartment. 119 Waverly Place in Greenwich Village had not only been their home, but it had also served as the national headquarters for the Faith during their years there. With a flood of memories and emotions, they closed the door and returned to their car. Horace started the engine and turned his automobile away from the curb into traffic. Driving through the city that had been their home for the greater part of their lives, they took last looks at familiar landmarks. When they crossed over the Hudson River to the mainland from Manhattan, more waves of emotions must have washed over them.

The era just passed had been full of tests. Throughout it all, their unshakable devotion to Bahá'u'lláh had been their salvation, the rock upon which they had fortified their family. But even there they had encountered severe challenges. As Horace put it, 'The Cause seems never to lack excitement, to say nothing of trouble.'[116]

There had also been an abundance of achievements in New York. Horace's pen had found its authentic voice. The Holleys had become a team knit tightly together through their dedicated service to the Faith. The New York Bahá'í community they were leaving was thriving. As the city's skyscrapers disappeared from the car's rear-view mirror, they knew that the hearts and best wishes of their New York friends were accompanying them as the car pointed towards the west.

The route ahead had become familiar to Horace during his countless visits to Chicago as blue hills of the Appalachian Mountains gave way to rolling farmland. The Upper Midwest, with its prairies and Great Lakes, would become their adopted home for the next two decades. Other trials and triumphs were awaiting them over the horizon, yet no leg of their lives' journeys would be as full of turbulent seas as those they had sailed through in New York. They were toughened mariners who had proven their seaworthiness.

12

SPIRITUAL CONQUEST IN THE MIDST OF WAR

> ***To-day***
> *So these, then are the violent times*
> *Of fiery mountains and sullen seas*
> *When starving people are stuffed with crimes*
> *And none has comfort, beauty and ease.*
>
> *For sure these days are those latter days*
> *That brewed so bitter in prophet's blood.*
> *We toil at end of our shameful ways.*
> *We shamble in vain from fire and flood.*
>
> Horace Holley[1]

The last of the painters and decorators had left the small but imposing white building on a bend along Sheridan Road. The remaining ladders had been taken down and velvet curtains were now hanging across the tall windows which gave the structure its classical look. This was to be the Holleys' Wilmette home from that point forward, even as it served its primary function as the Seat of the National Spiritual Assembly. For that reason, the Bahá'ís were beginning to refer to the edifice as the Ḥaẓíratu'l-Quds, meaning 'The Sacred Fold', the Bahá'í term for the headquarters of a Bahá'í Assembly. (That name was often shortened in conversation to 'the Ḥaẓírá'.) Built as the studio and residence of the architect of the House of Worship, Louis Bourgeois, its main room had two-storey-high arched windows and a balcony running along the other side of the room. From there Bourgeois could look across to the building site as he went about the task of creating architectural drawings for every detail of the majestic Temple which the Holleys could now view towering at its full height across the street.

Their move to the Ḥaẓírá raised the question as to what that building meant, for it was not simply a meeting place and administrative centre, it also had symbolic value as the visible embodiment of a divinely ordained institution. This was not merely a philosophical inquiry, for the nature of the building's use had practical applications. The National Assembly determined that the main room and the entrance hall should be decorated to reflect their use as its headquarters, and that the remainder would be the private home of the national secretary and his family.

After a day of unpacking and settling in, Horace paused to take a break from the ardours of moving half-way across the country to reflect, to survey his new surroundings, and to jot a hurried note to his old friend, Mountfort Mills, in New York. He could not help but tell Monty all that was running through his head during this turning point not only for his life, but for the institution he served.[2] It was a joyful letter full of musings. He related that decorum dictated that the meeting room should be attractive and appropriately respectable; consequently, Doris was instructed 'to shoot the works, & the works are shot'.[3] His wife's decorative sensibilities had created 'a place where anyone can enter & find [it] charming and dignified'.[4] The Holleys also purchased a refrigerator for the kitchen and furniture for the dining alcove which looked out on the lake. The new dining table was long enough to accommodate the National Assembly as a conference table. But what meant far more to him than simply having a spacious home after decades of cramped New York apartments was the spiritual meaning of the place he now occupied. He knew he needed to become spiritually detached in such a special home that was not really his.

> There's a wonderful blessing in this move, Monty, as well as heart aches. Sometimes it comes over me that for years I've dreamed of a studio with a gallery and here it is;* & it comes over me that I've neither a house nor hotel to live in any more, but a kind of symbolic, be-severed-damn-you place with too many implications to be thought about.
>
> ---
>
> *and under what conditions that never [came] into my dream![5]

Feelings of gratitude welled up within Horace because for the first time since his youthful years in Italy, he was surrounded by beauty. With maturity, he appreciated the impact which physical beauty has on the spirit.

So today, for us, is the day when we first began to feel settled & arranged. To step out on the gallery, & look down into the studio at night, with the curtains drawn, is a breath-taking experience. It makes the heart yearn for some not-yet-written drama in which the soul will have part – but the flesh be honored too, as the instrument for the realization of whatever beauty we have.[6]

As soon as they arrived in Wilmette, Horace realized that there was another bounty to living away from the noise and constant movement of New York. He wrote, 'Monty, there's time to think out here (which really means to feel). It's the combination of challenge & scare which appeals to me.'[7] He did not mention what must have been one of his favourite elements of the Ḥaẓíra. It sat on a bluff just above the beach. From the back of the building, he could scurry down an embankment and at once enjoy the moods of Lake Michigan – a vast inland sea with rolling waves. Seashores had always been one of the environments Horace preferred to rest and restore his spirit. On sweltering days in midsummer, no doubt both Holleys took advantage of the cool waters of the lake by walking the beach, wading, and swimming. In the middle of the worst of winters, inside the warmth of the Ḥaẓíra, they could gaze out of windows to watch waves whipped to a frenzy by arctic blasts, creating close to shore ice figures as waves froze solid in mid-air to create amazing shapes. With the ethereal beauty of the Temple on one side and the wild beauty of the lake on the other, their new residence must have seemed magical.

In the next edition of *The Bahá'í World*, Horace discussed the historic significance of the establishment of headquarters for all National Assemblies, for his move to the Bourgeois studio marked the establishment of a permanent seat for the National Assembly, linking that institution to the House of Worship. At about the same time as his move, five other National Assemblies acquired or built national centres. Now, less than two decades after the first election of national governing bodies, having a physical headquarters with all the responsibilities it entailed was a turning point signalling the increased capacity of National Assemblies.

The Assembly had approved a salary for Horace based upon his expected necessary expenses in Wilmette. Once the Holleys had been in their new home long enough to better estimate their expenditures, Horace informed the treasurer that costs had been overestimated, stating, 'Since I regard the financial arrangements as intended to meet living expenses and not as a source of profit, I am very glad to enclose a check . . . of the excess from the most recent payment.'[8] He asked that his salary be adjusted down to reflect the range of his costs, noting further that 'this amount covers the work of two persons and not one'. Instead of an augmented salary, 'Doris and I have the use of the house, heat, light and phone'. He concluded, 'We are both delighted to make possible a saving for the NSA of . . . a year.'[9]

Horace was not simply setting up housekeeping in Wilmette, he was establishing the National Centre. He had already recognized that, as the work became more complex, even national committees would require staff. In the early years of the National Assembly when it was based in New York, Bertha Herklotz, a professional stenographer, had been hired to assist part-time with clerical work. She sometimes attended National Assembly meetings to take notes – a practice that was discontinued in the 1940s when Shoghi Effendi informed the National Assembly that it was inappropriate for staff to be present when making decisions. Over the course of the next decade, Bertha's work shifted from assisting the secretary to assisting Roy Wilhelm with the Treasury paperwork.[10] Horace's salary when he was first employed by the National Assembly always included Doris's assistance, who served as another secretarial aid. (She was also the hostess and housekeeper of the Ḥaẓíra.) In 1940, Horace hired a believer from Chicago, Sophie Loeding, as the first full-time staff member of the secretariat. She was a capable, experienced executive secretary. Sophie had been privileged to be present when 'Abdu'l-Bahá laid the cornerstone of the Temple.[11] In the beginning, her job included attending National Assembly meetings to take stenographic minutes, just as Bertha had done in New York.[12] About six months after the Holleys established the secretariat in Wilmette, the National Assembly made the decision to move the Treasurer's Office and the Publishing Committee's Office from the New York area to Wilmette as well. Bertha, along with Tom and Clara Wood, who managed the actual printing and distribution of Bahá'í literature, was asked to relocate to Illinois.

The first question to arise because of the move to Wilmette was: where should the national offices be located? The Ḥaẓíra lacked adequate space for more than the Holleys' work. The temporary solution was to rent an apartment in a residential building. Within a few years, a small, frame, two-room building was erected on the Temple grounds[13] which would serve as office space for more than fifty years. Sophie, Bertha, and Clara made the best of it.

After Bertha was injured in an accident, she returned to New York, and Loretta Voeltz, a young woman from Kenosha, Wisconsin, was hired to replace her. Loretta was responsible for keeping the financial accounts and writing receipts. She came from a family of early believers who had hosted 'Abdu'l-Bahá during His visit to her hometown. Her sister had been among the local believers who served as volunteers at the National Centre.[14] Loretta would work for the Treasurer's Office until she retired more than forty years later.[15]

Under Horace's watchful eye, these first staff set about developing systems and procedures for the work of the national headquarters. He did his work at the Ḥaẓíra, but twice a day he would stroll across Sheridan Road and down Linden Avenue to the tiny office, where he would sign letters, chat with the staff, and pick up outgoing mail. He would then walk to the Wilmette post office substation at 4th and Linden and return to the office with the incoming mail. This routine became his primary source of exercise and sunshine. Loretta and Sophie remembered him as a kind, considerate, generous boss who was unfailingly thoughtful towards those he supervised.[16] He was greatly revered by the staff for his intelligence, vast knowledge of general facts and the Bahá'í Writings, which he retained within his extraordinary memory. He could be impatient, but never with them; nor was he demanding. The staff appreciated his sense of humour. He was able to draw out their best efforts.[17] Contrary to the social conventions of the time, Horace insisted that the staff address him by his first name.[18]

Horace's writing style for the routine correspondence of the National Assembly evolved over the years. In the beginning, his letters regarding Assembly business included a touch of informality, probably because most of them were addressed to individuals he knew personally. But over time, the tone shifted to the style of conventional business letters, perhaps because of Sophie's influence. She described his letters as consistently 'well-reasoned, concise, and always conveyed the exact meaning he had in mind'.[19] As the volume increased, the letters became shorter – even pithy.[20] On at least one occasion, the letter simply read 'yes'.

* * * * *

The Wilmette Bahá'í community in 1939 consisted primarily of believers connected to the House of Worship and the National Office, though as the population of the Chicago metropolitan area spread to the suburbs of Cook County, other Bahá'ís moved to Wilmette. Besides those working at the national office, there were the Hannen and Struven families who maintained the Temple and its grounds. Of all the believers in their new community, the one family the Holleys would associate with the most was the True family. Corinne True was an elderly well-to-do widow and the 'Mother of the Temple' – often referred to as 'Mother True'. 'Abdu'l-Bahá had charged her with the task of ensuring that the Temple be built, instructing her about its details during her 1907 pilgrimage. She never faltered in carrying out that directive. It became the focus of her life. Shoghi Effendi said of her that she had 'learned to be spiritual and at the same time get things done'.[21] Corinne had had eight children, only three of whom were still living in 1939. One daughter, Arna, was widowed with children and living in California. The other two, Edna and Katherine – neither of whom ever married – resided in Wilmette at their mother's expansive stucco home five blocks from the House of Worship and less than a block from the Lake. Katherine was a surgeon. Edna, a graduate of Smith College, was a successful businesswoman who owned a travel agency. The two sisters in Wilmette were among the most active believers in the country, and both would serve with Horace on the National Assembly. The Trues, like the Holleys, were amiable companions with gracious, patrician manners.[22]

In 1940, the village of Wilmette, situated on the western border of the city of Evanston, had a population of 17,233.[23] Evanston, which separated the village from the city of Chicago, boasted Northwestern University, which added a touch of culture and renown to the small suburban city. It was also the home of multiple national civic organizations, such as Rotary International and several fraternal organizations. With its high-rise downtown hotel and restaurants, it was the big city to Wilmette, and where most of the Bahá'ís found lodging when they visited Wilmette.

It was easy to travel to and from Wilmette. The commuter rail service of Chicago, locally referred to as the 'EL' due to its many elevated tracks, ended at Wilmette. Its terminus station was just two blocks from the Temple grounds. Also, a station for an interstate rail line was located in the centre of the village's business district. While having the 'second city' of the country – that is, the city second to New York – an easy train ride away, Chicago was still too distant to entice the Holleys. During the two decades they lived in Illinois, the village of Wilmette was transformed from a rural agricultural hub to a bedroom community for commuters to Chicago.

The Holleys looked for ways to make friends within Wilmette while living on an isolated spot on the lakefront. Joining a church was no longer an option, and their work required only minimal interaction with neighbours. One way Horace found to engage with members of the community was to join the Wilmette chapter of Rotary International, a service organization that promoted both good character and the betterment of the community through good works. At the time Horace became a Rotarian, membership was restricted to men. The one membership criterion that made it a prestigious and difficult organization to join was its requirement that each chapter accept only one representative from each profession or organization within its locality. In this way, each group broadly reflected the most influential, active citizens of a community. A club, for example, might have one physician, one member of the local government, one merchant, one manager of an industry, one insurance executive, and the like. Horace, as the only Bahá'í official in Wilmette, filled that slot. All Rotary clubs around the globe met weekly, and these gatherings usually included a meal and featured a talk, often delivered by a guest. Even if a Rotarian was away from home, he was expected to find and attend a meeting wherever he was. The organization became a blessing for Horace, not only because it put him in contact with notable people in Wilmette, but also because its weekly meeting requirement became an easy way for him to meet people when he travelled outside of the area or overseas on behalf of the Faith. Rotary chapters also provided venues where he could give speeches on topics related to the Faith. Years later when Horace was about to move from Wilmette, he recommended that Charles Wolcott, his successor as national secretary, replace him in the club's 'religion' slot. When Charles later gave a talk to the club based upon one of Horace's published essays, the members were astonished. In all of their two decades of chatting over lunch with Horace as a friend, never once had he mentioned he was a published author[24] – an indication that by the time he moved to the Midwest, his image of himself as a writer had been superseded by his desire to serve the Faith.

One fruit of his years of membership in Rotary was a friendship between the Alexander and Holley families. William Alexander, a fellow Rotarian, lawyer and President of the Wilmette Village Council, appointed him as the first chairman of the Wilmette Historical Commission in 1949. Alexander's wife also served on that Commission, further strengthening the bonds between the families. Horace had always been interested in history and relished this assignment. Through his efforts, the Wilmette Historical Society was founded. Always systematic as he went about any task, Horace steered the Commission to develop procedures for preserving significant historic locations and artifacts and to create a sense of appreciation for the history of the area among the citizens. These efforts led to the establishment of a museum to showcase the village's past. Between his work with Rotary and his leadership of the Commission, he became well known and liked in Wilmette, interacting with a number of local groups and officials. He also joined the Wilmette Conversation Club, perhaps one of his favourite groups, because it existed to have men of attainment meet in the homes of the members to hold erudite discussions about important topics.[25] All of his activity created a positive impression of the Faith.

* * * * *

When Europe was ablaze during World War I, 'Abdu'l-Bahá had laid out the blueprint for the spiritual conquest of the planet – the Tablets of the Divine Plan, and placed the primary responsibility for carrying them out upon the North Americans. From the time these Tablets were first promulgated, especially in 1919, Martha Root from Pennsylvania travelled the world under the watchful care of Horace on behalf of the National Assembly. Hyde and Clara Dunn also answered the call of the Tablets and moved from the West Coast of the United States to Australia, establishing the Faith on that continent. Despite these heroic responses, the focus of raising the Temple and establishing Bahá'í communities in the United States and Canada consumed the meagre resources of the North American Bahá'í community for many years, thus the mission set out in the Tablets was deferred in anticipation of a time when conditions were more favourable.

The Guardian understood that two processes had to be well established before the Divine Plan could be implemented. First, institutions capable of marshalling and directing resources had to exist, otherwise the efforts of even the best of teachers would be lost if gains could not be consolidated. Second, an army of teachers had to be trained before being deployed to the far corners of the earth. This educational process could not be carried out until core selections from the Sacred Texts were available in English. The burden of translation fell on Shoghi Effendi. Thus, during the 1930s, in addition to writing his all-important World Order letters, Shoghi Effendi used his extraordinary knowledge of the English language to translate many excerpts and lengthy Tablets from Bahá'u'lláh. These works are known in the West as *Gleanings from the Writings of Bahá'u'lláh*, *Prayers and Meditations*, *Epistle to the Son of the Wolf*, and *Kitáb-i-Íqán: The Book of Certitude*. Shoghi Effendi further understood that to arise and settle in faraway places his Western flock needed to be inspired to show forth courage and fortitude. To achieve that end, he also translated Nabíl's[26] immortal chronicle of the heroic first decades of the Faith, which was given the English title *The Dawn-Breakers: Nabíl's Narrative of the Early Days of the Bahá'í Revelation*. Horace was the one spear-heading the printing of these books.

Moreover, these important selections from the Sacred Texts had to be studied and absorbed; so the Guardian emphasized the importance of summer schools. He also directed that those schools include practical subjects that teachers would need such as courses on Bahá'í ethics and morality, the Spanish language (to facilitate the teaching work in Latin America), and the history, teachings, and customs of Islam. This last topic was indispensable grounding if the believers from Christian and Jewish religious backgrounds were to have a sound understanding of the Cause.[27] Horace, again, was intimately involved with developing these educational programmes.

Throughout his New York years, the rural Maine retreat, Green Acre, had captured a place in Horace's heart – he could not imagine a summer 'not spent at that blessed spot'.[28] He and Doris even rented and later purchased a small summer cabin there in the nearby town of Eliot.[29] They often spent the months of July and August at the school where Horace not only taught courses but enjoyed using his free time to further his own private study and writing as well as attending courses taught by others. For many years, the National Assembly held its July meeting at Green Acre, where its relaxed environment strengthened the friendships of the members.[30] When Horace moved to Illinois, he continued to teach classes at Green Acre, but also taught courses at a ranch in southeast Michigan which would later become the Louhelen Bahá'í School.[31] He was intimately involved in the changing curriculum needs of the Bahá'í summer schools, and, because of his unique vantage point, made recommendations based upon a broad picture of the needs of the Faith.[32] He offered his opinions about Bahá'í education in a letter to two of his colleagues, insisting that 'we should cease trying to bring pressure upon believers to attend study classes, as if we were responsible for overcoming reluctance to turn to divine truth, or truant officers preventing some children from running away, and concentrate upon the conception that Bahá'í study is the most exciting experience on earth and whoever stays away is missing a great privilege'.[33]

* * * * *

The earliest teaching plan devised and adopted by the National Spiritual Assembly during Horace's first years as a member, the Plan of Unified Action, was a plan in name only. Its two goals: raise funds to complete the House of Worship and expand the membership, were so broad that they were of little value in motivating the friends. During the years of that Plan, Horace became frustrated by the overall lack of active teaching by the generality of believers, so he wrote a short essay entitled 'Regarding Service (A suggestion for the believers and friends)' to address a problem he thought had persisted since the time of 'Abdu'l-Bahá – failure to rely on divine assistance. His description of the typical approach used to entice people to become seriously interested in the Faith no doubt accurately described teaching efforts in most North American communities. A believer would decide to host a meeting in his home and then invite other Bahá'ís to attend. The others were requested to invite their non-Bahá'í friends. Though this method led to the establishment of regular gatherings, it seldom attracted anyone who was not already a believer. Unfortunately, those community members who did not attend these meetings were often viewed as being unwilling to assist the Faith, sometimes leading to estrangement. Horace postulated that this approach was ineffective because it was not based upon the power of divine assistance.

> Why was this method doomed to failure? It may be for the reason that it meant dependence upon the <u>friends</u> and not dependence upon

God. Compare Miss Root's marvelous journey to South America, all alone, when such universal results were secured. She depended upon none of the friends, but her dependence was entirely upon the power of the Covenant. Verily, she was 'independ[ent] of all save God'. Was not this successful?[34]

Horace appealed to the friends to stop relying on their fellow believers to find interested souls and for them to instead 'go boldly forth among the strangers, carrying the Message to places where the Message is not known, and relying entirely upon the confirmation of the Covenant'.[35]

* * * * *

In 1935, the National Teaching Committee, under the adept leadership of Leroy Ioas, determined that twelve of the States in the United States did not have any Bahá'ís and most of the Canadian believers lived in either Vancouver, Montreal, or Toronto. Clearly, a revised, systematic approach had to be developed to open the virgin areas of both countries.

That same year, Allen McDaniel, from Washington DC and chairman of the National Assembly, travelled throughout New England visiting Bahá'í communities. He found small, struggling groups whose understanding of Bahá'í administration was shallow, and whose appreciation of the importance of obedience to Bahá'í institutions was limited. Many of the communities were also hampered by internal disunity. Nevertheless, ignorance of Bahá'í administration did not mean that the friends did not care about the Administrative Order; indeed, they expressed eagerness to learn and to follow guidance. He also found that most communities focused on their own membership and were not directed outward towards the wider community, perhaps because most of the locations he visited were populated primarily by elderly, long-time believers. He did encounter a few groups that were bringing in new believers, but these were the exception. In a word, the communities of one of the most active regions of the country were stagnating. Despite lack of growth, McDaniel reported that everywhere there was 'a spirit of hope, faith and courage' and nowhere did he find 'any feeling of hopelessness or despair'.[36]

McDaniel's report noted that the other members of the National Assembly, including Horace, had also visited many Bahá'í communities. Of New England in particular, Horace remarked, 'That's my native country',[37] and so it was hardly surprising that he concentrated his travels in that region. Communities were keen for him to come because his talks and personal interactions with them were inspirational and fruitful. Horace hoped to promote the use of radio to spread the Faith in New England, drawing up a plan to put that new communications media to use to spread the Faith. In New York, the Holleys' door had always been open to inquirers, often through the efforts of Doris. But these efforts, both by the Holleys and collectively by the friends in the Northeast, never resulted in steady growth. Similar frustrations led Leroy Ioas to develop a new teaching tool – the fireside – on the West Coast. These were introductory meetings held in homes, usually on a weekly basis. Welcoming hospitality and the building of friendships in an informal atmosphere were key elements that made them successful. Over time, with the encouragement of the Guardian, firesides would become the backbone of teaching efforts in North America.

After studying the 1935 report of the National Teaching Committee,[38] Shoghi Effendi surprised those assembled at the 1936 National Convention by announcing that after twenty-four years in abeyance, the time had arrived to carry out the Tablets of the Divine Plan. The opening stage would be to establish the Faith throughout the Americas. In only a few words, he set before them a Herculean task: 'Would to God every State within American Republic and every Republic in American continent might ere termination (of) this glorious century (1944) embrace the light (of the) Faith of Bahá'u'lláh and establish (the) structural basis of His World Order.'[39] The National Assembly lost no time in appointing an Inter-America Committee to coordinate the work of sending forth teachers to Central and South America and to the island nations of the Caribbean. It charged the National Teaching Committee with overseeing the systematic planting of the Faith in the States of the United States and Provinces of Canada which did not yet have at least one Local Spiritual Assembly.

In a cable sent to the next Convention in 1937, Shoghi Effendi added the completion of the outer ornamentation of the House of Worship as a third goal. Just as the Temple superstructure finally was in place and its outer adornment was underway, the Guardian announced 'The Seven Year Plan', beginning officially at Riḍván 1937 and concluding in 1944 on the 100th anniversary of the Declaration of the Báb – the inception of the Bahá'í Faith.[40] All of the goals would have to be won during this period. There was only one way that two of the goals could be met – believers would have to leave their homes and settle in targeted areas. Both the Inter-America Committee and the National Teaching Committee would have to think and act strategically, like generals mapping out a battle plan, if they were to accomplish the task before them in such a short span of time. Unlike the Plan of Unified Action, this teaching plan's tangible goals could never be won simply by a handful of itinerate public speakers. The National Assembly also immediately realized that the Plan required funds, not only for Temple construction, but to dispatch believers to unopened locales and support them until they could support themselves. Shoghi Effendi gave those who moved to goal areas a new name: pioneers, evoking the collective memory of Americans moving westward on foot and in covered wagons to settle and develop the sparsely populated regions of the continent. He could not have given them a more romantic appellation.

Horace shared his thoughts about the Seven Year Plan in a letter to an old friend, expounding upon what he believed it meant for the troubled times of the late 1930s. His thinking was apocalyptic, convinced as he was that much of what Shoghi Effendi warned would happen to the Bahá'ís and humanity in the World Order letters was near at hand.

> What I feel is a great change in the world, & more & more pressure on the believers to have a real faith <u>inside</u> or be exposed to all kinds of confusion. Sticking fast to the main things, & not worrying about details or personalities, is our job during these years as far as I can see. The nations are crystallizing anti-human policies & attitudes. The issue will find us out sooner than we realize, perhaps, but it will be a lot easier to cope with vital things than with the vague uneasiness that often permeates the Cause. Those who go along now, building up solid knowledge & working along on the 7 year plan as well as they can, are going to be ready, while those who revolve around their own egos are going to be unprepared when the big issue – the world vs. the Cause – occupies the scene.[41]

Horace was familiar with organized Christian missionary activities that took the Gospel to new regions of the United States and the world. As a child and youth attending his hometown church, he had listened to reports about how the Congregationalists had sponsored new churches in the Western regions of North America as the nation's population expanded toward the setting sun.[42] As a college student he would have often passed by a large stone monument on the Williams College campus commemorating the 1806 haystack incident. Five Williams students were praying together in the fields of the campus and discussing the spiritual welfare of the peoples of Asia when a fierce storm blew through the area. The tempest was so fierce that the terrified students thought death was upon them as they huddled for safety in a haystack. In gratitude for their deliverance, they pledged to take the Gospel of Christ to the peoples of the world who had not yet heard about their Saviour. The American Board of Commissioners for Foreign Missions was born from the group's pledge. The incident is commonly considered the spark that ignited the development of organized American Protestant missions to other countries. All Williams students of Horace's generation knew the story and what had been accomplished by Protestant foreign missionaries over the century that had passed. Horace would serve as the hub for information during the Seven Year Plan as Baháʼís spread out to complete the mission of bringing Baháʼu'lláh's Faith to all regions of the Western Hemisphere. He was on familiar turf.

The Seven Year Plan was executed like a well-conceived and coordinated battle plan. The committee appointed to dispatch pioneers to the locales within the United States and Canada was headed by Leroy Ioas who undertook it with gusto. Its success was in part due to the National Assembly's decision to appoint only members living on the West Coast, making it possible for the committee to meet frequently and for them to work closely together. This lesson of proximity was then applied to other aspects of the Plan. Sending individuals and families to unfamiliar places where they were expected to re-establish their lives required information about the target areas, careful analysis of needs, and knowledge of available volunteers. It became not only a question of dedication and willingness but also one of evaluating whether a prospective pioneer could find employment and adapt to a strange environment and perhaps a new language, especially those willing to go to other countries.[43] Most of the volunteers were single women. For Horace, this element posed a special dilemma, especially when any young woman offered to move to a goal community in Latin America. He had sincere concerns about their safety, confiding to a colleague that, 'it ought to be appreciated by the N. S. A. and the Inter-America Com., that single women simply can't be allowed to go to Mexico and South America representing the Cause – unless they are iron jawed and at least 65 years old'.[44] Fortunately, Horace's advice was not heeded: a handful of young, attractive, single women proved their worth as international pioneers.

Many of the goal areas of the Seven Year Plan were in the Southern United States, where enforced racial segregation and the legalized oppression of Blacks presented a difficult and risky environment for the pioneers. Courage and dedication were not enough to be successful; the National Assembly realized with experience that those pioneers sent to areas where the races were rigidly kept apart required comprehensive support from Bahá'í institutions. New believers drawn from the White segment of Southern towns and cities may have wished in their hearts for racial harmony, but many feared serious repercussions, including violence, if Bahá'í gatherings were racially integrated. This posed a spiritual and practical dilemma for the National Assembly. Was it wiser to begin introducing the Cause in the South at segregated gatherings in order to increase the number of believers and interested seekers, or was it more important to promote integrated meetings from the outset and risk losing many of the people attracted to the Faith and also stir up trouble? In a letter written on behalf of the National Assembly explaining this situation to Shoghi Effendi, Horace added that similar problems existed in northern cities, but there the divide was between the classes.[45] Shoghi Effendi approved of the approach proposed by the National Assembly to have separate gatherings in the beginning with the understanding that the two groups should be fused together as soon as possible and 'be given full and equal opportunity to participate in the conduct of the teachings as well as the administrative activities of the Faith'.[46] The Seven Year Plan forced the Bahá'í community to confront the deep-seated complexities of racial and class prejudices as it put into action the guidance of Shoghi Effendi. In the end, there could and would be no compromise of the cornerstone principle of the oneness of mankind. With the American believers confronting the black and white divide squarely as they went about spreading the Faith, the Guardian determined that it was time for him to provide the Americans with an education about what he termed 'the most vital and challenging issue'. It would become the most studied section of an important letter he wrote to North America in the midst of perilous times.

The letter's context is important to its understanding. Shoghi Effendi alone embodied the office of Guardianship. He had no children, and at that time there were no living Hands of the Cause of God to assist him or oversee a transition after he was gone. Though never one to flee from danger out of fear for his own well-being, he could not ignore the tenuous situation that threatened his unique position in 1938. The Holy Land became turbulent and dangerous as burgeoning numbers of Jewish refugees fleeing persecution in Europe made their way to their ancient homeland, with many of them settling in Haifa. The Arab population pushed back against this tidal wave of Jews who they knew claimed the land as their own. Both sides initiated violence and acts of terrorism. British authorities governing the country were caught in the middle as they tried to restore order. As the situation in the Holy Land became more volatile, Shoghi Effendi decided he could best serve the Faith by returning to Europe. But there too, dangers were rising.

While away, Shoghi Effendi began to draft a lengthy letter instructing the Americans as to what to do as the world situation darkened. After returning safely to Haifa that December, on Christmas Day he dispatched this highly significant work, addressed to the friends in the United States and Canada, to Horace as secretary of the National Assembly. The epistle was the size of a small book. It would long be considered one of the Guardian's most significant writings. Horace gave it the title: *The Advent of Divine Justice*. Its opening reminded the North American friends safely shielded by two oceans that their fellow believers in other parts of the world could no longer carry out most Bahá'í activities because of the rise of authoritarian regimes and the spread of war. The North American Bahá'í community was the last fortress standing. It was up to them to carry forward the work of the Faith until their sister communities were liberated. The narrative explored the earlier accomplishments of the North American community but also candidly elucidated the challenges and shortcomings of American society. Shoghi Effendi emphasized the importance of morality and warned the Bahá'ís against adopting the toxic racial attitudes and materialism of their fellow countrymen. His exploration of the racial situation in the United States was eye-opening and accurate. The Bahá'í Faith had begun in Iran not because of the virtues of that society, but because of its degradation. The same was true of the United States. It was chosen as the cradle of the Administrative Order because of the corruption embedded in American society. The last half of the work focused upon teaching the Faith, setting forth at length what was required, the traits teachers must mirror forth through their characters, the methods they should use and how the teaching work should be supported. The letter was a *tour de force*, perhaps written with the thought that the Holy Land might once again be cut off from the world. Shoghi Effendi left nothing unsaid. The North American Bahá'í army had its marching orders for spiritually conquering the Western Hemisphere. Horace described it as Shoghi Effendi's 'beacon of inextinguishable light ignited before the descent of final darkness'.[47]

Shortly after receiving *The Advent of Divine Justice* in late December 1938, the National Assembly announced it would make a concerted effort to put into practice the guidance found in the letter. The lengthy essay demanded a higher standard of conduct which placed upon the institutions of the Faith 'the obligation to encourage and protect the members of the racial, religious and class minorities'[48] within its communities. It would henceforth strive to adhere to this standard whenever it made appointments, giving preference to minority members.[49] Promoting race unity became a top priority for the National Assembly even after America entered the World War II in 1941. From that time on, the National Assembly never slackened its commitment to race unity and used every opportunity to promote it. For example, on 4 January 1944, five years after receiving *The Advent of Divine Justice*, Horace sent an open letter to President Franklin Roosevelt on behalf of the National Assembly which discussed America's race problem and praised Roosevelt for his efforts to stand up for the country's Black citizenry. It stated that his 'firm and powerful support of the principle of justice in race relations in connection with labor policy at this time, and your attitude of understanding and sympathy toward the economic and social hardship sustained by our Negro[50] citizens, have been noted with grateful appreciation by all American Bahá'ís'.[51] It asked, 'How can we exercise the concentration of material and spiritual power in America for world peace if we continue to abuse that power in dealing with our own most helpless minority?'[52] After quoting from one of 'Abdu'l-Bahá's statements on race unity, the National Assembly's letter asked the President to continue to make this issue a national priority.[53]

* * * * *

As gloom spread its shadow over more and more of the globe, Shoghi Effendi emphasized to the North American Bahá'ís that they should not do or say anything to side with any of the belligerents.[54] Weeks after Germany invaded Poland in September 1939, triggering a declaration of war from Great Britain, Horace suggested to the Green Acre Committee that it consider adding a course he had prepared on 'the Spiritual Life, the aim of which is to build the habit of meditation and that attitude of reverence to the Creative Word', because such a course might be 'suitable for a time of war and suffering. . . .'[55] It was obvious to Horace that the times were changing too rapidly to plan far in advance. In his letter to the Committee, he wrote, 'None of us can foresee the condition or the psychology of the summer of 1940 – it's an entirely different world than 1939 . . .'[56] From its beginning, the American Bahá'í community had been joined with Canada, a country which was part of the British Commonwealth. The believers in that country went into the War earlier than their friends in the United States; the Canadians joined when the Battle of Britain began in late 1939. From that time until the end of the War, plans were always tentative, or as Horace put it, 'Next summer is on the lap of Bahá'u'lláh. I hope the Divine Plan doesn't require too much difficulty for the schools . . .'[57]

In the run-up to the War, conscription was reinstated in the United States and Canada. The National Assembly, after consulting Shoghi Effendi, developed a policy that Bahá'ís should not resist the draft because they were not pacifists, but should instead seek non-combatant status on religious grounds. To facilitate this, the National Spiritual Assembly issued membership cards to all believers in the United States and Canada for the first time. Many Bahá'ís who served in the War did so as medical officers, still in danger, but not carrying weapons. Horace wrote a letter to the National Youth Committee six weeks before the United States entered the War, giving his own personal suggestion that they take advantage of the reinstatement of the draft to educate all Bahá'í youth of draft age not only about the Bahá'í policies towards conscription, but also about the Faith's teachings about war and peace as well as the duties of citizenship. This would better prepare them for teaching opportunities in the months ahead.[58]

Mobilization for war pulled the United States economy out of the Great Depression. The crash of 1937 was the last financial trauma, for once President Roosevelt recognized that war with Germany was likely, he ramped up production of war materials even as he massaged public opinion to accept America's support for its allies under siege, especially Great Britain. Even though many Americans sympathized with England when its cities were bombed by Germany, they continued to consider the conflict to be another peoples' fight. As with the early years of World War I, America relied on the two oceans to shield it and carried on with business as usual, though it was happy to provide supplies from its factories and farms to its overseas allies. If only the mainland of North America was considered, the United States could have remained aloof from the conflicts, other than to play the role of arms merchant. But America had colonies. The largest one was the Philippines, which Japan coveted, so it was eager to dislodge America from the Pacific. Japan's national ambition for Pacific hegemony turned to bitterness when Roosevelt crippled it with trade embargos. On 7 December 1941, Japan attacked the United States naval base at Pearl Harbor in another of America's colonies, Hawaii. Within a few days, the Axis powers in Europe, including Nazi-controlled Germany, declared war on the United States. There was nothing to be done but to fight.

Immediately after the attack on Pearl Harbor, the village of Wilmette prepared defences. The Bahá'í properties were near a US Coast Guard Station, a stone's throw from the Ḥaẓíra. The station's personnel increased from a handful to forty men.[59] The lake front behind the Holleys' home was lit with floodlights at night lest German submarines attacked through the Great Lakes. The Holleys became accustomed to air raid drills. When sirens went off, they were required to conceal the lights of the House of Worship and the Ḥaẓíra. Doris purchased groceries with government-issued rationing cards and had to reduce the staples in her cupboards, including Horace's last luxury – coffee.[60] In 1943, the darkest days of the war, Horace complained to Mountfort Mills that he missed sleeping on a nice warm beach along the Atlantic, to which his New York friend replied, 'How about one outside your back door!' adding that along the Atlantic, no one dared venture onto a beach without 'eternal vigilance', suggesting Horace look for relaxation in the Highlands.[61]

* * * * *

From 1941 through the end of World War II, the membership of the National Spiritual Assembly remained constant. And what an exceptional collection of giants it was! Seven of the nine would later be named Hands of the Cause of God. Louis Gregory, who had become the foremost Bahá'í champion of race amity, was again a member. Allen McDaniel, who used his professional expertise as an engineer to work with the contractors during the construction of the Temple, was still serving and focused upon the completion of the exterior ornamentation and the interior. Roy Wilhelm, the spiritual anchor and finance expert, brought his wisdom, folksy humour, and material resources to the conference table, even though ill health made it difficult for him to participate as fully as he had in the past. Fred Schopflocher's factory was busier than ever because the military needed his product. Leroy Ioas had become the primary engine driving the teaching campaigns from his perch in California. His knowledge and experience as a railroad executive became critical in determining the availability of public transportation for Bahá'í purposes during the war. George Latimer brought his lawyer's organizational skills to the work. Amelia Collins, a wealthy widow who lived part-time in Wilmette, travelled the world to promote the teaching work and in the process had become much beloved by the Guardian. The youngest member, Dorothy Baker, was a spiritual ball of fire who had picked up the race unity torch from the ageing Louis Gregory. This housewife from Lima, Ohio, added vibrancy and intense reliance on prayer to the work of the National Assembly. And, of course, its secretary, Horace Holley, continued to carry out the work he had been doing since 1924.

In the mid-1930s, Horace noticed that his colleague Fred Schopflocher seemed to be in a foul mood,[62] so unlike the sweetness which normally characterized him. When he first got to know Fred in the 1920s, Horace referred to him as 'one of the greatest Bahá'í souls in this country'.[63] Fred was born in Germany to an orthodox Jewish family with eighteen children. His family owned the world patent for producing bronze powder. He had taken that knowhow to Canada and become wealthy as an industrialist by setting up a second factory for the family business. Green Acre had provided him with a spiritual refuge and the souls who would nurture him at the start of his journey as a Bahá'í. But now he was critical of everything, even Green Acre. What Fred was not disclosing to his friends was the agonizing ordeal he was quietly experiencing. Other than his Canadian wife, most members of his large family were still in Germany where, because they were Jews, they were being persecuted and later rounded up and slaughtered by the Nazis.[64] His family's German factory was confiscated. Many of his relatives would not survive the war. At home in his grand house in Canada, Fred was helpless to come to their aid despite his plentiful material resources. For the most part, Americans were ignorant of the Holocaust as it unfolded. Only the liberation of the concentration camps by Allied troops at the end of the war would bring the full horrors of the Nazi regime and its systematic attempt to wipe out the Jews and other minorities to the attention of humanity. For Fred, the disaster unfolding in his homeland with the rise of the Nazis was personal, though he apparently never discussed it with his colleagues.

As the hot fires of the war ignited more and more of the world, Shoghi Effendi addressed the darkness of the age in another earth-shaking, book-length letter, which Horace titled *The Promised Day Is Come*. Issued in March 1941, before the United States entered the War, it was addressed to the world-wide Bahá'í community. The work included extensive excerpts from Bahá'u'lláh's letters to the main political and religious leaders of His time. These, according to Horace, armed the Bahá'ís against 'the psychic onslaught of war itself, and created an inner peace which nothing in the world can assail'.[65]

Throughout the War, the spirits of the North American Bahá'ís were raised again and again by the heroic activities of their fellow members as they achieved the goals of the Seven Year Plan. With bad news in the news media inundating everyone, stories of the experiences of travelling teachers or pioneers brought tangible confirmations that Bahá'u'lláh's promises for a brighter new world after a period of intense suffering were true. Miracles were happening. Despite restraints on civilian travel, the friends continued to move to goal areas, and gatherings such as summer schools and national Conventions were held as usual, except during the last months of the War. Horace was in the middle of this buzz of progress. If the previous decade had been about deepening and training the believers to enhance the quality of the community, the 1940s were a time of movement and growth. It was exciting.

* * * * *

Despite the greater travel distance, Horace and Doris continued to spend late summers each year at Green Acre, which also afforded them side trips to visit Horace's relatives. Their modest cottage was near one occupied by the Bowditch family, who spent the summers there to assist with the school's programmes. The Bowditchs kept a garden to supply the school's kitchen with produce, and Horace eagerly volunteered to tend it. He loved growing vegetables and had often planted little gardens, even amidst nooks and crannies of New York City. It was a refreshing diversion from his desk work. He would rise early in the morning and head to the patch to take care of chores such as pulling weeds and capping broccoli. To the Bowditchs, both Holleys were good fun. Doris and Nancy Bowditch would walk together to the riverbank and wade into the cool water, chatting away as the fast current swirled around their feet. The Holleys also took an interest in the young Bowditch grandchildren. One day, Horace invited their six-year-old grandson, Neddie, to accompany him on a hike at nearby Mt Savant, a hill blessed by a visit from 'Abdu'l-Bahá. They brought along a lunch and had a jolly time until Horace set the woods ablaze when he tried to build a cooking fire with dried leaves. Fortunately, the flames were extinguished before the fire department had to be summoned. That family remembered Horace's 'sweet smile, his joyful humour and great kindness'.[66] Doris, like Horace, was also funny, but they especially remembered her 'for being outspoken when the need arose, and for her devotion to Horace'.[67] One evening with the Holleys stood out in their memories. The Holleys paid a visit to the Bowditch cabin shortly after Horace's compilation, *Bahá'í World Faith*, was published. The two families huddled around a small wood stove taking turns reading aloud passages from that book. 'It was a magical evening.'[68]

* * * * *

In 1943, perhaps the worst year of the War, Shoghi Effendi again astonished the North American believers when he directed them to hold an Inter-America Conference in conjunction with a big celebration of the Centenary of the Declaration of the Báb. This event would serve as a befitting capstone to the first hundred years of heroic achievements of the Faith. It was to be held in Wilmette at the House of Worship, its exterior at last complete. Representatives from the new national communities throughout the Americas were to be invited. If most of the Bahá'í communities around the world could not hold major celebrations in

1944, the Americans would do so on their behalf.⁶⁹ Horace, of course, played a major role in the intricate planning and execution of this lofty and joyous undertaking. To maximize the impact of this occasion, the Guardian called for extensive nation-wide publicity before, during and after the event – something that the American community had never done before. Who among the National Assembly members had more expertise in advertising than Horace? He dove into it.⁷⁰

When the long-anticipated opening of the Centenary celebration arrived, the House of Worship stood in all its glory as a glistening jewel with its ground quartz ornamental panels sparkling in the sunshine. The lawns encircling the building were not yet fully laid out as gardens, but nonetheless they provided a pleasant setting, especially looking toward the lake. But once the exhilarated participants entered the auditorium beneath the enormous dome, the reality of the work yet to be done struck them. The main auditorium of the building was still a concrete shell, unadorned and unfurnished. Folding chairs had been placed throughout the vast space for the special programme. For those who had attended gatherings in the basement of the Temple for two decades, however, finally being seated beneath the great dome was a thrill, even if it continued to be a construction site.

The Centenary and All-America Program meetings were spread between 19 and 24 May. The Centenary's most important sessions were held on the evening of 22 May, the hundredth anniversary of the Báb's declaration to Mullá Ḥusayn that He was the long-awaited Promised One. The first of the three evening programmes began at 8:00 p.m. Horace, one of three speakers, spoke about, 'The World in Transformation'. The 9:40 p.m. programme was the actual dedication ceremony of the House of Worship. This was followed at 10:00 p.m. with another commemoration of the Declaration of the Báb, in alignment with the time the historic event had occurred that world-shaking night in Shiraz, Persia in 1844.

A highlight of those days of jubilation was 'The Meeting of the Americas' session devoted to the work of raising up communities throughout all of the nations of the Western Hemisphere. Twenty-three nations were represented, mainly by new believers from those countries. On the last day, a great banquet was held at the Hotel Stevens in Chicago and a portion of its after-dinner programme was broadcast live by radio.

Altogether, the 1944 celebration surpassed all expectations as a successful occasion. There was much to celebrate. The exterior of the Temple was, at long last, completed and breathtakingly beautiful – especially on the night when it was fully illumined for the first time for the Centenary. All but a handful of the goals of the Seven Year Plan had been met, resulting in growing Bahá'í communities spread throughout the hemisphere. The Faith had been planted in the southern-most town of South America and in the far north in Alaska. In the process, a handful of itinerate teachers visited the fledgling communities and isolated friends to educate them, boost their morale and inspire them to greater service. Among the pioneers, a cadre had acquired expertise in going into new communities to introduce the Faith, moving from place to place as needed – an invaluable new resource. The National Assembly had established a committee to promote the translation of Bahá'í literature into Spanish and Portuguese and to arrange for its publication and distribution. The Faith was on the move! Issue after issue of *Bahá'í News* was filled with reports of activities taking place throughout the Americas, including photographs of new groups in other countries – proof that the goals were being met.

Within the United States and Canada, more than a hundred households uprooted themselves and settled in new localities to win goals. Most of those who undertook this sacrificial service were single women. There were a few who relocated more than once after one community was firmly launched and another required attention. During the seven years of the Plan, the number of Local Spiritual Assemblies in the United States and Canada grew from 70 to 139 – a remarkable achievement. All of this was the fruit of careful coordination, of passionate appeals to specific believers to arise, and of settling the volunteers where they were most needed. If Shoghi Effendi noticed a slack in the momentum, he would issue an emphatic appeal that would inspire another wave of volunteers. It was a relentless process, for as soon as one goal was met, a pioneer already settled at another goal area would be forced to leave the post for personal reasons, requiring the recruitment of a replacement pioneer to fill the goal.

The rapid increase in the number of infant Assemblies necessitated the development and implementation of new tools to assist them. Naturally, Horace, who had become the acknowledged expert in Bahá'í administration, took on the task of producing a manual, *Bahá'í Procedure*, to supplement the compilation of Shoghi Effendi's letters, *Bahá'í*

Administration. It first appeared in 1937 and was revised in 1942.[71] Horace compiled it from material published in *Bahá'í News* as well as from policies found in the minutes of the National Assembly. Because administrative policies were organic and subject to change and expansion, Horace originally planned a loose-leaf format for the manual, with each section numbered separately. By the second printing, it had become an inexpensive paperback book.[72] Many copies were tucked way into the luggage of those taking the Faith to new areas where it provided the basis for the organization of nascent communities. In 1947, Horace followed up this work with an essay, 'Present-Day Administration of the Bahá'í Faith', which was published as a pamphlet by the Bahá'í Publishing Committee.[73]

Horace's masterful, inspiring summary of Bahá'í administration in the leaflet acknowledges at the outset that, 'Until one has made contact with the spirit of the Bahá'í teachings and desires to cooperate wholeheartedly with their purpose, the administrative phase of the Faith can have little real meaning or appeal.'[74] From the vantage point of a decade of active teaching work, the essay speaks to the new believer or the sincere seeker desiring a spiritual home. It gives hope to those friends struggling to establish a new point of light on the globe because, from his high perspective from which he could observe the whole of the Americas, he witnessed what wondrous happenings could spring from reliance on the powers of Bahá'u'lláh when coupled with unity.

> Where the community is small and insignificant, in comparison with the population of the city or town, the first condition of growth is understanding the Manifestation of Bahá'u'lláh, and the next condition is that of true humility. If these two conditions exist, the weakest soul becomes endowed with effective power in service to the Cause. The result of unity, in fact, is to share the powers and faculties of all with each.[75]

His overview of the elements of Bahá'í administration concludes with what Horace enunciated as four of its characteristics. The first is 'its completely successful reconciliation of the usually opposed claims of democratic freedom and unanswerable authority'.[76] Second is 'the entire absence from the Bahá'í Cause of anything approaching the institution of a salaried professional clergy'.[77] Third is 'the absence of internal factionalism, that bane of all organized effort and the sure sign of spiritual disease'.[78] Finally, the fourth was 'that the Bahá'í Cause has within it an inherent necessity operating slowly but surely to bring its administration into the hands of those truly fitted for the nature of the work'.[79] This last characteristic would be brought about through evolution as those who had the larger vision gradually replaced those lacking it, so that 'the result is an inevitable improvement in the qualities placed at the service of the Cause, until the highest attributes of humanity will be enrolled'.[80]

As the friends raced to fulfil the remaining goals of the Seven Year Plan, Shoghi Effendi paid homage to Horace and the National Assembly and the American community for their exemplary work during trying times. As with most of his letters to the National Assembly, it begins, 'Dear Horace', thanking him for reports he has sent.

> He is always happy to hear from you, as he has a great deal of sympathy for what he fully realizes must be your continuously overworked state. Hard pressed for time as he himself constantly is, he well knows what it means!
>
> He most deeply appreciated the way you devote yourself so entirely and single-mindedly to the service of our beloved Faith.
>
> The wonderful work the friends have done during these last two decades, more particularly under the Seven Year Plan, never could have been accomplished if the administration had not grown strong and efficient enough to carry the burden of organization required for the successful outcome of teaching and Temple projects. And you have certainly expended the major portion of your energies these many years in helping to establish this administration and facilitate its functioning. Now you can have the pleasure of watching your labors bear precious fruit.[81]

In a handwritten postscript at the bottom of the letter, Shoghi Effendi reiterated those sentiments and also paid homage to Doris, Horace's 'dear collaborator'.[82]

* * * * *

The great celebration of 1944 must have exhausted the Holleys, who were no longer young. Just weeks following it, most likely in early

July, Horace suffered a heart attack, requiring hospitalization and an extended rest during which he was not allowed visitors. Even after weeks of rest, his doctor would not even allow him to venture out of doors. Doris and Sophie Loeding did their best to continue the work of the Secretariat with the help of other Assembly officers.[83] One indication as to how much the American community depended upon Horace was a special notice atop the July 1944 *Bahá'í News* informing the readers that he had experienced a sudden illness requiring a complete rest, therefore that edition of the newsletter would be abbreviated. It ended with an update that he was back at home and improving.[84]

When Horace moved to Wilmette he quit smoking cigarettes, most likely as an acknowledgement of the exalted status of the building where he lived.[85] However, the habit of chain-smoking he had acquired as a teenager had already diminished his health. Though that first cardiac episode was not considered serious, it was a warning. His brother Irving blamed the heart attack on the Centenary celebration, certain the event had rested primarily on Horace's '"know how" and "see-it-thru' ability"'.[86] Horace had confided to his siblings that when the festivities were over he wanted to retire to Maine, where he would resume his own writing. Irving hoped that his younger brother would view the heart attack as a sign from God to do just that 'and transmute all his years of experience thru those keen eyes of his, and convert it all into some rare book of his life, seasoned as it would be with his rare wisdom'.[87] From that point on, Horace's greatest personal tests would be bouts of ill health springing from an assortment of medical problems.[88] When Shoghi Effendi learned of the heart attack, he wrote to Horace of his relief to learn that he was recovering and asked that he not over-tax himself, adding that he felt 'confident that you will render our beloved Faith services as outstanding and unique as those that will remain associated with your name during the Formative Age of the Faith of Bahá'u'lláh'.[89]

* * * * *

Despite government restrictions on travel during the War and the rationing of gasoline, far more than a majority of delegates attended the National Conventions between 1942 and 1944. But in 1945, the constraints of rationing and limitations on civilian travel on public transportation had reached such a level that the Convention had to be cancelled. For the first time, voting was carried out by mail, and a handful of tellers assembled in Foundation Hall to count the ballots. Horace and the other outgoing members who could get to Wilmette looked on as the tellers called the roll of delegates and deposited each ballot in a box.[90] Although the delegates were prevented from consulting in person, they were encouraged to consult with their local communities and then send comments and recommendations to the National Assembly. These were later published in *Bahá'í News*.[91]

* * * * *

During the 1930s, much of the Bahá'í community focused on economic issues in public meetings, publications, and other forms of outreach, and sought to apply the Faith's principles to the economic disaster of the Great Depression. With the onset of World War II, peace – a topic dear to Horace's heart – became the theme on which the Bahá'í community focused its attention. His compilation of talks and writings of 'Abdu'l-Bahá, *Foundations of World Unity*, which addressed peace among its subjects, was finally published in book form by the Publishing Committee in 1945.[92] Having pondered and studied how to achieve lasting peace for decades, Horace wrote an essay for *The Bahá'í World* summarizing attempts over the centuries to consolidate nations or groups, and analysing those that were successful, and which were not. He concluded that only those efforts which required members to relinquish sovereignty to a greater or higher organization lasted and had a positive effect. For him, this was at the heart of the failure of the League of Nations – relinquishing any aspect of national sovereignty was never a requirement of its membership.[93] Fear that it would become a requirement was the primary reason for the United States' hesitation to join the League.

As the end of World War II came into view, a few far-sighted leaders were determined to prevent such a catastrophe from ever afflicting humanity again. Even before the United States entered the War, President Roosevelt started to lay the groundwork for the establishment of a new organization of countries, to be called the United Nations, which would improve upon and replace the fading League of Nations. In August 1941 he met secretly with Winston Churchill, Prime Minister of Great Britain, on a battleship off the coast of Canada and devised what became known as the 'Atlantic Charter'. This significant agreement set out the war aims of the allies, stating that they were not fighting to expand territory. It also included lofty aims such as that the peoples of the world had a right to self-determination, the seas should be freely open to all nations, the abandonment of the use of force, and disarmament of aggressor nations at the end of the war and general disarmament afterwards. The charter was endorsed by a number of nations or their governments in exile. Roosevelt, with Churchill's blessing, came up with the name 'United Nations'. Details of the structure of the proposed organization were discussed with America's leading allies at the Dumbarton Oaks Conference in 1944. Months later, Roosevelt, Churchill, and Stalin, as the heads of the United States, Great Britain, and the Soviet Union respectively, agreed to most of the proposed elements of the United Nations when they met at the Black Sea port of Yalta. The United Nations would have the authority to deploy an international coalition of troops to maintain peace, a power denied to the League. The bi-cameral organization would have one of its chambers, the Security Council, composed of the most powerful of the nations, five of which would possess the right to veto any proposed action. There was a gaping hole in the proposal, for the issue of relinquishing national sovereignty was never addressed. Overall, however, the new organization represented a modest step forward towards the goal of a world federation that could truly maintain peace. Roosevelt was impatient to bring the new world organization into being and so a gathering was scheduled for late April 1945 at which its charter would be drafted and adopted. While making plans to attend that historic meeting, President Roosevelt died, twelve days before the United Nations conference convened.[94]

This historic conference of delegates from fifty of the allied nations[95] was held in San Francisco, California, thereby fulfilling 'Abdu'l-Bahá's prophetic words delivered years before in Sacramento that that region would be the first to hoist the banner of peace. Leroy Ioas's lifelong interest in international peace through international organization was rekindled as soon as the conference was announced in the newspapers. At his urging, the San Francisco Bay Bahá'í communities sprang into action immediately. Pleased by this initiative, the National Assembly supported and ratified their plans. Having already developed proficiency in the use of radio, the Bay area friends scheduled a series of broadcasts on the Bahá'í peace plan for the period of the conference and hosted events to which the delegates were invited. Two of their community members, Leroy's wife Sylvia Ioas, and Horace's young friend Marion Holley, were designated by the conference organizers as official observers representing the Bahá'í community at the United Nations sessions.[96] A number of delegates attended the Bahá'í-sponsored events. According to two San Francisco newspapers, the Bahá'í symposium on peace received the largest attendance of any peace meeting held during the period of the United Nations Conference.[97] Lessons learned, and contacts made twenty years earlier when the San Francisco Bahá'ís had held the first World Unity Conference no doubt led to this success.

The National Assembly, expecting President Roosevelt to attend the San Francisco Conference, sent him a telegram expressing its hope that the President 'would be spiritually guided and reinforced to lead the nations and peoples of the world in the inauguration of universal peace', ending the cable with a quotation from 'Abdu'l-Bahá, and the prayer, 'may the dire needs of humanity be met by the creation of a new world order through the effort of the forthcoming conference in San Francisco under your leadership'.[98] It was signed by George Latimer as chairman and Horace as secretary. A cordial response was received from the Department of State on behalf of the White House and Secretary of State.[99]

Several years after the War was over, Shoghi Effendi put the entire period of the two World Wars into historic perspective as part of the larger plan of God. By the time he wrote his narrative, New York, the City of the Covenant, had been chosen as the headquarters of the United Nations, making it an unofficial world capital. One of the United Nations' first consequential actions was the ratification of the establishment of the Jewish State of Israel to resolve the question of control over Palestine – important for the fate of the Bahá'í World Centre as well as for the world. In succinct language, Shoghi Effendi explained the background, rise and future significance of the United Nations as seen through the eyes of the spirit – the process known as the Greater Plan of God.

> The other process dates back to the outbreak of the first World War that threw the great republic of the West into the vortex of the first stage of a world upheaval. It received its initial impetus through

the formulation of President Wilson's Fourteen Points, closely associating for the first time that republic with the fortunes of the Old World. It suffered its first setback through the dissociation of that republic from the newly born League of Nations which that president had labored to create. It acquired added momentum through the outbreak of the second World War, inflicting unprecedented suffering on that republic, and involving it still further in the affairs of all the continents of the globe. It was further reinforced through the declaration embodied in the Atlantic Charter, as voiced by one of its chief progenitors, Franklin D. Roosevelt. It assumed a definite outline through the birth of the United Nations at the San Francisco Conference. It acquired added significance through the choice of the City of the Covenant itself as the seat of the newly born organization, through the declaration recently made by the American president related to his country's commitments in Greece and Turkey, as well as through the submission to the General Assembly of the United Nations of the thorny and challenging problem of the Holy Land, the spiritual as well as the administrative center of the World Faith of Bahá'u'lláh. It must, however long and tortuous the way, lead, through a series of victories and reverses, to the political unification of the Eastern and Western Hemispheres, to the emergence of a world government and the establishment of the Lesser Peace, as foretold by Bahá'u'lláh and foreshadowed by the Prophet Isaiah. It must, in the end, culminate in the unfurling of the banner of the Most Great Peace, in the Golden Age of the Dispensation of Bahá'u'lláh.[100]

There was one other event which set World War II apart from all earlier conflicts. On 5 August 1945, a single bomb dropped from the bay of an American war plane flying over the city of Hiroshima, Japan. At the moment it exploded, creating a gigantic mushroom cloud that instantly incinerated the city, mankind entered the Atomic Age. For the first time, a new technology – the splitting of the atom – had been harnessed, not for the betterment of the human race, but to create the most terrible weapon in the history of *homo sapiens*. Its initial development took place in secret beneath the stands of a sports stadium in the middle of Chicago. The airborne attack on Japan, ordered by Roosevelt's successor, President Harry Truman, did not immediately bring about Japan's unconditional surrender. It took a second atomic bomb to convince the Japanese leaders that capitulation was their only option, thereby bringing the War to an end. Fifty years later, a headline of the *New York Times* expressed succinctly what happened that day in the skies over Hiroshima: 'The Bomb: An Act That Haunts Japan and America'.[101] All of the urgent warnings of Bahá'u'lláh, 'Abdu'l-Bahá, and Shoghi Effendi of what awaited humanity if it did not turn its face towards its Maker, had proved prophetic. Horace placed the atomic bomb into a more complete context.

> The Bahá'ís have looked upon the development of the greatest concentration of human energy, science, mechanical equipment and social will the world has ever created, summoned by the dire urgency of battle – a massive force which nothing could withstand; a force able to move mountains and divert seas, command the ether and explode the universe within the atom, all for the victory of war.[102]

He lamented what a waste of the world's resources the War had been, how misguided, for, 'This energy they have seen dissipated, undone and turned into weakness when the supreme issue became not war, but peace.'[103] The nations had bankrupted the influence of the League of Nations because they did not really want peace. The United Nations seemed likely to follow its predecessor into irrelevance because, from its birth it was not organized in such a way as to bring about a lasting peace. Despite the praiseworthy elements of the United Nations Charter which appeared to reflect Bahá'í principles, its fine words would prove to be insufficient to achieve its noble goals. Only the Bahá'í principles were complete enough to bring about a true and lasting peace.

> . . . they have drawn parallels between the Charter of the United Nations and the Bahá'í principles of world order which indicate how far we still are even from the 'Lesser Peace'[104] which has been ordained in this age as the preliminary stage leading to the 'Most Great Peace' of divine intention and effect.[105]

But all was not forlorn gazing upon the ruins left by the Great Upheaval. When the ruinous fighting was over, Horace realized it had actually strengthened the sense of Bahá'í unity, rather than lessened it, and he wrote,

> War has established the conditions under which the followers of Bahá'u'lláh, losing their physical unity, have learned the true meaning of their unity in spirit and in truth. As communication and travel slackened and ceased, their realization of essential oneness quickened. As the pressure of a struggling society intensified, longing for the Kingdom of peace and fellowship filled their hearts.[106]

Further pondering the War's greater meaning, Horace concluded that the First World War had been a warning to mankind which went unheeded. Consequently, the War just ended was the punishment – divine retribution – for failing to learn the obvious lesson of the previous conflagration – namely, that humanity had to undergo a spiritual revival.

> The second world war released the flood of psychological as well as material destruction which can only be stayed by the power of a world religion. When men denied peace they denied themselves. Now we may have peace on God's terms or there is no peace.[107]

As much as the war-weary world wanted the victories against the other Axis powers, including Japan, to mark the beginning of a true era of peace, it was not to be. The malevolent forces of the twentieth century had unleased a God-less ideological movement, Communism. The most powerful empire under Communist control, the Soviet Union, ended the war with enhanced military technology and weaponry sufficient to make it an even greater menace than Fascism. Within less than a decade after the bombing of Japan, the Soviets had their own atomic bomb. Even before the guns fell silent, posturing between the Soviet Union and the Western countries, led by the United States, started what came to be known as the Cold War. To the end of his life, Shoghi Effendi addressed this conflict that threatened to go from cold to hot in an instant. Neither he nor Horace would live to see its conclusion. In the months preceding the cessation of World War II, Russian troops moved into eastern European nations with no intention of leaving. As Churchill would remark, an 'Iron Curtain' had descended over Europe, severing most of its eastern region from easy access to the rest of the world. Authoritarian, Communist governments answerable to Moscow were imposed by Russian overlords. Atheism became the only State-sanctioned religion. Bahá'ís in those countries, most notably Canadian pioneer to Bulgaria Marion Jack, were caught in this oppressive and dangerous situation. The National Assembly knew she was in trouble and tried desperately to come to her aid but was thwarted by the political situation.[108] Further spreading the Faith in the Communist-controlled regions of the world, which included the Chinese empire, became a hazardous endeavour.

* * * * *

With the War over, the North American Bahá'í community entered a new phase. Remarkably, it had been able to sustain its work of sending pioneers to Central and South America despite the restrictions on travel. It had even completed the exterior of the House of Worship. Peace held the promise that it could accelerate its efforts, especially with the country returning to pre-1930 prosperity. Soon, visits to the Holy Land could resume. There was much to look forward to.

The 1946 election of the National Spiritual Assembly of the United States and Canada was a watershed. For the first time, none of the members were drawn from those who had served on the Temple Unity Executive Board. Age and its infirmities had taken their toll on Roy Wilhelm and Louis Gregory. Roy's midterm resignation during the previous year generated the first by-election for a National Assembly seat. Louis was struggling with cancer.[109] Allen McDaniel, who had served almost as long as Horace, was not re-elected – his role as the engineer member overseeing the Temple construction was finished just as his health became a problem. This left Horace as the longest serving member amidst a new generation of Bahá'í leaders. It was also the first time that the Assembly elected a woman as chairman, Dorothy Baker, who through her previous years of membership had proved that she was a capable, organized administrator as well as an inspired, indomitable teacher and lecturer. And that year, one of the members had a secret which she kept from her colleagues. Amelia Collins was informed privately by Shoghi Effendi that he had named her a Hand of the Cause of God, the first to be appointed while living since Bahá'u'lláh's appointments of the first four Hands. How must that have affected her thinking as she participated in Assembly consultations?

The new members had not been part of the establishment of the

Administrative Order and generally knew nothing about the process and hurdles that had brought the institutions to the level of maturity they evinced two decades later. Horace remarked to George Latimer that, 'The balance between experienced and inexperienced members is very delicate this year at best. . .'[110] Horace was particularly concerned about what the new members understood of the relationship between the National Assembly and the Local Assemblies. He took Paul Haney aside and explained to him that his own frame of reference, having experienced the difficulties required to establish the institutions, was always based upon the Declaration of Trust and By-Laws. Therefore, 'when anything happened contrary to fixed constitutional principles,' Horace felt it was wrong, 'without regard to motive and intention'.[111] Paul understood. Horace said of Paul, 'I think he will turn out all right.'[112]

The younger members observed that, as Horace entered his sixties, he was no longer energetic, most likely because of his declining health. In 1949, one younger member commented to another that, 'Horace just plods along in the same speed all the time and I just cannot accommodate myself to this slow motion.'[113] The year before, Horace had confessed to Shoghi Effendi that he could no longer keep up with all of his responsibilities, including those related to *The Bahá'í World*.

> Answering your question about the publication of The Bahá'í World I confess that the major responsibility has rested upon me. Part of the international survey has not been completed. The work has called for a degree of concentration and a period of relief from other duties which I have lacked the capacity to distil from the passing days. It is a fault and a failure which no explanation can lighten. There could be no more creative and inspiring task for a writer in the Faith today; but the work has increased year after year and my strength has fallen behind the pace. The survey has become an honor for which I have no merit.[114]

The last line of Horace's letter to the Guardian read, 'I am filled with bitter regret.'[115]

During this period in the late 1940s, when Horace's health increasingly circumscribed his ability to carry out his duties, he was blessed with assistance from an ally and helper, Leroy Ioas, who had moved from San Francisco to Wilmette in 1946 because his employer had transferred him to Chicago. Whenever Horace could not tend to a matter, such as escorting an important visitor through the House of Worship or meeting with someone on behalf of the Assembly, Leroy was happy to step in on his behalf.[116] And, to Doris's relief, Sylvia Ioas replaced her as cook and hostess for the National Assembly when Doris needed her help.[117] Just as in New York where Horace could work closely with Roy Wilhelm and Mountfort Mills, in Wilmette he had the bounty of creating similar bonds with the Ioas and True families. That same year, Edna True was elected to the National Assembly. Her travel agency became vital to settling pioneers as a member of the Latin-America Teaching Committee and, after the War, with her service as the primary officer of the European Teaching Committee. Finally, Horace could easily consult about day-to-day National Assembly business with fellow members without the expense and time of long-distance communication.

During his 1949 annual visit with his brothers at Irving's mountain retreat, Sunnycroft, in Schoon, New York, Horace suffered another bout of ill health requiring hospitalization. From his hospital room, he wrote a short poem about the test of illness.

> ### *By This I Know His Love*
> *He seized me by the hair and held me over the dread abyss*
> *And made me pay with pain for every desperate breath.*
> *By this I know His wondrous love. I know by this*
> *He loves me more than earth and life, or heaven and death.*[118]

Less than a year later, Horace was back in a hospital – this time in Evanston – unfortunately, at the time of the 1950 National Convention. The delegates voted to send him a message which read in part, 'mindful of the valiant services you have rendered these many years . . . send unbounded love' and assurances of prayers for his speedy recovery.[119] Commenting to a well-wisher about his continued bouts of ill health, Horace wrote, 'How strange when one's intention to serve is thwarted by conditions beyond one's power! I suppose there is a mystery there, to be resolved through radiant acquiescence, but this is new territory for me.'[120]

* * * * *

Shoghi Effendi allowed the North American community a brief respite after the 1944 conclusion of the hectic, but fruitful, Seven Year Plan. In 1946 he gave them another Seven Year Plan that would conclude in 1953, at the centenary of the annunciation of Bahá'u'lláh's Revelation in the infamous Tehran dungeon, the Síyáh-Chál. The goals of the new Plan included the consolidation of the victories of the previous one, the establishment of many more Local Spiritual Assemblies, and the election of the National Spiritual Assembly of Canada, a Spiritual Assembly of Central America, and a Spiritual Assembly of South America. Furthermore, the interior of the House of Worship and the gardens had to be completed. Those goals alone would have stretched the community, but the Guardian added another major component: Europe. With the War over, it was time to raise up or restore communities in Europe, so the North Americans were assigned ten more countries on that continent still recovering from the War. These last goals were thought to be the most difficult, but proved to be the easiest to meet, in part because Bahá'ís from those countries residing in the United States were willing to return to their homelands. In response to those rapid victories, Shoghi Effendi gave the Americans additional goals in Africa. The completion of the Wilmette Temple was another goal carried out quickly, with the interior completed and the gardens laid out in 1951.

While the War was still raging, the Guardian had informed the Bahá'í world in 1944 that erecting the superstructure of the Shrine of the Báb was about to begin. At that time, the Shrine was a nine-roomed, square, one-storey building. It was an unremarkable stone edifice surrounded by a few modest gardens. The plan devised by Canadian architect William Sutherland Maxwell, Shoghi Effendi's father-in-law, was a superstructure with four parts: a square colonnade topped by an octagon and a drum upon which would rest a golden dome. The beautiful design blended styles from many cultures in one harmonious, uplifting effect. Shoghi Effendi was anxious to have it completed by 1953, the same year the Mother Temple of the West was to be finished. What a time to undertake such projects! When the War ended in 1945, construction materials and skilled workers were in short supply because the rebuilding of devasted countries on three continents was underway. One task the National Assembly officers had to accomplish was to find a way to get funds to Italy to pay for marble at a time when the international transfer of funds was especially risky.[121] Careful husbanding of scarce Bahá'í resources to meet the expansion goals while at the same time raising funds to complete both buildings was an immense challenge. In 1948, Shoghi Effendi imposed two years of financial austerity upon the United States and instructed that it must temporarily cease a number of activities, including summer schools and the publication of Horace's beloved *World Order* magazine. The friends contributed the funds, making it possible for all of the suspended activities to resume with the Guardian's consent.

* * * * *

Establishing a National Spiritual Assembly in Canada proved to be one of the more difficult goals to achieve. A decade earlier, the only active Bahá'í communities in that country were in three major cities. With a sprinkling of believers scattered in between, entire provinces did not have a single believer. During the first Seven Year Plan, the unopened provinces received pioneers, mainly from the United States. However, dispatching American citizens to Canada became increasingly challenging once Canada entered the War and entry to the country was restricted. The far east Maritime region was especially problematic due to its notoriously conservative citizenry. This was exacerbated by the War because the Atlantic Coast region was under military control as the launching point for troops headed to Europe and the main location of the defences against a possible invasion. It was consequently difficult for Americans to gain government permission to settle there.[122] Despite those impediments, enough Local Spiritual Assemblies were established during the Plan across the whole of the country to ensure a satisfactory underpinning for a National Assembly. Canadian travelling teachers as well as summer schools held within Canada fostered a sense of community among the Canadian Bahá'ís. 'Abdu'l-Bahá had given His Tablets of the Divine Plan to them as co-recipients with the United States – a responsibility they would now take on with greater fervour under the direction of their own administration.

In April 1948, Horace, along with four other National Assembly members, travelled to Montreal to represent the United States Bahá'í community and to hand the reins of the administration of the Faith in Canada over to the National Assembly about to be established. The historic first Canadian National Convention took place in a building already replete with Bahá'í history, the stately Maxwell home. It was a befitting spot to launch the Canadian community because it had been the residence of May Maxwell, 'the Mother of Canada' who in 1940 had passed away in Argentina working to meet the goals of the Seven Year Plan. Shoghi Effendi designated her a martyr. The beautiful townhouse had been designed by its owner, the architect of the Shrine of the Báb, William Sutherland Maxwell. Presiding that day was the wife of Shoghi Effendi, Mary Maxwell, daughter of May and Sutherland Maxwell, who was then called Rúḥíyyih Khánum. The spacious home was filled with 112 Bahá'ís. As the delegates and guests surveyed the special house, they could not help but reflect back upon the time when 'Abdu'l-Bahá stayed there in 1912.

Horace's long-time friend and colleague, Fred Schopflocher, was among those elected to the first National Assembly of Canada. A number of active believers from the United States, such as Horace's old friends the McKays, had pioneered to Canada and would remain there to ensure the success of the new national community, the ninth nation to establish a National Spiritual Assembly.[123] A year after that historic election, Horace received a letter of appreciation from the new National Assembly for his assistance with incorporating the nascent institution and for giving generously of his time and advice during those first days when that Assembly set about organizing its work.[124]

* * * * *

At some point in the late 1940s, a number of believers noted a marked change in Horace's bearing.[125] He seemed to have been inwardly transformed. The word most often used to describe him was 'luminous'. A softer, humbler side of him became more evident. He still had his wit, not always appreciated, but even those who had not much liked him before found themselves drawn to him, to that inner spirit that had risen to the surface.[126] He had turned his thoughts again to the question of personal transformation, proposing for example, that he give a course on that theme at Green Acre in 1948 which he wanted to title, 'God and You'.[127] He had stopped agitating within himself about how to set the world aright through social, political, and economic change. Peace, he concluded, would only come through religion.

In the Bahá'í writings, peace is revered because in essence it is a spiritual mystery in which humanity has been invited in our day, for the first time, to partake. Peace is a divine creation; a reconciliation of humanity and divine purpose. Peace appears first as a universal religion; as its influence gathers force and its principles spread then peace can permeate the body of society, redeeming its institutions and its activities and consecrating its aims.[128]

In late 1951, while he was in Peru meeting with the two Regional Assemblies,[129] a cable arrived from Haifa addressed to him rather than to the National Assembly. As his office assistant, Doris opened it. She was astounded by its contents. Hardly able to contain within herself what she had read, she drove through Chicago traffic to pick up her husband at the airport.[130] At that time, it was possible to meet arriving passengers on the tarmac at the base of the mobile steps pushed up to the airplane's door. As a weary Horace descended the staircase, she was no longer able to hold back the news from Shoghi Effendi. At the top of her voice, she yelled to him above the din of the airfield, 'You're a Hand!!!' Dumbfounded, Horace instantly dropped his suitcases, threw up his hands, and shouted back to her, 'No, not that!'[131]

13

INSTITUTION OF THE LEARNED

... our one task is to learn how to meet the inner spirit of the people.
Horace Holley[1]

When Horace studied Shoghi Effendi's telegram naming him a Hand of the Cause, he was baffled. He knew that Hand of the Cause of God was a high, important station and that he was unworthy of the title. Furthermore, he did not understand its implications in practical terms. The Guardian alone did.

It was only when 'Abdu'l-Bahá's Will and Testament was promulgated in 1922 that Western believers became aware for the first time of the importance of the institution of the Hands of the Cause. This essential Bahá'í institution did not originate with 'Abdu'l-Bahá, but was established by Bahá'u'lláh Himself, who had appointed four Persian believers to that position. However, as none of the four ever travelled outside of the Near East, the friends in Europe and North America had no working knowledge of their role in the Bahá'í community.[2] Three of the original group of Hands had passed away before 'Abdu'l-Bahá's death in 1921, and the fourth, Mírzá 'Alí-Muḥammad (Ibn-i-Aṣdaq) passed away in 1928 during the early years of Shoghi Effendi's ministry. Bahá'u'lláh had instructed these four to travel the length and breadth of Iran to raise up that Bahá'í community. In 1897, five years after His Father's passing, 'Abdu'l-Bahá directed those four Hands to appoint a group of trustworthy, capable believers to establish the first administrative body for Iran, the Central Spiritual Assembly of Tehran. He also stated that the Hands were to serve as lifetime members of the Tehran body. This institution, though unelected until 1913, carried out many of the same functions as a National Spiritual Assembly and was the precursor to the National Assembly of Iran and held the distinction as the first national Bahá'í governing body in the world.[3]

'Abdu'l-Bahá named additional believers to the station of Hand of the Cause, but posthumously. Shoghi Effendi continued this practice, beginning with the British believer John Esslemont, who was named a Hand of the Cause after his untimely passing in 1925. Others named after their deaths included Horace's friends Keith Ransom-Kehler, Roy Wilhelm, Louis Gregory, and Martha Root. These appointments, while edifying, confused many believers because the Will and Testament of 'Abdu'l-Bahá had set out specific functions and tasks for the Hands, assignments which remained unfulfilled. 'Abdu'l-Bahá's description of their responsibilities seemed beyond the capacity of any mortal – and Horace, who had studied the Will closely for decades, was well familiar with His words. They must have terrified Horace.

> The obligations of the Hands of the Cause of God are to diffuse the Divine Fragrances, to edify the souls of men, to promote learning, to improve the character of all men, to be, at all times and under all conditions, sanctified and detached from earthly things. They must manifest the fear of God by their conduct, their manners, their deeds and their words.[4]

Leroy Ioas, who had a strong down-to-earth streak, asked Shoghi Effendi to explain the duties of the Hands of the Cause, so that he could understand them in concrete terms. He made this request in 1935 when there were no living Hands of the Cause. Shoghi Effendi explained their future work in a response written on his behalf:

> Regarding the functions of the Hands of the Cause of God. They are numerous and varied, and include teaching as well as administrative work, and such activities as the Guardian may choose to ask them to perform. Their number has not been fixed by the Master. But as to their relationship to the Guardian, the Will is quite clear on this matter. 'The Hands of the Cause of God must be nominated and appointed by the Guardian of the Cause of God. All must be under his shadow and obey his command . . . This body of the Hands of the Cause of God is under the direction of the Guardian of the Cause of God.' It is clear, therefore, that they are directly responsible to the Guardian, and are not under the jurisdiction of any Assembly.[5]

Months prior to his appointment of Hands of the Cause, Shoghi Effendi took a preliminary step towards further expanding the Administrative Order; a step that would become intertwined with the duties of the Hands. On 9 January 1951, Shoghi Effendi surprised the Bahá'í world by announcing the formation of an International Bahá'í Council. What must have especially thrilled Horace was the Guardian's mention of the new body's 'efflorescence into [the] Universal House of Justice'.[6] From the time of his first encounter with 'Abdu'l-Bahá at Thonon-les-Bains, France in 1911, Horace had longed for and worked towards the establishment of that supreme institution. The Guardian explained that the Council's role in the beginning would be limited to fostering the construction of the superstructure of the Shrine of the Báb and serving as the face of the Faith to the new Government of Israel. It was the start of something monumental. The membership of the Council was composed primarily of Western believers, including Charles Mason Remey and Horace's close friend and colleague, Amelia Collins. The members were asked to reside in Haifa. About a year later, Leroy Ioas would be requested to serve as Secretary-General of that body. Amelia's and the Ioas's departure was profoundly felt in the Wilmette community and, certainly, Horace and Doris sorely missed their companionship and assistance.

Bahá'ís the world over were even more astonished when, on 24 December 1951 – Christmas Eve in the West – the Guardian appointed twelve living, breathing believers to join the ranks of the Hands of the Cause of God. Fellow National Spiritual Assembly members Leroy Ioas and Dorothy Baker were among that first contingent of appointees, along with Horace. Charles Mason Remey and Amelia Collins, who were by then living in the Holy Land. William Sutherland Maxwell, the architect of the superstructure of the Shrine of the Báb, was the first Canadian named a Hand. Horace's counterpart as long-time secretary of the National Assembly of Iran, 'Alí-Akbar Furútan, was among the Persians. Horace would always refer to 'Alí-Akbar as his 'co-worker' in acknowledgement of their mutual burden.[7] The only Hand not surprised by her own appointment was Horace's dear friend, Amelia Collins, who had been informed privately in 1946 of her elevation but had been asked not to divulge it.[8]

Congratulatory greetings flowed into Horace's mailbox. The Local Spiritual Assembly of New York City – which he had served as its first secretary – wrote to him with pride, noting. 'When one looks back over the tempestuous years of the Faith through which you have come, the long years of faithful service, the energy and initiative which you have poured out, you well deserve this happiness.'[9] None of the letters he received were probably more gratifying than that from the National Spiritual Assembly of Canada, which not only praised him for his years of service, but added that his presence among them as a Hand of the Cause would be a source of 'Celestial Strength' that would be a 'source of reassurance of the power of this Cause and those forces at our disposal if we are but channels for them'.[10]

For the first time in decades, serving as a Hand of the Cause allowed Horace to bring out his softer side, because he was no longer only the voice of institutions charged with administering justice. As a Hand, his job would be to uplift and nurture the friends, a role he carried out well. As one of his collaborators on Bahá'í publications told him, she felt that he 'had been a Hand of the Cause for a very long time, but now the Guardian has confirmed it . . .'[11]

Two months later, on 29 February 1952, Shoghi Effendi appointed seven additional Hands, including Fred Schopflocher and Corinne True, bringing the total to nineteen. One member of the first contingent, William Sutherland Maxwell, died in Canada shortly thereafter, so on 26 March, Shoghi Effendi appointed his wife, Amatu'l-Bahá Rúhíyyih Khánum, formerly Mary Maxwell, to replace her father, thereby retaining the same number of Hands.[12] On 29 March 1952, Horace attended Maxwell's funeral in Montreal as one of two designated representatives of the Guardian. He had been a friend to Sutherland and his late wife, May Maxwell, for many years.

The Guardian did not ask those Hands serving on National and Local Spiritual Assemblies to resign, instead he told them to continue their services even as they assumed other responsibilities; consequently, both Horace and 'Alí-Akbar Furútan continued to serve as secretaries of the two most important National Assemblies.

As Horace began this new stage of his life, he did so without many of the believers who had been his colleagues, friends, and even mentors. Amelia Collins and Leroy Ioas had departed for the Holy Land. Roy Wilhelm, Louis Gregory, and George Latimer had died. So had Horace's old friend, Mountfort Mills, the one person whom he had often turned to for advice and help. Within a year his intimate friend and colleague Florence Morton would also pass on to the next world. The membership of the National Spiritual Assembly continued to change. By 1952, most members were younger than Horace. Edna True and Paul Haney were the first non-Persian members who had grown up in the Faith as second-generation Bahá'ís. Fellow Hand, Dorothy Baker continued to serve as an officer. His new colleagues were energetic teachers of the Faith who brought a vibrancy to the work of the National Assembly, but they held different perspectives from Horace, because they had never experienced the early struggles he and his old friends had endured. Though only in his sixties, he was looked upon as an elder statesman, a relic of the past.

* * * * *

At Riḍván 1953, the world-wide Bahá'í community embarked on its first international plan, the Ten Year Plan, later referred to as the Ten Year Crusade. The decade encompassing the Crusade would become one of the most glorious – though also heart-wrenching – chapters in the history of the Faith. Crisis and victory would embrace.

This new plan was launched when the United States was in the middle of a spiritual revival, which, ironically, did not benefit the Faith. The country, having emerged from years of economic hardship and war, was experiencing a period of unprecedented prosperity. No generation in history accumulated wealth as quickly as did the middle class of America in the 1950s. The new President, Dwight David Eisenhower, was a calming grandfather figure embodying contentment and 'Americanism'. The traumatized American soldiers returning home from the War were drawn not to the fun craved by troops returning from World War I, but to the stability of the religion of their upbringing, to normalcy, and to family. After receiving government-funded college educations, the former warriors took advantage of government loans to purchase homes in suburban neighbourhoods which were springing up seemingly overnight throughout the country. They married and had large families, creating a 'baby boom'.[13] Then these flourishing families joined Christian churches. A widespread expression throughout the country was: 'The family that prays together, stays together.'[14] Young adults during the early 1950s were not interested in new ideas about religion; they were seeking the familiar, the traditional, the comforting, and the socially acceptable. Church membership in the United States had been in slow but steady decline for decades, but from the last years of the Great Depression through 1960 it rose sharply, especially during the 1950s.[15] It reached a record high of 69% in 1960 – up 14% from 1950.[16]

Sensitive to the nation's return to conventional Christianity, the film industry produced a number of blockbuster movies on Christian themes, such as *Ben Hur*, *The Robe*, and *The Ten Commandments*. Evangelists such as the young itinerate minister Billy Graham called the lost to Christ in fully packed stadiums, on television, and even in the salons of the White House. President Eisenhower, a hero of the War, was baptized – sparking the expression 'piety on the Potomac', implying a bland, comforting, well-meaning return to a generalized Christianity. Congress added the motto 'In God We Trust' to all coins.[17] In such an atmosphere, in which a feel-good version of Christianity was mixed with growing material comfort, gaining converts to the unfamiliar – even alien – Bahá'í Faith would be a frustrating challenge throughout the Ten Year Crusade. Lack of growth on the home front would vex not only the National Assembly and the Hands of the Cause, but Shoghi Effendi as well.

The goals of the Crusade which most excited many North American believers were the remote, exotic places mentioned specifically by 'Abdu'l-Bahá in the Tablets of the Divine Plan; these attracted Bahá'ís with a sense of adventure as well as dedication. Many goals were tiny islands. Other places included in the list of 131 countries and virgin territories which the Guardian specified had to be opened to the Faith during the Plan were ones with giant obstacles. Some posed special religious and cultural challenges, especially those countries that were predominantly Muslim or Orthodox Christian where religious leaders held tight control over the citizenry. Countries with authoritarian regimes presented other problems, especially the Communist-controlled Soviet Union and its satellite nations where atheism was the only state-sanctioned religious belief. The work carried out during earlier plans had already taken the Faith to many corners of the world; now the overall goal was to claim the remaining countries and territories for Bahá'u'lláh. But thinly spreading the Faith over the globe was not enough; the Administrative Order had to be firmly established in those countries which already had Bahá'ís, but which lacked functioning Assemblies. Strengthening these outposts required that Bahá'í literature be translated and published in many more languages. New believers needed to be confirmed and educated.

At least since 1936[18] and especially after the formal launch of the first Seven Year Plan in 1937, the American community had been sending out many of its most dedicated believers to other countries, and most had remained at their posts. This meant that, unless there were other strong believers to replace them, American communities were being depleted of their most active workers.[19] In 1953, five members of its National Spiritual Assembly resigned in order to pioneer to other countries, thrilling Shoghi Effendi.[20] Horace inadvertently found himself the anchor, the institutional memory, the one constant force of the American community at the national level. Even if his health had permitted him to entertain the possibility of pioneering, Shoghi Effendi had always made it clear that his assigned station was as an administrator in Wilmette. Horace could take solace in the handwritten words of the Guardian from the time when the first wave of pioneers had been sent forth throughout the Western Hemisphere in the 1930s.

> As to those whose function is essentially of an administrative character it can hardly be doubted that they are steadily and indefatigably perfecting the structural machinery of their Faith, are multiplying its administrative agencies, and are legalizing the status of the newly established institutions. Slowly and patiently they are canalizing the spirit that at once directs, energizes and safeguards its operations. They are exploiting its potentialities, broadcasting its message, publicizing its literature, fostering the aspirations of its youth, devising ways and means for the training of its children, guarding the integrity of its teachings, and paving the way for the ultimate codification of its laws. Through all the resources at their disposal, they are promoting the growth and consolidation of that pioneer movement for which the entire machinery of their Administrative Order has been primarily designed and erected. They are visibly and progressively contributing to the enrichment of their unique community life, and are ensuring, with magnificent courage and characteristic promptitude, the completion of their consecrated Edifice – the embodiment of their hopes and the supreme symbol of their ideals.[21]

* * * * *

One of Shoghi Effendi's first assignments for the Hands was to attend a series of conferences in 1953 that would mark the centenary of the annunciation of Bahá'u'lláh's mission and serve to rally the believers to arise and fulfil the goals of the Crusade. These historic gatherings were scheduled to be held in Kampala, Uganda; Chicago/Wilmette, United States; Stockholm, Sweden; and New Delhi, India. Horace had only travelled outside of North America once after his return to the United States in 1914. Months before he and Dorothy Baker were appointed Hands, they had journeyed to Panama together on behalf of the National Spiritual Assembly to attend the formation of the first Regional Spiritual Assembly for Central America, Mexico, and the Greater Antilles.[22] His first international assignment as a Hand was to travel back to Panama City, and to Lima, Peru, in 1952 to consult with members of the two National Assemblies in Latin America and assist them after their first year of functioning as Bahá'í institutions.[23] His overseas journeys were just beginning.

International travel was exciting for a man such as Horace, with his innate curiosity and the sensibilities of a world citizen. It was also significant to him that he made these trips in the 1950s by airplane rather than by train or ship. When he was a boy, he had loved the science fiction of Jules Verne, and now the technology Verne imaginatively wrote about as futuristic had become a reality. To understand how quickly the Age of Flight had progressed, consider that in October 1909, a few weeks before Horace and Bertha were married in New York City, the Wright Brothers[24] had flown down the Hudson River between Governor's Island and Grant's Tomb and back. At least a million New Yorkers watched this amazing spectacle. The excitement generated by this early demonstration of mechanized flight still hung in the air of the city the day Horace wed. Now, airplanes were crossing oceans. Flying was so noteworthy to Horace that he made a list of his international flights, including the airports he stopped at *en route*.[25] He had always been interested in the speed and effect of changing technology, and now he was experiencing the excitement of flight first-hand.

For many years, Horace had been a sought-after orator. In 1945, Shoghi Effendi had urged him to take up public speaking for the Faith, 'in spite of' his 'many other pressing tasks'.[26] Now, as a Hand of the Cause, he was in even more demand. With his 'rather high voice with a slight Yankee twang, which added spice to his clear, dry, gripping delivery', his talks combined intellect with inspiration cleverly sprinkled with wit.[27] His usual practice when preparing a speech was to write it out in full, then create an outline that he used at the time he delivered it, so it would flow as if he were speaking extemporaneously. Taking on his new responsibilities, all the while continuing his work as secretary of the National Assembly, left him little time to write essays, so the prepared texts of his talks became his primary literary achievement. These drafts were some of his most accessible, inspiring compositions because his ideas became clearer, more refined, and so much easier to articulate. For example, the talks he gave in other countries were never patronising, and while they lacked the scholarly traits of his North American talks, they offered spiritual truths with a simplicity that went straight into the hearts of the listeners. He used stories more and references to literature and history less. He became increasingly conscious that everything he did, including public speaking, was an extension of the world of the spirit. One time, for instance, he arrived at the scheduled venue to give a talk, but no one was there other than the woman who was to introduce him. He instructed her to deliver her introduction anyway, and then he proceeded to give his prepared remarks. As they drove home together, the woman remarked that it was a shame that no one was there to hear his wonderful address. He replied that the lack of an audience did not matter, as a great many souls in the next world were listening.[28]

Horace was often asked to furnish a photograph of himself for publicity, so Doris decided he needed an updated one. Her husband was not interested. In fact, searching for Horace in group photographs, he is invariably found in the back and often to one side – away from the centre focus. Doris became so determined that he should have his picture made that she set a trap by soliciting the help of a Wilmette friend, Jane Alexander, wife of the village President and fellow member of the Historic Commission with Horace. Jane admired Horace for his sense of history, inner spiritual calm, and ability to give interesting talks about the past that did not bore his audiences. She was an excellent amateur photographer who had just acquired a new camera. Doris asked her to come to the Ḥaẓíra with her gear while their husbands were together at a Rotary meeting, under the pretence of making a portrait of Doris. When Jane set up her equipment and began to take Doris' picture, she found her to be stiff and self-conscious; surprising because Doris – whom Jane described as a little wren – always projected a bright cheerfulness, even when serious. Then Horace arrived. How could he refuse Jane's kind offer to photograph him when her equipment was already set up in his living room? Doris wanted him seated on a radiator in front of a window with the House of Worship in the background. The sunny back lighting created a challenge, but in the end, the most iconic of all photographs of Horace was taken. Jane later remarked that as soon as Horace was together with his wife, he made her forget herself. The happy, relaxed expression on Doris's face as she posed beside her husband bespoke their close relationship. With the session complete, the Holleys asked if Jane would also be willing to take a portrait of Amelia Collins, which was quickly arranged and carried out.[29]

* * * * *

1953 was a banner year for Horace. The period between October 1952 and October 1953 was proclaimed a Holy Year to commemorate the centenary of the annunciation to Bahá'u'lláh as God's Messenger for this Day which occurred while He was a prisoner in Tehran. For Horace, it would be a year of experiencing cultures and places that were new and exotic to him. He would gain an enhanced appreciation of the diverse peoples of the world. More importantly, the four intercontinental conferences held that year provided the first opportunity for most of the Hands of the Cause to meet each other and become united through friendship. The Americans were all old friends, but Horace had not met most of the others, especially the Persians. Language still divided them, but their mutual love and devotion to the Cause quickly overcame that obstacle. Corinne True, already eighty-eight years old at the time of her appointment, was unable to travel, so Horace made many visits to her home a few blocks from the Ḥaẓíra to ensure that she was informed, consulted, and able to sign statements and letters being issued by the Hands as an institution. This drew them even closer as friends and colleagues.[30]

The first of the four conferences was held under a great tent in Kampala, Uganda, which was then still a British Protectorate. A stalwart group of pioneers from Iran and England had settled there, including Hand of the Cause Músá Banání. The pure-hearted African believers had been warned by suspicious friends and relatives to stay away from the conference, lest the white Bahá'ís use the occasion to take advantage of them or harm them. Fortunately, Africans from over thirty tribes ignored those admonitions and came anyway. They made up the majority of the more than 200 participants. What these new believers experienced was not exploitation, but sincere love, especially the love of Shoghi Effendi, conveyed to them by his representative Leroy Ioas, who had been instructed to greet each African believer personally on behalf of the Guardian. One unfortunate incident required Horace's skill as a wordsmith. Dorothy Baker gave a public talk which was attended by a hostile reporter. He twisted her words in his newspaper article to say that she had called upon Africans to rebel against the government. A delegation was dispatched to meet with the editor of the newspaper, but they failed to convince him to retract the false report. He reluctantly agreed, however, to allow them to submit a letter challenging the article. Horace was asked to draft it and the paper ran his defence of the Bahá'í Faith and Dorothy.[31]

The intercontinental conference for the Americas was held in Chicago and Wilmette during the Bahá'í festival of Riḍván. It was a spectacular gathering because it not only celebrated the centenary of the annunciation of Bahá'u'lláh's mission and the spread of the Faith to more and more regions of the world, but it also marked the completion of the House of Worship. Shoghi Effendi, who was too overwhelmed with work to attend, sent his wife, Hand of the Cause Rúḥíyyih Khánum, as his special representative. Horace was so elated by the occasion that he invited his brothers Frank and Irving and their families to attend the festivities. The three brothers and their wives happily posed together for a professional photograph in front of the Temple. His family did not fully understand his commitment to the Bahá'í Faith, but they were proud of him and his role in bringing the majestic edifice to completion. Corinne True, 'The Mother of the Temple', who could not take part in the other three intercontinental conferences, invited all the Hands of the Cause in attendance to come to her home for hospitality, further strengthening the *esprit de corps* beginning to emerge among that band of spiritual titans.

Travelling to Stockholm for the European Intercontinental Conference afforded Horace the opportunity to stop briefly in Holland and Norway where he connected with believers in Amsterdam and Oslo.

One highlight of the conference was his first meeting with fellow Hand George Townshend, from Ireland, which apparently occurred at a luncheon in Amsterdam. George, a former Anglican clergyman and an exceptionally gifted writer, had contributed many articles to Bahá'í publications, including *World Order* magazine, and had assisted Shoghi Effendi with his English translations. Horace admired Townshend immensely and must have found in him a kindred spirit. Townshend's health was precarious, so the Stockholm conference was the only one he attended, which was probably the sole opportunity the two writers had to spend time together.[32]

The most strenuous and lengthy journey for Horace that year was to the Intercontinental Conference for Asia held in New Delhi, India. It was the final conference of the four and a very exciting event – 'the first international Bahá'í gathering ever held in the East'.[33] Four hundred and fifty people attended from all over the world. The National Assembly of India not only did an excellent job planning the conference, but also hosted several impressive ancillary events for the public and high government officials, including a programme at the New Delhi Town Hall and a garden party hosted on the lawns of the Imperial Hotel.[34] It arranged for selected participants to meet with the Prime Minister, President and Vice-President of the country. Horace was among the delegation that met with the President.[35]

Judging from his handwritten notes, Horace found inspiration in the other talks, especially those of Mr Samandari, an elderly Hand who had been privileged as a teenager to be with Bahá'u'lláh during the last days of His life in 1892. This tiny man, but spiritual giant, recounted his memories of that precious time as well as stories from his encounters with 'Abdu'l-Bahá. Horace followed Samandari's talk with a brief account of his own first meeting more than forty years earlier with 'Abdu'l-Bahá in France.[36]

During the New Delhi Conference, the Guardian sent a cable requesting that the Hands, including Horace, extend their time on the subcontinent by at least a month to travel around India and to neighbouring countries. Horace was assigned specific communities to visit in South India and was requested to visit the Island of Ceylon (Sri Lanka).[37] This additional travel seems to have been the highlight of his time in Asia. During the first part of his trip, Hands of the Cause 'Alí-Akbar Furútan and Zikrullah Khadem were with him, as were a few other friends from the conference, including his New York protégé Mildred Mottahedeh. As he moved from place to place his travelling companions departed, leaving him in the care of local Bahá'ís who assisted and guided him. He visited Bombay (Mumbai), Poona (Pune) and other regions of Panchgani, Sholapur (Solāpur), Hyderabad, Secunderabad, Bangalore, Mysore, Trivandrum, Madras (Chennai), and finally in Ceylon: Colombo, Kalutara, and Kandy. He ended his tour by returning to Colombo.

After arriving in Hyderabad, Horace hurriedly scratched a brief note to Mildred Mottahedeh, who had attended all four conferences with him, but had left him for Italy. In his postscript, he commented, 'It's quite a shock to find I'm without your good companionship and wide experience. Friend you spoiled me!'[38] He said, 'I've fallen in love with this hotel and town. It's really charming, and the friends are giving me time enough for rest between meetings.'[39] He described the routine of each stop as 'press conference, public meeting, and meeting with the local Bahá'ís' and jokingly commented, 'I'm getting quite proficient at it! What a relief from the daily grind!'[40]

He accomplished a lot, especially when the local friends had enough advance notice to plan for his arrival, which was often not the case at the beginning. He toured the Bahá'í boarding school, New Era School – one of the first Bahá'í educational institutions, visited the 'Lucky Restaurant' in Poona owned by a Bahá'í which served as a Bahá'í gathering place, attended a Rotary meeting and brought along the secretary of the Local Assembly as his guest, and visited the Theosophical World Centre where he chatted about 'Abdu'l-Bahá's talks to Theosophist groups. He spoke to hundreds of people on a variety of topics, met with individuals and members of the press, and dined with the important politician, Sir Ramaswami Mudaliar. He also closely observed Hinduism in India and Buddhism in Ceylon and spoke as best he could about the need for the Bahá'ís – particularly the pioneers – to reach the followers of those religions rather than focusing on foreigners living in the country.

Horace's report to Shoghi Effendi included general comments and several specific recommendations. His first concern was that some of those who had enrolled as Bahá'ís had accepted the Faith before they had sufficient knowledge of its fundamentals. They did not understand important teachings and requirements, including the one prohibiting Bahá'ís from retaining memberships in other religions. It was disturbing to him to find pioneers controlling their communities instead of accompanying the local believers to give them the skills and knowledge to take charge. One solution to these problems would be to send more itinerate teachers.[41] Despite issues to be addressed, he told the Guardian that

> The Bahá'ís I met are kindness and hospitality itself. They go far beyond Western Bahá'ís in personal service to a fellow-believer, visiting their city, and they are prepared to undertake great sacrifices for the Faith. I emphasized the Master's words about the unity of East and West in this Day.[42]

Horace's last sentence well summed up his experience in India, saying, 'With grateful acknowledgment of the blessing I have received.'[43] Over the next year, he would receive letters from individuals in India whose hearts he had touched. One letter informed him that his words had led to her formal enrolment in the Faith.[44]

* * * * *

Horace was often asked why he had never made a pilgrimage so that he could meet the Guardian. Despite their years of constant correspondence, the two men had never met. His usual reply was, 'He doesn't want to know me. I don't feel worthy.'[45] The opportunity arose for him to make a pilgrimage to the Holy Land as a side trip of his journey to the New Delhi Conference. He arrived in the Holy Land in December 1953 on the way home from India and Ceylon.

Towards the end of the day, Horace's plane arrived at Lod Airport situated between Tel Aviv and Jerusalem. That principal airport for an ancient country was spartan, because the newly established State of Israel was struggling to survive in a hostile neighbourhood of states seeking its eradication, and so there were no funds available for fancy facilities. Young soldiers with rifles slung over their shoulders were everywhere. After collecting his luggage, Horace still had a journey of several hours up the coastal plain along bumpy roads surrounded on both sides by farmland. The looming long hulk of Mt Carmel, barely visible in the dark, must have thrilled him as he travelled north; for Haifa sat on the other end of that sacred mountain. By the time he arrived at the Western Pilgrim House on Haparsim Street, it was already late. He climbed the front stairs to the main entrance of the charming building with its small portico and double front doors. In the dim light, he briefly scanned the reception hall with its high ceilings and oriental columns. The building had an atmosphere of muted, dignified beauty. Turning to the left, Horace was shown to the sparsely furnished room that had been the residence of Amelia Collins, who was then staying across the lane in the House of the Master. Exhausted but excited, he tried to sleep.

Horace expected to meet Shoghi Effendi the next day but was informed that the one person he so longed to see was unwell. This did not mean the Guardian was ill in the conventional sense of that word. It meant that he had been overcome by bad news which forced him to take to his bed. In this case, a few believers and an Israeli government minister had caused his misery.

Even though Horace was disappointed to have his long-awaited meeting delayed, his first full day in the Holy Land was noteworthy. There was still much to explore, and he was eager to offer prayers for the first time at the Holy Places. Up the steep incline of Mt Carmel, the Shrine of the Báb, newly completed with its shining golden dome, beckoned him in the morning light. He was reunited with Leroy and Sylvia Ioas, who were living at the other end of the Western Pilgrim House. Another old acquaintance, Mason Remey, shared his sparse sitting area. Rúḥíyyih Khánum, Shoghi Effendi's spirited Canadian wife, whom Horace had watched grow up as the only child of the Maxwells, was also eager to greet him as his hostess. And dear Milly Collins, who had taken up residence in the Master's House, was there to make him feel at home.

The following day, Horace had his long-awaited meeting with the Guardian at dinner. The usual protocol was that the pilgrims and those living at the Pilgrim House had their evening meal in a dining room on the lower floor. The ends of the building were capped with graceful curves, which gave that room on the northeast side a delightful feel with its large windows looking down towards Haifa Bay. In the evening, Shoghi Effendi would unobtrusively cross the street from the Master's House and slip into the dining room through an outside door in that room. He never sat at the head of the long, plain wooden table, but to the side on the right of that place of honour, which was reserved for the most recent arrival, who was Horace. Everyone was instructed to wait upstairs until Shoghi Effendi had arrived and was seated. Through the glass window set in the door at the top of the staircase, Horace watched Shoghi Effendi enter and get settled. The first thing that struck him was Shoghi Effendi's small stature, thinking to himself, 'how could so much energy be generated in so small a frame!' He next observed the Guardian's face, especially his eyes, which radiated light and loving-kindness.[46]

Horace's pilgrimage was important not only to him, but to Shoghi Effendi. The commander was finally going to meet one of his generals. Rúḥíyyih Khánum wrote movingly about their meeting.

> My own impression of the significance of that meeting is, of course, personal, but it seemed to me that Horace, who had always been a man standing alone in his own wilderness, bowing only to his God, and vigorously protecting his inner independence, had been a little afraid, probably sub-consciously, of meeting this Shoghi Effendi. I think he suspected his soul would be seduced by that meeting, and to me that *is* what happened. Horace surrendered completely to love. As to the Guardian, he too had been aware of the intense independence of this rare Bahá'í giant and wondered what their meeting would be like. I remember the first night something prevented Shoghi Effendi from going over to the Pilgrim House and so he did not meet Horace until the second night of his pilgrimage; but then the last barricades of Horace's heart went down like a sand fortress when the tide comes in, and I suspect this must have been a great inner release for this essentially sensitive, deeply spiritual man.[47]

Over the course of Horace's pilgrimage, he dined several times with Shoghi Effendi. The Guardian did most of the talking. In fact, Horace could not recall him ever eating anything. Occasionally, someone would ask a question, or Rúḥíyyih Khánum would do so to clarify a point for a shy pilgrim. His fellow diners were Amelia Collins, the Ioases, the Revell sisters from Philadelphia who were administrative aids to Shoghi Effendi, and Mason Remey.[48] These meals were gatherings of old friends. What Horace remembered most about Shoghi Effendi's personality was his compassion, kindness, and softness. He never once observed the Guardian's justice.[49]

As Horace was a pilgrim, Shoghi Effendi did not burden him with talk about the business of the American National Spiritual Assembly or with a message to convey to it upon his return. He frequently used the term 'Citadel of the Faith' when referring to America and told Horace that the American community was entering a period of triumph as it won victory after victory. Of course, as new countries were opened to the Faith by North American pioneers, the infant Bahá'í Assemblies in those areas adopted the administrative procedures of the United States. Shoghi Effendi did not approve of this. He wanted the members of the institutions in other countries to find their own ways of carrying out administrative duties, thereby demonstrating unity in diversity. When Horace injected that the National Assembly had tried to create uniformity within the United States so that pioneers and teachers going from one community to another would not be burdened by local variations, the Guardian replied that that approach was fine within a country but should not be imposed on others.[50]

Shoghi Effendi provided Horace with dazzling insights into the role the Bahá'í institutions would play far into the future to create a better world – a prosperous world truly at peace. He also emphasized that the institutions at the World Centre must always take precedence over those at the national level. The Universal House of Justice would establish a constitution of its own, and existing constitutions of National Assemblies would have to be revised to conform to it. They discussed the codification of the Bahá'í laws – a goal of the Ten Year Crusade which only the Guardian could complete. He informed Horace that he would have to search all of Bahá'u'lláh's writings, even prayers, to create the codification because not all of them were included in the Kitáb-i-Aqdas. Horace gathered indirectly from hints of the Guardian that the Universal House of Justice would be established by the end of the Crusade.[51]

Shoghi Effendi touched upon a variety of topics in his discussions with Horace, such as the development of the Holy Places at the World Centre, the tests experienced by 'Abdu'l-Bahá, relations between the Faith and the State of Israel, and the other institutions to be established to surround the environs of the House of Worship in Wilmette. One overarching topic was the recently launched Ten Year Crusade. The Guardian emphasized that all the goals of the Tablets of the Divine Plan had been given to North America. Therefore, if another National Assembly was assigned a goal, it was still the responsibility of the North Americans to ensure it was met. He added that one lone pioneer did not

The National Spiritual Assembly during the height of World War II, 1944. First row left to right: Allen McDaniel, Amelia Collins, Dorothy Baker, George Latimer; Second row left to right: Horace Holley, Roy Wilhelm, Louis Gregory; third row left to right: Philip Sprague, Leroy Ioas

Representatives from Latin America with members of the National Spiritual Assembly, 9 July 1944. At the time, Horace Holley was recovering from a heart attack. Gayle Woolson, pioneer and Auxiliary Board member, is on the far right of the second row

Horace Holley, in the centre, serving in his role as chairman of the Wilmette Historical Commission at a 1952 event at the Wilmette Library. William H. Alexander, President of the Wilmette Village Council and friend to Horace, is on the left

Undated portrait of Horace Holley in later life

Horace Holley in front of the Hazira in Wilmette, Illinois, which served as both the headquarters of the National Spiritual Assembly, and his residence

Hands of the Cause at the First Intercontinental Bahá'í Conference in Kampala, Uganda, February 1953, with the Kampala Ḥaẓíratu'l-Quds in the background. Left to right: Musá Banání, Valíyu'lláh Varqá, Shu'á'u'lláh 'Alá'í, Mason Remey, Horace Holley, Tarázu'lláh Samandarí, Zikrullah Khadem, Leroy Ioas, Dorothy Baker, 'Alí-Akbar Furútan

Hands of the Cause at the European Intercontinental Conference in Stockholm, 1953. Note George Townshend, front row, fourth from left; this was the only Conference he attended, we see him here holding the arm of Mason Remey. Horace Holley is in the back row, far right, behind Amelia Collins and Adelbert Mühlschlegel

Hand of the Cause Horace Holley at the Intercontinental Conference in New Delhi, India in 1953 He became known for wearing white shoes during the last years of his life

Horace Holley with fellow Hand of the Cause Zikrullah Khadem, at the New Era School, Panchgani, India, 1953

Horace Holley in Africa, during his time at the Kampala Conference

Horace Holley meeting with Bahá'ís in Sholapur, India as a Hand of the Cause, 1953

Shoghi Effendi, whom Horace Holley finally met during a pilgrimage on his way back to the United States from India in 1953

The National Spiritual Assembly of the United States at the time of the inauguration of the Ten-Year Crusade in 1953. Five of these members resigned during that period to resettle in goal areas in different parts of the world. This so pleased Shoghi Effendi that he hung a copy of this photograph in the Mansion at Bahjí

Horace Holley with close friend, colleague and another Hand of the Cause, Amelia Collins

Portrait of Horace and Doris Holley taken in front of the Hazira windows by their friend, Jane Alexander

Amelia Collins, photographed by Jane Alexander at the request of the Holleys

The Holley brothers and their wives at the dedication of the House of Worship in 1953. Left to right: Horace Holley, Doris Holley, Frank Holley, Jennie Holley, Irving Holley, Mary Holley

Horace and Doris Holley during a moment of fun. This candid pose reflects Horace's playful personality, which was seldom photographed

Horace Holley, in back row, center, serving as representative of Shoghi Effendi at the first regional national convention of Brazil, Colombia, Ecuador, Peru and Venezuela, surrounded by delegates and friends. This historic gathering was held in Lima, Peru in 1957

The National Spiritual Assembly of the United States during the last year Horace Holley served on it, 1959. Front left to right: Edna True, Horace Holley, Katherine True. Back left to right: Charles Wolcott, Ellsworth Blackwell, Florence Mayberry, Borrah Kavelin, Charlotte Linfoot, Arthur Dahl.

constitute a community, so it was important to dispatch others to the same locale until a genuine community was firmly established. However, once a goal area was won, those following the first pioneer should not necessarily receive financial support to settle there. One profound insight Shoghi Effendi provided into the Ten Year Crusade was its true goal: not simply raising the numbers and locations of Bahá'ís but building a refuge for humanity when hope and faith in the old institutions of the world were gone. The important people of the world had not come to the aid of the Bahá'ís in carrying out this work, which had instead been accomplished by little-known, plain people of no consequence to the greater society. In retelling this point to a gathering of Bahá'ís, Horace said, 'God is God because He can make His Cause succeed with people such as you and I.'[52]

Of all the things Shoghi Effendi said during those magical days, one stood out in Horace's memory. The comment was made during one of their last conversations when they spoke about the kings and rulers of the world. Horace related that with great humility and dignity, Shoghi Effendi stated, 'I am the King of Kings.'[53] 'Abdu'l-Bahá had called Shoghi Effendi, 'the sign of God' and stated emphatically that he who obeys him obeys God.[54] Those words took on new meaning.

As important as his talks with the Guardian were, Horace was a pilgrim and so he spent many hours visiting the Holy Places where he prayed and meditated. The Shrine of the Báb was always especially beautiful at dusk, so Shoghi Effendi made arrangements for Horace to visit it at that hour to see it when it was most enchanting. Horace was also deeply moved by viewing the blood-soaked remnant of the clothing the Báb was wearing at the time of His martyrdom which was displayed in the International Archives.

Mason Remey and Leroy Ioas had to travel to Jerusalem to meet with Israeli officials to rectify one of the problems that had recently upset Shoghi Effendi, and Horace was asked to accompany them. While in that ancient city, revered as sacred by Judaism, Christianity, and Islam, he visited the Church of the Holy Sepulchre, the traditional site of Christ's martyrdom and tomb and the most sacred spot in Christendom. Horace commented that the Christians remained unaware that 'the tomb is empty, and the Spirit of Christ is walking the earth'.[55]

When he returned to Wilmette, Edna True asked Horace about his meeting with Shoghi Effendi. All he could say was, 'you want to give your life for him'.⁵⁶ He spoke about his pilgrimage to a gathering in Evanston, but otherwise never wrote about it and seemed reluctant to speak about it, especially his time with Shoghi Effendi.

Several days after Horace spoke at the Evanston meeting, he received the terrible news that Dorothy Baker's plane had blown up over the Mediterranean Sea as she was returning home from India. She had been thrilled to be travelling in a jet plane, a technology just coming into widespread use. However, it was an innovation that was not yet reliable. Over the previous two decades, she had shared many unforgettable experiences with Horace, and now she was gone in an instant. Just months before, Fred Schopflocher had passed away with little warning. In March, Paul Haney, then serving on the National Assembly as chairman, was appointed a Hand to replace Dorothy. As both the primary officers of the Assembly as well as Hands, Paul and Horace collaborated more closely than before. Paul's mother had worked with Horace for many years on Bahá'í publications, so he was another youth Horace had watched grow up. Paul would play an increasingly important role in Horace's life to the end. Along with Corinne True, Horace and Paul now constituted the three Hands responsible for all of the Americas.

*****

On 6 April 1954, Shoghi Effendi announced to the Bahá'í world a further development of the institution of the Hands of the Cause. He called for the establishment of a subsidiary institution to assist them: Auxiliary Boards for each of the five continents. The Hands for the Americas were requested to meet in order to select nine Auxiliary Board members for the Western Hemisphere who would report directly to them. For the first time, the Hands were also called upon to develop close relationships with the National Assemblies in their regions and report to the World Centre the progress of their activities – in essence, becoming the eyes and ears of the Guardian. In the same letter, Shoghi Effendi called for the initiation of five Continental Bahá'í Funds to facilitate the fiscal needs of the Auxiliary Boards and he designated Horace as the trustee for the Continental Fund for the Americas – one more addition to his myriad duties.⁵⁷ As the National Assembly explained, this cable from Shoghi Effendi set the Hands upon a new direction by 'forging ties' with the National Spiritual Assemblies in order to lend them 'assistance in attaining the objectives of the Ten Year Plan'.⁵⁸

The National Assembly's commentary on the Guardian's message emphasized the significance of the cable in its wider context. Shoghi Effendi's announcement and directives were simple, profound, and breath-taking because the second complementary component of the Bahá'í Administrative Order – the Institution of the Learned – was starting to reveal its form.

> What we witness now is the birth of a new Bahá'í Institution, a new instrument through which the Guardian's spiritual power can flow forth to the Bahá'ís, particularly those concerned with the Ten Year Plan.
> As a new Institution, its unfoldment will be gradual, from seed to tree.⁵⁹

This statement of the National Assembly was especially insightful, for the Administrative Order was always intended to be composed of both elected and appointed institutions. In the Kitáb-i-'Ahdí, the Book of His Covenant, Bahá'u'lláh said, 'Blessed are the rulers and the learned among the people of Bahá.'⁶⁰ Shoghi Effendi, exercising his role as interpreter, stated that the 'learned' were the Hands of the Cause and other Bahá'í teachers, and the 'rulers' were the members of the Universal House of Justice and the National and Local Assemblies. While there were overlapping responsibilities between the two elements of the administration, they each had separate roles. 'Abdu'l-Bahá's Will and Testament made the Hands of the Cause and those serving under them an auxiliary institution of the Guardianship. In 1968, the Universal House of Justice would expand the appointed institutions to include Continental Boards of Counsellors and assistants to Auxiliary Board members. Counsellors would serve fixed terms and assume responsibilities previously held by the Hands of the Cause because the House of Justice determined that it did not have the authority to appoint Hands, only the Guardian could do so. In 1973, the House of Justice established an international council, the International Teaching Centre, composed initially of selected Hands and Counsellors. Its mission was to oversee and foster the work of the Institution of the Learned – later referred to primarily as the 'Institution of the Counsellors'.⁶¹ Referring to the Institution of the Learned, the House of Justice explained: 'The existence of institutions of such exalted rank, comprising individuals who play such a vital role, who yet have no legislative, administrative or judicial authority, and are entirely devoid of priestly functions or the right to make authoritative interpretations, is a feature of Bahá'í administration unparalleled in the religions of the past.'[62]

Horace not only played a pivotal role in the establishment and development of local and national Assemblies, but he would also help to shape the appointed institutions. And he did so while serving on both at the same time. As secretary of the National Assembly, he began to write letters on behalf of the Assembly addressed to himself as a Hand of the Cause. In his own mind, compartmentalizing his roles was never a problem, no matter how many hats he wore. His office at the Ḥaẓíra became not only the headquarters of the National Assembly, but the address and centre for the work of the Hands for the Americas, including his role as Trustee of the Continental Fund.

One way in which Horace influenced the development of the new institution was by beginning the conversation with his two colleagues, Paul Haney and Corinne True, about how they should go about appointing the first Auxiliary Board members for the Americas. Using his extensive knowledge of the pioneers and teaching work, he wrote a detailed plan, dividing the hemisphere into regions and outlining how they could provide the Board members with practical guidance necessary to carry out their work. When it came time to select the Board members, he suggested that they 'choose them for quality and capacity, no matter what some may be doing in other fields of Bahá'í service'.[63] Regarding their work as Hands with the four National Assemblies in their region, he recommended they begin by sending each a letter. The tone of his comprehensive proposal was congenial, making it clear to the other Hands that he was only offering suggestions to begin the conversation.[64]

In their first letter to all the newly appointed Auxiliary Board members as they were about to embark on their service, the three Hands assured them they would prepare the way for every visit of an Auxiliary Board member to a community. They would first notify the appropriate Assembly or other relevant Bahá'í bodies so that the Auxiliary Board member could be confident of being warmly received, and so that the recipient community would understand the Auxiliary Board member's role. The loving and encouraging letter to the new Board members, replete with practical advice and instructions, ended by saying that the Hands welcomed suggestions and advice and pledged their support to their new helpers. They stated they had 'confidence that every mission undertaken will be confirmed', reminding the Board members that they and the Hands were channels 'through which the Guardian's sustaining power and inspiration can flow to the Bahá'ís and the world'.[65]

Among Horace's additional duties were training and supervising several of the newly appointed Auxiliary Board members – a new role for him. Though he had supervised staff before as an officer of a corporate body, as a Hand, he would function as an individual most of the time.

A member from the first contingent of the Auxiliary Board was Florence Mayberry from Missouri, who was a professional writer like Horace. She wrote detective stories for the Ellery Queen series, Horace's favourite type of leisure reading. She remembered years later how afraid she had been to meet him because she was both in awe of him and a little scared of him. She had heard that 'he could be bitingly, and cleverly, sarcastic and impatient of stupidity'.[66] During their six years of association when she served as a Board member and later as a fellow member of the National Assembly, she discovered, however, that he was not at all like his reputation. Instead, he was 'warm, gentle, spiritually perceptive and in the last years of his life, particularly the final year . . . he began to seem translucent with a light that came from within him'.[67] He made her feel at ease in his presence, and he instilled in her confidence and a feeling of security as she went about her service.[68]

Florence first met Horace at the 1954 National Convention when she was serving as a delegate. Everyone was excited because the first announcement of those chosen to serve as Auxiliary Board members was to be made. With all eyes in Foundation Hall fixed upon him, Horace rose from the table where he had been seated as secretary of the Convention, walked to the podium, took out the paper with the list and read the nine names on behalf of the three Hands of the Cause from the Americas. When he read her name, Florence was flabbergasted. She neither knew what to think nor to do. She heard whispers among the audience that the other names were familiar, but who was Florence Mayberry? After the session adjourned, she worked up the courage to go to the podium, where Horace was lingering to chat with well-wishers. Making her way through the crowd, she got his attention and said, 'I'm Florence Mayberry.' Smiling, he took her hand. She then thanked him and the other Hands for appointing her and promised to do her best. Horace waved away her thanks and instantly replied, 'Don't thank me, you'll be the one doing the hard work.'[69]

Early in her service as a member of the Auxiliary Board, Horace assigned Florence the special, delicate task of resolving a problem of disunity between believers. The fledgling institution she served lacked a history of managing such thorny matters, so she asked Horace what to do. He gently tapped her shoulder with his finger and said simply, 'Do what your heart tells you.' That unexpected advice gave her a sense of wonder and freedom – she was free to use her best judgement without fear of that she was not doing her job as Horace might want her to do. Through experience, she learned that heeding Horace's advice to follow her heart led to good results. It allowed the powers of the spirit to have their effect. Throughout the years ahead, she used his example whenever anyone she was guiding needed advice and encouragement. She continued to do so as a Counsellor member of the International Teaching Centre.[70] After three years of working with Horace, Florence felt compelled to express her admiration for him, saying that she thought of him not only as 'one of the most brilliant of Bahá'ís', but also as 'one who is a shining star of the spirit', noting that even though he had had 'the heaviest of problems', yet he was 'not imprisoned by self'.[71] She added that, 'Whenever I grow tired, I remind myself of all you do. And then you aid me to be released from my prison.'[72]

Horace's correspondence with another member of that first contingent of Auxiliary Board members, Gayle Woolson, an American pioneer to South America, demonstrates the strategic mindset of a military general. Gayle was able to serve the Faith full-time, so one of the first things the Hands did after her appointment was to arrange for another pioneer to relieve her at her post on the Galapagos Islands so that she could focus on strengthening the Regional Spiritual Assembly of South America.[73] During their first year of service, the first task given to the Board members was to meet with every pioneer in their assigned region to urge them to remain at their posts.[74] Gayle and the other Board member in South America travelled extensively to encourage and support the other pioneers. Just as during the first years of the Assemblies, there were lessons to be learned through experience. For example, when Gayle returned briefly to the United States to visit family, Assemblies there wished to take advantage of her experience by arranging teaching trips to a number of communities. These requests generated a letter from the American Hands to the National Assemblies informing them that they should not make plans for Auxiliary Board members without first consulting the Hands. Even though the Hands were grateful for this service in her homeland, as Horace explained to Gayle, 'The Institution of the Hands is separate from the Administrative Institutions, and we want the distinction maintained.'[75]

Shortly after Hand of the Cause Leroy Ioas began his work on the International Bahá'í Council in 1952 in Haifa, he sent Horace a letter which he hoped would be shared with the National Assembly and others.[76] It was noteworthy not only because of the sage advice it contained, but because it marked the beginning of guidance coming from Hands serving in the Holy Land to direct, guide, and inspire the other Hands as well as Assemblies and Auxiliary Board members. That means of disseminating guidance would become routine in the future.[77] The contents were based on informal statements of Shoghi Effendi, so Leroy stated explicitly that he had obtained the Guardian's permission. He had also solicited from his fellow Hand, Amelia Collins, her approval of the letter's contents. He straightforwardly discussed reasons the American community was not growing at home, even as the pioneers it dispatched to other countries met with success. Attracting new believers and establishing new Assemblies were crucial to carrying out the Tablets of the Divine Plan.[78]

> The Guardian says the reason the Faith has gone ahead so rapidly in Latin America and Europe is because the pioneers are consecrated to the teaching work. What has been done in foreign fields should be more than matched in America.
>
> The reason we are not achieving our goals on the home front is because the Friends are concentrating on so many things that there is little time for teaching. This must be reversed. The Friends – each and everyone – must be consecrated to teaching – and other things of lesser importance fall into their proper position. <u>Consecration</u> is the attitude and motive power of the individual in the teaching field. His whole interest and activity of life must be to teach the Faith. Complete dedication and consecration to teaching are the essential elements necessary now to gain the goals. The Guardian said if the Friends gain that ideal condition and <u>arise</u> and <u>act</u> and

<u>teach</u> such acts will become the magnet attracting the confirmations of Bahá'u'lláh."[79]

The letter provided specific advice, focused on the importance of individuals carrying out their own teaching work, especially by hosting introductory meetings (firesides) in their homes every nineteen days. The National Teaching Committee was urged to systematically promote and encourage the believers to take initiative as individuals. Shoghi Effendi felt that there were already more than enough teaching materials. What was required was action utilizing available resources, not developing new methods or more resources.

The letter also made a point about an issue that had concerned Horace for several years.[80] During the second Seven Year Plan which began in 1946, the National Assembly had increased the number of national committees to meet the new goals of sending pioneers to Europe, and of developing advertising and public relations at the national level. These added to the previous committees working on the North American and Latin American goals. Managing and coordinating multiple important national committees required capacities that the National Assembly had yet to master. Leroy brought this matter up because Shoghi Effendi was concerned by reports that the multiple national committees were each sending out conflicting appeals to all communities, confusing and upsetting the friends. Should a believer answer the call to travel to teach in Europe or the call to settle in South America or move to another state? Should the committee working on nationwide publicity also be available to help local communities with event publicity; that is, should national work be diverted? The work of the various committees had to be brought under control and coordinated, otherwise they would dilute the overall effectiveness of the efforts to meet the goals of the Crusade.[81]

Leroy concluded his comments by stressing the one thing which most occupied the thinking of Shoghi Effendi: increasing the membership through teaching.

> The Guardian feels so strongly about teaching that he stated the Propagation of the Faith is perhaps the most important of all the phases of the Guardianship – even more important than directing the administrative order – which he feels is now so developed locally and nationally that it should be the channel through which

the creative forces of the Faith can more effectively be spread to the world.[82]

Any guidance from Shoghi Effendi, no matter how it was conveyed, was of paramount importance to Horace and his fellow Hands. In a letter to the American Auxiliary Board members, they emphasized this to those assisting them throughout the Hemisphere.

> Little by little we must become aware of how potent is the Guardianship in all Bahá'í undertakings, and in all Bahá'ís wherever they live and work. His divinely-guided master hand plans and directs the unfoldment of successive stages of the Master's Divine Plan. Our supreme need and privilege is to respond with complete consecration to his peerless leadership and thereby fulfil the high destiny to which we have been called by the Center of Bahá'u'lláh's Covenant.[83]

Amidst this period when Horace was as busy as he had ever been, it was hardly surprising that he began to experience new health problems, in addition to struggling with earlier ones. It was as if the more he was asked to do for the Faith, the more hurdles he had to jump. A stoic, Horace seldom confided any of his personal troubles unless left with no choice. One time during 1954 when the forces unleashed by the Ten Year Crusade had generated a frenzy of activity needing to be managed, he was uncharacteristically late for a morning session of the National Spiritual Assembly. When he finally joined the meeting, he quietly made his apologies without any explanation. What he failed to tell his baffled colleagues was that he had awakened that morning blind in one eye and immediately sought medical care.[84] Sometime later, he reported to Leroy Ioas that his doctor believed his sight would return, but 'If not – well, I'm getting in good practice on doing the day's work with one eye. Things could be a lot worse.'[85] His eyesight eventually returned, to Shoghi Effendi's great relief.[86]

* * * * *

As Horace went about his work: giving talks, writing letters and statements for two institutions, and meeting with the friends, he had reason to revisit many of the ideas, spiritual insights, and commentaries on the state of world affairs he had wrestled with for over four decades. In 1956, he produced another book, a collection of his talks and essays from the previous forty-seven years. It was entitled *Religion for Mankind* and published by his friends in England, the Hofmans. Marion Holley[87] Hofman, originally from California, had worked closely with Horace on many projects prior to her marriage to the Englishman David Hofman, and was herself an accomplished writer and editor. The Hofmans had established their own publishing business, George Ronald. It would be the last book Horace published. Indeed, after that, he seldom wrote articles, even for *The Bahá'í World*, having left the editorial board of that publication in 1952. His relentless responsibilities for the Cause combined with the energy-draining effects of age had taken their toll. His pen when he picked it up, moved more surely, but also more slowly than before.

In his 1956 introduction to *Religion for Mankind*, Horace briefly recounts his own spiritual journey from the day he first received the book about 'Abdu'l-Bahá from Bertha through the period of his participation in the four intercontinental conferences during which he observed first-hand the worldwide development of the Faith. The two spiritual bookends of his life were his 1911 encounter with 'Abdu'l-Bahá at Thonon, France, and his 1953 pilgrimage to the Holy Land where he prayed in the 'Holy Places and Gardens' and 'felt the power of an advancing Faith express itself through the Guardian, Shoghi Effendi Rabbani'.[88] He affirmed that his own 'spirit of investigation brought prodigious reward beyond desert', and hoped that 'as others in their turn arise to seek a new Spirit, a new Guidance in this troubled age', they might 'find a few trails blazed and at least a faint path marked for them leading from the world of Self toward the world of Revelation'.[89]

* * * * *

In 1957 Horace flew to Lima, Peru, this time as the representative of the Guardian, to attend one of four Bahá'í Conventions being held simultaneously in Latin America. The Lima gathering included believers from Brazil, Colombia, Ecuador, Peru, and Venezuela. The crowning achievement of the Convention was the establishment of a Regional Spiritual Assembly that encompassed those five countries. It had been determined that it was time to bring into existence other National Assemblies for

South America and no longer have the entire continent under one entity. This was only an interim step, as a more significant goal was to establish National Assemblies for each of those five countries by the end of the Ten Year Crusade in 1963. Horace's mission was to hasten the fulfilment of that goal by inspiring the believers and providing guidance.[90]

Horace was given a very touching task to carry out in Lima during the celebration of a Holy Day, the First Day of Riḍván. After he finished telling the story of Bahá'u'lláh's announcement that He was the Promised One of all ages in the Baghdad Garden of Riḍván in 1863, the crowd lined up, and he anointed each with attar of rose, a gift to the Convention from Shoghi Effendi. The sweet scent of roses wafted throughout the room, creating a heavenly atmosphere that touched every heart. The next morning, Horace reconvened the Convention and read the Guardian's message aloud. That day, he also presented Shoghi Effendi's gifts to the newly formed Regional Spiritual Assembly: two albums bound in beautiful, hand-tooled Italian leather, full of photographs of Bahá'í Holy Places, Houses of Worship, and a variety of Ḥaẓíratu'l-Quds from around the world. When he was departing for home, the members of the new National Assembly, along with many other Bahá'ís, accompanied him to the airport. As one member of the Regional Assembly reported, 'His love and presence touched and opened every heart there.'[91]

Shortly after the Latin American Conventions, on 19 June 1957, the American Hands sent a letter to every believer in the United States expressing their concern about the deteriorating situation of the Bahá'í community on the home front. There had been little growth in membership or movement towards meeting the Assembly goals. They therefore called for fifteen gatherings across the country to rally the friends. Horace was the principal speaker at the one held in Wilmette. These well-attended conferences were 'the greatest gathering of American Bahá'ís ever held for concentration on one essential objective' other than the centenary celebrations in 1944 and 1953, and stimulated the friends to arise to meet the goals.[92]

The fifteen conferences were so successful that the National Spiritual Assembly called for another fifteen in other localities. This second wave again attracted large numbers of the friends and had the desired effect of generating action. Horace, however, was unable to take part in any of the second group, for he was stricken with another heart attack.[93] A year after his first heart attack in 1944, Shoghi Effendi had admonished him, saying that, 'He hopes you are yourself keeping in very good health and not over doing? – though he knows from long personal experience that it is almost impossible not to overdo when the work of the Cause keeps on steadily piling up!'[94] For Horace, rest continued to be a luxury until it became a necessity.

* * * * *

Until 1957, the Hands had focused almost exclusively on promoting the teaching work, but in June, in response to both external and internal threats to the Faith, the Guardian added the protection of the Cause to their duties and instructed them to work in close collaboration with National Assemblies.[95] Shoghi Effendi further refined the work of the Auxiliary Boards by expanding their membership and dividing the members between two areas of focus: protection of the Faith and teaching. The number of Board members in the Americas doubled to eighteen.[96]

That was not all. On 2 October 1957, Shoghi Effendi appointed eight additional Hands of the Cause, including two North American pioneers residing in Africa: an American, William Sears, and a Canadian, John Robarts. While Horace had never served with either of them, he was well familiar with both from their outstanding teaching work, especially as pioneers. Robarts had served on the Canadian National Assembly and attended the New Delhi conference with Horace. Shoghi Effendi added a statement about the Hands that would shortly take on great significance. He called them 'the Chief Stewards of Bahá'u'lláh's embryonic World Commonwealth', adding that they 'have been invested by the unerring Pen of the Centre of His Covenant with the dual function of guarding over the security, and of insuring the propagation, of His Father's Faith'.[97]

Shoghi Effendi announced in that same letter that to mark the half-way point of the Ten Year Crusade, five more intercontinental conferences would be held the next year and the Hands of the Cause were invited to participate. These conferences were 'for the purpose of accelerating the march of the institutions of His world-redeeming Order, and of hastening the establishment of His Kingdom in the hearts of men'.[98]

Thus concluded the last general letter from Shoghi Effendi to the Bahá'í world.

* * * * *

A little more than one month later, in early November, at about 2:30 in the morning, the telephone rang at the True home in Wilmette. Edna, probably assuming a call at such an hour was for her surgeon sister, answered it. The familiar voice on the other end was not calling from a hospital, but from London. It was Hand of the Cause Rúḥíyyih Khánum. The line crackled with the static of the slightly distorted international connection. Marshalling all the fortitude, all the self-control she could muster, Rúḥíyyih Khánum conveyed the heart-breaking news that the centre of her world, her beloved husband, the Guardian of the Cause, had passed away without warning from a heart attack after a brief illness. They were in London on business. Could Edna and Katherine inform their mother on her behalf? She also reported that she could not rouse anyone at Horace's home to answer the telephone. Katherine knew the Holleys were away in Wisconsin, where Horace was recuperating in a hospital from surgery, probably to relieve the constant pain in his legs which had plagued him for years. Edna promised they would notify his doctor, a Bahá'í.

It was then Dr Manucher Javid's turn to be disturbed in the middle of the night. A young neurosurgeon and chief of that department at the University of Wisconsin Medical School, he had been one of nine Persian Bahá'í youth Shoghi Effendi sent to the United States during the middle of World War II to further their educations. He had just performed back surgery on Horace. With tears streaming down their faces, the doctor and his wife drove to the hospital to inform Horace. Awakened suddenly from sleep, Horace reacted with surprise and grief when he heard the news. His first comment was that the Guardian's passing meant trouble ahead. He well remembered the aftermath of 'Abdu'l-Bahá's passing in 1921. Horace's assessment was accurate, but the trouble would come from an unexpected source.

Most of the other Hands of the Cause immediately arranged to travel to London as quickly as possible to attend the funeral, but such a lengthy journey was impossible for Horace. Yet he was determined to participate in a meeting of the Hands to be held in the Holy Land only a few weeks later, recovered or not.[99]

Just as in the waning days of November 1921, the question haunting all Bahá'í minds was: what now?

14

THE PROMISED LAND

Those who live in the depths of a small, narrow valley, and make no effort to climb the lofty mountains by which they are beset – such people never behold the landscape stretching beyond the hills; they know not what the mountains may conceal.

But he who makes the mighty effort, leaving behind him the narrow valley of human selfishness and ease; he who has the supreme courage and strength to gain the summit, for him the invisible becomes visible; for him the infinite divine horizons are unfolded, and that which was hidden behind the mountains is revealed.

Horace Holley[1]

At the time of Shoghi Effendi's funeral in a London suburb, there was one worrisome problem – no one in the Faith had the rank, station, or authority to initiate any international action in his absence. The International Bahá'í Council did not have that authority. There were no descendants of 'Abdu'l-Bahá left within the Faith. The Hands of the Cause of God were equal in rank. No one believed they had the right to lead the Faith to the next step, whatever that step might be. The Hands of the Cause, as much as any of the mourners, were visibly overcome with grief, many having fainted or come close to it when they learned of the Guardian's untimely death at age 60. It was at this crucial moment when the whole of the Bahá'í enterprise could have faltered, perhaps irreparably, when a heroine of the Faith stepped forward. Rúḥíyyih Khánum was shattered by the sudden loss of her adored husband, the depths of which she could only express privately through verse. She could have followed the well-worn path of widows and entered into seclusion to nurse her sorrow. Instead, in the midst of the funeral events, she put aside her own feelings of grief and invited the Hands to come to the Holy Land where they could consult together as a group. At that decisive hour, like Mary Magdalene calling the bereaved Disciples of Christ to action as they hid during the weeks following the Crucifixion, she saved the Bahá'í Faith from heading down a wrong path.[2]

* * * * *

After his back surgery, Horace continued to be in constant pain;[3] nevertheless, he rallied enough from his convalescence to travel to the Holy Land less than two weeks after the Guardian's passing to attend the first Conclave of the Hands of the Cause. His fellow Hand from Wilmette, Corinne True, was too old and infirm to join him on the journey. Amelia Collins wrote a letter to Doris, assuring her she was watching over Horace while he participated in the sessions.[4]

During the 1953 Intercontinental Conferences, the Hands of the Cause had got to know each other face to face, but the conferences were not meant to be occasions for them to consult among themselves because they continued to take their instructions from Shoghi Effendi. When they came together in Haifa four years later, there were unknown faces among them – the eight Hands appointed less than two months earlier. The final contingent of Hands was thankfully younger than their predecessors. Several of the first appointments had died while others, such as Horace, suffered from ill health. This band of stalwart believers from Persia, North America, Europe, and Africa was united in love and grief, but separated by language and culture. Once again, it was the Guardian's widow who capably bridged those deep chasms. She was a North American[5] who for the last twenty years had lived in a Persian household during which time she became conversant in Farsi. She also spoke other languages, including French, the language widely spoken as a second language in the Near East.

For the first time, twenty-six of the twenty-seven Hands of the Cause gathered together on 18 November at Bahjí in the majestic garden in front of the Shrine of Bahá'u'lláh – the Ḥaram-i-Aqdas[6] – laid out by Shoghi Effendi. There, amidst row upon row of scarlet geraniums brought into full bloom by the first rains of autumn, beneath the swishing cypress trees bending with the afternoon breezes, in the formal garden where statues of peacocks and eagles symbolically reminded the Guardian's ardent lovers of eternity and victory, a memorial service was held for their beloved Shoghi Effendi. It began at 2:00

in the afternoon to correspond with the time nine days earlier when the interment occurred in England. The same day that the Hands gathered at Bahjí, the entire Bahá'í world paused to hold memorial services. Following the recitation of prayers and sacred verses, the Hands arose and with eyes wet with tears proceeded to the entrance of the small stone building revered by all believers as the Bahá'í Qiblih, the Holiest Spot on earth because it held the sacred remains of Bahá'u'lláh. Beneath its portico, they each removed their shoes, and with heads bowed, one by one entered the Shrine to offer their personal prayers for divine assistance and for inspiration from on high to guide God's Faith through the troubled time they were experiencing.

Their hearts strengthened through intense prayer, the Hands then solemnly walked along the crushed red tile paths to the entrance of the imposing two-storey white building that dominated the garden – the Mansion – Bahá'u'lláh's warm-weather, country home[7] where He ascended to His other Kingdoms in 1892. Its huge, blue metal door stood open for them. With shoes removed again, these lieutenants quietly ascended the steep marble staircase and entered the magically beautiful central hall, decorated by Shoghi Effendi as a museum showcasing the history and achievements of the Cause. There in the southeast corner hung a velvet curtain on which was embroidered in gold thread the symbol, the Greatest Name, covering the entrance to the chamber where Bahá'u'lláh passed away. They took their seats, and the Conclave began.

But how to begin?

Their first order of business was to determine if the Guardian had left a will. Nine of their members were selected to make a thorough search of Shoghi Effendi's chambers. Horace was chosen to represent the believers in the Western Hemisphere. Having completed that task, the velvet curtain was drawn back, and they filed into the southeast corner room for more prayers, prostrating themselves around the pallet on the floor where Bahá'u'lláh had died. As the sun was setting, they adjourned until the next morning and headed back to Haifa.

* * * * *

As soon as Leroy Ioas received the telephone call with the terrible news of Shoghi Effendi's unexpected death, on 4 November, he, his wife and the Revell sisters – all members of the International Bahá'í Council – immediately made certain that Shoghi Effendi's chamber was locked and secured. Before departing for Europe, Shoghi Effendi had locked his apartment and office. After checking the locks, the friends barricaded the door and then locked the outer door to the upper living quarters, putting iron bars across it and padlocking them for good measure. All the keys to the apartment were then sealed in an envelope, which they all signed. The precious envelope was then placed in a safe in Leroy's office in such a way that it would be obvious if it was tampered with. Trusted believers were asked to sleep either at the entrance to the Guardian's private quarters or at the foot of the stairway leading to them.[8] As soon as Rúḥíyyih Khánum returned from London, accompanied by four other Hands of the Cause, she retrieved the envelope and then the five of them entered the Guardian's chamber. The first thing they did was to place seals over the safe in his office, the logical place to store a will. All five signed the tape on the safe. The keys to the safe were then placed in a separate envelope, which was likewise sealed with wax and signed by all five. The drawers of the Guardian's desk were also taped and sealed. This entire procedure took them about an hour and was carefully documented. The sealed envelopes with keys were delivered to Leroy to place in his safe.[9] The care, the integrity of protecting undisturbed the Guardian's personal space and possessions, was above reproach.

At the time Shoghi Effendi became the Guardian, his great-aunt, Bahiyyih Khánum, had arranged for a small suite to be constructed on the roof of the Master's House exclusively for her great-nephew's use. After his marriage in 1937, an additional room was added. Few people ever entered those rooms other than the Guardian and his wife, except to clean them. In the years Leroy closely served Shoghi Effendi as secretary of the International Bahá'í Council, only once did he visit the room Shoghi Effendi used as his office.

The next morning, 19 November, promptly at 9:00 a.m., the nine chosen Hands, including Horace, retrieved the keys from the safe, broke the seals, opened the locks, removed the iron bars, and entered the Guardian's private apartment. The other locks were opened, and seals broken. He and the other eight Hands searched everything and everywhere, looking from the top to the bottom of the office, but they did not find anything that appeared to be a will or instructions. Nothing had been disturbed since the chambers were locked and sealed.[10] Next, the search continued with Shoghi Effendi's lawyer and bankers. No last will and testament would ever be found.

The other Hands had already assembled at the Mansion that morning when the nine arrived from Haifa with their report. No deliberations could proceed until the Hands could collectively affirm with a high degree of certainty that there was no successor. After hearing the report, they certified that Shoghi Effendi had left no descendants and no testament.

Bahá'u'lláh's book of laws, the Kitáb-i-Aqdas, enjoined upon every Bahá'í the duty of writing a testament. Shoghi Effendi had said that his monumental work, *The Dispensation of Bahá'u'lláh*, was his true testament. Yet 'Abdu'l-Bahá's Will and Testament was clear about the succession of the Guardianship. Shoghi Effendi was obliged to select his successor from among his sons or other male descendants of Bahá'u'lláh. He could deviate from the law of primogeniture if his eldest son failed to be worthy of that spiritual station. The Hands of the Cause could not choose a successor; they could only ratify the Guardian's choice by serving as witnesses to it.[11] Shoghi Effendi left no children[12] and all Bahá'u'lláh's male descendants were either dead or expelled from the Faith as Covenant-breakers, and so, because of their actions, disqualified themselves. Shoghi Effendi owned no property other than a few personal effects, because the lands and buildings belonged to the Faith. In fact, had he written a will, legal complications might have arisen with the government regarding Bahá'í properties and taxes.[13]

The Hands of the Cause were aware that, for the first time since 1844, there was no longer any person with God-given infallibility, including conferred infallibility. The Universal House of Justice, when established, would have conferred infallibility, but in the meantime, the Hands determined that the only authority they had was to carry out the directives of the Guardian. The Will and Testament of 'Abdu'l-Bahá was clear on that point. After days of prayers at the Shrines and passionate deliberation, they determined they did indeed have clear directives to follow, especially the letters of Shoghi Effendi setting out the Ten Year Crusade which would not conclude for another five years. It also became apparent when considering many statements of the Guardian that once a significant number of National Assemblies was achieved, the Universal House of Justice could be elected. The only course of action was evident; they would work to complete the goals of the Ten Year Crusade and foster the advancement of the Administrative Order to create the conditions necessary for the election of the Universal House of Justice, which they hoped could be accomplished at the end of the Plan.

The Hands also considered the section of 'Abdu'l-Bahá's Will and Testament which called for the election of nine from among themselves to assist the Guardian. The Hands carried out this injunction by selecting those serving as members of the International Bahá'í Council, plus five others – including Horace's American colleague, Paul Haney – to serve as a body in the Holy Land. These nine would be called the Custodians. All the Custodians, not just the original five, would serve on the International Bahá'í Council, which continued to have members who were not Hands, and they were expected to live in Haifa.

During their sessions, his fellow Hands experienced a side of Horace that only those who had served with him on the National Spiritual Assembly were familiar with. Hand of the Cause 'Alí-Akbar Furútan remarked that Horace had 'an impressive ability to marshal proof and arguments in a clear and cogent pattern of reasoning and a propensity for embellishing his theme, from time to time, with the most delightful seasoning of wit'.[14] Rúhíyyih Khánum also commented that it was at the first Conclave that Horace 'crowned his lifetime of service to the Cause of Baha by producing the finest fruit of his knowledge and understanding of its teachings – the Proclamation issued by the Hands, the first draft of which and major portion, we owe to his pen alone'.[15]

Hand of the Cause John Robarts later confided to a friend that the Hands were apprehensive about writing a proclamation, fearing how it would be received by the believers across the world. It was a vital yet delicate task. As a professional writer, Horace was the logical choice to create a draft. Rúhíyyih Khánum knew John could type, so she directed that both men work together and sent them to Shoghi Effendi's room. John sat on the Guardian's bed with the Guardian's typewriter on his lap. Horace placed a hard-back chair at a right angle to the bed and sat down. Then Horace began to dictate the document to John, astounding his scribe at how the words just flowed with ease.[16] In a sense, Horace had been preparing his entire life to carry out that task.

The Hands' Proclamation of 25 November 1957 was an historic document, one that helped to save the Faith during the treacherous transition by providing both solace and the assurance that the Cause of God would continue to go from strength to strength. The believers were not captain-less, for their captain had left detailed instructions how to reach the next safe port – the establishment of the Universal House of Justice. His experienced officers could well carry out their assignments with the aid of the National and Local Spiritual Assemblies. These elected institutions would continue to manage most of the day-to-day work of the Cause.

There were both spiritual and practical matters for the Hands of the Cause to consider. How should they obtain permission from the National Spiritual Assemblies to carry out the central work of the Faith in the absence of a Guardian or the Universal House of Justice? How could they ensure that the Bahá'í institutions secured control of the properties and financial accounts that had been managed by Shoghi Effendi, many of which were in his name? How could they gain the recognition from the government of Israel and its courts that the administration of the Faith was now in their hands and that of the International Bahá'í Council? Most importantly, how could they best earn the confidence and cooperation of the friends? Who could make what decisions? Fortunately, as they studied the letters of the Guardian from the final months of his life, they realized he had referred to the Hands of the Cause as the 'Chief Stewards' in his last general message. This title had both spiritual and legal implications. That rank signified that he had designated the Hands to act on his behalf. They interpreted this to also mean that they could not deviate from Shoghi Effendi's instructions.

Over the course of the next week, Horace produced drafts of a number of documents. Several were legal statements. Horace not only had experience with composing formal by-laws and charters but had also learned from experience what it was to work within the confines of charters, including the challenges. Fortunately, as he proceeded with his work, he had access to the advice of the Guardian's Israeli lawyer. The first document he produced was entitled, 'Unanimous Proclamation of the 27 Hands of the Cause of God.' Written in the format of a legal declaration, it set out that Shoghi Effendi had died in London on 4 November 1957 without leaving a successor and that it had fallen upon the Hands 'as Chief Stewards of the Bahá'í World Faith to preserve the unity, the security and the development of the Bahá'í World

Community and all its institutions'. It affirmed that, consistent with the directives of 'Abdu'l-Bahá's Will and Testament, the Chief Stewards had selected nine of their number to serve as the Custodians. These were listed by name. It stated that, as Shoghi Effendi's Stewards, the Custodians were granted broad powers to carry out his instructions until the Universal House of Justice was established and would decide to bring their role to an end. All twenty-six Hands present affixed their signatures, and Corinne True sent a notarized affidavit affirming her consent.[17]

The most important of all the documents Horace drafted was a letter to the Bahá'í world from the Hands of the Cause. It opened by acknowledging the state of deep mourning throughout the Bahá'í community brought about by the passing of their beloved Guardian. It then reported what the Hands as the Chief Stewards of the Cause had decided during their Conclave in the Holy Land. After describing in detail the futile efforts to find a will from Shoghi Effendi, they determined they had no alternative but to come up with means to continue the forward movement of the Faith at least until 1963. The Proclamation of the Hands read in part:

> The first effect of the realization that no successor to Shoghi Effendi could have been appointed by him was to plunge the Hands of the Cause into the very abyss of despair. What must happen to the world community of his devoted followers if the Leader, the Inspirer, the Planner of all Bahá'í activities in all countries and islands of the seas could no longer fulfil his unique mission?
>
> From this dark abyss, however, contemplation of the Guardian's own life of complete sacrifice and his peerless services gradually redeemed our anguished hearts. Shoghi Effendi himself, we knew, would have been the first to remind the Hands, and the widespread body of the believers, that the Dispensation of Bahá'u'lláh has quickened those powers and resources of faith within mankind which will achieve the unity of the peoples and the triumph of His World Order. In this new light of understanding the company of the Hands could perceive with heightened gratitude the existence of those innumerable blessings which Shoghi Effendi had created and left as his true legacy to all Bahá'ís.
>
> Has not the World Centre, with its sacred Shrines and institutions,

been firmly established? Has not the Message been established in 254 countries and dependencies? Have not the National and Regional Spiritual Assemblies, forerunners of the Universal House of Justice, been implanted in twenty-six great areas of all continents? Has not the Guardian left us not only his incomparable translations for English-reading Bahá'ís of the Bahá'í Sacred Literature but also his own master works of interpretation which disclose to us the unshatterable edifice of an evolving Bahá'í Order and world community? Has not the Guardian, building upon the enduring foundation of the Master's Tablets of the Divine Plan, created the World Crusade to guide our work until 1963?

Has not the Guardian, moreover, in his mysterious insight into the present and future needs of the Bahá'í community, called into being the International Bahá'í Council and the company of twenty-seven Hands with their Auxiliary Boards, whom, in his final communication to the Bahá'ís, he designated 'Chief Stewards of the embryonic World Commonwealth of Bahá'u'lláh'?

Such reflections cannot but, in such a world-shattering experience as all Bahá'ís have this month endured, reveal to us how strongly Shoghi Effendi has laid the foundations of the World Order of Bahá'u'lláh through the appointment of Hands of the Cause and likewise the appointment of the International Bahá'í Council, the institution destined to evolve into the Universal House of Justice.[18]

The statement then turned to the future, with the sure knowledge that they were not walking a dark path, but one lit by the far-seeing Guardian before he departed this life, and before him by His Grandfather, 'Abdu'l-Bahá in His Will and Testament.

In our capacity of Chief Stewards of the embryonic World Commonwealth of Bahá'u'lláh, we Hands of the Cause have constituted a body of nine Hands to serve at the Bahá'í World Centre. This body of nine Hands will energetically deal with the protection of the Faith whenever attacks, whether from within or outside the Bahá'í community, are reported by Hands from their areas or by National or Regional Assemblies or whether they arise within the Holy Land. Correspondence will likewise be maintained with the Hands of the Cause working in the several continents. This same body will correspond with National Assemblies on matters connected with the prosecution of the objectives of the Ten Year Plan. On matters involving administrative questions this same body will assist National Assemblies by citing those passages of the Baháʼí Sacred Literature which direct the Assemblies to a sound solution.

As to the International Baháʼí Council, appointed by the Guardian and heralded in his communications to the Baháʼí world, that body will in the course of time finally fulfil its purpose through the formation of the Universal House of Justice, that Supreme Body upon which infallibility, as the Master's Testament assures us, is divinely conferred: 'The source of all good and freed from all error.' The main work of the Council has been to act as the Guardianʼs representative in matters involving the Israeli Government and its courts of law.[19]

The Hands of the Cause then raised a call to action. Steadfastness was the word of the hour. Through consecration, through spreading the Faith of Baháʼu'lláh, the Baháʼí world would bring in the victories that were the aims of Shoghi Effendi's life. It was time to strengthen all efforts to achieve the remaining goals of the Ten Year Crusade.

> Beloved friends! Is not the most precious legacy bequeathed to us all by Shoghi Effendi the privilege of constancy in the Faith of Baháʼu'lláh and devotion in teaching His Message? This is the heartfelt plea we direct to every Baháʼí; The hour has come, as it came with the passing of ʻAbduʼl-Bahá, when true Baháʼís will be distinguished by their firmness in the Covenant and their spiritual radiance while pressing forward the mighty work committed to every area of the world community – to every individual Baháʼí! For now our implacable opponents may, and probably will, unleash attacks, assuming in their ignorance that the Faith of Baháʼu'lláh is weakened and defenseless. By consecration of spirit we are armed against all manner of assault and we hold the weapon of Faith with which the triumph of the Guardianʼs aims and purposes is assured.
>
> The Hands of the Cause, determined to carry out every aspect of the Guardian's expressed wishes and hopes, call upon the National Assemblies to proceed with the holding of the Intercontinental Conferences which Shoghi Effendi has planned for 1958, and make

each of them a great rallying-point of determination to achieve the tasks of the next phase of the World Crusade. We are, moreover, to keep ever before us the other tasks fixed in the Ten Year Plan as objectives to be won by 1963.

Meanwhile the entire body of the Hands, assembled by the nine Hands of the World Centre, will decide when and how the International Bahá'í Council is to evolve through the successive stages outlined by the Guardian, culminating in the call to election of the Universal House of Justice by the membership of all National Spiritual Assemblies.

When that divinely ordained Body comes into existence, all the conditions of the Faith can be examined anew and the measures necessary for its future operation determined in consultation with the Hands of the Cause.[20]

Besides the letter to the Bahá'í world, the Hands of the Cause sent a separate letter to all National Spiritual Assemblies asking them to provide written statements pledging their loyalty and specifically consenting to the plan the Conclave of the Hands had arrived at to manage the Faith as Chief Stewards and interim caretakers. As time was of the essence, the requested statements quickly poured into the World Centre. Armed with affidavits from Assemblies from all over the world, as well as with the other documents produced by the Hands, plus the October 1957 letter from Shoghi Effendi containing the term 'Chief Stewards', the Hands were able to convince Israeli officials and courts to recognize the right of the International Bahá'í Council and the Custodians to assume control of all Bahá'í properties in the Holy Land, including the twin Holy Shrines, and bank accounts with the funds of the Faith. Disaster had been averted.

Once Horace returned home, he was informed that many friends continued to be disturbed by the question left unresolved by the Hands as to whether there could ever be another Guardian. Auxiliary Board members reported to the Hands the many questions that were raised about the Guardianship during their meetings held around the country. Waiting until the Universal House of Justice was elected seemed too distant during a period fraught with potential dangers.[21]

During the Conclave, the Hands had concluded from their study of authoritative texts that only the Universal House of Justice could make a definitive statement about the future of the Guardianship, and, as of 1957, a date had not been fixed for the establishment of the House of Justice. To Horace's mind, logic dictated that the door to a future Guardian was closed. He believed the conditions set forth in the Will and Testament of 'Abdu'l-Bahá could no longer be met. The Will had been widely disseminated for decades, making it possible for all Bahá'ís to study it and draw conclusions, as he had.

Concerned by various reports brought to its attention, the National Spiritual Assembly of the United States encouraged the Hands living in America to draft a statement to explain why there could not be another Guardian.[22] Horace produced a draft in consultation with Paul Haney and the National Assembly, giving it the title 'A New Bahá'í Era'. It opened by declaring that, since the passing of Shoghi Effendi, 'The landscape has changed; in some aspects it is unfamiliar; we pause in temporary confusion until we become accustomed to the new condition and can see its relationship to the eternal verities of the revelation we have accepted with all our hearts.'[23]

As this statement circulated, segments of it were sent to the Custodians in the Holy Land who immediately became alarmed, because they thought it interpreted the Proclamation issued by the Conclave. They cabled the American Hands to delete several sentences, specifically the ones stating that the door to another Guardian was closed and that the Custodians had the authority to expel individuals from the Faith. Horace responded quickly, asking his colleagues in Haifa to consider the full statement, not just the excerpts. After studying the document, the Custodians firmly insisted that 'A New Bahá'í Era' be removed from circulation at once and the matter dropped. Horace was shocked, not only because he believed the statement was a necessary prophylactic, but because he felt the Custodians were censoring believers who were making determinations based upon their own reading of 'Abdu'l-Bahá's Will and Testament. He wrote them a frank letter, begging them to reconsider.[24] The response he received showed that the Custodians had a broader view than the Hands serving in the field. Their concern was not the accuracy of the statement, but the wisdom of promulgating it. They wanted the crucial matter of the future of the Guardianship to be addressed with one voice taking into consideration how the message would be understood globally. The Hands in Haifa wrote,

The Custodians from East and West are aware of the wisdom of avoiding statements or points of view on basic issues which cannot be accepted equally by East and West, and indeed by all the Bahá'í world, especially in this period, so soon after the ascension of the beloved Guardian, when we are still unable to grasp the full implications of the present situation.[25]

They also added the aside that, 'It would have been a great help if you yourself could have served here in these early and critical months, and given us the benefit of your experience and clarity of thought on the many pressing issues with which we have had to cope.'[26] Nonetheless, it seems that there was a change of thinking, because on 12 June 1958, the Custodians issued a statement exploring the future of the Guardianship because questions persisted. It included a quotation from the 'A New Bahá'í Era' statement.[27]

* * * * *

In May, another Intercontinental Conference was held in Wilmette and Chicago. As one of the six Hands present, Horace eulogized the Guardian, speaking of how he transformed the Faith during his thirty-six-year ministry by providing a better appreciation of the mission of the Cause of Bahá'u'lláh.[28] The number and diversity of those who took part in the conference was visible proof of how far the Faith had advanced in the fifteen years since the 1944 Inter-America Conference. There were 1,652 people representing 29 countries in attendance. It was Horace who provided the surprising, unforgettable climax of the conference with his parting words. With emotions running high as the gathering was drawing to a close, he stood before the assembled crowd and with all the intensity he could muster cried out three times, 'Ya-Bahá'u'l-Abhá!' each time 'with great force and rising inflection'.[29]

In the month following that memorable and significant gathering, Horace suffered another heart attack. This time it was Borrah Kavelin, the chairman of the National Assembly, who admonished him not to drive himself so much. The note to Horace said that, 'We have so few giants left in the Faith at the present time that it frightens and disturbs me to realize that you, the number one Giant, must really exercise great care not to be completely overwhelmed by the great burdens that you must carry all by yourself,' adding that Horace owed it 'to the Bahá'í world and to History to avoid reaching the point of no return, no matter how inviting that might seem at times'.[30]

If Horace was not well enough to travel, he could still carry on the quiet work of reading and writing. During 1958 he created a compilation of the Guardian's last letters, which was published that year as *Messages to the Bahá'í World: 1950–1957*. In its introduction, Horace observed that during the first two decades of his ministry, the Guardian wrote primarily to specific institutions and individuals.[31] But after 1950, Shoghi Effendi increasingly addressed his letters to the worldwide Bahá'í community. This was a collection of those major letters. From the outset of Shoghi Effendi's ministry in 1921, Horace had become an expert in the writings of the Guardian, not only through the process of creating the compilations that became a significant addition to Bahá'í authoritative literature, but by conducting study classes and creating study guides. As Shoghi Effendi remarked to one pilgrim, he and Horace thought alike and wrote alike.[32] It was because Horace immersed himself in the writings of the Guardian.

* * * * *

Slowing with age, Horace found brief respites from his many burdens in small pleasures: a cup of coffee while visiting with a friend, a walk along the lakeshore, a game of bridge, or a good dime-store mystery novel. Doris liked attending musical shows, but these no longer appealed to him, so she went with friends. Horace did enjoy the festivities of patriotic celebrations, especially Independence Day, with its rousing speeches, parades and fireworks. And he discovered the wonders of television when the new technology became widely available in the 1950s. One evening, his surgeon and friend, Dr Javid, called to ask a question. Chattering along, the doctor suddenly remembered the day and hour and realized that he had called Horace during the middle of his favourite television show, the detective series 'Perry Mason'. He asked if he had interrupted Horace's enjoyment of that programme, and, with obvious pain in his voice, Horace said that he had indeed.[33]

Anyone trying to describe Horace never failed to mention his sense of humour, an element of his personality that stayed with him until the end of his life. Of course, there were those who did not like it, especially his sarcasm. He had an unfortunate tendency to use a humorous remark to let someone know that he had become impatient with them. Many times, his humour reflected his erudition, and that too was not always appreciated. The following examples of his wit provide a fuller picture of the man.

Horace's nephew, Irving Holley, Jr., recounted that his uncle was a master of the pun. Irving's mother came from Virginia where the pitchers of sweetened iced tea served at all meals except breakfast were often accompanied in summer by a plate of mint sprigs. One day, Irving's mother was hosting Horace and realized she had forgotten the mint. Embarrassed by this omission, she apologized and returned to the kitchen to retrieve it, whereupon Horace looked at his nephew with a twinkle of mischief in his eye and wryly commented, 'She mint to do it.' The family groaned but knew all too well that it was part of 'his irrepressible fun'.[34]

Another time, Horace accompanied his nephew to a ship to see him off. As they made their way through the narrow corridors of the Polish ocean liner to his nephew's cabin, they found it almost impossible to pass because of crowds of laughing Poles bringing enormous baskets laden with fruit to their departing relatives. Elbowing their way through the crowd, Horace turned to his nephew and said, 'You've heard of the problem of the Polish Corridor, no doubt.' Years later, his nephew remarked he hoped his own children would be learned enough to get the joke.[35]

On another occasion, when Horace was a presenter at a programme that also included a distinguished professor from Northwestern University, the evening concluded with a segment for questions. The professor asked Horace about a controversial topic in religious circles: the theory of evolution which proposed that there was an as yet undiscovered creature linking homo sapiens to apes – the so-called 'missing link'. The professor asked Horace, 'What do the Bahá'ís believe about the theory of evolution and especially the missing link?' Horace simply replied, 'We believe it is missing.'[36] This was not only funny but succinctly summarized the Bahá'í teachings on the topic.

A story that circulated among many Bahá'ís illustrated how he combined humour with wisdom. A believer telephoned Horace late one evening to complain about a member of her Local Spiritual Assembly who was dominating the community. After the caller expounded bitterly at length about the situation without so much as a pause, Horace finally interjected, 'You are very sincere, my dear. In this instance, however, you are sincerely wrong.' After changing the trajectory of the conversation with that bit of humour, he gave her a surprising alternative way to look at her community's problems. He said that 'the person who is running the affairs of the Assembly single-handed is not wrong. The other eight members of the Assembly who are allowing this to take place are wrong.' But that was not all; he said that the others were jeopardizing the spiritual health of that person. It was amazing to him that the friends in the caller's community would allow such a situation to exist and permit one of its members to go astray. He then directed the caller to stiffen her backbone and bring the matter to her Assembly for full and frank consultation. When this incident was related by the caller to Hand of the Cause Paul Haney, he commented, 'Well, he never asked anyone to do something he would not do himself.'[37]

Another example of his wit occurred during a luncheon when a believer called Horace 'Mister Holley', rather than by his first name. He told her, 'All of the disciples of Christ are known by only their first names save one, Judas Iscariot. Please call me Horace.'[38]

* * * * *

In the 1950s, Horace was looking toward the future and must have realized it was essential to groom a possible successor as National Assembly secretary. Charles Wolcott was elected to the National Assembly in 1953. He was a talented musician from California. He also had administrative capacity honed through his employment as head of music for a major Hollywood film studio. When Horace recognized special qualities in Charles, he began to quietly draw them out. At the close of an evening session of the National Assembly, Horace would often turn to Charles and say, 'How about joining me for a cup of coffee?' They would then retreat to the kitchen next to the meeting room where they would find that Doris already had a pot of the hot brew waiting for them. Sometimes, especially when Horace wanted to get outdoors and walk a bit, they would go to a nearby restaurant that was open late. There, the two would converse for hours. 'These were memorable moments,' Charles wrote years later, 'because they offered opportunities to relish his sparkling wit, to partake of his vast knowledge of the Sacred Writings and above all to listen to this keen perception of the affairs of the world which illuminated our conversations.' Charles attributed 'whatever abilities' he had as a speaker on behalf of the Cause to these late-night sessions.[39] Horace was right, for Charles would briefly serve as his successor as secretary before moving to Haifa where he served on the International Bahá'í Council and as a member of the Universal House of Justice.

The believers, with increasing confidence, turned to the Hands as individuals for advice. Horace was not constrained to working only in the United States, but also had to keep abreast of whatever was happening in the rest of the Western Hemisphere. He had been following and learning from the pioneers' reports since 1936. When he became a Hand, it was part of his job to pass on his insights from this big picture. For example, when the Canadian National Eskimo and Indian Teaching Committee asked for guidance regarding teaching the Eskimos (Inuits), he suggested that they be taught as families rather than individuals, an insight that would be widely implemented decades later but at the time was farsighted.[40]

From time to time, Corinne True still attended gatherings, but with the departure of Paul Haney for the Holy Land, Horace became for a time the most active Hand of the Cause resident in the United States, even as he continued to serve as the secretary of the National Assembly. Many believers could not remember a time when he was not the secretary. He had become a revered figure accorded the status of an elder statesman. This was apparent at the National Conventions. At the last one Horace would attend, in 1958, he was again elected secretary of the Convention and was seated at the front alongside the Convention's chairman, Borrah Kavelin. Horace sat quietly through the consultation but occasionally would subtly motion to the chairman that he wanted to speak. Borrah would nod that he had the floor. Horace would rise from his chair and walk slowly to the podium. A hush would fall over the assembled believers. Then Horace would extemporaneously make comments about whatever was the issue at hand. But these were not ordinary remarks. They were not just wise, learned remarks. No, they were of such a quality that one listener described them as 'confirmations of the Kingdom of God'. The sanctity of what he had to say, their depth based upon his extraordinary knowledge of the teachings, was stunning. He moved his listeners and transported them to another realm. Horace had become a channel for the Holy Spirit.[41]

* * * * *

On 21 November 1958, Horace was again in the Holy Land for the second Conclave of the Hands of the Cause. Carefully following the instructions left to them by their departed Captain, they had successfully steered the Faith through the first year of sailing through uncharted waters. The initial shock of the Guardian's unexpected death had passed, and, putting aside their own feelings of despair, the Hands had rallied the community, especially during the five Intercontinental Conferences. There was much left to accomplish, and, thankfully, the troubles they had expected never materialized.

In the months before his passing, Shoghi Effendi, like his Grandfather 'Abdu'l-Bahá before him, focused on the potential of opposition to the Faith and internal problems, warning the friends and making arrangements to strengthen the means of protecting the Faith. In both cases the internal trouble came from unexpected quarters – those who had been in trustworthy positions. Major transitions are usually laden with challenges because change is often not easy to accept and the ambitious and the duplicitous are always ready to take advantage of the uncertainty inherent in a change in leadership. The years immediately following the passing of the Guardian were especially unpredictable because there were no obvious candidates to assume the mantle of Head of the Faith. The Israeli War of Independence in 1948 had caused many of the expelled relatives from Bahá'u'lláh's family to flee Palestine; consequently, they caused very few problems in 1958, aside from stirring up issues regarding Bahá'í properties. Ahmad Sohrab was a spent force, defeated by the world-wide spread of the Faith that left his small group behind with little to show for their efforts; he would die a few months after the Guardian, having lived long enough to see Shoghi Effendi triumph. None of the Hands of the Cause would have guessed in November 1957 that the person scheming to seize control of the Faith would be one of their own. He bided his time, waiting for the right moment to reveal his ambitions. It came during the third Conclave of the Hands in 1959.

Charles Mason Remey had become a Bahá'í while a student in Paris just at the hour the new twentieth century began, New Year's Eve, 1899.[42] His middle name, Mason, the one by which people called him, was a reminder that he was a direct descendent of George Mason, the 'Father of the Bill of Rights' and one of the illustrious Founding Fathers of the American Republic. Remey's father was a high-ranking naval hero stationed in Washington DC, where young Mason ran in elite circles. His architectural business was never stellar, but that did not matter for he inherited wealth and also married into it. His wife died of suicide after one year of marriage, having given him no children. From his youth, Remey served the Faith continuously, travelling the world to spread it at the direction of 'Abdu'l-Bahá and later under the supervision of the Guardian. He was especially knowledgeable about the Covenant of Bahá'u'lláh, authoring articles exploring it in the first years after the promulgation of the Will and Testament. He chaired the Committee of Investigation of the Chicago Reading Room matter that had divided the American community on the issue of the Covenant during World War I. Even though he had been elected to the Executive Board of the Temple Unity for many years running, he was elected to serve only one year to the National Spiritual Assembly – the first year Horace served.

Remey had the bearing of a distinguished diplomat. Tall, imposing, extremely well-bred, he was dignity personified. He was also intelligent, well-travelled and well-educated. These qualities were ideal as President of the International Bahá'í Council because one of his most important tasks was representing the Faith to Israeli government officials.

When Shoghi Effendi called Remey to Haifa in the early months of 1922, the two consulted about buildings, especially the unfinished Western Pilgrim House. However, the Guardian did not invite Remey to take part in the discussions about the timing of the election of the Universal House of Justice. He did, however, make certain that Remey viewed the original copy of the Will and Testament and affirm that it was authentic. Over the years, Remey continued to provide Shoghi Effendi with advice about building projects and he was granted the commissions to design two of the Houses of Worship to be built during the Ten Year Crusade: the ones for Sydney, Australia, and Kampala, Uganda. Remey also drew up the blueprints for the International Bahá'í Archives, though the design for that first building of the World Centre was conceived by Shoghi Effendi himself. All in all, Charles Mason Remey was remembered by many who knew him as a proud man – proud of his family's history and his work as an architect.[43]

By 1957, Remey was 83, one of the oldest of the Hands, yet despite his age he fully participated in the Conclaves and signed all the statements issued by the Hands at the end of the First Conclave, including

Conclave of the Hands of the Cause of God gathered in the House of 'Abdu'l-Bahá, November 1957. Horace Holley is standing behind Tarázu'lláh Samandarí, to the right

Hands of the Cause of God at the 1958 Conclave. Horace Holley is in the middle row, second from the right. Charles Mason Remey is seen over Horace's left shoulder, the last person on the right in the last row

No 10 Haparsim Street, the Western Pilgrim House, Haifa, Israel. This hostel became the home for the Holleys as well as for others serving in the Holy Land. Horace passed away in that building in 1960

The members of the International Bahá'í Council in 1961 were elected by members of the National and Regional Spiritual Assemblies. Left to right: Sylvia Ioas (Vice-President), Charles Wolcott (Secretary General), Jessie Revell (Treasurer), Ethel Revell (Western Assistant Secretary), Ian Semple (Assistant Secretary), Borrah Kavelin (Member-at-large), Lotfullah Hakim (Eastern Assistant Secretary), 'Alí Nakhjavání (President), Mildred Mottahedeh

Horace Holley facing the Shrine of Bahá'u'lláh during the last months of his life in 1960

Resting place of Horace Holley at the Haifa Bahá'í Cemetery

the one stating that there did not appear to be a successor to the Guardian. At the end of the Second Conclave in November 1958, an intense period of day-long discussions of the progress of the Ten Year Crusade that lasted a week, he asked to speak to the group. This was his first request to address the Conclave, and though the other Hands wished to accommodate him, the time set for the meeting to end had passed and most had planes to catch. They agreed to give him unlimited time to speak at the beginning of their next Conclave the following year.

It was at the Third Conclave, in 1959, that the Hands began to think further into the future. They could oversee the completion of the Ten Year Crusade, but after Riḍván 1963 there was no guidance from Shoghi Effendi to enact. From that point on, the Hands determined, based on careful study of authoritative texts, that only two institutions were authorized in the Sacred Writings to carry the Faith forward at the international level: the Guardianship and the Universal House of Justice. Based upon their study, they decided the time had come to take the steps necessary for the election of the Universal House of Justice in 1963. Furthermore, they agreed that in 1961, the International Bahá'í Council would be reconstituted and its members elected for the first time by the National and Regional Assemblies, thus creating a trial run for the election of the House of Justice in 1963. This would change the International Bahá'í Council from being an appointed body to an elected one. They also revised its mandate by limiting it to planning the 1963 election and the Jubilee to be held in London that same year in accordance with the directive of the Guardian. The Hands made one other decision that was totally unexpected. The decision was something so momentous, so farsighted, so unheard of for a group wielding power, that it would shine throughout the ages as a pure, unselfish act. They made the collective decision to ask the electors to not vote for any of the Hands of the Cause of God for membership on either the International Bahá'í Council or the Universal House of Justice, because 'the Chief Stewards of the Faith are wholly occupied with specific tasks assigned them by the beloved Guardian and perforce assumed since his passing . . .'[44] All of their control of the Faith and its properties and funds would be willingly turned over to others. They were truly servants of the Cause of God.

Remey was incensed by this turn of events, especially the decision to exempt Hands from service on either the International Bahá'í Council or the Universal House of Justice. He had assumed that, as President of the

International Bahá'í Council, he would be elected to the Universal House of Justice and would become its President. Ranting during the proceedings, he went so far as to castigate the Hands for failure to fill the position of Guardian. At the conclusion of the Conclave, he refused to sign the statement of the Hands laying out their decisions, the only one to refuse to endorse it. His behaviour and pronouncements were proof to his colleagues that he was no longer suited to be among the nine Custodians, so they quickly agreed to replace him. Remey left Haifa for the last time.

In 1931, Shoghi Effendi had stated to an American family visiting the Holy Land as pilgrims, 'I don't know what I would do without Horace Holley.'[45] By 1959, the Hands of the Cause had reached the same conclusion and decided that he was needed more in Haifa than in Wilmette,[46] so they elected him to replace Remey as a Custodian. Horace returned home and immediately began to bring his service in America to an end.

* * * * *

Before the Holleys left Wilmette, a farewell gathering was held for them beneath the dome of the House of Worship in Foundation Hall. More than 200 well-wishers crowded the auditorium on 19 December to be with the couple they loved and admired one last time. During the programme, Horace spoke of his early years in the Faith in Paris and New York City. He drew contrasts between the situation of the Faith during his youth and its growth and maturation since the time 'Abdu'l-Bahá's Will and Testament was promulgated. As a witness to monumental changes, he could survey all that had passed with satisfaction. He concluded his remarks by challenging his audience, 'Let us be concerned in these crucial days, not with our petty differences, but with the glorious opportunities that are ours to help establish the beginning of the Kingdom of God on Earth.'[47]

Saying farewell to the staff who had served with such dedication at the National Office was more emotionally difficult for him than the programme honouring him at the House of Worship. Horace looked so frail and ill that those devoted assistants knew they were unlikely to see him again. He could not bring himself to say the word 'good-bye'; he just closed the door behind him.[48]

* * * * *

The Holleys' first stop on their journey to the Holy Land was Connecticut, where his brother, Irving, and his wife, Mary, anxiously awaited their arrival at the airport. They all no doubt sensed that this might be the last time they would be together.

The four enjoyed the visit, reminiscing and bringing each other up to date with the comings and goings of absent relations. As important as seeing his favourite brother was to Horace, he had another reason for visiting Connecticut: to visit his only remaining child, Marcia. She had never been able to fully function as an adult and spent her time in and out of facilities such as the one where she would pass away in 2002.[49] During that early winter visit in 1959, she was again staying in a home for impaired adults. Irving drove them there. It would be the last time Horace would see his daughter.

Horace's relatives were surprised and concerned when they learned he had agreed to move to volatile Israel. His health was so precarious that Irving had become reluctant to venture far from home, lest Horace have an emergency that required his immediate care. They knew that among the goods their brother was shipping to Haifa were portable oxygen tanks.[50] Too quickly, it was time to catch the plane to New York. Goodbye to his dear ones, goodbye to New England. Detachment, detachment, detachment. God was great and good and only asked His servants to do what was best for them.

The Mottahedeh family were among those who accompanied the Holleys to the New York City airport from which they would embark. More loving farewells enveloped them as they closed another chapter of their lives. Neither would ever live in the United States again. As the plane took off over the Atlantic before turning northeast, the Holleys must have taken one last look at the great metropolis that they had loved, the City of the Covenant.

* * * * *

Living in Haifa was like living on the edge of the world; situated where three continents meet, it had been mankind's strategic crossroads for millennia. Looking out over the eastern Mediterranean from the vantage point of the slopes of Mount Carmel, the whole of the world seemed stretched out at one's feet. It was exhilarating.

Yet Israel was a tiny country surrounded by hostile neighbours, so living there was like living on an island. After the 1948 United Nations partition of Palestine and the War of Independence, the Baháʼí Holy Places thankfully fell within the ceasefire lines that had become Israel's unofficial borders.[51] Even though Judaism had become the official state religion, the government was supportive of the Baháʼís, primarily because of the Guardian's careful development of cordial relations with the new government from its inception. However, the Arabs within and without Israel never accepted the Jewish homeland within their midst, and so the country was perpetually on a war footing. Haifa was one of the primary ports of Israel, and the Holleys could watch its expanding Navy coming and going in its harbour.

Haifa was the most diverse city in the country and its primary industrial centre. Away from the religious and political centres, it rarely attracted those with extreme points of view, unlike Jerusalem and Tel Aviv. Even though its Jewish population was its fastest growing segment, it still retained sizeable percentages of Christians and Muslims. Most of the time, the three groups tolerated each other, just as they had for centuries, and so there were fewer incidents of politically motivated violence than in other cities in the country.

*****

When ʻAbduʼl-Bahá built His home in Haifa, He chose a Christian neighbourhood between the old city walls and the German Templer Colony. Much of it was still farmland or gardens in 1900. The large home housed not only His growing family – His daughters married and had children – but also those serving Him and those whom He had taken under His care. Land was purchased adjoining this primary residence on which homes were later constructed for his daughters and their families. One of these had been donated by a son-in-law to serve as a pilgrim house for Western believers in the years before World War I, but within a few years, it became too small to accommodate the growing numbers of pilgrims. The local authorities named the lane bisecting the Baháʼí properties, Haparsim – 'the Persian Street'. This steep lane climbing the mountainside became a compact world for the Holleys.

Across Haparsim Street from the Master's House and slightly up the hill was another large plot that was also a Holy Place because it was one of the locations where Baháʼuʼlláh had pitched His tent during His

1891 visit to Haifa. 'Abdu'l-Bahá decided that it was a befitting location to construct a larger pilgrim house. Horace's friends, the Randall family, had provided the first funds to build it, and Amelia Collins had provided most of the rest. 'Abdu'l-Bahá Himself had conceived the plans and instructed Charles Mason Remey to create blueprints. When the Holleys arrived, this building was used as the headquarters of the International Bahá'í Council, yet it still accommodated pilgrims and visitors. It also served as a dormitory for some of the Hands and members of the Council. The Holleys were assigned a spacious room with high ceilings on the upper main floor and shared sitting areas with others. On the lower level, near the dining room where the Guardian used to meet with friends over dinner, was a small kitchen, shared by residents and visitors alike.

At the bottom of Haparsim Street, less than a block away from the Pilgrim House, was the beginning of the commercial area where Doris could buy groceries and other household necessities. Within the surrounding blocks there were Arab bakeries that had steaming mounds of pita bread and great varieties of treacly sweet baklava laid out on large trays. Tiny grocery stores with their bins of dried lentils, beans and chickpeas, and barrels of spices spilling out onto the sidewalk were squeezed next to produce stands or small food stalls selling falafel and shawarma. Pots and pans and other household items dangled from the awnings of hardware stores, and above it all was the din from haggling in Hebrew and Arabic combined with the sound of passing traffic. Even for a New Yorker like Doris, this new environment required acclimatization. At certain hours of the day the neighbourhood echoed with the chants of muezzins calling Muslims to prayer, or church bells summoning Christians to vespers. Fridays were the day of rest for Muslims, Saturdays were the day Jews rested, and Christians worshipped on Sundays, so any day of the week, at least one shop was open depending upon the religion of the proprietor. There was a rhythm to life in Haifa. Doris, who had a reputation as a good cook, made the best of these surroundings to keep her husband well and happy.

The Holleys arrived in the early days of winter, which, coming from Chicago, they could have mistaken for early spring. New green grass and a palette of wild crocuses, anemones, and cyclamens painted the hillsides. Winters in Haifa were generally mild, and snow a rarity, but the damp cold could penetrate to the bone during the rainy season.

Sometimes high winds buffeted the mountain side and sent towering waves crashing against the seawalls in the harbour. Most buildings lacked fireplaces or central heat and instead relied on small charcoal braziers – hammered metal plates on a stand – or small radiators. The Western Pilgrim House only had a kerosene radiator centrally located on the lower level by the kitchen. Surely, those first months in the Holy Land challenged Horace's precarious health.

The material comforts at the Pilgrim House were far below those of the United States. There was only one shower in the building which was shared by everyone, and it provided only cold water. Privacy was limited. The furnishings were basic and worn. But the formerly affluent residents from the United States[52] hardly noticed, for the blessings of living there were extraordinary – especially that of associating with such dedicated, knowledgeable believers. Visitors, including pioneers, staying there for a week or more would buoy the spirits of the residents with reports of Bahá'í adventures from their home communities. The residents especially loved hearing new teaching stories. Every morning, the residents, including the Hands of the Cause and their wives, would gather in the kitchen where, over coffee, tea, cereal, and toast, they would consult together about incoming correspondence from Western countries. The wives were as informed as their husbands, especially Sylvia Ioas, who served on the International Bahá'í Council. Leroy often started the discussion, having already perused the mail. The wives would enter the discussion. Then Horace would speak up in his soft voice with to-the-point comments sprinkled with some clever wit. Hand of the Cause John Ferraby would sit there without saying a word, listening intently to the others consult, until the discussion was reaching a conclusion, at which point he would finally speak up. John's comments invariably were brilliant points that no one had thought of, often taking the discussion in a new direction. Fortunate visitors would munch their bowls of cornflakes and milk, all the while imbibing this elevated breakfast conversation.[53]

When the Hands elected nine of their number to serve as Custodians, this group set up their office in a special room across the street from the Pilgrim House. Within the walled grounds of the Master's House, in the corner next to the main gate were two small buildings connected by a covered breezeway. The lower level of one was a garage containing Shoghi Effendi's automobile. On the upper floor of the building next to the gate was a room which 'Abdu'l-Bahá had lined in cedar so that the wood would absorb the dampness of Haifa winters. Until the last weeks of His life, 'Abdu'l-Bahá preferred to sleep in that room rather than in His chamber in the main house. It was this room that the Hands used as their collective office. Rúḥíyyih Khánum observed Horace's participation in the meetings of the Hands held there.

> It was very touching to see how Horace, so frail that one felt a breeze would blow him away, would cross the street and struggle up the short flight of steps to the Hands' meeting room. He listened attentively to the discussions, signifying agreement through a nod of his head or raising his hand, saving the very little strength he had left to express his opinion in words should the need arise. In spite of his extremely fragile condition he was still the old Horace, and his clear mind and wisdom were of inestimable help in our decisions and his personality a joy to me.[54]

After months of silence, in April, Charles Mason Remey issued a statement declaring he was the second Guardian. It was sent to many Bahá'í communities. He based his assumption of the Guardianship on his appointment by Shoghi Effendi to the position of President of the International Bahá'í Council. His reasoning was convoluted, twisting the words of 'Abdu'l-Bahá's Will and Testament from their obvious meanings to argue his case.

The other Hands of the Cause were shocked and dismayed. At first, many of them concluded that, as a man in his 80s, Remey was no longer mentally competent and his outrageous claim should be excused as nothing more than the ravings of an old man. In their first communication to the Bahá'í world discussing Remey's claims, they blamed his declaration on a 'profound emotional disturbance'[55] and said they hoped he would come to his senses so that he could be enfolded back into the community.[56] But when five members of the National Assembly of France as well as a few other believers accepted Remey's claim, evidence emerged that his declaration was not the product of mental instability, but an orchestrated, well-thought-out attempt to wrest control of the Faith. Yet several Hands, especially those in Europe, hesitated to take decisive action and to expel him and his followers from the Faith. The Hands were compassionate people who well understood the gravity, the spiritual damnation that came with the pronouncement that someone was a Covenant-breaker, and they were especially reluctant to expel Remey after his lifetime of distinguished service.[57] As the Hands equivocated, Horace spoke up at a meeting of the Custodians and said simply, 'Cast him out,' quoting the exact words of the Will and Testament. His forthrightness gave his colleagues the courage to take action.[58] A few months later, when the episode had reached a climax and the Hands unanimously expelled Remey from the Cause of God, his colleagues said, 'We are deeply grateful to Bahá'u'lláh that we had the valued, mature and wise advice of dear Horace during the most difficult period of this whole Remey affair and that he was able through his example and counsels, to render at the end of his life yet another great service to the Faith he had worked for so constantly, with such outstanding distinction and devotion, and for so many years – a Faith whose Guardian had heaped upon him so many honours.'[59]

* * * * *

Horace's heart had grown over the years as his understanding of the power of love deepened, but his physical heart was finding it increasingly difficult to keep pace with his spirit. On the evening of 12 July, he emerged from the washroom near his room in the Western Pilgrim House and collapsed onto the hard, tile floor. Others rushed to his aid, but he was gone. He was gone.

Death had chosen a worthy, symbolic spot to take Horace home. He passed away in sight of the room at the end of the central corridor where in less than three years the Universal House of Justice would hold its meetings – the room that would become its Council Chamber. The Western Pilgrim House would serve as its Seat for its first twenty years. Like Moses, Horace had been led to the top of Mt Nebo, where he could look towards the Promised Land, but he could not enter it. His lifelong goal – the supreme institution he so longed to help bring into existence – was almost ready to be born; but it was not his fate to be present at its birth, when, in April 1963, it was elected by the fifty-six National Spiritual Assemblies gathered in the Holy Land representing humankind.

Earlier that day, Hand of the Cause 'Alí-Akbar Furútan visited Horace and had found him confined to his sick-bed. Furútan had been hesitant to come close to Horace lest he disturb him, but 'found him calm and serene, his face illumined by a smile, his whole being suffused with radiance'.⁶⁰

Over forty years earlier, 'Abdu'l-Bahá had instructed Horace on how to think about the troubles of life, comparing his life's journey to the voyage of a ship. The traveller should welcome the waves for 'if the tranquility become permanent' it meant only one thing, 'the fact that one's journey has come to an end'.⁶¹ Relating Horace's days in Haifa to a friend in the United States, Amelia Collins said that Horace had never been happier than during his brief time in the Holy Land. His earthly spiritual journey – begun aboard a ship – had reached its tranquil harbour.

* * * * *

Word of Horace's passing quickly spread throughout the Bahá'í world. The grief-stricken Custodians immediately contacted Rúḥíyyih Khánum, who cancelled the rest of her visit to North America and returned to the Holy Land. Unfortunately, the Ioas family and Amelia Collins were also away from Haifa at the time, tending to their own health problems.

The following day, a befitting memorial service for Horace was held in the central hall of the House of the Master, a minor historic occasion in a building that had witnessed world-shaking events. From there, the Bahá'ís resident in the Holy Land, accompanied by visitors, followed his casket to the Bahá'í cemetery at the foot of Mt Carmel just below the Cave of the Prophet Elijah. There he was laid to rest next to both the Great Afnán, builder of the first Bahá'í House of Worship in the world in Ashqabat ('Ishqábád)⁶² and the immortal British Hand of the Cause, John Esslemont. Horace's remains would forever lie where generations of pilgrims could visit his resting place to pray and pay homage to one to whom they owed so much.

Charles Wolcott, secretary of the National Assembly of the United States, was surely overtaken by feelings of sorrow when he read the first line of the cable that arrived at the National Centre offices in Wilmette on 13 July from the Hands of the Cause in the Holy Land. It read:

GRIEVED ANNOUNCE PASSING HAIFA MUCH-LOVED DISTIN-
QUISHED HAND CAUSE GOD HORACE HOLLEY OUTSTANDING

CHAMPION FAITH SINCE DAYS MASTER PRAISED BY BELOVED GUARDIAN FOR UNIQUE CONTRIBUTION DEVELOPMENT ADMINISTRATIVE ORDER STOP HIS INDEFATIGABLE SERVICES PROTECTION TEACHING ADMINISTRATIVE FIELD CULMINATING SERVICE HOLY LAND INSPIRING EXAMPLE PRESENT FUTURE GENERATIONS BAHAIS STOP SHARE ABOVE MESSAGES HANDS ALL NATIONAL ASSEMBLIES STOP URGE HOLD MEMORIAL GATHERINGS TEMPLE LOCAL COMMUNITIES UNITED STATES.[63]

That same day, the National Assembly responded with a cable that began, 'DEEPLY GRIEVED LOSS REVERED HAND DEARLY BELOVED FRIEND HORACE HOLLEY'. In its letter to the American community conveyed through its institutions and agencies, the National Assembly said that 'Our feelings of loss at the passing of this distinguished servant who stood as a bulwark of inspiration and guidance to the American Bahá'í community are mitigated by the realization that his devotion to the teaching efforts on the home front will now be showered upon all of us in even greater abundance from the Abhá Kingdom.'[64]

Memorial services were held in many locations. Of note were the two special ones timed to be simultaneous at the Shrine of the Báb in Haifa and the House of Worship in Wilmette.[65] A tribute to Horace planned by the New York Spiritual Assembly was attended by about 150 people. As Mildred Mottahedeh wrote in her letter of condolence to Doris, 'we all knew for years that the moment was rapidly approaching when he would leave us but it was just as great a shock when he did'.[66] After saying that he was not just a friend but a mentor, she said, 'I feel that my development as a Bahá'í, if I have made any, was in a measure due to him,' and that 'Only future generations will be able to correctly apprise his tremendous work for [a] new world.'[67]

Doris, lost without Horace, remained for more than a year in Haifa, continuing to serve as a housekeeper and hostess at the Western Pilgrim house. She then pioneered, first to Switzerland and then to Ireland. Arriving in Limerick when youth were flocking to the Faith in that city, she became a favourite of the young, new believers because of her warmth, humour, and down-to-earth personality. She passed away in 1983 at her Irish pioneer post, much loved, revered and missed.

Horace left many legacies: his writings, the insights he provided which moulded Bahá'í institutions, his shining example of devoted, tireless service, and the hearts he touched. He also left behind protegées he mentored. For example, Charles Wolcott not only succeeded Horace as secretary of the US National Spiritual Assembly, but he and fellow officer Borrah Kavelin were among the first nine members elected to the Universal House of Justice in 1963. Florence Mayberry and Edna True were among the first contingent of Continental Counsellors appointed in 1968 by the House of Justice, and Florence was later named an original member of the International Teaching Centre when it was established by the House of Justice in 1973. Another of his close friends, Mildred Mottahedeh, was elected to the International Bahá'í Council in 1961 and spent years representing and fostering the Bahá'í International Community at the United Nations' New York headquarters.

Horace's greatest gift to posterity was his role in the development of the Administrative Order, the embryo of the future world government. He did not think that his most significant contribution was the role he played, along with Mountfort Mills, in drafting the charters and by-laws for the National and Local Spiritual Assemblies. As he saw it, his primary contribution was asking questions. In carrying out his work as an officer of the National and New York Assemblies, he would recognize the need for guidance on a particular point, and then write a letter putting a question to Shoghi Effendi. Horace gathered Shoghi Effendi's answers, and then disseminated them.[68] The compilations he created will forever serve as the foundational guidebook for the collective management of the entire human race.

Rúḥíyyih Khánum, who had assisted Shoghi Effendi as a secretary throughout their marriage, gave her own perspective of just how Horace contributed to the development of the Administrative Order in her moving tribute to him after his death. She prefaced it by extolling his 'comprehensive knowledge of the Teachings, his mastery of correct Bahá'í procedure, and the lucidity of his mind . . .'[69]

> This great servant of the Faith, with just that kind of mind, ground a lot of edges off the administrative machinery of the Cause in America and in this process, lasting thirty-six years, had a lot of the sharp edges ground off his own nature and mind. Undoubtedly the greatest factor in his life, next to his having accepted so wholeheartedly the Faith of Bahá'u'lláh, was Shoghi Effendi. Horace loved

Shoghi Effendi's ideas. He grasped, perhaps better than anyone else, just what the Guardian was constructing through the erection of the Administrative Order. He assisted in this through all the powers of his mind, giving, year after year, an unstinting service to its realization.[70]

While young, Horace had deeply pondered many aspects of the promised Universal House of Justice, exploring his insights in *The Bahá'í World* edition published in 1930.[71] His article postulated that the establishment of the House of Justice could not take place before 'certain requisite conditions . . . come into existence'.[72] He noted that two of those, the political liberation of the Persian Bahá'í community and the communities in the Soviet Union, were outside the control of the Faith. There was, however, one precondition which could be brought about through the exertions of the believers:

> The most favorable condition for the election of a thoroughly representative Universal House of Justice would be the active functioning of National Spiritual Assemblies in a sufficient number of countries to involve Bahá'ís of every religious and racial affiliation, supplying the broad basis for that superstructure crowning, with the Guardianship, the social reality of religion in the new age.[73]

He happily anticipated that this supreme Bahá'í institution would not be long in coming and would bring about the promised Day of God through the implementation of Bahá'u'lláh's teachings, saying, 'The existence of this body in the near future will demonstrate to the world most conclusively how Bahá'u'lláh has revealed a truth for the healing of the nations.'[74]

The 1963 edition of *The Bahá'í World* which contained Rúhíyyih Khánum's tribute to Horace also included the report of the establishment of the Universal House of Justice – 'the source of all good and freed from all error'[75] – by electors embodying the diversity of the human race. The decade-long Crusade had ended in triumph. The Faith of God for this day encircled the globe and its foundation was unassailable due to the firm planting of the Administrative Order throughout all the continents. That 'In Memoriam' article ended with Horace's own words. These same words seem the most fitting ending to this summary of his extraordinary life, a summary which will be improved upon in the future as mankind more fully appreciates the work of this ardent lover of God and humanity.

> Now what we have here is, indeed, a Divine creation. It is humanity being raised toward God and the Divine grace of God descending to humanity . . . therefore in our daily lives, when we have troubles and difficulties of an administrative nature, let us not be too impatient or too easily discouraged because we are in the process of making possible the formation of that spiritual body of the Universal House of Justice. There is the basis of the world's peace. There is the order and security of the world. There is the nobility and enlightenment of the human race . . . if by the purity of our motives, by the depths of our self-sacrifice, we could hasten by one year or one month the establishment of that body, the whole human race would bless us for that great gift.[76]

GOD MOST GLORIOUS

Beyond the sweep of farthest star
Beneath the beauty of the rose
His tokens shine remotely far
His glory stands ineffably close.
(Radiant the heart of him who knows.)

No longer weak as creed outworn
No longer dim as hope denied
His will proclaims celestial morn
Within the dungeon of our pride.
(His power no people can deride.)

A scourge He gives each bitter fear
He arms for death each sullen hate.
Destroying sin in man and state.
(The world is witness to its fate.)

His glory seizes East and West
Confounding nation, sect and clan
A fiery crucible to test
The soul committed unto man,
(The goal of life since time began.)

He builds upon our ruined age
A kingdom righteous, firm and sure.
Behold! Our ancient heritage
Summons the meek, awaits the pure.
(His peace forever will endure.)[77]

BIBLIOGRAPHY

'Abdu'l-Bahá. *Foundations of World Unity: Compiled from Addresses and Tablets of 'Abdu'l-Bahá*. Wilmette, IL: Bahá'í Publishing Trust, 1945, 1972.

— *Paris Talks: Addresses given by 'Abdu'l-Bahá in 1911* (1912). London: Bahá'í Publishing Trust, 12th ed. 1995.

— *The Promulgation of Universal Peace: Talks Delivered by 'Abdu'l-Bahá during His Visit to the United States and Canada in 1912* (1922, 1925). Comp. H. MacNutt. Wilmette, IL: Bahá'í Publishing Trust, 2nd ed. 1982.

— *A Traveler's Narrative Written to Illustrate the Episode of the Báb* (1891). Trans. E. G. Browne. Wilmette, IL: Bahá'í Publishing Trust, rev. ed. 1980.

— *Will and Testament of 'Abdu'l-Bahá*. Wilmette, IL: National Spiritual Assembly of the Bahá'ís of the United States, 1944.

Afnan, Elham. "Abdu'l-Bahá and Ezra Pound's Circle', in *The Journal of Bahá'í Studies*, 2 June 1994.

Ahlstrom, Sydney E. *A Religious History of the American People*. Foreword and concluding chapter by David D. Hall. New Haven: Yale University Press, 2nd ed. 2004.

Allen, Frederick Lewis. *Only Yesterday: An Informal History of the 1920s*. New York: Harper Perennial Modern Classics, 1931.

— *Since Yesterday: The 1930s in America*. New York: Harper & Row, 1939.

Armstrong-Ingram, R. Jackson. *Music, Devotions, and Mashriqu'l-Adhkár: Studies in Bábí and Bahá'í History*, vol. 4. Los Angeles: Kalimát Press, 1987.

Bahá'í Encyclopedia Project, The. https://www.bahai-encyclopedia-project.org.

Bahá'í Procedure. Comp. National Spiritual Assembly of the Bahá'ís of the United States and Canada. Wilmette, IL: Bahá'í Publishing Committee, 2nd ed. 1942.

Bahá'í Scriptures: Selections from the Utterances of Bahá'u'lláh and Ábdul'-Bahá. Ed. Horace Holley. New York: Brentano's, 1923.

The Bahá'í World: An International Record. Vol I (Bahá'í Yearbook, 1926–1926), vol. II (1926–1928), vol. III (1928-1930), vol. V (1932–1934); vol. VII (1936–1938), vol. IX (1940–1944), vol. X (1944-1946), vol. XI (1946–1950), vol. XII (1950–1954), RP Wilmette, IL: Bahá'í Publishing Trust, 1980–81; vol. XIII (1954-1963), Haifa, The Universal House of Justice, 1970.

Bahá'í World Faith: Selected Writings of Bahá'u'lláh and 'Abdu'l-Bahá. Ed. Horace Holley. Wilmette, IL: Bahá'í Publishing Trust, 1971 edition.

Bahá'u'lláh. *The Kitáb-i-Aqdas: The Most Holy Book.* Haifa: Bahá'í World Centre, 1992.

— *Tablets of Bahá'u'lláh Revealed after the Kitáb-i-Aqdas.* Comp. Research Department of the Universal House of Justice. Haifa: Bahá'í World Centre, 1978.

Balyuzi, H. M. *'Abdu'l-Bahá: The Centre of the Covenant of Baha'u'lláh.* Oxford: George Ronald, 1971.

— *Edward Granville Browne and The Bahá'í Faith.* Oxford: George Ronald, 1970.

Banani, Sheila. 'The Life and Times of August Forel', in *Lights of Irfán*, vol. 6, pp. 1–20.

Barry, John M. *Roger Williams and the Creation of the American Soul: Church, State, and the Birth of Liberty.* New York: Viking Penguin, 2012.

Beckley, Zoe. 'Women to Have War Wardrobe?', in *New York Evening Mail,* reprinted in *Los Angeles Evening Express,* editorial page, 23 March 1918.

Berg, A. Scott, *Wilson.* New York: G. P. Putnam's Sons, 2013.

Black's Law Dictionary. Online at: https://thelawdictionary.org.

Blomfield, Lady, *The Chosen Highway.* London: Bahá'í Publishing Trust, 1940. RP Oxford: George Ronald, 2007.

Bohn, Willard. '"O. W. Gambedoo", "H.H." et *Les Soirées de Paris*', in *Revue des lettres modernes : Guillaume Apollinaire 9,* nos. 249–253 (1970), pp. 13–41.

Bramson-Lerche, Loni. 'Some Aspects of the Development of the Bahá'í Administrative Order in America, 1922–1936', in *Studies in Babi and Bahá'í History,* vol. 1 (ed. Moojan Momen). Los Angeles: Kalimát Press, 1982.

Brandow, James C. *Genealogies of Barbados Families: from* Caribbean *and* The Journal of the Barbados Museum and Historical Society. RP 2001.

Bryan, William Jennings. *The Old World and Its Ways.* Thompson Publishing Company, 1907.

Buck, Christopher. *God & Apple Pie: Religious Myths and Visions of America.* Kingston, NY: Educator's International Press, 2015.

Bushnell, George D. *Wilmette: A History.* Wilmette, IL: Village of Wilmette, 1997.

'The Case of Ahmad Sohrab and the New History Society', in *Bahá'í News Letter,* no. 43 (August 1930).

Century of Light. Prepared under the supervision of the Universal House of Justice. Haifa: Bahá'í World Centre, 2001.

Chanler, Julie. *From Gaslight to Dawn: An Autobiography of Julie Chanler.* New York: New History Society, 1956.

Chapman, Anita Ioas. *Leroy Ioas: Hand of the Cause of God.* Oxford: George Ronald, 1998.

Churchill, Suzanne Wintsch. *The Little Magazine, Others and the Renovation of American Poetry*. London: Ashgate, 2006.

—; McKible, Adam (eds). *Little Magazines & Modernism: New Approaches*. New York: Routledge, 2007.

Collins, William P. 'Kenosha, 1893–1912: History of an Early Bahá'í Community in the United States', *Studies in Bábí and Bahá'í History*, vol. 1 (ed. Moojan Momen). Los Angeles: Kalimát Press, 1982.

The Compilation of Compilations, vol. II. Maryborough, Australia: Bahá'í Publications Australia, 1991.

The Continental Boards of Counselors: Letters, Extracts from Letters, and Cables from The Universal House of Justice. Comp. National Spiritual Assembly of the United States. Wilmette, IL: Bahá'í Publishing Trust, 1981.

Cooper, John C. Jr. (ed). *A Collection of Verse by Boys of the Lawrenceville School*. Princeton, NJ: Princeton University Press, 1910.

The Dawn-Breakers: Nabíl's Narrative of the Early Days of the Bahá'í Revelation. Trans. Shoghi Effendi. Wilmette, IL: Bahá'í Publishing Trust, 1932, 1974 edition.

Day, Anne L. 'Randall, John Herman', in *Biographical Dictionary of Internationalists*, pp. 595–7. Ed. Warren F. Kuehl. Westport, Connecticut: Greenwood Press, 1983.

Dyar, Harrison Gray. 'II: The Bahai Religion: The Will of Abdul Baha', in *Reality*, vol. VI, no. 7 (July 1923), pp. 16–20.

— 'IV: The Bahai Religion: An Episode in its History', in *Reality*, vol. VI, no. 9 (September 1923), pp. 40–46.

Egea, Amín. *The Apostle of Peace: A Survey of References to 'Abdu'l-Bahá in the Western Press 1871–1921*. Vol. 1: 1871 – 1912. Oxford: George Ronald, 2017.

Ellis, Edward Robb. *The Epic of New York City: A Narrative History*. New York: Old Town Books, 1966.

Fletcher, John Gould. *Autobiography of John Gould Fletcher*, originally published as *My Life is a Song*. New York: Farrar & Rhinehart, 1937, 1988.

Fowler, Penny. *Frank Lloyd Wright: Graphic Artist*. Rohnert Park, California: Pomegranate Communications, 2002.

Freeman, Dorothy. *From Copper to Gold: The Life of Dorothy Baker*. Oxford: George Ronald, 1983.

From Iran East and West: Studies in Bábí and Bahá'í History, vol. 2 (ed. Juan R. I. Cole and Moojan Momen). Los Angeles: Kalimát Press, 1984.

Gail, Marzieh. *Arches of the Years*. Oxford: George Ronald, Oxford, 1991.

— *Summon up Remembrance*. Oxford: George Ronald, 1987.

Gelernter, David. *Americanism: The Fourth Great Western Religion*. New York: Doubleday, 2007.

Glovsky, Norman E. *The Lake Superior Country in History and in Story*, by Guy M. Burnham. Park Falls, WI: Weber & Sons; RP Paradigm Press, 1996.

Gregory, Louis, 'Inter-racial Amity', in *The Bahá'í World*, vol. II (1926–1928).

—; Ober, Harlan. 'Alfred Eastman Lunt', In Memoriam, in *The Bahá'í World*, vol. VII (1936–1938), pp. 531–4.

Grun, Bernard. *The Timetables of History: A Horizontal Linkage of People and Events.* New York: Simon & Schuster, 3rd rev. ed. 1991.

Grundy, Julia M. *Ten Days in the Light of 'Akká* (1907): Wilmette, IL: Bahá'í Publishing Trust, 1979.

Ham, Paul. *1913: The Eve of War*. Endeavour Press, Ltd., 2013 (UK digital publisher).

Harper, Barron Deems. *Lights of Fortitude: Glimpses into the Lives of the Hands of the Cause of God.* Oxford: George Ronald, rev. ed 1997.

Hill, Candace Moore. *Bahá'í Temple (Images of America)*. Charleston, South Carolina: Arcadia Publishing, 2010.

Hills, William Henry (ed). *The Writer: A Monthly Magazine for Literary Workers*, vol. XXIV, Boston, August 1912. This difficult to find work can be accessed at: https://babel.hathitrust.org/cgi/pt?id=mdp.39015059398860&view=1up&seq=128&q1=Holley.

History of Waterbury and Naugatuck Valley, Connecticut, vol. III. Chicago: The S. J. Clarke Publishing Company, 1918.

Hitchcock, William I. *The Age of Eisenhower: America and the World in the 1950s*. New York: Simon & Schuster, 2018.

Hofman, David. *George Townshend: Hand of the Cause of God*. Oxford: George Ronald, 1983.

Hogenson, Kathryn Jewett. *Lighting the Western Sky: The Hearst Pilgrimage and the Establishment of the Bahá'í Faith in the West*. Oxford: George Ronald, 2010.

Holley, Horace. 'Aims and Purposes of the Bahá'í Faith', in *The Bahá'í World*, vol. III (1928–1930), pp. 7–12; and in several subsequent volumes.

— 'The Artist in America', in *The New Republic*, 5 June 1915, pp. 113–15.

— 'The Assurance of World Peace: The Evolution of Peace', in *The Bahá'í World*, vol. X (1944–1946).

— 'The Background of Matisse', in *The New Republic*, 20 February 1915, pp. 74–6.

— 'The Bahai Congress, the New Cycle, and Divine Command: Notes of Memory and Anticipation', in *Reality*, vol 1, no. 2 (June 1919).

— *Bahaism: The Modern Social Religion*. London: Sidgwick & Jackson, 1913.

— *Bahai: The Spirit of the Age*. New York: Brentano's, 1921.

— (ed.) *Bahá'í Scriptures: Selections from the Utterances of Bahá'u'lláh and 'Abdu'l-Bahá*. New York: Brentano's, 1923.

— *Creation: Post-Impressionist Poems* (Paris, January-October, 1913). London: A.C. Fifield, 1914.

— 'Current Bahá'í Activities', in *The Bahá'í World*, vol. III (1928–1930).

— *Divinations and Creation.* New York: M. Kennerley, 1916.

— 'Earth's Justice', poem embedded within commentary, in *Collier's: The National Weekly*, vol. 57, no. 6 (22 April 1916), p. 15.

— *The Inner Garden; A Book of Verse.* Boston: Sherman, French & Company, 1913.

— 'International Survey of Current Bahá'í Activities in the East and West', in *The Bahá'í World*, vol. IX (1940–1944).

— 'On the Spiritual Reality', in *The Egoist*, 1 May 1914.

— 'Our Unpublished Masterpieces', in *The Seven Arts*, vol. 1 (1916–17), pp. 419–25.

— *Present-Day Administration of the Bahá'í Faith*, leaflet. Wilmette, IL: Bahá'í Publishing Committee, 1947.

— *Read-Aloud Plays.* New York: M. Kennerley, 1916.

— *Religion for Mankind.* Oxford: George Ronald, 1956.

— "Religious Education for a Peaceful Society", in *The Bahá'í World*, vol. XI (1946–1950).

— *The Social Principle.* New York: Laurence J. Gomme and Marshall, 1915.

— 'The Spirit and Form of Bahá'í Administration', in *The Bahá'í World*, vol. III (1928–1930), pp. 9–16.

— 'The Stout Lady Buys a Dancer', in *The New Republic*, vol. 2, 24 April 1915.

Hussey-Arntson, Kathy; Leary, Patrick. *Wilmette (Images of America).* Charleston, South Carolina: Arcadia Publishing, 2012.

Jackson, Jeffrey H. *Paris Under Water: How the City of Light Survived the Great Flood of 1910.* New York: Palgrave MacMillan, 2010.

Jasion, Jan Teofil. *'Abdu'l-Bahá in France: 1911 & 1913.* Paris: Editions bahá'íes France, 2016.

— *'Abdu'l-Bahá in the West: A Biographical Guide of the People Associated with His Travels.* Paris: Editions bahá'íes France, [no date].

Johnson, Paul, *A History of the American People.* New York: Harper Collins, 1997.

— *Modern Times: From the Twenties to the Nineties.* New York: Harper Collins, rev. ed. 1991.

Kazin, Michael. *A Godly Hero: The Life of William Jennings Bryan,.* New York: Alfred A. Knopf, 2006.

— *War against War: The American Fight for Peace, 1914–1918.* New York: Simon & Schuster, 2017.

Knock, Thomas J. *To End All Wars: Woodrow Wilson and the Quest for a New World Order.* Princeton, NJ: Princeton University Press, 1992, 1995.

Kreymborg, Alfred. *Troubadour: An American Autobiography* (1925). New York: Sagamore Press, 1957.

Kuehl, Warren F. (ed). *Biographical Dictionary of Internationalists.* Westport, Connecticut: Greenwood Press, 1983.

—; Dunn, Lynne K. *Keeping the Covenant: American Internationalists and the League of Nations, 1920–1939*. Kent, Ohio: The Kent State University Press, 1997.

Lacroix-Hopson, Eliane. *'Abdu'l-Bahá in New York the City of the Covenant. Sydnea, Australia:* Bahá'í Publications Australia, 2nd ed. 2005.

Lee, Sze Wah Sarah. 'Aesthetics of Experiment: Imagism, Vorticism and the European Avant-Garde', Doctorial thesis, Goldsmiths, University of London, 2016.

Levenstein, Harvey. *Seductive Journey: American Tourists in France from Jefferson to the Jazz Age*. Chicago: The University of Chicago Press, 1998.

Loeding, Sophie, 'Eyewitness Impression of the Dedication', in *Bahá'í News*, no. 494.

Marchand, Roland. *Advertising the American Dream: Making Way for Modernity, 1920 – 1940*. The University of California Press, 1985.

Mayberry, Florence, *The Great Adventure*. Manotick, Ontario: Nine Pines, 1994.

McAuliffe, Mary. *Twilight of the Belle Epoque: The Paris of Picasso, Stravinsky, Proust, Renault, Marie Curie, Gertrude Stein, and Their Friends through the Great War*. London: Rowman and Littlefield, 2014.

McDougall, Walter A. *Freedom Just Around the Corner: A New American History 1585 – 1828*. New York: Harper Collins (Perenniel), 2004.

— *The Tragedy of U.S. Foreign Policy: How America's Civil Religion Betrayed the National Interest*. New Haven: Yale University Press, 2016.

McGroarty, John Steven. *Los Angeles: From the Mountains to the Sea*. Chicago and New York: The American Historical Society, 1921.

McKay, Doris. *Fires in Many Hearts*. Manotick, Ontario: Nine Pines, 1993; RP Oxford: George Ronald, 2021.

Meacham, Jon. *American Gospel: God, the Founding Fathers, and the Making of a Nation*. New York: Random House, 2006.

The Ministry of the Custodians 1957–1963: An Account of the Stewardship of the Hands of the Cause. Haifa: Bahá'í World Centre, 1992.

Momen, Moojan. *The Bahá'í Communities of Iran 1851–1921*. Vol. 1: *The North of Iran*. Oxford: George Ronald, 2015.

— (ed). *Studies in Bábí & Bahá'í History*, vol. 1. Los Angeles: Kalimát Press, 1982.

Morison, Samuel Eliot. *The Oxford History of the American People*. New York: Oxford University Press, 1965.

Morrison, Gayle. *To Move the World: Louis G. Gregory and the Advancement of Racial Unity in America*. Wilmette, IL: Bahá'í Publishing Trust, 1982.

Muhajir, Iran Furútan, *Siyyid Mustafá Rúmí: Hand of the Cause of God, Apostle of Bahá'u'lláh*. Wilmette, IL: Bahá'í Publishing Trust, 2020.

Munson, Gorham. *The Awakening Twenties: A Memoir History of a Literary Period*. Baton Rouge: Louisiana State University Press, 1985.

Nakhjavani, Violette. *The Maxwells of Montreal: Middle Years 1923–1937, Late Years 1937–1952*. Oxford: George Ronald, 2012.

Newcomb, John Timberman. '*Poetry*'s Opening Door: Harriet Monroe and American Modernism', in *Little Magazines & Modernism: New Approaches*, edited by Suzanne W. Churchill and Adam McKible, pp. 85ff.

Noll, Mark A. *The Old Religion in a New World: The History of North American Christianity*. Grand Rapids, Michigan: William B. Eerdmans, 2002.

Parisi, Joseph; Young, Stephen. *Dear Editor: A History of Poetry in Letters*. New York: W. W. Norton, 2002.

People from Salisbury, Connecticut: Horace Holley, Peter Buell Porter, Myron Holley, Orville L. Holley, Bird Beers Chapman. RP Books LLC, 2010.

Perry, Anne Gordon. *Green Acre on the Piscataqua*. Wilmette, IL: Bahá'í Publishing Trust, expanded 3rd ed. 2012.

Phelps, Myron H. *Life and Teachings of Abbas Effendi: A Study of the Religion of the Babis, or Beha'is Founded by the Persian Bab and by His Successors, Beha Ullah and Abbas Effendi*. New York: G. P. Putnam's Sons, 1903. Abridged ed. *The Master in 'Akká*. Los Angeles: Kalimát Press, 1985 (both the original and the 1985 edition were used).

Prothero, Stephen. *Religious Literacy: What Every American Needs to Know – and Doesn't*. New York: Harper Collins (Harper One), 2007.

Rabbaní, Rúḥíyyih (Rúḥíyyih Khánum). 'Horace Hotchkiss Holley', In Memoriam, in *The Bahá'í World*, vol. XIII (1954–1963).

— *The Priceless Pearl*. London: Bahá'í Publishing Trust, 1969.

— 'Twenty-Five Years of the Guardianship'. Wilmette, IL: Bahá'í Publishing Committee, 1948.

Rameshni, Omeed. 'Jinab-i-Fadil Mazindarini (Fadil Mazindarini)'. Website, 2009. https://sites.google.com/site/fadilmazindarani/thereproductions

Randall-Winckler, Bahíyyih. *William Henry Randall: Disciple of Abdu'l-Bahá*. Oxford: OneWorld, 1996.

Redman, Earl. *'Abdu'l-Bahá in Their Midst*. Oxford: George Ronald, 2011.

— *The Knights of Bahá'u'lláh*. Oxford: George Ronald, 2017.

— *Shoghi Effendi: Through the Pilgrim's Eye*. Vol. 1: *Building the Administrative Order, 1922–1952*. Oxford: George Ronald, 2015; vol. 2: *The Ten Year Crusade, 1953–1963*. Oxford: George Ronald, 2016.

Research Department of the Universal House of Justice. 'Passages Regarding the Constitutions of National and Local Spiritual Assemblies', February 2019,

Rodriguez, Suzanne. *Wild Heart, A Life: Natalie Clifford Barney and the Decadence of Literary Paris*. New York: Ecco (Harper Collins), 2003.

Rosenfeld, Lucy D. '3 Towns Where Creative Minds Congregated', in *The New York Times*, 22 December 1996. https://www.nytimes.com/1996/12/22/nyregion/3-towns-where-creative-minds-congregated.html.

Ruhe-Schoen, Janet. *Champions of Oneness: Louis Gregory and His Shining Circle*. Wilmette, IL: Bahá'í Publishing Trust, 2015.

Rutstein, Nathan. *Corinne True: Faithful Handmaid of 'Abdu'l-Bahá*. Oxford: George Ronald, 1987.

Ryrie, Alec. *Unbelievers: An Emotional History of Doubt*. Cambridge, Mass.: The Belknap Press of Harvard University Press, 2019.

Salpeter, Harry. 'A Note on Advertising', in *Liberator*, September 1918.

Schmidt, Leigh Eric. *Restless Souls: The Making of American Spirituality*. New York: Harper Collins, 2005.

Schweikart, Larry; Dougherty, Dave. *A Patriot's History of the Modern World: From America's Exceptional Ascent to the Atomic Bomb: 1898—1945*. New York: Sentinel, 2012.

Sears, William. 'In Memoriam: Horace Holley (1887–1960), Hand of the Cause of God', in *Canadian Bahá'í News,* January 1961.

Seelye, John. *Memory's Nation: The Place of Plymouth Rock*. University of North Carolina Press, 1998.

Shlaes, Amity. *The Forgotten Man: A New History of the Great Depression*. New York: Harper Perennial (HarperCollins), 2007.

Shoghi Effendi. *The Advent of Divine Justice* (1939). Wilmette, IL: Bahá'í Publishing Trust, 1984.

— *Bahá'í Administration: Selected Messages 1922–1932*. Wilmette, IL: Bahá'í Publishing Trust, 1928, 1974, 1980.

— *Citadel of Faith: Messages to America, 1947–1957*. Wilmette, IL: Bahá'í Publishing Trust, 1965.

— *Directives from the Guardian*. Comp. Gertrude Garrida. New Delhi: Bahá'í Publishing Trust, 1973.

— *God Passes By* (1944). Wilmette, IL: Bahá'í Publishing Trust, rev. ed. 1974.

— *Messages to the Bahá'í World: 1950–1957*. Wilmette, IL: Bahá'í Publishing Trust, 2nd ed. 1971.

— *This Decisive Hour: Messages from Shoghi Effendi to the North American Bahá'ís, 1932–1946*. Wilmette, IL.: Bahá'í Publishing Trust, 1992, 2002.

— *The World Order of Bahá'u'lláh: Selected Letters by Shoghi Effendi* (1938). Wilmette, IL: Bahá'í Publishing Trust, 2nd rev. ed. 1974.

Smith, Peter. '*Reality* Magazine: Editorship and Ownership of an American Bahá'í Periodical', in *From Iran East and West*, vol. 2.

Smith, Ryan. 'The Bizarre Tale of the Tunnels, Trysts and Taxa of a Smithsonian Entomologist', in *Smithsonian Magazine*, 13 May 2016. https://www.smithsonianmag.com/smithsonian-institution/bizarre-tale-tunnels-trysts-and-taxa-smithsonian-entomologist-180959089/.

Sohrab, Ahmad. *My Bahá'í Pilgrimage: Autobiography from Childhood to Middle Age*. New York: The New History Foundation, 1959. RP H-Bahai: Lansing, Michigan, 2004.

— *The Story of the Divine Plan*. New York: The New History Foundation, 1947.

Spring, Leverett Wilson. *A History of Williams College*. New York: Houghton Mifflin, 1917.

Stavitsky, Gail. 'Artists and Art Colonies of Ridgefield, New Jersey'. http://tfaoi.org/aa/4aa/4aa26.htm.

Stenstrand, A. J. 'Authorship of the Writings Attributed to Baha Ullah', in *Reality*, vol. VIII, no. 4 (October 1924), pp. 32-5.

Stockman, Robert H. *'Abdu'l-Bahá in America*. Wilmette, IL: Bahá'í Publishing Trust, 2012.

— *The Bahá'í Faith in America*. Vol 2: *Early Expansion, 1900-1912*. Oxford: George Ronald, 1995.

Szefel, Lisa. 'Beauty and William Braithwaite', in *Callaloo*, vol. 29 (Spring 2006), no. 2.

— *The Gospel of Beauty in the Progressive Era: Reforming American Verse and Values*. New York: Palgrave McMillan, 2011.

Taherzadeh, Adib. *The Covenant of Bahá'u'lláh*. Oxford: George Ronald, 1992.

— *The Revelation of Bahá'u'lláh*. 4 vols. Oxford: George Ronald, 1974–1987.

Thompson, Juliet. *The Diary of Juliet Thompson*. Los Angeles: Kalimát Press, 1983.

Tooze, Adam. *The Deluge: The Great War, America and the Remaking of the Global Order, 1916-1931*. London: Penguin, 2014.

Tuchman, Barbara W. *The Proud Tower: A Portrait of the World before the War 1890-1914* (1962). New York: Ballantine Books, 1994.

Van den Hoonaard, Will C. *The Origins of the Bahá'í Community of Canada, 1898-1948*. Waterloo, Ontario: Wilfrid Laurier University Press, 1996.

Walker, Williston. *A History of the Congregational Churches in the United States*. New York: Charles Scribner's Sons, 1894.

Watson, Steven. *Strange Bedfellows: The First American Avant-Garde*. New York: Abbeville Press, 1991.

Weinberg, Robert. *Ethel Jenner Rosenberg: The Life and Times of England's Outstanding Bahá'í Pioneer Worker*. Oxford: George Ronald, 1995.

— *Lady Blomfield: Her Life and Times*. Oxford: George Ronald, 2012.

Whitehead, O. Z. *Some Bahá'ís to Remember*. Oxford: George Ronald, 1983.

— *Some Early Bahá'ís of the West*. Oxford: George Ronald, 1977.

Whitmore, Bruce W. *The Dawning Place: The Building of a Temple, the Forging of the North American Bahá'í Community*. Wilmette, IL: Bahá'í Publishing Trust, 1984.

Williams, Tom. *A Mysterious Something in the Light: The Life of Raymond Chandler*. Chicago: Chicago Review Press, 2013.

Williams, William Carlos. *The Autobiography of William Carlos Williams*. New York: New Directions, 1967.

Wilson, A. N. *God's Funeral*. New York: W. W. Norton, 1999.

Winks, Robin W.; Neuberger, Joan. *Europe and the Making of Modernity: 1815–1914*. New York: Oxford University Press, 2005.

Witemeyer, Hugh (ed). *Pound/Williams: Selected letters of Ezra Pound and William Carlos Williams*. New York: New Directions, 1996.

Ybarra, T. R. 'Churches as Play Places: The Rev. Dr. Guthrie Says People Will Come to St. Mark's if He Offers Real Entertainment', in *The New York Times*, 20 February 1921.

Young, William H.; Young, Nancy K. *The 1950s*. Westport, Connecticut: Greenwood Press, 2004.

Journals

The American Review of Reviews and World's Work (ed. Albert Shaw).
Bahá'í News Letter: The Bulletin of the National Spiritual Assembly of the Bahá'ís of the United States and Canada
Callaloo
The Century Illustrated Monthly Magazine, vol. 82 (1910); vol. 84 (1912).
The Editor
The Egoist: An Individualist Review
The Forum
The Fourth Estate: A Weekly Journal for Advertisers and Newspaper Makers
The Freewoman
Good Furniture Magazine
The Journal of Bahá'í Studies
Lawrenceville Alumni Bulletin
Lawrenceville Yearbook, 1906
Liberator
The Little Review
The Masses
The New Freewoman
The New Orient
The New Republic
Others: A Magazine of the New Verse
Poetry: A Magazine of Verse
Printer's Ink
Publishers Weekly
Reality Magazine
Revue des lettres modernes, Guillaume Apollinaire,
Rhythm
The Seven Arts
The Smart Set
Smithsonian Magazine
Les Soirées de Paris
Star of the West: The Bahai Magazine. 25 vols. 1910–1935.

The Williams Record
The Writer: A Monthly Magazine for Literary Workers. Ed. Hill
World Order
World Unity

Newspapers

Los Angeles Evening Express
Smithsonian Magazine
The Register of Torrington, Connecticut (both morning and evening editions as well as special editions)
The New York Herald
The New York Times
Times Literary Review
The Times (London)

Interviews

Hooper Dunbar
Manucher Javid
Joanne Tahzib
Loretta Voeltz

NOTES AND REFERENCES

Prologue

1 *Star of the West*, vol. IV, no. 16 (31 December 1913), pp. 1–2.
2 This group of Hands of the Cause of God were the first appointed while still alive since the time of Bahá'u'lláh. Previously, other than the four appointed by Bahá'u'lláh, other Hands of the Cause had been named posthumously. Amelia Collins, who was among those named in 1951, had been told privately of her appointment in 1947, but it was not known until the first contingent was announced in a cablegram from Shoghi Effendi dated 24 December 1951. See Shoghi Effendi, *Messages to the Bahá'í World: 1950–1957*, p. 20.

1 The Book

1 Horace Holley, opening stanza of 'Sonnet: On the Occasion of a Birthday', in *Lawrenceville Alumni Bulletin*, 1 November 1909.
2 The trip was well documented. Irving Holley, Sr. wrote a number of letters to Joan Sanford with details of what the two brothers were doing. Horace kept a diary which recorded the itinerary. The letters are in the Holley Collection of the Connecticut Historical Society, which also contains photographs taken during the trip.
3 Letter from Irving Holley to Joan Sanford, written in Glasgow, Scotland, 14 April 1909, from the Irving Holley, Jr. collection shared with Claire Vreeland who passed it to the author.
4 Glovsky, *The Lake Superior Country in History and in Story*, pp. 143–5.
5 Engagement announcement, *Torrington Evening Register*, 25 October 1909.
6 An example of this is a letter to Bertha Holley answering questions about Tibetans and their culture from the Tibetan Friendship Group. Letter from Jared Rhotan at International Hostel, Sanskrit University in Utter Pradesh, India to Mrs Bertha Delia Holley, postmarked 13 March 1968. Original given by Irving Holley to Claire Vreeland whose family passed it to the author.
7 Letter from Irving Holley, Jr. to Claire Vreeland (misspelled on letter as Freeland), 29 January 1987. Original in possession of the author courtesy of the Vreeland family.
8 Torrington High School Report Card for the year 1903–1904 for Horace H. Holley, Torrington Historical Society Archives.
9 'The 1908–9 Lit.', in *The Williams Record*, vol. XXIII, no. 9, (Thursday, 22 April 1909) p. 2.
10 The hostess was Charlotte MacGregor Todd from Milwaukee, Wisconsin, wife of Swiss artist Lucien Monod. They are primarily remembered as the parents of

Jacques Lucien Monod, winner of the Nobel Prize for Medicine. The Monods were friends of the dancer Isadora Duncan, and held strong socialist political views. According to Jan Jasion, Charlotte Monod was included on a list of Bahá'ís in France around this time, which may explain why Bertha felt free to introduce the Faith at another person's party. Charlotte Monod's participation in the Bahá'í Faith may have been short-lived because she is less visible a few years later. See Jasion, *'Abdu'l-Bahá in France*, p. 3.

11 Lady Blomfield (1859–1939) (née Sara Louise Ryan in Ireland) played a pivotal role in the development of the Bahá'í Faith in the United Kingdom. For more about this significant early Bahá'í, see Weinberg, *Lady Blomfield: Her Live and Times*.

12 Blomfield, *The Chosen Highway*, p. 1.

13 Lady Blomfield did not bring the Bahá'í Faith to England, but it was largely through her efforts that it blossomed there.

14 Blomfield, *The Chosen Highway*, pp. 1–2.

15 Bryan, *The Old World and Its Ways*, p. 384.

16 Phelps, *Life and Teachings of Abbas Effendi: A Study of the Religion of the Babis, or Beha'is Founded by the Persian Bab and by His Successors, Beha Ullah and Abbas Effendi*, This book was republished in abridged form in 1985 by Kalimat Press of Los Angeles, under the title, *The Master in 'Akká*. The original introduction by E.G. Browne was omitted and replaced by one by the Bahá'í writer and translator, Marzieh Gail. The main body of the book was also edited to remove inaccurate content. Footnotes were added to bring the book up-to-date and to add explanatory information. Both were used in writing this chapter.

17 ibid. p. xxxi.

18 ibid. pp. xl–xli.

19 Beginning in the nineteenth century, as public schools became more secular, Protestant churches began to offer religion classes for all ages on Sunday mornings, usually preceding the worship service. These classes were commonly referred to as 'Sunday School'.

20 Spring, *A History of Williams College*, pp. 318–20. Williams students were required to attend worship services while Horace was at the college, however, this requirement was eliminated a few years after Horace left. Horace was also a member of the campus organization, the Young Men's Christian Association, which also held religious gatherings. Horace was well aware of the fact that the individual most responsible for the establishment of the American Board of Commissioners for Foreign Missions (ABCFM), Samuel John Mills, was inspired to do so with four other Williams students during a mystical experience during a thunderstorm referred to as the Haystack Prayer Meeting in 1806. Mills was the son of the Congregationalist Minister for Torrington and born in Horace's hometown. A large monument on the campus at Williams marks the location of the Haystack event. During the nineteenth century, ABCFM was the largest and most important of the American missionary organizations, sending devoted Christians to many corners of the world to spread Protestant Christianity.

21 Horace Holley's ancestry has been traced by the author through the records obtainable at www.ancestry.com.

22 For a captivating exploration of this period, including the persecution of the

NOTES AND REFERENCES

Puritans in England, their settlement of New England, and their subsequent persecution of other religious groups such as the Society of Friends (Quakers), see Barry, *Roger Williams and the Creation of the American Soul: Church, State and the Birth of Liberty*.
23 Holley, *Religion for Mankind*, p. 9.
24 ibid.
25 Shoghi Effendi, *Bahá'í Administration*, p. 80.
26 Holley, *Religion for Mankind*, p. 9.

2 Words, Words, Words, and an Encounter

1 Horace Holley, excerpt from an untitled poem dedicated to Willard Ansley Gibson, 1910, Williams College Archives. Gibson, who graduated from Williams in 1909, was a fellow poet and friend of Holley's.
2 Undated letter from Horace Holley to Irving Holley, Connecticut Historical Society, Holley Collection.
3 Juliet Thompson was travelling in Europe and in Palestine, and the Kinney family was also away from New York City.
4 The central business district retained the name Wolcottville.
5 *History of Waterbury and Nagautuck Valley*, vol. III, pp. 40–43.
6 The newspaper announcement of Horace's wedding in the *Torrington Evening Register*, 4 November 1909, did not mention Horace's parents by name but did name his grandfather, and that he had been president of the Warrenton Woolen Mills.
7 'Edward Hotchkiss Holley', in *Torrington Evening Register*, Thursday, 14 September 1899, p. 5.
8 See, for example, letters from Edward H. Holley to his Aunt Hattie, 23 June 1870 and 28 April 1871, Connecticut Historical Society, Holley Collection.
9 Letter from Horace Holley to Dr Curtis T. Prout, 13 May 1933. Copy provided by the Holley family to the Vreeland family, which provided it to the author.
10 ibid.
11 Edward Holley passed away at Dr Stearn's sanitorium on 14 September 1899 at the age of 51. His obituary stated that his death was not 'altogether unexpected'. 'Edward Hotchkiss Holley', in *Torrington Evening Register*, Thursday, 14 September 1899, p. 9.
12 'Mrs. N. W. Holley', in *The Register's Torrington Souvenir*, 1897, compiled by H. F. Donlan.
13 Letter from Irving Holley, Jr. to Claire Vreeland, 29 January 1987, original in possession of the author courtesy of Claire Vreeland. This was the Coe Brass Factory. The Coe relatives were very generous to the Holley children.
14 The Holleys had another son two years after Horace was born, Homer Rossiter Holley. Homer died at the age of 21 months.
15 Horace would dedicate one his books to his eldest brother, Frank, with the words *In Loco Parentis,* Latin for 'in place of the parent'. Holley, *The Modern Social Religion.*
16 Letter from Horace Holley to Irving Holley, 14 August 1914, written from France. Connecticut Historical Society, Holley Collection.
17 ibid.

18 See a fuller discussion of this, see McDougall, *Freedom Just Around the Corner*, pp. 144–5.
19 See, for example, letter from Horace Holley to Irving Holley, 10 July (no year), written in Paris, discussing their New England proclivities. Connecticut Historical Society, Holley Collection.
20 Undated letter from Horace Holley to Irving Holley, from Lausanne, Switzerland, most likely written in January 1910. Irving Holley, Jr. provided a copy to Claire Vreeland, and the Vreeland family provided it to the author.
21 The nature of this illness is unclear, but it is borne out by the sharp drop in Horace's grades on his report card for November 1903. At the time, his brother Irving was in Florida trying to recover from tuberculosis and wrote to their mother urging her to send Horace to him. Irving Holley, Jr. in a letter to Claire Vreeland dated 2 December 1987 gave the reason for his father's stay in Florida..
22 Undated letter from Horace Holley to Nellie Holley, postmarked June (probably 1906). Sent to the Hill Sanitorium in Watertown, Connecticut where Horace's mother was being treated for poor health.
23 Cecil Sherman Baker came from a family of career military officers. His great-uncle was the famous Civil War General William Tecumseh Sherman. Horace discusses the engagement with satisfaction in a humorous letter to Irving on 8 December 1903. Irving Holley, Jr. provided a copy to Claire Vreeland, and the Vreeland family provided it to the author.
24 Undated letter from Horace to Irving Holley, Lawrenceville. Irving Holley, Jr. provided a copy to Claire Vreeland, and the Vreeland family provided it to the author.
25 Letter from Horace Holley to Ellen Holley, 10 September 1904. Irving Holley, Jr. provided a copy to Claire Vreeland, and the Vreeland family provided it to the author.
26 The 1906 student yearbook at Lawrenceville stated, referring to Horace, that 'to him you owe every laugh or bright idea contained in these sketches of our classmates'. *Olla Podrida* (Lawrenceville Yearbook), 1906. His nephew, Irving Holley, Jr. wrote about Horace's quick wit and use of puns. He described his uncle as 'the life of the party'. Letter from Irving Holley, Jr. to Claire Vreeland, 29 January 1987, original in possession of the author courtesy of Claire Vreeland.
27 *People from Salisbury, Connecticut: Horace Holley, Peter Buell Porter, Myron Holley, Orville L. Holley, Bird Beers Chapman*, reprint by Books LLC, 2010. There are published biographies of Reverend Horace H. Holley as well as much information about him available on the internet. He was a friend of President John Adams and President John Quincy Adams. His wife, Mary Austin Holley, was the sister of Stephen Austin of Texas, and a person of note in her own right.
28 It is interesting to note that the brief announcement of Horace's engagement to be married, in the 25 October 1909 edition of the *Torrington Evening Register*, does not mention his parents or grandparents but does mention Reverend Horace Holley and that great-great-uncle's accomplished brothers, Orville Holley and Myron Holley.
29 See various Williams College publications including yearbooks and campus newspaper from 1906 to 1909.
30 Telegram from Frank Holley, 18 June 1908, original in possession of the author courtesy of Claire Vreeland.
31 Culebra, Virgin Islands.

32 Undated letter from Horace Holley to Nellie W. Holley, in the possession of the author courtesy of Claire Vreeland who obtained if from Irving Holley, Jr.
33 The Holley summer cottage, called Sunnycroft, was along Skroom Lake in the Adirondack Mountains of New York. It was purchased first by Irving Holley, who later sold it to Frank Holley. Horace would enjoy visiting it throughout his life despite its association with his mother's passing.
34 The telegram listed a stroke as the cause of death. Years later, Horace said it was due to 'shock'.
35 Letter from Nellie W. Holley to Horace Holley, 6 April 1908, original in the possession of the author.
36 Handwritten memoir of Irving Holley, Sr., 8 January 1939. A copy was provided by Irving Holley, Jr. to Claire Vreeland, and the Vreeland family provided it to the author.
37 State of New York, Certificate of Marriage for Horace H. Holley and Bertha D. Herbert, No. of Certificate 22156. The officiating clergyman was Melville K. Bailey, and the witnesses were Francis V. Holley and Myrta E. Herbert. Reverend Bailey had served as the minister for the Episcopal Church in Torrington that was located on the same city block as the Francis Newman Home. He had subsequently moved to New York but kept a friendship with the Holley family.
38 This information comes from the engagement announcement in the 25 October 1909 edition of the *Torrington Evening Register* and the wedding announcement in the 4 November edition of the same newspaper.
39 Undated letter from Horace Holley to Irving Holley. A copy was provided by the Holley family to Claire Vreeland, and provided by the Vreeland family to the author.
40 See Hogenson, *Lighting the Western Sky: The Hearst Pilgrimage and the Establishment of the Bahá'í Faith in the West* for the story of the establishment and early years of the Paris Bahá'í community.
41 Jasion, *Abdu'l-Bahá in France: 1911 & 1913*, p. 1.
42 The portrait of Bertha Herbert titled 'The Decorator', by Alice Pike Barney, is owned by the Smithsonian American Art Museum in Washington, DC., see americanart.si.edu/artwork/decorator-1163.
43 Redman, *'Abdu'l-Bahá in Their Midst*, p. 19.
44 Undated letter from Lausanne, Switzerland from Horace Holley to Irving Holley, copy provided by Irving Holley, Jr. to Claire Vreeland, and the Vreeland family provided it to the author.
45 Letter from Horace Holley to Irving Holley, 2 March [1910], Connecticut Historical Society Archives, Holley Collection.
46 In the 1830s, a handful of Irish immigrants began holding Catholic religious services in Torrington, establishing a Catholic Church in 1877. Catholic congregations which sprung up in the town later were the result of Polish, Italian and Slovakian immigration during the early years of the twentieth century after Horace no longer lived in Torrington. 'The Torrington Cluster of Roman Catholic Parishes is a group of four Catholic churches located in Torrington, CT', http://www.torrington.info/-torrington-cluster-of-catholic-churches.html.
47 Letter from Horace Holley written in Florence, Italy to Irving Holley, Easter Sunday [1910]. Copy provided by Irving Holley, Jr. to Claire Vreeland, and provided by the Vreeland family to the author.

48 The 'City on a Hill' image comes from a speech given by John Winthrop, Governor of the Massachusetts Bay Colony, as a flotilla of ships carrying a large number of Puritan settlers embarked from England in 1630. It has been used ever since as the image of the ideal of America as a shining example to the rest of the world, including by President Ronald Reagan.

49 Buck, *God & Apple Pie: Religious Myths and Visions of America*, pp. 56–60; Meacham, *American Gospel: God, the Founding Fathers, and the Making of a Nation*, p. 39.

50 In 1817, Horace's great-uncle, Reverend Holley, was the speaker at the annual celebration of the Pilgrims' landing at Plymouth, Massachusetts. During the course of the festivities, Holley's speech and visit to one of those propounding the provenance of the rock as that upon which the first settlers first set foot onto Massachusetts helped to cement the tale of its authenticity by linking it to the manner in which the story of St John was passed on to become part of the Gospels. Seelye, *Memory's Nation: The Place of Plymouth Rock*, University of North Carolina Press, 1998.

51 For a fuller discussion of this see Gelernter, *Americanism: The Fourth Great Western Religion*, pp. 21–36.

52 For a fuller discussion of this see Morison, *The Oxford History of the American People*, pp. 70–71.

53 For a fuller discussion of the Puritans and their influence on New England and, ultimately, the United States, see Noll, *The Old Religion in a New World: The History of North American Christianity*, p. 41; Prothero, *Religious Literacy: What Every American Needs to Know – and Doesn't*, pp. 213–14; Morison, *The Oxford History of the American People*, pp. 61– 4; Ahlstrom, *A Religious History of the American People*, pp. 1090–91; and all of Gelernter, *Americanism: The Fourth Great Western Religion*.

54 Ahlstrom, *A Religious History of the American People*, p. 1090.

55 Holley, 'The Little World', in *The Inner Garden*, p. 87.

56 Holley, 'In Italy', in *The Inner Garden*, p. 27.

57 *The Century Illustrated Monthly Magazine*, vol. 82 (1910), p. 606. That issue included three of Horace's poems: 'The Mirror', 'To Hertha', and Forget the Graves of Heroes'. In vol. 84 (1912), p. 28, the poem ' Holiday' was published with illustrations based upon drawings by Bertha. The fanciful drawings include a medieval castle surrounded by olive trees – based upon their surroundings in Siena, Italy.

58 Letter from Horace Holley to Irving Holley from Florence, Italy, 2 March (probably 1910).

59 Undated letter from Horace Holley to Irving Holley.

60 Winks, *Europe and the Making of Modernity: 1815–1914*, pp. 309–15. See also Szefle, Lisa, *The Gospel of Beauty in the Progressive Era: Reforming American Verse and Values*, throughout.

61 See, for example, "*Poetry*'s Opening Door: Harriet Monroe and American Modernism" by John Timberman Newcomb, pp. 85ff. *Little Magazines & Modernism: New Approaches*, edited by Suzanne W. Churchill and Adam McKible; Szefel, Lisa, *The Gospel of Beauty in the Progressive Era: Reforming American Verse and Values*, pp. 16–17, 111–15; *Dear Editor: A History of* Poetry *in Letters*

throughout this book for a big picture on Harriet Monroe's contribution to and influence on the evolution of American verse.
62 Braithwaite was a colleague of the Black activists and writers W. E. B. DuBois and James Weldon Johnson and among those who founded the National Association for the Advancement of Colored People (NAACP), whose national convention was addressed by 'Abdu'l-Bahá in 1912. In 1927, Braithwaite was one of the two speakers at a Race Amity gathering held by the Boston Bahá'í community. (Louis Gregory was the other speaker.) see Morrison, *To Move the World: Louis G. Gregory and the Advancement of Racial Unity in America*, p. 181.
63 Horace used the word 'race' quite often to denote the human race, not skin colour.
64 Letter from Horace Holley to William Braithwaite, 2 December 1915, Harvard University Library, Box 12, quoted in Szefel, 'Beauty and William Braithwaite', in *Callaloo*, vol. 29, no. 2, Spring 2006. See also Szefel, *The Gospel of Beauty in the Progressive Era: Reforming American Verse and Values*, pp. 17–18, 134–44 for a general summary of Braithwaite's life and contributions to literature.
65 For a general summary of the Imagist Movement and a scholarly assessment of it, see Lee, 'Aesthetics of Experiment: Imagism, Vorticism and the European Avant-Garde'.
66 'On the Borderland', in *The Times Literary Review*, 1 April 1914.
67 *The Egoist: An Individualist Review*, vol. 1, no. 11, 1 June 1914, p. 201. Note that Horace Holley used the title 'Hertha' for a number of different poems, most of which were not about his eldest daughter. The one Aldington is referring to is the one that appeared in *Creationism*.
68 *The Egoist: An Individualist Review*, vol. 1, no. 12, 15 June 1914, p. 236.
69 Very few poets met with Aldington's approval. Horace was not alone in receiving a bad review from this critic.
70 *The Editor*, vol. 43, 1 January 1916, p. 17.
71 *The American Review of Reviews and World's Work* (ed. Albert Shaw), vol. 51, p. 503.
72 'Divinations', in *Poetry: A Magazine of Verse*, vol. 11 (January 1918), p. 222.
73 Pound and Williams, *Selected Letters of Ezra Pound and William Carlos Williams*, p. 26.
74 Drafts of portions of Horace's unfinished manuscript on the arts were retained by Horace's family and passed on to Claire Vreeland who has provided them to the author. He began the book in Paris and continued working on it in New York City.
75 Holley, *Religion for Mankind*, p. 232.
76 ibid.
77 ibid. pp. 232–3.
78 The word 'awful' originally meant 'awe-inspiring' and had a positive connotation. Over time, its original meaning was altered, and it came to mean 'bad'.
79 Holley, *Religion for Mankind*, p. 233.
80 ibid.
81 The visit of 'Abdu'l-Bahá to Thonon is memorialized in detail by Juliet Thompson, a portrait artist from New York City, who probably knew Bertha Holley prior to 1911. It seems that during the time that the Holleys were there, Juliet

was away from Thonon at the nearby town of Vevey across the lake in Switzerland for a few days. She does not mention them in her detailed account. There were a few other American Bahá'ís vacationing at Vevey at the time, and it was the location of the second home of the Dreyfus-Barney family. See Thompson, *The Diary of Juliet Thompson*, pp. 159–87; Jasion, 'Abdu'l-Bahá in France: 1911 & 1913, p. 34.
82. Holley, *Religion for Mankind*, p. 233.
83. ibid.
84. ibid. p. 235.
85. ibid. p. 236.
86. ibid.
87. Interview between the author and Loretta Voeltz, 27 January 2012; letter from Claire Vreeland to Roger White, 26 September 1989, in which she reports her interview with Mildred Mottahedeh. A copy of the original was provided to the author by the Vreeland family.
88. Holley, *Religion for Mankind*, p. 237.
89. Horace dated the incident to 1911, but more likely it occurred on 19 May 1913. See Jasion, 'Abdu'l-Bahá in France: 1911 & 1913, p. 613, where it is noted by another chronicler that 'Abdu'l-Bahá spoke about the non-existence of time and space. There is no evidence that the Holleys visited Paris during the autumn of 1911 other than the date of the reminiscence.
90. Letter from Horace Holley to Mrs. Frank Baker [Dorothy], 11 August 1949.
91. Holley, *Religion for Mankind*, p. 234.

3 Paris

1. Holley, 'An Artist's Morality', in *The Forum*, vol. LIII, January 1915–June 1915, pp. 436–7.
2. Holley, 'Crisis', in *The Inner Garden*, p. 113.
3. Holley, 'An Artist's Morality', in *The Forum*, vol. LIII, January 1915–June 1915, p. 437.
4. ibid.
5. ibid.
6. ibid.
7. Ibid. p. 438.
8. ibid.
9. Holley, 'The Poets Return', in *The Forum*, vol. LIII, p. 759.
10. ibid.
11. ibid, p. 760.
12. The Holleys were probably unaware that the Bahá'í Faith prohibits the consumption of alcohol, even in food. This law did not become enjoined on Bahá'ís in North America until 1935.
13. Letter from Horace Holley to Aunt Jenny, from Castello dell Quattro Torri, Siena, 3(?) December (1911?). Given by the Holley family to Claire Vreeland who gave it to the author. The entire account of the Christmas celebration is taken from that letter.
14. 'A Visit from St. Nicholas', by Clement Clarke Moore, was published anonymously in 1823 in the Troy, New York, newspaper *The Sentinel*, which Orville

Holley edited. Holley gave the poem the name 'Account of a Visit from St. Nicholas'.

15 Beckley, "Women to Have War Wardrobe?" by Zoe Beckley in *New York Evening Mail,* reprinted in *Los Angeles Evening Express,* editorial page, 23 March 1918. Bertha Holley is quoted as saying, 'I contend that only an artist, gifted with a feeling for color and line, can create such a system [of dresses]. When I was a portrait painter in Paris seven years ago I began to work out a means whereby line and color as applied to portrait painting could be directed into the channel of dress design.'

16 Hills (ed), *The Writer: A Monthly Magazine for Literary Workers,* vol. XXIV (August 1912), p. 118. Horace provided this trade journal with a summary of his life and work as a writer.

17 For more on this significant event as well as 'Abdu'l-Bahá's 1911 visits to England and France, see Balyuzi, *'Abdu'l-Bahá: The Centre of the Covenant of Bahá'u'lláh,* pp. 140–68; Egea, *The Apostle of Peace: A Survey of References to 'Abdu'l-Bahá in the Western Press 1871–1921,* pp. 92–179; Redman, *'Abdu'l-Bahá in Their Midst,* pp. 17–49.

18 See Tuchman, *The Proud Tower: A Portrait of the World Before the War 1890–1914;* Winks and Neuberger, *Europe and the Making of Modernity,* for a less glowing view of Europe during the pre-WWI period.

19 For example, the Armory Show in 1913 introduced modern artists to the United States such as Braque and Picasso, who had already been accepted in Paris. The show marked the beginning of the American art culture moving fully into modernism.

20 Letter from Horace Holley to Irving Holley, 8 January 1911. Holley Collection, Connecticut Historical Society Archives.

21 Undated (1912?) letter from Horace Holley to Mary Sharp written in Paris. Copy provided by Irving Holley, Jr. to Claire Vreeland, and provided to the author by the Vreeland family.

22 Rue Boissonade has its own page in the French version of Wikipedia because of the large number of creative people of note who lived there during the early years of the 20th century.

23 It seems that the building where the Holleys lived may have opened at one end onto Rue Campagne-Première and on the other onto Rue Boissonade. The buildings were renumbered after they lived there, so there is no certainty, but number 16 seems to have been in the middle of the block where the buildings straddled the land between the two streets. Both were cul-de-sacs, one opening onto Raspail, the other opening onto Montparnasse. I am grateful to Mr Frederic Autret for this information. For more information about this neighbourhood, see McAuliffe, *Twilight of the Belle Epoque: The Paris of Picasso, Stravinsky, Proust, Renault, Marie Curie, Gertrude Stein, and Their Friends through the Great War,* pp. 242, 243.

24 I am grateful to Mr Jan Jasion for providing me with information about the Scotts.

25 Letter from Horace Holley to Irving Holley written in Paris, 10 July 1912. From the Holley papers provided to Claire Vreeland who passed it to the author.

26 Letter from Horace Holley to Mary Sharp, 7 July 1912. From the Holley papers provided to Claire Vreeland who passed it to the author. The second apartment was at 52 Boulevard St. Jacques.

27 Letter from Horace Holley to Irving Holley, 1 April 1914. From the Holley papers provided to Claire Vreeland who passed it to the author. The location of the studio is unknown.
28 Horace was also influenced by the Fauvists and wrote an article about Matisse, 'The Background of Matisse', in *The New Republic*, 20 February 1915, pp. 74-6. 'Matisse's work is permeated with energy, the stress of mass against mass, color against color', p. 75.
29 *New York Herald*, 9 March 1914: 'American Artist Holds Exhibition in Paris', regarding an exhibition Bertha Holley held at the Hotel Astoria in Paris. The article stated that 'Her creations are interesting as color studies.' Among those in attendance were two with the title 'Princess', one 'Marquise', and one 'Comte'.
30 Ashnur Galerie announcement, copy furnished to Claire Vreeland by Irving Holley, in the possession of the author.
31 McAuliffe, *Twilight of the Belle Epoque*, p. 243.
32 Notes to Horace from Pablo Picasso were found among his papers by his relatives. Correspondence from Polly Holley Doremus to Claire Vreeland which was passed on to the author.
33 Holley, 'The Stout Lady Buys a Dancer', in *The New Republic*, vol. 2, 24 April 1915, p. 301.
34 ibid.
35 Ibid. p. 302.
36 Horace Holley published an article written in French in the journal *Les Soirées de Paris*, no. 9 (1914), pp. 5-6. It was a discussion of literary trends in English publications. I am grateful to Jan Jasion pointing out to me his publications in French during this period.
37 Fletcher, *Autobiography of John Gould Fletcher*, pp. 50–51.
38 The other two Scottish colourists were Francis Cadell and Leslie Hunter.
39 See 'Anne Estelle Rice', http://www.hollistaggart.com/artists/biography/anne_estelle_rice/10/9/2011.
40 For more about Natalie Barney's literary salon, see Rodriguez, *Wild Heart, A Life: Natalie Clifford Barney and the Decadence of Literary Paris*, pp. 17 –83. Among those who attended were Ezra Pound and Richard Aldington, which may explain how they met Horace Holley.
41 For a detailed exploration of 'Abdu'l-Bahá's visit to North America see Balyuzi, *'Abdu'l-Bahá: The Centre of the Covenant of Bahá'u'lláh*, pp. 140-68; Egea, *The Apostle of Peace: A Survey of References to 'Abdu'l-Bahá in the Western Press 1871–1921*, pp. 92–179; Redman, *'Abdu'l-Bahá in Their Midst*, pp. 17–49; Stockman, *'Abdu'l-Bahá in America*, throughout.
42 Winks and Neuberger, *Europe and the Making of Modernity*, pp. 330, 333.
43 'Abdu'l-Bahá, *The Promulgation of Universal Peace*, pp. 16-17.
44 Hills (ed), *The Writer*, vol. XXIV (August 1912), p. 118.
45 Wilson, *God's Funeral*, p. 227.
46 Jasion, *'Abdu'l-Bahá in France: 1911 & 1913*, p. 739.
47 ibid. p. 335.
48 Redman, *'Abdu'l-Bahá in Their Midst*, p. 311; Jasion, *'Abdu'l-Bahá in France: 1911 & 1913*, p. 422.
49 Jasion, *'Abdu'l-Bahá in France: 1911 & 1913*, p. 423.

50 ibid. pp. 422–3.
51 Letter from Ahmad Sohrab to Harriet Magee, 19 May 1913. Quoted ibid. pp. 611–12; the original is held by the USBNA.
52 ibid. pp. 61 –13.
53 Letter from Ahmad Sohrab to Harriet Magee, 4 May 1913. USBNA, Magee papers.
54 Jasion, unpublished manuscript.
55 Holley, *The Modern Social Religion*, p. 178.
56 ibid. p. 1. For an excellent look at the march toward agnosticism and atheism among the English-speaking leaders of thought during the nineteenth century, see Wilson, *God's Funeral*.
57 Throughout his life, Horace Holley uses the term 'race' to usually stand in for the longer 'human race'. Since his time, the word 'race' has gained a narrower meaning and so twenty-first century readers may find his choice of words disconcerting.
58 Holley, *The Modern Social Religion*, p. 206.
59 ibid. p. 187.
60 ibid. Appendix III: Bibliography for Further Study, pp. 220–23.
61 *Star of the West*, vol. IV, no. 16 (31 December), pp. 1, 3.
62 Advertisement by Mitchell Kennerley, Publisher of New York.
63 John Peebles McClure, from Oklahoma (probably a member of the Chickasaw Tribe), was a poet born in 1893. He would move to New Orleans where he was one of the more significant members of the literary circle of that city as well as a journalist and bookstore owner. As a young man, he was drawn to the mystical poetry of William Blake.
64 Holley, 'On the Spiritual Reality', in *The Egoist*, 1 May 1914, p. 179.
65 ibid.
66 Afnan, "Abdu'l-Bahá and Ezra Pound's Circle', in *The Journal of Bahá'í Studies*, 2 June 1994, p. 8.

4 Turmoil

1 Kazin, *A Godly Hero*, pp. 217–18.
2 Letter from Ahmad Sohrab to Harriett Magee, 23 May 1913, pp. 4–5. USBNA. See also Jasion, *'Abdu'l-Bahá in France*, p. 626.
3 Letter from Ahmad Sohrab to Harriett Magee, 23 May 1913, pp. 11–12. This is quoted as it appeared in Sohrab's letter, not directly from the newspaper or how it was quoted in *Star of the West*.
4 *Century of Light*, p. 28.
5 Letter from Horace Holley to Irving Holley, 1 April 1914. Provided by Irving Holley, Jr. to Claire Vreeland, and then to the author.
6 An article written by O. W. Gambedoo vexed scholars of the Imagist Movement because they felt it would offer insights into the connection between that London-based school of English poets and the leading poets in French, especially Guillaume Apollinaire. Willard Bohn, in ' "O. W. Gambedoo", "H.H." et *Les Soirées de Paris*' in *Revue des letters modernes, Guillaume Apollinaire 9*, nos 249–253, 1970, pp. 135 – 41, deduces after much detective work that Horace Holley is Gambedoo, a word that plays on English words meaning 'escapade'. A

number of the clues point to Horace as the only possibility. It was undoubtedly a means of having some fun with the Imagists after their treatment of his poetry.
7   Schweikart and Dougherty, *A Patriot's History of the Modern World: From America's Exceptional Ascent to the Atomic Bomb: 1898–1945*, p. 69.
8   Holley, *The Modern Social Religion*, p. 93.
9   Ham, *1913: The Eve of War*, ch.2.
10 Horace does not give enough information to identify 'Princess Eristoff', but most likely she was Marie Erisoff, a noted Russian portrait artist and fashion model for the House of Chanel.
11 Letter from Horace Holley to Irving Holley, 1 April 1914. Provided by Irving Holley, Jr. to Claire Vreeland and then to the author.
12 ibid.
13 Schweikart and Dougherty, *A Patriot's History of the Modern World*, p. 81.
14 McAuliffe, *Twilight of the Belle Epoque*, p. 270.
15 Letter from Horace Holley to Irving Holley, 15 August 1919. Provided by Irving Holley, Jr. to Claire Vreeland and then to the author.
16 Letter from Horace Holley to 'Brother' from Poigny, Rambouillet, Seine et Oise, France, 1 August 1914. Provided by Irving Holley, Jr. to Claire Vreeland and then to the author. Based upon statements in letters from later that month, the letter was probably to Frank Holley.
17 ibid.
18 Letter from Horace Holley to Irving Holley, 14 August 1914. Connecticut Historical Society, Holley papers.
19 Letter from Horace Holley to Irving Holley, 15 August 1914. Provided by Irving Holley, Jr. to Claire Vreeland and then to the author.
20 Letter from Horace Holley to Irving Holley, 1 September 1914, en route from Paris to Havre 8:00 a.m. Provided by Irving Holley, Jr. to Claire Vreeland and then to the author.
21 ibid. The letter describes the atrocities, but they are so horrific that the author has chosen not to quote from the letter. They were bad enough to shock and scare Horace.
22 ibid.
23 ibid.
24 ibid.
25 ibid.
26 ibid.
27 ibid. Horace erroneously referred to the objects as torpedoes.
28 ibid.
29 ibid.
30 The Poetry Bookshop, at 35 Devonshire Street in London, both sold and published poetry. It was established and run by Harold Munro who had connections to Imagism poets Ezra Pound and Richard Aldington. The shop also had a few small rooms where poets could stay. Among those who took advantage of the rooms was American poet Robert Frost. The shop operated between 1913 and 1926, including during WWI while Munro was away fighting with the army.
31 The family's daughter was married to a Frenchman.
32 Letter from Horace Holley to Irving Holley, 1 September 1914, en route from

Paris to Havre 8:00 a.m. Provided by Irving Holley, Jr. to Claire Vreeland and then to the author. The letter was continued from London on 5 September 1914.
33 Winston Churchill's mother was Jennie Jerome Spencer-Churchill, an American heiress from New York City.
34 ibid.
35 Undated letter [1914] from Horace Holley to Irving Holley written at the Poetry Bookshop, London. Provided by Irving Holley, Jr. to Claire Vreeland and then to the author.
36 The ship sailed from London on 24 October 1914. Ship's passenger list obtained through ancestry.com.
37 http://www.atlantictransportline.us/content/32Minnetonka.htm.
38 Holley, 'War', written in August 1916 and never published. Provided by Irving Holley, Jr. to Claire Vreeland and then to the author.
39 Holley, *The Social Principle*, p. 13.

5 The Poet Returns

1 Holley, excerpt from 'Home', in *Divinations and Creation*, p. 13.
2 Ellis, *The Epic of New York City: A Narrative History*, p. 509. By 1917, there were more motorized vehicles than horses in New York City.
3 For a good summary of New York City and its history, see Ellis, *The Epic of New York City*.
4 See, for example, Holley, 'The Background of Matisse', in *The New Republic*, 20 February 1915.
5 Holley, 'The Artist in America', in *The New Republic*, 5 June 1915, pp. 113–15.
6 Holley, 'Our Unpublished Masterpieces', in *The Seven Arts*, vol. 1 (1916), pp. 419–25.
7 Undated 10-page summary in the handwriting of Horace Holley setting forth the events leading to his divorce from Bertha Holley. USBNA, Horace Holley papers, Box 24.
8 ibid; Whitehead, in his essay on the life of Horace Holley published in *Some Bahá'ís to Remember*, p. 225, relates the incident of Bertha attempting to leave Horace as Doris Holley related it to him many years later. The description here is a composite of the two sources.
9 Undated 10-page summary in the handwriting of Horace Holley setting forth the events leading to his divorce from Bertha Holley. USBNA, Horace Holley papers, Box 24.
10 This Tablet from 'Abdu'l-Bahá to Horace Holley appears to be the only one ever written to him alone. It is found in USBNA, Holley papers.
11 Letter from Horace Holley to Joseph Hannen, 21 June 2016. USBNA, Hannen papers.
12 USBNA, Holley papers.
13 ibid.
14 Holley, 'Statement Concerning My Invention, The 'Self-Tie' Collar', unpublished. USBNA, Horace Holley Papers, Box 10. Horace conceived of this invention after his separation from Bertha, but the document indicates that she assisted him by drawing the prototype. At the time, March 1919, Horace was residing in the Hotel Plymouth in New York City.

15 It is unclear when the Holleys moved to the house. It was apparently located within the boundaries of New York City, but provided green spaces for the children. They did not live in the house for long. Most likely, the studio they rented for Bertha on 49th Street in Manhattan was retained. Letter from Horace Holley to Irving Holley, 22 August [1916?]. Connecticut Historical Society Archives, Holley papers.
16 Kreymborg, *Troubadour: An American Autobiography by Alfred Kreymborg*, p. 187.
17 ibid. pp. 187–88.
18 Stavitsky, 'Artists and Art Colonies of Ridgefield, New Jersey' by Gail Stavitsky.
19 Kreymborg, *Troubadour*, p. 186.
20 Churchill, Suzanne, *The Little Magazine, Others and the Renovation of Modern American Poetry*, pp. 45–6.
21 Alfred Stieglitz, remembered not only for his own work but because he was a husband of the painter Georgia O'Keefe, was raised in nearby Hobokon, New Jersey. Stieglitz is credited with gaining acceptance of photography as a form of art as well as promoting modern art in general.
22 *Others, The Magazine of The New Verse*, was the child of Alfred Kreymborg and Walter Arensberg. Their goal was to publish lesser known talented poets, especially their experimental works. In addition to poems by Horace Holley, the famous first issue included works by William Carlos Williams, Mary Carolyn Davies, Mina Loy, Orrick Johns, Ezra Pound, and Wallace Stevens. Gordon Munson stated that '*Others*, in fact, became a focal center of the American resurgence [in poetry]. It was at the center of the free verse explosion of the decade, but it may be added that all the lines of the poetic revival passed through it' (Munson, *The Awakening Twenties: A Memoir History of a Literary Period*, p. 33). Over the course of the next four years, it would introduce a number of major poets or works. For a fuller discussion, see Munson, pp. 33–8; Kreymborg, Alfred, *Troubadour*, pp. 169–75, 186–90; Parisi and Young, *Dear Editor: A History of Poetry in Letters*, p. 118; Watson, *Strange Bedfellows: The First American Avant-Garde*, pp. 301–3.
23 Kreymborg, *Troubadour*, p. 188.
24 Williams Carlos Williams, *The Autobiography of Williams Carlos Williams*, p. 136. For more about these gatherings outside Ridgefield, see Watson, *Strange Bedfellows*, pp. 298–301.
25 'Announcement of Awards', in *Poetry*, vol. 9, no. 2 (November 1916), pp. 106–9.
26 *The Publishers Weekly*, vol. 90, p. 2083.
27 *The Social Principle* was published by L.J. Gomme & Marshall in New York in 1915, rather than by Horace's London publisher.
28 'Announcement of Awards', in *Poetry*, vol. 9, no. 2 (November 1916), pp. 106–9.
29 Holley, *The Social Principle*, p. 13.
30 ibid. pp. 80–81.
31 ibid. p. 36.
32 ibid. p. 82.
33 ibid. p. 84.
34 ibid. p. 47.
35 *The Forum* was published in New York between 1885 and 1950. It was known

for its articles by prominent guest authors on current events or social issues. It also published literature such as poems and fiction. Horace's New York publisher, Mitchell Kennerley, published this journal. Though nationally read and widely respected for its excellence, it was the only major publication that was accessible to Black Americans in the first decades of the twentieth century. This *Forum* should not be confused with a much later pornographic publication of the same name.

36 Holley, *The Social Principle*, p. 91.
37 ibid, p. 92.
38 Flyer for *The Social Principle*. USBNA, Horace Holley papers..
39 Letter from Horace Holley to Albert Vail, 4 June 1922. USBNA, Vail papers, Box 1.
40 Letter from Horace Holley to Irving Holley, 14 March [1917?]. Connecticut Historical Society Archives, Holley papers.
41 Holley, *Read-Aloud Plays*, pp. v–vi.
42 Letter from Horace Holley to Irving Holley, 14 March [1917?]. Connecticut Historical Society Archives, Holley papers.
43 Berg, *Wilson*, pp. 332–7.
44 While Horace was a student at Williams College, a new President of the school was ceremoniously inaugurated. As President of Princeton University, Wilson was one of the featured speakers. Horace would have been required as a student to attend that event.
45 Letter from Horace Holley to Alfred Lunt, 26 January 1917. USBNA, Lunt papers.
46 Rosenfeld, '3 Towns Where Creative Minds Congregated', in *The New York Times*, 22 December 1996.
47 Knock, *To End All Wars: Woodrow Wilson and the Quest for a New World Order*, pp. 66–7.
48 *The Masses*, while advocating socialism and communism (before the atrocities in Russia under Lenin and Stalin were known), also published many of the best American writers. It included poetry and innovative artwork as well as essays.
49 Much has been written about the persecution of Eastman during World War I. Two sources are Knock, *To End All Wars*, pp. 135–6 and Berg, *Wilson*, pp. 495, 498.
50 Salpeter, "A Note on Advertising', in *Liberator*, September 1918, p. 3.
51 After Eastman learned about the horrors of communism in Russia under Joseph Stalin, his opinions changed such that during the last decades of his life he was politically conservative. Much can be found about Eastman on the Internet, including a Wikipedia page. He is one of the historic characters featured in the 1981 Academy Award winning motion picture, *Reds*, directed by Warren Beatty.
52 Letter from Horace Holley to Joseph Hannen, 29 February 1916. USBNA, Hannen papers.
53 Ellis, *The Epic of New York City*, pp. 510–11. This is but one of many sources about this epidemic, many of which discuss its effect on New York because over 12,000 people died there. Interestingly, the Bahá'í sources and Horace's own surviving correspondence are silent about this influenza that killed millions and at least for several months disrupted the rhythm of normal society. One of the most

important American Bahá'ís to die from the effects of the disease was Phoebe Apperson Hearst, wealthy philanthropist who was responsible for the first pilgrimage of Western believers to meet 'Abdu'l-Bahá in the winter of 1898-99, for which she was given the title, 'Mother of the Faithful' by 'Abdu'l-Bahá. See Hogenson, *Lighting the Western Sky: The Hearst Pilgrimage and the Establishment of the Bahá'í Faith in the West.*

54 Holley, letter to the Editor under the title 'Protests Against Mr. Pelletien's Views on Americanism', dated 27 July 1919, in *The New York Times*, 30 July 1919, p. 8.
55 Balyuzi, *'Abdu'l-Bahá*, pp. 412-15.
56 Minutes of the Board of Council (Assembly) for New York, 22 January 1917. New York Bahá'í Archives.
57 Sohrab, *The Story of the Divine Plan*, pp. 40-42.
58 Khalil Gibran was a neighbour of Juliet Thompson, also an artist. The original of Gibran's portrait of 'Abdu'l-Bahá is owned by the Bahá'í World Centre. Gibran was attracted to the Faith but did not become a formal member of it.
59 Holley, 'The Bahai Congress, the New Cycle, and Divine Command: Notes of Memory and Anticipation', in *Reality*, vol. 1, no. 2 (June 1919), p. 29.
60 The Convention was covered extensively in *Star of the West*, vol. 10, no. 4 (17 May 1919), pp. 54-72. On the Paris Peace Conference, see the article by Joseph Hannen, p. 55: 'The fact that while we were gathered, discussing plans for spiritual union and harmony throughout the world, the delegates at Paris, in the Peace Conference, were meeting to establish the new world conditions politically, economically and socially, lent a peculiar power and significance to the gathering of the friends in the metropolis of the new world.'
61 'Recent Tablet to an Eminent Bahai in Persia', revealed 23 March 1919, translated by Dr Zia M. Bagdadi, April 1919, in *Star of the West*, vol. 10, no. 2 (9 April 1919), pp. 26-7. The Bahá'í Faith does not claim that President Wilson got his ideas for the Fourteen Points directly from the Faith. It is true that his eldest daughter, who filled the role of First Lady for a time after the death of her mother, was a friend of Ali-Kuli Khan and his wife, Florence Breed Khan. The Khans were living in Washington during the Wilson administration while Khan served as *chargé d'affaires* to the United States for the government of Iran. The Khans provided Wilson's daughter with Bahá'í literature. Nonetheless, Wilson was an eminent student of government and international affairs and had been considering many of the points for decades as a scholar. He and his closest aid, Colonel House, drafted the points together. During the last year of the War in anticipation of participation in the Paris Peace Conference, Wilson arranged for a group of experts working in New York City, known as The Inquiry, to consider matters such as those addressed in the Fourteen Points in detail. A number of members of this working group of experts accompanied the President to Paris.
62 Letter from Horace Holley to Irving Holley, 14 March [1917?]. Connecticut Historical Society Archives, Holley papers.
63 ibid.
64 Holley, *Divinations and Creation*, p. 31.
65 Holley, *Read-Aloud Plays*, pp. 44-5.
66 St Mark's sold this beautiful large chapel some years later. It is now St Nicholas Carpatho Church.

NOTES AND REFERENCES

67 Holley, *Read-Aloud Plays*, p. 46.
68 Letter from Horace Holley to Irving Holley, 17 May (probably 1918 or 1919) from 288 East 10th St., NYC. Irving Holley, Jr furnished a copy to Claire Vreeland and the Vreeland family provided it to the author.
69 Letter from Horace Holley to Albert Vail, 4 June 1922. USBNA, Vail papers, Box 1.
70 Holley, *Read-Aloud Plays*, p. 50.
71 Holley, 'Earth's Justice', poem embedded within commentary, in *Collier's: The National Weekly*, vol. 57, no. 6 (22 April 1916), p. 15.

6 The Early Days of the Bahá'í Faith in New York

1 Minutes of meeting between the New York Spiritual and General Assemblies, 7 August 1924, submitted by Bertha L. Herklotz, Recording Secretary, p. 3. New York, New York Bahá'í Archives.
2 During this period, key officers of the national governing bodies resided in the New York area. Furthermore, the Bahá'í community in Chicago area was not as strong as New York for a variety of complex reasons. This changed in 1939, when the Secretariat of the National Spiritual Assembly was moved from New York to the village of Wilmette, Illinois located in the Chicago outskirts, and once again, the Chicago area regained its position as the centre of the American Bahá'í community.
3 The New York Bahá'í community usually had about two hundred names on its voting list, but many of these were not active participants. Like most groups, probably twenty or fewer carried out most tasks for the community. Most other Bahá'í groups in the United States had fewer than twenty active believers.
4 Among the Holley papers are lists of the members of the New York community during the time that they were there. As with all communities, the numbers were higher if those who did not participate are counted. These lists can be found in USBNA, Horace and Doris Holley papers.
5 An undated letter [late 1930?] to Shoghi Effendi from the New York Spiritual Assembly stated that, 'The fact that our community is the largest and most varied Baha'i group in America surely creates special opportunities for service among believers of all races, classes and types.' New York, New York Bahá'í Archives.
6 Minutes of the New York Community Meeting, held at the St. Mark's in the Bowery Parish House, 29 November 1914, pp. 1–2. New York, New York Bahá'í Archives. The minutes mention Horace Holley by name as being present. The meeting was addressed by Reverend Doctor William Norman Guthrie. Horace read an opening prayer at the next meeting held on 13 December at the Kinney home, where there are unconfirmed reports that the Holleys were staying temporarily. Minutes of the New York Community Meeting, 13 December 1914. New York, New York Bahá'í Archives.
7 The Paris Bahá'í community, in the main, informally looked to the Dreyfus-Barney family to manage it, even though neither Hippolyte nor Laura put themselves forward. The multiple segments of the community, separated by language and culture, did not seem to gather frequently – perhaps not at all. Like New York, the Paris community had weekly meetings in homes that were open to both adherents and inquirers, but it did not have a Nineteen Day Feast like

New York. I am grateful to Yann Nochi for information on that community, especially Hippolyte Dreyfus-Barney.

8 *The Bahá'í World*, vol. III (1928–1930), pp. 84–5; vol. 4 (1931–32), pp. 118–19. As Guardian of the Bahá'í Faith, in 1930, Shoghi Effendi designated nineteen Western believers as Disciples of 'Abdu'l-Bahá. Nineteen were initially given this honour, and several more were added later. The honour was only ever bestowed posthumously.

9 'Dodge, Arthur Pillsbury (1849–1915)', in The Bahá'í Encyclopedia Project, https://www.bahai-encyclopedia-project.org/index.php?option=com_content&view=article&id=168:dodge-arthur-pillsbury&catid=37:biography; See also, Hogenson, *Lighting the Western Sky*, pp. 56, 182.

10 Collins, 'Kenosha, 1893–1912: History of an Early Bahá'í Community in the United States', in Momen (ed), *Studies in Bábí and Bahá'í History*, vol.1, pp. 228–9.

11 Stockman, *The Bahá'í Faith in America*, vol. 2: *Early Expansion, 1900–1912*, pp. 14-15. Note that Hudson County, New Jersey, across the Hudson River from New York City, may have had the first Bahá'í administrative body in the West, because in the autumn of 1899 they selected a small committee to manage the community, however, the members were appointed rather than elected. This committee, nonetheless, did not evolve into a strong institution due to the ups and downs of the Bahá'í membership in that New York suburb (ibid. pp. 11–13). Later, 'Abdu'l-Bahá changed the name of the Chicago Board of Counsel to the House of Spirituality.

12 Only men may serve on the international governing institution, the Universal House of Justice. Consequently, these teachers erroneously assumed that the same applied at the local and national level. Even though women many not serve on that House of Justice, they serve in all other Bahá'í administrative capacities and Bahíyyih Khánum, the sister of 'Abdu'l-Bahá, served for a time as head of the Faith. Service on elected institutions is not one of status.

13 *Robert's Rules of Order* was first published in 1876 and remains the authority for conducting meetings in many American organizations including church groups, local government commissions, non-profit and professional associations, school boards, and the like. The fact that many American Bahá'í communities continue to make motions and second them is a remnant from the use of this handbook for many decades.

14 From 1922 on, the Local and National Houses of Justice have gone under the title Local and National Spiritual Assemblies. This temporary title denotes the reality that they are not yet fully developed.

15 Taherzadeh, *The Revelation of Bahá'u'lláh*, vol. 1, pp. 289-91. See also Momen, *The Bahá'í Communities of Iran 1851–1921, Volume 1: The North of Iran*, pp. 92–4. This Central Committee of Tehran became not just the governing council for that city but, by default, assumed jurisdiction over the entire country. The Kenosha Wisconsin Bahá'í community in the United States may have had a governing council a year earlier, but it did not rival the Central Committee which not only oversaw the large Tehran community, but made decisions for the rest of the country.

16 Orosco Woolson, who changed his first name to Clement, was born in New Jersey in 1879 and became a Bahá'í in 1899. He was probably the youngest

NOTES AND REFERENCES

member of the Board of Counsel. In 1906, he left New York to study to become an osteopathic physician. He later settled in St Paul, Minnesota, where he continued to be an active participant in the Faith. See Stockman, *The Bahá'í Faith in America*, vol. 2, p. 331.

17 Charles E. Sprague was an active member of the New York Community, but in 1905 moved to Philadelphia where he helped establish the Bahá'í community there. See Stockman, *The Bahá'í Faith in America*, vol. 2, pp. 211, 215.

18 Undated and unsigned document providing a timeline of the important developments of the New York City Bahá'í community from 1898 through 1909. Archives of the New York, New York Bahá'í community. The other information about the evening comes from the written recollection of Louise Herman which she sent to D. C. Lincoln in about 1934. Archives of the New York Bahá'í community.

19 Hogenson, *Lighting the Western Sky*, pp. 13–14.

20 Written recollection of Louise Herman which she sent to D.C. Lincoln in about 1934. Archives of the New York, New York Bahá'í community. For more about the election, see also Stockman, *The Bahá'í Faith in America*, vol. 2, p. 36. With regard to the Women's Auxiliary, see ibid. p. 129.

21 Printed statement 'To the Followers of Bahá'í in the City of New York' announcing the formation of the Board of Counsel and its membership. The other information about the evening comes from the written recollection of Louise Herman which she sent to D.C. Lincoln in about 1934. Archives of the New York Bahá'í community.

22 Undated printed letter from the New York Board of Counsel to the Followers of Bahá'í in the City of New York. New York Bahá'í Archives.

23 'Notes taken at Acca by Mr. Montfort Mills, of New York, during the summer of 1909'. USBNA, Holley papers.

24 ibid. p. 4.

25 Letter from Bahá'í Temple Unity to 'Abdu'l-Bahá, 30 January 1910. USBNA.

26 Report [minutes?] of the annual election meeting of the New York Bahá'í Community held on 28 November 1917. The document is dated 5 December 1917. New York Bahá'í Archives.

27 Excerpt from a Tablet from 'Abdu'l-Bahá to Roy Wilhelm. USBNA, Roy Wilhelm papers, provided by Dr Joel Nizin to the author.

28 Minutes, 7 February 1919. New York, New York Bahá'í Archives. The membership of the committee to promote the work of the Tablet of the Divine Plan for the Northeast was announced in *Reality* magazine.

29 Minutes, 4 April 1917. New York Bahá'í Archives.

30 Minutes, 25 April 1917. New York Bahá'í Archives.

31 Minutes, 9 May 1917 show Horace co-hosting the gathering for the Temple. New York Bahá'í Archives.

32 See, for example, Minutes, 9 May 1917 in which Horace is asked by the Board of Counsel to give a talk at an upcoming meeting. *Reality* magazine also reported on Bahá'í gatherings in New York, including the talks. Horace and his talks are mentioned frequently.

33 Speech of President T. Woodrow Wilson before the United States Senate delivered on 22 January 1917, quoted in Berg, *Wilson*, p. 421.

34 Minutes of the New York Board of Counsel, 14 February 1917. New York Bahá'í Archives.
35 Soldiers were stationed around the complex of the House of Abdu'lláh Pá<u>sh</u>á, to watch 'Abdu'l-Bahá. He was allowed to move within the walls of the city of 'Akká, but not to go outside of the city.
36 Grundy, *Ten Days in the Light of 'Akká*, pp. 71–6. Some of the details come from the summary of the history of the Nineteen Day Feast prepared by Frank E. Osborne. New York Bahá'í Archives.
37 ibid. p. 76.
38 List and summary of documents from Frank E. Osborne which outline the early history of the New York Bahá'í Community. New York Bahá'í Archives.
39 Recollection of Etta Fleming prepared in 1933 for the New York Bahá'í Community. New York Bahá'í Archives.
40 Recollection of Andrew F. Fleming prepared in 1933 for the New York Bahá'í Community. New York Bahá'í Archives.
41 Stockman, *The Bahá'í Faith in America*, vol. 2, pp. 245–7.
42 Minutes of the New York Board of Counsel, 11 December 1916. New York Bahá'í Archives.
43 Ma<u>sh</u>riqu'l-A<u>dh</u>kár is the official name for the structure. In the Bahá'í Faith, Ma<u>sh</u>riqu'l-A<u>dh</u>kárs are institutions with their own purposes and goals. They combine worship with service.
44 In 1908, Dr Edward C. Getsinger, then residing in Washington DC, wrote to 'Abdu'l-Bahá about the need for a national governing body for the United States. Dr Getsinger, with his wife, Lua, were the first Western believers to meet 'Abdu'l-Bahá when they travelled to the Holy Land in 1898. Rather than focusing upon the establishment of such a body, 'Abdu'l-Bahá added a postscript in His own handwriting discussing the need to build the House of Worship, stating that the building must become the cause of uniting the American Bahá'í community. The reply made clear that it was not yet time to organize a National Spiritual Assembly because there were not yet enough believers in North America to justify it. But Dr Getsinger was assured that the time would come for the establishment of a National Spiritual Assembly. 'Abdu'l-Bahá's statement said, 'Every work must be undertaken in its own time and place and season.' USBNA, Edward Getsinger papers.

Corinne True of Chicago also wrote to 'Akká to discuss the possibility of creating an organization in order to construct the House of Worship. A member of 'Abdu'l-Bahá's family replied on His behalf in a letter dated 19 June 1908 that such an organization should be established through representatives sent from the Bahá'í communities and furthermore, that women would have the right to serve on the institution. USBNA, Corinne True papers, Box 1, folder 27.
45 Roy Wilhelm became a member a few months later in that year, probably due to resignations. For details about the establishment of Bahá'í Temple Unity, see Armstrong-Ingram, *Music, Devotions, and Ma<u>sh</u>riqu'l-A<u>dh</u>kár*, pp. 161–69.
46 For a more detailed account of the election of the Temple Unity Committee in 1909, see Rutstein, *Corinne True: Faithful Handmaid of 'Abdul'-Bahá*, pp. 81–3.
47 The replacement of the Temple Unity Committee with the National Spiritual Assembly was a process that took three years. Between 1922 and 1925, they overlapped.

48 The 'Souvenir Picnic' has been held annually at the Wilhelm property ever since 1912 to commemorate 'Abdu'l-Bahá's visit to the United States. It attracts hundreds of people from the surrounding region.
49 Transcript of talk, 'What is Happening to the Bahá'ís', by Horace Holley, delivered on 18 September 1954 at Foundation Hall within the Bahá'í House of Worship, Wilmette, Illinois (at the Central States Area Conference). USBNA, Holley papers.
50 *Baha'i World Faith*, pp. 384–5. This Tablet arrived in New York on 20 September 1920. USBNA, Roy Wilhelm papers.
51 Transcript of talk, 'What is Happening to the Bahá'ís', by Horace Holley (see note 49 above).
52 Ahlstrom, *A Religious History of the American* People, pp. 898–9.
53 Ruhe-Schoen, *Champions of Oneness: Louis Gregory and His Shining Circle*, pp. 166–8.
54 This period is not the same as the period during the early 1950s involving Senator Joseph McCarthy's investigation of Americans connected with Communism that is also sometimes called the Red Scare.
55 For discussions of this period, see Allen, *Only Yesterday: An Informal History of the 1920s*, pp. 39–65.
56 Letter from Horace Holley to Irving Holley, 19 June 1921. Connecticut Historical Society Archives, Holley papers.
57 Letter from Horace Holley to Irving Holley, 17 April [1919 or 1920?]. Connecticut Historical Society Archives, Holley papers.
58 Redman, *'Abdu'l-Bahá in Their Midst*, p. 310.
59 Wedding announcement on behalf of Annette Sterner Pascal of Horace H. Holley and Doris Pascal in 28 September 1919 edition of the *New York Times*. See also Connecticut marriage records for Horace Holley and Doris Bowen available through ancestry.com. At that time, New York laws made it difficult for divorced individuals to remarry, which probably explains why the marriage took place in nearby Connecticut.
60 Letter from Horace Holley to Irving Holley, 5 October [1919?]. Copy provided by the Holley Family to Claire Vreeland and the Vreeland family furnished it to the author.
61 Tom Williams, *A Mysterious Something in the Light: The Life of Raymond Chandler*, p. 72. Julian Pascal's second wife, Cissy, left him for the famous writer of detective stories Raymond Chandler. Gordon Pascal was a close friend of Chandler's.
62 http://chandlerbiography.wordpress.com/2010/06/24/julian-pascal/posted on June 24, 2010.
63 Ancestry.com records regarding the Pascal/Bowen family.
64 Grun, *The Timetables of History: A Horizontal Linkage of People and Events*, p. 694.
65 Annette Sterner's brothers were Frederick Sterner, a prominent architect, and Albert Sterner, a painter and illustrator.
66 'Mission of Mrs. Pascal', in *Good Furniture Magazine*, May 1920, pp. 202–3.
67 Ernest Pascal was one of the main screenwriters of his day, producing scripts for classic films such as *Kidnapped* (1937), *The Hound of the Baskervilles* (1939), *The Blue Bird* (1940), and *Wee Willie Winkie* (1937).

68 Letter from Horace Holley to Irving Holley, 1 June 1920, Connecticut Historical Society, Holley papers.
69 Letter from Horace Holley to Irving Holley, 25 August [1920?]. Provided by the Holley Family to Claire Vreeland and then to the author. It appears from letters around this period that Horace underwent an operation in Philadelphia at about the same time as the loss of his infant son. This saddled the grieving couple with additional medical expenses. There are no details as to why Horace required medical treatment. See, for example, letter from Horace Holley to Irving Holley 11 January [1921?]. Provided by the Holley family to Claire Vreeland and then to the author.
70 See, for example, a statement affirming Edward B. Kinney's membership in St Mark's. Harvard Divinity School, Andover Library, W. N. Guthrie papers. In a Tablet to Kinney translated on 23 February [1914?], 'Abdu'l-Bahá said, 'Convey infinite love and kindness on my behalf to the Rev. Dr. Norman G. Guthrie and say to him: "praise be to God that He hath chosen thee from amongst the ministers so that thou mayest harken to the Call of the Kingdom of God, listen to the heavenly melody, behold the light of Reality, act according to the advices of His Holiness the Christ, promulgate the principles of Baha'O'llah, become the cause of the illumination of the world of humanity and be ordained as the high priest of the Church of the Kingdom. All the ministers will be submerged under one of those periodic waves of the earth, leaving behind no name and no trace, but thou shalt unfurl the Standard of spirituality in the heavenly universe extolling and magnifying the Lord of Mankind with the music of the Kingdom. Thank thou God that thou has attained to this most great bestowal."' USBNA, Doris Holley papers, Box 1.
71 *Star of the West*, vol. V, no. 2 (9 April 1914), p. 25.
72 A committee of Bahá'ís associated with St Mark's was set up to organize the Bahá'í meetings at the church. They were called 'The Friends of 'Abdu'l-Bahá'. Minutes of the Organization Meeting of The Friends of 'Abdu'l-Bahá, 30 December 1916. New York Bahá'í Archives.
73 Tablet addressed to Edward B. Kinney, 23 February [1914?], which Kinney received on 8 March 1914 from 'Abdu'l-Bahá. It was translated by Mirza Ahmad Sohrab. USBNA, Doris Holley papers, Box 1.
74 When the Holleys first arrived in New York, they spent many hours with the family honoured with hosting both 'Abdu'l-Bahá's first meeting in America on the day He arrived and then, ten months later, His last meeting the night before He sailed – the Kinney Family: Edward and Helen (Carrie) and their young sons. 'Abdu'l-Bahá bestowed the names Saffa and Vaffa, respectively, on Edward and Carrie. Saffa, a talented musician and composer, taught music and was employed as organist and choir director for churches. As a youth, he had been privileged to study under the famous Czech composer Antonin Dvorak. Vaffa, a well-to-do heiress, served as hostess to many Bahá'í gatherings in their large Manhattan home. The Kinneys were important friends to Horace for decades.
75 Undated document on relationship with Bahá'ís. Harvard Divinity School, Andover Library, W. N. Guthrie papers.
76 The Dutch word 'bowery' means plantation or farm, which is how the Bowery neighbourhood of Manhattan got its name.

77 Letter from Karl Reiland, Charles L. Slattery, Percy S. Grant to Bishop Greer, 18 March 1918. Harvard Divinity School, Andover Library, W. N. Guthrie papers.
78 Ybarra, 'Churches as Play Places: The Rev. Dr. Guthrie Says People Will Come to St. Mark's if He Offers Real Entertainment', in *New York Times*, 20 February 1921.
79 Undated statement by W. N. Guthrie about the Bahá'í association with St Mark's. Harvard Divinity School, Andover Library, W. N. Guthrie papers.
80 Many years later, in 1948, Horace wrote to his former employers at *Iron Age*. In response, the owner's daughter said that 'I can't think of anybody that has made so permanent and so favorable an impression upon our organization as you have – an impression that has lasted for more years than I like to think of except that their very number shows how deserving you are of high compliment on your ability and friendly personality. You've got to be either very good or very bad to be remembered 25 years after.' Letter from Sandy at *Hardware Age* magazine to Horace Holley, 20 January 1948. USBNA, Horace Holley papers, Box 6.
81 Notice, 'Horace Holley Becomes Copy Chief', in an advertising industry trade journal, *Printer's Ink*, 29 September 1921, p. 27.
82 Horace discusses his positions and his growing responsibility at all three employers in letters to his brother Irving Holley between 1918 and 1925. The letters were either furnished by the Holley Family to Claire Vreeland or are in USBNA, Holley papers.
83 Marchand, *Advertising the American Dream: Making Way for Modernity, 1920–1940*, throughout. See also Allen, *Only Yesterday*, pp. 146–51; Schweikart and Dougherty, *A Patriot's History of the Modern World: From America's Exceptional Ascent to the Atomic Bomb: 1898–1945*, pp. 230–31.
84 Letter from Horace Holley to Irving Holley, 19 June 1921. Connecticut Historical Society Archives, Holley papers.
85 Holley, *Bahai: The Spirit of the Age*, p. 59.
86 Horace Holley's second book, *The Social Principle*, draws upon Bahá'í themes but is really a lengthy essay expounding upon Horace's conceptions of modern life without basing his writing exclusively upon Bahá'í teachings. It was not meant as an introductory book about the Faith but to reach a broad audience who could be persuaded by his ideas, if not attracted to his religion. For this reason, I have not compared *The Social Principle* with *Bahai: The Spirit of the Age*.
87 Holley, *Bahai: The Spirit of the Age*, pp. 3–42.
88 Ibid. p. 25. Horace Holley refers to there being three Manifestations of God in the Bahá'í Faith. He was unclear about the station of 'Abdu'l-Bahá.
89 According to Hooper Dunbar, one of his friends spoke with Horace during the last years of his life and found that he was conversant in Theosophy and owned a book about it that had been written by a Bahá'í. Multiple interviews with Hooper Dunbar by the author.
90 In the essay, '*Reality* Magazine: Editorship and Ownership of an American Bahá'í Periodical', by Peter Smith published in *From Iran East and West*, vol. 2, Smith argues that Horace Holley's attempt in *Bahai: The Spirit of the Age* to find common ground with groups such as New Thought and Theosophy was a reflection that he too was drawn to the metaphysical. While he did praise the efforts of these groups to develop new means of thinking to achieve a higher spiritual

consciousness, there is no evidence in Horace's life or his other writings that he endorsed any of the more extreme expressions of mystical practices such as the study of the occult, spiritual healing, seances and fortune-telling that some of the groups he addressed were drawn to. *From Iran East and West*, edited by Juan Ricardo Cole and Moojan Momen, pp. 135–56. For an in-depth look at the religious background of the early adherents to the Bahá'í Faith, especially the metaphysical groups, see Peter Smith's excellent survey of the first decades of the American Bahá'í Community, 'The American Bahá'í Community, 1894–1917: A Preliminary Survey', *Studies in Bábí & Bahá'í History*, vol. 1, edited by Moojan Momen, pp. 155–64.
91 Shoghi Effendi, *Bahá'í Administration*, p. 55.

7 The Covenant

1 Untitled statement of Horace Holley, in *Reality*, vol. V, no. 1 (January 1922), p. 3. Note that the statement is reproduced as it was printed in 1922 without the use of diacriticals.
2 According to the 1880 US Census and Juliet Thompson's US passport application, Juliet was born in New York City. She always gave New York as her birthplace. Many Bahá'í publications list her as being born in Washington DC, an erroneous statement which began with the posthumous publication of Juliet's diary. Her friend, Marzieh Gail, suggested without proof that Juliet was actually born in Virginia (Thompson, *The Diary of Juliet Thompson*, p. xvi.) Government documents are available through the website www.ancestry.com.
3 Juliet (and her mother) resided with Mrs Marguerite 'Daisy' Smythe, a woman of means who probably paid most of the expenses of the townhouse. Though Juliet was a boarder, her relationship to Daisy was more akin to that of a sister.
4 Thompson, *The Diary of Juliet Thompson*, pp. 312–13.
5 ibid. p. 313.
6 ibid.
7 ibid. p. 314
8 Stockman, *'Abdu'l-Bahá in America*, pp. 198–9.
9 Lacroix-Hopson, *'Abdu'l-Bahá in New York the City of the Covenant*, p. 99.
10 Shoghi Effendi, *God Passes By*, p. 288.
11 Holley, '"City of the Covenant": A Great Bahai Work started in New York City', in *Reality*, vol. I, no. 3 (July 1919), p. 28.
12 These events have been recounted in a number of publications, but in none more beautifully than in 'The Passing of 'Abdu'l-Bahá' by Lady Blomfield and Shoghi Effendi, extracts of which appeared in *Bahá'í Year Book*, vol. 1 (April 1925–April 1926), pp. 19–31. It was reprinted in later editions of *The Bahá'í World*.
13 Balyuzi, *'Abdu'l-Bahá*, p. 482. For more details of 'Abdu'l-Bahá's passing see ibid. pp. 452–82.
14 Roy Wilhelm 1922 Pilgrim's Notes. USBNA, Roy Wilhelm papers, Box 7. I am grateful to Dr Joel Nizin for generously providing his research into Roy Wilhelm.
15 Bahá'u'lláh instructed everyone to refer to 'Abdu'l-Bahá as the Master. Following His Father's death, 'Abdu'l-Bahá took on the name 'Abdu'l-Bahá as an indication of His own servitude, for it means 'Servant of Bahá'. As many who read this

book might assume other connotations from the title 'Master', this book refers to 'Abdu'l-Bahá by the name He chose for Himself. His given name was Abbas.
16 Shoghi Effendi, *Baháʼí Administration*, p. 15.
17 Rabbani, *The Priceless Pearl*, pp. 46–7.
18 The Guardian excluded the lengthy sections dealing with the history of Covenant-breaking as well as a few sections dealing with responsibilities of the Universal House of Justice which would not come into effect until well into the future. The abridged version of the Will and Testament can be found in Shoghi Effendi, *Baháʼí Administration*, pp. 3–12.
19 Weinberg, *Ethel Jenner Rosenberg: The Life and Times of England's Outstanding Baháʼí Pioneer Worker*, p. 204.
20 Note to Horace Holley, 27 February 1922, on the top of the record of the decision of the New York Board of Counsel at its emergency meeting of 26 February to consider what was to be done with the extracts of the Will and Testament it had just received. Two members of the Executive Board of Temple Unity were present. This meeting was discussed in the 1 March 1922 letter from Horace Holley to Alfred Lunt, secretary of the Temple Unity Executive Board. Lunt resided in Boston. USBNA, Alfred Lunt papers, Box 19.
21 Note from Alfred Lunt to Horace Holley, dated Monday [26 February 1922?] conveying the decision of the Unity Board to the New York Board of Counsel regarding the dissemination of the Will and Testament of 'Abdu'l-Bahá. USBNA, Alfred Lunt papers, Box 19.
22 This meeting was held at St Mark's Hall, part of the facilities of St Mark's-in-the-Bowery Episcopal Church.
23 Letter from Horace Holley to Alfred Lunt, 1 March 1922. USBNA, Alfred Lunt papers, Box 19.
24 Letter from Alfred Lunt to Horace Holley, 4 March 1922. USBNA, Alfred Lunt papers, Box 19.
25 Letter from Alfred Lunt to Horace Holley, 24 March 1922. USBNA, Temple Unity files, Box 1.
26 Letter from Horace Holley to Alfred Lunt, 22 March 1922. USBNA, Temple Unity files, Box 1.
27 In Charles Mason Remey's unpublished account of his time in Haifa in March 1922, he stated that Shoghi Effendi summoned him not to consult about setting up the Administrative Order, but to solicit his views as an architect about the buildings and grounds at the World Centre. He was excluded from the consultations, other than the informal ones that occurred during meals. Remey, 'A Pilgrimage to the Holy Land: CMR 1922', USBNA, Mary Rabb papers.
28 Muṣṭafá Rúmí, who carried the Faith to Burma (now Myanmar), would be named a Hand of the Cause of God after his passing. See Muhajir, *Siyyid Muṣṭafá Rúmí: Hand of the Cause of God, Apostle of Baháʼu'lláh*, pp. 159–74.
29 Letter from Roy Wilhelm to Ella Goodall Cooper, 26 February 1922. USBNA. I am indebted to Dr Joel Nizin for sharing his research into Roy Wilhelm.
30 Rabbani, *The Priceless Pearl*, pp. 55–6. See also Remey, 'A Pilgrimage to the Holy Land, CMR 1922', pp. 39–40.
31 Shoghi Effendi, *Baháʼí Administration*, p. 18.
32 ibid. p. 36.

33 Americans spelled Jináb-i-Fáḍil a variety of ways because there was not yet a standard for transliteration.
34 The most extensive information on Jináb-i-Fáḍil can be found through the website 'Jinab-i-Fáḍil Mazindarini (Fadil Mazindarini)', https://sites.google.com/site/fadilmazindarani/thereproductions by Omeed Rameshni, Melbourne, Australia, 2009.
35 Letter from Horace Holley to Albert Vail, 4 March 1922. USBNA, Albert Vail papers, Box 1.
36 ibid.
37 The committee was chaired by Charles Mason Remey, who had become the unofficial expert within the United States regarding all matters related to the Covenant of Bahá'u'lláh. The other members included George Latimer of Portland, Oregon; Louis Gregory of Washington DC; and Emogene Hoagg, from California (who often lived in Europe). Ironically, both Gregory and Latimer were lawyers, and so should have been trained how to carefully, appropriately and with all due consideration conduct an investigation. Many people blamed Remey, as Chair, for the heavy-handed way this was conducted.
38 Shoghi Effendi, *Bahá'í Administration*, p. 19.
39 Randall-Winckler, *William Henry Randall: Disciple of 'Abdu'l-Bahá*, p. 91.
40 Peter Smith, 'Reality Magazine: Editorship and Ownership of an American Bahá'í Periodical', in *From Iran East and West: Studies in Bábí and Bahá'í History*, vol. 2, pp. 135-56.
41 According to newspaper articles available on the internet, Deuth was a Baron.
42 Letter from Nellie French to Ella Goodall Cooper. USBNA, Ella Cooper papers.
43 The *Star of the West* was established in 1909 through the individual initiatives of Gertrude Buikema and Albert Windust at the suggestion of Ahmad Sohrab. Windust was in the printing business and Buikema provided funding. Windust served as the primary editor. What began as a modest newsletter grew to the point where these two dedicated believers were no longer capable of managing it, even with assistance. It also became clear by 1921 that it needed to come under the management of a national Bahá'í governing body. The Temple Unity Executive Board was already considering how to bring this about when the Guardian called for the establishment of the National Spiritual Assembly in 1922. Shoghi Effendi wanted the National Assembly to bring the *Star of the West* under its control as one of its first items of business. This entailed working out with the founders a legal arrangement to transfer its ownership. Both were grateful to be relieved of the burden of that vital publication. The National Assembly appointed a new editor and staff. This transition took several years to complete and resulted in an improved publication, which also changed its name to *The Bahai Bulletin: Star of the West*. Following the implementation of these changes, Shoghi Effendi stated in a letter to the National Spiritual Assembly dated 23 December 1922 that he was 'glad to note an encouraging improvement in its [the *Star of the West's*] management, its style, its general presentation and the nature and number of its articles'. Shoghi Effendi, *Bahá'í Administration*, p. 29. There was well-founded concern that *Reality* magazine would divert the limited resources available to produce the *Star of the West*.
44 Tablet received by Mrs. Florian Krug, in *Reality*, vol. IV, no. 8 (August 1921), p. 43.

45 Official Report of the 1921 Bahá'í Temple Unity Convention, (selections from the transcript of the proceedings sent to all believers by the Executive Board), p. 46. USBNA, National Spiritual Assembly papers.
46 Holley, '"City of the Covenant": A Great Bahai Work started in New York City', in *Reality*, vol. I, no. 3 (July 1919), p. 29.
47 The nature of Robinson's business relationship is unclear. He may have become a part owner, not an employee.
48 Peter Smith, '*Reality* Magazine: Editorship and Ownership of an American Bahá'í Periodical', in *From Iran East and West: Studies in Bábí and Bahá'í History*, vol. 2, p. 144. For more about Mary Hanford Ford, see the brief biography of her in Whitehead, *Some Bahá'ís to Remember*, pp. 145–52. There is also a lengthy Wikipedia article on Ford.
49 Ryan Smith, 'The Bizarre Tale of the Tunnels, Trysts and Taxa of a Smithsonian Entomologist', in *Smithsonian Magazine*, 13 May 2016.
50 ibid.
51 Letter from Horace Holley to Albert Vail, 12 August 1922. USBNA, Albert Vail papers, Box 1. Horace reported that Mary Hanford Ford had protested to Robinson about putting 'The Bahá'í Magazine' on the front cover, to no avail. After being apprised of the situation, Horace resigned immediately, severing all association with *Reality*. The lesson he learned from that experience was, 'Our only protection against such unwarranted uses of the Bahai name is to create a larger and deeper expression of the Cause in our own magazine.'
52 *Reality*, vol. V, no. 8 (August 1922), p. 1.
53 *Reality*, vol. V, no. 9 (September 1922), p. 1.
54 *Reality*, vol. V, no. 10 (October 1922), p. 56.
55 ibid. pp. 57–8.
56 ibid. pp. 4–7.
57 *Reality*, vol V, no. 12 (December 1922), pp. 55–6.
58 ibid. pp. 56–9.
59 Shoghi Effendi, *Bahá'í Administration*, p. 23.
60 Dyar, 'II The Bahai Religion: The Will of Abdul Baha', in *Reality*, vol. VI, no. 7 (July 1923), pp. 16–20. Dyar argued that the three sections of the Will should be treated as three separate Wills because they were written at different times. Based upon the legal logic that the latest Will is the only one that counts, he deduced that one of the three was written last, and so it was definitive and the other two should be disregarded. The one he chose only called for an elected Universal House of Justice and did not mention the Guardianship or Local and National Spiritual Assemblies.
61 Stenstrand, 'Authorship of the Writings Attributed to Baha Ullah', in *Reality*, vol. VIII, no. 4 (October 1924), pp. 32–5. The author of this article was probably the sole American to follow and advocate for Mírzá Yaḥyá (Azal) as the rightful successor to the Báb, a very unusual stand, even among those familiar with the Faith in the Middle East. However, it was the position of Professor E. G. Browne of Cambridge University, who wrote about the Faith and met both Bahá'u'lláh and Mírzá Yaḥyá.
62 See, for example, an article by Dyar discussing the matter of Dr Amin Fareed being declared a Covenant-breaker, that is, he was expelled from the Faith by

'Abdu'l-Bahá. Most likely, having been a part of the Washington DC Bahá'í community for many years, the Dyars knew Fareed as a friend. Dyar, 'IV – The Bahai Religion: An Episode in its History', in *Reality*, vol. VI, no. 9 (September 1923), pp. 40–46.
63   Undated account of verbal report given by Mrs Morton to the National Spiritual Assembly. Most likely this is from 1923. USBNA, National Spiritual Assembly files, National Spiritual Assembly Minutes. The woman giving the report could be either Marjory Morton or Florence Morton. The former is more likely.
64   Minutes of the National Spiritual Assembly of the United States and Canada, 26 and 27 July 1924, p. 3, plus the statement by Dr Harrison Dyar which was attached. USBNA, National Spiritual Assembly files.
65   Shoghi Effendi, Extracts from the *United States Bahá'í News*; and Letter from Shoghi Effendi to the National Spiritual Assembly of the United States and Canada, 27 November 1924, in Shoghi Effendi, *Bahá'í Administration*, p. 73. The name of the magazine is left blank in *Bahá'í Administration*.
66   Minutes of the Open Conference Meeting for the New York Bahá'í Community, New York, 3 September 1925, pp. 3-4. New York Bahá'í Archives.
67   ibid. p. 4.
68   Peter Smith, '*Reality* Magazine: Editorship and Ownership of an American Bahá'í Periodical', in *From Iran East and West: Studies in Bábí and Bahá'í History*, vol. 2, pp. 135-56.
69   See, for example, the report of Ahmad Sohrab's activities in New York City in 1919 which included the statement, 'He is always a great joy to all the friends of the Bahá'í movement.' USBNA, 'Some Bahai Activities', in *Reality*, vol. 1, no. 8 (December 1919), p. 34.
70   For example, he was credited with the idea for establishing the publication that became *Star of the West*.
71   Letter from Edward Getsinger to Albert Windust, 12 March 1911. USBNA.
72   Gail, *Summon up Remembrance*, pp. 170–71.
73   ibid. p. 171.
74   Sohrab, *My Bahá'í Pilgrimage: Autobiography from Childhood to Middle Age*, pp. 81–3.
75   Minutes of the National Spiritual Assembly of the United States and Canada, 23 and 24 January 1926, and 12 June 1926. USBNA.
76   Rabbani, *The Priceless Pearl*, p. 120.
77   It was reported to the New York Assembly that one of Sohrab's talks was lifted completely from H.G. Wells' 'The Salvaging of Civilization'. New York Bahá'í Archives, Minutes of the New York Spiritual Assembly, 12 April 1928.
78   Sohrab, *My Bahá'í Pilgrimage: Autobiography from Childhood to Middle Age*, pp. 124–7.
79   There was evidence that after Sohrab left Los Angeles, he continued to promote Fareed's participation in Bahá'í gatherings, despite knowing full well that anyone declared a Covenant-breaker by 'Abdu'l-Bahá was to be avoided unconditionally. Letter from Carl Scheffler to Horace Holley, 19 September 1925. USBNA, Scheffler files, Box 2.
80   Wikipedia has a lengthy article on Julia Olin Chanler.
81   Wikipedia has an article on Lewis S. Chanler.

82 Chanler, *From Gaslight to Dawn: An Autobiography of Julie Chanler*, pp. 119–21, 127–8, 131–7.
83 This Tablet was distributed to all Bahá'ís in the New York Metropolitan area by the New York Board of Counsel. It was translated into English by Shoghi Effendi in 1921 while he was still attending Balliol College, Oxford in England. Doris kept it among her papers. USBNA, Doris Holley files, Box 1, p. 3.
84 Chanler, *From Gaslight to Dawn: An Autobiography of Julie Chanler*, p. 161.
85 ibid. p. 162.
86 ibid.
87 ibid. p. 164.
88 New York Bahá'í Archives, Minutes of the Spiritual Assembly of New York, 1 March 1928.
89 The New York Assembly wrote to the National Assembly on 14 March 1929, letter attached to the letter from the New York Spiritual Assembly to the National Spiritual Assembly of the United States and Canada, 8 October 1930, attached to the National Spiritual Assembly Minutes of 11, 12, and 13 October 1930. USBNA, National Spiritual Assembly files.
90 Letter from the New York Spiritual Assembly to the National Spiritual Assembly of the United States and Canada, 8 October 1930, attached to the National Spiritual Assembly Minutes of 11, 12, and 13 October 1930. USBNA, National Spiritual Assembly files. The Local Assembly stated in its candid letter to the National Assembly that its chief difficulty was that the National Assembly took no action between the time Mrs Chanler rejected the National Assembly's overtures until June of the following year. In the interim, the New York Assembly was deferring to the National Assembly. During that period, the believers in New York made their own decisions on how to react to the New History Society and Sohrab without institutional guidance. The last paragraph of the letter to the National Assembly stated, 'we express the conviction that the entire problem of the N.H.S. must be regarded as an episode in the education of the collective body of American Bahá'ís'.
91 Cable from Shoghi Effendi to the National Spiritual Assembly of the United States and Canada, 3 December 1929. USBNA, National Spiritual Assembly files.
92 Minutes of the National Spiritual Assembly of the United States and Canada, 4, 5, 6 June 1927. USBNA, National Spiritual Assembly files.
93 Letter written on behalf of Shoghi Effendi to Horace Holley as secretary of the National Spiritual Assembly, 1 January 1930. USBNA, National Spiritual Assembly files.
94 In May 1930, Ali-Kuli Khan reported that when he travelled around the United States he was questioned about the New History Society and why there were two centres in New York. New York Bahá'í Archives, Minutes of the New York Spiritual Assembly, 14 May 1930. A letter from Shoghi Effendi also recounted the international agitation stirred by Sohrab's mailings. Letter written on behalf of Shoghi Effendi to Alfred Lunt as secretary of the National Spiritual Assembly, 30 August 1930. USBNA, National Spiritual Assembly files.
95 An American, Ruth White, tried to prove that the Will and Testament was a forgery. Ahmad allowed her and her husband to attend one of his New York

meetings. She caused troubles, including in Palestine with the government, but had a negligible influence within the New York community, indeed in America. Her greatest harm was to the German Bahá'í community.

96 Rabbani, *The Priceless Pearl*, pp. 120-21.
97 Letter from Shoghi Effendi to the National Spiritual Assembly of the United States and Canada, 27 February 1929, p. 1. USBNA, National Spiritual Assembly files.
98 ibid. p. 3.
99 Chanler, *From Gaslight to Dawn: An Autobiography of Julie Chanler*, pp. 179-82.
100 Letter written on behalf of Shoghi Effendi to the Spiritual Assembly of New York, 9 March 1931. New York Bahá'í Archives, New York Spiritual Assembly files.
101 'Annual Report of the National Spiritual Assembly of the Bahá'ís of the United States and Canada 1929-1930', in *Bahá'í News Letter*, no. 40 (April 1930), p. 4.
102 ibid.
103 Minutes of the National Spiritual Assembly, 27, 28, 29 June. USBNA, National Spiritual Assembly files. During the weekend meeting held in West Englewood, New Jersey, the secretary, Alfred Lunt, placed two telephone calls to Sohrab in one final effort to ascertain and change his attitude. An in-person meeting at the National Assembly's office was offered and rejected. Based upon this and the totality of information before the National Assembly, it drafted the statement at the meeting, with Horace among the three members assigned to craft the initial document.
104 'The Case of Ahmad Sohrab and the New History Society', *Bahá'í News Letter*, no. 43 (August 1930), p. 3.
105 ibid.
106 Cable from Shoghi Effendi to the National Spiritual Assembly, 27 July 1930, followed by a letter discussing the same topic in a letter written on behalf of Shoghi Effendi to Alfred Lunt as secretary of the National Spiritual Assembly, 30 August 1930. USBNA, National Spiritual Assembly files.
107 Supplement to the Minutes of the National Spiritual Assembly, 24 August 1930: 'Statement of a Group of New York believers at conference with the National Spiritual Assembly, Green Acre'. USBNA, National Spiritual Assembly files.
108 Letter from Horace Holley to the Members of the Spiritual Assembly of New York City, 29 August 2930. New York Bahá'í Archives; see also Minutes of the Spiritual Assembly of New York City, 28 September 1930. New York Bahá'í Archives.
109 See, for example, Minutes of the Spiritual Assembly of New York, 10 December 1930. New York Bahá'í Archives.
110 Letter written on behalf of Shoghi Effendi to Horace Holley as secretary of the National Spiritual Assembly, 1 January 1930, included in full in the Minutes of the Spiritual Assembly of New York, 14 May 1930. New York Bahá'í Archives.
111 Letter written on behalf of Shoghi Effendi to Roy Wilhelm, with postscript from Shoghi Effendi, 19 October 1930. USBNA, National Spiritual Assembly files.
112 Letter written on behalf of Shoghi Effendi to the New York Spiritual Assembly 9 March 1931, New York Bahá'í Archives.
113 Letter written on behalf of Shoghi Effendi to the National Spiritual Assembly

of the United States and Canada through its chairman, Mr Allen McDaniel, 9 March 1931. USBNA, National Spiritual Assembly files.

114 Letter from the National Spiritual Assembly of the United States and Canada to the Spiritual Assembly of New York, 27 April 1931. New York Bahá'í Archives. At the request of Shoghi Effendi, several believers of unquestioned wisdom and loyalty were asked to maintain their friendships with Mrs Chanler, in the hope of eventually drawing her away from Sohrab and back to the fold (National Spiritual Assembly Minutes, USBNA). However, those efforts never achieved the desired result. As Mrs Chanler mentions in her autobiography, a handful of formerly active believers remained loyal to Sohrab, but none of those she mentions were well-known Bahá'ís. May Maxwell was one of those asked to continue to be a friend with Mrs. Chanler.

115 Letter from the National Spiritual Assembly of the United States and Canada to the Spiritual Assembly of New York, 27 April 1931. New York Bahá'í Archives.

116 See, for example, the matter of an inquirer that was reported to the New York Assembly. Minutes of the Spiritual Assembly of New York, 24 February 1932. New York Bahá'í Archives.

117 USBNA, 'Notes of Haifa, May 12, 1932', p. 8. 'Combined notes of Lorol [Schopflocher] and Keith [Ransom-Kehler], dictated by Keith, typed by Lorol. Approved by Clara Dunn and Lyle Loveday.' Shoghi Effendi is quoted as saying that it was 'an excellent idea' of Horace Holley to have the name Bahá'í copyrighted'.

118 The American Hands of the Cause (Paul E. Haney, Horace Holley, Corinne True), 'Ahmad Sohrab and the New History Society', 13 January 1958. USBNA, Horace Holley files.

119 Letter written on behalf of Shoghi Effendi, 25 May 1941 quoted ibid. p. 5.

120 This was the first day of the Festival of Riḍván which began at sunset on 20 April. However, after the institution of the Badí' Calendar, the first day of Riḍván varies within a day or so from year to year. In 1958, Bahá'í communities across the globe would have been holding their annual elections on the evening of the day Sohrab died.

121 Even though the New History Society as an organization lost any remaining vitality it had with the death of Sohrab, its 'Bahá'í Library' remained open to the public for many years after that event.

122 He married Juanita Storch, a Bahá'í, and they had one daughter, Laila. The marriage was short-lived and within a decade or so of the separation both mother and daughter began to use the last name 'Storch'.

123 Letter written on behalf of Shoghi Effendi to the New York Spiritual Assembly, 10 September 1931. New York Bahá'í Archives.

8 New York City Paves the Way

1 Letter from Horace Holley to Albert Vail, 12 August 1922. USBNA, Albert Vail papers, Box 1.

2 The National Assembly appointed Horace Holley to the staff of the *Star of the West* (*The Bahá'í Magazine*) in 1922 and again in 1923. Minutes of the National Spiritual Assembly, 30 June to 1 July 1923. USBNA. Horace served only briefly in 1922, citing that he believed the staff could only carry out their functions if they

could consult in person, but as they were scattered around the country, they could not easily consult. He was willing to do whatever else was needed to assist the magazine, especially provide content. Letter from Horace Holley to the National Spiritual Assembly, 8 October 1922. USBNA, Alfred Lunt papers, Box 19.

3 *Bahá'í Scriptures: Selections from the Utterances of Bahá'u'lláh and 'Abdu'l-Bahá*, edited by Horace Holley (New York, Brentano's Publishers, 1923, copyright Bahá'í Publishing Committee 1928). Not until the second edition was it officially approved by the Bahá'í Committee on Publications because there was no review process when it first appeared.

4 Publishing *Bahá'í Scriptures* prior to the 1922 elections meant that it did not have to undergo the review process administered by the Assemblies at that time. The Temple Unity Executive Board tried to manage Bahá'í publications but did not have the authority to make definitive judgements or to require prior consent. The later review process would have slowed the publication of *Bahá'í Scriptures*, but probably had little effect on its contents.

5 Letter from Horace Holley to Irving Holley, 3 July [1923?]. Connecticut Historical Society, Holley papers.

6 *Bahá'í Scriptures: Selections from the Utterances of Bahá'u'lláh and 'Abdu'l-Bahá*, pp. vi–vii.

7 Letter from Horace Holley to Albert Vail, 11 July [1922?]. USBNA, Albert Vail papers, Box 1.

8 *Bahá'í Scriptures: Selections from the Utterances of Bahá'u'lláh and 'Abdu'l-Bahá*, p. ix.

9 Letter from Horace Holley to George Latimer, 17 April [1924?]. USBNA, Latimer papers.

10 Letter from Doris McKay to Claire Vreeland, 3 October 1985. Original in the possession of the author with thanks to the Vreeland family.

11 Shoghi Effendi, *Bahá'í Administration: Selected Messages 1922–1932*, p. 56. Since the compilation was published without going through a strenuous review process, it contained several translations that were not accurate and therefore misleading. Nonetheless, as most of the translations had previously been published in journals and newsletters before *Bahá'í Scriptures* became available, having the most important of these messages available in one volume was useful. Horace assured the Guardian (through his secretary), that he would happily make revisions in the second edition. Letter from Horace Holley to Azizullah S. Bahadur (secretary to Shoghi Effendi), 24 December 1923. USBNA, Holley papers.

12 Letter from Horace Holley to the National Spiritual Assembly of the United States, 22 February 1940. USBNA, Horace Holley papers. In his letter to the National Assembly, Horace discusses the changes that Shoghi Effendi wanted made in *Bahá'í Scriptures* as well as the evolving needs for compilations of the Bahá'í Writings and the recorded talks of 'Abdu'l-Bahá. He suggests three volumes, rather than one.

13 This book went through a number of editions, the last of which was in 1976. After that time, the volume of translated sacred texts increased such that a single volume no longer reflected the Holy Texts. Furthermore, many of the translations included by Horace Holley had been improved. After more than thirty years, it went out of print.

14 *Bahá'í World Faith: Selected Writings of Bahá'u'lláh and 'Abdu'l-Bahá*, edited by Horace Holley (Wilmette, Ill., Bahá'í Publishing Trust, 1971 edition), p. i.
15 Holley, 'The Writings of Bahá'u'lláh', in *Star of the West*, vol. 13 (August 1922), pp. 104–07.
16 ibid. p. 105.
17 ibid. p. 104.
18 ibid. pp. 105–06.
19 ibid. p. 106.
20 ibid.
21 ibid. pp. 106–07.
22 Before 1922, the word 'Assembly' was used in America to mean 'Bahá'í community', not the body which governed the community. This confusing use of the word continued for a few years after 1922 when the first Assemblies were established as governing institutions.
23 The original members of the Spiritual Assembly of the Bahá'ís of New York, New York elected in 1922 were: Mountfort Mills, chairman; Horace Holley, secretary; Albert W. Randall, Treasurer; Bertha Herklotz, recording secretary; Nellie Hope Lloyd; Roy C. Wilhelm; Hooper Harris; Richard Manuel Bolden; Edith Magee Inglis; Henry Grasmere. *Reality*, vol. V, no. 10 (October 1922), p. 56. This is an interesting mix of people drawn from throughout the metropolitan area, not simply from within the incorporated boundaries of the city. The Assembly included two single women who did clerical work, a wealthy businessman and two lawyers. Richard Bolden was the founder and minister of First Emanuel Church and an African-American. Henry Grasmere, like Bertha Herklotz, had a father from Germany. Grasmere was a professional jeweller (US passport application, ancestry.com). Albert W. Randall was working in the publishing business (US Census data, ancestry.com). Edith Inglis was the wife of editor and author William O. Inglis. Her husband is most remembered for his lengthy, unpublished interview with John D. Rockefeller.
24 The author is grateful to the Spiritual Assembly of New York for granting permission to study the minutes from the Board of Counsel and those of the first two decades of the Spiritual Assembly.
25 Undated report of the Nineteen Day Feast Committee of New York. A handwritten note at the top dates it as 21 April 1925. New York Bahá'í Archives.
26 Minutes of the New York Spiritual Assembly, 16 October 1924. New York Bahá'í Archives.
27 Minutes of the open conference meeting between the New York Bahá'í community and the New York Spiritual Assembly, 5 March 1925. New York Bahá'í Archives.
28 ibid.
29 Minutes of the New York Executive Board, 14 February 1917. New York Bahá'í Archives.
30 Minutes of the Spiritual Assembly of New York, 10 December 1925. New York, New York Bahá'í Archives.
31 24 December 1925 Letter from the National Spiritual Assembly to the Spiritual Assembly of New York, 24 December 1925. New York Bahá'í Archives. See also Minutes of the Spiritual Assembly of New York, 19 November 1925. New

York Bahá'í Archives. However, the Local Assembly was insistent in its request and was further advised to wait. 22 June 1926 Letter from the National Spiritual Assembly to the Spiritual Assembly of New York, 22 June 1926. New York Bahá'í Archives.
32 Minutes of the Spiritual Assembly of New York, 11 November 1931. New York Bahá'í Archives.
33 ibid.
34 Minutes of the Spiritual Assembly of New York, 6 January 1932. New York Bahá'í Archives.
35 'By-Laws of the Spiritual Assembly of the Bahá'ís of the City of New York', in *The Bahá'í World*, vol. V (1932– 1934), pp. 228, 235, 237.
36 Letter from Shoghi Effendi to the Spiritual Assembly of New York, 18 October 1927. Much of the contents of this letter were repeated word for word in another letter written on the same date to the National Spiritual Assembly of the Bahá'ís of the United States and Canada. The one to the National Assembly was published in *Bahá'í Administration: Selected Messages 1922–1932*, pp. 139–47.
37 Letter from the Spiritual Assembly of New York to the Local Spiritual Assemblies of the United States and Canada, 25 November 1931. New York Bahá'í Archives. It is unknown if or how the By-Laws were disseminated outside of the United States.
38 ibid.; see also Shoghi Effendi, *Bahá'í Administration: Selected Messages 1922–1932*, p. 143.
39 ibid.; see also Shoghi Effendi, *Bahá'í Administration*, pp. 143–4.
40 Letter from the National Spiritual Assembly to the Spiritual Assembly of New York, 5 February 1946. New York Bahá'í Archives.
41 Letter from the Spiritual Assembly of the Bahá'ís of New York to the Local Spiritual Assemblies of the United States and Canada, 25 November 1931. New York Bahá'í Archives.
42 Certificate of Incorporation, The Spiritual Assembly of the Bahá'ís of the City of New York. New York Bahá'í Archives. New York could not act as quickly as Chicago because of issues that had be solved regarding New York State law. Minutes of the Spiritual Assembly of New York, 24 February 1932. New York Bahá'í Archives.
43 Letter written on behalf of Shoghi Effendi to Horace Holley, 20 April 1932. USBNA.
44 Minutes of the Spiritual Assembly of New York, 30 December 1931. New York Bahá'í Archives; and Minutes of the Spiritual Assembly of New York, 20 January 1932. New York Bahá'í Archives.
45 Minutes of the Spiritual Assembly of New York, 11 June [1930?] . New York Bahá'í Archives.
46 Letter from the Spiritual Assembly of New York to Mr R. C. Collison, Chairman of the National Teaching Committee, 28 July 1930. New York Bahá'í Archives.
47 Letter from Horace Holley to Alfred E. Lunt, 29 July 1930. New York Bahá'í Archives.
48 Letter from the National Spiritual Assembly to Hooper Harris, 20 July 1930. New York Bahá'í Archives.
49 Letter written on behalf of Shoghi Effendi to the New York Spiritual Assembly, 20 February 1934. USBNA.

50 Minutes of the New York Spiritual Assembly, 26 March 1925, p. 1. New York Bahá'í Archives.
51 In 1931, the Local Spiritual Assembly praised and thanked Ophelia Crum for her tireless work as a volunteer to manage the centre. Minutes of the New York Spiritual Assembly, 16 April 1931. New York Bahá'í Archives.
52 Most of the Bahá'ís lived in Manhattan and Brooklyn. Brooklyn was an independent city until 1898 when it merged with New York. When the Faith was first introduced in New York, most of the meetings were held in large homes in Brooklyn, and New York and Brooklyn functioned as separate Bahá'í communities. This separation did not last long after the political merger.
53 Minutes of the New York Spiritual Assembly, 11 March 1927, p. 2. New York Bahá'í Archives.
54 Letter written on behalf of Shoghi Effendi to the New York Spiritual Assembly, 20 February 1934. USBNA.
55 Johnson, *A History of the American People*, p. 664.
56 'Abdu'l-Bahá, *The Promulgation of Universal Peace*, pp. 111–13.
57 ibid. p. 113.
58 Letter from Horace Holley to Agnes Parsons, 9 May 1921. USBNA.
59 The National Association for the Advancement of Colored People. At the time the NAACP was founded in New York in 1909, 'colored' was the polite term for Blacks. For more than a century it has been the premier civil rights organization in the United States fighting for racial justice.
60 Gregory, 'Inter-racial Amity', in *The Bahá'í World*, vol. II (1926–1928), pp. 282–3.
61 Minutes of the New York Spiritual Assembly, 23 June 1927. New York Bahá'í Archives.
62 'High Honor for Rev. R. M. Bolden: Thrifty Minister Delegate to Defense Convention: Well Known Civic Leader', in *The Indianapolis Recorder*, no. 31 (4 March 1916), p. 1.
63 'The Rainbow Circle', in *Reality*, vol. III (January 1921), p. 40.
64 Undated minutes of the New York Spiritual Assembly, probably 1925. New York Bahá'í Archives.
65 Minutes of the New York Spiritual Assembly, 26 May 1927, p. 2. New York Bahá'í Archives.
66 ibid.
67 Minutes of the New York Spiritual Assembly, 23 June 1927, pp. 2–5. New York Bahá'í Archives.
68 Minutes of the New York Spiritual Assembly, 30 June 1927, pp. 1–2. New York Bahá'í Archives.
69 ibid. pp. 2–3.
70 Undated letter [1930?] from the New York Spiritual Assembly to Shoghi Effendi,
71 Morrison, *To Move the World: Louis G. Gregory and the Advancement of Racial Unity in America*, pp. 192–3.
72 Holley, 'The Local Community', text of a talk given by Horace Holley to the New York City Bahá'í community on 24 (27?) February 1931, p. 7. USBNA, Horace Holley papers.
73 ibid.

74 ibid. pp. 7–8.
75 ibid. p. 10.
76 ibid. pp. 11–12.
77 Frances 'Fanny' Wright, born in Scotland, was a writer, feminist, abolitionist, and social reformer who was ahead of her time in her thinking and interests. She moved to the United States and died in Ohio in 1852. There is a lengthy article about her in Wikipedia.
78 Alhstrom, *A Religious History of the American People*, p. 777. William P. DuBose, described by Ahlstrom as 'probably his church's greatest theological mind' (ibid.) was the towering figure at Sewanee seminary during Guthrie and Townshend's time there.
79 Some items from the Townshend–Guthrie correspondence can be found in the W. N. Guthrie papers in the archives of Andover Library at Harvard Divinity School.
80 Schmidt, *Restless Souls: The Making of American Spirituality from Emerson to Oprah*, p. 203. According to Schmidt, Guthrie was part of the group that looked to the poet Walt Whitman as their spiritual leader.
81 First Draft of The Autobiography of William Norman Guthrie, "Green Acres; Second Season", 22 September 1935, pp. 24–32. Harvard Divinity School, Andover Library, W. N. Guthrie papers. For an in-depth look at Green Acre's role in spiritual movements in the late nineteenth and early twentieth centuries, see Leigh, *Restless Souls: The Making of American Spirituality from Emerson to Oprah*; and Perry et al, *Green Acre on the Piscataqua*.
82 Undated memoir by Dr William Norman Guthrie of his years in New York. Harvard Divinity School, Andover Library, W. N. Guthrie papers.
83 Letter from Irvin Ewing to William N. Guthrie, 6 January 1933. Harvard Divinity School, Andover Library, W. N. Guthrie papers.
84 'Bahá'í Service Easter Sunday at St. Mark's Church', in *Bahá'í News*, no. 19 (August 1927), p. 3.
85 Undated memoir by Dr William Norman Guthrie of his years in New York. Harvard Divinity School, Andover Library, W. N. Guthrie papers.
86 Letter from Bishop William Manning of the Diocese of New York to the Reverend William N. Guthrie, D.D., 18 April 1928. Harvard Divinity School, Andover Library, W. N. Guthrie papers.
87 'Dr. Guthrie Seeks Peace in New Jersey', in *The New York Times*, 15 December 1923, pp. 1 and 6.
88 Certification document that Horace Holley was duly elected Junior Warden of St Mark's in the Bowery Protestant Episcopal Church, October 1928, signed by W. N. Guthrie, rector. USBNA, Horace Holley papers, Box 26.
89 Horace's nephew, Irving Holley, Jr., remembered visiting his uncle and aunt at one of the apartments owned by St Mark's. He had the impression that they got the use of it rent-free in exchange for watching over the building, but he was not certain about that detail. Letter from Irving Holley, Jr. to Claire Vreeland, 29 January 1987. The original was given to the author by the Vreeland family.
90 'I am moving on Oct. 1 and have taken a really gorgeous apartment at 129 E. 10, which is one of the St. Mark's buildings, with a little garden in the rear, and lots of room for my other work. It is really the best place I have lived in New York...'

Letter from Horace Holley to John Herman Randall, 13 July 1927. USBNA, Horace Holley papers, Box 4.

91 In a letter to Wright, Horace complains that he misses his evening visits with him. The letter both solicits an article from Wright for *World Unity* magazine and speaks of the St Mark's apartment building commission. Letter from Horace Holley to Frank Lloyd Wright, 16 March 1928. USBNA, Horace Holley papers, Box 6.

92 Apparently, at the time Horace was developing the church endowment campaign, he received as stipend from the church for doing so because he was again doing work in advertising/public relations. Letter from Horace Holley to W. N. Guthrie, 25 February [1931?]. USBNA, Horace Holley papers, Box 26.

93 Examples of the doctrinal differences with the Roman Catholic Church derived from Protestantism include that the Anglican Communion does not require confession of sins to a priest, allows non-members to participate in the sacrament of communion, and allows women to be ordained.

94 Horace's brother Irving also left the Congregational Church and became an active member of the Episcopal Church in Torrington. Apparently, one of the clergymen of that church had been a friend of the Holley family, probably because its building was located near to the Francis Holley home.

95 Letter from William Norman Guthrie to Mr Coran Capshaw, 26 July 1932. Harvard Divinity School, Andover Library, W. N. Guthrie papers.

96 ibid.

97 'The Real Issue Raised by the Controversy between St. Mark's in-the-Bouwerie, New York City, and the Body and Soul Clinic', statement by Horace Holley, 23 July 1932. The letter was widely circulated. USBNA, Horace Holley papers, Box 26.

98 'Minutes of the Recessed Meeting of Rector, Wardens and Vestrymen of St. Mark's in the Bouwerie', 30 March 1933. USBNA, Horace Holley papers, Box 25. Horace also drafted a Bill of Particulars, outlining in a lawyerly fashion the situation and making specific recommendations to the vestry: 'A Policy and Plan of Action for the Vestry of St. Mark's in-the-Bouwerie, written by Horace Holley, and addressed to the vestry clerk, Coran Capshaw'. USBNA, Horace Holley papers, Box 26.

99 Statement by Horace Holley, Junior Warden, St. Mark's in-the-Bouwerie, "The Real Issue Raised by the Controversy between St. Mark's In-The-Bouwerie, New York City, and the Body and Soul Clinic", 23 July 1932. Harvard Divinity School, Andover Library, W. N. Guthrie papers; USBNA, Horace Holley papers, Box 26.

100 ibid. p. 2.

101 ibid.

102 Letter from William Norman Guthrie to Horace Holley, 25 July 1932. Harvard Divinity School, Andover Library, W. N. Guthrie papers. Also available in USBNA, Horace Holley papers, Box 26.

103 Letter from Horace Holley to W. N. Guthrie, 29 July 1932, pp. 3–4. USBNA, Holley papers, Box 26.

104 ibid. p. 2.

105 ibid.

106 See, for example, 'Dr. Guthrie Defies Vestry to Oust Him', in *The New York Times*, 18 April 1933, p. 18.
107 'St. Mark's Vestry Upheld by Court: Election that Turned Out Dr. Guthrie's Followers is Declared Legal, Church Announces', in *The New York Times*, 24 July 1933, p. 13.
108 Letter from Doris Holley to Ernest Pascal, 17 July 1933. USBNA, Doris Holley papers, Box 1.
109 Rabbani, *The Priceless Pearl*, pp. 318–20.
110 Shoghi Effendi, *Bahá'í Administration*, p. 101.
111 Rabbani, 'Twenty Five Years of the Guardianship'.
112 Shoghi Effendi, *This Decisive Hour: Messages from Shoghi Effendi to the North American Bahá'í 1932–1946*, no. 16, p. 9.
113 ibid.
114 'Concerning Membership in Non-Bahá'í Religious Organizations', in *Bahá'í News*, no. 98 (March 1936), p. 7.

9 The Birth Pangs of the New Ordering of the World

1 Holley, 'Current Bahá'í Activities', in *The Bahá'í World*, vol. III (1928–1930), p. 61.
2 Shoghi Effendi, *Bahá'í Administration*, p. 17.
3 ibid. p. 26.
4 ibid.
5 Determining which communities could send delegates and how many to be allotted to each was a dilemma. At first, a community had to have nine believers to be eligible to send a delegate. Larger communities were allocated delegates according to population. Those residing in communities smaller than nine had no voice. One year, the National Spiritual Assembly decided that the regional chairmen of the teaching committees should represent the believers from communities that did not have delegates, but this approach was quickly abandoned.
6 Holley, 'Map of Bahá'í Unity in North America: Mutualizing the Efforts of Believers throughout Canada and the United States to Fulfill the Principles as Set Forth by 'Abdu'l-Bahá in the Divine Plan', printed and drawn material in a jacket. USBNA, Holley papers.
7 Albert Hall, Hooper Harris, Alfred Lunt, and Mountfort Mills were lawyers. They did not all serve simultaneously during the thirteen-year period of the Temple Unity Executive Committee.
8 Official Report of the 1921 Bahá'í Temple Unity Convention, (selections from the transcript of the proceedings sent to all believers by the Executive Board), pp. 33–4, 38. USBNA, National Spiritual Assembly papers.
9 For many years there was a National Convention and a Congress, which took place consecutively. The first was a business meeting and the second was a gathering open to anyone. The Congress proceedings were filled with speeches, performances and, occasionally, workshops.
10 The three charters of the Bahá'í Faith are: The Book of My Covenant, that is, the Will and Testament of Bahá'u'lláh – the Kitáb-i-Ahd; the Tablet of Carmel authorizing the establishment of the World Centre on Mount Carmel; and the Will and Testament of 'Abdu'l-Bahá.

11 The National Spiritual Assembly later decided, based upon a letter it reviewed from 'Abdu'l-Bahá to Corinne True, that it would be better not to circulate such a letter. Letter from Mountfort Mills to Ella Goodall Cooper, 30 June 1922. USBNA, Ella Goodall Cooper papers. Cooper had hoped that gaining signatures on the circular letter of loyalty would also be a means of establishing a nationwide membership list. Those uncomfortable with the contents of the letter would probably not sign it. Letter from Ella Goodall Cooper to Mountfort Mills, 2 June 1922. USBNA, Ella Goodall Cooper papers.
12 Transcript of the Proceedings of the 1922 National Convention. USBNA, National Spiritual Assembly papers.
13 ibid,
14 A few weeks prior to the 1922 Convention, Horace addressed the issue of how the Constitution of Temple Unity could be made to conform to the new guidance contained within the Will and Testament of 'Abdu'l-Bahá. He believed it did not require an amendment, but, if he was mistaken, proposed a change in the By-laws. Letter from Horace Holley to Alfred Lunt, 22 March 1922. USBNA, Temple Unity papers, Box 1. This stimulated Lunt's thinking as a lawyer about the relevance of the Temple Unity Constitution to the new situation. 24 March 1922 Letter to Horace Holley from Alfred Lunt, 24 March 1922. USBNA, Temple Unity papers, Box 1. Horace did not attend the Convention that year.
15 ibid.
16 Official Report of the 1921 Bahá'í Temple Unity Convention, (selections from the transcript of the proceedings sent to all believers by the Executive Board), pp. 20, 24–5. USBNA, National Spiritual Assembly papers.
17 The previous year, only six individuals had received a majority of the votes, so a second vote was taken to determine the other three members. Two people received a majority with the second vote and the Convention decided by acclamation that the Secretary should cast the final vote on behalf of the Convention because the ninth member had not received a majority. Thus, Charles Mason Remey was re-elected to the Board. Horace Holley received the next highest number of votes after Remey. ibid. p. 38.
18 Transcript of the Proceedings of the 1922 National Convention. USBNA, National Spiritual Assembly papers.
19 Corinne Knight True was born into a prosperous family and her husband was successful in business. She always had paid help to take care of the drudgery of housework, freeing her, especially once her children were old enough to care for themselves, from those time-consuming chores. She therefore had leisure time to devote to Bahá'í responsibilities.
20 Ella Goodall Cooper was a 'society woman' whose wealth made it possible for her to participate in the upper class organizations for women in the San Francisco Bay area. Childless, she came from a prominent wealthy family which employed servants. She was married to a successful cardiac surgeon. Like her colleague and friend, Corinne True, she had the means, social status and free time to work on behalf of the Faith, though both were the managers of their households.
21 Gregory, 'The Thirteenth Mashreq'ul-Azkar Convention and Bahai Congress: The Feast of El-Rizwan – Convention and Congress Notes', in *Star of the West*,

vol. 12, no. 4 (17 May 1921), p. 90. The members from the 1921 election who were not elected in 1922 were Louise Boyle and George Latimer. Latimer would, however, subsequently serve on the National Assembly over several decades.
22 Letter from Ella Goodall Cooper to Mountfort Mills, 2 June 1922. USBNA, Ella Goodall Cooper papers.
23 ibid.
24 'Bahai Organization: Its Basis is the Revealed Word', by Louis Gregory, Agnes Parsons, and Mariam Haney on behalf of the National Spiritual Assembly of the United States and Canada, in *Star of the West*, vol. 13, no. 12 (March 1923), pp. 323–8.
25 ibid. p. 323.
26 Letter from Horace Holley to Alfred Lunt, 21 October 1922. USBNA.
27 Shoghi Effendi, *Bahá'í Administration*, p. 58.
28 Letter from Ella Goodall Cooper to Howard MacNutt, 23 June 1923, p. 3. USBNA, Ella Goodall Cooper papers.
29 ibid, p. 1.
30 Shoghi Effendi, *Bahá'í Administration*, pp. 37–9, 42.
31 At the time, the British Bahá'í community lacked people of the capacity of Horace and other American Bahá'í writers. Canada, part of the community with the United States, was a member of the British Commonwealth.
32 Minutes of the National Spiritual Assembly of the United States and Canada, 1 and 2 March, p. 3, USBNA, National Spiritual Assembly papers.
33 ibid. p. 1.
34 Letter from Horace Holley to Alfred Lunt, 9 March 1934. USBNA, Alfred Lunt papers.
35 Letter from Alfred Lunt to Horace Holley, 21 March 1924. USBNA, Alfred Lunt papers.
36 Notes of Baha'i Congress and 16th Annual Convention of the Baha'i Temple Unity, taken by J. E. Revell, p. 7. USBNA, Ella Goodall Cooper papers.
37 ibid. p. 14.
38 ibid. p. 13.
39 According to the US Census records found on the website www.ancestry.com, Bertha Herklotz was born about 1880 in New York City. The information in these records varies, but it appears most likely that her father was born in Germany and her mother in Holland. She never married and usually resided with family members.
40 Minutes of the National Spiritual Assembly of the United States and Canada, 1 & 2 August 1925, p. 3. USBNA, National Assembly papers.
41 ibid. p. 5.
42 Holley, unpublished one-act play, 'I want to live in Greenwich Village'. USBNA, Horace Holley papers.
43 For further reading on the little world of 'The Village' during Horace's years in New York, see Munson, *The Awakening Twenties: A Memoir-History of a Literary Period*; and Watson, *Strange Bedfellows: The First American Avant-Garde*.
44 The statue was of Alexander Lyman Holley, a brilliant engineer who adapted the Beemer process for steelmaking, greatly improving the production of iron and steel. Horace had clippings about this statue among his papers. USBNA.

45 Letter from Horace Holley to Charles Mason Remey, 28 April 1925. USBNA, Holley papers.
46 Letter written on behalf of Shoghi Effendi to the National Spiritual Assembly of the United States and Canada, 20 April 1926. USBNA, National Spiritual Assembly papers.
47 Rabbani, *The Priceless Pearl*, p. 92.
48 'Your personal contributions to so many aspects and phases of the movement, performed so diligently, so effectively and so thoroughly are truly a source of joy and inspiration to me. How much I feel the need for a similar worker by my side in Haifa, as competent, as thorough, as methodical as alert as yourself. You cannot and should not leave your post for the present. Haifa will have to take care of itself for some time.' Letter written on behalf of Shoghi Effendi to Horace Holley as secretary of the National Spiritual Assembly of the United States and Canada, 21 September 1926, with a handwritten postscript by Shoghi Effendi. USBNA, National Spiritual Assembly papers.
49 Letter from Horace Holley to Irving Holley, 26 November [1925?]. Provided to Claire Vreeland by the Holley family and by Vreeland to the author.
50 ibid.
51 Minutes of the National Spiritual Assembly of the United States and Canada, 3 May 1926, p. 1. USBNA, National Spiritual Assembly papers.
52 Minutes of the National Spiritual Assembly of the United States and Canada, 29 April 1928, p. 2. USBNA, National Spiritual Assembly papers.
53 For a brief period, the log cabin Roy Wilhelm built on his property at Teaneck, New Jersey served as the national headquarters. Between 1930 and 1932, while Alfred Lunt served as secretary, the headquarters was associated with him in the Boston area.
54 Letter from Horace Holley to John Herman Randall, 10 April 1927. USBNA, Horace Holley papers.
55 McKay, *Fires in Many Hearts*, p. 47.
56 Letter from Doris McKay to Claire Vreeland, 3 October 1985. In the possession of the author with thanks to the Vreeland Family.
57 McKay, *Fires in Many Hearts* p. 58.
58 ibid.
59 ibid.
60 ibid. pp. 59–60.
61 In 1929 he was also employed part-time for the World Unity Foundation's journal and as the person responsible for St Mark's-in-the-Bowery's real estate holdings.
62 Minutes of the National Spiritual Assembly of the United States and Canada, 28 and 29 April 1929, p. 1. USBNA, National Spiritual Assembly papers.
63 Cable from Shoghi Effendi to Carl Scheffler (Evanston, Illinois), 25 April 1929. USBNA, Horace Holley papers.
64 Minutes of the National Spiritual Assembly of the United States and Canada, 8 and 9 June 19, p. 9. USBNA, National Spiritual Assembly papers.
65 Letter written on behalf of Shoghi Effendi to Horace Holley for the National Spiritual Assembly of the United States and Canada, 18 April 1930. USBNA, National Spiritual Assembly papers.

66 Letter from Hertha Holley to Horace Holley, 26 April [1928?]. USBNA, Horace Holley papers.
67 Hertha must have travelled to Europe with her mother and sister because these two returned to the United States in September of 1928. Ancestry.com: List of United States Citizens arriving in Quebec, Canada from a ship which sailed from Le Havre, France on 7 September 1928. Bertha returned alone to France to check on Hertha in the spring of 1929. Ancestry.com: List of United States Citizens arriving in Quebec, Canada from a ship which sailed from Cherbourg, France on 9 May 1929. Arrangements were made for Hertha to remain under the care of a family friend in France – a fellow portrait artist, Madame da Cordoba.
68 Letter from Dr Forel to Horace Holley, 11 November 1929. Provided by the Holley family to Claire Vreeland, and then to the author; Report from Dr Henri Ernest regarding Miss H. Holley, 13 November 1929. Provided by the Holley family to Claire Vreeland and then to the author.
69 In letters dated 2 and 25 February, and 5 April 1933, Horace writes to Bertha about his finances and inability to continue meeting all the costs of Hertha's care because he has had to take cuts in pay due to the Depression. In the 2 February letter, he states that '. . . this depression has gone so far that I no longer have any margin, and indeed the future has become uncertain'. USBNA, Holley papers, Box 2.
70 An example of Mountfort Mills' correspondence to the Holleys reporting his visits to Hertha on Horace's behalf is one dated 19 September 1930 following a visit to Dr Forel's sanatorium. Letter provided by the Holley family to Claire Vreeland and then to the author. In an earlier letter to Horace dated 12 October 1929, reporting a visit to Hertha and consultation with those caring for her, Mountfort ended by saying, 'I know how hard this must hit you, Old Man, and sympathize with you with all my heart. But it is surely coming out all right.' Letter provided by the Holley family to Claire Vreeland and then to the author.

Mountfort Mills was an international lawyer who married a woman from France. The couple established a second home in Geneva, where his wife passed away in 1929. Mills alternated between Geneva and New York City where, after the death of his wife, he resided at the Harvard Club when in the United States. During this period, Mills worked tirelessly for Shoghi Effendi to resolve the issue of ownership of the House of Bahá'u'lláh in Baghdad. See *The New York Times* obituary for Mountfort Mills published on 25 April 1949, p. 23, and *The New York Times* obituary for Mrs. Adele M. Mills published on 17 December 1929, p. 31.
71 Dr Auguste Forel sent multiple reports to the Holleys. An example is a November 1929 letter from Dr Forel to Horace Holley. Letter provided by the Holley family to Claire Vreeland and then to the author. Dr Forel was not only a ground-breaking expert in the field of psychiatry, but a philosopher who was public about his atheism. 'Abdu'l-Bahá sent him a Tablet in which He proved to Forel's satisfaction the existence of a Supreme Being. A study of Forel's connection to the Bahá'í Faith can be found in Banani, 'The Life and Times of August Forel', in *Lights of Irfan*, vol. 6, pp. 1–20.
72 Minutes of the National Spiritual Assembly of the United States and Canada, 28 April 1930, p. 1. USBNA, National Spiritual Assembly papers. Horace would be

responsible for special letters and the *Bahá'í News Letter*. Nellie French would be responsible for correspondence with non-Bahá'í organizations and international Bahá'í centres. Everything else would be Lunt's responsibility.

73 Letter written on behalf of Shoghi Effendi to the National Spiritual Assembly of the United States and Canada, 30 May 1930. USBNA, National Spiritual Assembly papers.
74 Ancestry.com: List of United States Citizens arriving in New York from Cherbourg, France on 26 January.
75 Minutes of the National Spiritual Assembly of the United States and Canada, 28 April 1930, p. 14. USBNA, National Spiritual Assembly papers.
76 Letter written by Mountfort Mills on behalf of Shoghi Effendi to Horace Holley as Secretary of the National Spiritual Assembly of the United States and Canada, 11 December 1926. USBNA, National Spiritual Assembly papers.
77 Minutes of the Meeting of the National Spiritual Assembly, 12 to 15 November 1925, p. 3. USBNA, National Spiritual Assembly papers; Letter written on behalf of the National Assembly by Alfred Lunt to Miss Greenacre, attorney, 9 March 1926. USBNA, Alfred E. Lunt papers, Box 2.
78 *Black's Law Dictionary* defines Declaration of Trust as 'The act by which the person who holds the legal title to property or an estate acknowledges and declares that he holds the same in trust to the use of another person or for certain specified purposes. The name is also used to designate the deed or other writing embodying such a declaration.' https://thelawdictionary.org/declaration-of-trust/.
79 Bahá'u'lláh, *The Kitáb-i-Aqdas*, para. 30, p. 29.
80 Letter written on behalf of Shoghi Effendi to the National Spiritual Assembly of the United States and Canada, 25 August 1927. Research Department of the Universal House of Justice, 'Passages Regarding the Constitutions of National and Local Spiritual Assemblies', February 2019, prepared at the request of the author.
81 Letter written on behalf of Shoghi Effendi to the National Spiritual Assembly of the United States and Canada, 15 December 1926. ibid.
82 Letter from the National Spiritual Assembly of the United States and Canada to Shoghi Effendi, 9 July 1931. The Guardian used the American incorporation to create a Palestinian branch of that legal entity which could hold title to real estate. USBNA, National Spiritual Assembly papers.
83 Letter written on behalf of Shoghi Effendi to the National Spiritual Assembly of the United States and Canada, 15 December 1926. Research Department of the Universal House of Justice, 'Passages Regarding the Constitutions of National and Local Spiritual Assemblies', February 2019, prepared at the request of the author.
84 'Shoghi Effendi was astonished to see, however, that in the Certificate of Incorporation, you do not have the articles mentioned in the Declaration of Trust whereby the Assembly is empowered to enter into contracts, accept bequests, and act as a fully empowered legal person. He thinks that it is very essential to provide the Assembly with such a power, for it is sure that the need for it will arise in the future. Many undoubtedly will try to leave something for the Cause in their will and perhaps the Assembly will have to create institutions such as schools, hospitals and orphanages for these are among its essential activities.

Shoghi Effendi would very much like to know whether the Certificate of Incorporation will give the Assembly such powers.' Letter on behalf of Shoghi Effendi to the National Spiritual Assembly of the United States and Canada, 20 April 1932. Research Department of the Universal House of Justice, 'Passages Regarding the Constitutions of National and Local Spiritual Assemblies', February 2019, prepared at the request of the author.
85 Rabbani, *The Priceless Pearl*, p. 302.
86 Holley, 'The Spirit and Form of Bahá'í Administration', in *The Bahá'í World*, vol. III (1928–1930), pp. 9–16.
87 Shoghi Effendi, *God Passes By*, pp. 334–6.
88 Shoghi Effendi, *Bahá'í Administration*, pp. 142–3.
89 See, for example, letter from Florence Morton, treasurer of the National Spiritual Assembly, to Corinne True, treasurer for Temple Unity, 5 June 1925. USBNA, Carl Scheffler papers, Box 4.
90 Letter from Alfred Lunt to Corinne True, 5 November 1924, p. 2, USBNA, Carl Scheffler papers, Box 4.
91 Letter from Nellie French to Shoghi Effendi, 3 February 1929. USBNA, Nellie French papers, Box 1.
92 Letter from Horace Holley to Alfred Lunt, 8 September 1924, p. 1. USBNA, Temple Unity papers, Box 1.
93 ibid.
94 ibid.
95 Holley, Introduction to Shoghi Effendi, *Bahá'í Administration*, p. ix.
96 For example, see letter from Horace Holley, secretary of the National Assembly, to Carl Scheffler, secretary of the Temple Committee, 21 October 1925. USBNA, Carl Scheffler papers, Box 2. The National Assembly sent a letter to the believers to combine and coordinate the goals of the Temple and those of teachings. The foremost member of the Temple Committee objected that this was a usurpation of the authority of the Committee. Horace gently explained that 'the unifying of the various branches of the work is, of course, the particular function of the N.S.A.'.
97 Letter from Carl Scheffler to Horace Holley, 27 December 1925. USBNA, Carl Scheffler papers, Box 2.
98 Letter from Horace Holley to Carl Scheffler, 6 January 1926 (on National Spiritual Assembly stationery). USBNA, Carl Scheffler papers, Box 2.
99 Shoghi Effendi, *Bahá'í Administration*, p. 45. From a letter from Shoghi Effendi to the members of the American National Spiritual Assembly, 9 April 1923.
100 ibid.
101 ibid.

10 Building the World Anew Is a Messy Business
1 Shoghi Effendi, *Bahá'í Administration*, p. 108.
2 Minutes of the New York Spiritual Assembly, 15 July 1926, pp. 1–2. Juliet Thompson met with the Assembly to convey concerns of Shoghi Effendi on his behalf about the development of factions within the community due to differences of opinion regarding teaching. New York Bahá'í Archives.
3 Lua Getsinger, accompanied by her husband, Edward Getsinger, went to India to teach the Faith at the direction of 'Abdu'l-Bahá. See Hogenson, *Lighting the Western Sky*.

4 See, for example, Minutes of the National Spiritual Assembly, 3 and 4 October 1925, p. 6, in which Ella Goodall Cooper reported that the friends in England disapproved of the American community paying teachers. The National Assembly decided to continue the practice at that time. USBNA, National Spiritual Assembly papers. There are other pilgrim notes addressing the subject of paid teachers. While not forbidding the practice, Shoghi Effendi usually pointed out the spiritual principles that all should have a profession, and all should teach.

5 See, for example, letter written on behalf of the National Spiritual Assembly of the United States and Canada by Horace Holley to Albert Vail, 30 October 1925. USBNA.

6 Letter from Shoghi Effendi to the National Spiritual Assembly of the United States and Canada, 9 January 1932. USBNA, National Spiritual Assembly files. Green Acre was the first Baháʼí retreat facility hosting summer schools. By the 1930s, there was also a primitive facility in Geyserville, California, later named Bosch Baháʼí School, and a farm in Davison, Michigan, used for training sessions. This last location would become Louhelen Baháʼí School.

7 For a worthy account of the beginning of the Great Depression, see Johnson, *A History of the American People*. Both Johnson, and Shlaes in *The Forgotten Man* explore the change in understanding of the economics of the Great Depression. With the passage of time and better knowledge of economics, many economists have concluded that, had the Federal Government not tried to intervene, the economic downturn could have righted itself through the forces inherent in the business cycle. Manipulation of the economy by experimental government intervention made everything worse, especially unemployment. Absent Hoover's policies, many experts believe there would have been a short-lived recession such as in 1920 under President Harding, and not a depression. What made the situation especially disastrous were the imposition of tariffs and high government taxes on businesses and the wealthy that drained the capital needed to expand the economy and reduce unemployment. These policies stifled international trade. In the midst of the Depression, Shoghi Effendi pointed out in his World Order letters that the economic experiments by the government were disastrous. It took many decades before noted economists would arrive at the same conclusion.

8 Ancestry.com: 1880 and 1900 US Census.

9 Letter from Carl Scheffler to Shoghi Effendi, 14 July 1934, in which he states that members of the National Assembly were sending money through him to help Lunt with his living expenses because he was 'in dire need'. USBNA, Carl Scheffler papers, Box 1.

10 In a letter from Horace Holley to Allen McDaniel dated 2 May 1930, Horace laments that he had been included in the Secretariat because he felt he had no defined role. He was editor of the newsletter, and to him, that was sufficient. He comments how his name had been suggested for inclusion in the Secretariat with the hope that it would help him and Fred Lunt to get to know each other better. Horace commented that this seemed to him to be 'an artificial method of association', for 'There can be no stronger association than as fellow members of the N.S.A. . . .' McDaniel replied by saying 'Shoghi Effendi has great faith in your capacities and abilities in the administrative work. I have a very definite feeling that he would wish and would be happy to have you as a member of

the Secretariat.' Letter from Allen McDaniel to Horace Holley, 3 May 1930. USBNA, Allen McDaniel papers, Box 6.
11 During the first year of the National Assembly, two members contemplated resigning because they found Lunt and at least one other member difficult to work with.
12 *The New York Times*, 14 August 1937, p. 13. For brief summaries of the life of Alfred 'Fred' Eastman Lunt, see Gregory and Ober, 'Alfred Eastman Lunt', In Memoriam, *The Bahá'í World*, vol. VII (1936–1938), pp. 531–4; Whitehead, *Some Early Bahá'ís of the West*, pp. 121–9.
13 See, for example, letter from Carl Scheffler to Shoghi Effendi, 14 July 1934. USBNA, Carl Scheffler papers, Box 1. In his letter to Shoghi Effendi describing the years of problems between Lunt and the other members of the National Assembly, Scheffler states that 'he reasons sometimes entirely without logic'. He attributed this in part to the financial stress Lunt was under. See also letter from the National Spiritual Assembly of the United States and Canada to Shoghi Effendi, 11 August 1933, p. 1. USBNA, National Spiritual Assembly files. Horace gave his personal opinion, without giving Lunt's name, that Fred 'arrives at conclusions frequently based upon a personal impression which fails to consider all the facts. This type moreover once having arrived at a conclusion tends to retain it against all proof and argument.'
14 Morrison, *To Move the World: Louis G. Gregory and the Advancement of Racial Unity in America*, p. 316.
15 Minutes of the National Spiritual Assembly of the United States and Canada, 2 and 3 May 1932, p. 4. USBNA, National Spiritual Assembly papers.
16 It is doubtful that Horace believed that the teachers were only needed until the House of Worship was completed because he expressed several times in his correspondence with Florence Morton that the completion of the superstructure, especially the dome with its ornamentation, would require more concerted teaching efforts because the building was likely to attract positive attention.
17 ibid.
18 ibid.
19 Letter from the National Spiritual Assembly to Shoghi Effendi, 9 November 1933. USBNA, National Spiritual Assembly papers.
20 In response to the National Spiritual Assembly's decision to cease employing full-time teachers, in a letter written on his behalf Shoghi Effendi said: 'Concerning the abolition of the institution of paid national teachers, the Guardian wishes to reaffirm his former statements on this matter, and to stress once more that great care be taken to avoid the difficulties and the misunderstandings which in former days had caused so much trouble among the friends. *The main point to be emphasized in this connection is that of making the teachings of the Cause not the work of a limited group but the chief duty and responsibility of every Bahá'í. This why no salaried teachers should any longer exist.* But occasionally to defray the expenses of a teaching trip of a certain Bahá'í, particularly when it is done spontaneously, can cause no harm to the Cause. Such an action, provided it is done with care and only when circumstances make it necessary, constitutes no violation of the principle already referred to. The danger in all activities of this nature is to give the impression that the teaching of the Cause is an institution,

depending on the support of paid teachers. Those who willingly and with utmost detachment arise to promote the Cause should, undoubtedly, be helped in every way. But they have no claim whatever on the financial help which some friends may freely choose to extend to them.' Letter written on behalf of Shoghi Effendi to Leroy Ioas, chairman of the National Teaching Committee, 5 March 1934, published in *Bahá'í News*, no. 84 (June 1934), p. 12.

21 Letter from Sam G. McClelland, nephew of Albert Vail, to Claire Vreeland, 21 April 1989. I am grateful to the Vreeland family for providing this letter. Dr McClelland, despite his uncle's defection, was a devoted believer who served many years in the role of Auxiliary Board member for protection. See also the letter from Carl Scheffler to Shoghi Effendi, 14 July 1934, in which Scheffler describes the situation with Vail and his own attempts as well as that of others to reach out to him. Scheffler lived in the Chicago area, so knew Vail well over many years. USBNA, Scheffler papers, Box 1.

22 I am grateful to Mary J. Watson for her memories of Albert Vail as an elderly man.

23 Minutes of the National Spiritual Assembly of the United States and Canada, 24 and 24 September 1932, p. 16. USBNA, National Spiritual Assembly papers.

24 Letter from Louis Gregory to Horace Holley, 17 November 1932. USBNA, National Spiritual Assembly papers. Quoted in Morrison, *To Move the World: Louis G. Gregory and the Advancement of Racial Unity in America*, p. 234. Morrison gives a lengthy exploration of this episode from the point of view of Gregory, who found Horace's manner of speaking, especially his humour, to be sharp – even harsh. This probably reflected the different regions of the country and different social classes the two men came from more than Horace's sentiments, for at that time there were wide divergences in regional ways of speaking as well as etiquette in the United States. In other words, the two might as well have come from different planets. Gregory also had heard Horace make comments prior to the 1932 decision that led him to believe that Horace did not approve of paying teachers. Gregory's assessment of Horace's attitude is not borne out in Horace's correspondence with other people. For example, Horace did not question the wisdom of a wealthy believer providing financial support to Elizabeth Greenleaf so that she could travel as a teacher.

Morrison's portrayal of Horace's return to the role of secretary as a power play is inaccurate. The Guardian had made it clear to the National Assembly that he was upset when Horace asked to be relieved as secretary in 1930. His reason for resigning his office was the family crisis of his daughter's mental illness that required him to seek employment that paid more than his work for the National Assembly because of the high costs of her expenses. In 1932, the Holleys were finally able to arrange the return of their daughter to the United States from a hospital in Europe, making the situation less critical. At the same time, Lunt's law practice was suffering because of the Depression, therefore it required more of his attention. Thus, in 1932, it became possible for Horace to resume serving full-time as secretary, allowing Lunt to focus on supporting his family. The members of the National Assembly well knew that Shoghi Effendi wanted Horace to be secretary because he had reiterated that sentiment in several letters. It was an unusually stressful time in the lives of both men, which may explain in part the raw emotions and perhaps occasionally undiplomatic communications.

Louis Gregory had the right to appeal the National Assembly's decision to both the National Assembly and the Guardian, which he did. He did not, however, have a right to challenge the decision publicly because, by doing so, he undermined confidence in the National Spiritual Assembly as an institution. There is no doubt that Horace was a strong-willed person whom many people treated with deference because of his knowledge and experience, but several of his fellow Assembly members possessed domineering personalities and would never defer to another member. Overall, correspondence and minutes of the National Assembly during this period of the early 1930s show that his colleagues respected Horace's input but did not always follow his suggestions. Horace was in constant communication with Shoghi Effendi about not only National Assembly business, but also New York City and *The Bahá'í World* business. Given this constant interchange, it is not surprising that Horace's point of view increasingly conformed with the Guardian's.

25 Report, Twenty-fifth Annual Convention of the Bahá'ís of the United States and Canada, 1–4 June 1933. USBNA, National Spiritual Assembly papers. That year, the National Assembly employed a stenographer who produced a transcript rather than a summary.
26 Letter from the National Spiritual Assembly of the United States and Canada to Shoghi Effendi, 19 July 1933, p. 3. USBNA, National Spiritual Assembly papers.
27 Letter from Florence Morton to Horace Holley, 5 July 1933, p. 2. USBNA, Horace Holley papers.
28 Letter from Allen McDaniel to Horace Holley, 10 June 1933. USBNA, McDaniel papers, Box 6.
29 Letter from the National Spiritual Assembly to Shoghi Effendi, 10 June 1933. USBNA, National Spiritual Assembly papers.
30 ibid. p. 1.
31 ibid. See also Bramson-Lerche, 'Some Aspects of the Development of the Bahá'í Administrative Order in America, 1922–1936', in *Studies in Bábí and Bahá'í History*, vol. 1, edited by Moojan Momen, p. 286.
32 Letter from the National Spiritual Assembly to Shoghi Effendi, 19 July 1933, quoted ibid. p. 287. The fact that the vote for the change to the By-Laws was eight to one is in the letter from the National Spiritual Assembly to the Guardian, 10 June 1933. USBNA, National Spiritual Assembly papers.
33 Letter from the National Spiritual Assembly to Shoghi Effendi, 10 June 1933, p. 2. USBNA, National Spiritual Assembly papers.
34 Will and Testament of 'Abdu'l-Bahá, next to last paragraph.
35 Letter from the National Spiritual Assembly of the United States and Canada to Shoghi Effendi, 19 July 1933, p. 2. USBNA, National Spiritual Assembly papers.
36 Letter from the National Spiritual Assembly of the United States and Canada to Shoghi Effendi, 2 May 1934, p. 2. USBNA, National Spiritual Assembly papers.
37 Letter written on behalf of Shoghi Effendi to the National Spiritual Assembly of the United States and Canada, 12 August 1933, published in *Bahá'í News*, no. 79 (November 1933), pp. 9–10.

NOTES AND REFERENCES

38 ibid.
39 ibid.
40 ibid. p. 10.
41 ibid.
42 Letter written on behalf of Shoghi Effendi to Alfred Lunt, 12 August 1933. It was attached to the minutes of the National Spiritual Assembly of the United States and Canada, 23, 24, 25 September 1933. USBNA, National Spiritual Assembly papers.
43 Talk by Horace Holley, 'The Local Community', delivered on 24 February 1931 to the New York City Bahá'í community. USBNA, Horace Holley papers, Box 6.
44 Letter from Leroy Ioas and George Latimer to the other members of the National Spiritual Assembly through Horace Holley, 23 July 1934. This letter summarizes the understanding of the two West Coast members of the Lunt matter. They said: 'Mr. Lunt apparently understands the implications of Bahai Administration in an entirely different light than that held by the Assembly. He feels that centralized authority in a small group of people is detrimental to the interests of the Bahai Faith and of the developing social structure. We see that the only means of protecting the unity of the Bahai Faith, is in a strong centralized authority in the Institutions of Spiritual Assemblies (both Local and National), as outlined in the Will and Testament of the Master' (p. 2). USBNA, Carl Scheffler papers.
45 Letter written on behalf of Shoghi Effendi to Alfred E. Lunt, 11 November 1933, published in 'The National Spiritual Assembly', in *The Compilation of Compilations*, vol II, no. 1496.
46 Letter from Florence Morton to Horace Holley, 8 April 1935 p. 3. Morton, who lived in the Boston area, was informed of the details of what happened by members of the Boston Assembly, who were appalled by Lunt's letter. USBNA, Horace Holley papers.
47 Letter from the National Spiritual Assembly of the United States and Canada to Shoghi Effendi, 2 May 1934. USBNA, National Spiritual Assembly papers.
48 *Bahá'í News*, no. 85 (July 1934), p. 2, quoting a letter written on behalf of Shoghi Effendi on 19 May 1934 to an individual.
49 Letter from Horace Holley to Florence Morton, 3 May 1934. USBNA, Horace Holley papers.
50 When the Guardian appointed Hands of the Cause and later instituted the institution of the Auxiliary Board, these servants were able to assume the role of counsellor to those who were creating difficulties. Furthermore, the Universal House of Justice was empowered to intervene in cases such as the one of Fred Lunt. The Guardian was willing to guide, yet hesitant to insist, because the role of making administrative decisions belonged to the House of Justice.
51 Undated statement, 'To the Delegates of the 26th Annual Convention'. USBNA, National Spiritual Assembly papers. Both statements bear the hallmarks of Horace's pen, though they are certainly the fruit of the consultation of the National Assembly.
52 ibid.
53 ibid.
54 ibid. p. 5.

55 ibid. The National Assembly was quoting the personal note at the end of an letter to Allen McDaniel, chairman of the National Assembly, from Shoghi Effendi, 8 August 1933.
56 ibid.
57 Letter from the National Spiritual Assembly of the United States and Canada to the Delegates of the 1934 Convention, 'To the Delegates, 26th Annual Convention', p. 3. USBNA, National Spiritual Assembly papers.
58 ibid.
59 Letter from the National Spiritual Assembly of the United States and Canada to Shoghi Effendi, 9 July 1934, p. 2. USBNA, National Spiritual Assembly papers.
60 Letter written on behalf of Shoghi Effendi to the National Spiritual Assembly of the United States and Canada, 11 June 1934, in *Bahá'í News*, no. 85 (July 1934).
61 Letter from Allen McDaniel to Carl Scheffler, 2 July 1934. USBNA, Carl Scheffler papers, Box 2. Both were absent from the meeting and McDaniel was conveying what he learned about it. McDaniel commented that, 'Assuming that the Guardian confirms this action, it will require all of our faith and courage to meet the reaction of some of the believers who are still functioning on the personal plane and who fail to realize the importance of establishing the administration on a true and sound basis.'
62 Letter from Alfred E. Lunt to the National Spiritual Assembly of the United States and Canada, 3 July 1934. USBNA, Alfred E. Lunt papers, Box 2.
63 Letter from the National Spiritual Assembly of the United States and Canada to Shoghi Effendi, 9 July 1934. USBNA, National Spiritual Assembly papers.
64 ibid.
65 Cablegram from Shoghi Effendi to the National Spiritual Assembly of the United States and Canada, 13 July 1934, USBNA, National Spiritual Assembly papers.
66 Letter written on behalf of Shoghi Effendi to the National Spiritual Assembly of the United States and Canada, 7 August 1934. USBNA, National Spiritual Assembly papers.
67 ibid.
68 Letter from Horace Holley to Florence Morton, 14 July 1934. USBNA, Horace Holley papers.
69 Letter from Leroy Ioas and George Latimer to the other members of the National Spiritual Assembly through Horace Holley, 23 July 1934. USBNA, Carl Scheffler papers, Box 1.
70 Draft of cablegram from the National Spiritual Assembly of the United States and Canada to Shoghi Effendi, 11 August 1934. USBNA, National Spiritual Assembly papers.
71 *Bahá'í News*, no. 87 (September 1934).
72 Cablegram from the National Spiritual Assembly of the United States and Canada to Shoghi Effendi, 21 August 1934. USBNA, National Spiritual Assembly papers.
73 Cablegram from Shoghi Effendi to the National Spiritual Assembly of the United States and Canada, 25 August 1934. USBNA, National Spiritual Assembly papers.
74 Whitehead, *Some Early Bahá'ís of the West*, p. 129.

75 Undated letter from Horace Holley to Rouhanieh [Latimer?] written at Green Acre. USBNA, George Latimer papers, Box 9.
76 For an in-depth exploration of the Lunt matter, see: 'The Lunt Affair, 1933–34', pp. 284–95, in Bramson-Lerche, 'Some Aspects of the Development of the Bahá'í Administrative Order in America, 1922–1936'.
77 Notes at Haifa, 12 May 1932, pp. 1–7; combined notes of Lorol Schopflocher and Keith Ransom-Kehler approved by Clara Dunn and Lyle Loveday. USBNA.
78 Rabbani, *The Priceless Pearl*, p. 213.

11 Understanding the Quest for World Peace: The Continuing Education of Horace Holley

1 Holley, 'Introduction', *Foundations of World Unity: Compiled from Addresses and Tablets of 'Abdu'l-Bahá*, p. 5.
2 Letter from Polly Marlowe to Claire Vreeland, 24 February 1989. Original in the possession of the author with thanks to Claire Vreeland and her family.
3 The Guardian gratefully acknowledged that the suggestion for the yearbook came from Horace. Shoghi Effendi, *Bahá'í Administration*, p. 74.
4 Letter from Horace Holley to Irving Holley, 26 November [1925?]. Provided to Claire Vreeland by the Holley family and by Vreeland to the author.
5 Letter written on behalf of Shoghi Effendi to Horace Holley, 12 March 1926. USBNA, National Spiritual Assembly papers.
6 Letter from Shoghi Effendi to the Bahá'ís in the East and the West, 6 December 1928 published in *The Bahá'í World*, vol. III (1928–1930), p. xiv.
7 Horace drafted the section on the 'Aims and Purposes of the Bahá'í Faith' and then it was repeated with only minor revisions in many editions. This was true also of the section on the Administrative Order. Horace drafted a summary, and it was used again and again.
8 See, for example, letters written on behalf of Shoghi Effendi to Horace Holley, 1 June 1938 and 15 May 1940. USBNA.
9 Shoghi Effendi's secretaries wrote to key people in different regions of the world asking them to submit material and providing them with Horace's contact information.
10 For example, Nellie French, writing of her own experience serving on *The Bahá'í World* editorial board, said, 'What experience and training I have had has been due to the assistance of Mr. Holley . . .'. USBNA, Nellie French papers, Box 1: Unpublished Memoirs of Mrs. Stuart French, Chapter XIV, 'Services at Home', p. 73.
11 Letter written on behalf of Shoghi Effendi to Horace Holley, 22 March 1932. USBNA, Horace Holley papers.
12 ibid.
13 Talks of 'Abdu'l-Bahá do not have the same status as sacred literature as do His written works.
14 'Abdu'l-Bahá, *Foundations of World Unity*, p. 8.
15 Letter from Horace Holley to Florence Morton, 30 December 1933. USBNA.
16 These talks, except for the one given at Lake Mohonk, are all available in *The Promulgation of Universal Peace: Talks Delivered by 'Abdu'l-Bahá during His Visit to the United States and Canada in 1912*.

17 For a comprehensive biography of Leroy Ioas see Chapman, *Leroy Ioas: Hand of the Cause of God*.
18 Letter from Horace Holley to Leroy Ioas, 21 July 1936. USBNA, Leroy Ioas papers, Box 3.
19 An interesting side note to the Holley/Latimer friendship is that both attended Williams College at the same time and even resided in the same dormitory. Horace was a year ahead of George academically and three years older, and so they were no more than acquaintances at the time. They often mentioned the Williams connection in their correspondence.
20 *Bahá'í News Letter: The Bulletin of the National Spiritual Assembly of the Bahá'ís of the United States and Canada*, no. 12 (June–July 1926), pp. 6–7.
21 Letter from Horace Holley to Albert Vail, 21 October 1925. USBNA.
22 Letter written on behalf of Shoghi Effendi to Horace Holley, 29 November 1926. USBNA.
23 This was Agnes Macphail, who spoke at the Montreal Conference which was chaired by William Sutherland Maxwell. Nakhjavani, *The Maxwells of Montreal: Middle Years 1923–1937, Late Years 1937–1952*, p. 74.
24 Shoghi Effendi, *Bahá'í Administration*, p. 117.
25 Since Horace had fled Paris, France, with his wife and young child at the beginning of World War I in September 1914, he keenly understood the significance of 'Abdu'l-Bahá's prediction that another war was coming in His second Tablet to the Hague, written after the Great War. Letter from Horace Holley to Albert Vail, 21 October 1925. USBNA, Vail papers. Mary Movius, in discussing Dr Randall's upcoming role as primary spokesman for the World Unity Foundation with him, mentions her concern about where the coming war will start. Letter from Mary Movius to John Randall, 11 June [1927?]. USBNA.
26 *Bahá'í News Letter: The Bulletin of the National Spiritual Assembly of the Bahá'ís of the United States and Canada*, no. 20 (November 1927), p. 5.
27 Letter from Horace Holley to Shoghi Effendi, 30 June 1927. USBNA.
28 ibid.
29 ibid.
30 Mountfort Mills, a lawyer from New York City and former chairman of the National Spiritual Assembly, was also part of this consultation, but at the time he was engaged in frequent travels abroad on behalf of the work of the Faith. As much as possible, Mills served as an advisor to and promoter of the World Unity Foundation.
31 Randall was one of two white Christian clergymen in New York City who played active roles in the Bahá'í community during the 1920s and 1930s. Shoghi Effendi wrote, 'I am delighted to learn of the evidences of growing interest, of sympathetic understanding, and brotherly cooperation on the part of two capable and steadfast servants of the One True God, Dr. [John] H. Randall and Dr. [William Norman] Guthrie, whose participation in our work I hope and pray will widen the scope of our activities, enrich our opportunities, and lend a fresh impetus to our endeavors.' *Bahá'í Administration*, p. 82. (Two Black clergymen were also involved. See Chapter 8.) For a brief summary of Randall's life, see Day, 'Randall, John Herman', in Kuehl (ed.), *Biographical Dictionary of Internationalists*, pp. 595–97. See also 'John Herman Randall Sr.: Pioneer liberal,

philosopher, pacifist' by one of his grandsons [David Randall?] at http://freepages.rootsweb.com/~knower/genealogy/johnhermansrcareer.htm.
32 At the time in 1927, several ordained clergymen were members of the Bahá'í Faith; for example, Albert Vail was a paid Bahá'í teacher and Unitarian minister.
33 The Board of Trustees of the World Unity Foundation included the following Bahá'ís: Horace H. Holley, Mountfort Mills, Florence Reed Morton, and Mary Rumsey Movius. The other members were: Reverend John Herman Randall (non-denominational Protestant), Reverend Alfred W. Martin (Unitarian), and Melbert B. Cary (friend of Dr Randall). The members of the Honorary Committee for the Foundation were: S. Parkes Cadman, Carrie Chapman Catt, Rudolph I. Coffee, John Dewey, Harry Emerson Fosdick, Herbert Adams Gibbons, Mordecai W. Johnson, James Weldon Johnson, Rufus M. Jones, David Starr Jordan, Harry Levi, Louis L. Mann, Pierrepont B. Noyes, Harry Allen Overstreet, William R. Shepherd, Augustus O. Thomas. *Bahá'í News Letter: The Bulletin of the National Spiritual Assembly of the Bahá'ís of the United States and Canada*, no. 22 (March 1928), p. 8.
34 See 'Abdu'l-Bahá, *The Promulgation of Universal Peace*, pp. 147–50, for 'Abdu'l-Bahá's talk given at the Mount Morris Baptist Church where Reverend Randall was pastor at the time.
35 *'Abdu'l-Bahá in New York: The City of the Covenant: April–December, 1912*, ff. The foreword is by John Herman Randall.
36 Randall's correspondence with Horace during this period indicates that Randall and the head of The Community Church were no longer getting along, and so Randall welcomed the opportunity to begin different employment. This is discussed in a number of letters in 1927 by both Horace and Randall. USBNA, Horace Holley papers.
37 Letter from John Herman Randall to Horace Holley, 13 August 1927. USBNA, Horace Holley papers.
38 Letter from Horace Holley to John Herman Randall, 23 August [1927?]. USBNA, Horace Holley papers.
39 ibid.
40 Letter from Horace Holley to John Herman Randall, 10 April 1927. USBNA, Horace Holley papers.
41 ibid.
42 Letter written by Horace Holley to John Herman Randall, 23 August [1927?]. USBNA, Horace Holley papers, Box 4.
43 Letter from Horace Holley to Florence Morton, 24 August 1931. USBNA.
44 Letter from Horace Holley to Florence Morton, 7 July 1932. USBNA, Horace Holley papers, Box 3.
45 Printed announcement of the forthcoming World Unity Magazine to solicit subscribers. USBNA.
46 Frank Lloyd Wright and Horace Holley were friends. It was Horace who convinced Wright to submit an article. Wright then offered to redesign the magazine's cover. His design, with some modifications, was first used for the October 1929 edition of *World Unity*. Website: The Wright Library, http://www.steinerag.com/flw/Periodicals/1930-39.htm. (The article quoted on the website assumes that Holley and Wright met through their mutual friend, Dr Guthrie. Actually,

they first met in Italy in 1910. Letter from Horace Holley to Irving Holley from Florence, Italy, dated Easter Sunday [1910], in the possession of the author.)
47 Day, 'Randall, John Herman', in Kuehl (ed.), *Biographical Dictionary of Internationalists,* pp. 595–97.
48 Most of what is published about Dr Randall's work with the World Unity Foundation is derived from memorials to him written by his descendants or from his own books.
49 The decision to make the magazine more openly Bahá'í was taken in 1932. Letter from Horace Holley to Florence Morton, 28 October 1932, p. 2. USBNA. In a 1933 letter to Morton, Holley pointed out to her how he was trying to 'build a bridge of sympathetic understanding between World Unity readers and the Articles of the Cause which will be published later on' through his more recent editorials. Letter from Horace Holley to Florence Morton, 2 February 1933, p. 2. USBNA. See also an explanation of the careful transition to Bahá'í content in letter from Horace Holley to Mary Movius, 7 January 1933. USBNA.
50 Letter from Horace Holley to Florence Morton, 29 November 1933. USBNA, Horace Holley papers, Box 3.
51 Morrison, *To Move the World: Louis G. Gregory and the Advancement of Racial Unity in America,* pp. 160–62. See also letter from Florence Morton to Horace Holley, 4 July 1932. USBNA, Horace Holley papers, Box 3.
52 See, for example, letters from Nellie French to Shoghi Effendi, 7 May 1928 and 3 November 1928. USBNA, Nellie French papers, Box 1.
53 Shoghi Effendi, *Bahá'í Administration,* pp. 124–8.
54 ibid. pp. 124–5.
55 ibid. p. 125.
56 Shoghi Effendi, *The World Order of Bahá'u'lláh: Selected Letters by Shoghi Effendi.*
57 Letter from Horace Holley to Florence Morton, 9 November 1933. USBNA, Horace Holley papers, Box 3. In that letter, Horace describes the classes held in New York to study the World Order letters and that he had given a course on Bahá'í administration and was conducting a series of classes on the letters.
58 Bahá'u'lláh called 'Abdu'l-Bahá 'The Master' and encouraged others to do so as well. 'Abdu'l-Bahá took on the name Servant of Bahá; that is, 'Abdu'l-Bahá, after his Father's death. 'Abdu'l-Bahá preferred His new name. Because The Master may have other connotations to the modern reader, it is only used in quotations in this book.
59 Letter from Horace Holley to Florence Morton, 15 March 1934. USBNA, Horace Holley papers, Box 4.
60 ibid.
61 'Introduction', in p. vi.
62 Letter from Florence Morton to Horace Holley, 7 July 1932. USBNA.
63 Shoghi Effendi, *The World Order of Bahá'u'lláh,* p. 64.
64 Letter written on behalf of Shoghi Effendi to Horace Holley, 16 March 1933, in which the question of voting in civil elections was clarified. It stated: 'The friends may vote if they can do it without identifying themselves with one party or another.' USBNA, National Spiritual Assembly papers.
65 Letter from Mary Movius to Horace Holley, 12 January [1933?]. USBNA, Horace Holley papers, Box 4.

66 Holley, 'The Clue to World Strife', in *World Unity*, vol. 13, no. 1 (October 1933), pp. 1–11.
67 Letter written on behalf of Shoghi Effendi to Horace Holley, 7 November 1933. USBNA.
68 ibid, p. 4. This letter was handwritten.
69 Letter from Horace Holley to Florence Morton, 23 March 1933. USBNA.
70 Holley, 'Current Bahá'í Activities', in *The Bahá'í World*, vol. V (1932–1934), p. 21.
71 Letter from Horace Holley to Florence Morton, 7 July 1932, and letter from Florence Morton to Horace Holley, 29 September 1932. USBNA, Horace Holley papers, Box 3. Mrs Morton had made it clear to Randall that his resignation was desired. The directors were greatly disappointed in Randall's job performance.
72 Letter from Horace Holley to Florence Morton, 24 August 1931. USBNA.
73 Letter from Horace Holley to Florence Morton, 7 July 1932. USBNA, Horace Holley papers, Box 3.
74 Both Randall and Holley were paid for their services, but after the financial crisis started, Holley took a cut in salary even as his responsibilities increased. For a time, he drew no pay but funded the journal from his own savings. Letter from Horace Holley to Florence Morton, 1 April 1933; see also letter from Horace Holley to Mary Movius, 20 March 1933. USBNA, Horace Holley papers, Box 4.
75 For an engaging discussion of US foreign policy during the 1920s and early 1930s which includes the religious views of the American Presidents of the period, see McDougall, *The Tragedy of U.S. Foreign Policy: How America's Civil Religion Betrayed the National Interest*, pp. 182–99.
76 Holley, 'The New Internationalism and World Peace', in *World Unity*, vol. 12, no. 6 (September 1933), p. 321.
77 Letter from Mary Movius to Horace Holley, 11 March (no year). USBNA, Horace Holley papers, Box 4.
78 'World Order Magazine', in *Bahá'í News*, no. 99 (April 1936), p. 12.
79 Letter written on behalf of Shoghi Effendi to Horace Holley, 12 November 1933. USBNA.
80 For example, in a letter written on behalf of Shoghi Effendi to Horace Holley from early 1932 (handwritten date is undecipherable), the Guardian praises Horace for agreeing to serve as an assistant to the National Assembly treasurer, Roy Wilhelm, during the period Horace had asked not to serve as full-time secretary. The letter said in part: 'Shoghi Effendi fully appreciates your talents and wants them to be used wholly for the Cause' (p. 2). But the Guardian understood that some kinds of service appealed to Horace more than others – especially presenting the Faith to leaders of thought and the public. The letter reminded Horace that the drudgery work of the Faith was also important, and that he had the ability to do both well. While Horace might find the public presentation of the Faith to be more interesting, he should consider 'what is of greater consequence for the administration of the Cause'. Letter written on behalf of Shoghi Effendi to Horace Holley, 1932. USBNA.
81 Letter from Horace Holley to Florence Morton, 23 January 1934. USBNA, Horace Holley papers, Box 3.
82 Letter from Horace Holley to Mary Movius, 21 December 1932. USBNA, Horace Holley papers, Box 4.

83 *Bahá'í News*, no. 90 (March 1935), p. 8.
84 Letter from Horace Holley to Florence Morton, 17 March 1933. USBNA, Horace Holley papers, Box 3.
85 See, for example, letter from Horace Holley to Florence Morton, 22 November 1935, reporting comments about the combined magazines. USBNA.
86 Letter from Horace Holley to Allen McDaniel, 4 June 1935. USBNA, Allen McDaniel papers, Box 6.
87 Undated World Unity circular. USBNA.
88 Kuehl and Dunn, *Keeping the Covenant: American Internationalists and the League of Nations, 1920–1939*, p. 73.
89 ibid. pp. 100–101.
90 Day, 'Randall, John Herman', in Kuehl (ed), *Biographical Dictionary of Internationalists*, p. 596.
91 Letter from Horace Holley to Florence Morton, 14 December 1936. USBNA, Horace Holley papers, Box 4.
92 Undated note. USBNA, Leroy Ioas papers, Box 3.
93 Holley, *Divinations and Creation*, p. 5.
94 The Horace Holley papers held by the USBNA in Box 2 contain two undated letters and one from 6 March 1933 from Marcia to Horace Holley. There is also a fourth from 1952.
95 Fortunately, Horace's relatives assisted him with caring for Marcia. After His passing, one of Irving's children, Polly Doremus, assumed responsibility for managing Marcia's care up until the end of her life. Interviews and letters with members of the Irving Holley family. Marcia Holley (Betty) died on 25 October 2002 in East Windsor, Connecticut. See ancestry.com, US Social Security Applications and Claims Index entry for Marcia Herbert Holley.
96 Letter from Horace Holley to a friend, 1 January 1935. This letter has been kindly shared with the author by the family of the recipient who wish to remain anonymous.
97 The Pascal family problems from the 1920s and 1930s are documented in numerous letters between Doris, Horace, her brothers, and mother, which are to be found in the Doris Holley papers. These matters were emotionally and financially draining on both Doris and Horace. For a brief summary of these problems, see 'Memorandum', an undated [1933 or 1934?] summary of the problems related to one of Doris's brothers which was drafted for a lawsuit. USBNA, Doris Holley papers, Box 1.
98 Letter from Horace Holley to Florence Morton, 18 February 1937. USBNA, Horace Holley papers, Box 4.
99 Letter from Horace Holley to Florence Morton, 4 November 1932. USBNA.
100 Letter from Dorothy Baker to George Latimer, 13 December 1935. USBNA, George Latimer papers, Box 9.
101 In 1935, the Kitáb-i-Aqdas was available in an English translation produced by Professor E. G. Browne of Cambridge University. The translation, however, was considered inadequate and obtaining a copy was not easy. Shoghi Effendi translated excerpts of this greatest of Bahá'u'lláh's books and began work on a synopsis of it which would not be published until 1973, sixteen years after his passing. A full, official translation was published in 1992 by the Bahá'í World Centre.

102 Letter written on behalf of Shoghi Effendi to the National Spiritual Assembly of the United States and Canada, 1935, quoted in the introduction to *The Kitáb-i-Aqdas* by the Universal House of Justice, p. 6.
103 Shoghi Effendi, *Directives from the Guardian*, p. 2.
104 For a history of the construction of the Bahá'í House of Worship in Wilmette, see Hill, *Bahá'í Temple (Images of America)*, and Whitmore, *The Dawning Place: The Building of a Temple, the Forging of the North American Bahá'í Community*.
105 Letter from Horace Holley to Florence Morton, 15 March 1934. USBNA, Horace Holley papers, Box 4.
106 The author's primary sources for this period are: Shlaes, *The Forgotten Man: A New History of the Great Depression*, and Allen, *Since Yesterday: The 1930s in America*, September 3, 1929–September 3, 1939.
107 Letter from Annette Sterner Pascal to Doris Holley, 7 October [1937?]. USBNA, Doris Holley papers, Box 1.
108 Doris Holley's mother, Annette S. Pascal, returned to the United States on 6 November 1938. See ancestry.com, arriving passenger information.
109 Cable from Shoghi Effendi to Horace Holley, 16 April 1938. USBNA, Horace Holley papers.
110 Letter written on behalf of Shoghi Effendi to the National Spiritual Assembly of the United States and Canada, 28 January 1939. USBNA, National Spiritual Assembly papers.
111 Proceedings of the 1938 Convention, p. 1. USBNA.
112 Shoghi Effendi, *This Decisive Hour: Messages from Shoghi Effendi to the North American Bahá'ís, 1932–1946*, no. 57, p. 36.
113 Cable from Shoghi Effendi to the National Spiritual Assembly of the United States and Canada, 22 June 1939. USBNA, National Spiritual Assembly papers.
114 Minutes of the National Spiritual Assembly, 16, 17, 18, June 1939. USBNA, National Spiritual Assembly papers.
115 Cable from Shoghi Effendi to Doris and Horace Holley, 22 June 1939. USBNA, Horace Holley papers.
116 Letter from Horace Holley to Florence Morton, 4 December 1934. USBNA.

12 Spiritual Conquest in the Midst of War

1 Holley, 'To-day', unpublished and undated poem, provided by the Holley family to Claire Vreeland who provided it to the author.
2 After the architect Louis Bourgeois moved from the building which served as both a studio and residence, the family taking care of the House of Worship and its grounds resided there.
3 Letter from Mountfort Mills to Horace Holley, 12 November [1939]. I am grateful to Kenneth Bowers for sharing this letter. He owns the original.
4 ibid. p. 2.
5 ibid. p. 5.
6 ibid. pp. 5–6.
7 ibid. p. 6.
8 Letter from Horace Holley to Roy C. Wilhelm, treasurer, 11 April 1940. USBNA, Horace Holley papers, Box 4.
9 ibid.

10 Herklotz also assisted Roy Wilhelm in carrying out his tasks as treasurer. For a time, another young woman was also employed to help the officers while the Faith was administered from the New York City area.
11 Loeding, 'Eyewitness Impression of the Dedication', in *Bahá'í News*, no. 494, p. 5.
12 'A Note about the First Bahá'í News Editor', in *Bahá'í News*, no. 525, p. 7. Shoghi Effendi informed the National Assembly at some point that no one should be present at the meetings when decisions were being made other than the elected members, so Loeding no longer attended and instead, a tape recorder was used to record the proceedings.
13 Interview between Loretta Voeltz and the author, 27 January 2012. According to Voeltz, this building had been erected originally for the Publishing Committee.
14 ibid. Voeltz reported that when Horace first hired her, she was informed that she should be willing to board in a home (that is, rent a bedroom) because the salary the Faith could offer would be insufficient for her to live independently. According to Voeltz, two Bahá'í accountants who lived in the Chicago area did volunteer work for the treasury. Voeltz primarily wrote receipts and kept the books.
15 When the author worked for the US Bahá'í National Center between 1981 and 1983, she met Sophie Loeding and Loretta Voeltz. At the time, Sophie was elderly and infirm and unable to talk much about the early years working with Horace Holley. She did, however, consent to be interviewed by Claire Vreeland and the notes of that were furnished to the author by the Vreeland family. At the time, Sophie was blind and had difficulty hearing and communicating, so the main point she made was that Horace was wonderful.
16 Interview between Loretta Voeltz and the author, 27 January 2012.
17 'A Note about the First Bahá'í News Editor', in *Bahá'í News*, no. 525, p. 7. Eunice Braun, who worked at the National Centre on Bahá'í publications in the 1950s and was the first manager of the Bahá'í Publishing Trust, said that Horace Holley was always 'helpful and encouraging and eager to help others expand their own concepts and ability'. Letter from Eunice Braun to Claire Vreeland, 19 January 1992. The original letter was furnished to the author by the Vreeland family.
18 Interview between Loretta Voeltz and the author, 27 January 2012.
19 ibid. The author has read hundreds of business letters composed by Horace Holley held by the Bahá'í National Office and the USBNA.
20 Hugh Chance, who became secretary of the National Spiritual Assembly in 1961 and was elected to the Universal House of Justice in 1963, said that Horace's letters were 'invariably well written, pithy and to the point'. Letter from Hugh E. Chance to Claire Hart Vreeland, 23 February 1986. A copy of the letter was furnished to the author by the Vreeland family. A number of other individuals described Horace's letters as 'pithy'.
21 Rutstein, *Corinne True: Faithful Handmaid of 'Abdu'l-Bahá*, p. 206.
22 The author and Edna True were friends during the last years of Edna's life. What is written about the Trues throughout this book derives from her association with Edna.
23 Bushnell, *Wilmette: A History*, p. 171.

24 Letter from Charles Wolcott to Claire Vreeland, 10 April 1986. Original in the possession of the Bahá'í World Centre Archives, having first been furnished to the author by the Vreeland family.
25 Letter from W. H. Alexander to Claire Vreeland, 5 May 1986. The original was furnished to the author by the Vreeland family.
26 Nabíl was a poet and member of Bahá'u'lláh's entourage during His exile to the Holy Land. A chronicler, Nabíl gathered the accounts of those survivors who were part of the early days of the Faith and compiled them under the supervision of Bahá'u'lláh. Shoghi Effendi did not include the sections of the narrative that related the ministry of Bahá'u'lláh following His exile to Baghdad. Nabíl was named an Apostle of Bahá'u'lláh by Shoghi Effendi. See *The Dawn-Breakers: Nabíl's Narrative of the Early Days of the Bahá'í Revelation.*
27 Letter written on behalf of Shoghi Effendi to unnamed individuals, 24 August 1939. USBNA, Carl Scheffler papers. See also letter written on behalf of Shoghi Effendi to Mr and Mrs L. W. Eggleston, 2 November 1932. USBNA, excerpt in compilation 'Letters from the Guardian' addressed to Horace Holley.
28 Letter from Horace Holley to Roushan Wilkinson, Green Acre School Committee, 2 January 1942. USBNA, Horace Holley papers, Box 2.
29 While the source of the funds is unclear, most likely they were able to purchase the cabin after Doris came into a modest inheritance from her uncle.
30 In addition to the Holleys, Roy Wilhelm, Fred Schopflocher, and Louis Gregory had summer homes at or near Green Acre. It was possible to meet for longer than a weekend when the Assembly met there.
31 Louhelen Bahá'í School near Davison, Michigan was given to the Faith by the Eggleston family. It had been their family home and ranch. Most of the classes were conducted in a barn or under trees until facilities were completed in 1982. Most of those attending Louhelen came from the Midwest while Green Acre drew its participants primarily from the Northeast and eastern Canada. The school at Geyserville, California, served the friends along the West Coast.
32 See, for example, a memo he wrote to Dorothy [Baker?] and Leroy Ioas, 15 January 1940, as a 'Supplement to Memo for Special School Committee'. He suggested that the summer schools consider how important it was to include time for socializing among the participants. He also discussed his views on education in general. USBNA, Horace Holley papers, Box 4.
33 ibid. p. 2.
34 Holley, 'Regarding Service (A suggestion for the believers and friends)', undated. Most likely this was written in the early 1930s. USBNA, Agnes Parsons papers, Box 9.
35 ibid.
36 Letter/report to the National Spiritual Assembly of the United States and Canada by Allen McDaniel, 6 May 1935. USBNA, Carl Scheffler papers, Box 2.
37 Letter from Horace Holley to Florence Morton, 25 January 1939. USBNA, Horace Holley papers, Box 4.
38 Letter from Horace Holley to Leroy Ioas, 8 May 1936, in which Horace says he was certain that cables from the Guardian giving the new goals of the Seven Year Plan were a direct result of the report of the National Teaching Committee. He also said that Shoghi Effendi's goals were timely because of the firm

establishment of the administration and the upheavals in the world. USBNA, Ioas papers, Box 3.

39 Shoghi Effendi, *This Decisive Hour: Messages from Shoghi Effendi to the North American Bahá'ís 1932–1946*, p. 11. Horace filled in the telegram language for the publication of the cable in *Bahá'í News*, no. 101 (June 1936), p. 1.
40 Cable from Shoghi Effendi to the 1937 National Convention, 1 May 1937, in *Bahá'í News*, no. 108 (June 1937), p. 2.
41 Letter from Horace Holley to Carl Scheffler, 1 November 1938. USBNA, Carl Scheffler papers, Box 1.
42 Holley, 'The Foundation of an Organic Religious Community', typed, undated essay. USBNA, Horace Holley papers, Box 6.
43 For a fuller discussion of how the Seven Year Plan was carried out successfully, see Chapman, *Leroy Ioas: Hand of the Cause of God*, pp. 95–118.
44 Letter from Horace Holley to George Latimer, 9 September 1936. USBNA, George Latimer papers, Box 3.
45 Letter from Horace Holley as secretary of the National Spiritual Assembly to Shoghi Effendi, 23 January 1937. USBNA, National Spiritual Assembly papers.
46 Letter written on behalf of Shoghi Effendi to the National Spiritual Assembly of the United States and Canada, 22 March 1937, in *Bahá'í News*, no. 108 (June 1937), pp. 1–2.
47 Memo to the National Spiritual Assembly for the June Meeting, 1940, from Horace Holley, 4 June 1940. USBNA, Horace Holley papers, Box 4. Horace stated that *The Advent of Divine Justice* required that the National Assembly put aside petty matters and focus upon the call to action of the Guardian. He suggested that the Assembly spend time together in prayer before conducting any business. Thereby, 'the spirit of oneness in servitude to the Faith will become the foundation of that mutual integrity and respect essential to collective wisdom and achievement'.
48 'The Oneness of Mankind', statement by the National Spiritual Assembly of the United States and Canada, in *Bahá'í News*, no. 124 (April 1939), p. 1.
49 ibid. pp. 1–2.
50 At the time the letter was written, 'negro' was considered the most polite of all possible terms when referring to Blacks.
51 'Letter to the President on Race Unity', From the National Spiritual Assembly of the Bahá'ís of the United States and Canada to The President [Franklin D. Roosevelt], 4 January 1944, in *Bahá'í News*, no. 174 (April–May 1944), p. 12.
52 ibid.
53 ibid.
54 Cable from Shoghi Effendi to the North American Bahá'í community, 22 September 1938, in Shoghi Effendi, *This Decisive Hour: Messages from Shoghi Effendi to the North American Bahá'ís 1932–1946*, p. 25.
55 Letter from Horace Holley to Green Acre Program Committee, Marjorie Wheeler, secretary, 15 September 1939. USBNA, Horace Holley papers, Box 2.
56 ibid.
57 Letter from Horace Holley to Roushan Wilkinson, secretary, Green Acre School Committee, 2 January 1942. USBNA, Horace Holley papers, Box 2.
58 Letter from Horace Holley to the Bahá'í Youth Committee, 23 October 1940. USBNA.

NOTES AND REFERENCES

59 Hussey-Arntson and Leary, *Wilmette (Images of America)*, p. 98.
60 Bushnell, *Wilmette: A History*, pp. 175, 178.
61 Letter from Mountfort Mills to Horace Holley, 22 March 1943. USBNA.
62 See, for example, letter from Horace Holley to George Latimer, 9 September 1936. USBNA, George Latimer papers, Box 3; letter from Horace Holley to Florence Morton, 8 October 1936. USBNA, Horace Holley papers, Box 4; letter from George Latimer to Allen McDaniel, Horace Holley and Leroy Ioas, 26 May 1938. USBNA, George Latimer papers, Box 4.
63 Letter from Horace Holley to the secretary of Shoghi Effendi, Azizullah Bahadur, 13 February 1924. USBNA.
64 'Siegfried Schopflocher (1877–1953)', in The Bahá'í Encyclopedia Project, https://www.bahai-encyclopedia-project.org/index.php?option=com_content&view=article&id=69:schopflocher-siegfried&catid=37:biography.
65 Holley, 'International Survey of Current Bahá'í Activities in the East and West', in *The Bahá'í World*, vol. IX (1940–1944), p. 13.
66 Letter from Polly Marlowe to Claire Vreeland, 24 February 1989. Original furnished to the author by the Vreeland family.
67 ibid.
68 ibid.
69 Shoghi Effendi, *This Decisive Hour: Messages from Shoghi Effendi to the North American Bahá'ís 1932–1946*, no. 109, p. 83.
70 See, for example, Horace Holley's memorandum to his two colleagues Allen McDaniel and George Latimer, outlining how advertising and the lessons of advertising should be used and commenting upon the publicity carried out for the Centenary. Memorandum to the Members of the Public Relations Committee from Horace Holley, 5 January 1945. USBNA, Horace Holley papers, Box 4.
71 *Bahá'í Procedure*, compiled by the National Spiritual Assembly of the Bahá'ís of the United States and Canada, 1942.
72 Letter from Horace Holley to Allen McDaniel and George Latimer, 1 April 1937. USBNA, George Latimer papers, Box 3.
73 Holley, *Present-Day Administration of the Bahá'í Faith*.
74 ibid. p. 2.
75 ibid. p. 3.
76 ibid. p. 16.
77 ibid.
78 ibid. p. 17.
79 ibid.
80 ibid.
81 Letter written on behalf of Shoghi Effendi to the National Spiritual Assembly of the United States and Canada through Horace Holley, 23 July 1943. USBNA, Horace Holley papers.
82 ibid. p. 4.
83 See letters from Doris Holley to George Latimer, 21 July 1944, 2 August 1944, and 10 August 1944. USBNA, George Latimer papers, Box 3.
84 'Notice', in *Bahá'í News*, no. 169 (July 1944), p. 1.
85 Letter written on behalf of Shoghi Effendi to Horace Holley, 27 February 1940, in which the status of the National Office was discussed saying, 'The principle

that has guided your work, namely to combine dignity and beauty in establishing the National Office, is certainly in keeping with the spirit of the Teachings, and you should, in the discharge of your future functions as custodian of that office, continue to uphold that same principle.' It went on to say that if social functions were held in the building, care should be taken to maintain the building's dignity. USBNA, National Spiritual Assembly papers.

86 Letter from Irving Holley to Lillian Baker (his sister), 7 July 1944. Copy furnished to the author by the Vreeland family who received it from the Holley family.
87 ibid.
88 Horace had gall bladder problems, back problems, arthritis, and eye problems in addition to heart and lung problems. This list is derived from an interview with his surgeon and Loretta Voeltz, and from correspondence from Irving Holley, Jr. to Claire Vreeland. See also letter from Doris Holley to Amelia Collins, 10 September 1949, written at Moses Ludington Hospital, Ticonderoga, New York. USBNA, Amelia Collins papers, Box 1.
89 Rúḥíyyih Rabbani, 'Horace Hotchkiss Holley', In Memoriam, in *The Bahá'í World*, vol. XIII (1954–1963), p. 856.
90 *Bahá'í News*, no. 175 (June 1945), p. 3.
91 *Bahá'í News*, no. 176 (August 1945), pp. 2–4.
92 Prior to 1945, *Foundations of World Unity* was printed privately using funds provided by Florence Morton.
93 Holley, 'The Assurance of World Peace: The Evolution of Peace', in *The Bahá'í World*, vol. X (1944–1946), pp. 649–50.
94 The National Spiritual Assembly sent a letter of condolence to Mrs Eleanor Roosevelt, of course, signed by Horace Holley as secretary, 13 April 1945. 'Letter to Mrs. Roosevelt', in *Bahá'í News*, no. 173 (April–May 1945), p. 14.
95 The Axis powers, including Germany and Japan, were not included. The War was not yet concluded and many of the necessary new governments that would emerge after it were not yet in place.
96 'Bahá'í Peace Program at San Francisco During Allied Nations Conference', in *Bahá'í News*, no. 176 (August 1945), pp. 8–9.
97 ibid. p. 8.
98 'Telegram to the President on Peace', in *Bahá'í News*, no. 174 (April–May 1945), p. 13. It was dated 26 March 1945.
99 'Letter from the Department of State', ibid. It was dated 17 April 1945.
100 Shoghi Effendi, *Citadel of Faith*, pp. 32–3.
101 'The Bomb: An Act that Haunts Japan and America', in *The New York Times*, vol. CXLIV, no. 50,145 (Sunday, 6 August 1995).
102 Holley, 'International Survey of Current Bahá'í Activities in the East and West', in *The Bahá'í World*, vol. IX (1940–1944), p. 14.
103 ibid.
104 The Lesser Peace is the term used to describe the period when there is no longer armed conflict, even though tensions between nations continue.
105 ibid.
106 Holley, 'International Survey of Current Bahá'í Activities in the East and West', in *The Bahá'í World*, vol. IX (1940–1944), p. 13.
107 ibid. pp. 13–14.

108 Information provided by Edna True to the author.
109 Letter from Horace Holley to his colleagues on the National Assembly, 11 April 1945, informing them that Louis Gregory was in Cook County Hospital recovering from an operation. He and Doris visited him and found him in 'a beautiful spirit' though they did not think he had been fully informed of the seriousness of his condition. USBNA, Horace Holley papers, Box 4.
110 Letter from Horace Holley to George Latimer, 17 June 1946. USBNA, George Latimer papers, Box 3.
111 ibid.
112 ibid.
113 Letter from Philip Sprague to Elsie Austin, 26 January 1949. USBNA, Elsie Austin papers.
114 Letter from Horace Holley to Shoghi Effendi, 24 March 1948. USBNA, Horace Holley papers.
115 ibid.
116 Chapman, *Leroy Ioas: Hand of the Cause of God*, p. 146.
117 Letter from Doris Holley to Amelia Collins, 10 September 1949. USBNA, Amelia Collins papers, Box 1.
118 Holley, 'By This I Know His Love', unpublished poem, dated 12 September 1949, written at Ticonderoga Hospital. USBNA, Horace Holley papers.
119 Letter from the Forty-Second Annual Convention sent by its secretary, Leroy Ioas, to Horace Holley at Evanston Hospital, 29 April 1950. USBNA, Horace Holley papers, Box 4.
120 Letter from Horace Holley to Alice Cox, 5 May [1950?]. USBNA, Alice Cox papers, Box 1.
121 Interview between Loretta Voeltz and the author, 27 January 2012.
122 For a riveting first-hand account of the difficulties faced by the American pioneers to Prince Edward Island in the Maritimes, see McKay, *Fires in Many Hearts*, pp. 310–25.
123 The process of opening the unopened regions of Canada to the Faith and gaining a National Spiritual Assembly are set out in van den Hoonaard, *The Origins of the Bahá'í Community of Canada, 1898–1948*, pp. 177– 02, 265–76.
124 Letter from the National Spiritual Assembly of Canada to Horace Holley, 10 April 1949. USBNA, Horace Holley papers, Box 4.
125 In her 'In Memoriam' article on Horace Holley's life, Rúḥíyyih Khánum comments that her parents, who were friends with Horace for many decades, began to notice a change in Horace from the late 1930s. He had submerged his creative, mystical side during his first years as secretary of the National Assembly, but that aspect of his being began to re-emerge over time in a more mature and elevated way. Rúḥíyyih Rabbani, 'Horace Hotchkiss Holley', In Memoriam, in *The Bahá'í World*, vol. XIII (1954–1963), p. 852.
126 This comes from a number of conversations the author had with believers who remembered Horace or heard their parents' comments about him.
127 Letter from Horace Holley to Dorothy M. Fisher at Green Acre Bahá'í School, 19 April 1948. USBNA.
128 Holley, 'Religious Education for a Peaceful Society', in *The Bahá'í World*, vol. XI (1946–1950), p. 660.

129 The meetings in Peru concluded on 23 December.
130 Midway Airport (previously called Municipal Airport) carried most of the civilian air travel in and out of the Chicago area prior to the opening of O'Hara Airport in 1955. https://airwaysmag.com/uncategorized/chicago-ohare-history/.
131 Whitehead, *Some Bahá'ís to Remember*, p. 241. The account of how Horace learned he was chosen a Hand of the Cause of God by Shoghi Effendi was also related to Hooper Dunbar by Doris Holley, who shared the story with the author. Doris McKay related the story differently, but her version was second-hand. She related that Horace immediately dropped both suitcases. All three accounts have Horace saying something different, but what was clear was that he did not want the appointment. Of course, with reflection, he could not deny Shoghi Effendi anything.

13 Institution of the Learned

1 Holley, *Religion for Mankind*, p. 246.
2 A few early Western believers met Hands of the Cause of God while on pilgrimage.
3 Momen, *The Bahá'í Communities of Iran: 1851–1921*, vol. I: *The North of Iran*, pp. 92–4. Momen provides details about this body. The Bahá'í Temple Unity Committee Executive Board was formed in the United States in 1909, but only gradually took on responsibilities other than the building of the House of Worship in the Chicago area.
4 The Will and Testament of 'Abdu'l-Bahá, Part One, para. 21.
5 Letter written on behalf of Shoghi Effendi to Leroy Ioas, 14 November 1935. USBNA.
6 Shoghi Effendi, *Messages to the Bahá'í World: 1950–1957*, p. 8.
7 Letter from A. A. Furútan to Claire Vreeland, 31 May 1989. The original was furnished to the author by the Vreeland family who then gave it to the Bahá'í World Centre Archives. The full list of the first appointments included: Dorothy Beecher Baker (Ohio, United States), Amelia Engelder Collins (California, United States, and Israel), 'Alí-Akbar Furútan (Iran), Ugo Giachery (Italy), Hermann Grossmann (Germany), Horace Hotchkiss Holley (Illinois, United States), Leroy C. Ioas (California, United States), William Sutherland Maxwell (Canada and Israel), Charles Mason Remey (Washington DC, United States, and Israel), Ṭarázu'lláh Samandarí (Iran), George Townshend (Ireland), Valíyu'lláh Varqá (Iran).
8 Harper, *Lights of Fortitude: Glimpses into the Lives of the Hands of the Cause of God*, p. 206.
9 Letter from the Local Spiritual Assembly of New York, 7 January 1952. New York Bahá'í Archives. On 2 January 1952, the New York Assembly sent a letter to Hand of the Cause Ugo Giachery, who was named a Hand at the same time as Horace. Ugo, an Italian from Sicily, had spent the war years in New York City where he served on its Assembly. The Assembly was thrilled that two of its former members were among the twelve believers from throughout the world named Hands in the first contingent. New York Bahá'í Archives.
10 Letter from the National Spiritual Assembly of Canada to Horace Holley, 15 May 1952. USBNA, Horace Holley papers, Box 1.

NOTES AND REFERENCES

11 Letter from Marion Little to Horace Holley, 23 January 1952. At the time Marion was pioneering in Florence, Italy. USBNA, Marion Little papers, Box 3.
12 Cable from Shoghi Effendi to the Bahá'ís worldwide, 26 March 1952.
13 Ironically, though their parents did not embrace the Bahá'í Faith in large numbers in the 1950s, the members of the 'Baby Boom' generation did during their youth in the 1960s and 1970s. Thousands of youth enrolled annually during that period.
14 Young and Young, *The 1950s*, p. 8.
15 ibid.
16 Johnson, *A History of the American People*, p. 839. See also Ahlstrom, *A Religious History of the American People*, p. 952, which includes a chart of the level of church affiliation in the United States between 1910 and 1970. It also has figures on church construction during the period between 1945 and 1960 on p. 953. In 1960, the amount spent on church building projects exceeded one billion dollars.
17 Young and Young, *The 1950s*, pp. 193–4; Johnson, *A History of the American People*, pp. 839–40. For a fuller discussion of President Eisenhower's connection to religion and the credit he received for sparking a religious revival, see Hitchcock, *The Age of Eisenhower: America and the World in the 1950s*, pp. 246–52.
18 The first Seven Year Plan goals were announced in 1936 and the efforts to send pioneers began immediately. Shoghi Effendi named the goals of the Seven Year Plan in early 1937 when he set a formal starting date for it.
19 Letter from Mildred Mottahedeh to Horace Holley, 17 February 1954. USBNA, Horace Holley papers, Box 4.
20 These five were Mamie Seto, Elsie Austin, Kenneth Christian, Matthew Bullock, and Dorothy Baker. Dorothy was on the way to her post when she died in a plane accident. The other four all pioneered to other countries.
21 Letter from Shoghi Effendi, 22 May 1939, probably written to the National Spiritual Assembly of the United States and Canada. Shoghi Effendi, *This Decisive Hour: Messages from Shoghi Effendi to the North American Bahá'ís: 1932–1946*, p. 34.
22 'Sacred Relic Given', in *Bahá'í News*, no. 244 (June 1951), pp. 11–12. Paul Haney and Amelia Collins represented the National Spiritual Assembly at the formation of the Regional Spiritual Assembly of South America, held in Lima, Peru.
23 'Airplane Trips', undated and unsigned document in the handwriting of Horace Holley. USBNA, Horace Holley papers, Box 10.
24 Orville and Wilber Wright from Dayton, Ohio, are generally credited with inventing the first airplane powered by an engine.
25 'Airplane Trips', undated and unsigned document in the handwriting of Horace Holley. USBNA, Horace Holley papers, Box 10.
26 Letter written on behalf of Shoghi Effendi to Horace Holley, 10 August 1945, USBNA.
27 Rabbani, 'Horace Hotchkiss Holley', In Memoriam, in *The Bahá'í World*, vol. XIII (1954–1963), p. 855.
28 Memories of Horace Holley by R. Ted Anderson for Claire Vreeland, 24 January 1991. The original was furnished to the author by the Vreeland family.

29 Letter from Jane Alexander (Mrs. William H. Alexander) to Claire Vreeland, 6 May 1986. The original was furnished to the author by the Vreeland family.
30 Rutstein, *Corinne True: Faithful Handmaiden of 'Abdu'l-Bahá*, p. 209.
31 The Kampala conference is reported extensively in *The Bahá'í World*, vol. XII (1951–1953), pp. 121–32. The newspaper incident is discussed in Chapman, *Leroy Ioas: Hand of the Cause of God*, pp. 202–04 and in Freeman, *From Copper to Gold: The Life of Dorothy Baker*, p. 268.
32 Hofman, *George Townshend: Hand of the Cause of God*, pp. 353–4. Horace wrote out a daily agenda for the time he was in Europe which included a note that he had lunch with George Townshend and his wife under the heading 'Amsterdam. "Stockholm Conference"', undated document in Horace Holley's handwriting,. USBNA, Horace Holley papers, Box 10.
33 Holley, 'New Delhi: Spiritual Conquest of the Orient', 22 October 1953, in *Bahá'í News*, no. 273 (November 1953), p. 10.
34 ibid.
35 'Persons to Wait Upon the President of India on 14th October'. USBNA, Horace Holley papers, Box 10.
36 Notes from the New Delhi Conference for the afternoon of 15 October, in Horace Holley's handwriting. USBNA, Horace Holley papers, Box 10.
37 'The Guardian's Cable to the Hands of the Cause at New Delhi', in *Bahá'í News*, no. 273 (November 1953), pp. 4–5.
38 Letter from Horace Holley to Mildred Mottahedeh, 1 November [1953]. USBNA, Mildred Mottahedeh papers, Box 13.
39 ibid.
40 ibid.
41 Letter from Horace Holley to Shoghi Effendi, 23 November 1953. USBNA, Horace Holley papers.
42 ibid. p. 5.
43 ibid.
44 Letter from Banoo K. Jehani to Horace Holley, 4 October 1954. USBNA, Horace Holley papers, Box 3.
45 Letter from Claire Vreeland to Roger White, 26 September 1989, in which she reports her interview with Mildred Mottahedeh, a close friend to Horace Holley. Copy of the letter provided to the author by the Vreeland family.
46 Notes of an Address by Horace Holley, North Shore Hotel, Evanston, Illinois, 6 January 1954. USBNA, L & R Larocque papers, Box 4.
47 Rabbani, 'Horace Hotchkiss Holley', In Memoriam, in *The Bahá'í World*, vol. XIII (1954–1963), p. 857.
48 Notes of an Address by Horace Holley, North Shore Hotel, Evanston, Illinois, 6 January 1954. USBNA, L & R Larocque papers, Box 4.
49 ibid.
50 ibid.
51 ibid.
52 ibid. section XXI.
53 ibid, section XXIII.
54 Will and Testament of 'Abdu'l-Bahá, Section I.
55 Notes of an Address by Horace Holley, North Shore Hotel, Evanston, Illinois, 6 January 1954, section XX. USBNA, L & R Larocque papers, Box 4.

56 Telephone interview between Dr Manucher Javid and the author, 30 July 2015.
57 Message from Shoghi Effendi to the Hands of the Cause and all National Assemblies of the Bahá'í World, 6 April 1954, in *Bahá'í News*, no. 279 (May 1954), p. 1.
58 Commentary by the National Spiritual Assembly, ibid. p. 1.
59 ibid.
60 Bahá'u'lláh, *Tablets of Bahá'u'lláh Revealed after the Kitáb-i-Aqdas*, p. 221.
61 Letter from the Universal House of Justice to the Continental Boards of Counsellors and National Spiritual Assemblies, 24 April 1972, in *The Continental Boards of Counselors: Letters, Extracts from Letters, and Cables from The Universal House of Justice*, pp. 42–5.
62 ibid. p. 45.
63 Letter from Horace Holley to Corinne True and Paul E. Haney, 13 April 1954. USBNA, Corinne True papers, Box 2.
64 ibid.
65 Letter from the American Hands of the Cause (True, Holley, Haney) to the American Auxiliary Board, 25 May 1954. USBNA, Corinne True papers, Box 2.
66 Letter from Florence Mayberry to Claire Vreeland, 11 July 1988. Furnished to the author by the Vreeland family. The original has been given to the archives of the Bahá'í World Centre.
67 ibid.
68 ibid.
69 Mayberry, *The Great Adventure*, p. 132.
70 ibid.
71 Letter from Florence Mayberry to Horace Holley, 20 March 1957. USBNA, Horace Holley papers, Box 3.
72 ibid.
73 Letter from the American Hands of the Cause to Gayle Woolson, 27 May 1954. A copy of the letter was furnished by Gayle Woolson to Claire Vreeland and it was then provided to the author by the Vreeland family.
74 Letter from the American Hands of the Cause, 2 June 1954, announcing to each Auxiliary Board member their appointment and assignment. A copy was furnished by Gayle Woolson to Claire Vreeland and it was then provided to the author by the Vreeland family.
75 Letter from the American Hands of the Cause to Gayle Woolson, 2 October 1956. A copy of the letter was furnished by Gayle Woolson to Claire Vreeland and it was then provided to the author by the Vreeland family.
76 This important letter is discussed in Chapman, *Leroy Ioas: Hand of the Cause of God*, pp. 250–51.
77 For example, a letter from the American Hands to the Auxiliary Board members, 14 June 1956, quoted extensively from a letter from the Hands in the Holy Land who were indirectly conveying guidance from Shoghi Effendi. This system amplified the letters from the Guardian himself and allowed his guidance to be reiterated in less formal language which was more straightforward.
78 Letter from Leroy Ioas to Horace Holley, 25 March 1952. USBNA, Horace Holley papers, Box 3. Leroy states that his letter is based on not only his own notes of the Guardian's words, but also those of Glen Vasel. He also asked Amelia Collins to review them for accuracy.
79 ibid. pp. 2–4.

80 Holley, 'Bahá'í Coordination', 21 November 1947, pp. 5–7. USBNA.
81 Letter from Leroy Ioas to Horace Holley, 25 March 1952, pp. 6–7. USBNA, Horace Holley papers, Box 3.
82 ibid. p. 10.
83 'A letter from the American Hands of the Cause' [Corinne True, Horace Holley, Paul Haney] to the Auxiliary Board members, Undated [1955?]. Copy furnished by Gayle Woolson to Claire Vreeland, provided to the author by the Vreeland family.
84 This story was related to me by Hooper Dunbar, who heard it from former National Assembly members serving at the time.
85 Letter from Horace Holley to Leroy Ioas, 14 March [1958?]. USBNA, Leroy Ioas papers, Box 3. In a letter from Leroy Ioas to Horace Holley, 27 February 1954, Leroy reported how distressed Shoghi Effendi had been at the report of Horace's eye problem. He assured Horace that prayers were being offered at the Shrines for the healing of his eyes. USBNA, Horace Holley papers, Box 3.
86 Letter from Leroy Ioas to Horace Holley, 27 February 1954. USBNA, Horace Holley papers, Box 3. The author spoke with Horace's physician and friend, Dr Manucher Javid, who stated that by the time he treated Horace three years later in 1957, Horace's eyesight had returned.
87 Marion Hofman, born Marion Holley, shared her maiden family name with Horace. They speculated as to whether or not they were related and determined that they did have common ancestors in the distant past.
88 Holley, *Religion for Mankind*, pp. 9–10.
89 ibid. p. 10.
90 At Shoghi Effendi's request, all nine members of the National Spiritual Assembly of the United States, not just those who were Hands, were sent to Conventions where regional Spiritual Assemblies were being established that year. Paul Haney was the representative for the formation of the first National Spiritual Assembly of Alaska. Corinne True overcame the infirmities of age and represented the Guardian at the first National Convention of the Greater Antilles held in Kingston, Jamaica. She was accompanied by her daughter, Katherine True, a member of the National Spiritual Assembly, who served as the Assembly's representative.
91 'Brazil, Peru, Colombia, Ecuador, Venezuela Form National Assembly in Lima', in *Bahá'í News*, no. 317 (July 1957), pp. 7–8.
92 'Grave, Far-Reaching Implications' Nationwide Rally for Ten Year Plan', in *Bahá'í News*, no. 318 (August 1957), p. 3.
93 Letter from Paul Haney to Gayle Woolson, 21 August 1957. A copy of the letter was furnished by Gayle Woolson to Claire Vreeland. The Vreeland family provided it to the author.
94 Letter written on behalf of Shoghi Effendi to Horace Holley, 10 August 1945. USBNA.
95 'Station and Function of Hands of the Cause', in *Bahá'í News*, no. 318 (August 1957), p. 2.
96 Shoghi Effendi, *Messages to the Bahá'í World*, pp. 122–3.
97 ibid. p. 127.
98 ibid. p. 130.
99 Telephone interview between Dr Manucher Javid and the author, 30 July 2015.

14 The Promised Land

1. Horace, 'The Victory of Faith', in *Star of the West*, vol. VIII, p. 265.
2. This paragraph is derived from Hand of the Cause Dr. A. Vargha's oral tribute to Rúḥíyyih Khánum made in the presence of Hand of the Cause 'Alí-Akbar Furútan, at a banquet given by the Universal House of Justice to honour Rúḥíyyih Khánum on her 60th wedding anniversary. The author was present as a staff member and heard the remarks.
3. Letter from Horace Holley to Leroy Ioas, 22 February [1958?]. USBNA, Leroy Ioas papers, Box 3.
4. Undated letter from Amelia Collins to Doris Holley. USBNA, Doris Holley papers.
5. Rúḥíyyih Khánum was born Mary Maxwell in New York City to a Canadian father and American mother. She grew up in Montreal, but spent much time in the United States throughout her childhood and youth. Before marrying Shoghi Effendi, she was pioneering in Germany. She had traversed, with the Guardian, the length of Africa.
6. The Ḥaram-i-Aqdas is an Arabic term for the Most Holy Sanctuary (or Precincts). The Shrine of Bahá'u'lláh is encircled by gardens. The quarter of those gardens in front of the Shrine of Bahá'u'lláh (the northwestern quadrant) is the Ḥaram-i-Aqdas.
7. To the end of His life, Bahá'u'lláh spent the coldest months in the House of 'Abbúd in 'Akká.
8. Statement by Leroy C. Ioas, signed by Leroy Ioas, Sylvia Ioas, Ethel Revell, and Jessie Revell, 6 November 1957, in *The Ministry of the Custodians: An Account of the Stewardship of the Hands of the Cause 1957–1963*, p. 25.
9. Official Statement signed by Rúḥíyyih, Mason Remey, Amelia E. Collins, Ugo Giachery, and Leroy C. Ioas, 15 November 1957, ibid. p. 26.
10. Official Statement signed by Rúḥíyyih, Mason Remey, Amelia E. Collins, Ugo Giachery, Leroy Ioas, Hasan M. Balyuzi, Horace Holley, Músá Banání, and Dr. A. Vargha, 19 November 1957, ibid. pp. 27–8.
11. Horace asked Shoghi Effendi about the role of the Hands of the Cause affirming the selection of the successor to the Guardian while he was on pilgrimage. The sense of the answer he received was that the Hands did not have the right to veto the choice of the Guardian, they instead served as witnesses to it, affirming that it was indeed the choice of the previous Guardian. Notes from talk given by Horace Holley in Evanston, Illinois, 6 January 1954. USBNA, L. and R. Larocque papers, Box 4.
12. According to Dr Javid, a rumour circulated in Iran that Shoghi Effendi had a child who was raised in hiding. He asked Horace Holley about the veracity of the rumour the night he informed Horace of the Guardian's passing. Horace said that he did not think that was true, because if it was, Amelia Collins would have told him. Telephone interview between Dr Manucher Javid and the author, 30 July 2015.
13. When presented with the totality of the situation by the Hands of the Cause, the British officials administering Palestine accepted that the Bahá'í real estate holdings and bank accounts belonged to the Faith as a religious organization, and not to individuals.

14 Letter from A. A. Furútan to Claire Vreeland, 31 May 1989. The original was provided to the author by the Vreeland family and the author has given it to the Bahá'í World Centre Archives.
15 Rúḥíyyih Khánum, 'Horace Hotchkiss Holley', In Memoriam, in *The Bahá'í World*, vol. XIII (1954–1963), p. 857.
16 John Robarts, communication to May Hofman.
17 *The Ministry of the Custodians 1957–1963*, pp. 28–30.
18 ibid. p. 36.
19 ibid. pp. 36–7.
20 ibid. pp. 37–8.
21 Letter from Horace Holley to the Hands of the Cause in the Holy Land, 25 February 1958. USBNA, Horace Holley papers.
22 I am grateful to the Secretary of the US National Spiritual Assembly, Kenneth Bowers, for checking the minutes of that 1958 meeting to confirm that the need for a statement about successors to the Guardian came from multiple sources. The National Assembly was unequivocal about the need to clarify this issue for the friends.
23 'A New Bahá'í Era', Draft copy with Horace Holley's corrections. USBNA, Horace Holley papers.
24 ibid.
25 Letter from the Hands of the Cause in the Holy Land to Horace Holley, 10 March 1958, in *The Ministry of the Custodians 1957–1963*, pp. 66–7.
26 ibid. p. 67.
27 Statement regarding the Guardianship issued by the Hands of the Cause in the Holy Land, 12 June 1958, in *The Ministry of the Custodians 1957–1963*, pp. 100–02.
28 *Bahá'í News*, no. 329 (July 1958), p. 6.
29 ibid. p. 14.
30 Letter from Howard B. Kavelin (Borrah) to Horace Holley, 4 June 1958. USBNA, Horace Holley papers, Box 3.
31 Holley, 'Introduction', in Shoghi Effendi, *Messages to the Bahá'í World: 1950–1957*, p. vii.
32 Letter from Claire Vreeland to Roger White, 26 September 1989, which relates an interview with Mildred Mottahedeh. A copy of the letter was furnished to the author by the Vreeland family.
33 Telephone interview between Dr Manucher Javid and the author, 30 July 2015.
34 Letter from Irving Holley, Jr. to Claire Vreeland, 29 January 1987, p. 1. The original was furnished to the author by the Vreeland family.
35 ibid. pp. 1–2. Poland, separating Russia from Germany, was often the route used by invading armies. At the time Horace joked about it, it was much in the news because Hitler wanted to invade the Soviet Union through Poland.
36 Undated letter from Jean Randazzo to Claire Vreeland written at St Thomas, Virgin Islands. The original was furnished to the author by the Vreeland family.
37 ibid.
38 ibid. Judas Iscariot is the disciple who betrayed Jesus to the authorities, leading to His crucifixion.
39 Letter from Charles Wolcott to Claire Vreeland, 10 April 1986. Original sent

to the Bahá'í World Centre Archives by the author, who acquired it from the Vreeland family.

40 Memories of Horace Holley provided by R. Ted Anderson to Claire Vreeland, 24 January 1991. Furnished to the author by the Vreeland family.

41 Telephone interview, 18 April 2021, with Hooper Dunbar who, as a youth, attended the 1959 Convention and witnessed this phenomenon.

42 Hogenson, *Lighting the Western Sky: The Hearst Pilgrimage and the Establishment of the Bahá'í Faith in the West*, pp. 179–80. This book contains biographical information about Remey, as does Harper, *Lights of Fortitude: Glimpses into the Lives of the Hands of the Cause of God*, pp. 287–306.

43 The author has over many years spoken with a number of people who knew Remey. He was often described as aloof with a sense of entitlement.

44 Conclave Message from the Hands of the Cause to the Bahá'ís of the East and West, 4 November 1959, in *The Ministry of the Custodians 1957–1963*, p. 168.

45 Letter from Sylvia Parmelee to Horace Holley, 20 March 1956. USBNA, Horace Holley papers, Box 4.

46 At the same time Remey was removed, Hand of the Cause H. M. Balyuzi asked to be allowed to return home to England for personal reasons. John Ferraby from the United Kingdom, another Hand serving as National Assembly secretary, was asked to serve as Balyuzi's replacement.

47 'Horace Holley Reviews Growth of Administrative Order at Farewell Meeting on Eve of Departure for Holy Land', in *Bahá'í News*, no. 348 (February 1960), pp. 1–2.

48 Loretta Voeltz, 27 January 2012, telephone interview with the author.

49 Marcia 'Betty' Holley suffered from mental illness. A trust fund set up by one of Horace's brothers helped to support her. After the death of her mother, Bertha Holley, Horace's niece (Irving Holley's daughter), Polly Doremus, became Marcia's guardian. Correspondence and telephone calls between Claire Vreeland and Polly Doremus supplemented by telephone calls between the author and Polly's daughter.

50 Letter from Claire Vreeland to Dr Javid, 27 September 1988. Copy of the letter furnished to the author by the Vreeland family.

51 The original boundaries envisioned by the United Nations would have placed Bahjí in Arab-controlled hands, and Haifa in Jewish hands. The holiest Shrine of the Bahá'í world might have been endangered under the control of an Islamic state.

52 Leroy Ioas and Paul Haney had important jobs with high salaries before moving to Haifa.

53 Account of Richard Mereness, in Redman, *Shoghi Effendi through the Pilgrim's Eye*, vol. 2, pp. 234–5.

54 Rúhíyyih Khánum, 'Horace Hotchkiss Holley', In Memoriam, in *The Bahá'í World*, vol. XIII (1954–1963) p. 857.

55 Cable from the Hands of the Cause in the Holy Land to the Continental Hands and All National Spiritual Assemblies, 28 April 1960, in *The Ministry of the Custodians 1957–1963*, pp. 196–7.

56 Letter from the Hands of the Cause in the Holy Land to the Hands of the Cause of God and the National Spiritual Assemblies throughout the Bahá'í World, 10 May 1960, ibid. p. 198.

57 The documents from this period are found in *The Ministry of the Custodians 1957–1963*. While this unfortunate episode is discussed in many books, including Taherzadeh, *The Covenant of Bahá'u'lláh*, pp. 385–91, the best at the time of the writing is to be found in Redman, *Shoghi Effendi through the Pilgrim's Eye*, vol. 2, pp. 236–44. These and other works discuss Remey's assertions and refute them.
58 Loretta Voeltz, interview with the author. Amelia Collins related this to Voeltz. Hand of the Cause Collis Featherstone told the same story to others.
59 Letter from the Hands of the Cause in the Holy Land to the Hands of the Cause of God, 9 August 1960, in *The Ministry of the Custodians 1957–1963*, p. 227.
60 Letter from A. A. Furútan to Claire Vreeland, 31 May 1989. The original was provided to the author by the Vreeland family and the author has given it to the Bahá'í World Centre Archives.
61 Tablet attached to a letter, 20 March 1916. The Tablet was revealed by 'Abdu'l-Bahá on behalf of Horace Holley. USBNA, Horace Holley papers.
62 The first Bahá'í House of Worship was built in Ashqabat, Turkmenistan when it was part of the Russian Empire. After the Communist takeover, it was confiscated. After being badly damaged by an earthquake, it was demolished.
63 Cable from HANDSFAITH to BAHA'I WILMETTE, in *The Ministry of the Custodians 1957–1963*, p. 217–18.
64 Letter from the National Spiritual Assembly of the United States to Local Spiritual Assemblies, American National Teaching Committee, Area Teaching Committees, Intercontinental Teaching Committees, Bahá'í Summer Schools, 14 July 1960. New York Bahá'í Archives.
65 Sears, 'In Memoriam: Horace Holley (1887–1960), Hand of the Cause of God', in *Canadian Bahá'í News,* January 1961.
66 Letter from Mildred Mottahedeh to Doris Holley, 11 September 1960. USBNA, Doris Holley papers.
67 ibid.
68 'Horace Holley Reviews Growth of Administrative Order at Farewell Meeting on Eve of Departure for Holy Land', in *Bahá'í News*, no. 348 (February 1960), p. 2.
69 Rúḥíyyih Khánum, 'Horace Hotchkiss Holley', in *The Bahá'í World*, vol. XIII (1954–1963), p. 856.
70 ibid.
71 Holley, 'Current Bahá'í Activities', in *The Bahá'í World*, vol. III (1928–1930), pp. 60–61.
72 ibid. p. 60.
73 ibid.
74 ibid.
75 'Abdu'l-Bahá, Will and Testament, quoted in *Bahá'í World Faith*, p. 446.
76 Quoted in Rúḥíyyih Khánum, 'Horace Hotchkiss Holley', In Memoriam, in *The Bahá'í World*, vol. XIII (1954–1963), p. 858.
77 Undated poem by Horace Holley written while residing in Wilmette, Illinois. It was published in 1951 by the Wilmette local periodical, *Life*. The use of this poem for Bahá'í publicity was mentioned in *Bahá'í News*, no. 24 (May 1951), p. 6 under 'References to the Faith'. USBNA, Horace Holley papers.

INDEX

'Abdu'l-Bahá
  Centre of the Covenant 103, 125-7, 347, 350
  description by Horace Holley 30-31
  Disciples of 100, 103, 108, 138, 414
  and Hands of the Cause 322-3
  and Horace Holley *see* Holley, Horace
  House of, in Haifa 100, 103, 108, 132, 138, 336, 355, 374, 376-7, 379
  and Houses of Justice, Spirituality 102, 104-5, 136, 416
  and House of Worship, Wilmette 108-9, 217, 227-8, 277, 279, 285, 287, 416
  journeys to the West
    Austria, Germany and Hungary 55
    Canada 320
    England 41, 48-50, 60, 122
    Paris, France 34, 42, 47, 48-50, 51-6, 63, 71, 114-15, 217, 267
    Thonon-les-Bains, France 29-33, 403-4
    United States 48-50, 51-2, 62, 105, 110, 112, 117, 125-8, 141, 147, 174, 180, 203, 222, 227, 255-6, 260, 262, 286, 303, 310, 403, 417, 418
  life, in 'Akká and Haifa 4-8, 17, 57, 186, 416
    pilgrim visits 101, 104, 107, 110, 114, 126, 141, 173, 195, 230, 412, 416
  and Nineteen Day Feast 107
  passing of 123, 124, 128-30, 136, 194-5, 351, 361, 420
  portraits by
    Juliet Thompson 126-7, 403
    Kahlil Gibran 93, 412
  and race unity 112, 114, 172-4, 298
  and *Reality* magazine 140, 145
  station and title 4, 112, 126-7, 250, 265, 419
  Tablets 110-11, 127, 418
    of the Divine Plan 92-3, 106, 147, 181, 223-4, 289, 293, 319, 327, 338, 345, 360
    of Visitation 195
    to Dr Auguste Forel 438
    to Horace Holley xii, 58-9, 80-81
    to The Hague 257, 263, 448
  talks 34, 42, 50-55, 63, 121, 122, 174 218, 255-6, 260, 262, 265, 310, 334, 404, 428, 447
    Foundations of World Unity 255, 309, 458
    Promulgation of Universal Peace, The 63-4, 91-3, 110-11, 122, 257-8, 278, 313, 448, 255
    Some Answered Questions 17
  and war 6
    President Wilson 94
  Will and Testament 130-37, 141, 144, 154, 157, 195, 198-9, 234, 322-3, 341, 356-7, 359-60, 363, 370, 372, 377-8, 421, 425, 434, 435
  Writings, compilations of 161
  see also Shoghi Effendi; Sohrab, Ahmad
Addams, Jane 174
Adirondack Mountains 401
Afnán, Great 379
Africa, Africans 92, 172, 175, 273, 318, 331-2, 350, 353, 465

African-Americans 24-5, 112, 429 *see also* Black Americans
'Akká 4-6, 17, 62, 92, 101, 107, 129, 416, 465
Alaska 305, 464
Aldington, Richard 25-7, 403, 406, 408
Alexander, Jane and William 289, 330
'Alí-Muḥammad (Ibn-i-Aṣdaq) 322
Allen, Samuel A. 263
Allenby, Edmund, General 92
America, Americans *see* United States *see also* Latin America, South America
American Board of Commissioners for Foreign Missions 295, 398
Americanism 91, 326
American Republic(s) 238, 293, 311-12, 369
Amsterdam, Holland 332-3
Angell, Norman 262
Anglican Church (Church of England) 21, 182-3, 333, 433
Antilles 329, 464
Antwerp, Belgium 16
Apollinaire, Guillaume 64, 407
Ardennes, the 67
Arensberg, Walter 83, 410
Arnold, Matthew 52
Asadu'lláh-i-Qumí 32
Ashnur Galerie, Paris 44-7, 64
Ashqabat ('Ishqábád) 109, 379, 468
Asquith, Herbert H. 74
Astor, John Jacob 148
Atlantic 1, 16, 30, 64, 75, 76, 78, 82, 99, 180, 300, 319, 373
Atlantic Charter 310, 312
Austin, Elsie 461
Australia 153, 224, 289, 370
Austria 55, 63, 67, 111
Austro-Hungarian Empire 63, 67, 111
Auxiliary Boards 340-45, 347, 350, 360, 362, 443, 445
Axis powers 300, 314, 458

Báb, the 5, 53, 57, 107, 122, 131, 181, 250, 265, 339, 423
  Centenary of Declaration 293, 303-5, 308
  Declaration 293, 303-4
  Shrine of 129, 212, 318, 320, 324, 336, 339, 380 *see also* Bahá'í Holy Shrines
Bagdadi, Zia 112, 197
Baghdad 190, 200, 349, 438, 455
Bagnell, Robert W. 262
Bahá'í
  administration, Administrative Order xiv, 101, 136, 141, 143-4, 149-50, 153, 155, 166, 172, 182 188, 191, 195, 198, 201, 211, 213-14, 216-17, 232-3, 237, 241, 250-51, 292, 297, 305-6, 316, 324, 327-8, 341-2, 346, 357, 380-82, 421, 447, 450
  incorporation of institutions 104, 165-8, 188, 193, 196-7, 201, 210-14, 301, 439-40
  see also Auxiliary Boards; By-Laws; Continental Boards of Counsellors; Convention; Hands of the Cause; Holley, Horace; Houses of Justice; International Bahá'í Council; International Teaching Centre; National Spiritual Assemblies; Spiritual Assemblies, Local; Nineteen Day Feast; Universal House of Justice
  Holy Places 190, 336, 338-9, 348-9, 374
  Holy Shrines 128, 212, 356, 359, 362, 464
  International Community 381
  Publishing Committee 285, 306, 309, 454
  World Centre 99, 128-9, 197, 212, 253, 311, 338, 340, 359-60, 362, 370, 412, 421, 434, 454
Bahá'í Administration 216-17
Bahá'í Magazine 259, 271-2, 427 *see also Star of the West*
Bahá'í News 187, 216, 233, 241, 248, 259, 264, 267, 305-6, 308, 309, 439, 454
Bahai News Letter 155

Bahá'í Procedure 305-6
Bahá'í Scriptures 161, 208, 428
Bahá'í World, The 166, 213, 252-4, 268, 284, 309, 316, 348, 382, 444, 447
Bahá'í World Faith 161, 303
Bahá'í Year Book 252, 420
Bahíyyih <u>Kh</u>ánum 6, 123, 129-30, 192, 202, 355, 414
Bahjí 168, 353-4, 467
   Mansion 168, 354, 356
Bahá'u'lláh 5, 102, 131, 136, 178, 228, 237, 249, 250, 260, 331, 333, 361, 374-5, 420, 423, 450, 455, 465
   and Hands of the Cause 102, 322, 341
   Horace Holley's understanding of xiii, xiv, 41, 57-8, 122, 161-3, 183, 189, 22, 254-5, 264, 280, 306, 378
   House in Baghdad 190, 200, 438
   and Houses of Justice xiv, 102, 104, 125, 130, 136, 154, 190-91, 382
   and peace xiii, 94, 222, 312
   Shrine and Mansion of 190, 353-4, 465, 467 *see also* Bahá'í Holy Shrines
   World Order of 102, 159, 191, 269, 293, 359-60
   Writings 121, 136, 161-3
      Gleanings from the Writings of Bahá'u'lláh 290
      Epistle to the Son of the Wolf 290
      Kitáb-i-'Ahdí 341
      Kitáb-i-Íqán: The Book of Certitude 290
      Kitáb-i-Aqdas (Book of Laws) 102, 127, 136, 154, 211, 276-7, 338, 356, 452
      Prayers and Meditations 290
      Tablet of the Branch 127-8
   see also Covenant of Bahá'u'lláh
Baker, Cecil Sherman 400
Baker, Dorothy 301, 315, 324, 326, 329, 332, 340, 460
Balkans 67
Balyuzi, Hasan M. 465, 467
Banání, Músá 331

Bangalore, India 334
Barbados 115-16
Barney, Alice Pike 17, 401
Barney, Natalie 47-8
Battle of Britain 299
Bayfield, Wisconsin 2
Belgium, Belgians 67-8, 70, 72, 111
Bible 20-21, 50, 161
Black Americans 24-5, 111-14, 172-6, 296, 429, 431, 456
Blake, William 407
Blomfield, Lady 3-4, 134-5, 398
Blomfield, Mary 3-4
Blum, Jerome S. 47
Boards of Counsel 104
   Chicago 101, 414
   New York *see* New York
Boas, Franz 174
Bolden, Richard Manuel, Reverend 175, 429
Bombay (Mumbai), India 334
Book of Common Prayer 183
Boston 24, 104, 109, 134, 175, 197, 217, 226, 230, 231, 239-47, 249, 403, 421, 437, 445
   Spiritual Assembly 239-45, 445
Botticelli 'Primavera' 118
Bourgeois, Louis 282, 284, 453
Bowditch, Nancy, and family 303
Bowen, Goodridge Sinderby (Julian Pascal) 115-16, 417
Boyle, Louise 436
Braithwaite, William Stanley 24-5, 403
Brazil 348
Britain, British Isles, British 1-2, 4, 10, 41, 48-9, 61, 64, 69, 70-74, 02, 129, 135, 148, 182-3, 192, 297, 299-300, 309-10, 331, 465
   artists, poets, writers 4, 47
   Bahá'ís 3-4, 48, 133-5, 191-2, 323, 379, 436, 466
   National Spiritual Assembly 135, 192, 201, 466
British Empire 41, 43, 74
   Exhibition 201
Brittingham, Isabella 108, 222
Brittingham, James 108

Brooklyn 107-8, 172, 175, 188, 431
Brown, John 173
Brown University 258
Browne, Edward Granville 5-6, 423, 454
Bryan, Mary 62
Bryan, William Jennings 5, 62-3
Buddha, Buddhism 60, 118, 334
Buffalo, NY 206, 258
Buikema, Gertrude 422
Bulgaria 315
Bullock, Matthew 461
By-Laws
   Chicago 168
   Local Spiritual Assemblies 166-8, 211-12, 381, 430
   National Spiritual Assembly of the United States and Canada 211-14, 233-8, 242, 245, 316, 381, 444
   New York Board of Counsel 103
   New York Spiritual Assembly 166-8, 211-12, 381, 430 *see also* Declaration of Trust
   Temple Unity 194, 210, 435

California 105, 133, 152, 179, 197, 215, 222, 223, 224, 256, 262, 287, 301, 310, 348, 367, 422, 441, 455, 460
Calvin, John 20
Cambridge University, England 5, 14, 423, 452
Canada, Canadians 16, 196, 211-12, 222, 255, 258, 293, 295, 299, 301, 309, 319, 436, 459
   Bahá'ís 92, 99, 143, 166, 215, 217, 223, 239, 257, 289, 292, 297, 299, 301-2, 305, 315, 318-20, 324-5, 316, 350, 368, 436, 455, 460, 465
   Parliament 258
   National Spiritual Assembly 318, 319-20, 325, 350, 459 *see also* National Spiritual Assemblies/ United States and Canada
Cannéll, Shipwith 82-3
Caribbean 14, 115, 173, 175, 293
Catholic Church, Catholics 18-20, 41, 51, 172, 183, 401, 433
Central America 315, 318, 329

Cezanne 46, 60
Chance, Hugh 454
Chandler, Raymond 417
Chanler, Julie 148-52, 154, 156, 158, 425, 427
Chanler, Lewis Stuyvesant 148-9, 152, 154, 158
Chennai (Madras), India 334
Chicago 24-5, 105, 112, 174, 179, 206, 211, 247, 260, 280-81, 287-8, 304, 312, 317, 321, 375, 460
   Bahá'í community and events 99-101, 108-9, 112, 137-8, 168, 197, 201, 215, 217-18, 257, 285, 329, 332, 364, 413-14, 416, 430, 443, 454
   Board of Counsel (House of Spirituality) 101, 414
   Reading Room 137-8, 150, 217, 370
   Spiritual Assembly 168
   see also House of Worship; Temple Unity
China, Chinese 111, 278, 315
Christian, Kenneth 461
Christian Commonwealth, The 59
Christianity 7, 19, 50-51, 57, 86-7, 111, 131, 181, 185, 327, 339, 398
Christian Scientists 122
Christmas 15, 39-41, 150-51, 297, 324
Church *see* Anglican, Catholic, Congregational, Episcopalian
Churchill, Winston 74, 309-10, 314, 409
City on a Hill 19, 35, 402
Cleveland, Ohio 257
Cobb, Stanwood 271-2
Coffee, Rudolf I, Rabbi 262, 449
Cold War 314
Collins, Amelia 152, 301, 315, 324-5, 331, 336-7, 345, 353, 375, 379, 397, 460, 461, 463, 465
Colombia 348
Colombo, Sri Lanka 334
Columbia University 9, 141, 174, 256
Columbian Exhibition 24
Committee on Permanent Committees 193
Communism 113, 267, 314-15, 327, 411, 417, 468

Community Church, The 260, 449
Conclaves *see* Hands of the Cause
Congregational Church 7, 18, 40, 175, 185, 187, 294, 398, 433
  Nazarene 175
Connecticut vii, 1, 6, 9, 11-12, 18, 40, 43-4, 68, 74, 115, 120, 173, 204, 257, 373, 417
Continental Boards of Counsellors 341, 344
Continental Fund 340-2
Conventions, National Baháʾí
  Alaska 464
  British Isles 192
  Germany 192
  Canada 319-20
  Latin America 348-9
  North America (US and Canada) 54, 93-4, 109, 137-8, 192-7, 200-03, 207, 211, 215, 217, 223, 225, 227-8, 231-50, 267, 279, 293, 302, 308, 317, 343, 368, 434, 435, 467
Cook County 287, 459
Coolidge, Calvin, President 225, 259
Cooper, Ella Goodall 197-8, 435, 441
Cornell University 258
Covenant of Baháʾuʾlláh 125-8, 136-8, 146, 153, 218-19, 222, 236, 292, 341, 347, 350, 361, 370, 422, 434
  Centre of the Covenant 103, 126-7, 347, 350
  Covenant-breaking 138, 144, 356, 378, 421, 423-4
Crum, Ophelia 431

Darwin, Charles 51, 54
Davies, Mary Carolyn 83, 410
Dawn-Breakers, The: Nabíl's Narrative 290
Day, Anne L. 273
Dayton, Ohio 257, 461
Declaration of Trust 439
  National Spiritual Assembly 166-7, 211-14, 245, 316, 439
Depression *see* Great Depression
Detroit 206
Dieppe, France 48

Dispensation of Baháʾuʾlláh, The 250, 265, 356
Dodge, Arthur Pillsbury 100-01
Doolittle, Hilda (H.D.) 25
Doremus, Polly vii, 452, 467
Dreyfus-Barney, Hippolyte 17, 29-30, 42, 65, 413
Dreyfus-Barney, Laura Clifford 17, 29, 42, 47, 54-5, 413
Druze, the 92, 129
DuBois, W. E. B. 176, 403
DuBose, William P. 432
Duchamp, Marcel 83
Dumbarton Oaks Conferencce (1944), 310
Duncan, Isadora 398
Dunbar, Hooper 419, 460, 464, 467
Dunn, Clara and Hyde (John) 224, 289
Dvorak, Antonin 418
Dyar, Harrison Gray 140-46, 150, 158, 423-4
Dyar, Wellesca Allen (Aseyeh) 141

Eastman, Max 89-90, 113, 411
East River, New York 78
Ecuador 348
Eggleston family 455
Egoist, The 26, 59-60
Egypt 6, 29, 42, 48, 49, 147
  Baháʾís in 132, 185-6
Einstein, Albert 154
Eisenhower, Dwight David, President 326-7, 461
Elijah, Cave of 379
Eliot, Maine 202, 290
Ellis Island 176
Emerson, Ralph Waldo 27, 180
English Channel 72-3
Episcopal Church (es), Episcopalians 16, 96, 116-17, 170, 179, 182-5, 187, 401, 433
  of the Ascension 117
  Grace Episcopal Church, Manhattan 16
  St Mark's-in-the-Bowery 96, 116-18, 137, 170, 179-85, 187-8, 412, 418, 432-3, 437

Esslemont, John E. 323, 379
European Teaching Committee 317
Evanston, Illinois 287, 317, 340

Fareed, Amin 148, 423-4
Farmer, Sarah 180
Fascism 267-8, 314
Fatimah 131
Fleming, Andrew 108
Fauvists 44, 47, 406
Ferdinand, Archduke, of Austria 67
Fergusson, John Duncan 47
Ferraby, John 376, 467
First Emanuel Church 175, 429
Fletcher, John Gould 46, 64
Florence, Italy 18-19, 22, 182, 161
Florida 215, 400
Ford, Henry 77
Ford, Mary Hanford 140, 148, 221, 423
Forel, Auguste 210, 438
Formative Age 308
Forum, The, magazine 86, 410-11
Fosdick, Harry Emerson 272-3, 449
France 16, 18, 29-30, 49-51, 54, 56, 62, 75-6, 78, 134, 209-10, 333, 377, 438
  and World War I 64-5, 67-9, 72, 75, 88, 111, 448
  see also Paris; Thonon-les-Bains
French, Nellie 215, 439, 447
French Revolution 51
Friends, Society of 122, 399
Frost, Robert 408
Furútan, 'Alí-Akbar 324-5, 333, 357-8, 378-9, 460, 465

Gambedoo, O. W. 64, 407
Geneva, New York 207
Geneva, Switzerland 20, 29, 33, 41, 209-10, 229, 438
Germany, Germans 20, 61, 110-11, 128, 203, 278, 301-2, 429, 436
  Bahá'ís in 55-6, 132, 134, 192, 426, 460, 465
  Templers 374
  and World Wars 63-75, 87-92, 299-302, 458, 466
Getsinger, Edward 416, 440

Getsinger, Lua 126-7, 222, 416, 440
Geyserville Bahá'í School (now Bosch) 224, 441, 455
Giachery, Ugo 460
Gibran, Kahlil 93, 412
George Ronald, Publisher 348
Geyserville (Bosch) 441
Graham, Billy 327
Grant, Ulysses S. 82, 329
'Grantwood' 82-4, 89
Grasmere, Henry 429
Great Depression 183-4, 209, 225-6, 229, 268, 270, 277-8, 299, 309, 327, 438, 441, 443
Great Migration 172-3
Greece 312
Greeks, ancient 23, 50, 78
Greenacre, Alice 211
Green Acre 156, 179-80, 202-7, 224-5, 230, 252, 255, 273, 290-91, 299, 301-2, 320, 441, 455
Greenleaf, Elizabeth 223, 443
Greenwich, Connecticut 115, 417
Gregory, Louis 112, 173, 175, 176, 197, 222-3, 228-31, 263-4, 301, 315, 323, 325, 403, 422, 443-4, 455, 459
Grossmann, Hermann 460
Grundy, Julia M. 106-7
Guardian *see* Shoghi Effendi
Guardianship 194, 266, 297, 341, 346-7, 356, 362-4, 371, 377, 382, 423
Guérard, Albert Léon 262
Guildhall, London 74
Guildhall School of Music, London 116
Gulpáygání, Mírzá Abu'l-Faḍl 146-7
Guthrie, William Norman 117-18, 179-85, 275, 413, 418, 432, 448, 449

Haddad, Anton 103
Haifa, Israel 29, 49, 92, 114, 128-31, 133-5, 147, 190-92, 195-6, 202, 206, 212, 232-3, 237, 297, 321, 324, 335-6, 345, 353-4, 356-7, 363, 368, 370-72, 373-80, 437, 457
  Bahá'í cemetery 379
  Haparsim (Persian) Street 335, 374-5

Halpert, Samuel 82
Hand(s) of the Cause 297, 322, 327, 341, 352, 371
  appointed by
    'Abdu'l-Bahá 322-3
    Bahá'u'lláh 102, 322, 341
    Shoghi Effendi xiii, 138, 179, 301, 315, 321, 322-5, 340, 360
  Chief Stewards 350, 358-60, 362, 371
  Conclaves
    First 353-4, 357-63, 370-71
    Second 369, 371
    Third 369, 371-2
  Custodians 357, 359-64, 372, 376, 378-9
  duties and functions of 323, 340-41, 353, 350, 356-7
  Institution of the Learned 341
  and intercontinental conferences 329, 331-3, 350, 353
  Proclamation 357-9, 363
  service on National Spiritual Assemblies following appointment 325
  see also individual named entries
Haney, Paul 316, 326, 340, 342, 357, 363, 367-8, 461, 464, 467
Hannen family 287, 412
Harding, Warren, President 113, 441
Harlem Renaissance 112, 173
Harlem River, New York 78
Harris, Gertrude 103
Harris, Hooper 103, 429, 434
Hartford, Connecticut 11, 257
Harvard College, University 21, 180, 197, 227
Harvard Divinity School 223
Hawaii 300
Ḥaẓíratu'l-Quds (Bahá'í Centre) 279, 282-6, 300, 330-31, 342, 349
Hearst, Phoebe Apperson 412
Heist, Albert 207
Henry VIII, King 20-21, 182
Herbert, Bertha *see* Holley, Bertha
Herklotz, Bertha L. 203, 210, 285-6, 429, 436, 454
Hinduism 334
Hiroshima, Japan 312-13

Hoagg, Emogene 133, 422
Hoar, William H. 103
Hofman, David 348
Hofman, Marion Holley vii, 311, 348, 464
Holy Year 331
Holley, Alexander Lyman 436
Holley, Bertha Herbert 1-4, 9, 15-17, 29-30, 33, 39-41, 43-4, 53-4, 55, 66, 68, 70-75, 78-9, 81-2, 90, 93, 94-6, 100, 104, 114-15, 183, 210, 329, 348, 397, 398, 401, 402, 403, 409, 410, 438, 467
  career as artist and fashion designer 2, 44, 66, 78-9, 81, 90, 95, 126, 405, 406
Holley, Doris Pascal 114-17, 185, 203-6, 208, 275-6, 278-80, 283, 285, 290, 293, 300, 302-3, 307-8, 317, 321, 324, 330-31, 353, 365, 367, 375, 380, 417, 452, 455, 459, 460
Holley, Edward Hotchkiss 10, 399
Holley, Ellen Martha Wheeler (Nellie) 11, 14-15
Holley, Francis Newman 10, 173
Holley, Francis Newman II (Frank, brother of Horace) 10-11, 14, 16, 68, 73, 332, 399, 401
Holley, Hertha 21-2, 26, 30, 40, 52-3, 55, 66, 70-73, 75, 79, 209-10, 274-5, 438
Holley, Horace Hotchkiss
  and 'Abdu'l-Bahá xi-xii, xiv, 8, 29-34, 37, 40-41, 53-8, 71, 76, 80-81, 86, 114, 124, 205, 217, 255, 324, 333, 348, 379, 419
  descriptions of 30-31, 124
  Tablets from xii, 58-9, 80-81
  and advertising, publicity 97, 119, 200, 203, 304, 457
  and Ahmad Sohrab 150-52, 156, 158-9
  background
    family and early life 6, 7, 10-15, 69, 125, 173, 292-3, 402
    religious 3, 7, 14, 18, 19-21, 40-41, 52, 85-7, 162-3, 182, 294-5

475

Bahá'í World, The (Bahá'í Year Book)
213, 252-4, 284, 309, 316, 348
and Bahá'u'lláh, understanding of
xiii, xiv, 41, 57-8, 122, 161-3,
183, 189, 22, 254-5, 264, 280,
306, 378
and Bertha Herbert Holley 2, 9,
15-16, 21-2, 40-41, 43-53, 65-6,
68-73, 75, 78-82, 94-5
children 97, 204
Hertha 21-2, 33, 52, 53, 55, 70,
75, 209-10, 274-5, 438
Horace Junior 116
Marcia 82, 274-5, 373
compilations
Bahá'í Administration 216, 305-6
Bahá'í Procedure 305-6
Bahá'í Scriptures 161, 208, 428
Bahá'í World Faith 161, 203
Foundations of World Unity 255, 309
Messages to the Bahá'í World: 1950-1957
The World Order of Bahá'u'lláh 250, 265
development of
Bahá'í administration, institutions xiv, 110, 155-6, 158, 160, 165-9, 199, 206, 216-19, 249-50, 285-6, 305-7, 308, 320, 328, 338, 342-5, 367, 381-2, 451
Auxiliary Board 342-5, 347
Convention 193, 231-4, 239-40, 309
National Centre and Office 285-6, 457-8
see also Holley/service on Bahá'í institutions
Bahá'í community life 99, 100, 106, 108, 159, 168, 216, 237, 292
and Doris Pascal Holley 114-16, 203-6, 208, 276, 279-81, 282-3, 285, 302-3, 307, 321, 330-31, 367, 375, 380
editor, editorials 2, 15, 139-40, 155,
216, 252-3, 270, 272 *see also*
Holley/compilations; production and printing of Bahá'í literature
education 1, 9, 13-16, 23, 50
friendship with
Amelia Collins 324, 331, 336, 353, 465
Bowditch family 303
Doris and Willard McKay 207-8, 320
Fred Schopflocher 301-2, 320
Kinney family 418
Leroy Ioas 256, 273-4, 317, 324, 336
Mildred Mottahedeh 334, 373, 380, 381
Mountfort Mills 104, 109, 174, 210, 211, 283-4, 300, 325, 438
Roy Wilhelm 109, 110, 131, 317
True family 287, 317, 331
Wright, Frank Lloyd 449
see also Holley, Irving
and Green Acre 204, 206, 225, 252, 290, 303-4, 320
Hand of the Cause 321, 322-6, 329, 331-35, 340, 342-9, 353-78, 460, 465
Conclaves 353-63, 369-72
Custodian 372, 376-8
health 207, 308, 316-17, 347, 349-51, 353, 363
and House of Worship 56, 217, 278, 282
interest in
art and artists 44-7, 64, 66, 78, 82-8, 113
current affairs 64, 106, 256-7, 266-8, 272-3
oneness of mankind 177-8
organization 198-9, 218
peace xi, xiii, 34-5, 75, 86, 88-9, 90, 222, 309, 313-14, 320-21
racial justice 112-13, 173-6, 263, 296, 298
social teachings of Bahá'í Faith 222, 254-5
in Italy 18-19, 33, 37-41

and leaders of thought 254, 258-63, 272-3, 451
and Louis Gregory 228, 230-31, 443-4, 459
memorials to 379-82
New York, love for 9, 204-5, 280, 373
in Paris 16-17, 34, 41, 43-66, 70-72, 114
  Ashnur Galerie 25, 44-7, 64
personality xii-xiii, 2-3, 207-8, 276, 286, 303, 320, 325 329-30, 337, 343-4, 349, 357, 365-7, 377, 400, 419, 454, 459
photographs of 330-31
production and printing of Bahá'í literature 134, 139, 160-61, 200, 216, 252-4, 255, 261, 265, 290, 316
and *Reality* magazine 139-40, 255, 423
service on Bahá'í institutions
  committees 92, 93, 106, 193-4, 256-7
  National Spiritual Assembly 200, 211, 215, 218, 231, 249-50, 291, 307, 315-16, 319, 325, 328, 347, 372
    incorporation of 211, 213
    secretary 144, 150, 152, 166, 182, 187, 201-10, 223, 226, 232-4, 245-7, 251, 259-60, 264, 267, 283-6, 289, 298, 301, 307, 311, 325, 342, 367
  New York Board of Counsel 101, 103, 105-6, 108, 133, 137, 140
  New York Spiritual Assembly 103, 142, 168, 175, 255
    By-Laws 166-8
    secretary 142, 156, 159, 163, 166-8
and Seven Year Plan 294-6, 455
and Shoghi Effendi 123, 131-2, 158, 161, 206, 208-9, 216-17, 218, 232-5, 239-40, 245-6, 252-4, 257, 259, 265-8, 271-2, 278-80, 307, 308, 316, 328, 329, 334-5, 347, 349-50, 365, 372, 381-2, 437
  The Advent of Divine Justice 297-8, 456
  pilgrimage 335-40, 348
  The Promised Day Is Come
  World Order letters 250, 265-9, 272, 450 *see also* Holley/ compilations
spiritual character and development xii-xiii, 36, 37-8, 75-6, 80-81, 97, 120, 122-3, 177-8, 205, 266, 275-6, 293-4, 299, 317, 320, 337, 343, 368, 379, 459
and St Mark's-in-the-Bowery 116-17, 179-85
study classes, outlines 225, 290-91, 299, 320, 450
talks 176-8, 225, 237, 252, 258, 292, 329-30, 349, 415
travel 329
  Britain 1-2, 71, 73-4
  India 333-6
  Israel 335-40, 353, 369
  Panama 329
  Peru 321, 329, 348
  Uganda 331-2
  Sweden 332-3
  Switzerland 17
and the Universal House of Justice xiv, 86, 324, 338, 378, 381-2
and war 86, 257, 269, 299
  World Wars 68-75, 87, 88-91, 110-11, 122, 257, 299, 302, 313-14
and *World Order* magazine 272, 319
and *World Unity* magazine (and Foundation) 258-65, 267-72
writer xii, 22-8, 37-9, 42, 45-6, 52, 53, 55-7, 64, 78, 84-7, 96-7, 123, 139-40, 205, 213, 216, 252, 255, 286, 288, 332, 357-60, 363
  'Gambedoo, O. W.' 64, 407
  articles, essays, statements 22-3, 28, 45, 59-60, 78, 123, 139, 161-2, 201
    'Aims and Purposes of the Bahá'í Faith' 253, 447

'A New Bahá'í Era' 363-4
'The Art of the Dress' 81
'The Clue to World Strife' 267-8
'Present-Day Administration of the Bahá'í Faith' 306-7
'Regarding Service' 291
'The Return of Religion' 33
'The Writings of Bahá'u'lláh' 162
books
   Bahaism: The Modern Social Religion xi, 56-9, 64, 121
   Bahai: The Spirit of the Age 121-3, 419
   The Dynamics of Art 66
   Religion for Mankind 348
   The Social Principle 84-8, 419
plays 23, 66
   The Genius 96-8
   I Want to Live in Greenwich Village 204
   Read-Aloud Plays 87
poetry 3, 9, 22-8, 33, 37, 39, 46, 60, 77-8, 84, 139
   'By This I Know His Love' 317
   'Confession' 95
   Creation: Post-Impressionist Poems 26-8, 46
   'Cross Patch' 84-5
   Divination and Creation 28
   'Flight' 98
   'God Most Glorious' 384
   'Hertha' 274
   'Homeward' 62
   'In Italy' 22
   Inner Garden, The 23
   'New York (by an artist refugee)' 78
   Post-Impressionist Poems 46
   'Sonnet: On the Occasion of a Birthday' 1
   'The Mice' 26-7
   'The Return of Religion' 33
   'To-day' 282
   'War' 75
Holley, Horace, Junior 116

Holley, Horace, Reverend 13, 19, 40, 400, 402
Holley, Irving (brother of Horace) vii, 1-4, 10-11, 14-15, 161, 308, 317, 332, 373, 400, 433, 467
   correspondence with Horace 65-6, 69, 87, 94, 97, 115, 120-21, 206, 252, 419
Holley, Irving, Jr. (nephew to Horace) vii, 366, 432
Holley, Lawrence 11
Holley, Lillian 11, 13, 14
Holley, Marcia (Betty) 82, 210, 274, 373, 452, 467
Holley, Myron 400
Holley, Orville 40-41, 400, 404-5
Holocaust 302
Holt, Hamilton 262
Hoover, Herbert, President 225-6, 270, 441
Hotel du Parc, Thonon 30 *et seq.*
Hotel Stevens, Chicago 304
Houses of Worship, Bahá'í Temples 349, 370, 379, 468
   Wilmette, Chicago (Mother Temple of the West) 56, 93, 104, 106, 108-9, 137, 160, 192, 193, 194, 197, 200, 203, 205, 211, 214-15, 217, 221, 228-9, 240, 261, 277-80, 282, 284-7, 289, 291, 293, 300, 301, 303-5, 307, 315, 317, 318, 331, 332, 338, 372, 380, 416, 440, 442, 453, 460
   Foundation Hall 217, 232, 309, 343, 372
Houses of Justice, local and national 102, 104, 136, 414 *see also* Spiritual Assemblies, Local; National Spiritual Assemblies
Hudson River 9-10, 77-8, 82-3, 110, 180, 280, 329, 414
Hughes, Charles Evans 262
Hungary 55, 63, 67, 111, 139
Hus, Jan 20
Ḥusayn (son of 'Abdu'l-Bahá)
Hutchinson, Andrew 103
Hyderabad, India 334

Iliad 78
Illinois, State of 193, 196, 211-12
Imagist poets 25-7, 407, 408
India, Indians 132, 154, 329, 333-5, 340, 440
Inglis, Edith Magee 429
Institution of the Learned 341
Inter-America Committee 293-5
Inter-America Conference (1944) 303-4, 364
Intercontinental conferences 329, 331-3, 348, 350, 353, 361-2, 364, 369
International Archives 339, 370
International Bahá'í Council 324-5, 352, 355, 357-8, 360-62, 368, 370-72, 375, 376, 377, 381
International Teaching Centre 341, 344, 381
Inuits 368
Ioas, Leroy 247, 256, 273-4, 292-3, 295, 301, 310-11, 316-17, 323-5, 332, 336, 345-7, 354-5, 376, 460, 463, 464, 467
Ioas, Sylvia 311, 317, 336, 354, 376
Iran xi, 5, 17, 42, 49, 101-2, 132, 134, 137, 201, 297, 322, 412 *see also* Persia
National Spiritual Assembly 322, 324
Ireland, Irish 176, 179, 333, 380, 398, 401, 460
Iron Age journal 97, 119, 419
Iron Curtain 314
'Ishqábád (Ashqabat) 109, 379, 468
Islam, Muslim 5-7, 129, 131, 136, 186-7, 290, 327, 339, 374, 375, 467
Israel, Israelis 311, 324, 335, 336, 338-9, 358, 361-2, 369, 370, 373
War of Independence 369, 374
Istanbul, Turkey 29
Italy 17-22, 29, 39-41, 87, 132, 182, 283, 318, 334, 402, 450, 461
Bahá'ís in 132, 268
Ives, Howard Colby 108, 222
Ives, Mabel Rice-Wray 222

Jack, Marion 315
Jamál Páshá 91
Japan 132, 278, 300, 312-14, 458
Jasion, Jan 398
Jaurés, Jean 68
Javid, Dr Manucher 351, 365, 464, 465
Jerusalem 335, 339, 374
Church of the Holy Sepulchre 339
Jesus Christ 19, 32, 39-41, 50-51, 53, 56, 85, 101, 114-15, 163, 181-2, 250
Crucifixion of 353, 466
Disciples of 353, 367, 466
Jews, Jewish 65, 129, 172, 187, 212, 290, 297, 301-2, 374, 375, 467
Johns, Orrick 83, 410
Johnson, James Weldon 174, 403
Johnson, Paul 172, 441
Jordan, David Starr 262, 449
Judas Iscariot 367, 466

Kalutara, Sri Lanka 334
Kampala, Uganda 329, 331-2, 370, 462
Kandy, Sri Lanka 334
Kavelin, Borrah 364-5, 368, 381
Keller, Helen 154
Kelsey, Curtis 128-9
Kenosha, Wisconsin 101, 108, 286, 414
Khadem, Zikrullah 333-4
Khan, Ali-Kuli 146, 412, 425
Khan, Florence Breed 412
Kheiralla, Ibrahim George 100-01, 144
Kinney, Edward 'Saffa' (and family) 117, 179, 180, 399, 413, 418
Knobloch, Fanny 56
Korea, Republic of 262
Kreymborg, Alfred 82-4, 410
Krug, Florian and Grace 128-9
Kuehl, Warren F. 273

Lake Michigan 112, 200, 279, 284
Lake Mohonk Conferences 256
Latimer, George 247, 256, 301, 311, 316, 325, 422, 436, 448, 457
Latin America 290, 295, 317, 329, 345-6, 348-9
Lausanne, Switzerland 17-18, 30
Lawrenceville Academy 7, 13-14, 88, 400
League of Nations 94, 106, 113, 270, 309-10, 312-13
League of Nations Association 262

League of Women Voters 175
Lebanon 5, 103, 197
Le Havre, France 71-2, 438
Leland Stanford University 256
Leman, Lac (Lake Geneva) 29, 33
Lesser Peace 312-13, 458
Liberator 89-90
Lima, Ohio 301
Lima, Peru 329, 348-9, 461
Limerick, Ireland 380
Linden Avenue, Wilmette 286
Life and Teachings of Abbas Effendi, The 5-7, 17, 30, 58, 62, 398
Little, Marion 461
Liverpool, England 1-2
Lloyd, Nellie 133, 429
Locke, Alain LeRoy 112, 173
Loeding, Sophie 285-6, 308, 454
London, England 2, 4, 17, 24-6, 33, 41-3, 46-7, 57, 72-4, 77-8, 82, 115-16, 121, 123, 130, 351-2, 355, 358, 371, 408
Long Island 82
Los Angeles, California 116, 148, 196, 424
Louhelen Bahá'í School 291, 441, 455
Louis XIV 51
Lowell, Amy 25
Lunt, Alfred 109, 134, 169, 197, 199, 201-2, 210, 216, 225-8, 230, 231-50, 275, 426, 434, 435, 437, 439, 441-3, 445
Luther, Martin 20
Luxembourg 67

MacNutt, Howard 103, 106-7, 222, 255
Macphail, Agnes 448
Madras (Chennai), India 334
Manhattan *see* New York
Man Ray 82-3
Mansfield, Katherine 47
Marburg, Theodore 262
Marseilles, France 29
Mary Magdalene 131, 353
Mason, George 369
Massachusetts Institute of Technology 141

Masses, The, magazine 89, 411
Mathews, Loulie 148, 176
Matisse 44, 46, 406
Maxwell, May Bolles 16, 223, 237, 320, 325, 427
Maxwell, Mary 320, 325, 336, 465 *see also* Rúḥíyyih Khánum
Maxwell, William Sutherland 16, 318, 324, 448, 460
Mayberry, Florence 343-4, 381
Mayflower Compact 213
McCarthy, Joseph 417
McClelland, Sam G. 443
McClure, John Peebles 59-60, 407
McDaniel, Allen 231-2, 292, 301, 315, 441, 446, 457
McKay, Doris 207-8, 320, 460
McKay, Willard 207-8, 300
Mead, Edwin D. 262
Mead, Lucia Ames 262
Metropolitan Museum of Art 9
Mexico 89, 296, 329
Miami, Florida 196
Miller, Herbert Adophus 262
Mills, Mountfort 104, 108, 117, 134-5, 143, 166, 174, 179, 191, 197-8, 201, 210, 211, 283, 300, 317, 325, 381, 429, 434, 438, 448, 449
Mills, Samuel John 398
Minnetonka (ship) 74-5
Mírzá Mihdí 130
Mírzá Yaḥyá 423
Montreal, Canada 79, 196, 257, 292, 319, 325, 448, 465
Moore, Marianne 83
Monod, Charlotte (MacGregor Todd), 397-8
Monod, Jacques Lucien 398
Monod, Lucien 397
Morrison, Gayle 443
Morton, Florence Reed 257-9, 266, 268-9, 271, 273, 326, 442, 445, 449, 450, 451, 458
Moscow, Russia 314
Mottahedeh, Mildred 334, 373, 380-81
Mount Carmel 181, 190, 212, 335-6, 373, 379, 434

Mount Savant 303
Movius, Mary Rumsey 257, 259, 267-8, 271, 448, 449
Mudaliar, Ramaswami 334
Muḥammad-'Alí 133-4, 136, 144
Mullá Ḥusayn 304
Mumbai (Bombay), India 334
Munro, Harold 408
Munroe, Harriet 24, 28
Munson, Gordon 410
Mussolini, Benito 268
Mysore, India 334

NAACP (National Association for the Advancement of Colored People) 174, 176, 262, 403, 431
Nabíl 290, 455
Nantucket 75
Napoleon Bonaparte 51
Nash, Philip C. 262
National Eskimo aand Indian Teaching Committee (Canada) 268
National Race Amity Committee 175-6
National Spiritual Assemblies 135-6, 156, 167-8, 198-9, 213-14, 216, 219-20, 236, 249, 284, 318, 320, 325, 340, 342, 345, 348-9, 350, 356, 358, 360-62, 371, 378, 381-2, 414, 416
   British Isles 135, 192, 201, 466
   Canada 318, 319-20, 325, 350, 459
   France 377
   Germany 192
   India 333
   Iran 322, 324-5
   United States (from 1948) 319, 324-6, 327-9, 330, 337-8, 340, 341-2, 343, 347, 349, 363, 367, 379-80, 382, 423, 466
   United States and Canada (to 1948) 109-10, 141, 143, 179, 182, 192, 194, 196-9, 200-06, 208-9, 210-20, 221, 223, 252-4, 256, 265, 265, 271-2, 280-81, 282-6, 290, 292-6, 298-30, 309-11, 315-17, 318, 370, 381, 413, 422, 425, 434, 436, 443-4, 454, 456, 458, 469
   and Ahmad Sohrab, New History Society 147, 156, 158, 426
   and Alfred Lunt 225, 231-49, 441-2, 445
   and Chicago community 216-19, 247
   and House of Worship 216, 221, 279, 284, 291, 440
   and national headquarters, office 207, 279-80, 282-5, 287, 372, 457-8
   and New York Spiritual Assembly 143, 156, 166-9
   and racism 296, 298
   and Seven Year Plans 295-6, 305, 307, 346
   and teaching 221, 223-5, 228-31, 264, 291, 441-2
   and unity 219-20, 234, 248-9, 251, 456
   and World War II 299-300
   see also Holley, Horace
   see also Conventions; Regional Spiritual Assemblies
National Teaching Committee 169, 223, 292-4, 346, 455
National Urban League 175-6
National Youth Committee 299
Naugatuck River 10, 12
Nazarene Congregational Church 175
Nazis 300, 302
Neal, M. W. 103, 117, 133, 140, 163-5, 181, 415, 421, 425
Nebraska 62
New Amsterdam 117, 148
New Delhi, India 329, 333, 335, 350
   Imperial Hotel 333
   Town Hall 333
New England, New Englanders xii, 2, 7, 12, 17, 19-21, 27, 69, 87, 96, 226, 292-3, 373, 399
New Era School, Panchgani, India 334
Newhaven, Port of 48
New Haven, Connecticut 257
New History Society 154-9, 169, 176, 425, 427
New Jersey 82-4, 102, 110, 410, 414, 426, 437

New World Order 21, 102, 191, 277, 311 *see also* World Order of Bahá'u'lláh
New York
  Bahá'í community 97-118 passim, 126-8, 133, 137, 139-40, 145-6, 149-81 passim, 188, 216, 222, 237, 280, 413, 415, 426, 448
    Board of Counsel (House of Spirituality) 101-8
    Centre 140, 149, 152, 154, 157, 164, 170, 179
    Library 139
    Spiritual Assembly *see* Spiritual Assemblies, Local
  City
    Broadway 91
    Bronxville 79
    Brooklyn 107-8, 172, 175, 188, 431
    Carnegie Hall 102-3
    Central Park 79
    Churches *see* Catholic; Community; Congregational; Episcopal; First Emanuel; Nazarene; Riverside; St-Mark's-in-the-Bowery
    East River 78
    Garment District 79
    Governor's Island 329
    Grand Central Station 79
    Greenwich Village 83, 89, 117, 126, 204-5, 280
    Harlem 112, 172-3, 175-6, 188
    Hotel McAlpin 93
    Manhattan 9, 16, 78, 82, 99-100, 110, 117, 128, 139-40, 147, 158, 171-2, 176, 182, 204, 206, 208, 280, 410, 418, 431
    Metropolitan Museum of Art 9
    Morningside Heights 82
    Public Library 79
    Ritz-Carlton Hotel 154
    Wall Street 110, 113
    Wanamaker's Department Store 2
    Washington Square 205
  City of the Covenant 127-8, 139, 159, 311-12, 373

  metropolitan area 137, 139, 165, 170, 197, 425, 429
New York Herald 63, 134
New York Times 91, 118, 154, 227, 313
New York Urban League 263
New York World 134
New Zealand 153
Nineteen Day Feast 100, 106-8, 156, 164-6, 236, 277, 413
Nobel Peace Prize 262
Northwestern University 287, 366

Oglesby, Sadie 175
O'Keefe, Georgia 410
Osborne, Frank 103, 416
Oslo, Norway 332
Others: A Magazine of New Verse 83
Ottoman Empire 4-5, 29, 49, 92, 111
Oxford, England 2
  University 14, 130, 425

Pacific region 300
Palestine 4-5, 29, 80, 92, 114, 128-9, 135, 212, 311, 369, 374, 426, 439, 465
Palisades 82-3
Panama 329
Panchgani, India 334
Paris, France xi, 3-4, 16-17, 25, 41-56, 59-61, 63-72, 74-5, 77, 79, 82, 87, 92, 94, 100, 113-14, 126, 147, 150, 205, 217, 274, 369, 372, 404-5
  'Abdu'l-Bahá, visits to 34, 42, 47, 48-50, 51-6, 63, 71, 114-15, 217, 267
  Americans in 3, 16-17, 43-7, 49, 67, 82, 369
  Ashnur Galerie 44-7, 64
  Bahá'ís in 17, 41, 43, 49, 56, 65, 398, 413
  Baltimore Hotel 56
  Eiffel Tower 34
  Gare de l'Est 55
  Gare de Lyon 56
  Gare Saint Lazare 48, 71
  Latin Quarter 43-4, 65
  Seine River 17, 43, 71

Paris Pact (Kellogg-Briand, 1928) 262
Paris Peace Conference (Versailles) 94, 113, 412
Parliament of World Religions 260
Parsons, Agnes 112, 174
Pasadena, California 215
Pascal, Annette Sterner 116, 417
Pascal, Elsa 116
Pascal, Ernest 115, 417
Pascal, Gordon 115, 417
Pascal, Julian (Goodridge Bowen) 115-16, 417
Pearl Harbor 300
Peploe, Samuel John 46-7
Perkins, Dexter 262
Persia, Persian 6, 17, 29, 42, 49, 60, 101-2, 104, 134, 137, 147, 197, 214, 228, 304, 322, 324, 326, 331, 351, 353
   Bahá'í community in 94, 99, 102, 122, 134, 332, 324, 382, 460, 465
   language 17, 57-8, 126-7, 132, 133, 134, 161
Persian-American Educational Society 15
Peru 321, 329, 349, 461
Phelps, Myron 5-7, 17, 30, 58, 62
Philadelphia, Pennsylvania 1, 9, 10, 196, 337, 415, 418
Philip Kobbe Advertising Agency 119
Philippines 300
Picasso, Pablo 45, 405, 406
Pilgrim House
   Eastern 212
   Western 335-7, 370, 374-6, 378, 380
Piscataqua River 180, 203
Pittsburgh, Pennsylvania 224
Pius VI, Pope 51
Plan of Unified Action 221, 225, 291, 294
Plymouth, Massachusetts 19, 402
Poetry Bookshop, London 73, 78, 408
Poigny, France 68-70
Poland, Polish 299, 366, 401, 466
Popes, papacy 19-21, 51, 182-3
Portland, Oregon 247, 256
Portsmouth, New Hampshire 180, 203, 257

Portuguese language 305
Pound, Ezra 24-5, 28, 47, 60, 83, 406, 408, 410
Princeton University 88, 411
Proctor, Henry H., Reverend 175
Protestantism 7, 14, 18-21, 51, 58, 181, 182-3, 295, 398, 433
Puerto Rico 14
Pune (Poona), India 334
Puritans 7, 18-21, 35, 40, 182, 399, 402
Putnam, Edwin A. 103

Qiblih, Bahá'í 354

race, racial, racism xiv, 50, 86, 111-13, 172-6, 228, 256, 263-4, 296-8, 301, 382, 403, 431
Race Amity Conferences 112, 174-6, 403
Raffe. Mírzá 103
Rainbow Circle 175
Rambouillet, France 69, 70
Randall, John Herman 260-63, 268, 270, 275, 448-50, 451
Randall family 375
   Ruth 134
   William (Albert. W.) 197, 429
Ransom-Kehler, Keith 323
Reading Room 137-8, 150, 217, 370
Reagan, Ronald, President 402
Reality magazine 139-46, 148, 158, 170, 255, 415, 422, 423
Redfield Advertising Agency 119, 203-4
'Red Scare' 113, 417
Reed, Alice (Mrs A. I.) 105
Reformation, the (Protestant) 19-21, 51, 58, 182-3, 191
Regional Spiritual Assemblies 329, 342, 348-9, 360, 371, 464
   Brazil, Colombia, Ecuador, Peru and Venezuela 348-9
   Central America 318
   Central America, Mexico and Greater Antilles 329
   South America 318, 344-6, 461
Remey, Charles Mason 134, 197, 205, 324, 336-7, 339, 369-72, 375, 377-8, 421, 422, 435, 460, 467, 468

Republicans 227, 270
Revell sisters 337, 355
Rexford, Orcella 223-4
Rhee, Syngman, President 262
Rhythm magazine 47
Ridgefield, NJ 82-3
Rice, Anne Estelle 46-7
Riverside Church 272
Robarts, John 350, 357
Robert's Rules of Order 101, 164, 414
Robinson, Herold S. 140-44, 423
Romantic poets 39
Root, Martha 224, 229, 289, 292, 323
Roosevelt, Franklin D., President 226, 270, 278, 298-9, 300, 309-12
Rosenberg, Ethel 133-4, 191-2
Rotary Club, Rotary International 164, 287-9, 330, 334
Rúhá, daughter of 'Abdu'l-Bahá 49
Rúḥíyyih Khánum, Amatu'l-Bahá 186, 213, 250, 320, 325, 332, 336-7, 351-2, 355, 357, 377, 379, 381-2, 459, 465
Rúmí, Siyyid Muṣṭafa 134, 421
Russell, Bertrand 262
Russia, Russians 67, 71, 110-11, 176, 314, 408, 411, 466, 468

Salisbury, Connecticut 11
Samandarí, Tarázu'lláh 333 460
Sanderson family 49
Sanford, Joan 397
San Francisco, California 143, 247, 256-8, 262, 210-12, 317, 435
San Francisco Conference (1945) 262, 310-12
Sarajevo 67
Scheffler, Carl 440, 441, 442, 443, 446
Schlieffen Plan 67
Schopflocher, Lorol (Kitty) 223
Schopflocher, Siegfried (Fred) 301, 320, 325, 340, 455
Schwarz, Consul and Alice 134-5, 192
Scotland, Scots 2, 47, 406, 432
Scott, Edwin 43, 49, 53, 126
Screenwriters' Guild, Hollywood 116
Sears, William 350

Seattle, Washington 224
Secunderabad, India 334
Sedition Act 89
Serbia, Serbs 67
Seto, Mamie 461
Seven Year Plans
   1937-1944 (first) 243-6, 302, 305, 307, 318, 319-20, 328, 455, 461
   1946-1953 (second) 318, 346
Sewanee, University of the South 179, 432
Shakespeare, William 162
Sheridan Road, Wilmette 282, 286
Sherman, General William 400
Shoghi Effendi
   and 'Abdu'l-Bahá 126, 128, 131, 135, 230, 234, 338-9
   promulgation of Will and Testament 132-5, 137, 190
   successor to 125, 130-32, 136-7, 141, 144, 186-7, 194-5, 234, 356-7
   and Administrative Order, establishment of 135-6, 143, 167-71, 190-92, 195-6, 199-200, 213-14, 216-17, 241, 245-6, 297, 305-6, 328, 338, 340-41, 346-7, 349
   Convention 200, 232-40, 241, 244
   International Bahá'í Council 324
   National Spiritual Assembly of the United States and Canada 202-3, 211-14, 215, 219-20, 232-6, 238-40, 243, 245-9, 264-5, 279-80, 285, 296, 328
   and adherence to laws of the Kitáb-i-Aqdas 276-7
   and Ahmad Sohrab 147, 150, 152-7
   and Cold War 314
   descriptions of 131, 195, 337
   and Divine Plan of 'Abdu'l-Bahá 135-6, 289-90, 293, 318, 327, 338-9, 347, 356, 360
   teachers and pioneers 224, 229-30, 264-5, 290, 294, 298, 305, 328, 338-9, 345-7
   see also Seven Year Plan(s), Ten Year Plan

and Hands of the Cause xiii
    appointments xiii, 138, 179, 301,
        315, 321, 322-5, 340, 360
    and Auxiliary Boards 340-41, 350
    explains functions of 323, 340-41,
        353
and Holy Places and properties in
    the Holy Land 212, 318-19, 338,
    353-4, 358, 362, 370
and Horace Holley *see* Holley,
    Horace
and House of Worship, Wilmette
    192, 229, 279, 293, 318, 332, 338
and independence of the Bahá'í Faith
    186-7
and Inter-America Conference 303-4
and intercontinental conferences 329,
    332-3, 350, 353
interpreter 199, 341, 360
lack of successor to 356-60, 363
passing of 351, 352-6, 369
and racism in the United States 172,
    175-6, 296-7
and summer schools 289-90
in Switzerland 192
and United Nations 311-12
and World War II 299, 302-4, 311,
    318
writings and translations 130, 133-6,
    191, 198, 250, 290, 333, 360,
    365, 425, 452
    Advent of Divine Justice, The
        297-8, 456
    Dispensation of Bahá'u'lláh, The
        250, 265, 356
    God Passes By 128, 213
    Messages to the Bahá'í World:
        1950–1957 365
    Promised Day Is Come, The 302
    World Order of Bahá'u'lláh, The
        265-6, 269, 272, 277, 290,
        294, 441, 450
    see also Guardianship
Sholapur, India 334
Siena, Italy 22, 24, 29-30, 33-4, 37-41,
    402
Siyáh-<u>Ch</u>ál 318

Slovakians 401
Smith College 287
Smith, Peter 419-20
Smythe, Marguerite 'Daisy' 420
Sohrab, Ahmad 81, 92-3, 146-59, 275,
    309, 422, 424-7
Soirées de Paris, Les 64 406
Some Answered Questions 17
Sorbonne, University of 16
South America 292, 293, 296, 305, 315,
    318, 344
Southampton, England 73
South India 333-4
Soviet Union 267, 310, 314, 327, 382,
    466
Spain, Spanish 66, 71, 183, 278
Spanish language 290, 305
Spiritual Assemblies, Local 104, 135-6,
    137, 156, 157, 159 164-8, 170, 189,
    198-200, 211-12, 216-17, 223-4,
    227, 230, 236-40, 244, 293, 305,
    316, 318, 319, 327, 338, 341-2,
    344-5, 349, 358, 366-7, 381, 414,
    423, 429, 445
    Boston 239-45, 445
    Chicago 168
    Kenosha (governing council) 101,
        414
    Los Angeles 148
    New York 103, 108, 128, 141, 142-5,
        149-59, 163-72, 175-6, 179, 181,
        188, 203, 231, 216, 255, 324-5,
        380-81, 413, 424, 425, 429, 431,
        460
    Poona (Pune), India 334
    San Francisco 256
    Tehran, Iran 102
    Washington DC 141
    see also National Spiritual Assemblies
Sprague, Charles E. 102, 415
Sri Lanka 333-5
SS Celtic 48
SS Merion 1-2, 8, 9
Stalin, Josef 310, 411
Star of the West 42, 92, 123, 139-40,
    147, 161-2, 195, 198, 216, 223, 422,
    424, 427 *see also Bahá'í Magazine*

Statue of Liberty 75
Sterner, Albert 417
Sterner, Annette *see* Pascal
Sterner, Frederick 417
Stevens, Wallace 410
Stieglitz, Alfred 83, 410
St Mark's-in-the-Bowery 96, 116-18, 137, 170, 179-85, 187-8, 412, 418, 432-3, 437
Stockholm, Sweden 329, 331-2, 370, 462
Struven family 287
Stuyvesant, Peter 117, 148
Swinburne, Algernon Charles 52
Switzerland 17, 30, 53, 192, 209, 229, 380, 404
Sydney, Australia 123, 370

Tagore, Rabindranath 154
Tehran, Iran 102, 123, 131, 318, 322, 331, 414
   Central Spiritual Assembly 322
Tel Aviv, Israel 335, 374
Temple Unity (and Executive Board) 105, 109-10, 133-4, 193-203, 210-15, 217, 226-7, 230, 233, 240, 251, 315, 370, 416, 421, 422, 428, 434-5, 460
Ten Year Plan (Crusade) 326-7, 338-41, 347-50, 356-7, 361-2, 370-71
Theosophists 60, 122, 334, 419
Thompson, Juliet 117, 126-7, 399, 403-4, 412, 420, 440
Thonon-les-Bains, France 29-34, 41, 53, 126, 324, 348, 403-4
Thoreau, Henry David 27
Tibetan Friendship Group 397
Times Literary Review 26
Toronto, Canada 292
Torrington, Connecticut vii, 1, 10-13, 18, 173, 401, 433
Townshend, George 179, 333, 432, 460, 462
Transylvania, University of, Kentucky 13
Trivandrum, India 334
True, Arna 287

True, Corinne 109, 134, 197, 287, 325, 331-2, 340, 342, 353, 359, 368, 416, 435, 464
True, Edna 287, 317, 326, 339, 351, 381, 454
True, Katherine 287, 351, 464
Truman, Harry, President 312
Tudor-Pole, Wellesley 134-5
Turkey 312 *see also* Ottoman Empire
Turkmenistan 109, 468
Tuscany 18-19, 22, 38
Tyndale, William 20

United Nations 262, 309-13, 374, 381, 467
   Charter 313
   General Assembly 312
   Security Council 310
United States 5, 7, 12, 19-21, 24, 40-41, 112-13, 120, 125, 143, 172-6, 179, 193, 196, 208, 213, 226-7, 238, 255, 259, 270, 277, 279, 294-5, 299-300, 302, 309-10, 312-14, 326-7, 369, 398, 402, 414, 431, 433, 451, 461
   Bahá'í communities in xii, 29, 49-50, 51, 63, 64, 74-5, 78, 87-94, 99, 101, 103-5, 107-10, 114, 117, 125, 131, 144, 146, 150, 158, 166, 169-70, 172, 176, 187-8, 191-2, 193-5, 198, 200, 201-03, 213, 216, 217, 222-5, 229, 233-4, 239, 240, 242-4, 247-8, 250, 258, 289, 291-3, 295-9, 302, 303-5, 307-8, 315, 318-19, 320, 322, 327-8, 338, 344-6, 349, 370, 380, 381, 404, 413, 414, 416, 417, 422, 425, 429, 441, 460
   National Spiritual Assembly *see* National Spiritual Assemblies
   Congress 211
   Senate 196
   Supreme Court 262
Universal House of Justice, The xiv, 34, 86, 101, 125, 130, 135, 167, 199, 238, 265, 324, 338, 341, 356-62, 368, 370-72, 378, 381-3, 414, 421, 423, 445

universities
  Brown 258
  Cambridge 5, 14, 423, 452
  Chicago 179
  Cincinnati 179
  Columbia 9, 141, 174, 256
  Cornell 258
  Harvard 21, 180, 197, 227
  Northwestern 287, 366
  Oxford 14, 130, 423
  Smith College 287
  Stanford 256
  of the South (Sewanee) 179, 43
  Wesleyan 148
  Williams College 2-3, 7, 13-16, 89, 295, 298, 411, 448
  Wisconsin Medical School 351

Vail, Albert 222-4, 228-30, 257, 443, 449
Vancouver 292
Varqá, 'Alí-Muḥammad 465
Varqá, Valíyu'lláh 460
Vatican, the 51
Venezuela 348
Verne, Jules 329
Victoria Station, London 48
Voeltz, Loretta 286, 404, 454, 458
Vreeland, Claire vii-viii
Vreeland, Paul vii-viii

Wales 2
war 86, 91, 124, 262, 278, 297, 369, 374
  World Wars xiv 311
    First (Great War) 45, 61, 63-5, 67-75, 78, 80, 82, 87-94, 106, 110-15, 119, 120, 122, 137-8, 147, 172, 225, 257, 268, 270, 278, 289, 300, 311-12, 314, 326, 370, 374, 411, 448
    Second 158, 257-8, 269-70, 273, 278, 298-302, 308-10, 311-15, 317-19, 326-7, 351, 448
Washington DC 56, 57, 105, 112, 126, 140-41, 147, 154, 174-5, 196, 197, 217, 292, 370, 412, 416, 420, 422, 424
Wells, H. G. 424

Wesleyan University 148
West Coast (US) 138, 196, 215, 247, 289, 293, 295, 445, 455 see also California
West Englewood, NJ 110, 426
Wharton, Edith 67
White, Ruth 425-6
Whitman, Walt 26-8, 180, 432
Wilhelm, Roy 109-10, 113, 123, 128, 131, 133-5, 157, 174, 191, 197, 280, 285, 301, 315, 317, 323, 325, 416, 417, 429, 437, 451, 454, 455
Wilkinson, Roushan 210
Williams College 2-3, 7, 13-16, 89, 411, 448
  Haystack event 295, 398
Williams, William Carlos 83-4, 410
Wilmette, Illinois
  Baháʼí community in 287, 301, 316-17, 324, 339, 351, 353
  Conferences held in 303-4, 329, 332, 349, 364
  National Baháʼí Centre 280, 282-9, 308-9, 328, 372, 379, 413
  village 280, 287-9, 300, 413, 468
  see also House of Worship
Wilmette Conversation Club 289
Wilmette Historical Commission 289
Wilmette Historical Society 289
Wilmette Village Council 289
Wilson, Woodrow, President 88-9, 94, 106, 112-13, 225, 262, 312, 411, 412
  Fourteen Points 94, 312, 412
Windsor 2
Windust, Albert 422
Winzer, Charles 47
Wolcott, Charles 288, 367, 379, 381
Wolcottville 10, 399
Wood, Tom and Clara 285-6
Woolworth Building, New York 77
Woolson, Gayle 344-5
Woolson, Orosco C. (Clement) 102, 103, 414
Worcester, Massachusetts 257
World Order letters (*The World Order of Baháʼuʼlláh*) 265, 269, 272, 277, 290, 294, 441, 450

World Order magazine 272, 319, 333
World Unity Committee 258
World Unity Conferences 256-8, 261-4, 311
World Unity Foundation 258-73, 275, 437, 448, 449, 450
World Unity magazine 259, 262-72, 433, 449, 450
Wright, Frances (Fanny) 179, 432
Wright, Frank Lloyd 182, 262, 433, 449
Wright, Orville and Wilbur (Wright brothers) 329, 461
Wright, Philip Quincy 262
Wycliffe, John 20

Yalta 310
Young Men's Christian Association (YMCA) 14, 398

ABOUT THE AUTHOR

Kathryn Jewett Hogenson, a native of Virginia, resides in Florida with her husband, Gary Hogenson. She is a lawyer by training and an historian by choice. For many years, she served the Bahá'í Faith at both the international and national levels as a staff member. A frequent lecturer, she is the author of other books and articles, including *Lighting the Western Sky: The Hearst Pilgrimage and the Establishment of the Bahá'í Faith in the West*.

www.ingramcontent.com/pod-product-compliance
Lightning Source LLC
Chambersburg PA
CBHW060512230426
43665CB00013B/1485